Classical Mythology

Classical

Mythology

pp 9–308 first published by The Gresham Publishing Company.
pp 311–479 copyright © 1995 Geddes and Grosset Ltd.

Copyright © this edition 1997 Geddes & Grosset Ltd, David Dale House,
New Lanark, Scotland ML11 9DJ.

ISBN 1 85534 348 7

Printed and bound in China

Contents

List of Illustrations

Introduction

⁂

The Growth of Myths

In the childhood of our world the myth-making faculty seems so much matter of course that the Greek word $\mu\upsilon\theta\upsilon\varsigma$ primarily meaning a word or speech, took on its special sense as work of fancy. Ignorant minds are moved by fear and wonder to interpret their experience in parables, the personages of which will be shadowy or misty images of their own nature, distorted beyond mere humanity and released from the limitations of earthly life. At the early stage of mental development passed through by each man, as by his kind, religion, law, and poetry go hand in hand, sanctioning a love of personification expressed for our children by-such ideas as 'Father Christmas', the 'Man in the Moon', or the 'Land of Nod'. These playful myths are modified to edification by considerate elders; but from what tales will be hailed as satisfactory in the best-regulated nurseries we can guess how wild imaginations, without probability or proportion, may commend themselves to savage peoples whose growing perceptions can elaborate so rude sketches into a mythology.

In an age of comparative enlightenment such imaginations too long lay despised for nursery fables, to be forgotten in the schoolroom; but the new science of folklore has put them in their true place as important lessons in the history of the human mind. The first thing that strikes a student of them is the resemblances and coincidences found in 'old wives' tales' all over the world, obscured but not hidden under the differences of colouring thrown upon them by diversity of custom and environment. Two explanations of such marks of identity have been put forward. It may be that these stories took their outline in one cradle of races, which were afterwards so widely separated as to have lost trace of their origin. Or, can it be in the nature of man that, under varying climes and conditions, he is apt to hit upon similar explanations of the phenomena everywhere threatening and upholding his life?

"The same heart beats in every human breast."

9

The question between these theories is complicated by the consideration of migrations and conquests that all along have gone to mix blood and thought. Once a Persian child may have learned its first notions from a Mongol slave-nurse; and thousands of years ago the rape of a Helen or the selling of a Joseph into Egypt were everyday experiences all over the world. It is easy to see how the races round the Mediterranean came to share one another's legends and superstitions. But it seems much more of a puzzle when we find hints of like imaginations rooted in Australia, that through all historic time has been cut off from other homes of man, and in America, where for ages the human mind seems to have had its own independent development from savagery.

Non nostrum tantas componere lites, when ethnologists are not yet at one on such questions. Nor need we here go into controversies that have divided rival schools of folklore students, the deepest of them still a matter of enquiry. "I have changed my views repeatedly, and I have resolved to change them again with every change of the evidence", says Dr J G Frazer, confessing how the candid enquirer must play the chameleon upon the shifting colours of this freshly-turned-up ground. He is here speaking of totemism, meaning a special relation the savage believes himself to bear to some fetish object or ancestral beast. The word tot*em* is little more than a century old in our language, and it was only in our time that, from its being taken as the crest of a Red Indian clan, it has been promoted to rank as an index of primitive customs over the world, specially significant in connection with the law of exogamy that forbade marriage between sons and daughters of the same totem. Scholars have had their eyes opened to once neglected hints of totemism in ancient records; and Dr Frazer published four weighty volumes on a subject which to writers like Fenimore Cooper supplied picturesque features for fiction, till L H Morgan in his Lea*gue of the Iroquois* and J F M'Lennan in his *Primitive Marriage* began to point out the important bearings of what had seemed a mere primitive heraldry.

Some commentators on folklore are suspected of making too much of totemism as a key of interpretation. Similarly, in the last generation the theory was pushed too far that found a comprehensive formula for myths in the visible changes of the sky and the seasons. The blood-red giant whose strength declines after midday might well be the sun; the hero who sets out so briskly in the fresh dawn of life may find his career clouded by the mists of evening; the moon and the stars too had stories of their own, embroidered by fancy upon the background of night. This way of accounting for myths, helped out by dubious etymologies, was boldly extended till the four-and-twenty blackbirds baked in a pie were like to become in grave eyes the hours of day and night, and the maid hanging out clothes in the garden was dealing with clouds when the frost bit her nose. The sun-myth school, taught in Britain by Max Müller and the Rev Sir G W Cox, has now suffered eclipse. But there can, of course, be no doubt that the sun and moon, the changes of weather and seasons, the havoc of storms, floods, and droughts, played a great part in suggesting the personages and scenery of nascent imagination.

Some students, flying from the Scylla of universal sun-worship, appear drawn to the Charybdis of looking on the growth of vegetable life as a main source of mythology, one indeed fruitful in hints for marvel. Such superstitions as the 'corn baby', still lingering among our peasantry in half-jocular respect, such rites as those of our nearly obsolete 'Jack in the Green', are survivals of fancies once taken very seriously, as they still are in many parts of the world. From its most distant corners, missionaries, explorers, traders, renegade white men, and other not always competent witnesses, go on adding to the list of traditions, taboos, sacrifices, charms, divinations, and other savage notions and customs; thus we have a growing heap of evidence to be sifted, tested, and compared by scholars seeking some consistent theory, a question that would not greatly trouble the original shapers of myth and legend.

So much has been hinted to show how folklorists are still at work on their foundations. Enough for us to know primitive man as prone to wonder, to be moved by desires and fears 'as old at once and new as nature's self', to look on all he does not understand as mystery, then to express his fears, aspirations, and amazement in rude fables, which, shaped by priests and poets with more or less conscious purpose, soon grew to be at once phases of faith and essays in science. Dim-sighted fancies they were, misled by refractions and shadows, yet gropings after truth, that, when lit by the dawn of knowledge and culture, might lose much of their original grossness, and be refined to inspiring systems of religion. The day is gone by when we could complacently look down on all paganism as a dead-level of ignorant idolatry and deceitful priestcraft.

> "Each form of worship that hath swayed
> The life of man, and given it to grasp
> The master-key of knowledge, reverence,
> Enfolds some germ of goodness and of right;
> Else never had the eager soul which loathes
> The slothful down of pampered ignorance
> Found in it even a moment's fitful rest."

It is not difficult to see how ancient Greece gave a soil for the rich crop of religious imaginations that, embalmed by genius and artistic skill, have passed into the literature of the world, while kindred beliefs of other lands wither in oblivion or are preserved only as curious specimens in the collections of ethnology. That sea-broken peninsula, set about with islands which made stepping-stones to the mainland shores of the eastern Mediterranean, was from very early times a meeting-place of different races that here blended their stock of ideas as well as their blood. The indigenous inhabitants, Pelasgians, or whoever they were, could not fail to be touched by hostile and commercial relations with the seaboard states of Asia and Africa, far before them in culture. Since the beginning of this century, it has been made clear that Crete was from about 3000 BC a strong sea-power of comparative civilization. The horizon of Greek history has been widened by the digging up of the Mycenaean treasures in the north-east of the Peloponnesus, where a new kingdom rose to greatness as that of Crete fell into decay. Then this horizon becomes clouded by swarms of Aryan invaders or immigrants pushing from the north, as their kinsmen descended upon Hindustan through the Himalayan passes, and as the Goths afterwards overran the other peninsulas of Europe. Thus diverse influences from north and south met within the narrow bounds of Greece, whence they soon flowed back upon Asia in the prosperous Ionian and other colonies that kept their motherland in touch with the dreamy East, whose own developed superstitions, in turn, kept infiltrating into the minds of a race all along ready to absorb a variety of religious ideas.

There were repeated waves of Aryan immigration, the strongest of them the Achaean and the Dorian that fixed their main settlements respectively in the northern and southern part of this almost sundered land. The conquered and displaced tribes would not be exterminated, but to a large extent became absorbed among the invaders, if they were unable to preserve their independence penned up in rugged mountain fastnesses, as appears to have been the case in Arcadia, as was certainly the case with Dravidian stocks in India, and with the much-mixed Celts of our own Highlands. So here was a Medea's cauldron of flesh and blood, a hodgepodge which would boil briskly on the fires of time till there emerged a new national consciousness that by what seems accident took for itself the general names of Hellas and Hellenes, then had to use its faculty for story-telling by inventing a fabulous Hellen as ancestor.

Myth-making had naturally thrived among this jumble of clashing races and blending superstitions. Nor was the Grecian mind thus evolved to be shut up within itself. The new seaboard states, like the old ones, had relations of commerce with other shores, that soon became relations of conquest. Pressed for room in their narrow, not over-fertile bounds, the enterprising Greeks swarmed out into colonies upon the Black Sea, and round half the Mediterranean. The south of Italy came to be known as *Magna Grecia,* where the chance of a tribe of *Graii* coming in contact with the Romans fixed on the whole race the Latinized name of Greeks, by which they have been best known to the modern world, as in some parts of Asia all Christians came to be 'Franks', and among some Red Indian tribes the American colonists in general were 'Boston men'. Into Italy these intruders brought their religious notions to be grafted on often kindred roots already fixed in the soil by common ancestors, strayed from far and wide. Thus Latin mythology readily adopted variants of the Hellenic forms, more dearly shaped by the influence of Greek literature upon conquering Rome. And in Asia the Greek mind not only lent but borrowed new inspirations that went to make its religion singularly rich in ideas to be shaped afresh by a love of personification and a sense for the beauty of life. Later on was to come a more fruitful union between the clear-eyed genius of Hellenism and the sterner Hebraic conscience. The myths of Greek paganism themselves had been cross-bred from mingling stocks, which might belong to sundered families of human thought and speech.

It is, of course, not to be supposed that any such mythology sprang into the world full-grown, as Minerva from the head of Jove. Its embryo forms are hidden from us in a remote past, unless we can catch them reflected in the fables of savages at a stage of development passed through by forgotten ancestors of Homer and Pindar. The theophany of Olympus was an obscure and slow accretion; and to the end the materials of Greek faith remained imperfectly fused. Even in the Christian era time-honoured 'stocks and stones' were worshipped with more fervour than the statues of famous deities. The 'sweetness and light' supposed to characterize Greek conceptions came slowly to days of art and study, perhaps tinged mainly the cultured life of cities, while rude Arcadians and the like clung to their old bogeydom. The earliest objects of adoration, of propitiation rather, appear everywhere to have been shapes of dread and horror, begetting imaginary monsters, 'Gorgons and Hydras and Chimaeras dire'. It is a world-wide experience that such old superstitions persist through ages of higher faith, long after their origin has been forgotten. There were once peasants in Britain who professed to have advanced beyond the faith of Rome or of Anglicanism, yet unwittingly practised pagan rites of sun-worship, and with maimed observance kept the feasts of banished idols, themselves lingering unsuspected here and there, as in the shape of ugly obelisks approved among believers zealous to proscribe the sign of the Cross.

The serpent, the owl, and other animals represented as attendant on the Olympian gods were no doubt older than themselves, hallowed as totems long before Zeus took shape, still to pursue his earthly amours in such suggestive forms as a bull's or a swan's. An uncanny creature like the snake makes a very early object of reverence or abhorrence which it is long in losing. Even in Scotland, where more deadly snakes than adders are unknown, people will not eat an eel; and there is a lingering prejudice against pork, perhaps coming down from days when the pig was in such honour here as to name mountains and islands. In Greece, serpents were revered by the ignorant later than Lucian's day, whose exposure of the false prophet Alexander shows us a tame snake as chief 'property' of that impostor's hocus-pocus.

Superstition would not so readily try her 'prentice hand on man'. Early deities, after growing out of the totem stage, are apt to take female forms, as conceived in a matriarchal state of society, while rude morals exalt the certain mother above the dubious father of her children. Later, when the male has assumed his place as head or tyrant of the family, with woman for his drudge, he makes a god rather in the image of his own sex. The Cretan state seen flourishing from about 3000 BC appears to have had a female fertilizing spirit for its chief divinity, along with a special regard for the bulls that made a valuable asset to tribal wealth. Similar conceptions prevailed on the Eastern shores whence Greece drew the first seeds of culture. The Aryan invaders from the north must have brought with them the notion of a father in heaven, the shining *Dyaus,* whose name has passed into so many tongues. The marriage of this sky-god with the earth-spirit begot that brood of deities, for whom dominions could be found in the air, the earth, the sea, and the dark underworld, and who were fabled to mix their immortal blood with that of the national or local heroes making a link between god and man.

The Greek Pantheon was fortunate in finding more than one *vates sacer,* for want of whom so many gods as well as heroes have been buried in oblivion. Homer and Hesiod fixed for us the religious ideas obtaining nearly a thousand years before our era; and both of them mention bards who must have been handling the same theme for generations. The theogony of Hesiod, as Mr Andrew Lang says, was for Greek youth what the catechisms of our own Churches are for us, presenting a formal view of Greek articles of faith. The title of 'Greek Bible' has been given to the poems of Homer, which, whoever wrote them, appear to be earlier than Hesiod in their first form; yet it is remarkable that they put the gods in a loftier light, ignoring much of the grossness found in later stories; and this though the poet seems to be consciously archaizing, as when he sets his heroes in the age of bronze weapons, but here and there lets out that iron was familiar to his time. The *Odyssey,* too, evinces some more elevated conceptions and other manners than the *Iliad,* which have been variously explained as signs of a later date or of a separate origin. The *Iliad,* for example, shows the Oriental contempt of dogs as prowling scavengers; while in the *Odyssey* they are fierce but faithful guardians of a flock, and one hound, lit up to fame by a ray of sympathetic feeling, bears a name, Argos, such as in the *Iliad* is attributed to the horses of Achilles. All those questions as to Homeric personality, authenticity, date, and origin on the Ionian shores of Asia or elsewhere, must be passed over lightly here. There may have been one great poet whose mind made a refining crucible for the ore of legend; but scholars now rather incline to take Homer as no more real than his heroes —themselves perhaps half-real—his name covering a long process of welding together old fables and traditions into a final form where imperfect fusion is betrayed by careless inconsistencies; and the evolved moral ideas that hint a later date may perhaps have belonged to some false dawn of thought, clouded over by recurrent barbarism.

In those famous poems the Pantheon appears not quite complete; but all its chief members have taken their place, superseding an older generation of gods, whose history was less edifying. Local cults, no doubt, went on amalgamating, also perhaps arising afresh, and in some cases spreading far, as when Athena, the patron goddess of Athens, became reverenced over Greece, and across the Adriatic was transformed into the Latin Minerva. There were waves of foreign influence, like the enthusiasm of the worship of Bacchus introduced with the culture of the vine, whereas honey had made the nectar of the old gods. The Orphic spirit in Greek religion is a more mysterious infusion. It has been supposed that Orpheus was a real teacher, who sought to raise men's minds upon a cloud of mystic practices and to refine superstition into a rule of nobler life. Under his name, at all events, a movement of religious zeal spread over the Hellenic world, probably allied with the new doctrines of Pythagoras as to life after death, marking one tendency of the Greek mind, while another was manifested in the Ionian philosophers who would have turned attention rather on rationalistic enquiries into the nature of matter and its phenomena.

About the middle of the millennium before Christ, we come into the clearer light of Greece's great days, when its hurling back of the Persian hosts called forth a stronger sentiment of national life, and mental culture went hand in hand with martial pride. A rapid development of intellectual life seems marked by the first solid history, the work of Thucydides, coming close upon the legendary tales of Herodotus. Now Phidias almost breathes life into the statues of the gods; Pericles adorns their temples, whose priests, and the craftsmen to whom those shrines bring no small gain, are concerned to keep up the old beliefs; but moralists are eager to shake their heads over barbarous legends which the great Athenian dramatists shape into statuesque tableaux and choruses; while philosophy seems hard put to it in reconciling them with new conceptions of duty and piety. The philosophic mind, indeed, sublimating forms into ideas, finds much to apologize for and to explain away in the popular Pantheon, set in a new light by comparison with the gods of other lands. Pythagoras saw Hesiod bound to a pillar in Hades as punishment for the lies he had told about the gods; Plato was for banishing the fabling poets from his ideal state. To Homer himself, it will be remembered, Olympus furnished the most comic scenes of his story. Later poets show consciousness that their favourite themes need a good deal of 'editing', such as Homer, too, no doubt did in his day according to its lights. Euripides raised applause by dealing boldly with unedifying stories of the gods, the sophist Protagoras was prosecuted for professing himself an agnostic as to their very existence. Plato suggests nobler myths of creation, and purgatorial emendations on the incredible torments of Hades: he may still speak of gods, but what he has in his mind's eye is the archetypal godlike. More and more, thinking men come to look on the divine as a potency or tendency rather than a batch of personalities, while the vulgar cling to old superstitions or even adopt new ones with the

15

eclectic spasms of decadence we see at work among some of ourselves, who give up their orthodox faith to itch after exotic theosophies and wonder-workings.

About a century before our era, Apollodorus wrote in stolid prose a history of godlike and heroic doings, which has made *mémoires pour servir* for many more spirited writers. Theocritus and other poets of a later age give a shapely turn to the old legends, as did Ovid in his *Metamorphoses,* that handed them down to the medieval world. Prose writers like Apuleius, too, try their hand at fairy tales. Then, in the second century after Christ, comes a Lucian to assail Olympus with peals of laughter, and to caricature the absurd marvels of mythology. It is harder for us to understand the mental attitude of Pausanias, who, in the same century, made an alternately credulous and critical survey of the monuments of his ancestral superstition. By this time the wisest pagans were more or less unconsciously borrowing from Christianity, while early Christian teachers might take classic legends as texts for denouncing the works of the devil, but would not be concerned to put these stories in the best light. Purer morals brought new tests to bear. Modern moralists and poets are bound to pass lightly over the coarsenesses of a mythology that has offered many subjects for edifying discourse and enhancement by graceful fancy. Our artists, too, have touched up some of those time-worn myths, bringing out here a feature, and there covering up a fault, to fit in with their rules of composition or canons of the becoming.

So stands in what might be called ruinous repair that broken temple of the Grecian mind which, ages after it has seen a devout worshipper, makes one of the grandest monuments of the human instinct bidding—

> "Build thee more stately mansions, O my soul,
> As the swift seasons roll!
> Leave thy low-vaulted past!
> Let each new temple, loftier than the last,
> Shut thee from heaven with a dome more vast,
> Till thou at length art free,
> Leaving thine outgrown shell by life's unresting sea!"

Theogony and Cosmogony

"The cosmogony or creation of the world has puzzled philosophers of all ages", pronounced the Vicar of Wakefield's learned acquaintance; but ancient poets have been readier with explanations, not wholly consistent. The books that reach us under the name of Hesiod set forth a formal series of conceptions, to a great extent incidentally borne out by Homer. The protoplasm of all things was Chaos, where Love soon began to stir and to call forth reproductive shapes. Night brought forth Day; Earth, besides her brood of mountains and seas, was the parent of the sky, that easily passed into a personage, Uranus, whose marriage with Gaea, or Gé, another allegory of the earth, founded a huge family of Titans, Cyclopes, and the like gigantic beings.

This prologue presents a rather misty scene, but the stage is now set for an historical drama in which the dynasty of the gods shows to disadvantage by quarrels between father and son more bitter than those of our eighteenth-century Georges. Uranus hated his monstrous progeny so much that he imprisoned them in a cave, and thereby drove Gaea to a treasonable plot, carried out by her youngest son Cronos (Saturn). Armed with a sharp sickle, he attacked and shamefully mutilated his father, from whose blood sprang fresh monsters. Here Hesiod breaks the main thread of his story to record the birth of Aphrodite from the sea, and also the incarnation of the Fates, along with abstractions such as Necessity, Strife, Toil, and many of the other characters to figure in mythological romance.

We come back to the reign of Cronos, paired with his sister Rhea, who afterwards as Cybele became venerated as mother of the gods, representing the matriarchally conceived deity who was long supreme on the adjacent coasts of Asia. Her husband turned out a not less ruthless tyrant than his father. Warned that he should be dethroned by one of his own children, he made a practice of swallowing them at birth. The family thus suppressed were three sisters, Hestia, Demeter, and Hera, followed by three brothers, Pluto, Poseidon, and Zeus. He who was to be the heir is the youngest in Hesiod, like his father before him; but elsewhere Zeus is represented as the eldest son. Rhea, like her mother, was naturally ill-pleased by such treatment of her offspring; and when it came to the birth of Zeus, she played a trick upon the unnatural father by wrapping a stone in swaddling clothes, which he unsuspiciously swallowed, while the babe was smuggled off to be brought up in a cave on Mount Dicte in Crete. There reared to manhood, the young god fulfilled his destiny by coming back to dethrone Cronos, forcing him also to disgorge his brothers and sisters along with the stone representing himself, long treasured as a relic at the shrine of Pytho on Mount Parnassus, afterwards more famous as the oracle of Delphi.

The reign of Zeus was soon marked by civil war. He had released his gigantic uncles from their confinement; and a faction of Titans ill rewarded him by raising insurrection on behalf of Cronos. The ten years' conflict of Titans and gods is a famous episode, that suggested to Milton his conception of the battle with fallen angels. The scene of the struggle was imagined as the mountains of Thessaly, where Olympus made the fastness of the gods, while the Titans occupied the Othrys range to the south, and were fabled to have piled its summits on

17

one another in their attempt to scale heaven, but came to be beaten back by the thunderbolts of Zeus, on whose side fought the hundred-handed giant Briareus, the Cyclopes, and other monstrous warriors. Finally the rebels were conquered and driven down to confinement in Tartarus.

Zeus, now established as sovereign, gave to his brothers, Poseidon and Pluto, the kingdoms of the sea and of the dark underworld, while he kept earth and heaven as his own dominion. But not yet could he reign in peace. Fresh rebellion broke out under Typhon, a hundred-headed monster begotten by Gaea and Tartarus; then came another insurrection of giants; so not for long, Typhon being at last imprisoned under the burning mass of Mount Etna, were the gods free to dwell at ease beside their nectar; and henceforth the history of Olympus becomes rather a scandalous chronicle of despotism tempered by intrigues.

From heaven we turn to earth, the early story of which seems more edifying. Iapetus, brother of Cronos, had four sons, two of whom took part with the rebellious Titans, one being Atlas, punished by having for ever to hold up on his shoulders the vault of the sky, or the earth itself, as his doom came to be more easily pictured in an illustration made familiar in the frontispiece to early collections of maps, hence christened by his name. His brother Prometheus fought for Olympus, yet later incurred the anger of Zeus. While man is sometimes spoken of as autochthonous, generated from the soil, one story makes Prometheus his creator, who kneaded him of day in the image of the gods, shaping his body to look up to heaven instead of down upon earth, and endowing him with the best of the qualities distributed by his brother Epimetheus among mere animals. At all events, Prometheus (Forethought) figures as the patron and champion of man, on whose behalf he stole away from heaven the gift of fire, grudged by Zeus, and in a hollow reed brought it down to be treasured on earth. The angry king of Olympus punished his bold vassal by fettering him on a cliff of the Caucasus for thirty thousand years, daily tormented by an eagle tearing at his liver.

Hesiod has to add a more grotesque offence given by Prometheus to the lord of heaven. Sacrificing an ox, he made two parcels of its flesh, one chiefly consisting of the bones covered with a slight layer of fat under the hide, then invited Zeus to choose one for himself; and though the god saw through the trick, none the less he held himself for insulted, and took this excuse to refuse the gift of fire, which then had to be filched by man's presumptuous friend.

To balance the irrevocable boon of fire, Zeus gave man a curse in the shape of that scapegoat on which early priests and poets so readily load the sins of our race. Woman was created and sent down to earth by the hands of Epimetheus (Afterthought).[1] The name Pandora denotes how she was endowed by the gods with beauty and accomplishments, instructed and dressed by Athena, while Hermes bestowed on her artful wiles and Aphrodite seductive charms. As outfit, she brought a box filled with plagues and vices, which she was forbidden to open; but female curiosity was already as strong as in the days of Bluebeard: she raised the lid, and out flew the germs of widespread suffering for mankind. When she shut it up too late, only Hope remained at the bottom of the fatal casket to be a balm for all those woes.

Consistency seems too much to expect of poets, and from Pandora Hesiod goes on to give another history of man, afterwards made more familiar by Ovid. Our men of science tell us how we must have risen from a low estate through successive ages of stone tools and weapons, improved by the use of metals, hammering out more and more elaborate arts. The poetic mind reverses this progress, always looking back fondly on a golden dawn of innocence and happiness, from which man fell to the coarse realities of his present life. The classical age of gold was under Saturn, when the denizens of earth had no need to envy Olympus.

> " Like gods they lives, with calm untroubled mind,
> Free from the toil and anguish of our kind:
> Nor e'er decrepit age mis-shaped their frame,
> The hand's, the foot's proportions, still the same.
> Pleased with earth's unbought feasts, all ills removed,
> Wealthy in flocks, and of the bless'd beloved,
> Death as a slumber pressed their eyelids down;
> All nature's common blessings were their own;
> The life-bestowing tilth its fruitage bore,
> A full, spontaneous and ungrudging store:
> They with abundant goods, mid quiet lands,
> All willing shared the gatherings of their hands."

Hesiod's *Works and Days* (Elton's translation)

Next came the Silver Age, in which man became less pious and less blessed, incurring the anger of the gods, who now sent scorching winds and nipping frosts to blight that early Eden. In the Brazen Age that succeeded, men took to fighting among themselves. Between this and the more degenerate Iron Age from which he is looking back, Hesiod inserts an Heroic Age, when Zeus restored some of man's pristine virtue to carry him through the great Trojan war and other semi-mythological exploits of early Greek history. Ovid, not so much concerned with this period, reduces the ages from five to four, going straight on from the Brazen to the Iron Age, a change that has its basis of fact in the gradual substitution of iron for bronze weapons. The Roman poet's time gave him too plain a picture of human depravity.

> "Enfranchised wickedness dominion hath,
> And puts to flight truth, modesty and faith:
> Fraud and deceit, and treachery and greed,

And souls that covet others' good succeed:
The sailor spreads the sail on seas unknown;
From mountain slopes the patriarch trees fall down,
Supinely fall, and bound the wave upon;
And land which common was as air or sun,
Man metes and measures, marks and calls his own.
But not content to reap agrestan stores,
He delves below, and Stygian gloom explores.
Metallic ores—earth's secret heart within—
He drags to light, provocatives to sin:
The noxious iron, more pernicious gold,
Parents of war and blood and deaths untold.
Man lived by rapine: thresholds lost their awe,
Nor safety gave to guest or son-in-law:
Fraternal love was rare, and murders rife
Through nuptial infidelity and strife:
The step-dame culled the lurid aconites.
The son conspired against parental rights:
Prostrate was piety."

Ovid's *Metamorphoses* (Rose's translation)

So crying grew the sins of mankind that Zeus saw well to destroy the rebellious race. He who might have tried the experiment of setting a better example, at first was minded to use his celestial artillery, but feared to set the heavens on fire as well as the earth: immortals living in such glass houses could not safely throw thunderbolts. So he sent a deluge that is curiously analogous to our Bible story. The fountains of the sky were opened by a strong south wind; the deep, too, was stirred to wrath by the trident of Poseidon, called to his brother's aid; all the earth became submerged, so that fish swam in the highest branches among the nests of birds, and the most savage beasts of prey in vain huddled together seeking flight from a common fate.

The few men who could escape that flood perished by famine, all but one dutiful pair, able to find refuge on the last spot of dry land at the head of Mount Parnassus. These were Deucalion, the son of Prometheus, and Pyrrha, the daughter of Epimetheus. When the waters subsided under a north wind, they descended upon the general wreck, and tearfully sought counsel at a ruined altar of Themis, Titan-daughter of Uranus and consort of Zeus. There a dark oracle bade them veil their faces, ungird their garments, and throw behind them the bones of their mother. The pious Pyrrha shrank from such sacrilege; but Deucalion rightly guessed the riddle as meaning the bones of their mother earth. Obeying the oracle, they threw stones behind them that, taking human form like statues, began to breathe with life, turned into men and women according as they came from the hand of Deucalion or of Pyrrha. So arose a new breed of humanity that, whatever its other qualities, had at least the virtue of hardness and endurance to bear its lot.

The race thus re-created spread over the *orbis terranum,* taken to be not a globe but a round flat, environed on all sides by the boundless river Oceanus, in which stars and sun had their birth or setting. This disk was divided lengthwise by the broken line of the Mediterranean continued into the Euxine, an idea of which we have some trace in our use of *latitude* and *longitude.* To the north of this chasm Greece was fringed by Illyrians, Thracians, and other semi-barbarous folk, shading off into wilder Scythians and Sarmatians, beyond whom lay dark-dwelling Cimmerians, and still farther the fabulous Hyperboreans were understood to enjoy perpetual sunshine and bliss given them by ignorance; or perhaps we have here a hint of some glimpse of the far northern summer with its midnight sun. Far to the south, the 'blameless' Ethiopians were credited with some similar immunities; hence, too, came vague reports of pygmies who in our time have taken shape of flesh and blood; the shores of Africa were inhabited by more familiar races, while impassable deserts and mountains naturally made homes for giants and monsters. Atlas bore up the world near the Straits of Gibraltar, where the end of all known land was marked by the Pillars of Hercules, beyond which indeed were caught dim glimpses of Gardens of the Hesperides and blessed Islands of Atlantis, perhaps not mere dreams if it is indeed true that the Phoenicians circumnavigated Africa two thousand years before the Portuguese mariners. The eastern walls of the world were the Caucasus and Taurus ranges, hiding dusky peoples brought to knowledge by the Persian invasions, then more clearly by the conquests of Alexander. The cloudy prospect of Herodotus, who makes no doubt of Europe being larger than Asia or Africa, is bounded to the east by the deserts of Scinde, to the west by the Cassiterides, 'tin islands', that seem the southern end of our own country. In that direction classic views became extended, till Pausanias could tell how on that shore of Ocean 'live the Iberians and the Celts, and in it is the Island of Britain' – *toto divisos orbe Britannos.*

At the centre of all stood Greece, a focus of light for the outer barbarians, to whom yet she owed her strength and the seeds of her culture. The boss of the universe was the Thessalian Olympus, on which dwelt the gods in palaces of cloud turned by fancy to:

> "golden houses, girdled with the gleaming world:
> Where they smile in secret, looking over wasted lands,
> Blight and famine, plague and earthquake, roaring deeps and fiery sands,
> Clanging fights, and flaming towns, and sinking ships, and praying hands".

Several mountains took the sacred name of Olympus, and poets soon began to make this a mere figure of speech, raising their gods' home into the skies, with the Milky Way as a highroad of approach. In Homer, Zeus threatens to hang up the earth and sea in the air by a rope fastened to the crest of such a cloudy Olympus.

Either openly or in disguise, the immortals were much in the way of visiting our earth, and interfering with its affairs, as often as not selfishly or capriciously. Certain spots were taken as specially favoured by their resort, or as *penetralia* for the revelation of their will in mysterious oracles. One of the oldest of the oracles was the dark grove of Dodona in Epirus, where the sighing of the wind could be interpreted as the voice of Zeus. The most famous and influential came to be that of Apollo at Delphi on the slopes of Parnassus, a spot looked on as the earth's navel, the reverence of which went far beyond Greece, and must have been hoarier than the Olympian myths. In this theatre of stern scenery, walled by stupendous precipices, a cleft in the ground emitted mephitic vapour, rising about the tripod of the priestess who, when excited by the fumes, was understood to speak the god's mind. As in the case of other prophecies, her utterances were apt to be obscure, if not worded to fit more than one meaning that would cover doubtful events. Enormous treasures were offered at the temple of Delphi; and the profitable working of the oracle seems to have fallen into the hands of a local priestly caste, who in the end destroyed its credit by interfering too manifestly in politics, with a bias towards Sparta as against Athens. Another noted oracle of Apollo was that at Didyma, on the Ionian coast. The cave of Trophonius in Boeotia was also celebrated as a mouthpiece of oracular utterance.

The fur trader Alexander Henry gives an elaborate account of a Red Indian pow-wowing scene which strikingly matches with what we know of the classic oracles. The American Indians of the French and English wartime also drew omens from the bones and entrails of animals, as did those ancients at their sacrifices. All over the world the flight of birds has been interpreted in signs of good or ill luck, a notion surviving among ourselves, so feebly, indeed, that the appearance of such or such a number of magpies bears a different omen in separate parts of the country. How strong this particular superstition was of old is shown by the word *augur*, originally a diviner by birds; and, while the art was more regularly organized by the Romans, the Greeks also looked on birds as messengers of the gods, or as ministers of divine justice. Prometheus was not the only sinner fabled to be tormented by a vulture.

The legend of the Cranes of Ibycus is similar to us through Schiller's ballad. The poet Ibycus, on his way to the Isthmian Games, was murdered by two robbers, in sight of a flock of cranes, to whom he commended the charge of vengeance. Sure enough, the unknown murderers sitting in the open theatre, the conscience of one was moved to exclaim, "The cranes of Ibycus!" as the vengeful birds came hovering over their heads; then he and his comrade, seized on suspicion, saw nothing for it but to confess their crime, and paid with their blood for that of the beloved poet.

> "Scarce had the wretch the words let fall,
> Than fain their sense he would recall.
> In vain; those whitening lips, behold!
> The secret have already told.
> Into their Judgment Court sublime
> The Scene is changed; – their doom is seal'd!
> Behold the dark unwitness'd Crime,
> Struck by the lightning that reveal'd!"

Marching to battle against Carthaginians, a Greek army was dismayed to meet mules loaded with a herb used to wreathe tombstones; but their leader turned off the omen by pointing out how the same plant made crowns for victors at the Isthmian Games; and confidence was fully established by the appearance of two eagles in the air. Not every hero was strong-minded enough, like Epaminondas when the sacrifices went against him, to quote Homer, that "there could be no better omen than to fight for one's country". Not every poet cared to copy the boldness of Euripides: "The best seer is he who makes a good guess". In the time of Socrates and Thucydides the Athenian attack on Syracuse was ruined by an eclipse of the moon, as the Spartans connected their naval defeat at Cnidus with an eclipse of the sun. From Thales to Alexander, indeed, eclipses are recorded as repeatedly influencing Greek history. A dream inspired Xenophon to take a lead among the retreating Ten Thousand. Lightning on the right might be hailed as a lucky omen, while thunder on the left uttered a warning. A people whose leaders and warriors were so easily moved by signs and wonders, would not neglect such active machinery of bane and blessing as charms, curses, amulets, and the like. In our time have been unearthed leaden figures pierced with nails, by which, ages ago, spiteful Hellenic hearts practised upon the lives of their long-forgotten enemies, even as George IV's unloved queen, in less earnest mood, worked an ancestral spell upon a wax image of her husband.

Keenly as the Greek enjoyed the beauty and sunlight of life, his thoughts were much on death. Beneath the exultation of the paean and the rapture of the dithyrambic chorus, we catch, in recurrent undertone, the "still, sad music of humanity". The poets, who for him took the place of a priestly caste such as dominated Oriental minds, are seldom without a vein of melancholy moralizing, and do not shrink from straining their eyes into the darkness beyond the grave. The kingdom of the shades made a congenial scene for myths. Any gloomy cave or volcanic chasm seemed fit to be an entrance of the fearsome underworld to which man must come, for all his shuddering. In famous legends were explored the incoherent horrors of Hades, and its lower deep, Tartarus. Round this region coiled the black Styx, over which the souls were ferried by Charon to enter the gates guarded by Cerberus; and within flowed Phlegethon river of fire, Cocytus swollen with salt tears, and the black flood of Acheron, both real streams whose scenery suggested a dreary Inferno. In Tartarus certain noted evil-doers were described as bearing ingeniously protracted torments, while other unhappy souls suffered rather through misfortune than for crime. But for the common dead Hades made no place of active punishment: their sad lot was the privation of light and joy and all of life but a shadowy form keeping consciousness enough to know what it had lost. Then as now, man had his commonplaces of consolation; but when the Greek spoke out his mind, he would agree with the ghost of Achilles in the sentiment which Matthew Arnold transfers to the Balder of Northern Mythology.

> "Gild me not my death!
> Better to live a serf, a captured man,
> Who scatters rushes in his master's hall,
> Than be a crowned king here and rule the dead."

That the soul, unless stained by extraordinary guilt, had as little to fear as to hope in the homes of the dead, is shown by the obol placed in the mouth of each corpse as passage-money for Charon, without which he left the ghost wandering miserably on the farther side for a hundred years. Within the realm of shades the brightest spot was the weird garden of its queen—

> "No growth of moor or coppice,
> No heather-flower or vine,
> But bloomless buds of poppies,
> Green grapes of Proserpine,
> pale beds of blowing rushes,
> Where no leaf blooms or blushes
> Save this whereout she crushes
> For dead men deadly wine".

For exceptionally favoured heroes, Homer has a glimpse of some dim Elysian asylum far set in the western seas, a scene copied by Tennyson in his island valley of Avilion:

> "Where falls not hail, or rain, or any snow,
> Nor ever wind blows loudly, but it lies,
> Deep-meadowed, happy, fair with orchard lawns,
> And bowery hollows crowned with summer sea".

Later poets improved upon this vague hint; and Hades itself was furnished with a dark and a light side. There stood out of the shade three stern judges, Minos, Rhadamanthus, and Aeacus, distinguished for their justice on earth, before whom the trembling souls were led by Hermes to receive sentence according to their deeds.

Those who had done evil were scourged by the Furies to their appointed torment; but the good passed into blissful Elysian fields, where the joys of life lived again for them, and the water of Lethe blessed them with forgetfulness. Fame, indeed, rather than virtue appears as the title to a heavenly heritage, till philosophers like Plato made conscience the tormenting vulture and saw souls brought before those judges branded with the damning record of their sins; then laughing Lucian reports the tyrant Megapenthes sentenced by Rhadamanthus to go without the blessed draught of Lethe that he might be punished with memory of his past life. Such conceptions came to be complicated by the Pythagorean idea of transmigration of souls, as by vague hopes engendered in dreams of poetic prophecy and raptures of mystical initiation; but, unless for choice spirits, any prospect of a heavenly home would be dim and flickering in ages unwilling to look steadily through the gates of death.

How feebly the natural man pictures an abiding city for his soul, is shown by the importance the Greeks put on the body being laid to rest by funeral rites, without which the dead might wander disconsolate, exiled even from a home in Hades. In the wars that distracted their states, the victors would commonly let the vanquished bury their dead. The strange cruelty of Creon in forbidding the burial of Polyneices called forth the displeasure of gods and men; another case marked as exceptional is the insolence of Achilles upon Hector's body. In the Gaulish invaders who came to found Galatia, nothing seemed more barbarous than their carelessness as to what became of their slain comrades. The Greek practice varied between inhumation and cremation; the latter, as ensuring the body from outrage, apparently preferable, till Christian ideas of resurrection quenched the funeral pyre. Both forms of burial might be elaborately carried out for such a hero as Patroclus; but in cases of haste or necessity a mere sprinkling with dust, as in the story of Antigone, could seem enough to satisfy religious sentiment. Homer and other authorities have hints of an ancient custom of embalment in honey or oil.

As in other parts of the world, the rich and powerful might try to hoard up their memory in imposing tombs, like that famed *Mausoleum* erected for Mausolus of Caria; but the comparative want of slave labour in Greece and the democratic sentiment that, under one form or another, soon mastered its famous states, made such monuments less costly than those of the Asian and African kingdoms, while popular devotion and artistic skill filled this land with stately temples, palaces for the many deities, native or imported, crowding the Pantheon of its faith.

⚜

The Pantheon

In what might be called the Augustan age of Olympus, its dynastic founders had fallen into a shadowy background; and the divine family stood out in a new generation of dominant forms, shaped partly by differentiation of function and attributes, partly by accretion of kindred superstitions. The poets recognize twelve great gods and goddesses – sixteen is a fuller tale sometimes put forward – bearing over man and nature a rule limited by their own feuds, also now and then by a Fate mistily conceived as lord of all life, human or supernatural. Here follows a list of these divine personages, with some outline of their character and conduct, showing plainly how far man has since advanced in his religious ideas. Within brackets is given the, to us, more familiar name of the Latin deity, who, it must be remembered, had often undergone modification in the country of his adoption, or may have been originally a different personage adapted through the influence of that vassal that led the mind of its conqueror captive. But while Greek was long almost a dead letter to medieval Europe, the Roman poets supplied their mythological names to point the morals and adorn the tales of clerical scholarship that handed on the dimmed lamp of learning through the dark ages.

Zeus (Jupiter, Jove) was the king of earth and air, and overlord of Olympus, yet himself not wholly free from the power of what must be. He figures as a magnificent form, curled and bearded, sometimes crowned with oak leaves, holding in his hands the thunderbolts with which he scourged impiety. The 'Thunderer' made one of his most familiar epithets; and Mr J C Lawson tells us how in modern Greece – where Artemis has become St Artemidos and St Elias seems to have supplanted Helios the Christian God is still conceived of as aiming celestial artillery. An eagle attends him as minister of his will, and for page or cup-bearer he has Ganymede, a boy so beautiful that Zeus grudged him to mankind, and by the agency of his eagle had him stolen from Mount Ida to make him immortal in heaven. The serpent is an apt symbol going with any god, and not wanting to Zeus.

Besides Hera, his recognized sultana, the father of gods and men had half a dozen other immortal consorts, Metis, Themis, Eurynome, Demeter, Mnemosyne, and Leto. This family did not hinder him from seeking secret brides on earth, to whom he was in the way of appearing transformed into a satyr, a bull, a swan, a shower of gold, and so forth: with sly humour Lucian makes

Zeus (Jupiter)

From a sculpture

the god complain that women never love him for himself but always in some unworthy disguise. Of one of his illicit loves, Semele, daughter of Cadmus, it is told that she, prompted by Hera's jealousy, desired to see her lover in all his Olympian majesty, and was burned up by the awful glow of that revelation. Another mortal maiden hardly treated was Callisto, turned into a bear, and in that shape hunted down by her mistress Artemis at the instigation of jealous Hera; then all the Olympian seducer could do for his victim was to place her and her son among the stars as the Great and the Little Bear.

The god's visits to earth, indeed, are sometimes on errands of justice or enquiry. A pleasing story is that of Philemon and Baucis, the Phrygian Darby and Joan who entertained him as an unknown stranger in their humble home, and by divine gratitude were warned to fly from the wrath about to come on their impious neighbours. Moreover, this worthy pair, invited to choose a boon, asked nothing better than to end their days together after spending them as ministers in the temple to which their hospitable cot was transformed. More awful was the example of Lycaon's fate, that cruel and unbelieving king of Arcadia who, to test his guest's divinity, placed before Zeus a dish of human flesh, and for such impiety was turned into a wolf, his family being exterminated by lightning, as seemed not unfair to early moralists. Another victim of divine justice was Salmoneus, the overweening king of Elis, who had sacrifices offered to him as a god, and even haloed himself with artificial thunders and lightnings, amid which a veritable bolt from heaven scorched up this ape of divinity with his city and all its people.

To common men, Zeus was represented by many statues, the noblest of them the work of Phidias, which, forty feet high, in gold and ivory, passed for one of the Seven Wonders of the ancient world, and was hailed by the Roman conqueror, Aemilius Paulus, as "the very Jove of Homer". This adorned the rich temple at Olympia that became chief seat of the god's worship, while Dodona, as already mentioned, seems his oldest oracle. Another famous oracle was that of Jupiter-Ammon in the sands of Libya; under this title Zeus seems to have been fused with an Egyptian deity and is figured with horns. But indeed his epithets and attributes are innumerable. The Roman Jove, who bore a more solemn character than his Greek fellow-despot, was reverenced as Jupiter Optimus Maximus, his chief shrine being a temple on the Capitoline Hill, the St Peter's of pagan Rome.

Hera (Juno) was the legitimate queen of Olympus, who by all accounts led her husband a troubled life of it, through the jealousy for which he gave her but too much cause. Her other leading characteristics were a pride that kept her austerely virtuous, and a self-satisfaction that, when infused with anger, too often soured to vindictive hate; and always she proved quick to take offence at any slight on the part of gods or men. Her special handmaid was Iris, the rainbow, that carried her messages to earth; and her daughter Hebe served with Ganymede as cup-bearer at the celestial table. Another attendant came to be the peacock, when that gorgeous bird was brought as a novelty to Greece. The cuckoo was also a pet of hers.

The story goes that when Zeus courted Io, daughter of Inachus king of Argos, and transformed her into a white cow, the watchful Hera sought to foil her consort's intrigues by placing the animal under guard of the monster Argus, who had a hundred eyes, no more than two of them closed at a time. Zeus, on his side, employed Hermes to lull all the eyes of Argus to sleep with the spell of his Lyre, and then to slay him; and in memorial of his ineffective service, Hera placed his hundred eyes on the tail of a bird that made an emblem of her own pride. Also she sent a gadfly to drive the unfortunate Io through the world, wandering like the horned moon, till at last that persecuted maiden found rest in Egypt, where she bore a son who was the founder of Memphis. This myth is typical of the punishments often inflicted by a so impeccable and implacable goddess upon frail mortals.

A prettier story than most of those told of her makes an old priestess drawn to Hera's temple by her two sons, Cleobis and Biton, since befitting white heifers could not be found to yoke in the car; then the mother was so touched by their filial service that she prayed her patron goddess to grant them the greatest boon of heaven, and on coming out of the temple found them dead where they had lain down to sleep off their fatigue. On this fable of Herodotus, Addison in the S*pectator* rather cynically remarks that had their death followed an act of disobedience, the moral would have been reversed.

The 'ox-eyed Hera' is Homer's well-worn epithet to denote the calmly imperial looks attributed to the queen of heaven. She was worshipped specially at Argos, at Samos, and in a temple at Olympia, older than that of Zeus. The Roman Juno takes a more matronly form, and appears rather as the protector of married life than as the spiteful chastiser of illicit love.

Apollo – with Phoebus prominent among his many *aliases* – was the most beautiful and the most beloved of the Olympians, close kinsman to that radiant sun god who shines out in so many mythologies. Beside his sister Selene, the moon, he figures openly as Helios, the sun, with the by-name of Hyperion under which Hamlet contrasts him with a satyr. He was the son of Zeus and Leto (Latona), who, driven to Delos by the jealousy of Hera, there brought him forth with his twin sister Artemis, so that this island became their favoured sanctuary. The mother being still persecuted by jealous Juno, Apollo was reared by Themis so thrivingly that at the first taste of nectar and ambrosia he burst his swaddling clothes and stood forth a full-grown youth, demanding the lyre and the silver bow with which he is usually represented. His first great exploit was slaying the huge serpent Python, where afterwards arose the Delphic oracle; and he became peculiarly the god of prophecy, as, in a manner, the voice of heaven upon earth. He was also the source of life and healing, an attribute specially manifested in his son. Aesculapius, father of the medical profession, who was, indeed, slain by Zeus for presuming to restore the dead to life; but he handed down his science and practice to his daughter Hygeia The number of temples that came to honour Aesculapius, hints how this useful divinity was a double or deputy of the sun god in his healing power.

Yet where the benignant sun burns fiercely at times, 'far-darting' Apollo could hurt as well as heal, and his arrows might kindle pestilence, as in the camp of the Greeks before Troy. His chariot might be drawn by lions as well as by swans. He had a charge of flocks and herds, and generally of civilizing arts. But his chief renown was as the patron of song and music, hailed by the stirring chant of the paean. Orpheus was his son; and for attendants he had the nine Muses: *Clio* (history), *Euterpe* (lyric poetry), *Thalia* (comedy), *Melpomene* (tragedy), *Terpsichore* (dance and song), *Erato* (love song), *Polymnia* (sublime hymn), *Urania* (astronomy), *Calliope* (epic poetry). The favourite haunts of this choir were Mount Helicon and Mount Parnassus with its Castalian spring, in which so many poets have sought to bathe; and few bards of ancient or modern times fail to invoke Phoebus as their patron spirit.

Pindar tells how, in his character of *Hyperion* (the Sun), Apollo happened to be out of the way when the gods were dividing the earth by lot, and, thus left portionless, he asked of Zeus the volcanic Rhodes, which he foresaw would rise from the waves. So this island of roses became his special sanctuary, renowned by its Colossus, a brazen image of him, a hundred feet or so high, another wonder of the ancient world, overthrown by one of the earthquakes that have worked havoc here with later monuments. He had other local phases, like that *Smintheus* of the Troad, who seems to have been a mouse-god, the propitiation of destructive rodents flourishing here as among the Philistines.

The sculptors, for whom this comely god made a favourite model, usually show him as a naked form in the bloom of noble and graceful manhood, crowned with laurel, like the famous Apollo Belvidere statue of the Vatican. 'Ever young and fair'; Apollo seems to reflect the brightest side of Greek religion, and by his fine humanity to come closest in touch with its cultured worshippers. He had strongly marked traits of human nature, both good and bad. Celebrated was his affection for the fair boy Hyacinthus, whom he accidentally killed with a quoit as they played together, then as monument of him caused a blue flower to spring from his blood. Not less renowned was Apollo's love for the celibate nymph Daphne, who fled from him in vain, but was saved from his embrace by being turned into a laurel, to which the baffled god gave evergreen leaves. The gods seldom show to advantage in their love for mortal maidens, and this one was apt to treat his sweethearts too cavalierly, as in the case of Coronis, mother of Aesculapius, whom he slew on a report of her perfidy brought by a crow – originally a white bird, but now turned black as a punishment for scandal-mongering. Apollo was not only human but savage when he flayed Marsyas alive for presuming to compete with him in music. And his most unworthy exploit was joining his sister Artemis in the cruel revenge they took on Niobe by cutting off her whole flock of too loudly boasted darlings. But, on the whole, he appears in the beneficent character hymned by Shelley:—

> "I feed the clouds, the rainbows and the flowers
> With their ethereal colours; the Moon's globe,
> And the pure stars in their eternal bowers
> Are cinctured with my power as with a robe;
> Whatever lamps on Earth or Heaven may shine,
> Are portions of one power, which is mine.
>
> "I stand at noon upon the peaks of Heaven,
> Then with unwilling steps I wander down
> Into the clouds of the Atlantic even;
> For grief that I depart they weep and frown:
> What look is more delightful than the smile
> With which I soothe them from the western isle?
>
> "I am the eye with which the Universe
> Beholds itself and knows itself divine;
> All harmony of instrument or verse,
> All prophecy, all medicine are mine,
> All light of art or nature; – to my song
> Victory and praise in their own right belong."

Artemis (Diana), Apollo's twin sister, like himself, drew into her name the character of several foreign deities, one of them that renowned Diana of the Ephesians, whose temple ranked among the Seven Wonders. Her name was also given to the cruel goddess of Tauris, a congenial guest at Sparta, where the hardy lads scourged even to death before her altar look to be a softened form of human sacrifice. The native Arcadian Artemis, again, was a goddess of hunting and wild life, who went kirtled to the knee on wooded mountains, followed by nymphs of like tastes. She was chaste to a fault, as would appear from the stories about her victims; and her fatal jealousy would be most easily aroused not by love but by presumption on the part of mortals. Actaeon, who accidentally came upon her bathing, was turned into a stag to be torn in pieces by his own hounds. There is, indeed, some hint of tender passages between her and the giant hunter Orion; but varying stories of his fate make him the mark of her vengeful arrows; then he was set in heaven as a constellation along with the Pleiades, seven daughters of Atlas, her favourite attendants, whom this hunter had tried to pursue. A softer side to Artemis appears in her identification with the moon, in which character she let her coldness grow warm for the beautiful youth Endymion, kissed by her to sleep on Mount Latmus, to whom Zeus allowed a choice between death and perpetual youth in dreamy slumber, guarded by the enamoured goddess.

> "As I seemed to gaze on her,
> Nearer she drew and gazed; and as I lay
> Supine, beneath her spell, the radiance stooped,
> And kissed me on the lips, a chaste, sweet kiss
> Which drew my spirit with it. So I slept
> Each night upon the hill, until the Dawn
> Came in his golden chariot from the East,
> And chased my love away."
>
> —Lewis Morris

Athena (Minerva) was another virgin goddess, whose cognomen Pallas may have been derived from an Athenian hero of that name, while her chief Greek title shows her specially at home in the city that honoured her with the renowned Parthenon. The orthodox story about Athena's birth was that she sprang full grown and full-armed from the head of her father Zeus. She is often represented in armour, with helmet, breastplate, and shield, and so has passed for the goddess of war; but rather she fostered the patriotic defence without which civilization were fruitless, her true spirit being for invention, the care of the arts and crafts, and woman's handiwork especially. Justice and order grew up under her aegis, so that she was the protectress of cities. As to her particular regard for Athens, it is told that Poseidon being her rival for the place of its godfather, a council of the gods settled that honour on whichever should offer the most welcome gift to man. Poseidon struck the earth with his trident to call forth the horse, then Athena produced the olive, preferred as an emblem of peace and plenty, and bearing a quasi-sacred esteem in ancient Greece, as shown by the use of its wood for funeral pyres and of its leaves for crowns of honour.

The animals sacred to her were the serpent, the cock, and the owl, hence the proverb 'owls to Athens', translatable by our 'coals to Newcastle', a phrase that may have been prompted by the owl stamped on Athenian coins. She was grave, austere, dignified, and as a rule beneficent, free from the scandals fixed on other goddesses; even wanton Cupid stood in awe of this virgin governess. Once indeed she lost her temper with Arachne, the Lydian spinster who presumed to vie with her; and she appears in a ridiculous light when, on her invention of the flute, she set Olympus laughing by the queer faces she made in playing it. But she seldom showed feminine weaknesses; and her martial figure had masculine outlines. She plays the hero in Homer's battles, from which other intervening goddesses fly in tearful dismay at their first taste of bloodshed. The Roman Minerva rather emphasized her patronage of letters, when a poet's verse could not hope to flow smoothly *invitâ Minervâ*.

Aphrodite (Venus), the goddess of love, was a daughter of Zeus according to one story, but an older myth makes her spring from the sea in the cataclysm that followed the overthrow of Uranus. Her name, 'foam-born', bears out such an origin; and the fact of Paphos on Cyprus, Cythera, and other islands passing as her favourite homes, hints how she came across the Aegean, being no other than the lustful Astarte that scandalized the Hebraic conscience. To Greece she came dowered with soft charms, in a chariot drawn by doves or swans, adorned with flowers and fruit, and having as her special ornament the cestus or girdle, the loan of which was enough to inspire love, as when Hera borrowed it to enhance her charms in wheedling Zeus out of a favourable disposition towards the hated Trojans.

At first Aphrodite appears well dressed as becomes a matron; but soon her form made an excuse for sculptors and artists to display their mastery of the nude, in countless famous pictures and in statues like those known as the Venus of Milo and the Venus de Medici.

In song and story, too, the goddess of charms and caprice was bound to be familiar. The tritest tale of her loves, handled by Shakespeare, has Adonis for its hero, the beautiful youth incarnating, like Persephone, a myth of the alternation of growth and decay. For his sake Aphrodite abandoned heaven, and took to the woods like Artemis, where, instead of nerving the boy to hardy deeds, she would have had him hunt only such harmless animals as are the quarry of our noble sportsmen. But Adonis, not yet tangled in the wiles of love, was unwilling to toy in the shade with this fair charmer, and tore himself from her embraces to en-counter a boar by which he was wounded to death. So moving was the grief of the goddess that Hades yielded up her darling to pass half the year with her above-ground. Another form of this poetical conception of the seasons makes Adonis an orphan placed under charge of Persephone, who grew too fond of him to let him go, till Zeus compromised the dispute by decreeing that he should spend four months with the queen of Hades, four with Aphrodite, and four at his own will, barren winter being left out of account in this view of earth's recurrent life. The same notion occurs in the myth of Persephone herself, one variant of which divides her presence between three seasons, while another regards only the successive change of summer and winter.

Cupid, the Greek Eros, best known by his Latin name, who plays such pranks in myth, must have been born to Venus somewhat late in life; and still later she has about her in art a whole brood of such tricksy sprites. The original *Eros* was a more serious personage, who appears to have grown backwards into a fat and foolish boyhood. We find Love styled now the oldest, again the youngest of the gods. It is not very clear how Cupid came into the family; but poets as well as artists soon made much of this wanton imp, naked and winged, his eyes sometimes blindfolded, with his torch to kindle hearts, and the arrows he shoots in careless mischief, some tipped with gold to quicken, some with lead to palsy the pulse of love. The most famous story about him, that of Cupid and Psyche, is not found before Apuleius in the second century of our era, but no doubt came from ruder myths the doings ascribed to Cupid, that are of course much older than Hesiod or Homer. Eros had a less famous brother, *Anteros,* conceived as the avenger of slighted love.

A more staid attendant of Aphrodite was *Hymen,* who with his torch would lead the nuptial chorus. For handmaidens she had the naked Graces, *Euphrosyne, Aglaia,* and *Thalia,* daughters of Zeus, their Greek title *Charis* sometimes appearing identified with the goddess herself, who passed through a gamut of phases from the meretricious mistress of sensual pleasure to the august mother of all life. Her official husband was Hephaestus; but it seemed natural she should play this sooty clown false in her favour to other Olympians. The Latin Venus, originally of more humble rank, became exalted as mother of Aeneas, when Roman poets transfigured him into a national ancestor. And Plato reminds how there were two conceptions of the Greek Aphrodite, the Uranian who represents the purer spirit of Love, and the Pandemian, daughter of Zeus and the Titan Dione, who was more manifest to vulgar natures.

Demeter (Ceres) was the daughter of Cronos by Rhea, through whom she inherited the misty awe of Gaea, the earth, oldest of deities, that mother-spirit wedded by the invading sky-god. She figures most famously in the myth of her beloved daughter *Persephone* (Proserpine), known also as *Coré* ('the maiden'), who

> "Gathering flowers,
> Herself a fairer flower, by gloomy Dis
> Was gathered".

'That fair field of Enna' was in Sicily, recommended by its fertility as a favourite haunt of Demeter; but the scene of the rape of Proserpine is also put in Asia. Mother and daughter were highly honoured in Greece, especially at the Eleusinian Mysteries associated with Demeter's worship, which came to be the holiest rites of Greek religion, guessed at as a survival of its primitive awe developed into some mystic hope of immortality. This goddess of ancient date appeared one of the most beneficent, by her evident gift of growth, and by the agricultural arts she was fabled to have communicated to man through her nursling Triptolemus, who also gave the world a triple law called by his name: To honour parents; to reverence the gods with sacrifices of their boons; not to harm man nor beast. As inventor, or introducer, of the plough, he stands for father of civilization; so Scott was humorously reflecting a classic idea when he christened the unwelcome improver of Shetland farming by the name of Triptolemus Yellowley.

Hestia (Vesta), though named among the great gods, does not much appear in their intrigues, being modest and domesticated, as became her office of cherishing the family hearth. Yet her maidenhood implied no want of charm, if it be true that she was wooed in vain by Apollo and by Poseidon. She was probably akin to the deity still worshipped by the descendants of Persian fire-worshippers, who look on fire as so sacred that a Europeanized Parsee lights his first cigarette with a sense of doing something daringly profane. In the Prytaneum, or town hall of Greek cities, a public hearth was kept burning, from which emigrants carried sacred fire to be the seed of their colony's religion. The Roman Vesta seems a more conspicuous goddess, of great antiquity, well known to us through the Vestal Virgins bound, under severe penalties, to keep her fire burning and their lives as pure as that of their mistress.

Hephaestus (Vulcan) was the god of fire in its industrial applications, the Tubal-Cain of the classic world. Some accounts make him spring from Hera in a non natural manner, to match her husband's prodigious production of Minerva; but hers proved not a success, as the boy was born lame and so puny that she threw him out of heaven, to be reared by sea nymphs in a submarine grotto. Another story is that when Zeus chastised his nagging wife by hanging her from Olympus, her heels weighted with a pair of anvils, Hephaestus took his mother's part and was hurled down, to fall nine days – or only 'from morn to dewy eve' – till he came on the island of Lemnos with a broken leg; but he returned to heaven to reconcile the quarrelsome couple. There is also difference of testimony as to his marriage: various beautiful brides are ascribed to him, among them Venus herself, as if in mockery. For this lame and ugly fellow played the low comedian of Olympus, at whose hobbling gait the more elegant gods burst into unextinguishable laughter. Rough and begrimed as he was, there could be no question as to his usefulness. The palaces and jewels of Olympus were his handiwork, not to speak of the thunderbolts, as well as cunning devices like the net in which he caught Ares dallying with his faithless spouse, and for once turned the laugh on his side. For the heroes of myth he made such masterpieces as the shield of Hercules, the armour of Achilles, and the sceptre of Agamemnon. His workshops naturally came to be placed in volcanic islands, where the Cyclopes acted as his journeymen, the idea of them perhaps taken from craters, each with its burning eye. So Virgil places Vulcan's forge off the coast of Sicily, with the Aetnean fires as furnace:—

> "On their eternal anvils here he found
> The brethren beating, and the blows go round:

A load of pointless thunder now there lies
Before their hands, to ripen for the skies:
These darts, for angry love, they daily cast—
Consum'd on mortals with prodigious waste.
Three rays of writhen rain, of fire three more,
Of winged southern winds and cloudy store
As many parts, the dreadful mixture frame;
And fears are added, and avenging flame.
Inferior ministers, for Mars, repair
His broken axle-trees and blunted war,
And send him forth again with furbish'd arms,
To wake the lazy war, with trumpets' loud alarms.
The rest refresh the scaly snakes that fold
The shield of Pallas, and renew their gold.
Full on the crest the Gorgon's head they place
With eyes that roll in death and with distorted face."

—John Dryden

Ares (Mars), son of Zeus and Hera, was the god of war, apt to be at strife with his austere rival in that capacity, Athena, and indeed with all his Olympian kinsmen, among whom he gave his brother Hephaestus good cause for jealousy. In Greek mythology this blustering athlete cuts no noble figure, being beaten by Heracles and other earthly heroes, and showing something of the savage sullenness and stupidity that come natural to legendary giants. Even his father had a poor opinion of him, to judge by Homer's report of his reception in Olympus when he came complaining of his hurts got by meddling in the battle before Troy.

"Of all the gods who tread the spangled skies,
Thou most unjust, most odious in our eyes!
Inhuman discord is thy dire delight,
The lust of slaughter and the rage of fight;
No bound, no law thy fiery temper quells,
And all thy mother in thy soul rebels".

Mars rose to a loftier position at Rome, where, as father of Romulus and Remus, he took the same protecting part as Athena at Athens. But the Campus Martius of Rome was matched by the Areopagus of Athens, fabled to be so called because there the gods held a court to settle a dispute between Ares and Poseidon. At Sparta he would be made much of: it was there Pausanias found an image of him in fetters to prevent the god from deserting this martial state. In Italy he had for comrades *Quirinus,* a deification of Romulus, and *Bellona,* who seems to have been a native goddess adopted by the Romans; and in Greece, too, Eris, 'Strife', was his twin sister, while Terror and Fear were his sons.

Hermes (Mercury) was another son of Zeus, by Maia, the eldest of the Pleiades. His special function was as messenger and herald of the gods, in which capacity he is represented as a handsome and agile youth, with winged sandals and a broad-brimmed hat also winged, bearing the *caduceus,* a staff wreathed with serpents, which he got from Apollo under singular circumstances. No sooner was Hermes born than he took to stealing, and set out on a raid against cattle belonging to his brother Apollo. Among the precocious babe's adventures on this sally was the finding of a tortoise and turning its shell into the seven-stringed lyre. Having stolen fifty oxen, he stoutly denied the theft, and Maia stood up for her sleeping infant's innocence, till Zeus brought the truth to light; then Apollo was so delighted with the tortoise-shell lyre, that he not only pardoned his knavish little brother, but in return for that invention gave him a wand of magic power. Autolycus, the cunning robber of Mount Parnassus, might well be called his natural son.

Hermes came to be looked on as the god of herds, also of commerce and of theft, a pluralism of functions natural enough when cattle made the standard of value, as shown in the history of our word *pecuniary.* He was moreover the guardian of roads, of gymnastic exercises, of clever inventions, such as the alphabet attributed to him; of eloquence, and of games of chance; in short he appears a god of all work, who amused his leisure hours by playing sly tricks on his fellow denizens of Olympus, as when he stole the trident of Poseidon, the girdle of Aphrodite, and the arrows of Artemis; yet for all his mischievousness he appears a favourite in the family, and his father's chosen henchman in his excursions on earth. Of his own dealings with mortals, one is moralized by Ovid in the story of his love for Herse, daughter of Cecrops, whose sister Agraulos offered to betray her for a large bribe. But when Hermes came back with the money, Athena had punished Agraulos by setting the fiend Envy to poison her heart, so that she now stood out against letting the god pass to her sister's chamber, till he turned her into a black stone.

The most dignified office of Hermes was conducting the shades of the dead to the world below. The Roman Mercury seems originally to have been a patron of trade, his name connected with *merx*; but he took on the lighthearted and slippery ways of the Greek god, that have given an *alias* to the metal quicksilver. His most famous statue seems to have been that by Praxiteles, found in a mutilated state at Olympia. Small images of Hermes were very common in Greek life, set up on roadways and at the gates of houses, their faces sometimes painted black and white to symbolize the offices of the god above and below ground, and often perhaps mere fetish blocks such as that on which Lucian tried his prentice hand as a carver with sore result.

Poseidon (Neptune) should have been introduced earlier, as one of the oldest of the gods, brother of Zeus, against whom he sometimes ventured to rebel, but as a rule rested content with his satrapy of the sea, under which he had a marvellous golden palace, its grottos adorned with corals and sea-flowers, and lit with phosphorescent glow. Rejected as patron of Athens, in favour of his accomplished niece, he was understood to have a special regard for the Isthmus of Corinth, that focus of navigation from east and west. His sceptre was the trident fishing-spear of the Mediterranean; and he rode forth in a chariot drawn by dolphins, sea-horses, or other marine monsters. Horses came into his province as well as waves, an idea not far to seek in the comparison of leaping and rearing billows that has occurred to many a poet. Naturally, he had his moods, in some of which he could be very terrible to maritime mortals, for, besides storms, he raised disastrous floods and devouring monsters of plague and famine. His wife was the sea nymph *Amphitrite,* who still accompanies him on our crossing-the-line mummeries. By her he had *Triton* and other sons; but he would not have been a right god without giving her cause for jealousy, as against that unfortunate Scylla whom she got turned into a six-headed bugbear haunting the straits of Sicily, a caverned whirlpool opposite the rock Charybdis, into which a daughter of Poseidon had been transformed by angry Zeus. These perils, not now so apparent to sailors, were noted in the proverb, *Incidit in Scyllam qui vult vitare Charybdin.*

The powers of water take changing shapes, like that *Proteus,* son of Poseidon, who, guarding his herd of seals, had to be caught and held fast before he would give forth his oracles. He might be confused with *Nereus,* a benevolent Old Man of the Sea, who presided over calm weather, and with his fifty daughters the *Nereides,* was ready to help friendly mariners. *Oceanus* was an older god, son of Uranus, with an enormous family of Oceanides, among them the *Electra,* whose tears were drops of amber, through which her name passed to that force that has been so heavily enslaved by modern science. *Glaucus* seems a later deity, immortalized against his will by falling into the sea. The eldest son of Oceanus was *achelous,* guardian of the largest Greek river, and rival of Heracles for Deianira; he had some thousands of brothers, himself the most famous among a large family of river gods. *Thetis,* mother of Achilles, was daughter of one of those slippery beings, whom Peleus won by being able to hold her elusive form; then, *Eris* (Strife), not invited to their marriage, played the part of the wicked witch in our fairy tales, as appears in the Tale of Troy. But Thetis is connected with a legend of peace. She it was that, when Halcyone threw herself into the sea after her shipwrecked husband Ceyx, changed them both into the birds whose nest was taken to float upon the sea in the calm of 'halcyon days'.

Pluto, not having his seat on Olympus, hardly appears among the twelve great gods, large as this grim lord of the underworld must have loomed before superstitious minds. The name of *Hades* he shares with his realm; and *Dis* is another *alias* that at first seems to have belonged to Zeus. Another title of both realm and ruler, *Ortus,* is still very active in Italian folklore. The most dreadful of the gods was conceived as a dark-browed form, seated on an ebony throne, or driving in a chariot drawn by coal-black steeds; he brandishes a two pronged spear; and among his possessions is a helmet that has the property to cast a spell of invisibility. Sacrifices to him were offered at dead of night, the blood of victims being allowed to run into trenches from which it might trickle down to his underground palace. The one bright spot in his life was his love for *Persephone,* whom he carried off to share his gloomy throne. But this fair form became infected by the spirit of the dark abode in which she must dwell half the year, so that in a shadowy manner she seems to pass into the fearsome form of *Hecate,* the goddess of witchcraft and other weird doings that haunts crossroads or lonely scenes of murder. Such an ugly shade, indeed, appears to flicker as cast either by Artemis or by Persephone, while it is as 'handmaid' to the latter that Hecate appears in a so-called Homeric hymn.

Dionysus (Bacchus) was a god who came to Greece with the culture of the vine, and brought along with him eastern orgies that had their religious side. Son of Zeus by Semele, he was ever youthful, handsome and effeminate, clad in a panther skin, crowned with vine leaves and grape bunches round which his locks curled like tendrils, carrying as his sceptre the *thyrsus,* a wand wreathed with ivy or other vines; and his invocation was the excited dithyramb, contrasting with the sublime paean of Apollo Drama began with the choruses that celebrated his festival at Athens. The Dionysia, transported into Italy as Bacchanalia, were the Carnival days of the ancient world, when the Saturnalia of Rome gave a hint for our Christmas revelry. Bacchus had travelled far and wide, a long visit to India being one of his wanderings, on which he may have picked up the tigers, lynxes, or panthers that drew his chariot. His favourite attendants were goat-footed Satyrs, headed by the purple-faced Silenus, who made a disreputable boon companion. Also he led about a rout of wild women, who, as will be when women take to drink, were given to fits of scandalous excitement. These Maenads, Bacchants, or whatever they might be called, danced along intoxicated with a rabid frenzy that did not stick at the blood of any coldly prudent man who shunned their noisy enthusiasm. So it was with Pentheus, king of Thebes, who was for sternly putting down this exotic worship; but when he thought to spy on its rites in secret, the god beguiled him into shameful disguise as a woman; then his own mother headed the crew that pulled him from the tree in which he had ensconced himself, and tore him to pieces in their madness. Another king, Lycurgus of Thrace, who would have restrained such inspired excesses, was punished by being driven mad himself.

An amusing story is that of the pirates, who caught Dionysus and would have sold him as a slave; only their prudent steersman, guessing this to be a god, warned his comrades what might come of such impiety. Sure enough, the prisoner easily broke from their fetters, the ship's masts bloomed out in vines and ivy wreaths, the sails dripped perfumed wine, and all around rang the music of an invisible choir. By such prodigies the sailors' eyes were opened too late: their captive took the shape of a lion, backed by a bear that began by tearing the captain; then the rest jumped overboard to be changed into dolphins, all but that considerate steersman, who at the god's request set him ashore at Naxos, where he had his celebrated meeting with Ariadne. A rare hint of temperance principles appears in the legend of Icarius, an Athenian who entertained this strange god, and being taught in return the power of the grape, was beaten to death by his ungrateful neighbours, who took their first experience of intoxication to be no better than poisonous; then his daughter Erigone, led to his grave by the dog Maera, hung herself above it for grief, and as reward of her filial piety, she along with her father and the faithful dog were placed as stars in the Great Bear constellation.

Bacchus, like Cupid, belonged to a later generation of gods, their nature, indeed, in general so fissiparous that they had much power of adding to their numbers, while they were liable to a confusion of character and a multiplication of names. Zeus and the rest came to be regarded under a variety of attributes and epithets, which make them almost different personages in local worship. In the Greek world, confusion was confounded by the importation of avowed foreign deities like Isis and Serapis, till irreverent Lucian could represent the old gods as seriously disturbed through the intrusion of parvenu strangers, crowding Olympus with a mob of all nations and languages, so that nectar and ambrosia are like to run short. To abate this scandal, the satirist suggests a celestial committee of privileges, seven in number, three elected from the *ancien régime* of Saturn and four from the twelve great gods of the Jovian dynasty, who should be empowered to examine the titles of pretenders to godship. This task seems too hard for mere human patience; but before giving it up, we must at least mention certain divine or quasi-divine personages and conceptions that flit over the shifting background of classical mythology.

Plutus, the god of wealth, was a different personage from Pluto, understood to be in charge of the *irritamenta malorum* stored underground. He would not take his grimy form till the precious metals came into use as means of exchange; and the ancients made him blinded by Zeus, poets and moralists in all ages having reason to understand that riches do not always accompany merit. In the Theban temple of *Tyche* (Fortune) he appears as a child in her arms, she also being represented as blindfold, sometimes winged, sometimes standing on a slippery ball, holding the Cornucopia, or horn of plenty, from which she pours out her gifts so carelessly. Plutus belongs, of course, to the same family of abstractions as *Momus* (mirth), *Comus*, the presiding genius of revelry, and that *Priapus* whose figure did not strike the ancients as unfit for polite society, while he had serious functions as guardian of flocks, of swarming bees, and of fruitfulness in general.

A word should be said in passing as to certain other names apparently peculiar to Roman mythology, though perhaps handed down from Etruscan superstitions of kindred origin to those of Greece. The most renowned of these is *Janus,* the god of gates, whose principal shrine at Rome was closed in time of peace, twice or thrice only, it is said, during seven centuries, and notably at the birth of Christ, as Milton proclaims in his ode for the Nativity. He is represented with two faces, to look both ways. Janus has passed for deification of an ancient hero-king; but was probably a sun-god who opened the gates of heaven; and he appears to have been originally the chief god of Rome till supplanted by Jupiter. *Terminus* was the god of boundaries and landmarks, not left without work in a land of small encroaching communities. *Libitina* presided over funerals, as *Lucina* over childbirth. *Fortuna* seems here to have come to higher honour than did her sister Tyche in Greece. The *Lares* were the Roman spirits of ancestors; the *Penates,* household gods; the *Manes,* shades of the dead, who appear in more ghastly shape as *Lemures, Lamiae,* and *Larve;* then every Roman went through life attended by his *Genius,* as the Red Indian by his *manitou* or totem spirit. In Greece, also, man's body was shadowed by his *Ker,* a ministering wraith whose invisible activities are hard to catch; and he might believe himself guided by his *Daimon,* a guardian spirit that for us has taken uglier significance.

Manifold, indeed, were the bodiless shapes called into imaginary existence by the Greek aptitude for personification. There was *Ananke* (necessity), before whom the very gods must bow. *Ate* (the spirit of evil) sowed crimes among men. *Nemesis* (retribution) came after the wicked with slow but sure foot. *Nike* (victory), *Dike* (justice), and *Themis* (law) were all vaguely conceived as airy beings. Pausanias records altars or temples to such abstractions as Energy, Mercy, Shame, Rumour, and Persuasion. Death and his brother Sleep make a metaphor as old as Homer or Hesiod; and Dreams came from above as messengers, false ones issuing through a flattering sheet of ivory, but the true from a gate of horn, to whisper to mortals locked in the arms of *Morphens.* They were children of wide mantled Night, who readily became a personage, like *Eos* (Aurora), the Dawn; *Phosphorus* and *Hesperus,* the Morning and the Evening Star, and a host of other shining ones, attendants of the Moon and the Sun, whose four horses had their names and local habitation in the stables of the sky. So had the four winds, *Borcas, Eurus, Zephyrus,* and *Notus,* children of Eos and Astraea, the virgin star, those airy beings kept shut up in the cave of *Aeolus,* whence at command they issued forth as winged youths to do the will of the gods. The wife of Zephyrus was *Chloris,* who became more famous as the Roman *Flora,* the flower goddess, comrade of *Pomona,* whose spouse was *Vertumnus,* the Season god, wooing her successively as a ploughman, a reaper, a grape gatherer, and as an old woman white with winter snows, at last in the composite presentment of a beautiful youth. The Seasons *(Hore)* were also incarnated as lovely maidens, *Eunomia, Dike,* and *Irene,* daughters of Zeus and Themis, going along with the Graces in attendance upon Aphrodite or Apollo. The mostly animal signs of the Zodiac belong, of course, to older observation than that of Greek fancy.

The Seasons sometimes appear as two or four; but it has already been mentioned how the Greeks might leave winter out of account. It is noticeable how their imagination of female forms usually goes in triads, while the same tendency was less marked in the case of gods There were three Fates, *Moirai* (Parcae) – *Clotho, Lachesis,* and *Atropos* – to spin and cut the thread of life. Three also were the Furies – *Tisiphone, Alecto* and *Megera,* whose proper title was the *Erinyes,* but men gave them the flattering name of *Eumenides* (the Gracious Ones), as our mischievous fairies were styled 'the good people', or the 'men of peace'. The *Graiae,* grey cousins of the Gorgons, may have been originally represented as two, having one eye and one tooth between them, but they also pass into a trinity. The Muses are three times three. Three goddesses contend for the prize of beauty, and Psyche, like Cinderella, has two sisters.

Modern Greek folklore, that but blurredly reflects the ancient mythology, runs much to the sets of three brothers, so familiar in our *märchen,* of whom the youngest commonly is the lucky one; whereas this feature is not marked in the old Greek stories, so far as male characters are concerned. There are three supreme deities; but Pluto seems not to rank with his brothers; and of the three judges in the lower world, only Minos and Rhadamanthus appear as holding regular sessions. Two brothers seem more common than three in ancient stories. Miss Jane Harrison suggests that three figures would lend themselves to artistic composition; but this hardly explains why Greek heroes are grouped in triads less often than heroines; and a point for which several scholars can offer no explanation. Mr J C Lawson, in his scholarly comparison of ancient and modern superstitions in Greece, finds that there three has come to be a number of sinister associations.

It was a labour of Heracles to present a complete list of all those beings of earth and air, of water and darkness, that flickered into imaginary shape. Every river and fountain might have its nymph or Naïad, every tree its Dryad; the mountains were haunted by Oreades, as the forests by half-brutal Satyrs. Unknown regions, then, were readily peopled by Giants, Centaurs, Chimaeras, Amazons, Sirens, Cyclopes, Hyperboreans, or other fabulous creatures, such as long afterwards would be looked for across the Atlantic by the contemporaries of Columbus, in their turn taking omne *ignotum pro magnifico,* not to say *horrifico.*

Among what may be called the half-comic features of mythology, stands out one figure that grew to singular importance from humble beginnings. *Pan* (Faunus) seems to have been a country sprite like our Puck, a horned, sharp-

Pan

From the sculpture by Henry A. Pegram A.R.A.

eared, and goat-footed creature born among the wooded hills of Arcadia, where, angrily disturbed in his noonday sleep, he would sometimes appear to startle travellers, and no wonder, when the nymph who bore him to Hermes was dismayed at the sight of her misshapen offspring. His harsh voice was fabled to have served as volunteered artillery at the battle of Marathon, where it threw the Persians into *panic* fear. Another word we get from him is the pan-pipe, which he is said to have invented when the nymph Syrinx fled from his arms, and, on her prayer for rescue, was turned into a reed, which he adapted to such good purpose as to rival the music of Apollo's lyre. He came to be looked on as the god of woodland jollity, of herds and flocks, of fertility, and of country life in general. From being chief of the Satyrs, a hanger-on of Dionysus, Aphrodite, and other unedifying high society, he rose to rank as one of the most active of the gods. By a confusion, no doubt, of his name with the word *pan* (all), he was latterly looked upon as personification of nature; and at the dawn of a new era 'Universal Pan' had so far come to represent Olympus that a dubious legend makes the birth of Christ hailed by a supernatural voice proclaiming to Greece, 'Great Pan is dead'.

> "The oracles are dumb;
> No voice or hideous hum
> Runs through the arched roof in words deceiving.
> Apollo from his shrine,
> Can no more divine,
> With hollow shriek the steep of Delphos leaving".

But Pan was dethroned rather than dead, living on in Christian conceptions to shape the horned and cloven-footed devil of medieval mythology. Nay, so great loomed this vanished fame in after ages, that there are traces of strange comparison between him and his conqueror, so that Milton does not stick at using this name to hymn the advent of our religion—

> "Full little thought they than
> That the mighty Pan
> Was kindly come to live with them below".

⁂

Demigods and Heroes

The foregoing account of the gods indicates how Greek mythology included many semi-divine personages, of whom less need be said here, since they figure largely in the tales that follow. A salient instance of this double nature is supplied by the *Dioscuri,* Castor and Polydeuces (Pollux), hatched from the same swan's egg with their sister Helen, that *teterrima causa* of so many souls going down to Hades before their time. Though they had Zeus for father, fate did not provide immortality enough to go round this family; and an oracle let the two brothers know that one of them was destined to rank among the gods, while the other must share the common lot as putative son of the Lacedaemonian king Tyndareus. The brothers, devotedly attached to each other, and ignorant which of them was mortal, had no wish but to die together. *Dis aliter visum:* in a quarrel with rival suitors Castor was slain, and all Zeus could do for him was to strike down the slayer with a thunderbolt. But Pollux took his brother's loss so much to heart, that means were found to compromise with the decree of fate by sharing the boon of divinity between them, so that they spent together day about on Olympus and in Hades. These semi-immortal personages were also inconsistently placed among the stars as the *Gemini*. On earth they rose to quasi-divinity, first at Sparta, the place of their human origin, and their worship spread far over the Greek world into Italy. Castor having been renowned as a charioteer and Pollux as a boxer, they were looked on as patrons of public games, along with Hermes and Heracles. It is less obvious how they came to be the special protectors of mariners, like that 'sweet little cherub' sitting up aloft as agent of the modern Neptune's goodwill to poor Jack: sailors of the Latin nations still connect with their name the flitting gleams sometimes seen on a ship's rigging. On land, they appear as goodly youths nobly mounted on white chargers, who came to help of favoured armies at a critical moment. As Theseus rose from the dead to give aid to his Athenians on the plain of Marathon, so at the battle of Lake Regillus the Roman Dictator found that princely pair riding beside him to victory.

> "Back comes the Chief in triumph,
> Who, in the hour of fight,
> Hath seen the Great Twin-Brethren
> In harness on his right.
> Safe comes the ship to haven,
> Through billows and through gales,
> If once the Great Twin-Brethren
> Sit shining on the sails."

Pausanias mentions a case of this belief being turned to hostile account: when the Spartans were celebrating the feast of Castor and Pollux, two young Messenians, dressed for the part in white tunics and purple cloaks, rode into the camp to be received with awe as immortals, then galloped through cutting and stabbing the deceived worshippers.

Three hundred years or so before our era, the Greek writer Euhemerus boldly applied to the national mythology an explanation identified with his name: that the gods had been magnified out of renowned men. The process appears in the case of Alexander the Great, who claimed descent both from Achilles and Jupiter-Ammon, and, out of policy or vanity, made a point of having his quasi-divinity recognized in Greece. We know how cheap deification came to be when not only emperors were thus raised to the skies as matter of course, but Antinous, the minion of Hadrian, had a temple built in his honour, and sacrifice was offered to the images of the famous physician, Hippocrates. A grateful pupil of the Academy erected an altar to Plato. In earlier times any benefactor or terror of men would readily take on a supernatural character, at whose tomb sacrificial rites seemed due. Everywhere the first sketches of history show heroic personages, real or fictitious, looming out in proportions that seem more than mortal, like Achilles and Aeneas. Romulus and Remus precede our own Arthur in having ascribed to them some origin or end distinguished from that of common men. Hiawatha was a Red Indian Triptolemus who played the same part in bringing the sacred boon of corn among his fellow barbarians.

All over the world indeed the tomb of any hero tends to become a shrine. In Greece this hero-worship was manifolded by the number of rival states, each of them eloquently concerned to exalt its legendary worthies, whose names, if not invented by local pride, came down from a distant age when the gods were understood to move freely upon earth. The bards who sang before and after Homer had to earn praise or pudding by extolling the ancestors of their hearers – Homer himself had several legendary birthplaces, but not so many as Zeus. The Catalogue of the ships in the *Iliad* appears to have been inserted that no Greek state should be left out of that roll of ancient glory. Much later, Pindar's odes were addressed to victors in the athletic games of his day; and he takes every chance of bringing in allusions to such legendary fame as might tickle the ears of his numerous patrons. Not that the lauding bard need have been mercenary: admiration is the natural attitude of dithyrambic chroniclers, as in the case of one whom in our own time we have seen working himself up to extol dubious heroes from Dr Francia to Frederick the Great. But many a true worthy must have gone down into endless night, for lack of a sacred trump to sound his exploits.

> "For not to have been dipt in Lethe Lake,
> Could save the son of Thetis from to die;
> But that blind Bard did him immortal make
> With verses dipped in dew of Castalie."

Nor had the bards to please only limited audiences. Contests in music and song made part of the meetings for athletic prowess. The influence of the arts in ancient Greece, reflected in the fame of Apollo, went to refine and to illustrate its early legends. They were no barbarians among whom so many stories show poetry in high honour. The names of Sappho and Anacreon are remembered better than their works. When Alexander destroyed Thebes, he bid spare the house reputed as Pindar's. It is told that the Spartans being directed by an oracle to seek a leader in war from their rival Athens, the Athenians sent them the lame schoolmaster Tyrtaeus, as least likely to be of use to an enemy; but they had reckoned without his gift of impassioned song, that so inspired the Lacedamonian soldiers as to lead them on to victory singing the chants of which some fragments have come down to us under his name. Terpander of Lesbos is famed as the inventor of the seven-stringed lyre, in its simpler form ascribed to the precocious infant

Hermes. A more mythical minstrel appears Arion, said to have earned a fortune at musical meetings in Sicily.

Whatever poetical gains may have been, we owe a debt of gratitude to the 'rhapsodists'[2], actors in monologue, indeed, rather than poets, through whose chanting or recitation were handed down to us the strains attributed to Homer, which seem to have been finally stereotyped in the form given them by ceremonial delivery at the Panathenaic gatherings, whether or no they were edited under the direction of Pisistratus. We have specimens, or at least the titles of other epics, sometimes ascribed to Homer, that were authority for some traditional characters and incidents of legend. And as there were heroes before Agamemnon, so after Homer there were esteemed poets, such as Archilochus, Stesichorus, and Simonides, whose works, though lost to us, unless in fragments or allusions, no doubt went to colour the old stories, not to speak of extant but neglected poems like the *Argonautica* of Apollonius, an epic that should be better known as model for Virgil's *Aeneid*.

It will not be amiss to say a word about those primarily athletic contests that did so much to foster a national life and common religion among the jarring cities of the Greek world, the competitors coming not only from Greece but from its colonies in Asia and Sicily. The great meetings of the Greek world were:—

The *Olympic Games,* held on the templed plain of Olympia, near Pisa in Elis, where the Alpheus flows to the western coast of the Peloponnesus. These seem the oldest of all, traced back to the eighth century BC, but their origin is lost in immemorial antiquity; one fond tradition made them founded by Zeus in honour of his prevailing over Cronos. Other Panhellenic meetings apparently date from the sixth century.

The *Pythian Games* at Delphi, its old name Pytho, were given out as founded by Apollo. Like the Olympic Games, they took place every four years, whereas the next mentioned were at intervals of two years.

The *Isthmian Games,* held on the Isthmus of Corinth in honour of Poseidon.

The *Nemean Games,* in Argolis, taken to be founded or revived by Heracles after his killing of the Nemean lion.

There were also the *Panathenaic Games*, peculiar to Attica and her dependencies, and doubtless many other local celebrations which did not succeed in establishing themselves as national and historical landmarks.

Among these the famous Olympic Games were the most important as a festival at once social, political, and religious, held at intervals of four years, which period, styled an *Olympiad,* was used in dating events, like the five-year *Lustrum* of the Romans, the successive Olympiads running from 776 BC, when the games first appear as fully organized. We know how, in the effort to make a 'living Greece' once more of the modern kingdom, they came to be revived at the end of the nineteenth century, having died out in the fourth century of our era

> "You have the Pyrrhic dance as yet—
> Where is the Pyrrhic phalanx gone?"

The ancient ceremonies lasted for a month, beginning with the first full moon of the summer solstice. Both place and period were held as sacred, no armed force being suffered to approach. This national truce, indeed, might be disturbed by an old quarrel between Pisa and Elis for the presidency of the meeting, which once, in 364 BC, came to be broken up by a collision of implacable feuds, turning the games into a battle.

In the athletic contests which filled the first half of the month, all freeborn Hellenes might compete; but they were not open to barbarians, a word implying all people who did not speak Greek. 'Pot-hunting' and 'gate-money' did not corrupt the sport of early days, though something like 'professionalism' seems to have been developed. The prize was a simple crown of wild olive; but the winner deemed himself rich in the general applause and in that of his fellow citizens, who hailed his victory as a special triumph for his native state, where henceforth he lived in honour and privilege; and more substantial rewards were not always wanting, while his fame might be embalmed in a statue. The first and chief contest would be the foot race, followed by wrestling, boxing, hurling the spear and the discus, horse races, chariot races, and other exercises, altered or modified at different times. There were competitions for boys only, and at one time a race for girls; but as a rule women were held aloof from the lists. The *pancration* made a medley of boxing and wrestling, and the *pentathlon,* a succession of five separate contests, victory in either of which came to be the ardent ambition of athletes. Nor was personal prowess the only title to fame. Rich men, and magnates of outlying colonies, trained horses for races, where their success gave the owner such pride as comes from possession of a Derby winner. But the excitement of our Epsom or Newmarket faintly reflects the eagerness with which the Greek world fixed its eyes on the contests of Olympia

The second half of the month was taken up with processions, sacrifices, and such religious ceremonies, ending with a banquet to the successful competitors. During the festival it was customary for authors to read their compositions as at a Welsh Eisteddfod; and the History of Herodotus is doubtfully said to have been published in this manner. The huge concourse attracted on such an occasion lent itself, likewise, to commercial dealings, which gave it the character of an interstate fair. Works of art, also, were exhibited at what made the Greek form of an Exhibition, while such sanctuaries as Olympia and Delphi became permanent museums of national art and history.

The whole scene was thickly set with temples and statues, in part votive offerings, but often furnished by fines for bribery or foul play, which seem not to have been unknown. Besides metal, wood, clay, and stone, ivory was used in combinations, like the famous chryselephantine (gold and ivory) statue of Zeus by Phidias. Pausanias, who plays Baedeker for us among the memorials as they stood at his day, mentions one athlete, Theagenes, as having won 1400 crowns at the various games of his time. He began his career as a schoolboy by taking down a brazen statue in the marketplace and carrying it home on his back; but when he came to have a statue of his own after death, an enemy was less lucky in dealing with it, who used to vent his spite by scourging the brazen image every night till it fell over and crushed him. Milo of Croton is the competitor whose name has come down to us most renownedly, for his feats of strength and for his miserable end: trying to hold open a split trunk, he got his hands wedged into it, and was held a helpless prey for-wolves. Sometimes a town appears hard up for a hero, as that one whose boxing champion, having killed his adversary at the Games, was sentenced to lose the prize, then went so far out of his mind for grief, that after returning home he performed Samson's exploit with the pillars of a school and pulled down the roof upon threescore children. The indignant people pelted him with stones to take refuge in the temple of Athena, where he hid himself in a chest that when broken open was found empty; and an oracle bid his fellow citizens honour him as no mere mortal. Even in such sports, we see how hero-myths might take shape; then where minstrels and priests met, as well as athletes and lovers of horse-flesh, the occasion naturally made an exchange for legends jumbled together from the superstitious imagination of different districts.

These intercommunications go to explain the form in which many myths have come down to us, their outlines blurred, their colours run together, and sometimes changing like a chameleon with the ground on which they are set. The confusion would be increased by migrating tribes bringing their legendary heroes to new seats. There seems to have been a movement both of amalgamation and differentiation of traditions. Local heroes got to be identified with more widely famed ones, whose exploits in turn might be adopted to swell the renown of some minor champion, while new sprouts of glory could find credit by being grafted on to a time-honoured heroic stock.

The characters and deeds of the heroes had, of course, to fit local pride and jealousy, as when Minos, who in general mythology presents the type of a just judge, figures in the story of Theseus as a cruel tyrant wreaking his spite against Athens. "Thus it seems ill to earn the hate of a city great in eloquence and poetry", remarks Plutarch, whose life of Theseus is strikingly critical in tone. The recent discoveries in Crete, showing this island to have been a seat of maritime enterprise before the rise of the Greek states on the mainland, pave the way to some historic basis for Athens having been in such a tributary position towards the powerful Minos dynasty, as might well leave a grudge against their name. The vengeance of Minos, by the way, is attributed to the fact of his son

Androgeos having been murdered by resentful competitors whom he had beaten at the Athenian games.

The Muses are not to be trusted as historians. If heroes were promoted to godship, phantoms might take vague heroic form, like that of Pelops, legendary lord of the Peloponnesus, who appears in fable as boiled by his father Tantalus to make a sacrilegious meal for the gods, and again as winning an Olympic race by bribing his opponent's charioteer to run foul. For further instance of how we must pick and choose among variant legends, four different impieties are alleged as cause of the punishment to which Tantalus was so famously doomed. Nor can we be sure that we have all the versions once current. Some tales are known to us only by casual allusions in the poets; and some are best known as freely handled for the Athenian stage. Here and there we may surmise the moralizing or refining touch of an author. The brutal Polyphemus of the *Odyssey* must have grown softer of heart when he combed and shaved himself for love of the fair Galatea, though indeed his savage nature came out in the revenge he took on his favoured rival, Acis, as the happy pair sat listening to the love-lorn Cyclops' song. The painful stories of Niobe's children, and of Philomela, might both seem blended less shockingly in that of Aedon, the jealous sister, who would have slain Niobe's first-born, but by mistake killed her own son Itylus, a tragedy she laments for ever in the plaintive notes of the nightingale; and this tale also takes more than one form. Sometimes a patch can be detected as let in to an old story, the fable of 'The Choice of Heracles' for example, ascribed to a sophist of the fifth century BC, and evidently out of keeping with the sanguinary tissue of the original legend.

The figure most like a national hero is that of Heracles, who varyingly appears as born at Tiryns and at Thebes, but never settled down at any city that could take the full credit of his exploits, his wanderings carrying him far and wide, beyond the bounds of Greece. Outside of it was he honoured, as in his great temple at Tyre; but indeed Herodotus notes two separate incarnations of this great name. His descendants the Heraclidae are made to conquer the Peloponnesus, dividing its kingdoms between them – probably a mythical view of the Dorian invasion – and the list of that progeny, as enumerated by Apollodorus, is so long that it could have supplied heroic worthies enough to serve all the Greek states.

Many an ancient bard may have done violence to his conscience by ennobling liberal patrons with the blood of such an illustrious ancestor; and Heracles strangling the snakes in his cradle came to be a favourite device on the coins of Greek cities and colonies. The story of Perseus, still more that of Theseus, look like local variants of the long list of prodigious exploits that from many quarters came to be tacked on to a more widely famous name.

Thus we may have similar exploits recorded of different personages, and varying, often contradictory versions of what seems the same tale. That, of course, is no new thing in mythology. The classical writers who had to handle this medley of tradition, were more or less free to 'edit' it according to their own tastes and prejudices. Wild work was made of chronology by the need of bringing such and such a hero to some place at a certain time, and of putting certain heroes together on the same scene. Tiresias, the blind seer, for instance, figures like a Methusaleh in many generations. The charms of Ninon de L'Enclos did not hold out so long as Helen's, who for a century or so, if all poets are to be trusted, might by generations be prayed 'make me immortal with a kiss!' Heracles appears a contemporary of many heroes, some of whom must have been too old or too young to be very serviceable among the Argonaut crew that had him for a shipmate. The enterprise of the *Argo*, by the way, suggests how some early commercial voyage to the inhospitable Euxine may have made a core for such a snowball tale of marvel and adventure, as the siege of Troy very probably was a real prelude to the later struggles between Greece and Asia. Several cities, indeed, are now seen to have stood successively on the site of Troy, always likely to be a scene of collision between eastward adventurers and the holders of a stronghold commanding the entrance to the Hellespont.

Homer stands above other bards in appealing to a national patriotism, though there may be some trace of *particularismus* in his opposition of the northern Achilles to the Peloponnesian lord of Argos. Not less remarkable is the *Iliad's* advance from the barbarism of less refined legends. Poisoned arrows have gone out of common use, while there are hints of these in the *Odyssey* and in the cureless shafts bequeathed by Heracles to Philoctetes; warriors exchange courtesies as well as insults when about to engage; woman is no mere thrall; and human sacrifice occurs only in the exceptional case of the funeral of Patroclus, whose death indeed rouses Achilles for once to insult the body of a gallant foe, yet he repents before the grief of a suppliant father.

So much being hinted as to the Protean nature of the materials here to be handled, in the following stories the critical attitude must be laid aside. We have to take these legends as we find them. The writer's task is to reproduce the chief features of this mythology, treated on a given scale, usually after the best-known version, yet sometimes with an eye to the taste of readers who will not so readily stomach the grossness that did not offend ancient hearers. In a certain amount of selection or suppression, one is justified by classic example; but, as far as may be, the attempt is to present the Greek mind as shown in its famous fables, and to make familiar the names and characters so often cited in poetry, oratory, and history.

¹ (p.18) Plato relates a queer myth that man was originally created in a round shape, with eight limbs, and that, to abate his pride, Zeus cut him in two, dividing the race into male and female halves.

² (p.47) In the literal meaning of *rhapsodist*, 'stitcher together', seems to be a hint of argument for controverters of "Lewis Carroll's" opinion, that the works known as Homer's, if not written by him, were by "another man of the same name".

Phaëthon

A proud youth was Phaëthon when his mother Clymene let him know how for father he had no mortal man, none less than the god Phoebus-Apollo that daily drove across our world in the Sun's dazzling chariot. But the lad's companions mocked him when he boasted such high birth; then, at his mother's bidding, he sought out that heavenly sire to demand a boon through which all should know him as of divine race.

Before dawn he came to the golden palace of Phoebus, where the purple-mantled god sat on his ivory throne, amid a rainbow sheen of jewels. Round him stood his ministers and henchmen, the Hours, the Days, the Months, and noblest of all, the Seasons: Spring wreathed with fresh blossoms, naked Summer clothed in leaves and crowned with ears of corn, Autumn stained by the clusters of fruit he held in his sunburnt arms, and shivering Winter with snow-white locks. Phaëthon's eyes were dazzled before such magnificence, so that he dared not approach the throne till his all-seeing father called him by name.

"Welcome, my son, to the halls of heaven!" quoth Phoebus, laying aside the crown of sunrays on which mortal sight could not bear to gaze. "But say, what brings thee from earth?"

Thus encouraged, the beardless boy drew near to falter out his request, and soon waxed bolder in the god's smiling face. He made his complaint that men would not believe him Apollo's son, unless his father gave him a pledge of his birth that might be seen by the whole world.

"Before the whole world," cried the god, "will I own you for my son. Well hast thou done to seek a proof of favour, which your father grants unheard: so I swear by the Styx, that oath that binds even the gods. Ask, then, and have!"

"Father," exclaimed Phaëthon eagerly, "grant me my dearest wish, for one day to be trusted to drive the chariot of the Sun!"

A shade fell on the radiant face of Phoebus, and once and again he shook his glowing head before he answered.

"Rash boy, that knows not what he would dare! That charge is too great for heedless youth, indeed, for any mortal, since not even to the gods may it be safely committed. Jupiter himself takes not in hand the reins of the Sun's coursers. Among all the sons of Olympus, I alone can stand firm in the burning car and rule aright its fiery steeds on their steep and toilsome path. Renounce, I beseech thee, such a perilous boon. Ask anything else in heaven or earth, and again I swear by Styx it is thine."

But the forward youth, with pouts and entreaties, held fast to his audacious wish, and would not let himself be moved by fatherly counsels. So at last, the lord of the Sun, bound by his oath, was fain to consent, though sorely fearing what would come of trusting such steeds to so weak a hand.

It was time to be off on that daily journey, for already Aurora began to draw back the rosy curtains of the East, as Phoebus led his son to Vulcan's masterpiece, the golden chariot studded with sparkling gems, all so rich and beautiful that Phaëthon's head was turned by his good fortune to be its master for one day. The vanishing of the stars and the fading of the moon's horns were signal to lead out the four coursers of the Sun, pawing and neighing to show how, full fed with ambrosia, and refreshed by the night's rest, they came eager for their accustomed task. While the swift-fingered Hours fitted on their clanking bits, and harnessed them to the chariot-pole, fond Phoebus anointed the youth with a sacred balm that would enable him better to bear the heat of his glowing course. Meanwhile the god plied him with warnings, to which his impatient son hardly gave ear.

"Keep heedfully the straight path marked by fearsome signs of beasts. Beware in going by the horns of the Bull and the mouth of the roaring Lion, and the far stretched claws of the Scorpion or the Crab. Shun the South Pole and the North Pole; hold the upper arch of the sky from east to west; safest ever is the middle way. Sink not too far down, lest the earth catch fire; rise not too high to scorch the face of heaven. Spare the goad, and draw tight the reins, for my horses fly of themselves, and all the labour is to hold them in. Now mount the car – or no, dear son, think in time! It is not honour you shall win, but punishment and destruction. Leave the chariot to me, and be content to watch its course like your fellow men!"

But already the presumptuous stripling had sprung up to grasp the reins; and when Thetis drew the bar of heaven, he let the chafing horses bound forth, throwing back a hasty word of thanks and farewell to his anxious father.

Boldly Phaëthon urged that mettlesome team through the morning mists, with the east wind following to sweep him on his proud career. But soon the swiftness took away his breath, while under his light weight the car shook and swayed like a keel without ballast, till his head began to turn. And too soon the fiery coursers felt how their reins were in an unpractised hand. Rearing and starting aside, they left their wonted way; then all the earth was amazed to see the glorious chariot of the Sun speeding crookedly overhead as a flash of lightning.

Before he had gone far, the rash charioteer sorely repented his ambition, and

would have asked no greater boon than to be saved from that perilous honour
Too late he saw how wisely his father had warned him. His head whirled, his
face grew white, and his knees shook as he looked to earth and sea spread out
beneath, and to the boundless sky above. In vain he tugged at the tangled bridles;
in vain he cried to the horses which he could not call by name. Heated by the
wild course, they no longer minded his unmasterful hand, but took their own
way through the air, prancing hither and thither at will. Now they soared up towards the sky, so that the clouds began to smoke, and the Moon looked out with
dismay to see her brother's car so strangely guided. Then turning downwards, as
if to cool themselves in the ocean, they passed close over a high mountain, that in
a moment burst into flames.

Thus fearsome disaster fell upon the earth. The Sun, instead of holding his
stately beneficent course across the sky, seemed to rush down in wrath like a
meteor, blasting the fair face of nature and the works of man. The grass withered;
the crops were scorched away; the woods went up in fire and smoke; then beneath them the bare earth cracked and crumbled, and the blackened rocks burst
asunder under the heat.

The rivers dried up or fled back to their hidden fountains; the lakes began to
boil; the very sea sank in its bed, and the fishes lay gasping on the shore, unless
they could gain the depths whence Poseidon thrice raised his head and thrice
plunged back into his shrinking waves, unable to bear the deadly glow. Scythia
was not shielded by its frosts, nor Caucasus by its snows, licked up beneath the
passage of that scorching whirlwind. Mighty Atlas, they say, had all but let the
red-hot world fall from his writhing shoulders. On that day the negroes were
burned black, and, ever since, one stretch of our earth has lain a sandy desert,
where neither man nor beast can thrive. But all over the habitable world the
Sun's charioteer spread woe and ruin, as its cities were consumed one by one,
and the people in their torment swarmed here and there, like ants, among the
ashes of their homes. Never had such a calamity fallen on man since Zeus and
Poseidon drowned his impiety under the flood in which only Deucalion and
Pyrrha found dry land!

By now the wretched Phaëthon had given up hope to check or guide his baleful course. Blinded by terror and by the glare spreading beneath him wherever he
sped, seared by the heat till he could not stand on the glowing car, he threw down
the useless reins, to fall on his knees with a pitiful prayer for his father's help.
But his prayer was lost in the cry that went up from the whole earth, calling upon
the lord of heaven to save mankind from destruction.

Not unheard rose that cry. All-powerful Zeus was sleeping away the noonday
hour; but quickly he awoke and raised his head and saw what had befallen.
Snatching a thunderbolt that lay ready to his hand, he hurled it through the
smoky air, and struck senseless Phaëthon from this chariot he could not control.

Down the youth dashed with blazing locks, swift as a falling star, to be quenched like a firebrand in the river Eridanus. Then the horses of the Sun shook off their yokes, breaking loose to seek their stalls in the sky; and for once at noon night fell upon the earth, lit only by the flickering fires kindled through Phaëthon's folly.

So, on that woeful day, ended the vainglorious son born to Phoebus-Apollo, who was fain to hide his countenance for shame of his fatherly fondness. But some there were who mourned the rash youth's end. When the nymphs of the Eridanus had buried him on its banks, his mother, frantic with grief, came thither to pour out her heart's blood in sorrow. His three sisters, too, wept so bitterly, that the pitying gods changed them into poplar trees dropping tears of amber upon the water. And his friend Cygnus dived so often into the river to gather up Phaëthon's charred members, that when he pined away for grief, it was granted him still to haunt the stream in the shape of a swan.

Apollo Belvidere

From a statue

Perseus

1 The Gorgon

Acrisius, king of Argos, was sorely troubled through an oracle declaring that by the hand of a grandson he should die; then, having but one child, his fair daughter Danaë, he thought to cheat that doom by keeping her unmarried. To make sure, he shut her up in close prison, a cave underground, or, as some say, a brazen tower, never to see the face of man while she lived. But the gods can make their way even where the light of day is shut out. Danaë was visited by Zeus in the form of a shower of gold, and here she bore a son, who was to be the famous hero Perseus.

When the infant's crying came to the ears of the king, and he learned how a grandson had been born to him for all his watchfulness, his cowardly soul was filled with dismay. Not daring to have the boy's blood on his hands, nor yet to let him live, he had mother and child put together in a chest and sent drifting out to drown or starve upon the stormy sea. But Zeus watched over them; and at his bidding Poseidon stilled the winds and waves that gently bore their frail ark eastward, till it came washed ashore on the island of Seriphus in the Aegean archipelago.

Here Danaë and her babe were found by a fisherman named Dictys, who treated them kindly, and took them to his house to bring up Perseus as his own child. And so well throve this young stranger that the men of Seriphus could guess him to be of royal birth, nay, son of a god. In sports and combats he soon vanquished all his playfellows, and grew up to full strength and stature, his mind set on brave deeds by which he might prove himself a hero among men. In dreams he was inspired by Athena, who strung his heart to choose the deadliest perils in the flower of youth, rather than inglorious ease and safety.

Soon he was to have his desire. His foster-father Dictys had a brother, Polydectes, the chief of the island, but of less noble nature. He, at first friendly to the strangers cast on his shore, came to love Danaë, and would have forced her to be his wife. But all her heart was given to her son, and such a wooer seemed unworthy of one who had been loved by a god. The cunning Polydectes bethought him how to get rid of this manly youth who stood as a guard to his mother's honour. To have Danaë in his power he set Perseus upon a fearful adventure, from which the bravest man was little like to come back alive.

The task given him was to slay the monster Medusa, one of the three Gorgon sisters, she alone of them mortal, but her very looks deadly to the best-armed foe. For, to punish an impious outrage on Athena, her hair had been turned into vipers writhing about a face so horrible that whoever set eyes upon it was stiffened to stone before he could strike a blow. Yet Perseus did not fear to face the Gorgon, when his patron Athena gave him wise counsels how he should accomplish that perilous quest.

"Not without help of the gods can the bravest man assail such a foe," she bid him know, when the bold youth would have made light of all he must dare.

For now the goddess appeared to him in radiant majesty, accompanied by her brother Hermes, and they lent him certain powerful talismans in proof of their favour. Hermes girded on to him his own crooked sword that could cut through the strongest armour, and fitted the youth's feet with his winged sandals to bear him swiftly over land and sea. Moreover, from the realm of Pluto he brought him a wonderful helmet that made the wearer of it invisible. Athena gave him her polished shield, which he must use like a mirror so as to strike Medusa without looking straight in her horrific face. Also she provided him with a goatskin bag to hide the Gorgon's head, that even in death would freeze the blood of all who beheld it, friend or foe.

Thus equipped, he was bidden first to seek out, in their icy home of the north, the frostbound Graeae, half-sisters of the Gorgons, who alone could tell him the way to the far-off isle where Medusa had her lair. Not an hour did he lose in setting forth, only begging of Athena to watch over his mother till he brought back Medusa's head. With such heavenly aid, he could make no doubt of victory.

Springing into the air from the cliffs of Seriphus lightly he flew to the north, till he came among snows and mists and mountains of ice where no mortal man can dwell. There, on the edge of the Hyperborean sea, he found the Grey Sisters huddled up together, dim and shapeless forms, of which his eyes could hardly tell whether they were two or three. Clothed only in their long hair, white and bristling with ice, so old were they and so doting that they had but one eye and one tooth left between them, which their fumbling hands passed from each to other with groans and murmurs, as in turn they needed to munch the snowflakes or to peer through the blinding mists. This Perseus knew from Athena; and as she had bidden him, he stole up to the old hags, invisible in his helm of darkness, then suddenly snatched away their eye, as they wrangled which should have it to see whose steps came clanging on the frosty shore.

"Tell me the way to the Gorgons," demanded he, "or I take your tooth also, and leave you to starve in this wilderness."

A miserable outcry those Grey Sisters made, when they found themselves thus robbed by an unseen hand. With threats and curses they bid him give up their eye; but he held it firm, till, since so it must be, they mumbled out directions by which he might find the Gorgons' Isle. For thanks he gave them back their eye, but they saw him not, for he was gone before they could nod their feeble heads, falling asleep like blocks of ice.

Now he must fly far to the south, where the mists and snows soon melted away, and the earth lay green with fields and forests, and the blue sea shone and sparkled under a glowing sky. Hot and hotter grew the air as he flew over land and sea towards the other end of the world, all its rivers and mountains stretching out below his feet, and at last a great ocean upon which no sail was spread. There, following the course given him to steer by the sun and the stars, he spied out the island whereon lived those hateful sisters, among lifeless images of men and beasts whom their looks had turned to stone.

Swooping down in the brightness of noonday, he saw the three Gorgons fast asleep, Medusa in the middle. But on her he did not dare to fix his eyes. As Athena had bidden him, he drew near with his back turned, holding her shield so as to make a mirror for that bloodcurdling head, with its mane of vipers curling and writhing about it even in sleep. Fearfully beautiful was Medusa's face as well as horrible; but as she tossed to and fro in her dreams, Perseus saw how her body was clad in loathsome scales and brazen plumage, and how her limbs ended in crud claws; and her mouth open in a bitter smile showed fangs like a serpent's, bristling round her forked tongue.

He dared not look longer for fear she should open her blood-freezing eyes. Marking in his mirror how she lay, he struck backwards, and with one sweep of the crooked sword of Hermes had cut dean through her neck so swiftly as to choke her one shrill cry. Then with averted looks and shuddering hands he stowed away the bleeding head in his goatskin bag, and rose into the air with a shout of triumph.

That cry awoke the two sister Gorgons to find Medusa's headless body lying between them, and to hear the exulting voice of the foe who had done this deed. Hissing and howling, they spread their wings like monstrous birds of prey to seek him out with their iron talons. But Perseus, hid from them by his helm of darkness, was soon beyond reach of those revengeful monsters, that, unlike their sister, could not be slain by mortal hand.

Fast and far the hero flew with his prize, the way soon leading over a boundless desert on which he could see no green thing nor any living creature. But as the Gorgon's blood oozed through the goatskin, gouts of it dropped upon the thirsty sand, and there bred venomous snakes and scorpions, ever since to plague that barren soil. Huge pillars of whirling sand rose up to mark how the raging Gorgons chased him in vain; for Perseus soared above them invisible, nor set foot on earth till he came at evening to the westernmost bounds of the known world.

Here night and day knelt the old giant Atlas, holding up by pillars the weight of the sky. Of him Perseus, wearied by his long travel, begged leave to stay and rest in the famed garden of golden apples which Atlas kept jealously enclosed under guard of a dragon. But the churlish giant bid him to be gone.

"I am a son of Zeus, and I have done a deed to earn better welcome," pleaded Perseus.

"A son of Zeus is fated to rob my garden!" growled the giant, remembering an oracle of old, which was indeed to be fulfilled by Heracles.

"If so chary of what is yours, take a gift from me!" And with this Perseus drew forth the Gorgon's head to hold it full in the giant's face.

Not another word did Atlas speak. This hugest of Titans had in an instant been turned to a stony peak, his tall head white with snows, his beard stiff with ice, his rocky ribs bristling with forests. And so he stands to this day, a lifeless mountain bearing up the clouds.

Perseus and the Grey Sisters (Graiae)

By Sir Edward Burne-Jones

❦

2 Andromeda

His face set to the east, Perseus held an airy way, feeling himself truly invincible, now that to the god-given talismans he had added the spell of Medusa's head, which even in death could appal the strongest foe. When he had passed over the desert, and crossed the green edges of the Nile, he came next to the land of the Ethiopians, and other strange peoples; and soon the rising sun showed him a marvellous sight. Against a black rock on the seashore washed by every wave, the form of a sunburnt maiden stood like a statue, nor moved as he swept down towards her, so that but for the tears in her eyes and her long locks stirred by the wind, he might have taken her for carved out of stone. He saw how, veiled in sunlight and spray, she blushed at his approach, faintly struggling as if she would have covered her face with her hands, but could not, for she was fast chained to the rock.

"Fair maiden, how come that you are in such a plight?" he cried, wondering at her beauty, not less than her woe. "Why these chains for a form more fitly arrayed in wedding garlands? Your name and race? asks one who would set you free from such unworthy bonds."

The maiden strove to speak, but once and again tears choked her voice, and shame tied her tongue. But, when the hero put on his helm of darkness and thus became invisible to her downcast eyes, she at last found voice to answer.

"I am Andromeda, only daughter of Cepheus the king; and here am I set to suffer for words not my own. It was my mother Cassiopeia who, in her pride, boasted of me as fairer than the Nereïds, daughters of the sea. They, out of spite, worked on Poseidon to send a cruel sea-monster, ravaging our coasts, and scaring the people from their homes. Then my father sought the oracle of Ammon in the Libyan sands, and had for answer that by the sacrifice of his daughter alone could the pest be stayed. Long my parents were loath to devote me thus; but the people cried out so sorely that they were fain to obey the oracle. So here I stand helpless, awaiting the monster, that is to devour me at sunrise, then leave the land in peace. And there he comes!" she ended with a shriek, as afar off rose a shapeless black bulk from the sea depths.

"Not helpless, fair Andromeda!" said Perseus, and with his magic sword cut the chains that bound her as lightly as if they were thread. " By heavenly aid, I have slain the Gorgon, and so will I do to this monster, be it ever so fearful."

Now the maiden stood still and calm, trusting that here must indeed be a son of the gods sent to deliver her. But her cry of alarm had come echoed back from the cliffs, on which stood the woeful parents with a crowd of people, waiting to see her cruel end. Their warning shouts told how that the monster made speed towards the victim, who closed her eyes when she saw its back cleaving the waves like a swift galley.

With one word of cheer to Andromeda, Perseus made ready for the fight that should deliver her. He laid aside Medusa's head, veiling its horror in seaweeds that afterwards were found changed into coral branches. Drawing his sword, he sprang lightly into the air, and flew to meet the monster as it rushed upon Andromeda with foaming jaws and grinding teeth. But when from above the hero's shadow fell upon the sea, the creature checked its course to rage against this unlooked for enemy. Down swooped Perseus like an eagle, piercing its scaly neck with his keen blade. The monster roared and lashed and writhed, turning on its back as it vainly tried to get him into its horrid jaws, while again and again the sword goaded it to fresh fury upon the waves purpled with its blood; and to those looking on with affrighted eyes it seemed as if the whole sea were stirred by a storm.

At last, when all was still, the weeping parents ventured down from the cliff to see what had befallen. They found their daughter trembling but unharmed, and beside her Perseus stood wiping his sword, where out of the heaving red water stood up the monster's body, now still as a huge black reef.

"Dry your tears and take back your daughter, loosed by my sword," was the greeting of Perseus. "But her whom I have won from death, I claim for a kinder embrace. I am son of Zeus and Danaë, one whom you might not despise for her husband, even were she free to choose."

The grateful parents willingly agreed to give such a champion not only their daughter, but all the kingdom if he desired it as dowry. With tears, now of joy, they led him to their palace, where a feast was soon prepared to grace the marriage of Perseus and Andromeda, more lovely than ever in her bridal array.

But their wedding feast was troubled by a clang of arms, when into the hall burst Phineus, kinsman of the king, by whom the maid had before been sought in marriage. Backed by a throng of armed henchmen, he demanded his promised bride, hotly defying the favoured lover.

"No stranger is worthy to win the daughter of our land!" he declared; and not a few of the guests cried out on his side.

"You did not woo her when chained to the rock!" taunted Perseus. "Neither suitor nor kinsman stood by her against the monster from whose jaws I won Andromeda to be mine."

For answer Phineus hurled his spear, that stuck quivering in a post beside Perseus as he stood with his shield held over Andromeda. His sword flashed out like lightning, and in a moment the hall was filled with uproar. Song and mirth gave place to the dash and hiss of weapons, and the tables ran red with blood

Perseus and Andromeda

From the painting by Lord Leighton P.R.A.

instead of wine. So many were the followers and well-wishers of Phineus that the king's men could not withstand them; then over the din rose the hero's voice:

"Let all who are my friends turn away their eyes!"

He held up the Gorgon's head, and in the twinkling of an eye those enemies had been turned to stone as they stood, one brandishing a sword, one flinging a dart, and Phineus, last of all, upon his knees as he fell to beg for his own life when he saw what befell his comrades in rebellion. Not thus could they now disturb the marriage banquet.

> "Beautiful, eager, triumphant, he leapt back again to his treasure;
> Leapt back again, full blest, toward arms spread wide to receive him.
> Brimful of honour he clasped her, and brimful of love she caressed him,
> Answering lip with lip; while above them the queen Aphrodité
> Poured on their foreheads and limbs, unseen, ambrosial odours,
> Givers of longing, and rapture, and chaste content in espousals."

—Charles Kingsley's *Andromeda*

3 The Minister of Doom

Men say that the rock from which Perseus loosed Andromeda may still be seen at Joppa below Jerusalem. However that may be, in the kingdom of Cepheus he built a ship, on which to carry home his bride to Seriphus. He reached the island to hear heartstirring news. His mother was still alive, but Polydectes had made her a slave, persecuting her with his hateful love, so that she had been driven to take sanctuary from him in Athena's temple. Spurred by wrath, Perseus strode to the hall of that tyrant, and found him revelling among his drunken companions.

"Ha, foundling, whom we never thought to see again!" was his scornful welcome. "Have you brought the Gorgon's head?"

"Behold!" said Perseus sternly, as he uncovered the blood-curdling trophy, before which those mockers were forthwith turned to stone; and there they stand in a ring, washed evermore by wind and weather.

In place of Polydectes, Danaë's son made the good Dictys chief of the island. Now, from his joyful mother he learned how he was grandson of the king of Argos, and set out forthwith to claim his rightful heritage. But first he piously restored the magic gifts of the gods; and to Athena he gave the head of that Gorgon foe of gods and men, to be set as a boss in her dazzling shield, and serve her as the dread Aegis thrown over the innocent in the eyes of those who would do them wrong.

Acrisius had heard with dread of his grandson being still alive and on his way to Argos. Always bearing in mind the words of the oracle that he should die by this hand, he waited not his coming, but fled to Larissa in the land of the Thessalians. Thither Perseus followed, hoping to persuade his grandfather that he meant him no harm. He came to Larissa when its king was holding games, at which old Acrisius sat among the onlookers. The young stranger joined in these sports, and all wondered how easily he bore off the prize in racing and wrestling. But when his name ran from lip to lip, Acrisius shrank into the shade and covered his face, fearing to be known by that fated offspring.

It came to throwing the quoit, and again Perseus hurled far beyond all his competitors. But there rose a sudden gust of wind that carried his strongest cast aside, so that the quoit struck Acrisius, him and no other among the throng; and such a hurt was enough to end his old and feeble life.

Perseus stood horror-struck to learn how by chance he had been the death of his own grandfather. After burying the body and purifying himself by due rites from his unconscious guilt, he went back to Argos, but could not with a quiet mind keep the inheritance thus won He exchanged his kingdom with the neighbour king of Tiryns, and built for himself the great city Mycenae. There his life was long, in honour and welfare, when

> "Peaceful grew the land
> The while the ivory rod was in his hand,
> For robbers fled, and good men still waxed strong,
> And in no house was any sound of wrong,
> Until the Golden Age there seemed to be,
> So steeped the land was in felicity".
>
> —William Morris

Many famous heroes sprang from one whom men came to look on as half-divine; and after their death, Perseus and Andromeda, with Cepheus and Cassiopeia, were placed by the gods among the bright stars that guide wandering manners.

Arachne

The Lydian Arachne, daughter of a famed dyer in purple, was herself still more famed for rare skill in weaving. Not common country folk alone, but nymphs of the woods and the streams came to watch how deftly she plied her loom, and with what wonderful art she used the needle to embroider rich patterns on her webs. So high rose her name that it reached Athena, the goddess of such arts, to whose inspiration, men said, this humbly-born maiden must owe her skill. But to say that she needed any teacher hurt Arachne's pride.

"Athena, indeed!" she would cry, tossing her head. "There is none in heaven or earth with whom I fear to compete. Let Athena come, if she will, to try her hand against mine!"

"No, speak not so rashly," said a grey-haired old woman who stood by leaning on her staff, as the boastful damsel once uttered such a challenge. "Age and experience ever bring wisdom. Be ruled by me and own the power of the goddess, for she has graces to give to mortals who bend before her. No human work is so good that it cannot be bettered."

"Foolish old crone, keep your counsel till it be asked for!" hotly spoke back Arachne. "Folks lose their wits, also, by living long. To your slave or your daughter, play the mistress. For me, I need no lessons from doting age, nor yet from Athena. Why shrinks she from a contest of our skill?"

"She is here!" rang out a queenly voice; for lo! the seeming grandam had changed to Athena herself, who stood forth with flashing eyes and majestic bearing. In that disguise of feeble age, she had come to spy on her earthly rival's handiwork; and now, stung to haughty disdain, she offered to match her art against the Lydian spinster's.

Arachne had at first flushed for astonishment, but soon she recovered her confidence and boldly accepted the challenge. The contest began forthwith: two looms were set up, at which these eager rivals plied their best craft and cunning, with such swiftness that ere long on each the growing tissues shone in all the hues of the rainbow woven into marvellous devices, and shot with threads of gold.

For her design Athena chose the gods ranged upon the Acropolis at Athens, Zeus's awful majesty in the midst, Poseidon smiting the rock with his trident, herself in full panoply among the rest, who was shown calling forth the olive tree that made her best gift to man. About this central group were pictured scenes of impious mortals brought to confusion, rebellious giants turned to mountains, and, for a hint to her presumptuous rival, prating girls changed to screeching fowl. Round all ran a border of olive foliage, as sign of whose handiwork this was, with which few would dare to vie!

The irreverent Arachne, for her part, had picked out stories that cast shame or derision upon the gods. Zeus and his brethren were shown wooing mortals in unworthy form, Apollo humbly serving as a shepherd on earth, Dionysus playing his drunken pranks, nay, scandalous memories of old Cronos himself. From such ancient tales she could choose but too many to fill out her picture, all enclosed by a border of ivy leaves and flowers.

But these scenes were worked in with so cunning art, that one could believe to see real animals and real waves standing out before the eye upon that accusing web, the more offensive for its truth.

So Athena felt when she rose to examine the other's work. With a cry that was half envy and half indignation, she snatched at the too faithfully coloured cloth, tearing it to pieces, and showering blows upon the sly maker of such a masterpiece.

How might mortal maiden stand before the fair-haired goddess when her eyes blazed with wrath? Thus unfairly beaten, Arachne could not bear her spiteful shame. She stole away to hang herself in despair.

Nor even then was the wrath of Athena satisfied. She bid her rival live, yet in what hateful form! For a spell was woven round her bloated body, her human features disappeared, her hair fell off, her limbs shrunk up, and thus poor Arachne hung as a spider, doomed for ever to spin as if mocking the skill that had moved Olympian envy.

Meleager and Atalanta

1 The Boar Hunt

In Calydon, fair country of Aetolia, to King Oeneus and his wife Althaea was born a son whom they named Meleager. And when the babe was not a week old, there came to the house three lame and wrinkled old women, busy night and day with their distaffs, spinning the thread of men's life. For these were no other than the Fates, who, as they bent over the child, croned out his fortune thus—

"He will grow a goodly man, like his father," said the first.

"He will be a hero renowned through the world," murmured the second.

"He will live," muttered the third, "only so long as that firebrand on the hearth remains unconsumed."

The anxious mother's ear caught those words; then no sooner had the weird sisters vanished, than she rose from her bed to seize the firebrand, quench it in water, and hide it away among her most secret treasures.

Young Meleager grew up, as had been foretold, a son to be the pride of any mother. He made one of the band of heroes who went with Jason to seek the Golden Fleece; and when they came home, another feat of arms awaited him to celebrate his name by the slaying of the Calydonian boar.

In his son's absence, King Oeneus had drawn upon himself the wrath of a goddess. As thanksgiving for a fruitful year, he loaded the altar of Demeter with corn, to Dionysus he poured out wine, and to Athena oil; but he forgot any sacrifice to Artemis, and that haughty maiden avenged herself on the mortal who had failed in doing her honour. She sent into his country a monstrous boar with glowing eyes and foaming jaws, its bristles strong and sharp like sword points, its tusks long as those of an elephant, its breath so fiery as to scare man and beast when it broke crashing through the woods. Wherever it ravaged, the crops were trampled down, the herds scattered at its onset, the shepherds fled from their flocks, and the farmers dared not venture out to pluck the fruit of their vines and olives, left to hang rotting on the trees.

So when Meleager came home from Colchis, it was to find his father's land laid waste by the fear of this monster. At once he set about gathering hunters and hounds to track it to its lair, as no man had yet dared to do. He was readily joined by several of his fellow venturers on the *Argo*, not yet tired of perilous quests; and in all Greece could be seen no such gallant band as now joined together to hunt down the Calydonian boar.

Among the rest came the maiden huntress, Atalanta, of whom strange tales were told. Her father, too, was a king, and had hoped for a son like Meleager to be his heir; so, when a daughter was born to him, in his anger he threw her out to die upon a wild mountain. But there the child, men say, was suckled by a she-bear, then in its den found by hunters, who brought her up to their own rude life. Thus she grew manlike and hardy, careless of wind or weather, not less bold than beautiful, skilled to handle bow and spear, and more willing to face the fiercest beast than to listen to tender words. All her heart was set on hunting and strenuous exercises, and she thought of men only as comrades in sports, at which few youths could surpass her by strength or courage. More than one, rashly seeking to woo her, had rough handling to take for his answer.

"Happy the man who can find such a mate," was Meleager's first thought when he saw Atalanta, with her brown face like a lad's, her hair loosely tied back upon her broad shoulders, bearing a spear as lightly as if it were a spindle, and carrying bow and quiver slung about her sturdy sun-tanned limbs. But others murmured that their quest was none for women; and grudges rose against this unknown companion, who only asked a chance to prove her prowess. It was no time, indeed, for wooing nor for quarrelling, so without delay the whole band set forth to seek their fearsome quarry.

No hard task was theirs to find the boar, that soon came raging through the forest to meet those champions. The nets were spread to catch it; the hounds were turned into the thorny thickets; but the monster needed no rousing. Out of a bed of reeds it broke upon them, a grisly sight that set the dogs turning tail, when their masters stood fast to hurl a cloud of darts, and the first spear-point that drew blood was Atalanta's.

Maddened by wounds, with heaving sides and gnashing jaws, the boar dashed among them like a thunderbolt, laying low three or four with its dripping tusks before they could fetch a blow. One was forced to save himself by swinging up into the boughs of an oak, on the trunk of which the horrid foe sharpened its deadly tusks in vain, till a rash hound came within reach to be tossed howling into the air. One dog after another, too, was hurt by their own masters, as the spears flew amiss. Running on with axe heaved above his head, one bold hunter slipped upon the grass, wet with blood, and lay a helpless victim in the monster's way. But when the men gave ground before its charge, Atalanta's arrow flew with so true an aim that the bristling boar again stopped short to rage out its pain.

"Verily, maiden, you are the best man of us all!" cried Meleager; and the rest, ashamed to be outdone by a woman, once more closed to the attack.

A score of wounds in turn brought the monster to the ground; and when it got to its feet it was to stagger and turn round and round, blinded by blood. Red froth poured out of its jaws, choking its angry growls; its fiery eyes grew dim; and when at length Meleager thrust his sword to the hilt in its reeking sides, the huge beast lay writhing in its own gore mingled with that of its conquerors, never more to be a terror to the land.

The boar's death-throes were hardly at an end before Meleager planted his foot on its neck with a shout of exultation. Making haste to cut off the bleeding head and to strip away the bristly skin, he offered these trophies to Atalanta as the one that of all had best deserved them, though they fell to himself whose fortune was to give the fatal stroke. But against this some of the hunters cried out in displeasure, loudest of all the two Thestiades, brothers of Althaea and uncles to Meleager.

"This is no woman's work, nor is its prize for a maiden!" clamoured the jealous men; and those sons of Thestius made bold to tear the spoils from Atalanta's hands.

Thus began a brawl in which the heroes turned on one another their weapons still warm from the boar's blood. So hot waxed the quarrel, that Meleager in his own defence shed the life blood of both those kinsmen, who would have scorned the fair huntress. So all their jubilation was changed to bitterness and grief for friends slain over the body of their foe.

An ill day it was for the house of Oeneus, on which its brave son made an end of the boar. When the news came to Althaea, she had gone out to the temple to give proud thanks, but on the way fell in with a mourning train that bore her dearly loved brothers to their funeral pyre. Too soon she learned by whose hand they had fallen; then, beside herself for sorrow, she was moved to curse her own son. Beating her breast and tearing her hair with wild outcry, she broke open the secret place in which she kept hidden away that quenched firebrand that measured his days of life. Furiously she ran with it to where the sacrificial fire burned on the altar. In her madness she scarce knew what she did, yet three or four times, she drew back from her unnatural purpose, the mother and the sister warring in her breast. But as her eyes fell on the blood-stained corpses of her own mother's sons, with shuddering hand and averted face she hurled that brand upon the flame. Quickly was it burned to ashes; then as quickly her rage melted to heartbreaking repentance. When soon she heard what came of her vengeful frenzy, the woebegone mother saw nothing for it but to end her own days, dying with her brothers, beside the embers on which she had quenched the life of her son.

For as Meleager came home in triumph bringing the spoils of the great hunt, suddenly his steps had faltered and his eyes grew dim as if blinded by the smoke of that consuming firebrand. A hot fever filled his veins, while his heart dried up and his spirit withered away as a dead leaf. With a groan of amazement he fell like the trunk of some thunder-stricken oak, to breathe his last without a wound, nor ever knew how he had come to so untimely death And thus was accomplished the decree of those fatal sisters that looked upon his birth.

2 Atalanta's Race

When the boar of Calydon had been quelled by Meleager's doughty band, Atalanta would have gone back to her savage haunts, caring not to consort with men since he was dead who alone had stirred her heart. But that feat had come to the ears of her harsh father Iasus, who might well be moved to pride in such a daughter. He sought her out and brought her home to his kingdom, still without an heir.

Many were the suitors willing to win a bride so fair and so famous, daughter of a sonless king, and well able to hold her own in arms. But Atalanta would have none of them, choosing to remain a virgin, like the goddess of hunting to whom she was vowed. Still she practised manly exercises, scorning all softness, and having no skill in women's work. When her father pressed her to wed, she made one and another excuse; then at last agreed to take the wooer who could outstrip her in running; but death to be his lot if he failed to win the race.

Even on such hard conditions, brave and agile youths came forward to run for their lives against Atalanta's hand. She, fleet as a fawn, lightly outran the swiftest footed; and one after another they paid their rashness by a cruel end, for, while the suitor must run naked and unarmed, the fierce maiden bore a spear, with which she goaded them not to victory but to death. Still, the sight of their heads set up as a warning by the goal did not chill the hearts of other adventurers, hoping to win the prize where so many had shamefully failed. Among the rest was young Hippomenes, who, while acting as judge at such a contest, had let his own heart be inflamed by Atalanta's scornful eyes.

Before he offered himself to the trial, not trusting wholly in his breath and sinews, like the rest, Hippomenes had implored the favour of Aphrodite on that strange course of love. And the goddess heard and helped him with a gift, that by her counsel should serve him well. Three golden apples she gave him to carry in his hands as he ran, and what he was to do with them came from her knowing the heart of woman better than was open to man's wit.

Away went the youth and the maiden, racing towards the goal. Before long Atalanta was about to pass her competitor, who then slyly threw down one of the golden apples to roll across her way. Tempted by wonder or curiosity, she stooped to pick it up, while Hippomenes pressed swiftly on. After brief delay it was easy for her to catch up with him, but now he threw away the second apple, and again she halted to seize it. Again she followed hot-foot, when he, panting towards the goal, let the third apple fall before her. And lo! while once more she stopped to gain that glittering prize, her wily suitor had won the race.

Thus taken in her own snare, the man-like maiden could not but give her hand to Hippomenes, who hoped to win her heart also. But he, poor youth, had short joy in his fortune. For, as Oeneus neglected to propitiate Artemis, so this exultant bridegroom forgot to give thanks to Aphrodite for her favouring aid. Thereon the resentful goddess no longer smiled but frowned upon their love. She led them into offence against Rhea, mighty mother of the gods, who transformed that bold runner and his ungentle bride into a pair of lions, harnessed to her chariot when she drove forth amid a wild din of horns and cymbals.

Atalanta's Race

After the painting by Sir E. J. Poynter P.R.A.

Heracles

1 His Youth

Heracles, whom the Romans called Hercules, was the strongest man on earth, being indeed of the blood of the gods. Amphitryon, king of Tiryns, passed for his father, who had married Alcmene, granddaughter of Perseus; but his true father was Zeus himself, who had deceived this queen in the form of her husband. When his birth was at hand, the ruler of Olympus proclaimed that the child born that day should be lord over all Greece. Then Hera, in hatred of her secret stepson, brought about that his birth was hindered, and that his cousin Eurystheus came into the world before him, whereby afterwards Heracles was doomed to serve that unworthy kinsman.

Alcmene so well guessed how the jealous mistress of heaven would plot against her son, that she dared not nurse him at home, but had him exposed in a field, trusting that Zeus would not fail to protect his own offspring. There, then, came by Hera and Athena, wondering at this sight of a naked, new-born child. Hera, unaware who it was, caught up the babe to hold it to her breast, but it sucked so violently that she threw it down in anger. Athena, more patient and pitiful, carried the unknown Heracles to the city, and gave him to his own mother to be brought up as a foundling.

Joyfully Alcmene undertook to rear her child, hoping that the few drops of Hera's milk he had sucked would save him from the goddess's ill-will. But when Hera came to know who the babe was that she had saved from death, her heart was hot with spite. She sent two snakes to kill him in his cradle. While his mother slept, those ministers of her vengeance had twisted themselves about the child's neck. The nurse sitting by could not move nor speak for horror. But Heracles awoke with a shout that roused his anxious mother to see how her lusty babe had caught one snake in each hand, and laughingly strangled them before they could do him harm. Alcmene's cries in turn brought in her husband with drawn sword, who might well stand amazed at such a feat of infant strength. He sent for Teiresias to cast the child's fortune; and that blind seer now let him know the origin and destiny of Heracles.

Henceforth Amphitryon spared no pains on the bringing up of so wonderful a foster-son. He himself taught the boy to tame horses and to drive a chariot. The most famous teachers of arts and exercises were sought out for him all over Greece, among them Linus, son of Apollo, to be his master in music. But when Linus one day would have chastised this sturdy pupil, Heracles smote him to death with one blow of the lute, thus early indulging the hot temper that was to cost him dear. After this Amphitryon sent him from home to dwell among his herdsmen on the mountains, where he grew taller and stronger than any man in Greece, able to fell an ox with his fist, and never missing his aim with the bow or the spear. He is also said to have made one of that fellowship of young heroes who were schooled in the cave of the wise Centaur Cheiron.

There came a time when the full-grown youth must choose whether his strength should be turned to good or evil. Wandering alone, he met two beautiful women, each beckoning him to follow her on a different path. She who spoke first was full-fed and richly arrayed; her eyes shone with pride and lust; and her wanton charms seemed heightened by meretricious art.

"My name," spoke she, "is Pleasure, loved by the most of men. See, my path is broad and easy and soft to the feet! Take this way and you shall never want rich food and drink, nor fine raiment and soft beds, nor any cheer of life, and all without pain or peril. For I lead my friends far from strife and suffering, and give them only sweet things for which other men have toiled. Come, then, with me!"

The youth looked willingly at this fair temptress, yet before taking her hand, he turned to the other, who pointed out an opposite way. She appeared more modest and maidenly, clad in simple white without gauds or jewels, and in a low voice she spoke thus:—

"My name is Duty, whom no man dares to scorn, yet few learn to love. My path indeed will prove steep and thorny, and on it I promise not ease and pleasure, but labour and smarting, without which no man gains the best gifts of the gods. Yet pain bravely borne shall turn to joy and pride for him who faces the foes of life, wrestling with his own fate, and bearing the burdens of weaker men. So shall he who follows me win honour and peace upon earth, and at last his birthright among the gods."

"Say rather how he may come to die betimes on that perilous path of yours!" cried Pleasure with a mocking laugh.

"Aye," whispered Duty, "but those worthy to go with me think noble death better than to live in sloth and folly."

For a moment the hero stood in doubt, then his swelling heart went out to Duty, and he gave her his hand. Thus was made the Choice of Heracles, whose sorest sufferings would come when he strayed from that toilsome path.

2 His Labours

Having chosen Duty as his guide, Heracles followed her to become the most famous champion of his age. He slew cruel giants, he exterminated fierce wild
beasts; everywhere he hastened to help the oppressed. Gods as well as men
hailed his mighty deeds. Athena equipped him in armour from her own temple;
Hermes gave him a resistless sword; Apollo furnished him with sharp arrows;
and he bore a famous pictured shield, the work of Hephaestus at the bidding of
Zeus. Thus arrayed, he flew to the aid of Thebes when it was threatened by an
invader haughtily demanding tribute. This city, indeed, was dear to Heracles,
since his reputed father Amphitryon, his own kingdom given up, had made his
home there. In the battle for its defence Amphitryon fell; but the prowess of his
son gained the victory. The grateful Creon, king of Thebes, gave Heracles his
daughter Megara in marriage; and it seemed as if he had no more to wish for on
earth.

But nothing could make Hera forget her hatred to this son of Zeus. She sent
upon the hero a furious madness, in which he threw his own children upon a fire
and drove his wife from him in horror. When his frenzy passed away, letting him
know what he had done, he fell into deep melancholy, and for a time was seen no
more among men, while he sought pardon and healing from the gods. As penance it was appointed him to become vassal to his kinsman Eurystheus, he who,
by Hera's cunning trick, had gained the birthright promised by Zeus. Humbly
Heracles stooped his pride to serve that poor-spirited and faint-hearted lord,
spending now the best years of his manhood in labours beyond the power of any
but himself. On ten weary errands must he go at the bidding of Eurystheus, before he could be his own man again – such was the decree given forth from the
oracle at Delphi.

The first task set him was to slay the Nemean lion, a savage monster that had
long kept the land of Argolis in dread; it was invulnerable to all weapons, being
of the blood of that hundred-headed Typhon buried by Zeus beneath the roots of
Etna. Armed only with his bow, and with a wild olive tree he tore up by the roots
to make him a club, Heracles hunted through the forest of Nemea where the lion
had its lair. Before long its fearsome roar led him to a thicket, from which it burst
towards him open-mouthed, with jaws and mane dripping blood. Heracles drew
his bow with true aim, but one and another arrow fell harmless from the creature's hide, that could not be pierced by the sharpest point. But with his club the
hero laid it low in the act to spring; then, flinging away his weapons, he threw

himself upon the writhing beast, cast his arms round its neck, and choked it to death. He had much ado to tear off its skin, hard as iron; but when he had flayed it with its own sharp claws, he hung the skin about him as a garment and helmed himself with its head. By these spoils and by his huge club, this lion-killer was henceforth known wherever he went. So terrible did he appear bringing back such trophies, that the cowardly Eurystheus shrunk from meeting him face to face, but sent out his further commands for Heracles by another's voice.

The second task laid upon Heracles was to quell a monster haunting the marshes of Lerna. This was the Hydra, that huge snake with nine heads, one of which could not be hurt by any weapon, and the others would grow again as fast as they were cut off. Accompanied by his nephew Iolaüs, the hero set out for Lerna in a swift chariot, and soon found the wooded hill where the Hydra kept itself hidden. Leaving his nephew beside the horses, with fiery arrows he fetched the creature from out of its hole, to swoop upon him, hissing and spitting from all its heads, that waved like branches in a storm. Undaunted, Heracles met its onset and mowed down the twisting heads one by one, yet as fast as he cut them off two grew up in place of one, while it twined its loathsome body round his limbs and almost stifled him with its foul breath. He was forced to call for the help of Iolaüs, who ran up with a torch; then as Heracles shore off the bristling heads, his nephew seared each bleeding wound, so that they could not grow again. At last the raging Hydra was left with that one head no iron could wound; but he crushed it with his club, and tore it off and buried it in the ground under a heavy rock. In its poisonous blood the conqueror dipped his arrows, to make the hurt from them henceforth incurable.

His third labour was to bring in alive the golden-antlered and brazen-hoofed stag Cerynitis, that roamed free upon the Arcadian hills. A bold man he would have been who should slay that beast, sacred as it was to Artemis. For a year Heracles chased it in its native haunts and far beyond; it led him out of Greece to Thrace; and on over barbarous wildernesses, and deep into the northern darkness. Foiled again and again, he had nothing for it but to lame the agile stag with a dart, then could catch it to bear home on his shoulders. By the way he fell in with Artemis, wroth against him for hurting a beast under her protection. But a hero can soothe even an offended goddess; and she let him carry the stag to Eurystheus.

The fourth labour was to catch a grimmer beast, that boar that ravaged the Erymanthian mountain ridge between Attica and Elis. On his way to this adventure, Heracles brought on a strange battle, against his will. He was entertained by a Centaur named Pholus, who set before him meat enough but no wine, for he had only one cask, the gift of Dionysus, which belonged to the Centaurs in common, and must not be opened unless all the race were there to share it. Yet Heracles persuaded his host to broach that cask; and when the fumes of strong wine spread through the woods, the other Centaurs came trampling up, armed with rocks and fir branches. In their anger over the broached cask, they would have fallen upon the stranger, who stoutly defended himself, and his invincible arrows drove them to take shelter in the cave of Cheiron, his old teacher. That good Centaur, in the fray, was hurt by a chance arrow, which, dipped in the Hydra's poisonous blood, killed him in slow agony, all his own arts of healing being in vain. Pholus, too, the kindly host, died from handling one of those deadly arrows, which he let fall on his foot. Having mournfully done the last offices to those friends on whom he had brought such suffering, Heracles held on to the haunts of the Erymanthian boar, which he drove from the forests up to the bare crests, and wearied it out with chasing in deep snowdrifts till he could bind it with cords to bring it alive to Eurystheus.

His fifth labour was to cleanse in a single day the stables of Augeas, king of Elis, who kept three thousand cattle, but for thirty years had not taken the trouble to clear out the enclosures heaped with their filth. When he saw Heracles present himself for a task so unworthy of a hero, Augeas laughed, and lightly promised him one-tenth of his herds, if he would do the work that seemed beyond a giant's power. But Heracles was crafty as well as stout. He saw how the rivers Peneus and Alpheus flowed hard by, and whose waters he brought by a new channel to sweep through the Augean stables, and thus cleansed them out in a day. Now that Augeas heard how he had been sent by Eurystheus for this very task, he was for refusing the promised reward; but Heracles held him to his offer, calling to witness against him his own son Phyleus, in whose presence it was made; and when Phyleus testified truly, the angry father drove him from home, along with the hero who had done him so good a service. Years later, Heracles came back to teach that churlish lord how ill he had done in breaking his word with such a servant.

The sixth labour was hunting out the Stymphalanian birds, those same arrow-feathered birds of prey that troubled the voyage of the Argonauts. Lake Stymphalus in Arcadia was their breeding place, which Heracles found black with such a throng of the mischievous fowl that he knew not how to deal with them. But Athena, goddess of invention, came to his aid, giving him a huge pair of brass clappers made by Hephaestus, to raise a rattle louder than all the screeching of the birds. Taking post on a hill, Heracles startled them up by the clappers, then, as they rose in the air, shot them down with his deadly arrows; and those that flew away were so scared as never again to be seen in Greece.

The seventh labour was to master a bull wandering madly about the island of Crete. Minos, its king, willingly gave him leave to chase down this pest that worked havoc through his dominions, and no man had yet been able to tame it. But Heracles caught the bull, and mounted its back, and rode it through the sea to Greece. There Eurystheus turned it loose, again to be a terror to the people, till it was hunted down on the plain of Marathon by Theseus, he who ever took pride in doing deeds after the pattern of his great kinsman.

The eighth labour of Heracles was to catch the mares of Diomedes, a Thracian chief, who reared his horses to be as savage as himself by feeding them on human flesh. The hero first took Diomedes captive and gave him as food to his own wild mares, which after devouring their master, let Heracles drive them away quietly as kids. Yet they were not wholly weaned from their fierce nature, as, while he made a stand against the Thracians pursuing him, the troop of mares tore in pieces his companion Abderus, set to guard them; and Heracles had to tame them afresh. Men say that a horse of this breed was that Bucephalus long afterwards mastered by Alexander of Macedon.

The ninth labour was to win for Eurystheus's daughter the belt of Hippolyte, gift of Ares to that queen of the war-like Amazons, who lived far away in Asia. So un-womanlike were they as to kill all their male children; and they burned away their right breasts so as not to be hindered in the use of the bow. Hippolyte was so charmed by the looks and bearing of this foe that she offered to give up her belt freely. But Hera, taking the form of an Amazon, stirred up the women against him and they attacked him. Her stepson bring off that trophy without a hard battle and he killed Hippolyte, thinking that she had betrayed him. As he carried it back to Greece, Heracles passed by Troy, and there saved the daughter of its king, Laomedon, from the claws of a monster, as Perseus freed Andromeda. This king, also, cheated the hero of his promised reward; then Heracles vowed to come back and leave no stone of Troy standing upon another, as he did years later.

The tenth labour for Heracles, that should have been the last, was to bring a herd of red cattle belonging to the giant Geryon, from the island Erythia by the western ocean, where they fed under guard of the two-headed dog Orthus; and Geryon himself was so monstrous that he had three bodies, three heads, six arms, and six feet, being the son of Chrysaor, a giant engendered from the blood of Medusa, who was slain by Perseus. The more Heracles toiled for his kinsman, the more that cowardly king hated him, envying his prowess, and now Eurystheus hoped to be rid of him, sent so far against such a foe. But Heracles set out cheerful and undaunted, undertaking by the way exploits that would have appalled most men. Reaching the straits of Gades, he there set up two landmarks henceforth famed as the pillars of Heracles. Thirsty after long wandering through waterless deserts, the heat of the sun so irked him that he dared to point his arrows against Apollo, lord of the sky. Yet noble Apollo took no offence at his boldness, but favoured him with a golden boat in which he passed over to Erythia, where he slew the three-headed giant and his two-headed dog.

He then drove Geryon's herd home over seas and rivers and mountains, yet not without fresh perils on the way. As he passed through Italy, the fire-breathing giant Cacus stole part of the cattle while their keeper lay asleep. To leave no plain trace of the theft, he dragged them into his cave backwards by the tail. Deceived by this trick, when he had searched all round, Heracles gave them up for lost; but as he drove the rest of the herd past that hidden cave, the beasts shut up within called back to their fellows. To seek them out was to put himself face to face with Cacus, who found too late how ill it was to rob such a stranger. Having slain the thievish giant, Heracles went on with the herd, and still had much ado to keep them together, for Hera sent a gadfly to drive them wild among the hills; and she flooded a water on his way, which he could not cross till he had filled up the channel with stones. It was then that he wandered far into the wilds of Scythia, and there dealt with another monster, half-woman, half-serpent. But in the end he brought the herd safe to Greece, to make for Eurystheus a rich sacrifice to that ungracious queen of heaven.

When now the hero hoped to be free, that mean-minded king still claimed his service. Two of the tasks he had accomplished Eurystheus refused to count among the ten: the slaying of the Hydra, because then Heracles had his nephew's help; and the cleansing of the Augean stables, because for that he had taken hire. So he must undertake two more labours, making twelve in all; and the last were the worst.

He was next sent to pluck three golden apples from a garden given by Gaea, the earth-mother, to Zeus and Hera on their marriage. The Garden of the Hesperides it was called, from those four nymphs, daughters of Night, who kept it; and for warder it had a sleepless hundred-headed dragon. No man even knew where this garden lay; and Heracles, in search of it, had to wander far and wide, everywhere slaying giants and monsters with his mighty club. Once he came to blows with Ares himself, but Zeus by a thunderbolt parted those kinsmen of Olympian blood. At last the friendly nymphs of the Eridanus advised the hero to ask his way from Nereus, Old Man of the Sea, who knew all things. So Heracles did, coming upon Nereus while he slept clad in dripping seaweeds, to bind him and hold fast his slippery body for all the changing forms it was his way to take, till, weary of the struggle, he told how to find the island Garden of the Hesperides in the western ocean.

Further directions he should get from Prometheus, who now for thirty years had been chained to an icy crag of the Caucasus, exposed by turns to scorching sun and freezing winds, while daily tormented by the talons of an eagle, or as some say, a vulture, the minister of Zeus. As Heracles strode across those giant mountains, he saw this bird flying on its cruel errand, and shot it with one of his fatal arrows. Thus guided to the place of punishment that should last for ages, it was easy for the hero to tear Prometheus loose; nor did Zeus resent that boldness of his son, but laid aside his anger against the friend of man. The grateful prisoner, wise with age and lonely sorrow, repaid his release by good counsels for

The Garden of the Hesperides
By Sir Edward Burne-Jones

Heracles, bidding to seek out Atlas and ask him to fetch the golden apples from the Hesperides, who were thought to be his children.

So the messenger of Eurystheus went on to Africa, and first he came to Egypt, where the king, Busiris, had harsh welcome for strangers. Years before, a famine falling on his land, a certain soothsayer from Cyprus told how the gods' anger might be turned away by yearly sacrifice of some man not born on the soil. Busiris made this soothsayer his first sacrifice; and every year some stranger was marked for death. So Heracles, taken as a goodly victim, was brought to the sacrifice with laughter in his heart, for he burst the bonds like thread, killed the king at his own altar, and went his way from among the terrified Egyptians.

In Africa he overcame a doughtier foe, the giant Antaeüs, who challenged all-comers to wrestle with him for life or death, and could vanquish most men by the fresh strength it was his nature to draw in as often as he touched his mother-earth. But the hero had craft as well as strength to hold Antaeüs up in the air and there choke the breath out of him, so that he troubled travellers no more. Heracles also cleared the Libyan sands of wild beasts, as was his wont wherever he came.

So, after long travel, he found Atlas, where that weary giant bears up the weight of the world. Heracles offered to take the burden for a time on his own shoulders if Atlas would go for the golden apples, as he consented to do. But when he came back with three apples robbed from the garden, Atlas was unwilling to shoulder his heavy load again, now that he had felt what it was to stretch his limbs freely. The hero had to use cunning when force would not serve him. Pretending to be content, he only asked Atlas to hold the world for a little, while he wound cords about his own aching head to ease the pressure. The dull-witted giant did so; but no sooner had he the world on his back again, than Heracles made off with the golden apples, leaving Atlas taken by his own trick.

When once more he came back safe and successful, his unkind kinsman saw with despair how from all the perilous labours laid upon him Heracles but won more glory and goodwill as a benefactor of men. To make an end of him, Eurystheus chose a task that seemed beyond the might of any mortal; he sent his ever-victorious champion to fetch from the nether world Cerberus, the three-headed hound of hell. For this enterprise, Heracles piously prepared himself by visiting Eleusis, there being initiated into its mysteries and cleansed from the guilt of the Centaurs' blood. He then went to Taenarum the southern-most point of the Peloponnesus, where a dark cave opened as one of the gates of Hades. The god Hermes led him below into that chill underworld, where the thin shades fled in affright from a being of flesh and blood; but Medusa stood to face him, and he would have drawn his sword upon her, had not Hermes held his hand, bidding him remember how ghosts could no more be hurt by iron. The shade of Meleager, too, ventured up to whisper to him a message of love for his mourning sister Deïaneira, of which more was to come than he knew.

Near the gates of Hades, Heracles was amazed to find two living men chained to the black rock, and still more when he recognized them as his old comrades Theseus and Peirithoüs. For Peirithoüs, king of the Lapithae, who fought their great battle with the Centaurs, had been so exalted with pride that he ventured to woo Persephone in hell itself, and his dear friend Theseus accompanied him on the too daring errand; then, seized by Pluto, they were both condemned to endless prison among the dead. Hope shone in their eyes at the sight of Heracles; pitiably they cried to him for help, which he did not grudge. He caught Theseus by the hand to tear him loose from his chains; and the king of Athens could thus win back for a time to the upper world. But when the hero would have freed Peirithoüs also, the rocks shook as from an earthquake, and he was forced to leave that presumptuous man fast bound to his fate.

Yet so bold was he that he slew a bull of Pluto's cattle, pouring the blood into a trench for the wan ghosts to get a taste of life; and when the herdsman would have hindered, Heracles crushed his ribs, hardly letting him go but at the entreaty of his mistress Persephone. In such manner the hero stormed through hell till he came at last face to face with its dark-browed king, who barred his further passage. The undaunted one shot an arrow into Pluto's shoulder, making him roar for pain never felt before. Thus aware that this was an asker not to be denied, on learning his errand grim Pluto gave him leave to carry away Cerberus, if he could master it with his hands alone, using no weapon. Then at the mouth of Acheron, Heracles gripped that hellish watchdog by the throat, and, for all the terror of its three barking heads, its poison-dripping teeth, and its stinging tail like a scorpion's, he swung the loathly monster over his back and brought it up to earth to cast before the feet of Eurystheus.

This king, aghast at the very sight, could do nothing with Cerberus but let it go. As for Heracles, triumphant in every ordeal, Eurystheus gave up in despair his mastership over such a hero, and set him free on condition that he put back the monster at its fearsome watch post.

3 His Death

Thus released from his long servitude, Heracles still wandered about the world doing mighty deeds of strength to aid his fellow men. Yet ever Hera's ill will followed him, clouding his mind, so that here and there he turned aside from the chosen path of virtue. Athena for her part stood by him with help and counsel; and Zeus looked kindly upon the feats of his son, nor did he spare to chastise his spiteful queen when she took on her to send storms upon the hero's course. How he sailed with the Argonauts, how he dealt with the false king of Troy, how he brought back Alcestis to the house of Admetus, are famous tales often told.

Long ago, he had parted from his wife Megara, when he killed her children in a fit of madness; and in time he sought another bride, Iole, daughter of King Eurytus, who in his youth had taught him the use of the bow. This renowned archer offered his daughter's hand as prize to whoever could shoot better than himself and his three sons. Heracles came to the trial and beat his old master. But when he claimed Iole, Eurytus was unwilling to let her marry a man known to have brought such woe on Megara. Among the king's sons, Iphitus alone took the part of him whom he loved and admired beyond all men; then, his bride being denied him, Heracles went away in wrath.

Forthwith it happened that certain oxen of Eurytus were stolen by the noted thief Autolycus. The king was sure that this was done by Heracles in revenge; but Iphitus would not believe such villainy of his friend. He sought out Heracles, and they joined together to hunt down the true robber. On their chase they had mounted a tower to look out for the stolen herd, when the hero's old madness returned upon him, and holding Iphitus to blame for the ill will of his father, he hurled him from the tower in sudden fury.

When he came to himself and found that he had killed his best friend, Heracles passed into melancholy remorse. He pilgrimaged from one shrine to another, seeking to be purified from that sin. The oracle at Delphi at first refused to answer so blood-stained a suppliant; whereupon he threatened to rob the temple, to carry off the tripod and to set up an oracle of his own; then Zeus had some ado to make peace between his fierce son and the offended Apollo. In the end Heracles wrung from this god's priestess a sentence that his guilt could be purged away only by selling himself as a slave for three years, and giving the price to the children of Iphitus.

Willingly the hero stooped to this penance. In charge of Hermes, taking ship for Asia, where he was little known, he let himself be sold for three talents to Omphale, queen of Lydia. She soon found out what a strong slave she had, who rid her land of robbers and beasts of prey as easily as another would bear wood and water. But when she knew that this was no other than the world-renowned Heracles, she would have kept him for a spouse rather than a servant. Then, alas, in the softness and luxury of eastern life, the hero forgot his manhood, and let Omphale make sport with him. While she took his club and lion-skin as toys, he put on woman's clothes and gauds to sit at her feet spinning wool, or amusing her and her maids with stories of how he had strangled snakes in his cradle, and laid low giants, and quelled monsters, and gone down to face the king of death in his dark abode.

So three years passed away in shameful ease; then at once Heracles came to his right mind, like one awakening from a dream. He tore off the womanish garments in shame; he dropped the distaff from his knotty hands; and, turning his back on the idle court of Omphale, strode forth once more to seek deeds that might become a hero. But again a woman as fated to be this strong man's undoing.

In his later wanderings he came to Calydon, and saw Deïaneira, daughter of King Oineus, to whom he bore a message from her brother Meleager in Hades. From him Heracles had heard of her beauty; now he loved her well and carried her away as his wife, after a hot fight for her with a rival wooer, the river-god

Acheloüs, who changed himself into a snake and a bull, but in any form could not withstand the son of Zeus.

As if that beaten river-god would still do him an ill turn, his road brought him to a stream in flood, where the Centaur Nessus stood offering to carry wayfarers across on his back. For himself Heracles scorned such a ferry; he flung over his club and lion-skin on the farther bank, that he might lightly swim the swollen water; but his wife he trusted to Nessus. Then that rude Centaur, inflamed by her beauty, would have borne her off; but Heracles heard her cry, and with one of his poisoned arrows brought Nessus to the ground. In his death throes, the vengeful monster whispered to Deïaneira a lying tale: he bid her dip a shirt in his blood, and if ever she lost her husband's love, that should prove a charm to bring it back.

Heracles ended his labours by taking amends from those who in past years had done him wrong, among them King Eurytus, whom he conquered and slew, and made his daughter Iole a captive. When Deïaneira heard how her husband's old love lay in his power, she was moved by jealousy to try the spell of the Centaur's blood, which in truth had been poisoned by the hero's own deadly arrow. She sent him a shirt dipped in this venom, begging him to wear it as it was made by her hands. Without suspicion he put it on, when he came to offer sacrifices of thanksgiving for his victory.

Then, as soon as the fire on the altar had warmed the poisoned blood, burning pains seized him and shot through every vein, till, for once in his life, he could not but roar for agony. Vainly he struggled to pull off the fatal garment; it stuck to his skin like pitch, and he was fain to tear away the tortured flesh, beneath which his veins hissed and boiled as if melted by inward flames. In his rage he caught the servant who had innocently brought this gift from his wife, and hurled him into the sea. Seeing that he must die, with his last strength he tore down tree trunks to make a funeral pyre, on which he stretched himself, begging his companions to kindle it beneath his still living body. His armour-bearer, Philoctetes, alone had heart to do him this sad service, which Heracles rewarded with the gift of his deadly bow and arrows, that should one day be turned against Troy.

"Hera, you are avenged: give me a stepmother's gift of death!" were his last words, as the flames rose crackling about him; and a terrible storm of thunder and lightning broke out above, through which Athena's chariot bore the demigod to Olympus.

On the pyre lay the ashes of what part of him came from his mother. The immortal part he had from Zeus now dwelt in heaven. There even Hera's hatred died away, so that she welcomed him among the gods, and gave him in marriage her daughter Hebe, the spirit of eternal youth.

When poor Deïaneira knew what she had unwittingly done to her dearly loved husband, she killed herself for remorse, goaded by the upbraiding of her own son Hyllus. By the dying wish of Heracles this son married Iole; and from them sprang a famous race of heroes, later known as the Heraclids.

But the children of Heracles long inherited their father's hard fortunes. They were chased from city to city by the hatred of Eurystheus, so that they were forced to wander over Greece under the guardianship of Iolaüs, now grown old and feeble, yet ever faithful to the memory of his dead comrade and kinsman. At last Demophon, son of Theseus, gave them refuge in Athens, and with Hyllus gathered an army to defend them against Eurystheus. An oracle declaring that a maiden of noble birth must be sacrificed as the price of victory, Macaria, daughter of Heracles and Deïaneira, did not fear to devote herself to death. And in the hot battle Iolaüs prayed to Zeus to give him back for one day the strength of his youth; then, his prayer being heard, no foe could stand before a champion worthy to follow that peerless hero. The army of Eurystheus was set to flight, and its lord brought to a miserable end.

Still the Heraclids found themselves dogged by evil fate, as if the sins of their great father rose up against them. It was long before the curse of the race seemed to have worn out. Not till generations had passed, were warriors of the blood of Heracles able to conquer the Peloponnesus and divide its kingdoms among their chiefs.

Alcestis

Time was when great Apollo had so grievously offended his father Zeus that as punishment he had, for nine years, to serve as a mortal upon earth. Thus the god became herdsman to the Thessalian king Admetus, who made such a good master to him that, his term of service up, as parting gift Apollo won for Admetus from the Fates a boon never yet granted to man. When his day came to die, this king might live on if he could find any soul who loved him so well as to go down to Hades in his stead.

The day dawned when Death's messenger brought to the house of Admetus that word that strikes dumb king as well as beggar. Then eagerly he sought one willing to take his place. None of his friends would go down into darkness for his sake. His people had no more to give him than due pity and lamentation. His old father and mother clung fast to the few dim years they might yet have to live. Only his wife Alcestis, in the bloom of her beauty, joyful mother of children as she was, declared herself ready to sacrifice her life for his; and so it was to be.

As the black shape of Death drew near the doors to lead her away, the noble queen washed herself in running water, put on her festive attire and choicest ornaments to come forth for the last time into the light of day. With heartbroken woe she embraced once more her tearful children; of her servants too she took kind farewell; and these were her last words to Admetus—

"Since thy life is dearer to me than my own, I die willingly, not caring to take another husband, nor to abide with your orphaned children, as well loved by you as by me. One thing only I ask: give them up to the grudge of no second wife, for a serpent may be kinder than a stepmother."

The weeping king vowed that in death as in life Alcestis should be his only bride; and with this promise of comfort she fell into a mortal swoon.

While all the house was now busy with preparing her funeral rites, there arrived an ill-timed guest – Heracles bound on one of his mighty errands! Struck by the signs of mourning that met his eyes, he would have turned away; but Admetus, true to the duty of being hospitable, dissembled his grief, giving Heracles to think that the dead woman was only a visitor. Led into the guest chamber, crowned with flowers, and well supplied with wine, the hero carelessly fell to boisterous drinking and singing, till an old servant rebuked him for such unseemly riot in a house whose mistress had just been carried out to burial. Struck sober by contrition, and by the generosity of his host, Heracles asked which way Death had gone, then hurried after, bent on wresting from him his victim; and the house of Admetus was left hushed in its woe.

> "Night wore away
> Mid gusts of wailing wind, the twilight grey
> Stole o'er the sea, and wrought his wondrous change
> On thing unseen by night, by day not strange,
> But now half seen and strange; then came the sun,
> And therewithal the silent world and dun
> Waking, waxed many-coloured, full of sound,
> As men again their heap of troubles found,
> And woke up to their joy or misery."
>
> —William Morris

Admetus was sitting alone at daybreak in his silent home, overwhelmed by sorrow, also by shame that his wife had shown him the courage to die. Now again Heracles entered his gates, this time leading a veiled woman at his side.

"Oh, king!" he greeted Admetus, "it was ill done of thee to hide from me that thy wife lay dead; and I did thee wrong by revelling in a home darkened by such a loss. Here, to make amends, I bring a woman whom I won in a hard contest. Take her for thine own; or at least keep her for me till I come again."

"Lead her to some other friend!" cried Admetus, waving her away; and as he fixed his eyes on the veiled figure, he broke out: "I could not bear to see in my house one whose form so strongly recalls my own wife, that the very sight of her sets me weeping afresh."

"Nay, dry these tears," said the jovial hero. "Mourning brings not back the dead; but for the living there are still gifts of joy. Take, then, this woman to wife, and forget what has gone before."

"Never can I love any woman save Alcestis!" vowed the king; but his voice rose in a cry of joyful amazement, as Heracles drew off the veil to show him the living face of her he loved so well.

Alcestis it was and no other, whom for once a half-divine hero had been able to tear out of the arms of Death. Three days she lay breathing yet speechless, as if dazed by the dread of what she had seen through the gate of Hades. Then she rose and spoke, and went about the house which her life filled again with gladness.

Pygmalion and Galatea

Pygmalion, king of Cyprus, had more fame as a sculptor than as a warrior. So devoted was he to his art that he did not marry, declaring that no living woman could be so beautiful as the figures he fashioned with his own hands. And at one ivory statue he worked so long and so lovingly that it became the mistress of his heart, till he would have spent all he had in the world to give it breath as well as silent grace and beauty. All day he laboured to put new touches of perfection to the form; and all night he lay sighing for the power to make it flesh and blood.

Galatea was the name he gave his statue, in vain hoping to call it to life. He sought to kiss warmth and movement into its shapely limbs. He decked it with costly clothes, made its neck and arms sparkle with precious jewels, wreathed its cold head with flowers of every hue; but all in vain. The image remained an image, that seemed less fair the more he hid its white form in gold and purple.

There came the feast of Aphrodite, the great goddess of the island. Then Pygmalion presented himself in her temple, bearing rich offerings and sending up a passionate prayer with the incense smoke that rose from the altar.

"Queen of love, take pity on one who has too long despised your power! Give me for bride the work of my own hands; or, if that may not be, a maiden of earth as lovely as my Galatea!"

As if in favourable answer, three times the altar flame leaped up in the air, making Pygmalion's heart beat high with joyful hope. He hastened home to stand before the statue that a hundred times had almost cheated his eyes into belief it might be alive.

"Galatea!" he cried for the thousandth time, stretching out his arms; then had almost shrunk back in dread of what he so long desired.

For now as he gazed, a change came over the ivory shape. Its breast heaved; its veins ran with blood; its eyes no longer stared upon him like stones. It was no cheat. He pressed the hand that grew warm and soft in his. He could feel the pulses throbbing under his touch. He smiled to the face that smiled back again. He spoke, and his Galatea's lips had breath to answer—

"Aphrodite has worked her miracle!"

"Speechless he stood, but she now drew anear,
Simple and sweet as she was wont to be,
And once again her silver voice rang clear,
Filling his soul with great felicity;
And thus she spoke, 'Wilt thou not come to me,
O dear companion of my new-found life,
For I am called thy lover and thy wife'."

— *William Morris*

Pygmalion and Galatea
By Sir Edward Burne-Jones

The Rape of Persephone

An ill trick it was Aphrodite played on gods and men when she bid her mischievous son to shoot his dart at Pluto, that even in his gloomy kingdom should be known the power of love. From such a mountain mouth as breathes fire and smoke over Sicily came forth the stern King of Hades, to drive ;n his iron chariot across that fair isle, where the ground heaves beneath fruitful crops, and ruin is strangely mingled with the richest green.

There, in the Vale of Enna, his lowering looks fell upon Persephone, sweet daughter of Demeter, blooming like the flowers she plucked among her sportive companions. But she dropped her lapful of violets and lilies when that fearsome wooer caught her up into his chariot, striking his forked spear upon the ground, that opened in a dark cleft though which he bore her away to his dwelling in the nether world. A cry for help, too late, brought up Demeter to see that her beloved daughter had vanished from the face of the earth.

"Persephone! Persephone!" she cried in vain. No answer came but the rumble of the earthquake and the stifled roar of the volcano hailing that tyrant's retreat to his kingdom underground.

All day the sad mother sought her child, and at night she called Persephone's name, lit by torches kindled at the fires of Etna. Many a day she wandered over land and sea, but neither sun nor moon could show her the darling face, never forgotten in her heart. At last, in Sicily, she found a trace of Persephone – her girdle floating on a stream into which one of the girl's playmates had wept herself away, and could give only such silent token of her friend's fate!

But the nymph of another stream had power to speak, fair Arethusa, who, pursued by the river-god Alpheus under the sea, had fled to Ortygia, and there was changed by Artemis into a sacred fountain. She in pity told Demeter how, when drawing her springs from the deep caverns underground, she had seen young Persephone throned by Pluto's side as the queen of Hades, adorned with gems and gold in place of flowers, and had through that chill darkness heard her sighing for the sunlit vale whence death's king so roughly snatched her away. What power could bring her back from his cold embrace?

In wild despair Demeter cursed the earth, and chiefly the soil of Sicily that had swallowed up her child. Her tears fell as a plague upon field and grove, so that they no more yielded fruit for man or beast. The people wasted away in famine, crying upon the gods, who feared to lose the reverence and sacrifices due to them. Zeus himself pled with Demeter in vain: she would not return to her seat on Olympus, but went madly up and down the world, scathing and blighting where she was wont to bless.

"If a mother's tears touch you not, be mindful of a father's pride!" was ever her prayer to Zeus. "She is your daughter as well as mine, doomed to so untimely fate; and your honour as well as my woe calls for redress against the insolent robber of our child."

At last the father of the gods was fain to appease this ceaseless suppliant. He

The Return of Persephone
From the painting by Lord Leighton P.R.A.

sent Hermes to fetch Persephone from the nether world and restore her to her mother's arms; yet so it might be only if she had eaten nothing in the kingdom of Pluto. Alas! that very day she had been tempted to taste the seeds of a pomegranate, and thus was she still held in the power of her grudging spouse.

Once more the miserable mother filled heaven with her entreaties, and earth with her wrath. Again Zeus gave a decree that should content both his brother and the goddess of fruitfulness. Persephone's life must henceforth be divided between her mother and her husband, and with each of them she should spend half the year: no alternative might there be than life and death for her in turns.

Joyful was Demeter to clasp her fair daughter, brought back from the gloomy realm of Pluto; and glad was the earth of her joy. For now again the land grew green like a jewel set in its rim of blue sea; the withered trees budded and blossomed; the naked mountains were clothed with leaves; sweet flowers sprang up in valleys for children to gather freshly; the fields and gardens bore goodly food for man, and all the world smiled back to the bright sky of summer.

But, in turn, came year by year their darkening days, when the goddess gave up her daughter to that tyrant of the shades. Then all the earth must mourn with Demeter, laying aside the gay garlands of summer and the rich robes of autumn for wan weeds that ill kept out the winter cold, till again the welcome heralds of spring let men hail Persephone returning to her mother's arms. And so it goes with the world, while men still live and die.

Other wondrous tales men tell of what befell Demeter in those weary wanderings, to and fro, when long she sought her vanished child over the face of the earth. As this: that coming one day to a cottage, disguised as an old beggar woman, she was scornfully given a bowl of mush at the door, where the son of the house, like the rude boy he was, laughed to see how hungrily she ate such humble food; then the seeming crone flung the bowl in his face with an angry word, at which, lo! he had been changed into a spotted lizard, to teach him and his that poverty may hide a goddess.

But another home gave less churlish welcome to this beggar, old and poor. At Eleusis, in Greece, it was that a kindly housewife took her in, and would have had her stay as nurse to the new-born son, named Triptolemus. Bereaved Demeter came to love this child almost as her own, so that she was minded to bestow on him in secret the gift of immortality. His own mother, waking up one night, stood amazed to find that nurse holding her babe in the flames of the fire; then with screams of terror she snatched him away, not knowing how his limbs had been bathed in nectar, and a charm breathed over him so that the fire should but temper his life to deathlessness. Now the stranger shone forth by the hearth as a goddess, to tell what purpose it was had thus been brought to nought; and forthwith she passed away upon her long quest.

But when her mind was set at ease by the return of Persephone, Demeter sought out that nursling at Eleusis to show through him new favour to mortals. In her dragon-chariot she sent Triptolemus out with the gift of corn for men, and to teach them the use of the plough and the sickle, so that no more should they be in danger of famine. And in his native land she set on foot the sacred Eleusinian festival, by which for ages to come its people should remember Demeter and Persephone.

Orpheus and Eurydice

Orpheus the Thracian was famed as sweetest minstrel of old. Son of the muse Calliope, he was born under Mount Rhodope, yet often wandered about Olympus, home of the gods, enchanting also with his song the wooded slopes on Parnassus and the sacred spring of Helicon. The tale goes how when, with the skill taught by his mother-muse, he struck the golden lyre given him by Apollo, fierce beasts of the forest would come forth charmed to tameness; the rushing streams stood still to listen; and the very rocks and trees were drawn after that witching music, that softened the hearts of savage men.

The singer who could breathe life into a stone, readily won the heart of fair Eurydice, not the less since he had shown himself brave as well as gifted when he followed Jason on the quest of the Golden Fleece. But all too short was the happiness of that loving pair. As she danced at their bridal feast, a venomous snake, gliding through the grass, stung the heel of Eurydice, her only among the merry guests, so that she died on the night she was wedded.

The lamenting husband bore her to the grave, playing mournful airs that moved the hearts of all who followed that funeral train. Then, life seeming to him dark as death without his Eurydice, Orpheus pressed on to the very gates of Hades, seeking her where no man might enter till the day of his own doom.

But at this man's tuneful strains, Charon silently ferried him across the Styx, that black stream that divides our sunlit world from the cold realms of Pluto. So moving were the notes of his lyre that the iron bars slid back of themselves, and Cerberus, the three-headed guard of death's gloomy portal, sank down without showing his teeth, to let the lulling music pass. Without challenge Orpheus stole boldly into the world of the shades, flitting about him from all sides to fix their dim eyes on the man who could work such a spell even among the dead.

Fearsome and gruesome were the sights he saw in the dark caves of Tartarus, yet through them he held on undaunted, straining his eyes after Eurydice alone. He came past the daughters of Danaüs, who, all save one, had stabbed their husbands on the wedding night, and for such a crime must do eternal penance by vainly pouring water into a sieve; but, as the Thracian singer went by, they had a brief respite from their bootless task, turning on him looks which he gave not back. So, too, his music made a moment's peace for Tantalus, that once rich and mighty king, that for unspeakable offence against the gods was doomed to suffer burning thirst in a lake whose waters ever fled from his lips, and in his hungry eyes bloomed clusters of ripe fruit withering as he stretched out his hand to clutch them; and over his head hung a huge stone threatening in vain to crush him out of his misery. Again, Orpheus passed where Sisyphus, for his life's burden of wickedness, had to roll uphill a heavy rock always slipping from his arms to spin down to the bottom: he, too, could pause to wipe his hot brow as the singer's voice fell on his ears like balm. Nor did the spell of music fail to stop Ixion's wheel, bound to which that treacherous murderer must for ever whirl through the fiery air in unpitied torment. Then for once, they say, were tears drawn to the dry eyes of the Furies, those three chastising sisters, whose name men fear to speak.

> "Heavenly o'er the startled Hell,
> Holy, where the Accursed dwell,
> O Thracian, went thy silver song!
> Grim Minos with unconscious tears,
> Melts into mercy as he hears—
> The serpents in Megaera's hair
> Kiss, as they wreathe enamoured there;
> All harmless rests the madding throng;—
> From the torn breast the Vulture mute
> Flies, scared before the charmed lute—
> Lulled into sighing from their roar
> The dark waves woo the listening shore—
> Listening the Thracian's silver song!—
> Love was the Thracian's silver song!"
>
> —Schiller

But Orpheus looked not aside, and the thin ghosts ever made way for him as he pressed on till he came before the throne where the dark-browed king of Hades sat beside his queen Persephone, her fair face veiled by the shadows of that dire abode. Then, striking his softest notes, the minstrel raised a chant to stir the hardest heart, beseeching its sovereign for once to loose the bonds of death.

"Love," he sang, "gives me strength to seek the shades before my time; love, that if tales be true, has had power even here, when stern Pluto came forth to win a bride snatched from the world of life. Let me take back my loved one, doomed too soon by fate! Or, if that may not be, oh! dread king, in mercy accept two victims for one, nor bid me return alone to the upper air."

Black-browed Pluto nodded to his prayer, when Persephone whispered a pitiful word in her consort's ear. Then the lyre of Orpheus was silenced by a hollow voice proclaiming through the vaulted halls a boon for once granted to mortal man. All Hades held its breath to hear.

"So be it! Back to the world above, and Eurydice shall follow you as your shadow! But halt not, speak not, turn not to look behind, till you have gained the upper air, or never may you see her face again. Begone without delay, and on your silent path you will not be alone."

In grateful awe, the husband of Eurydice turned his back upon death's throne, taking his way through the chill gloom towards a faint glimmer that marked the gate of Hades. Willingly he would have looked round to make sure that Eurydice came behind him, he would have halted to listen for her footfall. But now all was still as death, save his own hasty steps echoing dreadfully as he pressed on to the light that shone clearer and dearer before him like a star of hope. Then doubt and impatience clouded his mind, so that he could not trust the word of a god. He had not yet gained the gate, when, giving way to eager desire, he turned his head and saw indeed behind him the shrouded form of her he loved so fondly.

"Eurydice!" he cried, stretching out his arms, but they clasped the thin air; and only a sigh came back to him, as her dim shape melted into the darkness.

In vain the twice-bereaved lover made Hades ring with Eurydice's name. He was never to see her more while he lived. Out of his senses for despair, he found himself thrust into the daylight, alone. There he lay like an image, for days unable to speak, or to sing, with no desire but to starve himself back to death.

At last he rose and took his way into the world of men. Now he went silent, the strings of his lyre broken like his heart. He shunned all dwellings and scenes of joy, nor would he look upon the face of women, though many a maid smiled kindly to bid him forget his lost Eurydice. Henceforth, his solitary haunts were the mountain forests of Thrace, where beasts rather than men would be his companions among the rough thickets.

But ere long, as he would have retuned his lyre to strains of woe, the rocks rang with a clamorous din, and forth upon him burst a troop of Maenads, women frenzied by the rites of Dionysus, to whom, with jangling cymbals and clanging horns, they yelled a shrill chorus E*voe, Evoe!* Clothed in fawnskins, and garlanded with vine leaves, they danced towards the stranger; but he rose in horror to fly from their flushed faces, nor heeded the wild outcry with which they called on him to join their revel. Furious at this affront, the maddened votaries of Bacchus followed him like fierce hunters closing on a deer. They stoned him to the ground, they broke his lyre in pieces, and, their drunken rage heated by the sight of blood, that ruthless crew ended by tearing their disdainer in pieces. His limbs were flung into a stream which bore them to the sea; and they tell how his head, still breathing Eurydice's name, was washed ashore on the isle of Lesbos, there to be buried by the Muses in a tomb that became a sacred shrine, on which the nightingales sang more sweetly than elsewhere.

Midas

Midas, king of Phrygia, was rich above all men in the world, yet, like others who have much, his heart was set on more. Once he had the chance to do a service to a god, when in his garden was found old Seilenus, who, strayed from the train of his patron Dionysus, had lain down here to sleep off a drunken bout. Midas sportively bound the wandering reveller with roses, and, after filling him with the meat and drink he loved, took him back to the god of wine; then so well pleased was Dionysus to see that jovial companion, that he bid the friendly king choose any reward he liked to ask. Midas did not think twice.

"Grant me this boon then," he cried eagerly: "that whatever I touch may turn to gold!"

"So be it!" laughed the god, pledging him in a cup of wine; and Midas left his presence exulting to know that henceforth his wealth was boundless.

Impatient to test his new-given power, as he walked through the woods he tore off a twig, and lo! at his touch it had turned to yellow gold. He picked up stones from the path, then they, too, became pure gold, and every clod he handled was at once a glittering nugget; he grasped an ear of corn to find it hard as gold; and when he plucked fruit or flowers they were like the apples of the Hesperides, so that soon his attendants went groaning under the burden of gold he gathered on the way. Weighed down by his golden robes, he himself would willingly have been borne along, but when he mounted a mule it stood a lifeless image, and the litter on which they laid him was too heavy for the strength of all his men. Almost beside himself with pride and greed, he got home to his palace, where, as he brushed through the portal, its posts turned to golden pillars; and when he threw himself on the nearest seat, it was henceforth such a costly throne as any king in the world might envy.

Fatigued by his journey and its excitements, Midas called for food. Obedient menials made haste to spread a table, while others brought basins in which as their lord plunged his hands, the water froze forthwith into golden ice. So it was when he sat down to eat. He smiled to see how his plates and bowls changed to gold, as beseemed; but his smile became a frown when the first savoury mouthful met his lips as tasteless metal. In vain he tried to swallow such rich fare; the sweetest morsel crunched between his teeth like ashes; and when he would have drained a cup of wine, the drink was solid gold.

Tormented by hunger and thirst, he rose from that mockery of a banquet, for once envying the poorest kitchen-boy in his palace. It was no comfort to visit the growing mass of his treasures; the very sight of gold began to sicken him. If he embraced his children, if he struck a slave, their bodies turned in an instant to golden statues. All around glared hateful yellow in his eyes. It was a relief when darkness came to hide that now abhorred wealth. Then, flinging off his heavy golden robes, he sank with a sigh upon a soft couch that at once grew hard and cold; and there he tossed restless all night, the richest and the most wretched man alive.

In sleepless despair, with the first light of dawn he hastened to Dionysus, earnestly beseeching him to take back his gift of splendid misery.

"So men's dearest wishes often prove unwise!" railed the god. "But once more I grant you your desire. Seek out the source of the Pactolus, and by bathing in its pure waters you may undo the spell laid upon you."

Scarcely waiting to thank him, Midas set off for that healing stream. Driven on by the gnawings of hunger, over mountain and plain he panted till he came to the Pactolus, whose sandy bed was streaked with gold wherever he trod; and men say that scales of gold may still be turned up to mark his footsteps. When he reached its cool fountain and hurled into it his fevered body, the crystal water was stained as if by gold. But no sooner had his head plunged beneath it, than that fatal gift was washed away; and to his unspeakable joy Midas came out able to eat and drink like other men.

This king was not always so fortunate in his dealings with the gods. Cured of his greed for gold, yet no wiser in his mind, he took to roaming the green woods, and there came upon Pan at strife with the great Apollo. For that rude Satyr had presumed to boast his pipe of reeds against the god's lute; and they asked Midas to judge which of them made the sweetest music. After listening to their strains, the dull-eared mortal gave judgment for Pan; then Apollo, in displeasure, punished him by decking his head with the ears of an ass, even as the Muses spitefully turned the daughters of Pierus into birds, when these mortal maidens would have contended with them in song on Mount Helicon.

The first pool into which Midas looked showed him how shamefully he had been transformed; but this time he could hope no favour from an angry god. Slinking into his palace by night, the king would have hid from all that he bore those long, hairy ears. His head he kept wrapped night and day in a turban such as makes a shield against the sun for men of the hot East. None knew why Midas went thus arrayed, save only his barber, to whom he could not but disclose the truth, binding him by oaths and threats never to breathe it to human ear.

But the barber, for his part, could not bear the weight of such a secret which he must not tell. Itching to let it out, yet fearing his master's wrath, he stole down to the lonely bank of the river and scooped out a hole, into which he whispered *"Midas has ass's ears"*, hoping to be heard by no man. But where he had opened the ground, there grew up a dump of reeds that, as often as they were stirred by the wind, kept on murmuring, *"Midas has ass's ears"*.

Scylla

Of Megara, Euclid's birthplace, it is told how in old days it was besieged by Minos of Crete. Long the siege lasted, for the Fates had decreed that the city should not be taken while it contained a talisman, which was no other than a lock of purple hair growing on the head of Nisus, its king; and that secret he had told to his daughter Scylla. So, month by month, the Cretan army lay encamped without the walls; but all their attacks were thrown away.

From the highest tower of the city, Scylla so often looked down on her father's foes, that she came to know the leaders by sight and by name. Always her eyes sought out Minos, the famous king, who, enemy as he was, seemed to her the most goodly and gallant man she had ever seen. Her heart followed her eyes, and her dreams kept the hero's image in mind by darkness as by daylight, till the love-sick maiden thought more of this stranger than of her own country or kin.

"Were it not well to end the weary war?" she told herself. "With me for a captive, would not the King of Crete grant us peace? And what could he refuse to her who put into his hands the secret of victory?"

Brooding over such thoughts, at last poor Scylla strung herself up to betray her native city, for the sake of one whose voice she had never heard, save raised in menace against its defenders. At the dead of night she stole to her sleeping father's couch. Softly she shore off the shining purple lock that glittered like a star among his grey hair. Cautiously she slipped out from the gates, and made her way to the enemy camp, demanding of the sentinels to lead her into the presence of Minos.

With beating heart she knelt before the king, whose love she hoped to buy at such a price. But when she held out to him the purple lock, explaining how on it lay the safety of her father's kingdom, and by looks rather than speech would have given him to know why she thus played traitress to her own people, the noble Minos repelled that gift with scornful indignation.

"A treacherous daughter is worthy of no brave man's love!" he declared. "Begone from my sight, dishonour of your race and your sex! Minos gains not victory by baseness."

Now that Megara lay at his mercy the generous foe offered it peace, and, without striking another blow, made ready to sail away to Crete. Scylla, wild with shame and remorse, not daring to face her father, begged in vain to be taken on board the fleet.

"The ship that bore you would never come safe to port," answered Minos sternly. "Such a one as you must be cursed by the gods, to find no resting place on sea nor on land."

"I deserve indeed to die," pleaded the miserable maiden; "yet for you it was I sinned against father and country – leave me not to their wrath!"

The proud king turned away without a word. When she saw his ship set sail, Scylla in despair leaped into the water, clinging to its rudder as it sailed away from her native shore. But down swooped an eagle to strike her with its beak and claws, so that she let go her hold and would have been drowned, had not some god changed her into a sea-bird. In that form she is doomed to fly homeless and restless over the waves, ever pursued by the eagle, that is none other than her betrayed father, to whom the gods granted such endless vengeance. So say some; but others tell how the traitorous daughter was transformed into a cruel monster haunting the strait between Italy and Sicily.

Bellerophon

It seemed as if a curse rested on the house of Sisyphus, the king of Corinth, who for his tyranny and treacheries had been doomed to endless labour in Hades. His son Glaucus was famed for his love of horses, which at last brought him to a cruel end, when the mares which he had fed on human flesh turned madly upon their master and tore him in pieces. The son of Glaucus was Bellerophon, a valiant and comely youth, who yet could not escape the evil fate of his race. For, having slain one of his countrymen in a chance fray, he was forced to fly from Corinth, to take refuge with Proëtus, king of Argos.

This king gave him kindly welcome, sheltering him from the avengers, and offering solemn rites to cleanse his guilt of bloodshed. Bellerophon's youthful charm won not only the favour of Proëtus, but the sinful love of Stheneboea, the dark-eyed princess whom he had brought from Asia to be his queen. But in vain she tempted the loyal guest to secret wickedness. When all her wiles could not make him untrue to honour and hospitality, her love turned to hate, and with a lying tale she would have stirred her husband's wrath against his foully slandered friend. The deceived Proëtus was in a strait what to do. He had come to love this gallant youth so well, that he could not bear to have him slain in his own sight. Yet, the false wife poisoning his mind, he was moved to wreak his jealousy by another's hand.

Without letting Bellerophon guess his changed mood, he sent him to visit his father-in-law, Iobates, king of Lycia, charged with a tablet on which was written in secret characters the bearer's doom.

All unsuspicious of harm, Bellerophon made the long journey by sea and land, that at last brought him to the city of the Lycian king. Iobates received the stranger like a courteous host, asking not who he was, nor whence he came, nor on what errand. Nine days he entertained his unknown guest freely with feasts and games, since Bellerophon's noble bearing showed him worthy of honour at a king's hands. Not till the tenth day did he declare his name, giving over to Iobates the tablet on which Proëtus had drawn a secret message, to be interpreted by his wife's father alone.

"He who bears this token comes deserving death at thy hands. See to it!"

The king of Lycia, in turn, had come to love that winsome Greek so well that he was dismayed to learn how he had been sent here for execution. To his son-in-law, who gave him such a charge, Iobates was so beholden that he dared not refuse to do his bidding; yet loath was he to punish, for an unknown crime, one who had already become his friend.

Unwillingly, he cast about for some plan of having Bellerophon killed without shedding his blood by his own hands; nor had he long to seek. The outskirts of Lycia were then being ravaged by a fire-breathing beast called the Chimaera, that had devoured every champion sent out against it. Indeed the very sight of it was enough to appal the stoutest heart, for it had the head of a lion, the hinder parts of a dragon, the body of a monstrous goat, rough with scales and bristles; and with its breath it scorched all who ventured to face it. Iobates, then, believed himself giving up Bellerophon to certain death when he begged him to rid the land of such a plague; and his heart smote him to see how gladly the gallant youth took upon himself that fatal adventure.

The very gods had pity on an innocent man thus sent to so cruel a death; however, he invoked their aid on his perilous quest by pious sacrifices. Before going far he came upon the winged horse Pegasus, sprung from the blood of that Gorgon slain by Perseus. Bellerophon would eagerly have made his own such a goodly steed; but Pegasus, never yet ridden by man, reared and flung and sprang, and would not let itself be caught. Tired out by his vain efforts to tame it, he had fallen asleep beside a fountain, when Athena appeared to him in a dream, and seemed to lay a golden bridle at his side and to whisper in his ear; "*Wake, take, tame*".

He woke up, and lo! beside him lay the golden bridle, while Pegasus was still feeding by the fountain. As he softly stole up to it, the horse did not now dash away from him, but, lowering its proud neck, let him slip the bit into its mouth, and stood still for him to leap upon its back. By divine aid he had mastered the horse of heaven.

Mounted on such a courser he soon reached the haunts of the Chimaera, that came out raging against him, vomiting fire and smoke. But now that monster had to do with an invincible foe. Soaring in the air beyond reach of hurt, Bellerophon shot down sharp arrows, till the ground, burning under the creature's breath, was quenched in its blood. Then the hero dismounted to cut off its hairy head and scaly tail, which he bore back in triumph as proof of his victory.

Iobates, half-glad to see him return with such spoils, half-concerned to find the victim still alive, soon took excuse to lay upon him another perilous adventure. He charged him with war upon the Solymi, a race of fierce mountain robbers who infested the borders of Lycia, and had slain the king's bravest fighters in many a battle. But they could not stand against the darts of this flying champion; and when he had routed them out of the land, he again came back unhurt.

Next, Iobates sent him far off against the Amazons, that nation of women warriors who had overthrown kings and their armies. But they, too, Bellerophon conquered, and again came back in triumph. On his way home an ambush was laid for him by Iobates, still striving to do his son-in-law's desire; then the hero slew these assailants as easily as he quelled all other enemies.

"This can be no evildoer deserving punishment, but rather a man dear to the gods," the heart of Iobates told him; and when once more Bellerophon came back victorious over every foe, the king no longer sought his death. Joyfully he hailed him as worthy of all honour, gave him his daughter as a wife, and shared with him his kingdom and riches, as if the stranger were his own son.

Thus raised to power and wealth, Bellerophon might surely rest in peace after the trials of his youth. But he who had borne himself so well in adversity, fell away from virtue when life became smooth and soft for him. It seemed as if that old guilt of bloodshed ever rose up against him. With years he grew not wise but proud, forgetting the gods to whom he owed his good fortune, that therefore came to be clouded by their ill will. His eldest son grew up a brave champion like the father, only to fall in battle with savage robbers. His daughter was slain by a shaft of offended Artemis. Heedless of these warnings, Bellerophon thought to fly to heaven on his winged steed. Then Zeus sent a gadfly to sting Pegasus, so that it reared in the air and threw off its presumptuous rider, tumbling to earth alive but sorely hurt. Now made aware of the gods' anger, the down-fallen hero henceforth shrunk from the looks of men. Crippled and feeble, he wandered about like a madman in solitary places, till at last death ended his miserable age, of which Homer has to tell how—

"Woes heaped on woes consumed his wasted heart."

Arion

After Orpheus, fabled as son of a Muse, the most famous singer in ancient Greece was Arion, who lived much with his chief patron, the wise Periander, king of Corinth. But Arion had a mind for showing his skill in other lands, and, for all Periander could say to keep him at Corinth, he sailed away to take part in a great musical contest held in Sicily.

There this minstrel gained such prizes and rich gifts that it was a treasure of gold and silver he had to take back from the land to which he brought nothing but his harp. To carry his wealth safe home, he hired a ship of Corinth, trusting Periander's countrymen rather than strangers not to play him false. But the sailors were covetous and treacherous; and the sight of that treasure turned them to pirates.

All went well with the ship; and Arion little guessed that he were safer on the stormiest waves. Halcyon weather and gentle breezes were bearing him round the southern point of Greece, when at once those wicked men threw off the mask of kindliness. With drawn swords they fell upon their passenger, declaring how they had hatched a plot to rob him of all he possessed

"Take my gold, but spare my life!" he entreated them to no purpose.

"Then how should we face Periander?" was their mocking answer. "Your gold will we bring safe to Corinth, but not the owner, who might tell tales. Choose forthwith: either slay yourself and get from us the boon of a grave on shore, or we throw you overboard without more ado."

All his promises and prayers being lost on them, the poor rich man asked one last grace, that he should be allowed to deck himself in his costliest robes, and to sing to the harp his sweetest song; then he would leap into the sea and save them the guilt of bloodshed. To this the rough sailors agreed, not unwilling to hear for once the strains of a renowned minstrel who had won all that wealth they hoped now to make their own.

So Arion robed himself in purple, and perfumed his hair, crowned with a triumphal wreath he took as the noblest of his winnings. Thus arrayed, he stood upon the poop to sing his death-chant. Poets tell that, when he sang in wood and field, the lamb and the wolf would stand together to listen, indeed, the stag and the lion, the hare and the hounds, while overhead the dove and the hawk hung still to listen in the air. Now, so sweetly his golden harp resounded over the sea, that not only were those cruel men half-stirred to pity, but a shoal of dolphins gathered about the ship, drawn after the music as if by a cable. When it came to an end, taking one last look at the bright sky, harp in hand, Arion leapt overboard.

The pirates let their sail fill and stood on for Greece, pleased to be so well rid of him. But Arion had not sunk under the waves. He was caught on the back of an admiring dolphin, that carried him safe and dry over the sea to Taenarum, the nearest point of land. So works the magic of song for men favoured by Apollo.

Thus set on shore, Arion travelled through the Peloponnesus and came to Corinth a day before the ship. The returned minstrel was gladly welcomed by Periander, who, indeed, could barely believe his story of his strange escape from drowning. When now the ship sailed into harbour those robbers, summoned before the king, were asked for news of Arion. Boldly they declared that they had left him honoured and prosperous in the new Greece beyond the sea. But as the false words came from their lips, he stepped forth before them clad as they saw him lost overboard, and still bearing the harp of marvellous power.

The amazed sailors no longer dared deny their crime but fell on the ground praying for mercy, and for pardon from their victim, whom they took for a god. The harper's heart was not tuned to vengeance; but the king was stern in justice. He ordered the treacherous crew to a death more cruel than they had designed for Arion, in memory of whose wonderful preservation was erected at Taenarum a brazen monument of him riding on the dolphin's back.[1]

---

[1] Pausanias speaks as if he had seen this monument, and adds that he had himself known "a dolphin so full of gratitude to a boy, by whom he had been healed of wounds received from some fishermen, that he was obedient to his call and carried him on his back over the sea whenever he wished."

The Argonauts

1 Jason's Youth

In a cave high up the rocky and snowy sides of Mount Pelion dwelt Cheiron, oldest and wisest of the Centaurs, that wondrous race that were half-horse and
half-man. When the brute strength of his lower part began to fail, the white-
bearded Centaur's head was richly stored with knowledge and experience, and
his hands had rare skill in playing on a golden harp, to the music of which he
gave forth wise counsels in human speech. So great was his fame that many a
king's and hero's son came to be trusted to his care for rearing in all that befitted
a noble youth. From him they had lessons in duty, to fear the gods, to reverence
old age, and to stand by one another in pain and hardship. He was a master of the
healing art, and this they learned as from the lips of Aesculapius himself. He
taught them to sing, to make music, to bear themselves gracefully in the dance,
but also to run, box, and wrestle, to climb the dizzy rocks, and to hunt wild beasts
in the mountain forests, laughing at all dangers as they scorned sloth and gluttony, and cheerily facing the sharpest storms of winter as they plunged into
foaming torrents under the hot summer sun. So in all the world there were no
better lads than they who grew up under the care of Cheiron to be both skilful
and strong, modest as well as brave, and fitted to rule by having rightly known to
obey.

Among that youthful fellowship, best in his day was Jason, a boy of princely
race, and a king's son by right. For his father Aeson had been born heir of Iolcus,
yet had let this kingdom be stolen from him by his wicked half-brother Pelias,
who would have slain Jason to make that wrongdoing sure. But Aeson had saved
the child by flight, hiding him in Cheiron's cave, where for years he little
guessed how it was his own heritage of rich plain and well-peopled seashore on
which he looked down from the cloud-wrapped ridges of Mount Pelion; nor did
Pelias know what a champion was growing up within sight of his usurped realm.

But when the sturdy lad had shot to full stature, and his mind, no longer set on boyish sport and mirth, turned eagerly to the wide world in which he might prove his manhood, old Cheiron saw the time come to let him know the secret of his birth, and how he was destined to avenge on Pelias the wrong done to his father. The young hero heard in amazement; then not a day would he delay in setting out on the adventure in store for him. Taking leave of his envious playmates, he dutifully received his old master's parting counsel.

"I need not wish you fearless before enemies; but remember how it becomes a king's son to be friendly to all other men, and helpful in their need."

The youth's heart beat high with hope, as under the bright morning sun he made his way down the mountain, where every step brought him nearer in view of the unknown world below. Lightly clad in a close-fitting vest beneath a panther's skin he had won by his own spear, his feet shod with new sandals, his long hair streaming in the wind, Jason bounded from rock to rock, and stepped out under the cool shade of pine woods, and pushed through thickets of tangled shrubs, all familiar to him, for Cheiron had taught his scholars to know every flower and leaf on their mountain home. But when the steep paths had brought him down to the lowland country, he found it covered with fields of corn, lush meadows, groves of fruit trees, and such signs of human habitation. Yet it was his chance to meet no soul to bid him speed, till on the bank of a rushing river he found an old woman in mean rags, who rocked herself feebly as she sat and cried out beseechingly—

"Alas! who will carry me across?"

With disdain Jason looked at this poor crone, and with doubt at the foaming torrent, swollen by the melting of the snows above. But to his mind came Cheiron's words that he must be helpful to all kindly folk; and the youth was ashamed of himself that he had turned proudly from one who rather called on him for pity.

"My shoulders are broad enough for such a light load!" said he heartily. "Up with you, old mother, and, the gods aiding, I will bear you safe!"

Without more ado, before he could raise a hand to lift her up, the seeming helpless beggar sprang on his back; and with her arms clinging round his neck, he strode boldly into the stream. He slipped, he staggered as it took him to the knees, to the waist, to the shoulders; and he had almost been put to swimming for it, while the old hag moaned and shrieked for terror, crying out that he was drowning her, and abusing him crossly for wetting her worthless rags.

"Hold on fast!" was his cheery answer, though she half-choked him by her clutching fingers.

For a moment he had a mind to throw off this thankless stranger, and take his own chance of buffeting the flooded torrent. But he knew that thought was unworthy, and struggled on sturdily to gain at last the further bank. Here as he scrambled to shore, all dripping and breathless, and would have gently laid down his burden on the grass, she sprang from his back to take on a wondrously altered guise. For when he looked to see a wrinkled and bent crone, with hardly a word to thank her helper, lo! there stood before him a tall and stately form, like no daughter of woman, her rags changed to jewelled robes, and her eyes now smiling on him so radiantly that he knew her as of divine race.

"Yes," she said, reading his mind. "I am indeed Hera, the queen of heaven, to whom you have done such service unaware. Not in vain was your spirit humbled and your back bowed for one appearing to be poor and helpless. In your own hour of need, call upon me, and see if a goddess can be grateful."

Speechless, the youth fell upon his knees, his eyes dazzled by the vision of glory that, as he gazed, went up in a shining cloud; and when he could see dearly, he was alone on the river bank.

Thanking the gods that he had been true to his better nature and to the teaching of his master, Jason took his way onwards to a city whose towers stood out before him upon the plain. But now he limped along more slowly, for he found he had lost one of his sandals, left sticking in the slimy bed of the torrent, where a sharp stone had cut his bare foot. Schooled as he had been to make light of such mishaps, he bound up his hurt with soft leaves, and held on through shade and sunshine till towards evening he reached the gate of Iolcus.

There he found all astir with a great feast held by Pelias in honour of the gods. Many an eye was cast curiously on this comely youth, as he wandered through the streets, sun-tanned and dusty from the long way. He thought these smart citizens despised him for being but half-shod, for he knew not what was known to them, how an oracle had foretold that Pelias should lose his ill-gotten kingdom to a stranger who came wearing but one sandal.

Seeking his way to the palace, he presented himself before Pelias, who, amid all his royal state, might well start at the sight of this half-barefooted youth, since night and day his guilty mind never forgot what sign was to mark the avenger.

"Your name and lineage?" he faltered forth.

"I am Jason, son of Aeson, come to claim my rightful heritage," declared the youth boldly.

The king's heart sank within him, for he was as full of fears as of falsehood and cruelty. But, hiding his dismay, he made a show of welcoming this nephew with joy, and bid him sit down at the feast beside his own fair daughters. Tomorrow, he said, would be a better time to talk about the affairs of the kingdom. Meanwhile, let all be joy and mirth to hail the return of a nephew long given up for dead.

Simple and honest himself, Jason was won by his uncle's fine words and by the charms of his new-found cousins. Their seeming kindness turned his head, so that he let his heart go out to them, believing Pelias must have been slandered as a faithless usurper. He ate and drank among them friendly, then, flushed with wine, listened eagerly to the minstrels who cheered the banquet. A song that set his pulses beating was the tale of the Golden Fleece: how Phrixus and Helle, a king's son and daughter, were persecuted by their cruel stepmother Ino; how they fled from her on a golden ram, sent by a friendly god; how poor Helle, turning giddy as they flew over land and sea, fell from its back into the Hellespont, that has ever afterwards been known by her name; but Phrixus safely reached Colchis at the farther end of the dark Euxine Sea; how he sacrificed the ram to Zeus, and hung up its fleece in a sacred grove by the river of the Colchians, among whom henceforth he lived and died. There it was jealously treasured by Aeëtes, king of that distant land, whose own life, said an oracle, depended on its safe keeping, so that he had it guarded night and day by a sleepless serpent, as by other perils no hero had been found bold enough to face; but never would the ghost of dead Phrixus be laid till the Golden Fleece were won back to his kinsmen in Greece. This song had been sung by command of Pelias; and keenly he watched his nephew's flashing eyes as the moving tale was told.

"Ah!" exclaimed the crafty king, "time was when I would have dared all for such a prize. But I am old, and the sons of our day are not as their fathers. Where lives the man who will venture to bring back the Golden Fleece?"

"Here!" cried Jason, leaping to his feet. "I will seek the Fleece, if I have to pay for it with my life."

His cunning uncle made haste to embrace him, with feigned pride and joy in a youth worthy of their heroic stock. Yes, let him bring the Golden Fleece to Iolcos; and he himself would gladly give up the kingdom to the hero of such a deed! So he promised, secretly trusting that his brave kinsman would never come back from that perilous errand; and thus by guile and flattery he hoped to make himself sure of his stolen power.

When, after a night's sleep, he came to think calmly over his undertaking, Jason might well see its rashness, and maybe he suspected how his uncle had thus schemed to get rid of him. But the old Centaur had taught him never to draw back from his word, and what he had spoken in haste he must strive to perform by dint of courage and prudence. He sought the aid of a cunning shipwright called Argus, who from the tall pines of Mount Pelion built him a fifty-oared ship, so strong that it could bear the buffeting of winds and waves, yet so light that it might be carried on the shoulders of its crew. This was named the *Argo*, after its builder. To man it, Jason sent out to his old schoolmates and to other heroes of Greece, summoning stout hearts and arms ready to join him in the quest of the Golden Fleece.

While they came together, Jason took himself to Hera's sacred grove at Dodona, beseeching her promised favour, of which he was assured by the Speaking Oak that made her oracle. As proof of her gratitude, he was bidden to tear away a limb of that oak to make a figurehead for his ship; and this lifeless wood had the power of speech, through which, when in doubt or danger, he might be counselled by the goddess. Moreover, she procured the goodwill of wise Athena to inspire Argus in building the ship, which should set out under such high auspices.

For comrades he had the best and bravest of the Grecian youth, sons of gods and men, a band henceforth to be known as the Argonauts. Among those heroes were names of fame – Heracles, the twin-brothers Castor and Pollux, Theseus, Orpheus, Peleus, Admetus, and many more, fifty in all, one to each oar of the galley, in which their seats were fixed by lot. Argus himself made one of the crew, and Acastus, the son of Pelias, stole off to join them against his father's will. Tiphys was their steersman; sharp-eyed Lynceus their pilot. With one voice they would have chosen Heracles for captain; but he gave the leadership to Jason, and all were content. After due sacrifices to the gods, and farewells to their friends, they launched forth the *Argo* into the blue sea, its prow set towards the clouds hiding that far-off eastern land whence they must tear the Golden Fleece. Orpheus put heart into them with his songs; but there was a tear in Jason's eye, as he saw the mountains of his fatherland fade away behind their track.

2 The Voyage to Colchis

Now to tell of all that hindered those heroes on their far course, and how one and another were cut off by mishaps, never to reach the Colchian land. Turning from the shores of Thessaly, they stood across the Aegean Sea to the rocky island of Lemnos, where a strange snare was set for them. The women of the island, maddened by jealousy, had slain all their men folk, and, now vainly repentant, hailed the newcomers as husbands for their defenceless need. Jason and most of his crew, going among them, gave way to their endearments, and amidst pleasures and feasting were tempted to forget what work they had on hand. But stouthearted Heracles had stayed by the ship; and when he came on shore to chide his comrades, they took shame for their softness, and tore themselves away to face the cold sea winds like men, who for a moment had been caught by womanly wiles.

Bending afresh to their oars, they passed through the Hellespont and came to a haven in the Propontis Sea, where Cyzicus, the young king of the Doliones, received them gladly and would have them stay to his wedding feast. But Heracles, again on watch in the ship, saw how here too there was a snare set. For a race of giant savages came down from the hills, and were blocking up the harbour mouth with huge stones, when Heracles gave the alarm, and with his arrows kept off these foemen, who fell or fled when the whole band had gathered to defend their ship. And worse was to betide here, for when the *Argo* steered forth into the open sea, a storm drove her back by night, and their late friendly hosts, the Doliones, taking them for enemies, set upon them in the darkness, so that Jason unaware slew the young king at whose marriage he had sat as a guest. Daylight showed both bands how they had mistaken each other; then for three days the Argonauts stayed to celebrate the funeral rites of those unhappily slain.

But soon they were to lose stout Heracles, who more than once had served them so well. As he tugged at his oar in the stormy waves, it broke, and not easily could another be found to match his brawny arms. When next they went on shore and his companions were being feasted by the hospitable Mysians, Heracles strode off into the forest to cut for himself a new oar from some tall pine tree. With him went the beautiful boy Hylas, whom he loved like a son, and also another of the crew named Polyphemus. While Heracles stripped himself to fell the tree he had chosen, young Hylas turned aside to a spring from which he would have drawn water for their supper. In this spring dwelt a bevy of water nymphs, who, as they saw the boy leaning over with his brazen pitcher, were so taken by his beauty, that they cast their arms round him and dragged him down into the water, never again to be seen of men. Polyphemus heard his last cry, and hastened to tell Heracles that the lad was being caught by robbers or wild beasts.

In vain these two searched for him through the forest, shouting and raging against the unseen foe who had laid hands on the hero's darling. Meanwhile their shipmates impatiently awaited them, for the wind had turned fair. When the hours passed and Heracles did not come, they fell to quarrelling among themselves, for some said they should not go without that tower of strength, but others were for leaving him behind. So, in the end, they did, and with quiet minds after the sea-god Glaucus had risen from the waves to disclose to them how Heracles was not destined to share the gaining of the Golden Fleece. That hero had glory enough awaiting him elsewhere.

On their next landing, Heracles might have found a task worthy of him, for this was the country of the Bebrycians, whose brawny king's humour was to challenge all strangers to box with him, never yet having met his match. But Pollux took up the challenge, and after doughty blows on both sides, smote the boaster to the ground; then his angry people would have avenged him with their weapons; but the Argonauts drove them away like wolves.

A more unfamiliar combat it was they undertook on coming to the home of the blind king Phineus, who was tormented by winged Harpies that pounced upon his food to snatch or defile it ere he could carry a morsel to his mouth. But two of Jason's band were winged men, able to rise in the air and drive away

Hylas and the Water Nymphs
From the painting by J. W. Waterhouse R.A.

those monstrous birds, letting the blind old man eat in peace his first meal for many a day. In gratitude, he warned them of dangers on their course, and first of the Symplegades, two islands of floating ice-rock that would open like a monster's jaws to close upon their ship and crush it, unless they could speed through at the nick of time. By his advice they took a dove on board to show them the opening of the perilous passage. Loosing the dove, they saw it fly through those heaving rocks, that closed to snap off but its last feather and again drew asunder in haste; then the Argonauts pulled hard at their oars, and their wary steersman brought them darting between the icy walls that in another moment would have clashed upon them.

Holding their way along the coast of the black Pontus, they met with other mischances and delays. Where king Lycus entertained them at the mouth of the Acheron, Idmon, the diviner, blind to his own fate, was slain by the tusk of a wild boar. Here, too, their steersman Tiphys died after a short sickness; and days were spent on the funeral rites. Well for the heroes, it may be, that they did not linger in the land of the Amazons, for these fierce women were more ready to wield sword and spear than distaff or needle; yet with them some of the crew would have tried a bout, as if they had not perils enough that could not be passed

113

by! Also they skirted the coast of the Chalybes, those sooty ironsmiths that night and day forge arms in the service of Ares. Next, standing out to sea, they were attacked by a flock of prodigious birds, that cast their brazen feathers from them like darts to wound the men at their oars. But while half of them rowed on, the other half stood on guard, and raised such a din by smiting spear upon shield, that the birds were scared away, and the *Argo* could anchor safely by an island near the east end of this sea.

Here they drew near to their goal, and now they fell in with new comrades that would serve them well. For, shipwrecked on this island, they found four naked youths, the sons of Phrixus, him who had brought the Fleece to Colchis. Clothed and fed by Jason, these four agreed to guide his company to the home of Aeëtes, yet not without dread, for they knew how jealously that cruel king guarded the Fleece on which hung his own life. But the Argonauts, who had come safe through so many perils, made light of all Aeëtes could do against them; and with the sons of Phrixus for pilots, they stood across the sea to where the ice-topped Caucasus echoed the groans of Prometheus chained upon a cloudy crag. And so at last the Argo entered the Phasis, river of Colchis, and by its bank her crew saw the dark grove sacred to Ares, in which gleamed that Golden Fleece they had come to fetch away.

3 The Winning of the Fleece

Leaving most of his men to guard their ship, Jason went forward to the city with a few companions, among them the four sons of Phrixus, who were here at home. King Aeëtes came forth to meet them, for from his towers he had seen the Argo reach the Colchian shore; and an evil dream had warned him of her errand. With him came his young son Absyrtus, also his two daughters, Medea the witch-maiden, and Chalciope, the widow of Phrixus. She was very glad to see her sons, whom she had mourned as lost. As her sister had done on Phrixus years before, Medea looked kindly upon Jason, for in a dream she had foreseen his coming, and no such goodly man could she see in Colchis. Their dark-minded sire had little joy to hail those strangers, yet hiding his ill will, he led them to the lordly halls of his dwelling, and set food and drink before them.

Not till the guests had eaten, did he ask what brought them to Colchis. Then with Medea's eyes ever fixed upon him, Jason told of their voyage, and all the perils they had come through for the sake of the Golden Fleece, which he boldly demanded as their reward. To this the frowning king made answer—

"Verily, it is a vain errand to come on from so far. What you have borne is but child's play to that which the man must dare who would prove himself worthy of such a prize. Listen, stranger, if you have the heart even to hear the trial appointed for that rash hand that may not touch sacred things till he have proved himself more than man. Two brazen-hoofed bulls, breathing fire from their nostrils, must he tame and yoke to a plough. Thus must he plough four acres of stony field, and sow the furrows with the teeth of a venomous dragon. From these teeth will spring up forthwith a crop of armed foemen, to be mowed down before they can slay him. All this must he accomplish between the sun's rising and setting; then if he still dare, he may strive with the serpent that guards the Fleece night and day. Are you the man?"

Jason's heart quailed within him as he listened to this tale of terrors, that indeed seemed more than mortal strength could affront. But he showed no fear, and, trusting in the favour of Hera and his own arm, he let the king know that he was ready for that ordeal, the sooner the better. Since it must take the whole day, this was put off till next morning; and the hero went back to his ship to rest before meeting those unearthly adversaries.

But while he slept, others in Colchis were wakeful. Chalciope wept in sore dismay, fearing that, if Jason failed in his attempt, Aeëtes would slay all the Argonauts, and among them her sons who had guided their ship to Colchis. Therefore she sought the aid of her witch sister to work some spell on behalf of the strangers.

Nor did Medea need persuading to pity, for at first sight she had loved Jason, and was minded to save him from the death designed by her cruel father. At nightfall she wandered among the woods gathering herbs and roots, out of whose juices she knew the art to make a magic salve, that for one whole day could keep a man scathless from fire and sword, and temper all his arms against the doughtiest stroke. Her charms duly worked, wrapped in a veil she went towards the harbour at the earliest peep of dawn, and there met Jason coming forth to see the sun rise once more, if never again.

"Will you go to death?" whispered a veiled woman in his ear.

"I had not come to Colchis, did I fear death," answered Jason.

"A bold heart alone will not avail. But you have one friend in this land, else you were lost," murmured the witch-maiden; and Jason knew her voice for that of the king's daughter whose dark eyes had met his so kindly.

Hastily she gave him to understand how by her aid he might pass through the sore ordeal unhurt. Then the longer he listened, the more ready he was to trust her counsels, daughter of an enemy as she was. When in whispers she had told him all he must do, Medea put into his hands the magical salve, and fled back to her father's house as day began to break.

Jason lost no time in putting her spell to the proof. After bathing in the sea, he anointed himself from head to foot with that salve, also his shield, his helmet, and all his weapons. This done, he let his comrades try their utmost upon him arrayed in the charmed armour The strongest of them hacked at his spear without being able to break it with the sharpest sword; the mightiest blows made no dint on his polished shield; and he stood like a rock against the brawniest wrestler of the band. Seeing, then, how Medea had been true with him so far, he did not doubt to follow out her bidding to the end; so his heart was high as he presented himself to the king at sunrise.

"Have you not repented?" asked Aeëtes with a sneer. "I had hoped to find you stolen away through the night with all thy presumptuous crew. It is no will of mine that a stranger must perish miserably. Think once again!"

"The sun is in the sky; and I am ready," answered Jason.

Without more ado, the king led him to a field where were laid out the brazen yoke, the iron plough, and the goad with which he must tame those fiery bulls, whose bellowing could be heard from their stable underground. All the beholders drew back, while Jason stuck sword and spear in the earth, hung to them his helmet, and, throwing off his mantle, stood nude like a marble statue with only his shield in hand.

Out came the brazen-footed bulls so suddenly as seeming to rise from the ground, that shook beneath them as they bounded upon Jason, snorting red flames from their nostrils, and roaring like thunder amid a cloud of hot smoke. But the hero neither fled nor flinched at their onset. He held up his shield, against which they dashed their iron horns in vain, and behind it he stood unhurt by their scorching breath. All other eyes were half-blinded in the smoke and dust, but they could then see how the hero caught one bull by the horn to bring it on its back by sheer strength, and how he flung down the other to its knees, wrestling against both of them with hand and foot. They being thus overthrown, he forced upon their necks the strong yoke, and harnessed them to the heavy plough, and, goading them forward, though they bellowed and struggled like a storm wind, he ploughed up the field with deep and straight furrows to the wonder of all looking on and the secret joy of Medea, who in the background kept muttering magic spells on his behalf.

Even scowling Aeëtes could not but marvel at such feats. But wrath was in his heart as he saw half the appointed task done, and still it was but noon. Yet he trusted that the other half were beyond this bull taming champion's strength. When the weary beasts had been driven back to their underground cave, he gave Jason a helmet full of dragons' teeth to sow in the fresh furrows. Strange seed that was, for no sooner had the earth covered it than the whole field began to stir and swell as if it were alive, and from every heaving clod glistened blades that were not green grass but sharp bronze and iron, the bare ground quickly bursting forth with a crop of helmets and spears which rose higher every moment, and grew up above shields and clanging mail till every furrow bristled with a rank of armed warriors, to be mowed down by Jason ere the sun sank over the sea.

And now Medea's secret counsel served him well for he took not spear nor sword in hand, but, when the warriors were full grown and stood like bearded corn ripe for the sickle, he pitched amidst them a huge stone, such as might have made a quoit for a giant. The rattle and crash of it was drowned by the yells of the armed men, turning here and there to ask who had cast this missile against them. So hot for fight were they that forthwith they fell blindly upon one another, wrestling together and plying sword and spear on the joints of each other's harness. Thus madly and blindly they fought, some springing up from the ground only to be reaped in death. So, while Jason leant on his spear to watch how these prodigious foes struck down their own brothers, the fight went on till the furrows were filled with blood and the field lay strewn with corpses, laid low as under a hailstorm. And when the sun set, the earth had swallowed up that monstrous brood, where now green grass grew over their bones.

Black were the brows of Aeëtes as Jason came to demand the Golden Fleece, since he had fulfilled the hard task set him.

"We will speak of that tomorrow," answered the king, turning away sullenly to his halls, while the Grecian heroes, proud and glad, went back to their ship.

There, as they sat at supper, into the blaze of their fire stole Medea with breathless haste to warn them what was afoot. Her father, she disclosed, was secretly gathering his warriors, and meant to set upon them next morning with overwhelming might. If they would win the Fleece, it must be now or never. She herself would guide Jason to the grove where it hung, and by her spells she could lull its fearsome guardian to sleep. Then he must seize it and fly before the sun rose.

This witch-maiden having already schooled him so well, Jason could not doubt again to do her bidding. His comrades left to unmoor the *Argo* and make all ready for instant flight, he alone let Medea guide him to the sacred shrine. With her had come her young brother Absyrtus; and he too followed, trembling for fear.

At dead of night they entered the gloomy grove of Ares, where at once they heard the blood-curdling hiss of that watchful serpent, whose coils glittered like lightning about the tall tree on which hung the Golden Fleece, turned to silver in the moonlight. Lightly as they trod through the tangled thicket, before they came in sight by flitting moonbeams, the monster had raised his fearsome head and opened his poison-breathing jaws. But Medea stole up to him with a soft, low chant that charmed his ears, and she sprinkled his eyes with a magical potion brewed from honey and herbs, and let its drowsy odour rise through his jaws, till soon this potent drug filled him with sleep. The serpent stretched out his measureless coils to lie still as any fallen branch, overpowered by the arts of the murmuring enchantress When his hissing had changed to deathlike silence, Jason stepped warily over the scaly bulk, nor did that fierce guardian stir as he laid hands on the Golden Fleece and tore it down from where it had hung since Phrixus nailed it there.

"Away!" was now the word, before the grisly serpent should awaken from the spell cast upon him. But as Jason turned exutlingly towards his ship, Medea held him back, and her song broke into lamenting.

"Well for you that can speed homeward to friends and honour! But woe is me, poor maiden, whom an angry father will slay when he knows how I have helped the stranger against him!"

"No stranger to one for whom you have played such a friendly part!" quoth Jason. "Fly with me, Medea, as my bride, without whose aid I might have gone back dishonoured. Thus I shall bear home two treasures for one, and be most envied among the sons of Greece. Speak, will you share my fortune?"

She answered not, but a maiden's silence may be more than speech. So, bearing up the Fleece with one hand, he cast the other around her, and it needed no force to draw away the daughter of Colchis, who might never see her father's land again. Side by side, the pair hastened down to the harbour; and the weeping boy Absyrtus clung to his sister, knowing not where she went.

With the first beam of dawn they came to the Argo, where the crew, sitting ready at their oars, hailed the Golden Fleece with a shout of joy to waken all Colchis. Medea and her brother being led on board, and the trophy fastened to their mast, Jason cut the cable by one stroke of his sword, then away went the *Argo* like a horse let loose, soon bounding beyond sight of that eastern shore.

4 Medea

King Aeëtes was awake early, arming himself and his men to fall upon those presumptuous strangers when they should come to demand the Fleece. But daybreak showed him the *Argo* flying across the sea; and hot was his wrath to learn that she had carried off his daughter and his son along with the chief treasure of Colchis, on which hung his own life. Quickly making ready his fleet, he launched forth to follow with so many ships that they covered the dark water like a flock of seagulls.

The Argonauts, seeing themselves pursued, hoisted every sail and tugged their best at the oars. But now it was ill for that crew that they had lost stout Heracles as well as other strong arms. For all they could do, the Colchian ships gained upon them so fast that one-half of Jason's men had to stand on guard grasping spear and shield, while the other half rowed with all their might.

"On, on!" ever cried Medea, fearing to fall into her father's hands; and when his ship drew so near that she could see his stern face and hear his threatening voice, the cruel witch did a deed from which Jason might know, as he would know to his sorrow, what a fierce and ruthless bride he had stolen away. In spite of the boy's tears and entreaties, she hurled her brother Absyrtus overboard; indeed, some say that she had him torn in pieces and thrown upon the waves that their father might be delayed by gathering up the dead body for pious burial.

So it was; and thus the *Argo* escaped from mortal foemen, soon to be hidden in a cloud of thunder with which the gods proclaimed their wrath against that hateful crime. Henceforth, for long, Jason's crew wandered as under a curse, abandoned for a time, it would seem, even by Hera's favour, when the king of heaven frowned upon them. They were driven astray by storms, blinded in mists, and tossed on many a strange sea, ere the guilt of innocent blood could be washed away from their ship. Broken and befouled, it came on the rocks of an unknown land; and no man can well tell how and where its crew made their way onward. Some say that Medea had enchantments to drive it over the land as on the sea.

With no guide, unless it were that marvellous figurehead speaking as an oracle, the Argonauts travelled now up a great river and across mountains and deserts, their ship dragged with them, till once more they could launch it in the Mediterranean Sea, repaired and rigged afresh for another voyage. Still trouble and danger were their penance, even when by sacrifices and holy rites they had appeased the gods for the death of Absyrtus. Many strange adventures befell them among the same perilous straits and giant-haunted islands as were afterwards known to the wandering Odysseus; they had to steer past Scylla and Charybdis and the luring Sirens; then but for Medea's crafty spells those stout hearts might never have won home to Greece. They were wrecked on the desert shore of Libya, and once more had to drag their battered *Argo* over its barren sands. Launching again, they came past Crete, to find this island guarded by the giant Talus, whose monstrous body and limbs were of red-hot brass, but for one vulnerable vein in his heel. When the Argonauts would have landed for food and water, from the cliffs he hurled mighty rocks at their vessel, that would have been sunk had they not sheered off in haste. But Medea, boldly going on shore, laid Talus fast asleep by her magical incantations, then wounded his heel of flesh to spill all his life-blood, so that the heat went out of his huge body, and it rolled from the rocks, crashing and splashing into the sea.

So many years had passed, that when at last they saw Iolcos, the band of hopeful youths who followed Jason came back weary and toilworn men, grown old before their time. They were hardly to be known by their friends, as they

The Golden Fleece
From the painting by Herbert J. Draper

stepped on shore amid cries of amazement, welcome, and triumph at the sight of the Golden Fleece they brought as proof of their achievement.

Pelias had long given them up for dead, never having thought they could come back alive with such a trophy. He himself was now drawing near to death, yet his palsied hands clung to the ill-gotten sceptre, and, for all his promise, he would not yield up the kingdom to Jason. But Medea had wiles deeper than his own. He and his looked askance on the Colchian witch, till she offered by her magic to make him young again, as she did for a ram which, boiled in a caldron with certain herbs, came forth under strange incantations a tender lamb. Thereby she persuaded the daughters of Pelias to do the like with their old father, who thus perished miserably, slain by the hands of his own children. But some tell how Aeson, Jason's father, was indeed restored to youth by the Colchian witch, and that he reigned again at Iolcos.

Jason himself had no mind for a kingdom gained by so wicked arts; and it might well be that his heart grew cold to such a cruel wife. Once more wandering from home, he fell in love with Glauce, the daughter of Creon, king of Corinth. He hoped to make Medea content with his second marriage; but not yet did he know the stern-hearted stranger he had taken to his side. Concealing her hate, the enchantress sent to Glauce a rich wedding robe, steeped in poison, which was the death of that woeful bride, vainly striving to tear the splendid torment from her flesh. Then, in the madness of jealousy, Medea slew her three young sons with her own hand; and when Jason furiously turned from their bodies to take vengeance on the unnatural mother, he saw her for the last time borne away through the air in a chariot drawn by dragons.

So a hero's life on which such bright suns had risen, was to set in dark clouds of affliction. Some say that in his frenzy he killed himself by the corpses of his children and of his murdered bride. But others tell how, as he sat by the seashore beside his good ship *Argo*, thinking sadly on the glorious days when she had borne him to Colchis, the rotten figurehead broke off and crushed him: so his protecting goddess sent death as the best gift to a man whose work was done.

Pyramus and Thisbe

In neighbouring houses lived Pyramus and Thisbe, he the briskest youth, and she the fairest maid of Babylon. Long had their eyes spoken what from childhood grew in their hearts; but the fathers of both frowned upon their wooing and forbade them to meet, as they could not be forbidden to love. Nay, love's flame burned but the hotter for being covered up, till it lit for them a way by which they could at least promise each other to be faithful to death.

The two houses were parted by a wall of sun-baked clay, in which the lovers found a chink to let them hear one another's voices from side to side. Daily, when all else was still, through this chink they exchanged sighs and whispers, and spoke of kisses that could not meet. Often they complained against the rough wall sundering each from the other's eyes; yet again were they fain to be thankful for the cleft where lip and ear were pressed by turns.

So for a time they nursed their secret love, yet could not bear for ever to be denied what both would buy at any cost. Through the wall at night was agreed them to give their guardians the slip: singly and by separate ways, they should steal from home, to meet at the tomb of Ninus, that known landmark in the woods outside the city; then never more would they consent to be parted.

So was agreed, and so was done. Thisbe, in her impatience, set out before the hour. With her veil wrapped close about her, slinking hurriedly through the streets in dread of every shadow, she first reached the place of meeting, where the moonlight showed a fountain shining beside the tomb, and over it hung a tree loaded with white mulberries. She looked round for Pyramus, but he came not yet by the silvered glades of the wood. She bent her head to catch the tread of his footstep; then what horrid sound of a sudden broke upon her ears, echoed by a shriek of womanish terror!

It was a roaring lioness that bounded out of the thicket where it had been gorging on its prey. The startled maiden did not wait to see its fiery eyes and its dripping jaws. Throwing off the long veil that hindered her flight, with screams she ran wildly through the trees, and never stopped till she could hide her beating heart and trembling limbs in a dark cavern which offered a refuge.

The full fed lioness did not care to give chase. But that savage creature fell upon Thisbe's white veil, left on the grass, befouling and tearing the fine stuff with blood-stained fangs, before it passed on to quench its thirst at the fountain, then took itself to its hidden lair among the rocks.

As he hastily drew near from the city, Pyramus had heard the fierce roaring and the cry of that voice he knew so well. Drawing his sword, he sped forward to the tomb, where now all was still.

"Thisbe!" he murmured; "Thisbe!" he exclaimed. But no answer came, and no living form moved under the moonlight.

Soon, to his consternation, he saw the ground freshly marked by a lion's claws. And there, beside the fountain, lay Thisbe's veil, all stained and torn. Horrified to frenzy, he made no doubt that the lion had borne away his beloved. Rashly he searched the dark wood, calling on the fierce beast to seize him for its prey rather than that helpless maid. Bitterly reproaching himself for not having been first at the meeting-place, he came back to shower tears and kisses on the veil of her he took for dead.

"Let me not live, after leading you into such peril!" he cried. "At least our hearts' blood may be mingled together, now we are free to meet in death!" With desperate hand he drove the sword deep into his breast, and fell dying at the foot of the mulberry tree. His blood gushed out upon the roots that sucked it up to turn the white berries into dark purple, as if the tree itself mourned for those unhappy lovers.

Day was breaking when Thisbe found courage to come forth from her hiding-place, and, starting at every crackle of a twig beneath her feet, made her way back to the tomb where she hoped to be safe beside the arm of Pyramus. All her fear now was he might think she had played him false. Her heart throbbed with joy as she saw him lying beneath that tree as if asleep; but misgiving fell upon her with the sight of the white mulberries turned black, and she stooped down to know him writhing in his death-throes upon her veil wet with his blood.

"Pyramus!" she cried wildly, raising his head. "Speak to me! Say this is but an ugly dream!"

At her voice he opened his dim eyes, he tried to smile and speak, but that effort was his last.

When no answer came, she tore her hair, she filled the wood with lamentations, she mingled her tears with his blood she laboured to kiss him back into life; and when all was in vain, she saw the sword sheathed in his breast.

"Death, too, sought to part us, but that neither death nor the living can do. Ah! cruel parents, at least ye will not grudge us to rest for ever side by side. And you, oh! pitying tree, stand ever with black berries as a monument of Pyramus and Thisbe."

With these words she drew the blade from her lover's wound and plunged it, still warm, into her own heart. Thus were they found locked together under that mournful tree; then the gods moved their parents to grant Thisbe's last prayer. They lay side by side on the funeral pyre; and their ashes were mingled in the same urn.

> "Here may ye se, what lover so he be,
> A woman dare and can as well as he."

Ion

Cecrops, Pandion, and Erechtheus were the first kings of Athens, under whom it chose Athena for its guardian deity. This race was said to have sprung from the earth, so deep in the past darkness, that men knew of them no more than their names, nor even clearly how they stood to each other in descent. But there came a time when their children seemed like to die out. For Erechtheus had only daughters, and all but one fell victims to Poseidon, who bore a grudge against the city that had preferred Athena to himself.

The one survivor was Creüsa, who passed for childless. But she in secret had been wooed by Apollo, and to him bore a son, whom, dreading her father's wrath, she had abandoned, hidden in a dark cave, where she laid him swaddled in a basket, thus trusted to the protection of Apollo. Herself deserted by that faithless celestial spouse, in time she was openly wedded to Xuthus, a neighbour prince who had done service to Athens in war, and thus seemed worthy to be its king. Years went by without an heir being born; then often Creüsa thought wistfully of that babe she had left to die, as seemed like, for she knew not what had become of him.

But the child was not dead. Apollo felt more compassion for his helpless offspring than for the betrayed mother; and by the hands of Hermes he had it carried to Delphi to be laid as a suppliant on the steps of his own temple. There it was found by the priestess, who adopted and reared this boy under the name of Ion. He grew up dedicated to the service of the temple, sprinkling its pavements, sweeping them with laurel branches, and scaring away birds from the consecrated offerings. Then early he showed such piety and dutifulness as to endear him to his foster-mother, not less than did his winsome looks and modest bearing.

When Ion had grown to his full stature, there came to the temple a train from Athens, its leaders no other than Xuthus and Creüsa, seeking at the oracle some remedy for their childless lot. Creüsa stood without, and talked with that fair-faced acolyte, whose voice and looks so stirred her heart that fain she would have learned how he had been brought up in the god's service. But he knew nought of his origin, and as yet she could not guess that he was her lost child. Meanwhile, Xuthus had entered the inner shrine, where, putting his case to the inspired priestess, he was bidden take for his own son the first he should meet on leaving the temple. He rushed out, then his eyes fell upon Ion, whom he made haste to embrace, hailing so goodly a stripling as a welcome heir given to his prayers.

But Creüsa did not share her husband's joy. Now she looked askance on Ion, her mind darkened by suspicion that this temple sweeper must be a natural son of Xuthus, whom he had planned with the priestess to pass off on her as a gift of the god. So strong was her mistrust that she began to hate the youth to whom at first her heart had gone out kindly. She took counsel with an old servant of her house, a man to stick at nothing for his mistress; and he engaged to poison Ion at a feast with which the king would have celebrated his adoption. A deadly poison the queen had about her in two drops of the Gorgon's blood given to her father by Athena.

Ion, at first troubled and amazed by the embraces of one he took for a madman, had come to understand that in some sort he must look on himself as the king's son. When the wine-cups were filled at the banquet, Creüsa's servant, as if to do him honour, handed to the new-made heir a rich golden bowl in which he had mingled one drop of the Gorgon's fatal blood. Then, before drinking, the pious youth poured on the ground part of the costly wine as libation to his guardian god. A flock of sacred pigeons were ever fluttering about the precincts of the temple, and now one of them lighted down to taste this offering. No sooner was its beak wet by the envenomed wine than it beat its wings with a shriek of pain that drew all eyes to see it quivering in deadly convulsions. At this sight Ion flung down the cup, tearing his garments and indignantly demanding who sought to take his life. He turned on the old man that had offered him the poisoned draught; then Creüsa's servant, seized by the other guests, under wrathful threats confessed that he had done this at her bidding. A cry arose against the stranger woman; and the elders of Delphi declared that she must be stoned to death as having planned to violate the sanctity of the temple by making away with its innocent minister.

When she heard how the executioners were in search of her, Creüsa fled as a suppliant to Apollo's temple, and, crouched at the altar, took sanctuary amidst a crowd clamouring for her blood. Then as Ion stood plying her with reproaches and questions why she had conceived such wicked intent against him who had never done her wrong, from the shrine burst forth the Pythia, for once deserting her tripod to speak openly before all. Amid reverent silence she disclosed the secret of her nursling Ion being laid on the steps of the temple, a nameless babe, and brought forth the basket in which she had found him.

Creüsa's heart began to beat, as she heard how this boy was of the same age as her own child; and she uttered a cry at the sight of the swaddling clothes she had wrapped about him years ago. The recognition was complete, when on these garments she traced patterns worked by her own hands. Ion, whom in jealous anger she would have murdered, could be no other than her long-lost son.

The youth proved slower to believe that this must be his mother; but the proofs were clear; and with proud astonishment he heard how his father was Apollo himself. Thus at last mother and son came to each other's knowledge; and all doubt was ended by an appearance of Athena sent to speak for her brother god, who might well shame to tell his own tale. Bidding Ion go to Athens and take up the heritage of its kings, the goddess foretold that he should be the father of a widespread people known after him as Ionians; and to Xuthus and Creüsa she promised another son named Dorus, from whom would spring the Dorian race. And so it came to pass, if poets tell true.

Theseus

Aegeus, the old king of Athens, was believed to have no children, so the sons of his brother Pallas, known as the Pallantids, looked to seize the throne on his death. But years ago, Aegeus had made a secret marriage with Aethra, daughter of Pittheus, king of Troezen, moved thereto by an oracle that also promised him from that union a son destined to rare renown. Yet soon he left poor Aethra, taking leave of her at a huge rock on the seashore which he rolled away to hide beneath it his sword and his sandals. "Should the gods grant us a son," he charged her, "let him not know his father till he be strong enough to move this stone; then let him seek me out at Athens, bearing the sword and sandals as tokens."

In due time Aethra bore a son named Theseus, whom she kept in ignorance of his race, and among her own people he passed as being the child of Poseidon, to whom special reverence was paid at this seaport of Argolis. The boy, indeed, grew up so lustily that he might well be thought of more than mortal birth. While he was still a child, Hercules visited Troezen, who was his kinsman by the mother's side; and the sight of such a famous champion and the tales of his exploits filled young Theseus with longing for the like adventures. While other children shrank from the lion's skin the hero wore, he flew upon it with his little sword, taking this for a lion indeed, when one day Hercules had thrown it off his brawny limbs. All through his youth Theseus kept that hero before him as pattern of what he would be; later he held it an honour to be friend and companion of Hercules.

Deserted by her husband, the mother's comfort was in a son known as the stoutest and boldest lad in the land, prudent, too, and trustworthy beyond his years. For all that Theseus was loved by Aethra, she did not forget how the time for their parting drew on. When he was full grown, she took him to the rock by the shore and bid him roll it away, as he did with ease, to find beneath it the sword and sandals hidden here by Aegeus. Then first she told him his true father's name, and that he must seek out the king at Athens, taking the sword and sandals as tokens of his birth.

Full of pride to know himself the son of such a king, and of eagerness to see the world, Theseus made light of his old grandfather's counsel that he should go to Athens by sea. Greece in those days had sore trouble from tyrants, robbers, and wild monsters; and the youth's heart was set upon ridding the country of pests such as he might expect to meet on his way by land.

"So shall I be like Hercules," he told his anxious mother, "and come more welcome to my father if I bring his sandals worn by travel and his sword stained with blood."

The mother sighed, but let him take his way. He would not even choose the easiest road, but went up into the mountains behind Epidaurus on the east coast of Argolis. He had not gone far, when out of a wood rushed the robber Periphetes, brandishing a huge club and calling on him to stop. Theseus stood firm, sword in hand, and when they closed in hot tussle, that club-bearer for once met his match. The youth nimbly avoided every crushing blow, drove his sword through the robber's heart, then went forward bearing the club of Periphetes and his bearskin cloak as trophies.

With this cloak he felt himself like his model Hercules; and before long it served him well, when he came to the isthmus of Corinth, haunted by a wretch named Sinis, of whom men spoke with dread as the 'pine-bender', for it was his wont to slay what unfortunates fell into his hands after a cruel manner: bending down two pines he would fasten the man between them, and let them spring up to tear his members asunder. But when he would have so dealt with Theseus the young hero felled him to the ground, bound him with his own cords, and let his bones be shot into the air to feed the kites.

Before leaving the isthmus, Theseus turned aside to hunt down a wild sow that ravaged the fields and had been the death of all other hunters. The country people, glad to be rid of this pest, warned him of another foe upon his way. Going from Corinth to Megara, on a narrow ledge of rock above the shore he would pass the giant Sceiron, whose humour was to bid wayfarers wash his feet, and to kick them over into the sea while so obeying him. To hear of such a peril was enough for Theseus, who now would not be persuaded to take any road but this. He went to meet that churlish giant, and, when called on to wash his feet, hurled him into the sea, to be changed into a rock washed for ever by the waves.

Next he came to Eleusis, where the people, pitying so gallant a youth, would have had him slink past with out being seen by their tyrant Cercyon, who, trusting in his mighty bones and sinews, challenged every stranger to wrestle with him, and none had yet come alive out of his clutch. But Theseus was not one to pass by such an adversary. He went up to the palace, ate and drank with the king, and willingly stripped for a struggle in which the insolent Cercyon fell never to rise again; then the citizens, delivered from that oppressor, would have had Theseus stay with them as their king.

But Theseus would not stay, hastening on to Athens past the den of another monstrous evildoer, to fall in with whom he was all the readier for the warnings given him. This was Procrustes, or the 'Stretcher', who would lie in wait for harmless travellers and with friendly words lure them to his dwelling as guests, there to divert himself upon them with a cruel device. He had two beds, one over long, the other too short for a grown man's body. Were the stranger short of stature, this giant's way was to put him into the longer bed and stretch out his limbs to fill it; but if tall, he was laid on the smaller one and his legs were cut down till he fitted that.

"Such a one were well brought to an end by his own tricks," said Theseus to himself, when, as his wont was, Procrustes came out offering hospitality to this wayfarer.

The youth, pretending to be deceived, cheerfully turned aside with him, then staggering and gaping as if he were tired out, let himself be led into the torture chamber.

"Friend," chuckled the giant, "you see how it is! This other bed of mine is too short for a youth of your inches; yet can I soon make that right."

But as he would have laid Theseus on the shorter bed, suddenly he found himself caught in a grasp of iron, flung off his feet, thrown down and bound for the stranger to hack and hew him with his own axe, and so he came to the miserable death he had wrought on many another.

This was the hero's last exploit on his way to Athens. On the banks of the Cephissus, he next fell in with friendly men, who refreshed him after his toils, washed him clear of blood and dust, and sent him on with good wishes, nor without pious rites and sacrifices to purify him if he had done aught amiss on that adventurous journey.

Yet a deadlier danger than all awaited him when at last he came to his father's home. Aegeus, wellnigh in his dotage, was no longer master at Athens. Treason and rebellion filled the streets of the city, where his nephews the Pallantids took on themselves to rule with insolent pride, while in his palace the old king had fallen under the power of Medea, that wicked witch woman, who lighted here after flying from Jason at Corinth. By her magic arts she had foreseen the coming of Theseus; and she knew at once who must be the noble youth that now presented himself in the king's hall. It was easy for her to make the feeble old man take this for some secret foe bent on his harm. Then the enchantress mixed poison in a bowl of wine, which she offered the stranger as welcome, whispering to Aegeus that thus they should be surely rid of him.

But before Theseus drank, he drew forth the sword glittering in his father's sight, not so dim but that Aegeus remembered it as his own; and his dull eyes grew bright as he guessed this goodly young man for his long-forgotten son. Coming to himself, he dashed the poisoned drink on the ground; and in a moment father and son were in each other's arms.

The cunning witch-queen might well scowl at their happy meeting. She felt that her power over the doting king was gone; and in her dragon-chariot she fled away from Greece for ever. Theseus, hailed as his father's heir, was soon able to quell the disorders of the kingdom. He drove out of Athens the insolent Pallantids, who already bore themselves as kings; and, young as he was, he showed himself so worthy that all the citizens were content to obey a ruler blessed with such a son to uphold him. The first service he did to his new country was to rid it of the fierce bull of Marathon, the dread of which had long kept the husbandmen from tilling their lands. Many a hunter had sought that monster to his own hurt, before Theseus, setting out alone against it, brought the bull alive from its lair, led it as a show through the streets, and offered it as a sacrifice to the gods that had given him such strength and valour.

Before long, the heir of Aegeus had the chance to do a greater deed for Athens, a deed never to be forgotten in song and history. Years before, on Athenian ground had been treacherously slain Androgeos, son of the mighty Minos, king of Crete. Some say that this crime sprang from jealousy, since the Cretan prince had beaten the athletes of the country in their own games. The father, to avenge his blood, had made war on Athens, to which he granted peace at the price of a sore tribute. Every nine years, seven of its finest youths and fairest maidens must be sent to Crete, there to be delivered to the Minotaur, a fearsome creature, half-beast and half-man, by which they were savagely devoured. Now, for the third time, this tribute had to be paid, the victims chosen by lot among the noblest families of the city. But when it came to drawing lots, Theseus stood forth to offer himself freely.

"The lot falls first on me, as son of your king!" he declared. "I will head the tribute band, and let the Minotaur taste my sword first of all, that has slain as fierce monsters."

His generous devotion filled the citizens with gratitude, but the old king was loath to risk his only son on such a perilous chance. In vain he begged Theseus to hold back; the hero's spirit was keen and steadfast as his sword. So on the appointed day, he embarked for Crete among the tale of luckless youths and maidens, followed by the prayers of their woeful parents. His own father, hardly hoping to see him again, made him promise one thing. The ship that bore this doomed band was wafted by black sails in sign of mourning; but if it should be their lot to come back safe, they were to hoist a white sail, that not an hour should be lost in showing good news to those on the watch for their return.

With winds but too fair for so forlorn an errand, the ship came safe to the city of Minos. There he kept the Minotaur in his famous labyrinth, a maze of winding passages in the rock, made or him by Daedalus, that cunning artificer of old, who when he had served the Cretan king long and well, offended him to such wrath, that with his young son Icarus he had to fly away to Sicily. The crafty Daedalus

131

knew how to fit wings to their shoulders, fastened by wax; and thus they sped over the sea, the father coming safe to land, but when heedless Icarus flew too near the sun, the wax melted, and, losing his wings, he fell into the sea thenceforth called the Icarian, after his name. His body was wafted far away over the waves, to be in time drawn ashore by Heracles, who gave it burial on an island also named from him, Icaria. Daedalus, grateful for this friendly service, fashioned and set up at Pisa a statue of the hero so lifelike, that when Heracles saw it in the twilight, he took it for a threatening foe and dashed it to pieces with a stone. Such an artist was the Daedalus whose name became a proverb for skill; and the world knew no other such work as he left behind him in the Cretan labyrinth.

The Lament for Icarus
From the painting by Herbert J. Draper

Minos might well be proud to see the prince of Athens offer himself to glut his revenge; yet even his stern heart took pity on this noble youth, so boldly claiming as a right to be first to face the ravenous monster.

"Think, before it is too late," he warned Theseus. "Naked and alone, you must seek out the Minotaur, that has torn in pieces every victim turned into its haunt. And even you could escape such an enemy, no stranger, venturing within the labyrinth, has ever been able to find his way out of its dark secrets."

"So be it, if so it must be!" answered Theseus; and that night was set for his dreadful ordeal.

But not in vain had the hero, at the bidding of an oracle, invoked for his enterprise the protection of Aphrodite, goddess of love. One friend he had in Crete, before ever a word passed between them. Ariadne, daughter of King Minos, looked with kind eyes on this gallant stranger, and her heart was hot to save him from so miserable death. Seeking him out by stealth, she whispered good cheer and counsel in his ear, giving him a clue of thread which he should unroll as he passed on into the labyrinth's windings, then, his task done, he might follow that helpful clue till it brought him back to the free air. Moreover, she put into his hand a magic sword, with which, and with none other, the Minotaur might be slain. And, if he came out safe, she made him promise to carry her away from her father's anger, as Theseus willingly agreed, when the very favour of so bright eyes seemed a charm to bring him safe through all dangers.

Thus equipped and heartened, he took his way alone into the mouth of the labyrinth, leaving the youths and maidens, his comrades, to await what should befall him. With tearful eyes they saw him swallowed up in the darkness, and heard his steps die away within. Then all was silence, till there burst forth an awful roar echoing through those hollow windings, to show how the Minotaur was aware of his foe. The time seemed long while fearfully they stood listening to a distant din of bellowing and clattering and gnashing, as if a thunderstorm were pent up in the cavern's remotest parts. Again, all fell silent; and, quaking at the knees, his companions hardly hoped to see their leader come back from that chill gloom that in turn should be their own grave. But what was their joy at last to catch his voice raised in triumph, then he strode forth into the starlight, his sword dripping with blood!

The hero threw himself on Ariadne's neck to thank her for the aid without which he would never have overcome that monster, nor made his way out of its darksome lair. But she bid him lose no moment in hastening beyond the power of her father and all his men. The watchmen she had made heavy-headed after draughts of strong wine; and now, by her counsel, the crew of Theseus bored holes in the Cretan ships that they might be in no state to pursue. This done, and taking Ariadne with them, the Athenians got on board their own vessel, and had hoisted sail before Minos awoke to see them already far at sea.

And now the pair who had loved each other at first sight would happily have been wedded; but their love went amiss. For Theseus became warned in a dream that his Ariadne was destined as the bride of no mortal man, but of a god. So he hardened his heart to put her ashore on the island of Naxos, and there left her asleep by the strand, sailing away without a word of farewell. Some say that when poor Ariadne awoke to know herself thus deserted, she fell into such despair that she saw nothing for it but to take her own life. But the tale as told by others is that on Naxos she was found by Dionysus, who kissed away her tears and made her his wife, and so she came to shine among the stars.[1]

However the truth be, Theseus held on his course with a heavy heart, the joy of victory all overcast for him by Ariadne's loss. And in that sorrow he forgot his father s charge to hoist a white sail if he should come back safe. Day after day, when the ship might be expected, old Aegeus sat upon a high point, straining his weak eyes on watch for her return. At last she came in sight, and lo! the sails were black as death. The king gave up his son for lost. With a cry of despair he flung himself over a cliff into the waves, still known by his name as the Aegean Sea.

So mournful news met Theseus when he sailed into the harbour in triumph, all Athens pressing down to learn how it had fared with him. With thanksgiving to the gods for their speeding, he had to mingle the funeral rites of his father; and never could the son pardon himself that fatal forgetfulness that made him king of Athens.

As king, Theseus ruled wisely and well, so that in his reign Athens first began to grow great. Many more adventurous feats he did far and wide, of which the most celebrated is his war against the Amazons, and the wooing with his sword of Antiope to be his loving wife. After her death he married Phaedra, daughter of Minos, who revenged on him his desertion of Ariadne, when the time came that his glory set in clouds of misfortune. Deceived by that wicked stepmother, he cursed his innocent son Hippolytus, who came soon to a violent end, flung out of his chariot and dragged to death on the seashore when Poseidon sent a monster out of the waves to scare his horses; then too late the mourning father learned how false Phaedra had beguiled him. In his old age the fickle citizens of Athens turned against the hero to whom they owed so much; and so deep did he lay their ingratitude to heart, that he turned his back upon the city, betaking himself to an island where a treacherous enemy did him to death. Not till ages had passed were his remains brought to Athens, and a famous temple came to be built there to his memory.

---

[1] Among the various apologies for Ariadne's desertion, Plutarch includes a most unromantic one of her being so seasick that Theseus had to put her on land, then himself was blown out to sea by a storm – an accident common enough in fact on those squally waters. A modern commentary, suggested by the recent discoveries in Crete, is that the vast rambling palace built for its Minos kings may well have suggested the poetical idea of a labyrinth.

Philomela

At Athens was told an older tale, and a sadder, than that of Theseus. The founder of the city was taken to be one Cecrops, from over the sea, whose grandson Pandion had two daughters, Procne and Philomela. In his reign Athens was hard beset by barbarians and delivered only by help of Tereus, a fierce king from Thrace, to whom grateful Pandion could only offer as reward either of his daughters in marriage.

Tereus chose Procne, the elder; and the wedding was held forthwith, yet with evil auspices, for though Tereus had the god Ares for father, Hymen came not to bless the feast, nor Hera and her attendant Graces; but the chief guests were the dread Furies, and a hoarse owl hooted on the roof of the bridal chamber. The rude Tereus, making light of these omens, bore his bride away to Thrace. They had one son, named Itys, and for years they lived together without mischance.

But, when years had passed, Procne began to weary among the half-savage Thracians, who could not make her forget Athens and her dear sister Philomela. At last, her longing grew so strong that she coaxed Tereus to let her go home on a visit. He harshly denied her request; but by dint of tears and kisses she won him over to consent that Philomela should be brought to see her sister in Thrace.

Tereus sailed to Athens, where he found the old king loath to part with his other daughter, even for a time. With misgivings he gave way to the plea of Procne's love of her sister, who for her part was not less eager to see Procne once more. Before letting her go, Pandion made Tereus swear to keep his dear child from harm, and to send her back safe to Athens; then he took leave of her with tearful farewells, as if fearing never to embrace her again.

Too truly he feared, for the barbarous Thracian's oath was as false as his love. No sooner had he set eyes on Philomela in the bloom of her maidenhood, than his heart took flame, and he repented his choice of the elder sister. As they sailed across the sea, he set himself to woo the younger, who, in her innocence, took all his endearments as offered for Procne's sake, and smiled upon him in the joyful hope soon to meet her sister. But once he had her on land in his own wild forests, Tereus no longer disguised his wicked desire to put her in her sister's place.

The sorrowful Philomela would have none of his hateful love; but she cried in vain for help to the gods; and when with drawn sword he would have forced her to his will, she fell on her knees begged him for death rather than dishonour. From that one crime the fierce tyrant shrank, yet with his cruel blade he cut out her tongue that it might not betray his falsehood. To make sure of her silence, he shut her up in a lonely prison far among the woods, where Procne might never learn that she still lived.

He told Procne that her sister was dead; and when this news came to Athens, the old father died of grief. Philomela guessed how Procne had been deceived; but her watchful keepers gave her no chance to escape, so for a year the queen mourned both sister and father as lost to her in the tomb, till at last with horror she learned the truth. Dumb Philomela's wits were free, and so were her hands. She got leave to spend her prison hours in weaving, then on a white web she wrought with purple threads the story of her woeful case. When her work was done, for pity, or bribes, she found a messenger to carry it to the queen.

Tereus was away from home when this woven letter came to Procne's hands, painting for her how she had been deceived and how her beloved sister was still alive. With the messenger for guide she hurried to the prison, tore Philomela from her keepers, and brought her home, the miserable sisters mingling their tears, while Procne alone could raise her voice in threats of vengeance against the husband who had so foully wronged them both. She, once so gentle and loving, now vowed to slay Tereus in his sleep, to burn his house, to curse him before the gods who too long had let such wickedness go unpunished.

As they reached the gates there ran out to meet them Itys, Procne's son, the darling of his rough father, and his image in features. That likeness to Tereus inflamed the mother's wrath, and when she saw how her sister could not speak a word to greet the wondering boy, her fury broke out upon this innocent one. Like a tigress she sprang at him, and, maddened by woe, struck a dagger into the throat of her own son. One wound was enough; yet Philomela, also, fed her heartburning on the boy's blood. These two raging women tore Itys limb from limb, and boiled his flesh in a cauldron, all their minds hot for revenge on the father. When Tereus came home, Procne set before him that horrid meal. He ate unsuspecting, and only when gorged to the full, thought of asking what game this was she had cooked so well.

For answer burst in speechless Philomela, to fling the gory head of his son at the king's feet, and Procne brandishing the torch with which she had kindled their marriage bed. The looks of the two wronged women told their tale as plainly as a hundred tongues. With cries and imprecations the father leaped to his feet, overturning the table in his blind horror of the unnatural food. He drew his sword upon the sisters, who fled before him from the accursed house, now filled with smoke and flame.

Tereus fiercely followed them into the woods, where, as minstrels tell, the gods worked a miracle to mark the guilt of this house. Procne was turned into a swallow, and Philomela into a nightingale, flying ever pursued by a long-billed hoopoe that was no other than the false husband with his blood-rusted sword. But old Pausanias has another tale: "Procne and Philomela melted away in tears, lamenting what they had done and suffered, and the story of their being changed into a nightingale and swallow comes from these birds having a sorrowful and plaintive note"—such as well might tune the unhappy sisters' song.[1]

---

[1] This painful story is told in different ways, Procne and Philomela exchanging their parts in one version.

The Tragedies of Thebes

1 Cadmus

It is told of Cadmus, the Tyrian, that he first taught the use of letters to Greece. A strange errand it was that brought this stranger from his home beyond the sea.

His father, king Agenor, had one young daughter, Europa, on whom fell the eyes of Zeus, and he plotted to bear her away to be his own. As Europa was sporting with her companions on the seashore, the god appeared to her in the shape of a milk-white bull, so gentle and goodly that she fell to stroking it and decking its head with flowers, while it licked her neck, lowing as if to breathe a spell upon the Tyrian maid that gave back a kiss to this kingly creature. As it lay down on the grass, the playful girl made bold to mount its broad back. But she screamed with fright when at once it leapt to its feet, and galloped away with her like a spirited courser. Europa did not dare throw herself off, still less when the bull plunged with her into the sea. Heedless of her cries, it bore that light burden across the waves, clinging to its flower-wreathed horns and looking back wildly to the shore, soon lost for her in tears. She would see her native land no more.

With dolphins and Nereïds gambolling on the track, and Tritons blowing their horns in bridal glee, all night the bull swam swift and strong as a galley, then at daylight set Europa on an island, which indeed was Crete. There the bull vanished, Zeus taking his own godlike form to tell her how he had done this for love. Aphrodite, too, appeared to comfort her with a promise that a whole new quarter of the world should be called after her name. So the maiden let herself forget her Asian home, and in time became the mother of Minos and Rhadamanthus, who were to sit in Hades as stern judges of the dead.

But Agenor never ceased to mourn his lost daughter. When her scared playmates came running back, crying out what had befallen her, he was beside himself for wrath and grief. Bitterly reproaching his three sons, Cadmus, Phoenix and Cilix, with having kept no better guard over their sister, he sent them out in search of her, and bade them not return home unless they brought back Europa.

The three youths set out together, and with them went their woeful mother Telephassa, who could not rest while her dear daughter was so strangely missing. For weeks they hastened here and there, for months and years, seeking everywhere to hear of Europa, but no one had seen her in any haunt of men. First Phoenix grew tired of their long quest, dropping off from it to make himself a home in the land Phoenecia, which was called after him. Then Cilix in turn wearied of long fruitless wandering, and fixed himself in the country of Cilicia. But Cadmus and his mother held on, till she, worn out by sorrow and travel, lay down to die, her last words a charge to him not to give up the search.

With a few faithful servants who had followed him from Tyre, Cadmus crossed the sea, and came into Greece; but there he could still hear no news of his sister, so that at last he lost all hope to find her alive Without her he might not see his father's face, and he knew not where to turn for a home. Coming to the renowned Delphic oracle of Apollo, he sought its counsel, and was bidden to follow a cow he would find feeding alone in a meadow nearby: where the cow first lay down he should build a city and call its name Thebes.

He soon found the cow, that walked on before him, leading him and his men through fields and hills, into a land of mountains and plains which came to be called Boeotia. There at last the cow, lowing to the sky, laid itself upon the grass as token for Cadmus that his long wandering was at an end. Thankfully he fell down to kiss the strange earth that a god seemed to give him for his own.

But the place had a fearsome lord with whom he must reckon. Proposing to offer sacrifice to Athena, that she might be favourable to him, he sent his servants to draw water from a stream which rushed out of a dark cave, its mouth hidden in a thick grove of mossy oaks never touched by the axe. The men entered the grove, but came not back; and from within he heard a sound of hissing, and saw wreaths of foul smoke spreading among the trees. He bounded forward to find his servants lying dead before the cave, scorched by the breath of a huge dragon that stretched towards him its three fiery heads, each bristling with three rows of teeth through which it breathed poisonous fumes, its eyes shining like fire, and its red crests glowing in the shadow of the cave mouth, as it pushed out its long neck to lick the bodies of the slain.

"Ah! poor companions, either must I avenge you, or be your mate in death!" cried Cadmus, and snatched up a heavy rock to hurl it at the monster, from whose horny scales it bounded back without doing them harm; but all the dark wood echoed with an angry roar.

Undaunted, the hero flung his spear so straight and strong that black blood gushed from the dragon's breast to mingle with the foam of its fury. Now it uncoiled all its monstrous length, and issuing from the cave, reared its horrid heads like trees to fall upon the man who dared to face its wounded rage. But Cadmus held his ground, smiting with all his might at the fiery jaws, till he drove his sword through one poison-swollen throat to nail it to an oak trunk. The monster twisted its necks and lashed its tail so as to bend the thick tree double, but the roots held firm, and the sword stuck fast; so there it writhed helplessly while its fiery breath was quenched by its own blood.

All unhurt, Cadmus stood over the dead body, when he was aware of Athena at his side, come down from Olympus to found a city that should grow great under her aegis.

"Sow the dragon's teeth in the earth," she bid him. "From them will spring up a race of warlike men to do your will."

Wondering at such advice, Cadmus did not disobey. He dug deep furrows with his sword; he plucked out the dead dragon's teeth; he sowed them in the earth drenched by its gore. Forthwith the ground began to heave and swell and bristle with spear points; then quickly there sprang up a crop of armed men, their weapons clashing together like corn beaten by the wind. Cadmus, in amazement, made ready to defend himself, but again a divine voice murmured in his ear—

"Sheathe your sword: let these do after their kind."

No sooner were the new-born warriors full grown out of the furrows, than they fell on each other in their lust for battle. So fiercely they fought that, before the sun was set, all but five had fallen dead on the bosom of their mother earth. These five, weary with bloodshed, dropped their weapons and offered themselves to serve Cadmus in place of his followers slain by the dragon.

With their aid he built here the citadel that came to be called Thebes, and thus founded a kingdom in the Boeotian land. There are those who say that this Cadmus, "man of the east", came not from Tyre, but from famed Thebes in Egypt, whose name he brought into Greece. But others have it that the name was given by Apollo's oracle.

The new city thrived, yet its first lord had to suffer from foes, both in heaven and on earth. The dragon-serpent slain by him was sacred to the god Ares, who long bore ill will to Cadmus for its death. In time Cadmus seemed to have made amends for that sacrilege, so that he took as his Harmonia, daughter of Ares and Aphrodite. All the gods came to the marriage; and among the gifts were a necklace and a veil made by Hephastus for Aphrodite's sake, gauds that became famous heirlooms as they were charged with misfortune for whoever wore them. And though Ares, at the bidding of Zeus, appeared to be reconciled with Cadmus, a curse rested on his house. His children and his children's children came to evil ends, among them Ino, who drowned herself after her husband in madness killed their son, and Semele, consumed by the fierce glory of Zeus, when she became the mother of Dionysus.

Cadmus himself, they say, was dethroned by his own grandson Pentheus. In his old age, the troubled king had again to go forth homeless, yet not alone, for with him went his faithful wife Harmonia. They wandered into the wild northern forests, till this once dauntless hero, bowed down by infirmities and burdened with the curse of that dragon's blood, was heard to murmur—

"If a serpent be so dear to the gods, would I were a serpent rather than a man!"

At once he sank upon his breast, his skin turning to scales and his limbs to speckled coils. As Harmonia saw how her husband was transformed, she prayed that she too might become a serpent; and her prayer likewise was answered. There they lived among the rocky woods, hurting no man, nor hiding from the sight of men who were once their fellows.

❧

2 Niobe

Thebes, thus founded in bloodshed, had a long history written in letters of blood by the hate of rival gods. It was the fate of Pentheus to be torn in pieces by the women of his house, his own mother their leader, because he frowned on their wild worship of Dionysus.

Another queen who worshipped the wine-god was Dirce, wife of the usurper Lycus. The daughter of the rightful king was Antiope, beloved by Zeus, to whom she bore twin sons, Amphion and Zethus, brought up humbly as shepherds on Mount Cithaeron, while their mother wandered in lonely exile, and in the end, they say, went mad through her misfortunes. At one time she fell into the power of Dirce, who in her hatred for the captive she had wronged, ordered her to be dragged to death by a wild bull at the hands of Amphion and Zethus. But when they knew the victim for their mother, they led a band of herdsmen against the city, slew Lycus, and tied cruel Dirce to the horns of the bull to make her perish by her own device.

So Amphion became king at Thebes, which he walled about through the power of music, being so skilled to play on a lyre given him by Hermes, that at its enchanting sound the very stones were drawn to move as he bade them. But on his children, too, fell a curse of wrath and woe.

Amphion had married Niobe, daughter of the doomed Tantalus, who was himself a son of Zeus. She bore seven noble sons and seven fair daughters; then, too proud of this goodly brood, she made bold to exult over Leto, as mother of twins and no more. But these twins were the divine Apollo and Artemis, on whom their despised mother called to avenge her against that presumptuous queen.

"Enough!" Apollo cut short her tearful tale. "Complaining but delays chastisement."

Wrapped in dark storm-clouds, brother and sister flew to overlook Thebes, where on an arena outside the walls, the seven sons of Niobe were exercising themselves in chariot racing, wrestling, and other sports. They had no warning, other than the the clank of the god's quiver, before the eldest was pierced to the heart by an arrow from the sky, and fell without a groan among the feet of his horses. The second turned his chariot to fly, but that did not avail him, struck by Apollo's unerring aim. So, also, it went with the third and fourth brothers, transfixed by a single shaft. The fifth and sixth sons ran to raise the bodies of their fallen brethren, but were themselves laid low before they could embrace the dead. The youngest only remained, a long-haired, fair-faced stripling, who, guessing how he had to deal with an angry god, threw himself on his knees to beg for mercy, but the fatal point was already winging to his breast.

The news of this sudden slaughter quickly spread through the city. Amphion stabbed himself for despair at the loss of his sons. Niobe, gathering her scared daughters about her, as chickens under the wings of a bird, hurried out to the field on which her seven boys were stretched lifeless around the altar of Leto. At the sight of them, rage spoke louder than grief, and raising her head against the gods who had so avenged their mother, she cried bitterly—

"Triumph, cruel Leto; but even now my offspring surpasses yours!"

For answer twanged the bow of Artemis, and the eldest daughter fell as she stood tearing her hair over her slain brothers. Next, the second with a sharp cry put her hand to her heart; then the third sister, who would have held her up, sank beside her, bleeding from an invisible arrow. One by one, all the daughters were shot down, till only the youngest in terror hung to her mother, whose pride now gave way; tears burst forth, and she stretched out her hands in suppliant prayer—

"Spare me but one, the last of so many!"

As she spoke, the last shaft of pitiless Artemis reached the child on the mother's bosom. Without a wound, Niobe herself sank as dead, her heart broken, her limbs motionless, her eyes staring, the blood gone from her face, where only her tears did not cease to flow. Sorrow had turned her to stone. For ever, they say, as the hot rays of the sun and the cold moonbeams pour down on that stone image, it weeps for the children of whom Niobe had boasted against the jealous gods.

⚜

3 Oedipus

After the destruction of Amphion's race, Laïus was brought back to his forefathers' throne, from which he had been driven into exile. Among all the descendants of Cadmus, the most famous and the most unhappy was this king's son, doomed by an oracle to be the death of his own father and the husband of his mother. Forewarned of such a fate, when his queen Jocasta bore a boy, Laïus had him cast out on Mount Cithaeron, with his feet tightly bound to make the child more helpless against speedy death. But the goatherd charged with this cruel errand took pity on the wailing infant, and, though he told the king that his bidding was done, in truth he had given it to another herd, who took it to his master Polybus, king of Corinth. By him the boy was kindly received, and brought up under the name of Oedipus ('Swollen foot'); while Laïus and Jocasta, making sure he had been torn to pieces by wild beasts, believed themselves to live childless, and thus hoped to cheat the oracle.

Polybus and his childless wife Merope adopted the outcast boy as their own son; then, as years went on, few at Corinth remembered how he was not so in truth. Oedipus grew to manhood never doubting but that these foster-parents were his father and mother, till one day, at a feast, some drunken fellow mocked at him for a baseborn foundling. In wrathful concern he sought to know from Merope whose son he truly was. She tried to put him off, yet could not deny that he was a stranger by birth. The dismayed youth turned to Polybus, who also gave him doubtful answers, bidding him ask no more, since it would be a woeful misfortune if ever he came to know his real parents.

But these hints only made Oedipus more eager to learn the truth, and he thought of Apollo's oracle. Leaving Corinth secretly, he travelled on foot to Delphi, where the priestess gave no plain answer to his question, but only this fearful warning—

"Shun your father, ill-omened youth! Should you meet with him, he will fall by your hand; then, wedding your own mother, you will leave a race destined to fresh crimes and woe."

Oedipus turned away with a shudder. Now he believed he understood why Polybus and Merope had made a mystery of his birth. Fearing affliction for them, who loved him well, he vowed never to go back to Corinth, but to seek some distant land, where, if madness came upon his mind to drive him to such wicked deeds, he might be far from the parents he took for threatened by a curse.

From Delphi he was making towards Boeotia, when in a narrow hollow way where three roads met, he came upon an old man in a chariot, before which ran an arrogant servant ordering all to stand aside to let it pass. Oedipus, used to ordering rather than to be being ordered, answered the man hotly, and struck him to the ground; then his master flung a javelin at this presumptuous youth. With his staff Oedipus struck back, overturned the old man from the chariot, and left him dead by the roadside. In the pride of victory Oedipus went his way, ignorant that the proud lord he had slain in a chance quarrel was no other than his own father, Laïus. A traveller who found the king's corpse buried it where it lay; and the news was brought to Thebes by the charioteer, who, having fled from that one bold assailant, to excuse his own cowardice gave out that a band of robbers had fallen upon them in the hollow pass.

Wandering from city to city, Oedipus reached Thebes, to find it all in mourning not only for the death of its king, but from the dread of a monster that haunted the rocky heights beyond the wall. This was the Sphinx which men took to be a sister of Cerberus, that three-headed hound of Hades. To anyone coming near it, the creature put a riddle, which if he failed to answer, it devoured him on the spot. Till some man should have guessed its riddle, the Sphinx would not be gone; and so long as it brooded over the city, blight and famine wasted the fields around. One or another Theban daily met death in setting his wit against this monster's, and its last victim had been a son of Creon, Jocasta's brother who for a time ruled the kingless land. Seeing himself unable to get rid of the Sphinx, Creon proclaimed that whoever could answer its riddle, were he the poorest stranger, should have as reward the kingdom of Thebes with all the dead king's treasures, and the hand of the king's widow, Jocasta, in marriage.

As Oedipus entered the city, a herald went through the streets to make this proclamation, that set the friendless youth pricking up his ears. Life seemed not dear to him; all he desired was to escape that destiny of crime threatened by the oracle. At once he presented himself before Creon, declaring that he was not afraid to answer the Sphinx.

They led him outside the walls to the stony wilderness it haunted, strewn with the bones of those who had failed to guess its riddle. Here he must seek out the creature alone, for its very voice made men tremble. Soon he was aware of it perched on a rock, a most grisly monster, with the body of a lion, the wings of an eagle, and the head of a woman. But Oedipus, caring little whether he lived or died, shrank not from its appalling looks.

"Put your riddle!" he cried; and the Sphinx croaked back—

"What creature alone changes the number of its feet? In the morning it goes on four feet, at midday on two, in the evening on three feet. And with the fewest feet, it has ever the greatest strength and swiftness."

Fixing her cruel eyes on the youth, she frowned to see him not at a loss – indeed, he smiled in her stony face, answering—

"The riddle is easy. It is man that in childhood goes on all-fours, then walks firmly on two feet, and in his old age must lean upon a staff."

Furious to hear her riddle guessed for the first time, the Sphinx gave a shrill scream, flapped her gloomy wings, and threw herself from the rock to her death. With shouts of joy the watching citizens poured out to greet that ready-witted youth that had delivered them from such a scourge. They hailed him as their king; and he was married to the widowed Jocasta, the more willingly on his part, as he believed himself thus made safe against the unnatural union predicted by the oracle, for he believed Merope to be his mother, for all her denial.

Years, then, he reigned at Thebes in peace and prosperity, gladly obeyed by the people, who took this young stranger for a favourite of the gods. He loved his wife Jocasta, older than himself as she was; and they had four children, the twin-sons Eteocles and Polyneices, and two daughters, Antigone and Ismene. But when these were grown to full age, the fortune of the land seemed to change. For now a sore plague fell upon it, so that the people cried for help to their king, who sent to Delphi his brother-in-law, Creon, to ask of the oracle how the pestilence might be stayed.

The answer was that it came as punishment for the unatoned blood of Laïus. Now, for the first time Oedipus set on foot enquiries as to his predecessor's death. Vowing to do justice on the criminal, whoever this might prove to be, he consulted Tiresias the seer struck with blindness in his youth because he had spied upon the goddess Athena, who again, taking pity on him for the loss of his eyes, gave him marvellous sharpness of ear, so that he understood the voice of all birds, also she filled his mind with mystic knowledge of things past and of things to come. But the blind seer was loath to tell what Oedipus sought to know.

"Bitter is knowing when ignorance were best. Let me go home, with a perilous secret hid in my bosom."

In vain the people begged him, in vain the king ordered him to speak. At last Oedipus angrily reviled him as having himself had a hand in the murder he would not disclose. This rash accusation made the old man speak.

"Hear then, oh king, if you must learn the truth. You are the man that slew Laïus in the hollow way to Delphi. For your sake, and no other, this curse is come upon the city."

Now with a start Oedipus remembered that old lord in the chariot whom he had slain in quarrel as he came from Delphi. Anxiously he pressed Jocasta with questions about her first husband. She described his grey hair, his haughty bearing, his black steeds; she told that he had been killed by robbers in a hollow pass where three ways met; and every word made Oedipus surer of the truth. But his wife mocked at the seer's wisdom.

"Even the god's oracle may speak falsely," she said, "for Laïus was warned at Delphi that he should fall by the hand of his own son, who, moreover, should marry his mother. Yet we never had but one child, and he was thrown out to die on Mount Cithaeron when not three days old, that thus our house should escape so dark a doom."

Among the bystanders chanced to be that goatherd charged long ago with the child's death; and him Jocasta called to confirm her words. But the old man fell on his knees, confessing how he had not had the heart to leave a helpless babe to be torn by wolves and eagles, but had given it alive to a servant of the king of Corinth.

Jocasta raised a cry, for she knew her husband passed for a son of that king, and she began to guess the truth, now clear to the awestruck Oedipus, that he and no other had unwittingly fulfilled the oracle by slaying his own father and wedding his mother. While he stood aghast, veiling his face for shame and horror, she fled to her chamber, like one out of her senses, barring herself in with her unspeakable woe. When the door was broken open, she had hanged herself with her belt rather than look again upon the husband who was no other than her son.

"Thy sorrows are ended; but for me death were too light a punishment!" he wept upon her dead body. And with the buckle of Jocasta's belt he tore both his eyes, so that night came upon him at noon.

A blind old man, his hair grown suddenly grey, Oedipus groped his way out of the palace, poorly dressed as he had entered it a travel-worn youth; and leaning on the staff with which he had been the death of his father. His people turned away from him shuddering. His own sons held aloof. Only his daughters, Antigone and Ismene, followed him tearfully, begging him to stay. He would not be entreated; and when they had led him out of the city, Ismene took leave of him and went back to her brothers, already quarrelling over the kingdom.

But Antigone vowed that she would never desert her father, and with him she wandered away from her birthplace. Led by her, he went from city to city as a blind beggar, till they came to Athens, where Theseus was king. He gave the exiles refuge in a temple at Colonos. In this sanctuary Oedipus lived on for some years, poor and sorrowful, pitied by his neighbours as a victim of fate, and gently tended by Antigone till death came to end his strange misfortunes.

4 The Seven against Thebes

After the death of her old father, Antigone went back to Thebes, where she found her twin-brothers at hot strife. Eteocles and Polyneices had agreed to share the kingdom between them, ruling year about, but always they looked jealously on each other, and their uncle, Creon, could not keep them friends. By and by Eteocles, in his turn of office, drove his brother from the city, where he henceforth reigned alone.

Thus exiled, Polyneices sought refuge at Argos, hoping for the help of its king, Adrastus. As by night he came before this king's palace, he ran against another fugitive, Tydeus of Calydon, son of King Oeneus and brother of Meleager, who through chance slaying of a kinsman had also had to fly from his native land. In the darkness these two strangers took one another for enemies and drew their swords; then the clash of arms brought out Adrastus and his men to part

Oedipus at Colonos
From the sculpture by Hugues

them. As soon as the torch light showed those warriors' shields, the king uttered a cry of amazement.

"Who are you and where are you from?"

This Adrastus had been troubled by an oracle, giving out his two daughters as destined to marry a lion and a boar. Now Polyneices bore a lion's head on his shield, and on that of Tydeus was a boar's, recognition of his part in the great Calydonian boar hunt led by his brother. On seeing their devices the king of Argos joyfully hailed the strangers as sent to fulfil that oracle in a manner not to be feared. He made them welcome to his house; and, learning that they were of royal birth, he forthwith married them to his daughters, Argia and Deïpyle, both glad to have so gallant husbands in place of fierce beasts.

Grateful for such a son-in-law, Adrastus eagerly took up the cause of Polyneices against Eteocles, and called on kinsmen and allies to gather an army for restoring him to his kingdom. Seven were the captains of that host – Adrastus, his brothers Hippomedon and Parthenopaeüs, his nephew Capaneus, his brother-in-law Amphiaraüs, Tydeus, and Polyneices himself, they who came to be famed as the Seven against Thebes.

One only of these heroes had hung back from the enterprise – Amphiaraüs, renowned both as warrior and as seer. Divining by his art that only one of the Seven would come back alive from Thebes, Amphiaraüs, to escape the king's importunities, hid himself in a secret place known only to his wife Eriphyle. When Adrastus would not march forth without one whom he esteemed the eye of the army, Polyneices thought that he should try to win Eriphyle, believed to have power on her husband's will to make him do whatever she desired. The son of Jocasta had brought from Thebes an ancestral treasure, no other than that fatal necklace made by Hephaestus for Harmonia, wife of Cadmus.

With this dazzling gaud he bribed Eriphyle to disclose her husband's hiding-place and to persuade him to go against Thebes. Unwilling at heart, Amphiaraüs then joined the host; but so resentful was he of his wife's treacherous vanity that, before setting out, he made his son Alcmaeon swear to kill Eriphyle, if the father should not come back alive.

In sight of Thebes, the allied army encamped on Mount Cithaeron; and Tydeus went forward as a herald to demand that Polyneices should be received into his kingdom. Eteocles sent him back with an insolent answer of defiance, for the city, full of armed men, was fortified by a high wall with seven gates, behind which the usurper felt sure of his defence. Yet to hearten the citizens, he called on the blind soothsayer, Tiresias, who gave out a dark foreboding—

"Thebes stands in dire peril, to be averted only by the youngest son of its royal house; his life alone is the sacrifice that, freely offered, can save the city."

At this utterance, none was more dismayed than Creon, Jocasta's brother, for he thought how his darling son Menoeceus was the youngest of the fated family.

He proposed, then, to send him off to Delphi, there to be kept safe under sanctuary of Apollo. But the brave stripling had at once devoted his life to his native city. The oracle no sooner heard, he hastened to the highest tower of the walls, and hurled himself over among the assailants.

And that sacrifice seemed to avail for the safety of Thebes. Each of the seven heroes stormed at a different gate; but all were driven back by the defenders, who, sallying out, spread death and rout among their enemy. So many brave warriors fell, that when once more the Argive host came on, Eteocles sent a herald to propose that the quarrel should forthwith be settled by single combat between him and Polyneices.

Thus it was agreed: the brothers met outside the walls, and fought before the two armies with such fierceness, that sweat burst in thick drops on the brows of the onlookers, loud in uproar as each party shouted to hearten its own champion. They clashed together like boars; they broke their spears on one another's shields; they took to their swords, closing in desperate thirst for a brother's blood that poured out from all the joints of their armour, till both sank dying on the field.

Both sides now claiming the victory, in their dispute they fell to fighting with more fury than ever. Again the invaders were routed, and fled, all their leaders, save Adrastus, having fallen, as Amphiaraüs had foretold. The Thebans, too, suffered such loss that a battle won so came to be known as a Cadmean victory.[1]

⚜

5 Antigone

The sons of Oedipus being no more, Creon again took over the kingdom, as he had done after the death of Laïus. His first order was that, to mark the infamy of Polyneices in warring against his mother's city his body, and those of his allies, should lie unburied, a prey to dogs and vultures. So, while they bore Eteocles to the tomb with royal ceremony, his brother's corpse was left to be parched by the sun and drenched by the dew, a guard set over it night and day to see that, on pain of death, no friend should give it a burial.

But Antigone, faithful to her brother as to her father, had stood beside the dying Polyneices; and with his last breath he had made her promise to do for him those funeral rites without which his soul might not rest in peace. No threats of Creon could change her sisterly heart. Ismene wept with her over their brother's fate, but had not the boldness to share her pious task. Alone, in the moonlit night, Antigone stole forth to the field strewn with corpses, among which she searched out her brother's. Washing it with tears, she strove to drag it away; but her strength failed her, and she must make haste, not to be seen by the watchmen. All she could do was softly and silently to sprinkle the body with dust; but that seemed enough to save it from miserable wandering on the bank of Styx.

In the morning, one of the guards came in fear to tell Creon that, for all their watchfulness, Polyneices' body had through the night been lightly covered with earth, by whose hands they knew not. Creon angrily ordered them to uncover it, and keep better watch, for their own lives should be forfeit if they again let anyone touch the body. With this threat the man went back to his post, glad to get off so lightly; for the king's resentment against Polyneices was so well known, that the guards had cast lots which of them should take on himself the perilous office of bringing news of his command set at nought.

Through the day sprang up a mighty whirlwind, filling the air with dust. Antigone again ventured out, to find, as she feared, that her brother's body had been stripped of its thin coat of earth. Again, now in broad daylight, she was trying to cover it, when the guard seized her and brought her, bound, before Creon, who stormed like a tyrant on learning by whom he had been thus defied.

"Rash girl!" he cried, "do you not know the law made but yesterday?"

"I know a higher law that is neither of yesterday nor today," she answered with unshrinking eye, "the eternal law of pity, that forbids me to leave the dead son of my mother unburied."

"If such be your love for a brother, you shalt go to love him in Hades!" stormed the king.

"Death is the worst you can do to me; but my name shall live as that of one who feared not to do a sister's duty. And to die before my time were welcome in a world of such woes."

Enraged by her boldness, Creon gave command that she should be walled up in a cave and there left to die. He was obeyed, for the shuddering citizens did not venture to cross his vindictive mood, though all men whispered against him that there was no honour in warring upon the dead. But Ismene now found heart to withstand him, clinging to her sister, falsely accusing herself as an accomplice in the pious crime, and demanding to share her fate. Then came another to plead for her, Creon's son Haemon, who was betrothed to Antigone, and loved her more than his life. Reverently addressing his father, he begged him to consider how all men would cry shame on him for such cruelty: the Thebans murmured, though they dared not speak out, mourning over the sister that little deserved death for her care not to leave a brother's body to wild beasts. King as he was, let him remember that he could not scorn his people's goodwill, as the tree that holds stiff against winds and waves comes to be uprooted, yet might stand firm by bending.

"Would the boy teach me wisdom?" his furious father cut him short. "I see how love for that traitress blinds thee; but thou shalt not have my foe for a bride. Too late shall she learn it is better to obey the living than the dead."

Antigone Strewing Dust on the Body of Polyneices
From the painting by Victor J. Robertson

When Antigone had been borne off to her doom, there came yet another to bend Creon's stubborn will. This was the blind Tiresias, whose inner vision warned him of fresh calamities for Thebes, polluted through the innocent fate of Antigone and the sacrilegious exposure of Polyneices to beasts and birds. The gods were wroth, he declared, at the wrong thus done to a king's children. But, like Oedipus, the king spoke bitterly to the rebuking soothsayer.

"Who has bribed you to scare me with lying auguries?" And that insult stung the old man to speak plain.

"Before the sun sets, you shall pay for double impiety – yes, two corpses for one! Their blood be on your head! Lead me far from him who defies the gods!"

Without another word, the seer turned away, leaning on a boy who had brought him into the king's presence. So solemn had been his warning, that Creon, left alone, began to falter in his ruthless purpose. He called the elders of the city into council, and of them deigned at last to ask what he should do.

"Bury the body of Polyneices, and set Antigone free from her living tomb!" they answered with one voice.

Since all men were against him, Creon sullenly gave way. He ordered Polyneices to be honourably buried beside his brother, and went himself to the cave in which Antigone had been walled up. Haemon, her lover, ran on first of the crowd bearing axes and bars to set her free; then peering through a cleft, he uttered a lamentable cry for what he saw within. Too late the wall was broken down, letting all see how the noble Antigone had strangled herself with her veil twisted into a noose. Haemon in speechless despair drew his sword, and, before the father could hold his hand, had fallen upon it over the body of his beloved.

When his mother, Creon's queen, heard what had befallen, she, too, killed herself for grief; thus Tiresias spoke truly that, before the sun set, the king's house should pay two corpses for one. All the city was one cry of mourning, amid which the bereaved Creon hardened his heart, and in his gloomy rage, once more forbade the burial of those slain foes about the city.

But again the widowed and childless king had to bend his obstinate will. Adrastus, by the swiftness of his horse, had escaped to Athens, and as a suppliant sought help from its king, nor was Theseus deaf to his prayer. With a strong army he marched to Thebes, summoning Creon to let the dead be buried, that their spirits should have rest. The Thebans were in no heart for further fighting; and their tyrant had nothing for it but to consent. The fallen followers of those seven heroes were heaped into seven piles, to be solemnly burned on the field, with due rites. Of Evadne, the widow of Capaneus, it is told that woe drove her to hurl herself upon her husband's funeral pyre. Over the ashes, Theseus built a temple to Nemesis, goddess of Retribution; then he withdrew with his allies; and for a time Thebes had peace to lament its evil destiny.

6 The Fatal Heirlooms

Thebes was still to suffer from the bane laid on its kingly house, that spread far beyond its own soil. Polyneices had left a son, Thersander, to grow up in exile at Argos. When years had passed, he and other sons of the heroes slain before

Thebes began to hatch revenge upon the hated city, and made against it a new war known as that of the Epigoni, or offspring of the Seven.

Of those Seven, Adrastus was still alive, but too old to lead the army. He sought counsel of the oracle at Delphi, that bid choose as chief Alcmaeon, son of Amphiaraüs, the seer. But Alcmaeon shrank from this honour put upon him, while also the oracle reminded him how he had pledged himself to revenge upon his mother Eriphyle the death of his father, betrayed by her to death for the bribe of that fatal necklace, but his dreadful vow was still unfulfilled. Eriphyle had some strange spell to throw over the will of her son, as of her husband. And, as against her husband, so she could be bribed to persuade her son. Thersander had one more Cadmean heirloom to bestow, the rich veil which was another wedding gift of Aphrodite to Harmonia. With this he bought from Eriphyle that she should win over her son to lead the Epigoni.

Alcmaeon, then, consented to be their chief, putting off his dark purpose to slay that bewitching mother. He marched to Thebes, where this time the war went for its invaders. The Thebans came out to meet them, but were driven back with the loss of their leader Laodamas, son of Eteocles. The blind Tiresias, now over a hundred years old, gave forth the worst auguries. He bid his fellow citizens send out a herald to propose terms of peace, and under this pretence, to fly from their walls by night. So they did, escaping to seek new homes elsewhere. Thersander entered in triumph the abandoned city, where now he ruled as the last heir of Cadmus, and lived to fall in the great war against Troy.

His fate was happy beside that of Alcmaeon, who went back victorious, brooding over the secret vow to slay his mother. To this fell duty, he believed himself urged by the oracle; and it steeled his heart when he came to learn how she had been bribed by the veil of Aphrodite to send him forth in arms. He slew her with his own hand, thus at last performing the long-deferred pledge to his father. But no more could he live in the home made horrible to him. He left Argos and wandered forth alone, taking with him those crime-inspiring gifts.

Then, wherever he went, the gods frowned on him as profaned by his mother's blood, and he was haunted by the Furies into restless madness. In time he seemed to be at peace in a city of Arcadia, whose king Phegeus did purifying rites to cleanse him from his guilt, and gave him in marriage his own daughter Arsinoë. But though his madness had left him, the curse he bore from place to place fell upon the land that thus granted Alcmaeon asylum. It was blighted by famine, through his pollution of it; so said the oracle, declaring that this exile could find rest only on ground which should have arisen since he took his mother's life.

Once more he wandered into the world, leaving with Arsinoë those fatal gifts. After a long search, he found at the mouth of the river Acheloüs an island newly sprung above the water, unseen by the sun when he raised his hand against

Eriphyle. Here he fixed himself, and seemed now to be free from his curse.

Yet fresh troubles came with relief from the Furies' scourge. Forgetting his wife Arsinoë, he married Callirrhoë, daughter of the river-god Acheloüs, and she bore him two sons, Acarnan and Amphoterus. They might have lived happily but for Callirrhoë hearing of the famous necklace and veil he had left with Arsinoë, which she coveted so as to give her husband no peace till they should be her own.

Driven by her importunity, Alcmaeon went back to Arsinoë, and demanded those fatal gifts on pretence of offering them to Apollo at Delphi, as a sacrifice by which he might be purged of the madness that, as he feigned, alone kept him apart from her. Arsinoë readily gave up her treasures, which he was for carrying off to his new home. But a disloyal servant betrayed to her father how his master had another wife, to be decked with the gifts of Aphrodite. Arsinoë's two brothers followed Alcmaeon, slew him taken at unawares, and brought back the necklace and the veil to their sister. She, who loved her false husband still, gave them such bitter thanks for that service, that her also they sent to death, cruelly and shamefully, in their wrath at the dishonour done to their house.

And still the flow of blood was not staunched. When Callirrhoë came to know how she had been deceived and bereaved, beside herself with rage, she prayed Zeus, by her kinship with the gods, to make her two boys grow up at once to men that they might lose not a day in avenging their father. Zeus nodded consent; and the sons who lay down careless children rose next morning bearded men, stern and strong. Setting out forthwith on their errand of bloodshed, they fell upon Arsinoë's brothers carrying her necklace and veil to Delphi. Acarnan and Amphoterus killed them both, before they knew they were in danger; then went on to root out their father's house.

Thus the fatal gifts at last came to Callirrhoë. But her father, the wise Acheloüs, would have none of their baneful charm. He bid carry them, after all, to Delphi, to be hung up in the temple of Apollo; and this being done, the curse, passed on through the Cadmean house, was charmed away from the race of Amphiaraüs, whose grandson, Acarnan, settled the Acarnanian land, as Cadmus had been founder of Thebes.

---

[1] (p.149) The heavy losses of Pyrrhus, in one of his Roman battles, gave the same significance of the phrase 'a Pyrrhic victory'.

Echo and Narcissus

To the river-god Cephissus was born a son named Narcissus, who seemed to his fond mother the most beautiful of children, and anxiously she sought from the blind prophet Tiresias to know his fate.

"Will he live to old age?" she asked; to which the dark-seeing prophet made answer, "If he shall not have known himself!"

What these mystic words meant, time only would show. The boy grew up rarely beautiful, not only in his mother's eyes but in the eyes of all that were not blind. There was no maiden who did not cast loving looks upon him; and less favoured youths envied the charms that, alas, made Narcissus vain above all sons of earth. Blushes, sighs, and sparkling eyes were heeded by him but as tributes to his loveliness; and when he had bloomed to the flower of manhood, he was in love with himself alone.

Shunning all who would fain have been his companions, it was his wont to walk apart in solitary places, lost in admiration of the graceful form which he thought no eye worthy to behold but his own. One day, as he wandered through a wood, he was spied by the wood-nymph Echo, who loved him at first sight, but was dumb to open her heart till he should ask its secret. For on her a strange fate had been laid: Hera, displeased by her chattering tongue, took away from her the power of speech unless in answer to some other voice. So now, when Echo slunk lightly among the thickets, shadowing the steps of that beautiful youth, eager as she was to accost him, she must wait for him to speak first, nor dared she show herself but at his desire. But he, given up to his sweet thoughts of self, strolled on silently, and the maiden followed him lovingly, unseen, till at last, as he halted to drink from a cool spring, his ear was caught by a rustle in the branches.

"Who is there?" he exclaimed, raising his eyes to peer into the green shade.

"*There!*" a voice back; but he did not see who spoke.

"What do you fear?" he asked; and the invisible voice answered—

"*Fear!*"

"Come here!" he cried in amazement, when thus his words were given mockingly back to him; and still the voice took no shape.

"*Here!*" was the reply; and now glided forth the blushing Echo, to make as if she would have thrown her arms round his neck.

But in the crystal pool the youth had caught another form that better pleased his eyes; and he roughly brushed away the enamoured nymph, with a harsh word.

"What brings you?"

"*You!*" she faltered, shrinking back from his frown.

"Begone!" he bid her angrily. "There can be nothing between such as you and the fair Narcissus."

"*Narcissus!*" sighed Echo, scarcely heard, and stole away on tiptoe to hide her shameful looks in the deep shade, breathing a silent prayer that this proud youth might learn for himself what it was to love in vain.

When left alone, Narcissus turned eagerly back to that spring in which he believed to have seen a fairer face. Like a silver mirror it lay, shining in sunlight, framed by a ring of flowery plants, as if to guard it from the plashing tread of cattle. On his knees at the edge, he stretched himself over the bright well, and there looked down upon a face and form so entrancingly beautiful, that he was ready to leap into the water beside it. A priceless statue it seemed, of one at his own blooming age, every limb chiselled like life, with features as of breathing marble, and curling locks that hung above ivory shoulders.

"Who are you that has been made so fair?" cried Narcissus; and the lips of the image moved, yet now came no answer.

Echo and Narcissus
From the painting by J. W. Waterhouse R.A.

He smiled, and was smiled back to. He flushed for delight, then the face in the water was overspread with rosy blood, its eyes sparkling like his own. He stretched out his hands towards it, and so the beautiful form beckoned to him; but as soon as his touch broke the clear surface, it vanished like a dream, to return in all its enchantment while he was content to gaze motionless, then again growing dim beneath the tears of vexation he shed into the water.

"I am not one to be despised," he pleaded with his coy charmer, "but such a one as mortal maidens and nymphs, too, have loved in vain."

"V*ain!*" resounded the sad voice of Echo from the woods.

Again and again he leaned down to clasp that lovely shadow in his arms, but always it eluded him; and when he spoke entreating it to his embrace, it but simulated his gestures in unfeeling silence. Maddened by so strong allurement of his own likeness, he could not tear himself away from the mirror in which it ever mocked his yearning fancy. "Alas!" was his constant cry, that always came sighing back from the retreats of the woeful nymph. Hour after hour, day after day, he hung over the pool's brink, nor cared to let food pass his lips, crying all in vain for that imaginary object of adoration, till at last his heart ceased to throb with despair, and he lay still among the water lilies that made his shroud. The gods themselves could not but be touched with pity for so fair a corpse; and thus was Narcissus transformed into the flower that bears his name.

As for poor Echo, who had invoked such punishment on his cold heart, she gained nothing but grief that her prayer was heard. Out of sight, she pined away for despised love, till all left of her was an idle voice. And that still haunts the rocks where never since can she be seen by startled eyes; but always she must be allowed the last word.

This was not the only tale told of Echo's fruitless love, for of old, too, love went often blind and deaf.

> "Pan loved his neighbour Echo – but that child
> Of Earth and Air pined for the Satyr leaping;
> The Satyr loved with wasting madness wild
> The bright nymph Lyda, – and so three went weeping:
> As Pan loved Echo, Echo loved the Satyr,
> The Satyr, Lyda – and thus love consumed them.
> And thus to each – which was a woeful matter –
> To bear what they inflicted, justice doom'd them;
> For inasmuch as each might hate the lover,
> Each loving, so was hated. – Ye that love not
> Be warn'd – in thought turn this example over,
> That when ye love, the like return ye prove not."
>
> —*Moschus*, translated by Percy Bysshe Shelley

The Sacred Oak

Every forest tree was held in respect by the men of old, for they could not be sure but that it was the home of some Dryad or other woodland nymph, whose life hung upon its flourishing. So poor Dryope learned to her woe, when, plucking a bright blossom for her child, she saw the sap run red, then found her own limbs putting forth leaves and flowers, as on the spot she became turned into a tree by the wrath of a nymph she had unwittingly wounded. In vain she struggled to fly, but rooted to the ground, she felt her voice failing, as with her last human words she begged that the child might often be brought to play beneath the sighing shade of her branches. Of many another hapless maid was it told that she suffered the same fate, like Daphne who, as a laurel, escaped the pursuit of Apollo, or like that Thracian Phyllis, betrothed to Demophon, son of Theseus, but when he tarried away from her too long she killed herself in hasty despair, and was transformed as a tree, hallowed by her overpowering love.

Bold was the crime and prodigious the punishment of Erysichthon, he that recklessly laid low a huge and venerable oak sacred to Demeter, in honour of whom the light-footed Dryads came often to dance round it in a moonlit ring. A giant it was among trees, towering high above its fellows, as they above the bushes, its branches thickly hung with votive tablets and garlands in sign of gratitude to the beneficent goddess. Yet that presumptuous churl bid his servants hew it down; and, when they hesitated in awe, himself snatched an axe to fetch the first stroke, crying—

"Were it the goddess herself, to the ground her tree shall come!"

The mossy bark gave out a deep groan as it felt the blow; the leaves turned pale; the branches trembled and dripped with sweat; blood burst from the trunk at every wound. The horrified bystanders vainly besought Erysichthon to throw down the axe. He struck one of them dead who would have held his hand, and kept urging on his thralls to the impious task, till at last the sacred oak fell with a crash echoing far around to drown the dying voice of the nymph that was its indwelling spirit.

To Demeter hastened the mourning Dryads of the grove; nor was the goddess deaf to their prayers for vengeance on the destroyer. She sent an oread to fetch Famine from the ice-bound deserts of the north; and this gaunt shape she charged to plague the life of Erysichthon. As, weary from his day's bad work, he lay dreaming of costly banquets, Famine hovered over him and breathed into his vitals a madness of insatiable greed.

He woke up with a raging hunger which no food could satisfy. The more he devoured, the more ravenous he felt, as if every mouthful added fuel to the flame of his appetite. In vain his table was loaded with all the fruits of the earth, with the flesh of every creature that ran, or swam, or flew; whatever he ate was lost like the rivers in the sea, and he never could have enough to appease the greed that tormented him night and day. When he had swallowed what would feed whole towns, he still felt hungry, as he vainly toiled to fill himself with emptiness. Thus the Dryads were avenged, while their beloved tree went to feed cooking fires that burned not so fast as his unquenchable voracity.

"More! More!" was his cry, if ever he had to wait a moment for the morsels that choked him into silence.

The once rich man was not long in eating himself poor. He had to sell his land, his goods, his house; and still unavailing gluttony preyed on him like a vulture. The day came when he had nothing left but his only daughter; and her, too, he sold as a slave to buy food with the price of her. And this resource she could spin out through the favour of Poseidon, who had bestowed upon her the power of changing herself into whatever form she pleased. Once in the hands of a master, she could soon slip out of them in some transforming disguise – a horse, a cow, a hind, a bird, or what not – and make her way back to the famishing father that he might sell her again to play the same trick on some other purchaser.

But at last her tricks wore themselves out, the story says not how; and the unhappy man had nothing for it but to devour his own flesh, consuming himself in less time than it had taken to hew down that sacred oak. So he perished miserably; but his name lives as a warning to men who mind not what is dear to the gods.

The Tale of Troy

1 Paris and Helen

The father of the Trojan race was Dardanus, who wandered across the Hellespont into Mysia, and married a daughter of the shepherd king Teucer. Their grandson Tros had a son named Ilus; and on a height by the river Scamander he built a city named Troy, or Ilion, the 'tower', its people known as Teucrians, Dardanians, or most famously as Trojans. For his new seat Ilus besought of Zeus some sign of favour; and in answer fell from heaven an image of Athena which, under the title of the Palladium, was to be treasured as the luck of Troy.

But soon Troy had ill luck, brought upon it by the son of Ilus, Laomedon, a crooked-minded king dealing falsely both with gods and men. He it was who gave walls to the city, and for that task hired Apollo and Poseidon, when, driven from Olympus by the displeasure of Zeus, they had been condemned for a year to serve some mortal upon earth. Poseidon surrounded Troy with strong walls, while Apollo pastured the king's herds in the valleys of Mount Ida. But after the year was up, Laomedon denied them the promised reward, driving them away with threats and insults, so that, when restored to their place in heaven, these gods bore a bitter grudge against Troy, by one of them never forgotten.

Before long, Poseidon's ill will was shown, for he sent to lay waste the land a ravening monster that could be driven away, spoke an oracle, only by the sacrifice of the king's daughter Hesione. She was already chained to a rock as its trembling victim, when to Troy in the nick of time came Heracles, who undertook to deliver her, as he did, by slaying the monster among his many feats and labours. For this deliverance Laomedon had promised him a team of matchless horses given by Zeus to his grandfather Tros. But, the monster slain, again this deceitful king broke faith, and Heracles angrily went his way without the horses, being bound to the service of Eurystheus

Years later, the hero came back to take vengeance for that deceit. He stormed the city, killed its faithless king, and gave Hesione to his own follower Telamon, who carried her away to Salamis in Greece. But at Hesione's entreaty he let her ransom one of her brothers, Podarces, 'the swift-footed', who, now under the name of Priam, 'the ransomed', became king of Troy.

Priam and his wife Hecuba had many children. The noblest of the sons was Hector, but the most handsome was Paris, before whose birth Hecuba dreamed that she bore a firebrand. That dream being interpreted by a seer as foretelling destruction for Troy, Priam and Hecuba agreed to save the city by exposing the babe to death on Mount Ida; and so was done through the hands of a slave.

But Paris did not die. Suckled by a bear, the child was found alive after some days, and reared among their own sons by the herdsmen of Mount Ida. He grew up hearty, handsome, and strong, a youth of mark above his fellows, though ignorant that he was a king's son. When he came to manhood he did such feats against the robbers of the mountains, that he won for himself the by-name of Alexander, 'helper of men'. He married the mountain nymph Oenone, and for a time lived happy among the herds, content with his simple lot and humble home.

> "There lies a vale in Ida, lovelier
> Than all the valleys of Ionian hills.
> The swimming vapour slopes athwart the glen,
> Puts forth an arm, and creeps from pine to pine,
> And loiters, slowly drawn. On either hand,
> The lawns and meadow ledges midway down
> Hang rich in flowers, and far below them roars
> The long brook falling thro' the clov'n ravine
> In cataract after cataract to the sea.
> Behind the valley topmost Gargarus
> Stands up and takes the morning: but in front
> The gorges, opening wide apart, reveal
> Troas and Ilion's columned citadel,
> The crown of Troas."
>
> —Alfred, Lord Tennyson

One day, as Paris fed his flocks in such a leafy glen of Mount Ida, there appeared to him three stately and beautiful women, whom, even before hearing their names, he was aware of as more than mortal. With them came a noble form, whose winged feet and the herald's staff he bore showed him no other than Hermes, messenger of the gods. In their presence the shepherd stood with beating heart and awe-struck eyes, while Hermes thus addressed him—

"Fear not, Paris; these are goddesses that have chosen you to award among them the prize of beauty. Zeus himself bids you to judge freely which of the three seems fairest in your eyes; and the father of gods and men will be your shield in giving true judgment."

With this the god put into his hands a golden apple.

161

At the wedding of Peleus and Thetis, parents of Achilles, Eris alone among the immortals had not been invited to the feast; then the slighted goddess of strife threw among the guests this golden apple, inscribed *For the fairest!* As was her design, three daughters of Olympus had quarrelled as to which of them it should belong; and now they came agreed to take the judgment of that bright-eyed shepherd, who stood before them scarcely daring to raise his eyes till they heartened him with appealing voices.

"I am Hera, the queen of Olympus," spoke the proudest of the three, "and I have queenly gifts to bestow on the humblest mortal. Give judgment for me, and, shepherd lad as you are, yours shall be the richest realm on earth!"

"I am Athena, goddess of arts," said the second. "Adjudge the prize to me, and you shall be famed as the wisest and bravest among men!"

"I am Aphrodite," said the third, with an enchanting smile, "and I have gifts sweeter than these. He who wins my favour need only love to be loved again. Choose me for the fairest among gods, and I promise you the most beautiful daughter of men as your wife!"

Paris might well stand in doubt before three so dazzling claimants; but he did not hesitate long. He gave the golden apple to Aphrodite, the goddess of love, who thanked him with a radiant smile, and confirmed her promise by an oath such as not even gods may break. But Hera and Athena frowned and turned away, and henceforth were enemies to all the Trojan race.

The glorious vision having vanished, it now seemed to Paris like a dream amid the toils of his daily life, in which he might have forgotten the promise of Aphrodite. As yet he knew no woman fairer than his loved wife. But soon came a change in his fortunes, when he despised poor Oenone, and left her to weep out her broken heart upon the wild mountain side.

For the first time since his birth, Paris went down to the city of Troy to try his strength in games held there by King Priam. As prize of one of the contests was proclaimed the herdsman's favourite steer, and he could not bear to think of its passing into the hands of a stranger. Not only that prize he won but others, surpassing even the king's sons, his own brothers as they were, had he but known it. They, for their part, might guess him to be no common clown, that bore himself above them all. One of his sisters, Cassandra, had the gift of divination; and she it was who recognized in this sunburnt mountaineer the child cast forth to die; then his parents were too glad of such a fine son to remember what had been foretold of him by the oracle.

Thus restored to his birthright, Paris came to stand so high in Priam's favour, that the king sent him to Greece in command of a great fleet, charged to demand that Hesione, borne off by Heracles, should be given back to her home, after many years. Alone Cassandra denounced this expedition, foretelling how a quarrel with the Greeks would bring them against Troy; but Apollo, who had

The Judgment of Paris
From the painting by Solomon J. Solomon R.A.

bestowed on her the gift of prophecy, had again cursed it with the fate that her warnings should never be taken for true.

Paris sailed forth, full of hope and pride, on an errand he did not perform. For he turned aside to visit Menelaüs, king of Sparta, married to Helen, the most beautiful woman on earth. At the first sight of this handsome stranger, richly arrayed in purple and gold, Helen was ready to forget her marriage vows. And when his eyes met hers, he forgot his true wife Oenone, weeping alone on Mount Ida, forgot his father's commands, forgot his own honour; he forgot all but the enchanting face which he was ready to take for that of the goddess herself – alas! to be famed for ages as

> "The face that launched a thousand ships,
> And burnt the topless towers of Ilium."

163

The honest heart of Menelaüs was so trustful that, going upon some expedition, he left his guest with his queen, to steal one another's love by soft words and kindling looks. He was soon to learn how ill that longhaired Eastern prince could be trusted. Before the king came back, Paris had fled, after breaking into his house by force, carrying off its treasures to the Trojan fleet, among them the dearest of all, the wife so little unwilling to follow a new master, that she left behind the young daughter Hermione she had borne to Menelaüs

With such a prize on board, the prince no longer minded the mission on which he had been sent by his father. Now that Aphrodite had fulfilled her promise, he gave himself up to dalliance with her. It was long before he steered for Troy to show her with pride to his own people. Spending the stolen wealth of Menelaüs in idle pleasure, these two would happily have forgotten their kin and country. Yet Paris went not without warning. As he sailed over a summer sea, it suddenly grew so calm that the ship seemed nailed to the water, from which rose the sea-god Nereus with dripping hair and beard, to utter fearful words.

"Ill omens guide your course, robber of another's good! The Greeks will come across this sea, vowed to redress the wrong done by you and to overthrow the towers of Priam. How many men, how many horses I foresee dead for your sin, how many Trojans laid low about the ruin of their city!"

⚜

2 The Gathering at Aulis

Helen's matchless beauty had drawn about her in youth so many hot suitors that they prudently bound themselves by an oath to honour whatever husband might be chosen for her, and to stand by him against any who should wrong his wedlock. So when Menelaüs learned how his wife had been stolen, he could call on a host of fellow rulers to take arms for recovering her and punishing that violator of his home. He and his elder brother Agamemnon, king of Argos, sons of Atreus and descendants of Pelops, were the mightiest lords in the Peloponnesus. Agamemnon, husband of Helen's sister Clytemnestra, stood out as greatest above all the kings of Greece; and when he summoned its princes to gather their ships and men for war with Troy, few ventured to slight his command. Two of the chiefs, indeed, held back at first, yet they were the two who in the end would be most famous among the champions of that war.

One of these was Odysseus (whom the Romans called Ulysses), who, having married a loving wife, Penelope, was reluctant to leave her and his young son Telemachus for a war which he foresaw as long and toilsome. So when

Palamedes, friend of Menelaüs, came with Agamemnon's summons to the rocky island of Ithaca, its crafty chief feigned to be out of his mind, in token of which he was found ploughing with an ox and an ass strangely yoked together, and sowing salt in the furrows. But Palamedes, too, was wily. He brought out the child Telemachus to lay him in front of the plough, then the father so carefully turned it aside as to show himself no madman. It is said that Odysseus never forgave that trick, though he seemed to forget it, and that years afterwards he took a chance of working fatal vengeance on Palamedes. But now, betrayed out of his pretence, he had to go with him to the gathering host, for which he soon could enlist a nobler champion.

Achilles was son of Peleus, a mortal married to the goddess Thetis, at whose wedding Eris threw down among the gifts that golden apple whoch was to be the seed of so much strife. His mother foretold that either he might die young after heroic deeds, or live long in ignoble ease; and eagerly the boy chose a short and glorious life. She sought to make him invulnerable by dipping him in the water of Styx; then the heel by which she held him remained the one mortal spot in his body. He was brought up with other heroes by old Cheiron, who fed him on the hearts of lions and the marrow of bears, and taught him gentle arts as well as the stern trade of war. Among all his companions he was noted for courage and pride, for generosity and hot temper, as for strength, beauty, and activity that won him such epithets as the 'swift-footed', and the 'yellow-haired' Achilles.

When the Trojan war was hatching, Thetis, aware that it should lead him to his death, would gladly have kept her son away. So she sent him, dressed as a maiden, to be hidden among the daughters of the king of Scyrus. There cunning Odysseus sought him out in the disguise of a merchant, who among rich clothes and other womanish gauds carried a store of bright weapons; then, while the true women had eyes only for adornments, Achilles revealed himself by snatching at sword and spear among all those wares. His sex thus discovered, it was not hard for Odysseus to bring him to the army, leading a band of warlike and devoted Myrmidons from his native Thessaly.

Another service the Ithacan prince undertook in going with Palamedes and Menelaüs as an embassy to demand of Priam that Helen should be given back. The king of Troy and his people heard them with amazement, as now for the first time they learned what Paris had done in Greece; and Priam would give no answer till his son came home to speak for himself. For his part, he had to complain of his sister Hesione held captive, for whom Helen might rightly be kept a hostage, if she were brought to Troy. And while the father tried to speak them fair, to the threats of these Greeks the Trojan princes gave back high words, so that they had almost come to blows had not grey heads checked the hot blood of youth. The ambassadors, courteously treated and put under guard against the insolence of the common folk, had to depart without their errand, bearing messages of defiance that made not for peace. As to Hesione, they told Priam how she was long happily married in Greece, and that her son Teucer was among the leaders of the host gathering to take vengeance on Troy.

After lingering long in foreign lands and seas, Paris brought home that bewitching bride, over whom the old king shook his head, and would have frowned on the darling son who had so ill done his mission in Greece. But his brothers, bribed by the wealth Paris had stolen from Sparta, and by the smiles of Helen's handmaidens had given to those still unmarried, were loud against letting her go back to Menelaüs. Their mother Hecuba was set to learn from her own lips whether she followed Paris by free will; and when Priam heard that it was so, he agreed with his sons to defend her against all the power of Greece. His people feared the trials of the war that now threatened; and as Paris strode through the streets of Troy, many a stifled curse followed him, who cared not that he brought such woe upon the city; yet even the grey-beards who frowned on Helen could not but turn their heads to look after so lovely a stranger. But the princes were deaf to the ominous warnings of their sister Cassandra. Among them Hector stood out as chief leader, now that his father was too old for war; and of the allies Troy called to its aid, the most illustrious was Priam's son-in-law, Aeneas, prince of the neighbouring Dardanians, who had no less a mother than Aphrodite.

Meanwhile, the Greek ambassadors had returned to Aulis, a harbour on the Euripus, where more than a thousand ships were gathered to carry a hundred thousand warriors across the sea. Years had passed before this mighty host could be brought together. All being at length ready, and the Trojans having shown no submission, the chiefs were for setting sail. But Agamemnon, their leader, going on shore to hunt, had hurt the pride of the goddess Artemis, by killing a hind sacred to her. The offended goddess brought about a dead calm, so that for weeks not a ship could stir from the strait, on whose shore so many warriors chafed in idle impatience. Then Calchas the diviner, in virtue of his art, gave out that Artemis would not be appeased without the sacrifice of Agamemnon's eldest daughter, Iphigenia: only at the price of her blood could they buy a fair wind.

The horrified father at first would have chosen rather to lay down the command than devote his daughter to such a doom. But Menelaüs, eager for revenge on Paris, hotly upbraided his brother's soft-heartedness, till Agamemnon was won to concede the cruel sacrifice.

He sent for his wife Clytemnestra, bidding her bring Iphigenia to Aulis, on pretence that she should be married to Achilles. Then, relenting in his purpose, he sent another message bidding her pay no heed to the first. But that second message was intercepted by watchful Menelaüs, who again heaped reproaches on the wavering Agamemnon as untrue to the common cause. As they stood quarrelling, it was announced that Iphigenia and her mother were at hand. So moving was the father's distress, that now Menelaüs himself pressed him to forego that sacrifice; but when the brothers had been reconciled with tears, the elder declared his heart steeled to let the maiden die.

Soon arrived Clytemnestra and Iphigenia with her infant brother Orestes; and again the king's heart was wrung by the joyful embraces of his daughter, who could not understand why they called forth no answering smiles. Clytemnestra better knew her husband; and his gloomy looks filled her with suspicion, the more so when, seeking out Achilles, she heard from him that he knew nothing of the feigned betrothal to Iphigenia. Next she fell in with the slave prevented by Menelaüs from carrying her husband's second message, and he told how Iphigenia was doomed for sacrifice.

When the queen had wrung all the truth from Agamemnon, loud was she in wrath and woe. The daughter clung about her father's knees, praying for mercy. Achilles burst into the tent, offering to shield her against the whole host already clamouring for her blood. But Agamemnon now stood like a rock against threats and entreaties: he remembered that he was a king as well as a father, nor yet a despot, but one who must consult with those who followed him in war. And Iphigenia rose to stand upright before him, saying with firm voice—

"Since so it must be, I am willing to die; then shall I be called the honour of Greek maidenhood, who have given my life for the motherland. Let the fall of Troy be my marriage feast and my monument!"

She turned away, her young brother Orestes clasped in her arms, leaving their mother prostrate on the ground in helpless despair. Iphigenia's last words were a promise to stand still as a lamb when brought to the altar; while Achilles, who had come verily to love this patient victim, spoke hotly of rescuing her by force under the knife of the priest, yet must fear that even his fierce Myrmidons would shrink from violating a sacred rite.

> "I was cut off from hope in that sad place,
> Which yet to name, my spirit loathes and fears;
> My father held his hand upon his face;
> I, blinded with my tears,
>
> "Still strove to speak: my voice was thick with sighs,
> As in a dream. Dimly I could descry
> The stern black-bearded kings, with wolfish eyes,
> Waiting to see me die.
>
> "The high masts flickered as they lay afloat;
> The crowds, the temples wavered, and the shore;
> The bright death quivered at the victim's throat;
> Touched; and I knew no more."
>
> —Alfred, Lord Tennyson

The Grecian host had been drawn up on a plain beside Aulis, where stood the altar of Artemis decked for ceremony. Iphigenia was led forth. Calchas unsheathed his sacrificial knife. The anguished father hid his face. A herald had proclaimed reverent silence, but not a man could speak or move as the noble maid stretched forth her neck to the blade that already glittered above her like the hard eyes of the slaughterer. However, Artemis took pity on this innocent victim. Iphigenia vanished, borne off by Artemis in a cloud to serve in perpetual maidenhood as priestess of her temple at Tauris. In the maiden's place, a fawn lay writhing before the altar, sprinkled with its blood. Calchas, with glad astonishment, proclaimed Artemis to be appeased. The victim she had sent was burned with fire upon her altar; then, as the last spark died out, a breath from heaven moved the air, and the ships could be seen tossing on the water where they had so long lain becalmed. A wind was springing up that at once set the camp astir.

Clytemnestra heard how her daughter had been carried away, never to see her more. Without waiting to take leave of her husband, she set out for his city of Mycenae; ill blood rankling in her heart that in later years was to work long woe for the house of Agamemnon. But he and his warriors, delivered from the spell cast on them, joyfully embarked, to sail with a fair wind for the coast of Troy.

There another victim was called for. The Greek who first set foot on Trojan soil, so an oracle had declared, was doomed to die. Even the bravest might well fear to defy fate, till dauntless Protesilaüs first leaped on shore, to fall forthwith by a spear flung by Hector. Long his faithful wife Laodamia mourned that he sent no word home; and many a hero who now hailed the bristling walls of Troy, would never again see wife or child. They had vowed not to cut their hair till these walls fell before them; but little thought the 'long-haired Achaeans' that the siege of this strong city would take them ten toilsome years.

⚜

3 The Wrath of Achilles

On the Trojan shore, at the confluent mouth of the rivers Simöeis and Scamander, the Greeks hauled up their ships, placing them orderly in rows, propped on beams and stones, with lanes between the squadron from each city; and each leader lived among his own followers, in tents or in huts of wood and earth, thatched with reeds, so that the camp was like a town, built over against the high-set battlements of Troy. In the midst was left an open space for public gatherings and for the altars of the gods. At either end it was guarded by Achilles

168

The Sacrifice of Iphigenia
From the painting by Reginald Arthur

and by the huge Ajax, as trustiest champions of the besiegers. Agamemnon, that 'king of men', had his quarter in the centre, among the tents of Odysseus, Menelaüs, Diomede, Nestor, and other warriors from all parts of Greece.

> Oh! say what heroes, fired by thirst of fame,
> Or urged by wrongs, to Troy's destruction came.
> To count them all demands I thousand tongues,
> A throat of brass and adamantine lungs."

Between the city and the camp, the two rivers enclosed an open plain that made arena for many a fray. Again and again the Trojans sallied forth to hot battle beneath their walls. Each army was led on by its champions whirling up the dust in their war-chariots, from which often they would spring down to meet one another hand to hand in single combat, while all the rest stood still to look on, mingling their shouts with the clang of arms. Now one, now the other party got the better, and drove its enemy out of the field. But when years had passed, and many souls of heroes had gone down to Hades before their time, not yet were the Greeks able to break through the walls of Troy.

Besides battles before the city, the invaders plundered far and wide in the countries around. In one such foray was captured Chryseïs, daughter of Chryses, a priest of Apollo, and she fell to Agamemnon's share of the booty. Her old father came to the camp seeking to ransom her; but the haughty king refused to yield up his captive, and harshly bade the sacred elder begone. Then as Chryses turned away sorrowful along the moaning shore, he prayed the god whom he served to reward his devotion by avenging him upon those arrogant strangers.

> "Such prayer he made, and it was heard. The god
> Down from Olympus, with his radiant bow,
> And his full quiver o'er his shoulders slung,
> Marched in his anger; shaken as he moved,
> His rattling arrows told of his approach.
> Like night he came, and seated with the ships
> In view, despatched an arrow. Clanged the cord,
> Dread sounding, bounding on the silver bow.
> Mules first, and dogs, he struck, but aiming soon
> Against the Greeks themselves, his bitter shafts
> Smote them. The frequent piles blazed night and day."
>
> —Cowper[1]

When the pestilence had raged for nine days, the Greeks met in council, and Calchas was called on to reveal the cause of the god's anger against them. The seer knew, but was loath to tell what might offend one he feared. Only when Achilles bid him speak out, promising to be his shield against any man in the host, were it Agamemnon himself, did Calchas declare how Apollo's wrath was on account of Chryseïs and the wrong done to her suppliant sire; nor would the plague be stayed till she had been freely restored with sacrifices and prayers to appease the god, injured in the person of his priest.

On this, Agamemnon flared into wrath, for he had come to love his fair captive well. Not less hotly did Achilles demand that the maid should be given back; and thus broke out a quarrel between those heroes, long jealous of each other. Since the general voice was against him, the king sullenly agreed to resign his prize; but in return he masterfully claimed Briseïs, another captive damsel who had been given to Achilles as his share of the spoil.

Such a demand stirred Achilles to quick anger; and before all the chiefs, he denounced the selfishness of their leader.

> "O, impudent, regardful of thy own,
> Whose thoughts are centred on thyself alone,
> Advanced to sovereign sway for better ends
> Than thus like abject slaves to treat thy friends.
> What Greek is he, that, urg'd by thy command,
> Against the Trojan troops will lift his hand?
> Not I: nor such inforc'd respect I owe;
> Nor Pergamus I hate, nor Priam is my foe.
> What wrong from Troy remote, could I sustain,
> To leave my fruitful soil and happy reign
> And plough the surges of the stormy main?
> Thee, frontless man, we follow'd from afar
> Thy instruments of death, and tools of war.
> Thine is the triumph; ours the toil alone:
> We bear thee on our backs, and mount thee on the throne.
> For thee we fall in fight; for thee redress
> Thy baffled brother, not the wrongs of Greece.
> And now thou threaten'st with unjust decree,
> To punish thy affronting heaven on me.
> To seize the prize which I so dearly bought;
> By common suffrage given, confirm'd by lot,
> Mean match to thine: for still above the rest,
> Thy hook'd rapacious hands usurp the best,
> Though mine are first in fight, to force the prey;
> And last sustain the labours of the day.
> Nor grudge I thee the much the Grecians give;
> Nor murmuring take the little I receive.
> Yet even this little, thou, who wouldst ingross
> The whole insatiate, envy'st as thy loss.
> Know then, for Phthia fix'd is my return:

Better at home my ill-paid pains to mourn,
Than from an equal here sustain the public scorn."

—John Dryden

"Let him go," haughtily retorted Agamemnon; "the host would be well rid of such a quarrelsome and wilful comrade."

"We need not such a friend, nor fear not such a foe."

But in any case he must give up his Briseïs, if the king had to tear her away with his own hands. At this threat the wrath of Achilles could not readily find words. He leaped to his feet, he laid hand upon his sword, and he stood torn between rage and loyalty, half in a mind to unsheathe against the leader of the host, when Athena swiftly descended to his side, visible to him alone, as she held him back by his yellow hair, bidding him restrain his hasty rage, and promising that prudence should not go without reward. Thus secretly counselled, the son of Peleus put up his sword, yet in bitter words he vented the swelling of his heart against that insolent king.

"Swoln drunkard! dog in eye but hind in heart,
Who ne'er in war sustain'st a warrior's part,
Nor join'st our ambush; for alike thy fear
In war and ambush views destruction near,
More safe, 'mid Graecia's ranks th' inglorious toil,
To grasp some murmurer's unprotected spoil.
Plunderer of slaves – slaves void of soul as sense—
Or Greece had witness'd now thy last offence.
Yet – by this sceptre, which, untimely reft
From its bare trunk upon the mountain left,
Bark'd by the steel, and of its foliage shorn,
Nor bark nor foliage shall again adorn,
But borne by powerful chiefs of high command,
Guardians of law, and judges of the land:
Be witness thou, by this tremendous test
I ratify my word, and steel my breast—
The day shall come, when Greece, in dread alarm,
Shall lean for succour on Pelides' arm:
Then, while beneath fierce Hector's murderous blade
Thy warriors bleed, and claim in vain thy aid,
Rage shall consume thy heart, that madd'ning pride,
Dishonouring me thy bravest chief defied."

—Sotheby

In vain Nestor, oldest and wisest of the Greeks, grey with experience of three generations of men, and reverenced as the familiar friend of bygone heroes – in vain with weighty words he strove to reconcile the threatening leaders. Vowing to fight no more for any woman's sake, Achilles, with his bosom friend Patroclus, withdrew to his tent, where presently he had the pain of seeing Briseïs fetched away by the messengers of Agamemnon. The other chiefs consented to let it be so, since now Chryseïs was given back to her father, and the god being duly propitiated, his fiery arrows ceased to fall upon the camp.

Such open indignity had driven Achilles beside himself. Going far apart along the shore of the sounding ocean, with tears of spite and sullen groans he called up his goddess mother from its depths. She rose like a mist to hear his tale of hurt honour and rankling pride. Thetis wept in sympathy with her injured son, whose cause she willingly agreed to further in the court of Olympus. He asked her nothing less than this, to make interest with Zeus that the Greeks should now suffer such loss as might teach them what it was to serve so hateful a king, and to want the help of their bravest champion.

Thetis promised to fulfil his mission as soon as Zeus should have returned from a feast he was holding among the blameless Ethiopians. After twelve days, then, she soared to Olympus, clasped its king by the knees, and begged of him to avenge her son's disgrace. Zeus, at first unwilling, gave way to her entreaties, consenting it should be as she desired, yea, confirming his decree with a nod that shook the skies. But he bid her go in haste, not to be spied by his jealous queen, who, not forgetting the slight put on her by Paris, was eager for the fall of Troy.

Hera indeed had marked the coming of the silver-footed Thetis, and she distrusted that resounding nod; but when she would have questioned her spouse what favour he had thus granted, Zeus sternly silenced her curiosity. There had nigh been a quarrel in heaven, but for Vulcan's handing round a bowl of nectar with such awkward goodwill, that his hobbling gait sent all the gods off in peals of laughter; and the rest of the Olympian day went merrily by in feast and song.

Soon would it be known on earth what Zeus planned against the Greeks. When all the other gods slept he lay awake, turning over in his mind how to carry out that promise wrung from him by the fond mother of Achilles; and it seemed best to send a false dream to Agamemnon, by which he was bidden lead out the host for a battle that should humble the walls of Troy.

> "For now no more the gods with fate contend;
> At Juno's suit the heavenly factions end.
> Destruction hangs o'er yon devoted wall,
> And nodding Ilion waits the impending fall.
> Awake; but waking this advice approve,
> And trust the vision that descends from Jove!"

Roused by such a lying phantom, the exultant king called all the chiefs to council. Then, to try the men's temper, he first spoke of their toils, their losses through nine fruitless years: he asked if it were not well to give up this weary siege and hasten back to the wives and children who pined for them in their homes over the sea. To his dismay, the Greeks heard him but too gladly. With loud applause they hailed his feigned retreat; and the whole army moved towards the shore in rushing waves, eager to embark. Already they had begun to launch their rotting ships, when Athena, sent by Hera, swooped down to hold them back. Odysseus she found still steadfast, and him she stirred to check the shameful flight. Into his hands Agamemnon gave the sceptre of authority, with which the hero flew among the broken ranks, reproaching, commanding, or beating back the dastards and laggards, crying on them to obey their leader's voice alone, and not

"That worst of tyrants a usurping crowd".

One man only ventured to speak out against him. The squint-eyed Thersites, that hobbling hunchback, was ever a mocker and reviler of his betters. He now spitefully raised his voice to ask why men like him should fight for a rich king, who grasped the rewards of war, but left its toils to harder hands. With a threat to have him stripped and scourged to the fleet, Odysseus laid the heavy sceptre on his crooked back so sturdily that Thersites shrank into tearful silence; and that example cowed all discontent.

The rout thus stayed, Odysseus eloquently called to his comrades' minds their vows, their hopes, the favourable omens that promised the fall of Troy. Old Nestor also addressed the warriors, bidding them forbear all strife but against the foe. Agamemnon no longer wasted his breath on crafty speech, but plainly ordered battle array. After offering sacrifice to the gods, and taking a meal that for many a man might be his last, the Greek host, as was their wont, advanced silently and sternly in close ranks, wrapped in a cloud of dust, while the Trojans came out to meet them like a noisy flock of cranes, with boastful cries and idle clash of arms. But he who should have led the Achaeans on to victory, now sat sullenly in his tent.

4 The Battles of Gods and Heroes

The armies being drawn up face to face, ready to set on, Paris, wearing a panther's skin over his bright armour, stepped gracefully forth from the Trojan ranks to challenge the bravest of the Greeks. At the word, Menelaüs sprang from his chariot and bounded forward like a lion upon the spoiler of his home. But when Paris, once as brave as he was beautiful, saw the hero in all the fierceness of his wrong, conscience turned him coward; he flinched from the encounter, and would have shrunk back among the thick of his own people, had not Hector sharply upbraided him for shirking the foe he had brought on their native city by his womanly tricks and graces.

> "Thou wretched Paris though in form so fair
> Thou slave of woman, manhood's counterfeit!
> Would thou had'st ne'er been born, or died at least
> Unwedded; so 'twere better far for all,
> Than thus to live a scandal and reproach.
> Well may the long-haired Greeks derisive laugh,
> Who think thee, from thy outward show a chief
> Among our warriors; but thou hast in truth
> Nor strength of mind, nor courage in the fight.
> How was't that such as thou could e'er induce
> A noble band in ocean-going ships
> To cross the main with men of other lands
> Mixing in amity and bearing thence
> A woman fair of face, by marriage ties
> Bound to a race of warriors; to thy sire,
> Thy state thy people, cause of endless grief,
> Of triumph to thy foes, contempt to thee!
> Durst thou the warlike Menelaüs meet,
> Thou to thy cost should learn the might of him
> Whose bride thou didst not fear to bear away:
> Then should'st thou find of small avail thy lyre
> Or Venus' gifts of beauty or of grace
> Or, trampled in the dust, thy flowing hair.
> But too forbearing are the men of Troy;
> Else for the ills that thou hast wrought the state
> Ere now thy body had in stone been cased."
>
> —Lord Derby

His brother's scorn goaded Paris back to pride; and he nerved himself to fight out the quarrel in single combat with Menelaüs, its issue to decide the war. A meeting was called, a truce proclaimed, and the two armies ranged themselves about the lists in which that eventful duel should end so much slaughter. From the walls of Troy, old Priam looked anxiously on; and to him came Helen, who, as she sat weaving her story into a web of golden tapestry, had been called to witness the battle between her rival husbands. Sitting by Priam's side, she named to him the chiefs of the Greeks, once her familiar friends, kingly Agamemnon, gigantic Ajax, wise Odysseus; but she looked in vain for her brothers Castor and Pollux, cut off by fate since she left their Spartan home.

175

Helen on the Walls of Troy
From the painting by Lord Leighton P.R.A.

When all was ready, Priam turned away, for he could not bear to behold the peril of his darling son. But Helen kept her place, gazing through tears upon her first husband, who now again seemed dear to her in his manly wrath. Lots being drawn for which of her lovers should cast the first javelin, the chance fell to Paris, and her eyes followed the shining dart as it sped through the air to bound back from the Greek's ringing shield. With a prayer to Zeus to guide his weapon well, Menelaüs next threw with such forceful aim that the point pierced through shield and armour and garment, and but for drawing deftly back, Paris had felt a deadly wound. As he staggered under the shock, the son of Atreus was upon him with drawn sword. The keen blade splintered against the prince's crest, and broke off short in the hand of Menelaüs, who then grasped Paris by the helmet and would have dragged him off among the exulting Greeks.

Already their shouts hailed the downfall of Troy's champion, when Aphrodite came to the aid of her favourite. With an unseen touch she burst the golden strap of the helmet, that came away empty in the grasp of the Greek, who flung it hastily down, again to aim a dart at the Trojan's breast. But as it whizzed to its mark, the goddess had caught up Paris and carried him off hidden in a cloud, to lay him fainting on the bridal bed, where Helen then came to tend him, her heart torn between love of the winsome form, and contempt for the craven spirit.

The Greeks now claimed the victory, as well they might after the flight of Paris; and in Olympus the gods held council about putting an end to the war. Zeus was for having Helen surrendered to the besiegers without more ado; but Hera pressed her ill will against Troy, offering her spouse in return for its destruction to let him ruin her own best-loved cities, Argos, Mycenae, and Sparta; and for the sake of peace in heaven its king gave way. Athena was sent down to rekindle the war, as she did by stirring the archer Pandarus to aim an arrow at Menelaüs, that drew blood from a hurt quickly stanched. That treacherous shot broke the truce; then Agamemnon, filled with grief and rage when at first he took his wounded brother for dead, cried on the Greeks to battle.

Hot was the combat in which gods took part as well as men. The hero of that day was Diomede, whom Athena healed, at a touch, of a mortal wound, so that he had strength to heave a stone, not to be lifted by two men of his degenerate posterity. He hurled it at Aeneas, brought to his knees by its crushing weight, to be saved by his mother Aphrodite, who screened him behind her veil; but he saw his god-given chariot horses carried off as trophies to the Greek camp. Diomede did not fear to assail the goddess herself, and wounded her with a dart, not less keenly with insolent words.

> "The field of combat is no scene for thee.
> Go, let thy own soft sex employ thy care,

> Go, lull the coward or delude the fair.
> Taught by this stroke, renounce the war's alarms,
> And learn to tremble at the name of arms!"

Giving her son to be guarded by Apollo, the queen of love fled horror-struck to Olympus in the chariot of Ares, who, fighting for Troy, got a hurt that made him bellow for pain. Hera herself had come down to join in the fray, taking the form of Stentor, the loudest lunged of the Greeks, and with his voice taunting them for cowardice, while Athena, hidden under her helmet of darkness, served Diomede as his charioteer to charge against Ares. But when the god of war, sorely pierced by his own darts, fled to Olympus with groanings and complaints, the goddesses, too, saw well to leave the field.

The earthly warriors went on fighting till Simöeis and Scamander ran red with blood. It was then that Diomede encountered the Lycian prince Glaucus, grandson of Bellerophon; but on learning of the old guest-fellowship of their sires, they forbore to shed each other's blood, and even exchanged armour, the brazen mail of the Greek for the golden trappings of the other, worth ten times as many oxen, thus plighting faith to be friends, foemen as were their people. But there was no compassion nor kindness in the heart of Ajax, as he raged among the Trojans, smiting down young and old, great and small, so that for a time Achilles went unmissed by friend as by foe.

From the heat and dust of that hurly-burly, Hector hastened back to Troy, where he vainly set Hecuba and her attendants upon a solemn procession to the temple of Athena, that she might be besought to check the doughty Diomede's career. In the palace Hector found Paris idly polishing and playing with his arms at Helen's side; then once more he broke out upon that unworthy brother, for whose sake so many brave men were meeting death, while he carelessly sat apart among the women. Stung by sharp reproaches, Paris promised to follow him to the battle; and his wife herself spurned the laggard forth, with warm words to Hector.

> "Brother of me the abominable, accurst!
> Would that from heaven a sweeping storm had burst,
> And wrapt me away for ever to the hills,
> In that day when my mother bore me first,
> Or, where the wave roars and the hurricane shrills,
> Had in the deep waste drowned me, ere I bred these ills!

> "But since the gods ordained them, why not then
> Give me a husband better and more fit
> That knew shame, and the burning tongues of men?
> This hath not, will have never, a sound wit,
> And he will reap his folly. But now sit

On this chair, O my brother, for our crime
Hath most thy soul to ceaseless sorrow knit;
And now with him I to such misery climb,
Men shall make songs upon us in the after-time."

—Worsley

But Hector would not stay; before all he must seek out his own wife
Andromache for one short greeting that might be the last. He found her not in
their home, but on a tower of the walls, eagerly watching the turns of a battle in
which her husband's life was exposed to the same swords that had already slain
all the men of her father's house. Beside her, borne in the arms of his nurse, was
her young son Astyanax. In vain she pled with her husband to remain within the
walls, as guard for Troy and for his dear ones.

"While Hector still survives I see
My father, mother brethren all in thee!"

It could not be, he told her; his part was to stand foremost in the field; and
much as he loved her, honour was dearer still. So, with heartfelt forebodings of
disaster, he took farewell of wife and child, perhaps doomed to slavery, did his
arm fail to shield them.

"So said the glorious Hector and stretch'd out his arms for the infant—
But back-shrinking, the child on the deep-veil'd breast of the damsel
Cower'd with a cry, and avoided in horror the sight of his father
Scared at the shine of the brass and the terrible plumage of horse hair
Tossing adown, as he stoopt from the crest of the glittering helmet:
Then did the father laugh right forth – and Andromache also;
But soon glorious Hector had lifted the casque from his temples,
And on the ground at their feet it was laid, the magnificent head-piece;
Then in his hands he receiv'd him and kist him and tenderly dandled;
Which done, this was his prayer unto Zeus and the rest of the godheads:—

"'Zeus! and ye deities all! may your blessing descend on mine offspring!
Grant estimation to him, as to me, in the land of the Trojan!
Gallant in arms may he be and his reign over Ilion mighty.
Let it be spoken of him when they see him returning from battle,
Bearing the blood-stain'd spoils, having slaughter'd his enemy fairly;—
This is the first of his lineage more excellent far than his father.
Such be the cry – and in him let the heart of his mother gladden'd!'
"Thus pray'd he, and surrender'd the child to the hands of the mother
And she receiv'd him and prest to the fragrant repose of her bosom,
Smiling with tears in her eyes; and the husband beheld her with pity,
Gently caressed with his hand, and bespake her again at departing:—
'Dearest and best! let not trouble for me overmaster thy spirit.

179

Captive Andromache
From the painting by Lord Leighton P.R.A.

None contravening the doom prematurely to Hades shall send me
Nor full sure can the sentence of Fate be avoided by mortals,
Whether for good or for ill firm fixt from the hour of our birthtime.'"

—J. G. Lockhart

With this, bidding her return to her household tasks, he laced on his helm and strode away, while Andromache went home to weep with her maids for the well-loved lord she had seen for the last time alive.

Hector and Paris having come back to the fray, it soon blazed up afresh, and for a time victory was bandied about by stirring feats of arms on either side. It was Hector that now defied the bravest of the Greeks to single combat; and Menelaüs would have taken up the challenge, had not his heedful brother Agamemnon held him back- from encountering such a peerless champion. But when old Nestor called shame on the warriors for faint hearts, minding them of the dead heroes of his own time, they were spurred on to agree that their nine mightiest should draw lots which must face the Trojan leader. The lot fell on huge Ajax, the very man who would have been chosen by every voice; and he with joy and pride armed himself for the trial.

More fiercely than when Paris was the skulking foe, these two met before the gazing armies. Long and mightily they fought with spears and darts and flaming swords, and when these were broken or blunted, with big stones caught up to crush the other beneath their shattered shields; but before either had got the bet-ter, darkness fell upon them, and they drew apart with courteous salutations and exchange of gifts, promising to fight out their duel some other day, now broken off at the bidding of sage elders on either side.

"Forbear, my sons, your further force to prove,
Both dear to men, and both beloved of Jove!
To either host your matchless worth is known,
Each sounds your praise, and war is all your own;
But now the Night extends her awful shade;
The goddess parts you: be the Night obeyed."

There was little rest that night for either army. A truce had been agreed upon that each should gather its dead for burning and burial in honoured mounds. The Greeks, warned by their losses, had made haste to throw up a wall and trench round their camp, where before long they might find themselves besieged in-stead of besiegers. The Trojans held confused council, in which it was proposed that Helen should now be given back, that with her their land might be freed from the plague of war. Paris could by no means consent to part with his bride, but he was willing to yield up the treasures of Sparta, if so much would content the enemy; and the doting Priam sent a herald to offer this wealth, and more, as

181

the price of peace. But the Greeks were not to be bribed by gold; and now fortune brought them a fleet of ships freighted with generous wine to warm their hearts into forgetfulness of pains suffered and to come.

Meanwhile, Zeus called a council of the gods, whom with threats he forbade to take further part on either hand. Yet, when daylight again awoke the war, moved by his promise to Thetis, he himself interfered with thunders that dismayed the Greeks. The battle raged all day and after fresh slaughter and countless heroic deeds, at nightfall the once exulting invaders were driven back behind their new-made defences, and the Trojans lay on the field they held as victors.

"Many a fire before them blazed:
As when in heaven the stars about the moon
Look beautiful, when all the winds are laid
And every height come out, and jutting peak
And valley, and the immeasurable heavens
Break open to their highest, and all the stars
Shine, and the Shepherd gladdens in his heart:
So many a fire between the ships and stream
Of Xanthus blazed before the towers of Troy,
A thousand on the plain; and close by each
Sat fifty in the blaze of burning fire;
And champing golden grain the horses stood
Hard by their chariots waiting for the dawn."

—Alfred, Lord Tennyson

While the Trojans already looked forward to spoiling the Grecian camp, those within it were beset with dismay. Agamemnon sent out whispering messengers to summon the chiefs, who found him tearfully downcast; and in words broken by sighs he put to them, now in good earnest, that there was nothing for it but to embark and fly, since the very gods fought for their foe.

He was heard in silence; but then up started Diomede, keenly reproaching the king with cowardice. Let him to whom the gods had given power and wealth but not a steadfast soul, let him and those like-minded take to craven flight! He himself would stay and fight out the fate of Troy, and one friend he had, Sthenelus, who would not let him fight alone. His bold words stirred outspoken assent, amid which rose Nestor to take the right of age in declaring to Agamemnon's face that all their misfortunes were owing to him, in that he had wronged Achilles and estranged their bravest warrior.

The contrite king listened meekly, and answered by confessing his fault, for which he was now willing to make amends. To the hero who held sullenly aloof in his secluded tent, he proposed to send an embassy of reconciliation, with gifts worthy of his fame, ten talents of gold, twenty golden vases, seven sacrificial tripods and twelve matchless steeds. Moreover, Agamemnon would allow him to have back his Briseïs along with seven more fair captives, and twenty others he might choose from the captives of Troy; then, when they had returned home in triumph, Achilles should marry any one of the king's very own daughters, with seven cities for her dowry; only now let him come to help against the terrible Hector.

Nestor spoke the general approval, naming three chiefs to carry such princely offers, the wise Odysseus, the bold Ajax, and Phoenix, who had been tutor of Achilles in youth. Attended by two heralds, those ambassadors took their way along the wave-beaten shore to that silent end of the camp, where the Myrmidons had lain in idleness while the tide of war rose and fell close at hand. They found Achilles in his tent playing the lyre as if all were peace, and singing to Patroclus, the friend of his heart, who alone kept him company. At the sight of the messengers he laid aside his lyre, rose to give them courteous greeting, made them sit down on richly spread couches, and bid Patroclus fill out wine for his guests. Nor would he listen to their errand till they had eaten as well as drunk the best he had to set before them.

> "Princes, all hail! whatever brought ye here,
> Or strong necessity or urgent fear.
> Welcome, though Greeks! for not as foes ye came,
> To me more dear than all that bear the name."

Supper over, Odysseus rose to drink the health of their noble host, and went on to lay before him those royal offers as proof of Agamemnon's repentance. If the hero despised such gifts, let him remember that on him lay the weal or woe of his people; and if that did not move him, could he bear to hear proud Hectors boasts that no Greek was his peer.

Achilles listened regardfully, but answered with unrelenting pride. He rehearsed his wrongs: the Greeks had chosen to affront him, and must do without the aid of his arm; for shield against Hector let them trust to the wall they had been fain to build, now their best champion had left the open field; for leader let them look to the insolent king, whose hateful gifts he spurned; had he come to Troy to seek wife or wealth, he could win them for himself. In vain old Phoenix tried to move him by memories of his docile youth. In vain blunt Ajax reproached his sullen obstinacy. Courteously, but firmly, Achilles dismissed them with a parting cup; and they went back to tell Agamemnon that the hero's heart was still hardened against him.

Diomede alone was undismayed by the news, for he felt in himself a champion to match Hector. While the common men slept, Agamemnon went restless from tent to tent, taking counsel with the leaders; and Odysseus and Diomede stole among the drowsy foe to spy out their strength and to bring back a trophy of snow-white horses, after slaying Dolon, an adventurous young Trojan whom they encountered bent on a like errand of darkness, and forced him to disclose, in vain hope of mercy, the position of the hostile army.

The next morning Agamemnon, donning his richest armour, with the courage of desperation, led forth the Greeks to battle that at first went in their favour. But the king, wounded by a spear, had to withdraw from the field; stout Diomede too was injured; and Hector in turn charged so hotly that he swept all before him. Paris this day shook off his softer mood to play the warrior.

The Greeks were driven back behind their wall, which already the storming enemy had almost broken through, when Poseidon came to its defence, passing sea and land in just a few bounds of his chariot. Never had the god of ocean forgotten his old grudge against Troy; and now, taking the form of Calchas, their reverent soothsayer, he heartened the Greeks to rally about Ajax the Great, and his namesake, Ajax the Great, who for a time kept off the assailants with showers of arrows.

Nor was Poseidon the only god that strove against Troy. Fearing lest Zeus should after all grant victory to the city of hated Paris, Hera beguiled her spouse by borrowing the girdle of Aphrodite to throw round her such a spell of enchanting smiles that the Thunderer sank to sleep in her arms. When he awoke he found the Greeks once more led on by Poseidon to victory, the Trojans flying, Hector lying senseless, stunned under a stone hurled at him by Ajax. But again Zeus made haste to turn the scale. Angrily reproaching his wife for her deceit, he sent Iris to bid Poseidon back to his own watery domain, and Apollo to revive Hector and cheer on the Trojans. With the sun-god for their leader, they again pressed the Greeks to their entrenchments, through which they burst in pursuit, so that soon a hot fight raged about the ships, last hope of Greece, and the prowess of Ajax and his brother Teucer was hard put to it to keep their fleet from being set on fire.

From the prow of his own ship, Achilles had watched the battle, unmoved to take part other than sending Patroclus to seek news. But Patroclus could not bear to stand idly by, and watch the ruin of Greece. With tears of rage he beseeched his friend at least to let him lead forth the Myrmidons, who even yet might turn the day, now that Ajax's galley could be seen flaming at the farther end of the camp.

Still feigning indifference, Achilles gave him leave, even equipped him in his own armour and mounted him on his chariot, driven by the famed charioteer Automedon. He charged him, indeed, to do no more than beat back the Trojans from the ships, the burning of which would cut off the Greeks' return; but when he saw the fierce Myrmidons as eager to be let loose as a pack of famished wolves, the hero's stubborn heart began to warm within him, and he sent his friend forth with a prayer for victory and safe return, a prayer that was to be half granted and half denied. Another heartfelt prayer he had made in the martial passion he strove to conceal; and his charge to Patroclus was to forbear facing Hector, worthy to die by no sword but his own.

> "Oh! would to all the immortal powers above,
> Apollo, Pallas and almighty Jove,
> That not one Trojan might be left alive,
> And not a Greek of all the race survive;
> Might only we the vast destruction shun,
> And only we destoy the accursed town!"

At the head of the Myrmidons, Patroclus rushed forth; then the very sight of him, mistaken for the champion whose armour he wore, was enough to strike panic among the Trojans. Driven from the ships, they fled before his onset, streaming back over the wall and the ditch choked with broken chariots and wounded horses.

Once more the tide of battle had been turned. With red slaughter, Patroclus chased off the enemy to Troy, indeed, he even strove to break through its walls, but drew back in wonderment when here he was confronted by the blazing aegis of Apollo, proclaiming that neither by him nor by Achilles was the city fated to be overthrown. He drew back, yet only to rage afresh against mortal enemies, and forgetful of Achilles' charge, he met Hector face to face. It was the god himself that, hidden in a cloud, stunned the Greek hero by a crushing blow, and laid the borrowed plume of Achilles in the dust. Before he could save himself, Hector was upon him, whose lance made an end; and with his last breath Patroclus gasped out a warning to the exultant foe, that ere long his soul would follow to the shades.

> "I see thee fall, and by Achilles' hand."

A crowd of champions closed over the body of Patroclus, for which strove the Trojans led on by Hector, now proudly clad in the stripped armour; and the Greeks, rallied round mighty Ajax, would have borne it off under cover of their shields locked together. So fierce was this tug-of-war that Zeus hooded it beneath thundering darkness, in which the slaughterers groped blindly, and Ajax cried with suppliant tears—

> "If Greece must perish, we thy will obey,
> But let us perish in the face of day!"

At his prayer, the god let daylight return; then at last the Greeks were able to drag away their hero's corpse out of reach of insulting hands. And when on the walls of the camp the Trojans saw arise the dread form of Achilles, and heard his voice uplifted thrice like a trumpet, they fled in such confused rout as to crush one another to death under the press of chariots and armour.

Soon they would have the whole Greek host sweeping forth upon them in waves of steel—

> "As from air the frosty north wind blows a cold thick sleet
> That dazzles eyes, flakes after flakes incessantly descending;
> So thick helms, curets,[2] ashen darts and round shields never ending,
> Flowed from the navy's hollow womb; their splendours gave Heaven's eye
> His beams again; Earth laughed to see her face so like the sky;
> Arms shined so hot, and she such clouds made with the dust she cast,
> She thundered – feet of men and horse importuned her so fast."

—Chapman

The prince of heroes was arming himself for battle.

5 Hector and Achilles

In his lonely tent, which was rather a spacious hall built by the Myrmidons of pines and reeds, its entrance barred by a huge trunk that only he could lift aside, Achilles had sat awaiting the triumphant return of Patroclus. But when instead of him came Antilochus, son of Nestor, an unwilling messenger for heavy news, who shall tell how the hero heard of his friend slain and his own armour gone to deck the proud Hector!

> "He grasp'd the ashes scatter'd on the strand,
> And on his forehead shower'd with either hand,
> Grimed his fair face, and o'er his raiment flung
> The soil that on its splendour darkly hung,
> His large limbs prone in dust at large outspread,
> And pluck'd the hair from his dishonour'd head;
> While all the maidens whom his arm had won,
> Or gain'd in battle with Menetius' son,
> Left the still shelter of their peaceful tent,
> And round Pelides mingled their lament,
> Raised their clasped hands, and beat their breasts of snow,
> And, swooning sunk on earth, o'ercome with woe;
> While o'er him Nestor's son in horror stood,
> And grasp'd his arm, half-raised to shed his blood.
> Deep groan'd the desperate man, 'twas death to hear

> Groans that in ocean pierced the sea-nymph's ear,
> His mother's ear, where deep beneath the tide,
> Dwelt the sea-goddess by her father's side.
> She heard, she shriek'd while, gathering swift around,
> Game every Nereid from her cave profound."

Thetis had hurried to comfort her son, promising to bring him new celestial armour, in which he might take vengeance on Hector; and Iris, sent by Hera, stirred him from his abject misery to make that appearance on the walls that had scared the Trojans like the aegis of some god. But again the hero seemed beside himself when they brought in the body of his friend. All night he lamented over it like a lioness robbed of her young, washing with his tears the cold limbs, begrimed and gory, which now could be laid out for a funeral to be bathed in Trojan blood.

> "One fate the warrior and his friend shall strike,
> And Troy's black sands must drink our blood alike.
> Me too, a wretched mother shall deplore,
> An aged father never see me more!
> Yet my Patroclus yet a space I stay,
> Then swift pursue thee on the darksome way.
> Ere thy dear relics in the grave are laid,
> Shall Hector's head be offered to thy shade!"

Meanwhile Thetis had hied her to Vulcan's smithy, where, at her entreaty, in one night the god of fire forged for her son matchless armour of mingled metals, and a wondrous shield on which were wrought pictured labours of peace as well as war. Such a godlike gift she brought to Achilles at dawn, and the very sight brightened his eyes like the shining mail, while the clanging touch thrilled his heart as a trumpet.

Without delay he sped to Agamemnon, calling chiefs to arms as he went. Face to face with king, Achilles briefly spoke out how his heart was unburdened from a wrath that had cost so dear to the Greeks. Agamemnon, too, owned his fault, laying it on a mind blinded by fate. Amid general acclaim, the heroes made friends. The king again offered atoning gifts; but all Achilles asked was instant battle, that might wipe out in blood the woe of their quarrel Prudent Odysseus proposed delay, ceremonies of reconciliation, and a hearty meal to strengthen the warriors for fight. Let who would feast, vowed Achilles, he himself would neither eat nor drink till he had avenged his dead friend.

Now hungering for slaughter, he hurried back to his tent, dressed in the flashing armour of Vulcan, and snatched up his mighty spear, which Patroclus had left untouched, not to be wielded but by the hero's own hand. Much roused to fresh fury by the sight of restored Briseïs weeping over that lifeless friend, he mounted his chariot, with a sharp word to those noble steeds, demanding of them not to leave him on the field as they had left Patroclus. For a moment the mettled coursers stood still, then lo! a marvel, when one of them was inspired to answer its master back in human speech with a warning that, if they bore him safe that day, his doom was yet not far off. The horse spoke, but the dauntless hero cried—

> "So let it be!
> Portents and prodigies are lost on me:
> I know my fates: to die, to see no more
> My much loved parents and my native shore—
> Enough – when heaven ordains, I sink in night.
> Now perish Troy!"

When like a storm the Grecian host poured out on the plain, Achilles flashing at their head in a golden halo shed upon him by Athena, on Olympus was held high council, at which Zeus, unable to control Fate, gave leave for the gods to range themselves openly on either side in this greatest of battles about Troy, else, the Thunderer saw, it must fall forthwith before that hero's rage of grief. Hera, Athena, Poseidon, Hermes, and Hephaestus fought now for the Greeks, while Ares, Aphrodite, Apollo, and Artemis shone in the Trojan ranks. And men strove like gods, high above all Achilles, from whose sword Aeneas was saved only in a mist thrown over him by Poseidon, in pity for this Dardanian prince that shared not the offence of Troy. So, too, Apollo for a time hid Hector in clouds from his fiercest enemy. Raging like a conflagration, and with his chariot wheels smoking in blood, Achilles charged through the routed Trojans, and he spared neither sup-plicant nor fugitives, neither old nor young, other than twelve chosen captives set aside, bound with their own belts, for sacrifice at the tomb of the slain Patroclus.

So great was the carnage he made, that the river-god Scamander, his stream choked with corpses, rose against him in gory flood, before which the hero was fain to turn and fly, and had been swept away but for catching at an elm to swing himself on to the bank. Even then, the offended river pursued him over the plain, calling his comrade Simöeis to aid, till Hephaestus helped Achilles by sending fire to scorch up the wooded banks; and the hissing waters fainted before the breath of flame. What wonder this, when Athena herself, heaving a huge bound-ary stone, threw down with it Ares, his mighty limbs sprawling over acres of ground; and Aphrodite coming to help him up, was laid low by a touch from the same doughty goddess; and scornful Hera buffeted and scolded Artemis to fly in tears to the throne of Zeus, who meanwhile looked down careless on the dreadful arena that was sport for him. But Apollo could disdain the ire of his fellow dei-ties, for to a challenge from Poseidon he replied—

> "To combat for mankind
> Ill suits the wisdom of celestial mind;
> For what is man? Calamitous by birth,
> They owe their life and nourishment to earth;
> Like yearly leaves that now, with beauty crowned,
> Smile on the sun, now wither on the ground.
> To their own hands commit the frantic scene,
> Nor mix immortals in cause so mean!"

Yet Apollo stood to guard the gate of Troy, when the beaten Trojans poured through it, flying wildly before the terrible Achilles. Hector alone stayed at bay without, though from the walls his father and mother stretched their hands, imploring him to seek shelter. The hero himself, rearing his head, like a trodden snake's, felt his heart quail as that mightiest of foes came on: prudence and policy bid him draw back, while shame and despair held him fast. But when he stood face to face with the irresistible Achilles, suddenly panic-stricken, Troy's champion turned and fled, as he had never thought to fly before mortal man.

Like a panting dove before a falcon he fled. Through their tears his parents and comrades saw him run thrice round the walls of Troy, pressed hard by Achilles, who bid the Greeks stand aside, since this prey was for no meaner hand. Apollo nerved Hector's limbs for that desperate race; and the gods, watching from Olympus, hesitated whether or no to snatch him from death, till Zeus weighed his fate in golden scales that sank the hero's soul to Hades. Then Hector, with one vain look at the gate from which Achilles always cut him off, turned for his last fight, Athena, indeed, deceiving him to his doom, for she stood beside him in the false form of his brother, Deïphobus, on whose help he vainly relied. As he confronted Achilles, he sought a moment of parley: now that one or other of them was to die, let the victor swear not to dishonour the corpse of the vanquished. To this his furious foe:

> "Accursed, speak not thou to me of compact, or of troth!
> No faith 'twixt men and lions, 'twixt wolves and lambs is none;
> But ever these the other hate to harry or to shun:
> So love and peace shall never 'twixt me and thee be blent,
> Till thou or I on earth be strew'd,
> And we the War-god rough and rude with the rud-red blood content."
>
> —Dean Merivale

Without more ado they hurled darts that went amiss, then closed upon each other. Achilles, all aflame, burned more fiercely to see that adversary wearing his own armour torn from Patroclus. Ere long his blade found a joint to pierce between neck and throat. Hector fell, gasping out his life with a bootless prayer for pious burial. The last words he heard were Achilles' bitter threat that his body should feast the dogs and vultures; and his own last murmur warned the Grecian hero that he too was doomed to die before Troy.

All who saw held Troy already fallen, from whose towers rose a din of lament, drowned in the exultation of the Greeks, pressing round as Achilles stripped the body; yea some who dared not have looked on Hector living were now forward with blows and spurns upon his noble corpse. Achilles himself, still maddened by lust of revenge, bored through the fallen chief's feet to tie them by thongs behind his chariot; then holding up to view the gory spoils, he dragged the naked limbs in the dust, before the eyes of his old parents, shrieking and tearing their thin locks. Andromache was sitting at her loom when she heard the mournful outcry, to bring her in haste to the walls, half-guessing what she should see, that when seen, blinded her eyes in swooning misery.

Hector's mangled and defiled body was cast on the shore beside the bier of Patroclus, round which Achilles made his chariots and Myrmidons circle thrice in honour of the dead hero, before they took food or rest. When the weary chief lay down to sleep, his friend's restless shade appeared at his side, urging him no longer to delay due rites of burial.

> "Sleep'st thou, Achilleus, nor rememberest me?
> Living, thou lov'dst me; dead, I fade from thee:
> Entomb me quick that I may pass death's door;
> For the ghosts drive me from their company,
> Nor let me join them on the further shore:
> So in the waste wide courts I wander evermore.
> Reach me thy hand, I pray; for ne'er again,
> The pile once lit, shalt thou behold thy mate:
> Never in life apart from our brave train
> Shall we take counsel: but the selfsame fate
> Enthralls me now that by me cradle sate.
> Thou too art doomed, Achilleus the divine,
> To fall and die by sacred Trioa's gate.
> Yet not my bones in death lie separate from thine."
>
> —Conington

The haunting ghost was soon to be laid. Next day Agamemnon sent out a band of men to hew down wood for a wide-piled funeral pyre. On this the body was laid, strewn over with locks of hair which his comrades cut from their own heads as offerings to the shade. Oxen and sheep, four noble steeds, and two household dogs were sacrificed to be thrown on the heap, and with them the twelve hapless Trojan captives. The pile was slow to light till the son of Thetis prayed for favouring winds, Boreas and Zephyrus, that flew to fan it into crackling blaze. Oil and wine were poured upon the flames burning all night, while beside them Achilles watched restless; then in the morning he quenched the ashes with wine to gather them in a golden urn, above which should be heaped a mound hiding the remnants of the fire.

Nor was this all. Funeral games must be held, with rich prizes given by Achilles, for which Agamemnon himself did not disdain to contend in honour of the dead. Henceforth the two chiefs were friends; and Achilles led the host when again it marched forth against Troy.

Within Troy now all was woe and wailing, as day after day the insatiable avenger could be seen dragging the body of its champion thrice round the pile sacred to Patroclus. Pitying gods preserved Hector's corpse from decay, and when twelve days had gone, Zeus was moved to save it from dishonour. He sent Thetis to soften her son's heart that he might agree to let it be ransomed. Then from the walls, in a chariot loaded with rich gifts, carne forth old Priam to throw himself at the feet of Achilles, clasping his knees and praying him, as he revered his own father, to give up the body of that noblest son.

He bent his grey head, ready to take death for an answer, and those looking on feared that the rage of Achilles might burst forth upon this helpless suppliant of the hated race. But all at once the stern hero's mood was turned by gentle compassion. He raised the old king, he granted his request, he had a couch laid for him in his tent, where Priam slept for the first time since Hector's death. Yet early in the morning, fearing to fall a prey to the pride of Agamemnon, he stole away with the body, now washed and anointed, and brought it safe within the gates of Troy.

The generous Achilles had promised a twelve days' truce, that Hector's body might be duly buried. So this hero's spirit, too, could sleep in peace, honoured by solemn rites and warm tears. And among all the farewells of his friends and kindred, none spoke from the heart more than the stranger Helen, for whose sake he had died.

> "Ah, dearer far than all my brothers else
> Of Priam's house! for being Paris' spouse,
> Who brought me (would I had first died!) to Troy,
> I call thy brothers mine; since forth I came
> From Sparta, it is now the twentieth year,
> Yet never heard I once hard speech from thee,
> Or taunt morose, but if it ever chanced,
> That of thy father's house female or male
> Blamed me, and even if herself the Queen,
> (For in the King, whate'er befell, I found
> Always a father,) thou hast interposed
> Thy gentle temper and thy gentle speech
> To soothe them; therefore, with the same sad drops
> Thy fate, oh Hector, and my own I weep;

For other friend within the ample bounds
Of Ilium have I none, nor hope to hear
Kind word again, with horror view'd by all."

—Cowper

Here ends the story of Homer's *Iliad*. But others tell how fresh heroes came to take the place of Hector as shield of Troy. There came the warlike Amazons, led by their queen Penthesileia, before whom the Greeks could not stand, till she fell by the spear of Achilles. But on tearing off her helmet, he stood as if spellbound in sorrow for the withering of so fair a face; and when Thersites, after his kind, jeered at the hero's compassion, Achilles struck this vile mocker dead with a single buffet.

Next Priam's nephew Memnon, the noble Egyptian, brought a band of dusky warriors to the aid of Troy. He, too, the son of Peleus overthrew after a hard contest; but Zeus for the sake of his mother Aurora, granted to him, as to his father Tithonus, immortality; and on earth was raised in his honour that colossal statue that, men say, gave forth a voice as often as it struck by the rising sun.

Then at last dawned Achilles' day to die. Nine past, Poseidon, friend as he was to the Greeks, had vowed vengeance against their champion, when, in one of their first onsets, he slew the god's son, Cycnus, fighting for Troy. The lord of ocean now charged Apollo with the fate of a foe his trident could not pierce. One spot in the hero's body was alone vulnerable, the heel by which his mother held him when tipped in the water of Styx. To that spot the archer-god guided a chance shaft of Paris; and thus unworthily fell the warrior that had sent so many souls down to Hades. But, if poets tell true, he himself had nobler fate, borne away by his mother to endless life in same happy island far from the eyes of common men.

Sore was the mourning for Achilles in the Grecian camp.
"Ten days and seven, with all their space of night,
Both gods and mortals we bewailed thee there.
But on the morning of the eighteenth light
We gave thee to the fire, and victims fair
Slew round thee, sheep and oxen; and the air
Hung sweet with smoke, thou burning in rich state
Of robes divine, sweet honey, and unguents rare,
While with a noise of arms about thee wait
Horsemen alike and footmen; and the cry was great.

"At sunrise, when the fire had ceased to burn,
They cinders white in oil and unmixed wine
We gathered, and thy mother gave an urn
All-golden, calling it the gift divine

Of Dionysus, moulded from the mine
By work-renowned Hephaestus: there abide
The ashes of Patroclus, mixed with thine;
Antilochus lies separate at thy side,
Best loved of all thy comrades, when Patroclus died."

—*Odyssey,* Worsley

As Troy had seemed ready to fall with Hector's death, so the loss of their champion for a time disheartened the host of Agamemnon. And even in death, Achilles had left among them a legacy of strife. His marvellous shield and armour, wrought by Hephaestus, were to go to the bravest of the Greeks – a gift nigh as fatal as the golden apple from which grew all that woe. For when by the voice of Trojan captives such a prize was adjudged to Odysseus, as their doughtiest foe in valour as in wisdom, great Ajax went mad for vexation, and killed himself by his own, hand on a hecatomb of harmless sheep he had taken for threatening warriors But that priceless armour Odysseus gave up to the ruddy-haired son of Achilles, who, grown to manhood beside his mother, Deïdameia of Scyrus, was now brought to the war in obedience to an oracle declaring that without his young arm Troy could not be overthrown.

⚜

6 The Fall of Troy

Still Troy did not yield, for all the heroes battering ever at its gates. Achilles' son, Neoptolemus ('new in war'), whom the Romans named Pyrrhus, showed himself a true branch of heroic stock; but neither for him did the walls fall that had held out against his father. Then Calchas the seer, offering sacrifice, read in the entrails of the victim that Troy would not be taken without the arrows of Heracles, given in legacy to his friend Philoctetes.

This hero had indeed sailed from Aulis with the rest of the Greeks, but going on shore he had been bitten by a serpent, and the wound festered so loathsomely, seeming like to breed a pestilence, that, to be rid of his ceaseless cries, his shipmates set Philoctetes on the isle of Lemnos, and there left him to shift for himself. Ten years having passed, he might well be dead long ago; but when Odysseus and Neoptolemus sailed to Lemnos, they found him still alive, gaunt and ragged, and full of rancour against the Greeks who had deserted him to make his solitary abode in a cave, killing game with the bow and arrows that should have been aimed at Troy. These messengers had much ado to gain his goodwill, but by persuasion and by threats of force they brought him away to the camp in the Troad, where at last a skilled physician healed him of his grievous hurt. But no healing could help a wound made by the arrows of Heracles, poisoned in the Lernaen hydra's black blood; and by one of them it was that Paris now met a miserable death.

Again spoke an oracle that Troy could not fall so long as it treasured its Palladium, that image of Athena fallen from heaven. Again Odysseus showed himself bold as well as cunning. He and Diomede, in beggars' weeds, slunk by night within the walls of Troy, known to none in that disguise save only to Helen, but she, for fear or shame, did not betray her old friends, though well aware that they came on no friendly errand. Her heart was now going back to her true husband, whose feats of arms she beheld daily from the walls; and she even helped his comrades to steal from the temple of Athena that sacred image. So unhurt they brought it at daybreak to the camp, to be hailed by the exulting Greeks as a sure sign of victory.

Yet still those oracles seemed to befool the army, against which Troy held out stoutly as ever. When the chiefs could no longer bind their followers to the weary war, Odysseus hit on the device that was at last to make an end. By his counsel they framed a huge horse of wood, moved on wheels, and hollow inside to hold twelve men, of whom he made one, along with Diomedes, Neoptolemus, and other chosen warriors. Leaving this fabric full in view, charged with its baleful freight, the Greeks sailed away through the night, as if they had given up the siege in despair; but they cast anchor under the isle of Tenedos, in sight of the Trojan shore.

Those so long cooped up within Troy at first could hardly trust their eyes when in the morning they saw the enemy's camp deserted behind its smouldering watch fires. Then like bees they came swarming out of the gates to spread freely over the fields that for ten years they had trod but in hasty sallies. Eagerly they roamed from one scene to another of the quenched war, the wall raised about the Greek camp, the shore still furrowed by vanished keels, the site of Agamemnon s tent, the quarters of Achilles and of Ajax, the towering burial mound of Patroclus, the banks of the Scamander erstwhile choked by corpses. But nothing held their thankful eyes like that strange shape of a wooden horse: what could it be, and why left behind by the retreating enemy? Some were for dragging it off into the city, even if the gates had to be broken down to give it passage; but others cried for caution, and loudest of all Laocoön, the priest of Apollo, who ran up to warn his countrymen that here must be some deceit.

> "Deem ye the foe hath passed away? Deem ye that Danaan gifts
> May ever lack due share of guile? Are these Ulysses' shifts?
> For either the Achaeans lurk within this fashioned tree,

Or't is an engine wrought with craft, bane of our walls to be,
To look into our very homes and scale the town perforce:
Some guile at least therein abides: Teucrians, trust not the horse!"

—William Morris[3]

"The very gifts of the Greeks are dangerous," he ended, and flung a spear piercing the hollow wood to stir a rattle of arms within; then, were not the Trojans blinded by their fate, that trick would forthwith have been disclosed and Priam's kingdom stood firm as of old.

While some spoke of cutting the ominous gift to pieces, and some of hurling it over a rock into the sea, there went a rumour through the throng that drew all eyes away, turned on a prisoner whom certain shepherds had found lurking in the sedge by the shore, and he gave himself up to be led bound before Priam. This was Sinon, a young Greek self-devoted to play a treacherous part, sure of death if it failed. Trembling and tearful he bemoaned his lot as a victim both of friends and foes, till the Trojans, taking pity, urged him to say who he was, and how he came into such sorry plight. Feigning to lay aside his fear, he let himself be heartened into telling an artful tale, which seemed borne out by his unarmed nakedness. He spoke his name, and did not deny his race.

"Though plunged by Fortune's power in misery,
'T'is not in Fortune's power to make me lie."

He had come to the war, he said, a boy in charge of his father's friend Palamedes, against whom Odysseus ever bore a grudge. By his wiles, it was the fate of Palamedes to be accused of treason and put to death; then Sinon, faithfully holding to the innocence of his lord, had threatened revenge on Odysseus, so as to bring on himself the ill will of such a powerful chief. Let the Trojans kill him, and they would do a pleasure to that enemy, and to the leaders of the Greeks, whose minds a hateful tongue had poisoned against him.

But Priam's people, touched by compassion, encouraged the unfortunate youth to have no fear; and he went on with his lying tale.

The Greeks, weary of the war, had designed to withdraw for a time; but contrary winds hindered them from setting sail for their native land; and celestial prodigies warned them of divine power to be appeased. An oracle declared that as Iphigenia had been doomed at Aulis, so now another victim must be offered to buy a favouring homeward wind. Calchas, won over by Odysseus, pointed out Sinon as the chosen sacrifice; and all who feared the lot might fall elsewhere, were content to let him die. Already the altar and the sacrificial array were prepared, when he broke his fetters, and fled for hiding to a swamp, from which he had the joy of seeing the Greek ships sail away, leaving him still alive on the hostile soil.

Hostile no longer, Priam bid him believe, ordering the prisoner to be freed from his bonds; for the Trojans made him welcome as an ally, who had so little cause to love his own countrymen. And now they pressed him to declare what meant that wooden horse, as he glibly did, raising his unbound hands to heaven in protest that he spoke the truth.

The goddess Athena, they were to know, had taken dire offence at the Greeks for stealing her image from Troy. Before sailing for Greece, with purpose to return anon under better auspices, the soothsayer Calchas bid them placate her by forming and dedicating this figure, made so huge by cunning design, that it might not enter the city gates, for if once it could be placed as an offering in Athene's temple, it must prove a shield for the Trojans like that robbed Palladium, whereas if they dared to injure it by fire or iron, their own profane hands would bring ruin on Troy.

> "With such deceits he gained their easy hearts,
> Too prone to credit his perfidious arts.
> What Diomede nor Thetis' greater son,
> A thousand ships nor ten years' siege had done—
> False tears and fawning words the city won!"

Then, lo! a portent seemed to confirm Sinon's lies. As Laocoön now stood in act to sacrifice a steer to Poseidon, over the sea came skimming two enormous serpents, that drew themselves on land and, with hissing heads upreared, slid straight for the altar. They first fell upon the priest's two young sons standing there too scared to fly, till the scaly coils were wound about their limbs. While the other spectators stared in speechless amazement, Laocoön with a cry ran to plunge his knife into those throats already gorging on his boys' flesh; but him also the monsters involved in their loathsome embrace, twisting twice round his neck and his waist, to crush all three, laced together in helpless torment. Laocoön and his sons being thus choked to death, the serpents glided on to hide themselves in the temple of Athena, without harming any other Trojan, so that they seemed sent as ministers of divine vengeance on the priest who had thrown a spear at that consecrated image.

The cry arose that Laocoön was justly punished, and that the Horse should forthwith be taken in, as an offering grateful to the goddess. The infatuated Trojans harnessed themselves to that fatal machine, dragging it up to the town with songs and shouts of welcome, else at every jolt they might have heard the clash of arms in its hollow womb. They even broke a breach in their wall to let it pass; and, when it was stowed in the temple, all the people gave themselves up to feast and jollity, their weapons thrown aside as no longer needed, and the gates left unguarded on what was to be the last night of Troy.

With the rest had entered that false Sinon, who, as soon as darkness fell, from the highest tower made signals with a torch to the Greek fleet at Tenedos. The ships stood back to the Trojan shore, and poured out their freight of warriors to steal up to the walls, unseen and unheard by those careless revellers. While all Troy sank to sleep, heavy-headed with wine, Sinon let out the warriors hid inside the fatal Horse. They hastened to open the gates for their friends without; but that was hardly needful, since the enemy themselves had broken down their own wall; then at dead of night a sudden din roused the Trojans, alas! too late to save their city.

Aeneas, become Priam's chief defence since Hector's death, was disturbed in his sleep by the pale ghost of that hero, who, all befouled by dust and blood, seemed to bid him fly, since now it was useless to fight for Troy. He started up to hear the streets alive with a tumult of clashing arms, clanging trumpets, exulting shouts, cries of amazement, entreaty, and lamentation, all mingled with the crackle of flames. He looked out to see a glare of fire spreading through his neighbours' houses, already crashing in ruin. He ran forth to meet a priest, burdened with the sacred things of his god. "Troy is no more!" exclaimed this fugitive, and breathlessly told how the Greeks were upon them.

Such as he might think only of escaping for their lives; but Aeneas made rather for where the fight raged loudest, and soon fell in with a small band of his comrades, willing like himself to make a desperate stand. So confused were the deeds of darkness, that presently they became mixed up with a band of plunderers, who hailed them as Greeks and could be cut down before they saw their mistake. Taking all advantage of such disorder, Aeneas and his followers hastily stripped the fallen men, to put on their shields and helmets; and thus disguised, they slew so many of the enemy, that some straggling bands fled back towards their ships or hid themselves within the Wooden Horse. On the other hand, the Trojans might well mistake these friends for foes; and when they ran to rescue Cassandra dragged along by her hair in ruthless hands, they were overwhelmed under a hail of stones flung down from the walls of a temple held against the Greeks.

The Greeks soon rallied and came swarming back; then, one by one, Aeneas saw his brave comrades fall in the medley. He himself courted death in vain; but be was borne away in the throng of fighters and flyers to where, above all, a fresh uproar broke out around Priam's palace, hotly stormed, and as hotly defended. Intent on saving the king, he made his way inside through a secret postern, then sprang towards the highest tower, already shaking under the battering of the assailants. Soon their axes burst open the gate, and in they poured, young Pyrrhus raging like a beast of prey at their head, before whom maids and matrons fled shrieking from court to court, and from chamber to chamber, in vain seeking to escape death or slavery.

The queen Hecuba and her attendants had taken refuge with Priam at his household altar, the old king encumbered with hastily donned armour and weapons he could no longer wield. Here came flying their young son Polites, hard pressed by the raging Pyrrhus, whose spear laid him dead at his father's feet. Crying out to the gods against such cruelty, Priam, beside himself for grief, with shaking hand threw a dart that jingled harmlessly on the rabid warrior's shield, and but challenged him to savage bloodshed. He dragged down the old man, butchering him at his own altar beside the body of his son.

> "And never did the Cyclops' hammers fall
> On Mars his armours, forged for proof eterne,
> With less remorse than Pyrrhus' bleeding sword
> Now falls on Priam."
>
> —William Shakespeare

Aeneas had come in time to witness this slaughter, which he would fain have avenged. But he stood alone; and the gruesome sight recalled to him his own helpless father in peril along with his wife and child. His comrades were dead or fled; some had even leaped into the flames in the horror of despair. There was nothing for it but to turn while escape was yet open. As he sped away, the glare of the conflagration showed him Helen crouched in a porch, her face muffled from the two peoples to whom she had wrought such woe. Aeneas had a mind to slay this curse of his country and hers. But between the sword and its graceless victim came a radiant apparition of his goddess-mother, who urged him forthwith to save his family, since hostile deities were invisibly upheaving the stones of Troy and stirring the conflagration kindled by Achaean hands.

Leaving Helen to face her wronged husband as she could, the son of Venus turned away with swelling heart, and under his divine mother's protection, came safe through flames and fights to his own house. But there old Anchises refused to be a burden to him: let the doughty warrior escape, taking with him his wife Creüsa and his son Iülus, for whom the grandfather foretold high destinies; he himself did not care to outlive the fall of Troy; he would stay and perish like Priam, in the tide of flames that came already raging up to their doors. But the dutiful Aeneas would not leave his father behind; he took the old man on his shoulders, giving him to carry the most sacred relics of the hearth, which the hero dared not touch with his own blood-stained hands. Little Iülus be led along; and Creüsa followed behind. His servants be ordered to escape separately, saving what they could, and taking each his own way, a cypress-shaded temple beyond the walls being appointed as meeting-place.

Thus Aeneas left his home, picking out dark and devious passages through the burning city, for he, late so fierce in fight, was afraid of every shadow now that these helpless dear ones were in danger at his side. Silently they slunk to a broken gate, but there Anchises cried that he saw the glittering arms of Greeks close at hand; then his son hurried on to plunge into the darkness outside the walls. When he ventured to halt and look round, he missed his wife, gone astray in their confused haste; and when he reached the temple at which they should meet, Creüsa was not there.

Distracted by anxiety, Aeneas left the band of fugitives and ran back to the city. Sword in hand, he dashed through smoke and sparks, retracing the line of his flight in a vain search for Creüsa, whose name he recklessly kept calling into the darkness. He pushed on as far as his house, to find it on fire and full of plundering foes. He flew to her father Priam's palace in faint hope she might have taken shelter there. Alas! before the temple of Hera, he saw a flock of weeping mothers and children standing captive beside a heap of rich spoil, guarded by Odysseus and old Phoenix. Was this the lot of his hapless spouse; or was hers among the bleeding corpses over which he stumbled at every step? Then suddenly she stood before him; not indeed her living self, but a glimmering and looming shape that struck him dumb for dread. His hair standing on end, he listened aghast to a voice which death inspired with prophecy.

> "Why grieve so madly, husband mine,
> Nought here has chanced without design:
> Fate and the Sire of all decree
> Creüsa shall not cross the sea
> Long years of exile must be yours;
> Vast seas must tire your labouring oars;
> At length Hesperia you shall gain,
> Where through a rich and peopled plain
> Soft Tiber rolls his tide:
> There a new realm, a royal wife
> Shall build again your shattered life.
> Weep not your dear Creüsa's fate,
> Ne'er through Mycenae's haughty gate
> A captive shall I ride,
> Nor swell some Grecian matron's train –
> I – born of Dardan princes' strain
> To Venus' seed allied;
> Heaven's mighty mother keeps me here.
> Farewell, and hold our offspring dear."
>
> —Conington

With these words, she seemed to glide away. He would have held her, throwing his arms round the beloved neck, but they clasped empty air: Creüsa had vanished like a dream.

The night passed in such scenes of agitation and amazement. Day began to break as the hero, still unhurt, made his way back to that temple outside the walls, where in his absence were gathered together a band of Trojans, men, women, and children, pale in the glare of their burning homes. Already dawn showed the walls of the city guarded by its triumphant foes. The ten years' warfare was over, the decree of fate fulfilled. There being no more hope in fight, these hapless fugitives turned their backs on the ruin of Troy, and followed Aeneas to the sheltering wilds of Mount Ida.

Thence they gained the seashore, to build ships and launch forth in search of the new home foretold by Creüsa's shade. For seven years were they driven here and there upon the sea, for still Hera followed them with her implacable hatred of Troy, enlisting the winds and waves to war against its wandering sons, as is told in Virgil's *Aeneid*. But at last, with a choice band of heroes, Aeneas landed in Italy, was betrothed to Lavinia, the only child of old King Latinus, slew his rival Turnus in battle, and so came to found a second Troy on the banks of the Tiber.

And what was the end of Paris, that winsome deceiver that had brought so much misery on his kin and country? Ere this last slaughter, he had been wounded by one of the fatal arrows of Heracles. While Helen made ready to throw herself at the feet of Menelaüs, praying for forgiveness which was not denied her, her ravisher, sick at heart and tormented by pain, had crept away to Mount Ida, seeking out his deserted wife Oenone. He entreated her to forget the wrong he had done her, and to heal him of his mortal hurt by herbs of which she knew the secret. And some say that she did forgive him, after all, and that their old love rekindled in the forest solitudes. But others tell how she bitterly repulsed the man who had wronged her a score of years before: "Go back to your adulteress and die!" He turned away miserably to die in the dark woods; and there his body was found by those herdsmen that had been foster-brethren of his happier childhood.

> "One raised the Price, one sleek'd the squalid hair,
> One kissed his hand, another closed his eyes;
> An then, remembering the gay playmate rear'd
> Among them, and forgetful of the man,
> Whose crime had half-unpeopled Ilion, these
> All that day long labour'd, hewing the pines,
> And built their shepherd-prince a funeral pile;
> And, while the star of eve was drawing light
> From the dead sun, kindled the pyre, and all
> Stood round it, hush'd, or calling on his name."
>
> —Alfred, Lord Tennyson

As the flames sank and paled in the dawn, who but Oenone came wandering that way, already half-repentant of her heart's bitterness. She asked the shepherds whose ashes were here burning; and when they spoke her husband's name, with a cry she leapt upon his funeral pyre and perished in the same flames. But Helen went back unhurt to Sparta, she who had brought destruction for her dowry to Troy.

---

[1] (p. 170) The Wrath of Achilles, The Battles of Gods and Heroes and Hector and Achilles make the theme of Homer's *Iliad*. Quotations of celebrated passages, where not marked with the translator's name, are from the familiar version of Pope, which, with all its faults, remains one of the most spirited: in the selection of versions, the aim is to illustrate the different manners in which Homer has been treated.

[2] (p. 186) Breastplates.

[3] (p. 195) Where another translator is not named, the citations here are from Dryden's *Aeneid*.

The House of Agamemnon

1 Clytemnestra

Troy had fallen; and the princes of Greece could sail away, each with his share of its spoils borne by a train of woeful captives. But many of those heroes had no joyful home-coming after so long toils and perils. Even before leaving Asia they fell out among themselves; and when they launched forth for Greece, it was to steer different courses among the Aegean isles. Some were wrecked or driven astray by a storm on the way, for Poseidon, who had aided them against his foes, was ever fickle of favour. Some came back to find themselves forgotten, or supplanted, and to fall into unnatural strife. Some never reached home, but were fain to abide upon distant shores among barbarous folk. And darkest of all was the fate of Agamemnon, king of men, whose glory had paled on the field beside the prowess of outshining heroes. Better were it for him that he had perished before Troy, like Achilles and Hector!

> "Stabbed by a murderous hand, Atrides died,
> A foul adulterer and a faithless bride."

Never had Clytemnestra forgiven her husband for consenting to the sacrifice of her daughter Iphigenia. Sister of Helen as she was, she too played false to the brother of Menelaüs, and in the long absence of Agamemnon she took for her lover Aegisthus, his kinsman, who had meanly stayed back from the war. There was ancestral hatred between these two. Their fathers, Atreus and Thyestes, were brothers, yet did one another such wrong as to leave a legacy of revenge among their children. Aegisthus had murdered his uncle; and now he usurped his cousin's wife and kingdom, giving out among the people that Agamemnon was dead.

But well the guilty pair knew it was not so, and in fear they looked for the day when the king should come back to his own. They had laid a train of beacons that, blazing from rocky isle to isle, and from wave-washed cape to cape, should

202

bear to Mycenae the news that Troy was at last taken. There came the night when an exulting watchman roused them to see those signals flashing across the sea – a cheerful sight to other Greeks, but a boding message for Aegisthus and Clytemnestra, who must now face the husband so long deceived, so terrible in his wrath.

Agamemnon's approach was announced: the joyful people poured out, hailing their triumphant king; and foremost came Clytemnestra to greet her lord with feigned gladness and treacherous smiles. While he threw himself prostrate, first of all to kiss his native earth, she looked askance at the captive woman by his side, who was indeed Priam's daughter Cassandra, bowed down by the burden of slavery, and speechless among these men of strange tongue. The queen spoke falsely of forlorn distress in her husband's long tarrying afar from home, often slain by rumour, always exposed to wounds. Now she welcomed him back, as should befit a hero, and bid him enter his halls, in which was a feast was being prepared to mark this happy day.

Thanking the gods for safe return, Agamemnon crossed a crimson carpet spread upon his threshold. One warning cry was raised by Cassandra, whose prophetic eye saw that bright web dyed with blood. No one heeded the muttering captive, taken to be crazy for grief; but she shrank back, refusing to enter the house, through whose walls pierced her gifted sight. And soon her voice was echoed by a dreadful sound from within.

Agamemnon had asked for a bath to refresh himself before the banquet; and his wife showed herself busy to serve him. But the traitress threw a mantle of web-work round his head, and quickly twisted it about his sturdy limbs in case he could see who lurked behind the door. Standing thus hooded and caught as in a net, out upon him sprang Aegisthus with an axe, to fell that lordly man like a steer, so that he sank into the silver bath filled with his own blood. Thus unworthily died the conqueror of Troy, lamented loudest by the stranger Cassandra, till she, too, perished by the queen's jealous hatred.

The people of Mycenae hardly dared to speak their minds, when they knew the great king murdered by a tyrant whose guards held them in dread; or he bribed the elders to silence from the rich booty brought back from Troy. Aegisthus and Clytemnestra boldly avowed their deed, which they put on the score of the crime of Atreus against Thyestes. They openly proclaimed their marriage, and Aegisthus took the kingdom for his own, making nought of secret curses as of the rightful heirship. Agamemnon had left a son, the boy Orestes, still too young to stand up for himself. All he and his sister Electra could do was to weep in secret at a tomb raised by the hypocritical hands of that mother and stepfather before whom these children had to hide their heartfelt horror.

For them Clytemnestra had no such love as for the vanished Iphigenia, her eldest born. Slighted and suspected in their father's house, they were as stepchil-

203

dren to their own mother. Electra, wise beyond her years, kept her lips shut, but her eyes and ears open, so that she came to learn how Aegisthus had in mind to kill her brother before he should grow old enough to avenge their unforgotten father.

The loving sister saw but one way to save the boy, already past his twelfth year. She charged a faithful old servant of Agamemnon with carrying off Orestes by stealth. They fled from Mycenae and the young prince found welcome and refuge with Strophius, king of Phocis, akin to his father by marriage, out of pity, too, willing to protect him against Aegisthus. Electra was left alone to watch

Clytemnestra
From the painting by the Hon. John Collier

over the hero's tomb, living in her mother's family as a slave-girl rather than a daughter, for the stepfather would not have her find a noble husband, who also might take on him the inheritance of hate.

Strophius had a son named Pylades, of the same age as Orestes. These two grew up together, sharing their sports and tasks, and coming to love one another like true brothers– indeed, better, for they cared not to be apart, even for an hour; and, with the keenest rivalry to excel, they kept side by side in every exercise of virtuous youth, both surpassing all their companions, while neither could nor would outstrip the brother of his heart. So devoted were they to each other, through good and ill, that the friendship of Pylades and Orestes passed into a proverb for Greece, as in Sicily did that of Damon and Pythias.

⚜

2 Orestes

The murderer of Agamemnon might well frighten Orestes, whose mind was set on avenging his father, as seemed the duty of a pious son. He had no secrets from Pylades, and all their desires were as one, so in this undertaking the friends swore to stand by each other for life and death. No sooner had they reached manhood than they set out together on the deadly errand, first seeking the oracle at Delphi, that not only encouraged their purpose but counselled artful means for carrying it out.

To Mycenae, then, they went in disguise, bearing an urn they were to give out as filled with the ashes of Orestes, that Aegisthus might believe himself safe from his blood-foe. They spent the night in pious rites at the tomb of Agamemnon; and there in the dawn they met Electra coming out to keep fresh her father's memory, cherished by her alone in the house where another had taken his seat. Years having gone by since they parted, the brother and sister did not know each other, so when these strangers declared themselves to be from Phocis, she eagerly asked for news of Orestes.

"Alas! he is no more," answered the unknown brother, little thinking how he wrung her heart; and he went on to tell a false tale: how Orestes had been dragged to death through an accident in a chariot race, and how they came charged to lay his ashes beside his father's. But over the urn said to contain all that was left of him, Electra broke into such a passion of grief that now he knew his sister, and had not the heart to keep her deceived. He dried her tears by declaring himself to be no other than Orestes, in proof of which he showed Agamemnon's ring she herself had placed on his finger to keep him in mind of

205

his filial charge. With his bosom friend Pylades to aid him, and by the counsel of Apollo, he was here to slay the slayers.

Boldly they went up to the palace, and kindly were they received by Aegisthus when he heard their story of the feigned death of Orestes, the man he had such cause to dread. No welcome could be too warm for the bearers of that urn. The guests, unarmed but for hidden daggers, sat down to eat with the king and queen, while Electra made some excuse for sending away the servants. As soon as they were alone together, these strangers started to their feet, Pylades seizing Aegisthus, Orestes his mother; and out flashed the daggers.

"Remember Agamemnon! I am his son and yours. The hour of vengeance is come!"

These were the last words Clytemnestra heard as she fell by her son's hand beside the body of the usurper. The servants, rushing in at the noise, made no stir to defend their hated master, nor were the citizens loath to be rid of a tyrant; and for the moment it appeared as if Orestes might now take his father's place un-challenged.

But soon grey heads were shaken over such a deed: however guilty, a mother's blood shed by her son must surely bring a curse on the city. And when the first flush of his exultation had passed off, Orestes himself began to be moved by remorse. A malignant fate it was that had laid on him a duty so dreadful. At his mother's grave, horror came upon him, so that by turns he raved madly with wild words and glaring eyes, or lay speechless like a dead man, tended by Electra; but neither she nor Pylades could bring him back to his right mind. No other Greek would sit with him at a meal, or even sleep under the same roof. Some elders of the people were for stoning him to death, that thus might be averted the anger of the gods. But the most part voted for banishment; and so was Orestes driven forth from the city, accompanied by his faithful friend and his sister.

Bitterly now he reproached the god that had spurred him on to a crime in guise of a pious office. Then Apollo appeared to him in a dream, bidding him go into the wilds of Arcadia, and there he endured his fate for a year till he should be called before a council of the gods, that might purge him from the stain of his mother's blood. Meanwhile, abhorred by gods and men, with every door shut against him, he was given over to the Furies, to be hunted like a beast by blood-hounds of hell. Even Strophius, the father of Pylades, turned his face from his son, as sharer in the guilt of Orestes; but the youth willingly bore banishment rather than leave his friend. Electra became his wife; and they went with her brother into a savage wilderness.

For a year Orestes wandered, mad and miserable, among desert mountains, everywhere followed by the sister Eumenides, tormenting him with their scourges and torches, and haunting his restless nights in visions of dread, till he was ready to kill himself but for the loving care of Pylades and Electra. When his punishment seemed greater than he could bear, once more he sought the shrine of Apollo, and had laid upon him a heavy task to fulfil in expiation of his sin. He must sail to Tauris in the Scythian Chersonese, and from its temple carry off the image of Artemis, so jealously guarded by a rude people and a cruel king, that even to set foot on their land was death for a stranger.

Such an errand was given in answer to the frenzied prayer of Orestes—

> "O king Apollo! God Apollo! God
> Powerful to smite and powerful to preserve!
> If there is blood upon me, as there seems,
> Purify that black stain (thou only canst)
> With every rill that bubble from these caves
> Audibly; and come willing to the work.
> No; 't is not they; 't is blood; 't is blood again
> That bubbles in my ear, that shakes the shades
> Of thy dark groves, and lets in hateful gleams,
> Bringing me . . . what dread sight! what sounds abhorr'd!
> What screams! They are my mother's: 't is her eye
> That through the snakes of these three furies glares,
> And make them hold their peace that she may speak.
> Has thy voice bidden them all forth? There slink
> Some that would hide away, but must turn back,
> And other like blue lightnings bound along
> From rock to rock; and many hiss at me
> As they draw nearer. Earth, fire, water, all
> Abominate the deed the Gods commanded!
> Alas! I come to pray, not to complain;
> And lo! my speech is impious as my deed!"
>
> —W. S. Landor

Agamemnon's son asked no better than thus to risk his ruined life; and Pylades was eager to share with him that perilous adventure. In a galley manned by fifty men, they set out for the cloudy shores of the Euxine Sea, whose very name made a word of ill omen.[1]

3 Iphigenia

Orestes knew not how the priestess of that Taurian shrine was no other than his eldest sister Iphigenia, carried away in his infancy from Aulis, where the Greeks would have sacrificed her to buy a fair wind. And Iphigenia, long exiled to serve Artemis among barbarous folk, had heard nothing of her kin and country through a score of dark years. No word came to that remote land of the fall of Troy, of the death of Agamemnon, of his son's vengeance. Often she longed for news from her old home, even to hear its once-familiar speech; and though held in honour, even reverence, by Thoas, king of Tauris, and his people, she would have welcomed any ship that might carry her back to Greece. But no Greek came to their stormy shores, unless by luckless shipwreck, for well was known the cruel custom of this people to sacrifice strangers in the temple of their goddess.

One day as its sad priestess stood gazing across the gloomy waves that made her prison, with secret horror was she brought face to face with victims for the shrine. A band of herdsmen exultingly dragged before her two youths they had caught lurking about the temple, of foreign speech and dress, and giving themselves out for castaway mariners. Her heart thrilled within her when at their first words she knew them for countrymen.

"Unhappy ones, I cannot welcome you!" she cried in the same speech. "Know you not the law of Tauris, that every stranger treading its soil shall be sacrificed to Artemis, and alas! by my hands?"

"How can a people that honours the gods have such barbarous law!" exclaimed one of the captives; but his companion stood silent, with eyes fixed on the ground, or stared wildly around him as if aware of invisible foes. "We are cast on this shore by misfortune; we claim pity, shelter, aid from pious men."

"You must die," spoke the priestess; and the eyes of the Taurians spoke for them. "Would, indeed, that you spoke another tongue! Your names and place?"

"My name is Misery," sighed the one, and said no more; while the other threw himself at her feet, praying for mercy, like a man to whom life was dear.

"This much stands in my power," answered the priestess. "The king will consent to release one victim at my entreaty, but the blood of one is demanded as offering to the goddess. Which of you shall go back to Greece to tell the fate of his comrade?"

"Let me die, I care not to live," murmured the downcast captive.

"No," cried the other eagerly, "send my friend home, for I have sworn never to abandon him."

"He is worthy to live, as so am not I!"

"Hear him not! He is the last of a great race; and you know not what a stock must perish in his death."

"To me, then, death is lighter by far. None will weep for me; but this man has a new-married wife, and parents living to mourn his loss. Spare their grey hairs and the helplessness of his unborn son!"

"Strange pair, who are you?" asked Iphigenia, moved by the warmth with which these two friends seemed to court death, each for the other's sake.

"I am Orestes, son of Agamemnon, hateful to gods and men since these hands shed my mother's blood."

"I am Pylades, who aided his friend thus to avenge the great Agamemnon."

A cry rose to the lips of the priestess, as she heard that it was her brother who stood before her, praying for death rather than life. It was all she could do to hold herself back from falling into his arms under the eyes of the Taurians, who stood by in watchful suspicion for this talk in an unknown tongue. Hastily she questioned Pylades, and from him was amazed to learn how Agamemnon died, and how Clytemnestra, and what penance had been laid on Orestes, soul-sick to madness for such a crime.

Could she bear to see slain, to slay with her own hand, the brother she had nursed as an infant, or the friend so devoted to him in his evil plight? In her heart she planned to save both those generous youths; but before her barbarian acolytes, thirsting for their blood, she would not trust herself to let Orestes know who she was. Hiding her inward feelings for the time, she haughtily ordered the captives to be led to prison in bonds.

There they lay lamentably, looking for nothing but death together, each blaming himself for having betrayed the other by some avowal that had changed the merciful mood of that priestess. But at the dead of night their dungeon door was opened, and in stole Iphigenia, no longer with stern voice and threatening mien. Alone beside the Greeks, she told them her name and birth; and now in turn Orestes had the amazement to hear that his sister still lived, while she for the first time learned all the woes that had fallen on her father's home.

But they had to think of present danger rather than of that troubled past. The Taurians were clamouring for the sacrifice of the prisoners; and Iphigenia told with a shudder how it was her duty to officiate at this cruel rite, most hateful even were the victims not of kindred blood and speech. When she heard that they had a stout and well-manned galley waiting for them on the shore, her ready wit devised a way of escape. She went to the king with horrified looks: these captives, she declared, were outcasts so deeply stained in guilt that they would bring pollution to the temple of her chaste goddess. Before they could be rendered an acceptable offering, she must purify them with sea water that washes away all offence of man; and the image of Artemis, too, must be cleansed from the taint brought upon it by the very sight of such malefactors.

The unsuspicious king let it be so, for he had come to look up to the foreign priestess as an oracle. While he and his chiefs stayed at the temple, making ready for that sacrifice, Iphigenia went down to the shore alone, bearing the sacred image, and leading the two prisoners by a cord that bound them fast together. Then soon from the cliffs above rang out a cry of alarm, when a strange ship was seen making out to sea, carrying off victims, priestess, and image.

Men ran to tell Thoas, who angrily ordered the launch of his swiftest galleys in pursuit, and from the cliffs would have hurled stones and darts on the fugitives, tugging hard at their oars, against the wind and tide that washed them back towards the shore. But lo! a dazzling light blinded the king's eyes, and from high overhead pealed out the voice of Athena.

"Thoas, it is the will of heaven that these strangers shall go free; for my sister Artemis can no longer dwell among a barbarous people that honour her with human bloodshed! When you have learned to think more nobly of the gods, she will return. Till then a new shrine is provided for her and her priestess in my own chosen seat, that famed city of the violet crown."

The Taurians heard with trembling, and now did not dare to stay the Grecian ship. So Iphigenia brought the image to Athens, to be there worshipped more worthily. And there, when his year's penance was up, the Areopagus was appointed as her brother's place of judgment, to which he came still led by the Furies, those stern ministers of Nemesis.

In the temple of Athena was the court held, a solemn array of gods sitting in the likeness of old men. On his knees at the altar, as beseemed a suppliant, Orestes told his story without deceit, making his plea for mercy on the score of a father's death set against a mother's. The votes were taken by white and black stones cast into an urn. When they came to be counted, white and black, for pardon or punishment, were equal in number. Orestes covered his eyes, and the Furies made ready to throw themselves on their victim.

"Stay!" cried Athena, appearing in her own form. "My vote is still to come."

She cast a white stone into the urn; and beneath her aegis held above his head Orestes rose a free man, while the angry Furies sank howling into the earth.

Thus absolved, the avenger of Agamemnon went home to Argos, where now the people welcomed him to his father's kingdom. They say that he married Hermione, the daughter of Menelaüs and Helen, after winning her in mortal combat from the son of Achilles, to whom she had been betrothed. And so these two fought out the quarrel of their fathers, a generation after so much blood began to flow for that false queen's fatal beauty.

---

[1] (p. 207) The Pontus Euxinus (hospitable) seems to have originally had the more fitting name of 'Inhospitable' (Αξενος), changed by some such superstitious euphemism as style the Furies Eumenides to aver their anger. The Scythian Chersonese (peninsula) was the Crimea, and Tauris appears to be represented by Balaclava, that has had its hecatomb of victims in modern ways.

The Adventures of Odysseus

1 His Perilous Voyage Homewards

A much-tried hero was he who had left his island home so unwillingly for the ten years' war, then, after Troy had fallen, was ten years on a wandering way back. All those years his faithful wife Penelope waited patiently for news of him, while their son Telemachus grew up to hopeful manhood without having known his father. Meantime, persecuted by Poseidon but protected by the care of Athena, Odysseus went from one misadventure to another, brought about by adverse fortune, by his own fault, and by the folly of his men, who perished here and there miserably; but on their captain the gods took pity, and at last let him reach Ithaca, where he found his house given up to greedy neighbours, wasting his substance and persecuting his wife to choose one of them in place of the husband taken for dead.

> "The fate of every chief beside
> Who fought at Troy is known:
> It is the will of Jove to hide
> His untold death alone.
>
> "And how he fell can no man tell;
> We know not was he slain
> In fight on land by hostile hand,
> Or plunged beneath the main."
>
> —William Maginn's *Homeric Ballads*.

When he set sail homewards with a small fleet of ships, at the very outset Odysseus and his company ran into mishap. Not content with the glory and the spoils they had won at Troy, they must needs land on the coast of the fierce Ciconians, whose town they plundered and held a feast on the booty. Their prudent leader was for making off at once; but his careless crews sat gorging and swilling, till the Ciconians came back upon them with a fresh force of warriors

211

from the inland parts of their country. The carousing Greeks had to stand to arms for a battle that lasted all day, then at evening were forced to escape on board their ships, with the loss of several men from each crew.

Putting out to sea, they must next contend with winds and waves, more ruthless enemies than men. They had nothing for it but to run before a storm that drove them out of their course and tore their sails to tatters. On the tenth day they made an unknown land, where, going on shore for fresh water, Odysseus sent three scouts to spy out the people of the country. These were the Lotus-eaters, living on a plant named lotus, which so dazed their senses that they cared for nothing but dreamy idleness, in the languid air of that land, "where all things always seemed the same", and no stranger had the heart to move away from it who had once tasted its flowery food, freely offered by those mild-eyed melancholy Lotus-eaters.

> Branches they bore of that enchanted stem,
> Laden with flower and fruit, whereof they gave
> To each, but whoso did receive of them,
> And taste, to him the gushing of the wave
> Far, far away did seem to mourn and rave
> On alien shores; and if his fellow spake,
> His voice was thin, as voices from the grave;
> And deep-asleep he seem'd, yet all awake,
> And music in his ears his beating heart did make.
>
> "They sat them down upon the yellow sand,
> Between the sun and moon upon the shore;
> And sweet it was to dream of Father-land,
> Of child, and wife, and slave; but evermore
> Most weary seemed the sea, weary the oar,
> Weary the wandering fields of barren foam.
> Then some one said, 'We will return no more';
> And all at once they sang, 'Our island home
> Is far beyond the wave; we will no longer roam.'"

—Alfred, Lord Tennyson.

The messengers sent forward had alone tasted of that entrancing food. But when Odysseus saw what a spell it worked on these men, he had them dragged away by force and tied fast on the benches of the ships, while the rest of the crews he hurried on board before they should fall under the same charm, to be bound for ever to a life of inglorious ease.

Toiling at their oars, they left the Lotus land behind, and crossed the sea to fall upon perils of another sort on a rugged shore overhung by the smoke of fiery mountain tops. Here dwelt the Cyclopes, a race of hideous and barbarous giants that neither planted nor ploughed, but lived on their half-tamed flocks and on wild herbs; nor did they hold any intercourse with other peoples, having no use of sail or oar. Even in form they were monstrous, each having one huge eye flaming across his forehead; and in nature they were as cruelly fearsome as their looks. At an island nearby, Odysseus left his ships safely beached, all but one, with which he himself stood across to the rocky coast of the Cyclopes.

As he was coasting along, there came to view a deep cave, its dark mouth overhung by shrubs, above a yard walled in with rough stones and tree trunks as a fold for sheep and goats. Here was the home of a Cyclops named Polyphemus, so inhuman that he chose to live apart even from his fierce fellows. Drawn ashore by curiosity, the bold hero had a mind to explore this gloomy haunt. His ship left hauled up on the beach to await his return, with twelve of the bravest men picked for companions, he climbed to the mouth of the cave, carrying some food in a wallet, and also a goatskin full of rich wine which he had brought away from Troy, now to serve him better than he knew.

When they reached the cave, they found it full of lambs and kids penned up within, along with piles of cheeses and great vessels of milk and curds. The giant being out on the hills where he herded his flock, these strangers made bold to feast on his stores; then the men were for making off before he came back; but now it was their leader's turn to be reckless, and he waited to see the owner of such wealth, in hope to find him not less generous than rich. Bitterly was he to repent of his rashness.

At nightfall Polyphemus came home, shaking the ground under his tread, and flinging down a crashing stack of firewood from his broad back as he darkened the mouth of the cave. The very sight of this one-eyed monster was enough to scare his unbidden guests into its deepest recess. When he had driven all the ewes and she-goats inside, he closed the entrance with a rock that would make a load for a score of wagons; then before turning in the mothers to their young, he milked them for his own use, setting aside part of the milk to make cheese, and keeping part for his supper. Last, he lit a fire, the glare of which soon disclosed those trembling lookers-on.

"Who are you?" he bellowed. "Pirates, or traders, or what?"

Odysseus alone had heart to answer, and told his tale of how they were on their way home from Troy, appealing for hospitality in the name of Zeus, the protector of helpless travellers. Polyphemus, laughing scornfully at the notion that the like of him cared for gods or men, asked where their ship was moored, which Odysseus, cunning as well as bold, knew better than to tell, but would have him believe that they had been wrecked on his coast. Without another word, the greedy giant snatched up two of the men at random, to dash them on the ground and devour their bleeding carcasses, washed down by mighty gulps of milk, after which he stretched himself out to sleep.

But there could be no sleep for his luckless prisoners, fearfully aware of the same horrible fate awaiting them in turn. Odysseus thought of falling on the heavy-headed monster with his sword; but how then could they move the stone that barred the entrance? When daylight began to peep in, the giant rolled it away with ease; but when he had driven out his flocks, he carefully put it back, shutting up those captives as if by a lid clapped to. And the first thing he had done on getting up was to grab two more of them for his breakfast.

All day the rest lay there in quaking dread, but their artful captain was scheming out a plan to get the better of that cruel host. Within the cave he had left lying a great club of olive wood, which was large enough to be the mast of a ship. The end of this Odysseus cut off, and made his men sharpen it to a point and harden it in the fire; then he hid it away in the dirt that lay thick over the floor. Lots were cast for four men to help him in handling such an unwieldy weapon; and the lot fell on the very four he would have wished for strong and stout-hearted comrades.

Again the giant came back at evening; again he milked his flock; and again he caught up two of the sailors to make a cannibal feast. Then Odysseus brought to him a bowl of dark-red wine, filled from his goatskin, humbly offering it as a drink fit to wash down the heartiest supper. Polyphemus tasted, smacked his lips, drank down every drop, and asked for more, promising the giver something in return for a liquor which, he declared, was far better than any made in his country.

"What is your name?" he cried, as three times the bowl was filled for him and emptied.

"My name," said the sly Odysseus, "is Noman. What gift have you for me who offers you such noble wine?"

"Be this your reward, then!" hiccuped the drunken giant. "I will eat up your fellows first, and Noman last of all."

With that he rolled over on the ground, stretching himself out to snore off the fumes of the wine. As soon as he was fast asleep, Odysseus heated in the fire the sharp stake he had made ready; then with four men bearing a hand, he suddenly drove it into the monster's eye, turning it round to be quenched in bubbling and hissing blood.

The blinded Cyclops got to his feet with such howls of rage and pain that his assailants fled out of reach, but in vain now he groped and stumbled about to catch them. The outcry he made before long brought up his neighbour giants in haste to the entrance of his cave, where they could be heard tramping and shouting through the darkness.

"What ails you, Polyphemus, to disturb us with such a din at dead of night? Who is hurting you in sleep? Who is driving away your flocks?"

"Noman is robbing me! Noman is attacking me in sleep!" bawled the furious giant; then his neighbours stalked away with surly growls, taking it that he must be unwell, and might be left to his prayers for help.

So far, so good; but for the plotters crouching at the back of the cave now came the question how they were to leave it safely. Their groaning jailer, indeed, pushed away the stone, but he sat down at the entrance, stretching his hands across it to catch them when they should try to slip out, for he thought these men as stupid as himself. But Odysseus had another trick in his bag. He tied together the big rams by threes, a man fastened hidden among their fleecy bodies. The biggest and woolliest ram he took for himself to ding on to, face upwards, below its belly.

As soon as it was light, the rams pressed out to their pasture, their master feeling their backs as they passed, with fearful threats against that scoundrel Noman who had worked him such a mischief. But one by one, the prisoners slipped undetected through his fumbling clutches; then, once got well outside, Odysseus untied his comrades, and, driving along the pick of the flock, they hastened down to the shore, to be joyfully received by their shipmates, who had given them up for lost.

Hurriedly they put their booty on board and were launching from the beach, when Odysseus in his exultation raised a shout that brought the giant out on the cliffs, where he stood like some tall peak reared in the smoky air. Tearing up a mass of crag, and taking aim at the voice, he blindly hurled it so close to the ship as almost to crush her, and the wash of it would have swirled her back to shore, had not Odysseus sheered off with a pole, while his men needed no bidding to row their hardest. As they pulled away, in vain they begged him to be silent; he could not keep in the satisfaction of taunting that inhuman monster that had murdered his comrades.

"Cyclops, eater of men, if any ask who put out that eye of thine, to make you uglier than ever, say it was done by no less a hand than that of Odysseus the Ithacan!"

At that Polyphemus gave a dreadful groan, for it had been prophesied to him that he should lose his sight at the hands of this very Odysseus he had so little suspected in the castaway guest. There he stood as long as they could hear him, breathing after them curses that were not lost on the wind. For this monster, barbarous as he was, had no less a father than Neptune, to whom he now prayed for calamity and destruction on those hateful strangers; and Poseidon would hear his prayer. But the last stone the giant threw, largest of all, raised a swell that carried them out of his reach; then safely they reached the isle where the other ships lay awaiting their return.

Before setting sail, Odysseus fed his men on the Cyclops' fat sheep; and the best of all he sacrificed as a offering of thanks for his escape, vainly hoping to propitiate the heavenly powers that were already brewing mischief against him.

"So till the sun fell we did drink and eat,
And all night long beside the billows lay,
Till blush'd the hills 'neath morning's rosy feet;
Then did I bid my friends, with break of day,
Loosen the hawsers, and each bark array;
Who take the benches, and the whitening main
Cleave with the sounding oars, and sail away.
So from the isle we part, not void of pain,
Right glad of our own lives, but grieving for the slain."

—Worsley

The next land they made was the floating island of Aeolus, king of the Winds, where they found no lack of hospitable entertainment. Aeolus and his sons were keen to hear about the siege of Troy, that filled all the world with rumour, so they kept those welcome guests for a whole month of eating, drinking, and talking. When at length Odysseus grew restless to continue his voyage, Aeolus did him a rare favour by tying up all the winds but one for him in an ox-hide bag, which he might carry on board. Only the gentle west wind did he leave free to waft the ships straight to Ithaca.

They sailed on, then, for nine days on a smooth sea, and had at last come so close to their native island that already they could see fires glowing on its shore as if to beacon them home. All that time Odysseus had never left the helm, so eager was he to greet his wife and son; now he lay down to rest, believing himself out of all peril. But while he slept, his crew put their heads together, asking one another what treasure could be hid in that bag on which their leader kept so close an eye. Making sure it must be full of gold and silver, they opened it to look, then out flew the howling winds that in a trice drove them back from their haven, tossed upon stormy gusts stirred from all quarters at once.

Odysseus had almost thrown himself into the sea, when he awoke to learn what his foolish men had done; and they too repented bitterly of their meddlesomeness, for now the conflicting tempests carried them helplessly back to the island of Aeolus. There disembarking, their leader explained how it had gone with him; but this time he found the king of the Winds in no generous mood.

"Begone, ill-starred wretch!" was his reply. "I have no more help for him who is abhorred of heaven."

There was nothing for it but to put out to sea again, and row on at a venture, for now every wind failed them. For a week they toiled in a dead calm, and on the seventh day made the rocky harbour of the Laestrygonians, where most of the ships entered to moor themselves in a row; but Odysseus was heedful enough to tie up his own vessel to a rock outside, whence he climbed a point to spy out the land. And he did wisely, for this people, too, turned out to be cannibal giants, who flocked down in crowds to crush the ships under a shower of rocks and spear the poor sailors like fishes, so that every one of those venturing in went to feed such cruel ogres. In the nick of time, Odysseus himself cut his cable, and his men rowed off for their lives, amid the splash of rocks the Laestrygonians pelted at them till they were clear of that fatal haven.

This one crew, thus far lucky, but sad for the loss of their comrades, held on till they reached another island, so tired that on coming to shore they lay two days without being able to stir or caring to know who lived here. It was indeed the home of the fell enchantress Circe, sister of Medea, a place to which the Argonauts had found their way years before. Not till the third day did the doughty Odysseus rouse himself to mount a hill behind, coming back with a fine stag he had killed for dinner, and news that he had seen smoke rising from a thick wood to show the island inhabited.

Their misfortunes having made them prudent, they now divided themselves into two equal bands, under the captain and his lieutenant Eurylochus, the one to stay by the ship, the other to go forward in search of the natives. Lots were cast in a helmet, and it fell to Eurylochus to take on this dangerous quest, so off he set with twenty-two men, fearful of coming into the clutches of some other ogre, while their comrades were left behind lamenting over them as if never to be seen again.

And on reaching that wood to which the smoke guided them, in the middle of it the explorers saw a fine stone house, guarded, to their dismay, by a troop of lions and wolves; nor were they less troubled when these fierce beasts ran up frisking and fawning about them like dogs, wagging their tails and rubbing their noses against the sailors as if in friendly welcome. Since none of the beasts of-fered to bite, the men presently took heart and went forward till they could hear a woman's voice singing within as she worked at her loom. Out she came at their call, and kindly bid them enter, as they did, all but Eurylochus, who hung about outside in cautious suspicion. And well that was for him, since the enchantress entertained his mates with bewitched meat and drink on which they fell like pigs, and soon ran out scampering, grunting and squealing, every one of them turned into a bristly hog by a stroke of her wand, to join the lions and wolves that had all been men transformed by her spells. Eurylochus only waited to see them penned up in sties, fed with acorns and beechnuts; then he fled back to the ship, in too great consternation to have breath or words for at once telling what had hap-pened.

The others having at last got the story out of him, Odysseus snatched up his sword and bow, for he was no leader to leave his men in such a plight. He bid Eurylochus go along to show the way, but as he flatly refused to risk being turned into a pig, the hero set out by himself. Then he had not gone far when he fell in with a noble youth, whose errand was to give him friendly warning.

> "On his bloomy face
> Youth smil'd celestial, with each opening grace.
> He seiz'd my hand and gracious thus began:
> Ah! whither roam'st thou, much enduring man?
> O blind to fate! What led thy steps to rove
> The horrid mazes of this magic grove?
> Each friend you seek in yon inclosure lies,
> All lost their form, and habitants of sties.
> Think'st thou by wit to model their escape?
> Sooner shalt thou, a stranger to thy shape,
> Fall prone their equal: first thy danger know:
> Then take the antidote the gods bestow.
> The plant I give, through all the direful bower
> Shall guard thee, and avert the evil hour.
> Now hear her wicked arts. Before thy eyes,
> The bowl shall sparkle and the banquet rise.
> Take this, nor from the faithless feast abstain;
> For temper'd drugs and poison shall be vain.
> Soon as she strikes her wand, and gives the word,
> Draw forth and brandish thy refulgent sword,
> And menace death: those menaces shall move
> Her alter'd mind to blandishment and love.'"[1]

This was in truth the god Hermes, sent by the guardian care of Athena; and the charm he gave to Odysseus was the sacred herb *moly*, that has a black root but a milk-white flower, and can be plucked only by celestial hands – an antidote to keep men safe against all the spells of Circe.

In spite of the god's assurance, it was with misgiving the hero drew near that house of enchantment, and called out its mistress. She invited him in, set him on a lordly seat and gave him a golden goblet full of honey, meal and wine, mixed with her magical drugs. No sooner had he drunk this potion than she struck him with her wand, crying, "Off to the sty with your mates!" But the virtue of the herb *moly* was stronger than that her potion; and Odysseus not only kept his feet, but, as Hermes had bid him, drew his sword upon Circe, making as if he would kill her. Amazed and terrified, she fell down to clasp his knees, praying for mercy.

"Who are you, proof to my spells? Surely no other than the great Odysseus! Sheathe your sword, and let us be loving friends."

Odysseus would not trust this witch till he had made her swear by the gods to do him no harm; nor would he eat in her house till she agreed to undo the spell she had laid on his men. Forthwith she anointed the pigs with a balm that rid them in a trice of their bristles, and they stood up taller and manlier than ever. After this proof of goodwill, Odysseus fetched the rest of the crew to share her

hospitality, though he had to threaten Eurylochus with death before the lieutenant would again venture himself in Circe's power.

But now she was all smiles and bounty. Bathed, anointed, and dressed in fresh
clothes, the weary sailors were set down to a good dinner. So well did they fare,
that they were content to stay with her for days and weeks and months, fattening
like pigs in manlike form while they forgot all the perils and hardships gone by,
and the charms of Circe made Odysseus forget how Penelope would be awaiting
him at home.

Circe
By Sir Edward Burne-Jones

2 From Circe's Isle to Calypso's

Thus a whole year passed by in careless ease for those wanderers that had escaped the arms of the Ciconians, and the snare of the Lotus land, and the maw of
the Cyclops, and the giant Laestrygonians, and the cruelty of winds and waves
stirred up against them. But in the end the sailors grew tired of having nothing to
do but eating and drinking and sleeping off their gluttony; then they moved
Odysseus to break away from the too dear delights of this enchanted isle. It was

time to be off, said they, if ever they were to see their wives and children again.

So now at last the hero roused himself as from a dream. Taking Circe in a favourable mood, he let her know how his men were longing to get home; and she did not turn a deaf ear to his prayer. Not her will but the decree of fate, she said, kept him back. So far from refusing to let her guests go, she showed herself ready to speed them with guidance and advice. But to their dismay, she told them that they must first sail for Hades, there to seek counsel from the ghost of the blind prophet Tiresias, who even among the dead was counted wise above his fellows.

Bold as he was against earthly foes, Odysseus might well shrink from nearing the abode of the dead, and his men bemoaned themselves as already lost; but there was nothing else for it. Circe took leave of them kindly, gave them directions how to steer for that gloomy haven, and put on board a ram and a ewe for sacrifice to the powers of the under world. So with many misgivings they put to sea again, all but one, the youngest and most foolish of the crew, Elpenor, who, sleeping off a fit of drunkenness on the housetop, when roused by the bustle of departure had jumped up in such a flurry that he tumbled over to break his neck and go straight to Hades without more ado.

Away they sailed before a fair wind raised by Circe, that as darkness fell brought their ship into the deep water of Oceanus, where dwell the Cimmerians in endless night. Here drawing to land, they went on foot along the shore as far as a rock, beneath which the rivers Phlegethon, Cocytus, and Styx rush together. At this weird spot, as the enchantress had bidden, they dug a deep trench, and over it cut the throats of the sacrificed victims, so that the blood ran into it; and Odysseus poured libations of honey and milk and wine, all sprinkled with barley meal, calling on the name of Tiresias, for whom he promised his best heifer, with other worthy offerings, as soon as he got safe to Ithaca. When the pale shades sniffed the blood, they came crowding up from every nook of Hades, eager to get a taste of life.

> "All the ghosts of the dead departed from the Nether Dusk 'gan fare.
> And brides there were and younglings, and burdened elders there,
> And there were tender maidens still bearing newborn woe,
> And many a man death-smitten by the brazen spear did go,
> The very prey of Ares, yet clad in blood-stained gear;
> And all the throng kept flitting round the pit from here and there
> With strange and awful crying, till pale fear fell on me.
> So therewith I bade my fellows, and urged them eagerly
> That the sheep that lay there slaughtered by the pitiless brass they should flay,
> And make them a burnt offering, and so to the Gods to pray;
> Unto Hades the almighty and the dread Persephone."

—William Morris

Odysseus had to draw his sword to keep back all other ghosts from the blood till Tiresias should have answered his summons. The first that pressed forward was young Elpenor, the latest come to Hades, flitting about disconsolate because his body still lay unburied at the halls of Circe; but he took cheer when his captain promised to burn it and build a tomb for him, and set up as a monument the oar at which the youngster had tugged in life. Next, to the further side of the trench came Anticleia, mother of Odysseus, whom he had left alive when he sailed for Troy, and knew not till now of her death; but though he saw her with tears, his sword held his own mother back from the trench over which she stretched her shadowy arms. At last came the blind Theban Tiresias, leaning on his golden staff; and he first was let stoop to drink that blood that gave him voice to prophesy as of old.

"Odysseus," said he, "your homecoming will be no halcyon voyage, since Neptune bears a spite against the man that blinded his Cyclops son. Yet all may go well if, when you reach the Thrinacrian shore, you harm not the herds of the Sun that pasture there. But to slay them will bring wreck on ships and men; and if you yourself should escape in sorry plight, it will be to find your house full of trouble. And in the end death will come to you from the sea."

Other charges he gave for the hero to treasure in mind; then Tiresias went back to his place, and the mother of Odysseus in turn might come forward to taste the blood and in the strength of it speak to her son, eagerly asking how he came to Hades while still alive. Not less eagerly did he ask for news of home, and heard that Anticleia had died of grief for his absence, but that his father Laërtes was still on earth in feeble and woeful age, and that Penelope his wife never ceased to await him with tears. Moved by the very sight of her, three times he would have embraced the mournful ghost; but each time she melted out of his arms like a dream.

And now thronged round him many a shade, all so wild for a taste of blood, that again he had to threaten them with his sword, letting one only drink and speak at a time. Many a beautiful woman he beheld, and many a famous hero, among them his comrades at the siege of Troy. What was his amazement to recognize Agamemnon, so mighty of limb, now flitting among the feeble ghosts, and to hear from him how, after escaping all chances of war and weather, he had been done to death at home by his false wife Clytemnestra! But when that king of men asked after his son Orestes, Odysseus could tell him nothing of the youth's hatching revenge against his father's foes. It was not so when Achilles came to view, for in him the living man was able to breathe a flush of pride by relating the deeds of Neoptolemus, a son worthy of his sire. That was one spark of cheer to the hero, who had so little joy in his own fate that when Odysseus saluted him as a king among the shades, the once high-souled Achilles made bitter answer—

> "Talk not of ruling in this dolorous gloom,
> Nor think vain words, he cried, can ease my doom.
> Rather I'd choose laboriously to bear
> A weight of woes, and breathe the vital air,
> A slave to some poor hind that toils for bread,
> Than reign the sceptred monarch of the dead!"

Other old friends he hailed, and foes: Ajax for one frowned on him, remembering their rivalry even in death; and when Odysseus would have appeased him, the resentful ghost turned away without a word. Great ones of old he saw, Minos and Orion and Heracles; also arrant sinners, Tantalus and Sisyphus groaning in their endless torment, and Tityus stretched out upon roods of ground for a deathless vulture to prey upon his vitals. But so thick grew the crowd of doleful ghosts, and so loud their lamentation, that soon Odysseus turned away with a shudder, fearing to come face to face with the very Gorgon if he tarried longer. Back he sped to his ship, and bade the men be quick to unmoor from this dark haven of the dead.

With a will they rowed down the Ocean river, that took them into the open sea; and here again the wind was fair to waft them back to Circe's isle. There the first thing they did was to burn and entomb the body of young Elpenor, that his soul might have rest among the shades. Again the enchantress gave them friendly entertainment; but Odysseus she drew aside to learn how he had fared in Hades, and to ply him with warnings against the further perils of his course.

And well her warnings served him when they again took the sea, still with a favouring wind that soon brought them to the isle of the Sirens, those sisters of enticing song. So sweetly they sang that all who heard them were drawn on shore to where they sat in a field of flowers, blooming among the bones of men thus lured to their death. But on Circe's counsel, before they came within earshot, Odysseus stopped the ears of his men with wax, and made them bind himself fast to the mast, charging them by no means to unloose him, however he might beg or command when his ears were filled with the fatal voices.

Thus prepared, winged by their oars they flew past the beach on which could be seen the Siren Sisters, and over the waters came their tempting strains, heard by the captain alone.

> "Come, pride of Achaia, Odysseus, draw nigh us!
> Come, list to our chant, rest the oar from its rowing:
> Never yet was there any whose galley fled by us,
> But, sweet as the drops from the honeycomb flowing,
> Our voices enthralled him, and stayed his ongoing,
> And he passed from that rapture more wise than aforetime:
> For we know all the toil that in Troyland befell,

When the will of the Gods was wrought out in the war-time:
Yea, all that is done on the earth can we tell."

—A. S. Way

Their song so thrilled his heart that Odysseus struggled hard to get loose, and by cries and signs would have bidden his men undo the cords; but they tied him up all the tighter, and deaf to him as to the Siren music, rowed their best till they were far out of hearing. Then only they unbound him, and took the wax from their ears; and for once the Sirens had sung in vain.

But, that peril hardly passed, another arose before them where the waters boiled with a fierce roaring that made the men drop their oars, staring aghast into the smother of spray and foam. It was all Odysseus could do to hearten them for rowing on, and he dared not tell them the worst he had learned from Circe of this fearful passage, beset by two monsters hungering for the lives of luckless mariners. For now they must tug swiftly and steer deftly between the two rocks, no more than a bow-shot apart. Under the lower rock was prisoned Charybdis, hate-

Ulysses and the Sirens (detail)
By Herbert J. Draper

223

ful daughter of Poseidon, that three times a day belched out a whirlpool, and three times sucked it back with all that came into its resistless gulp. Still more dreadful was the opposite den of Scylla.

> "High in the air the rock its summit shrouds
> In brooding tempests and in rolling clouds.
> Loud storms around, and mists eternal, rise,
> Beat its bleak brow, and intercept the skies.
> When all the broad expansion, bright with day,
> Glows with th' autumnal or the summer ray,
> The summer and the autumn glow in vain.
> The sky for ever lowers: for ever clouds remain.
> Impervious to the step of man it stands,
> Though borne by twenty feet, though arm'd with twenty hands.
> Smooth as the polish of the mirror rise
> The slippery sides, and shoot into the skies.
> Full in the centre of this rock display'd
> A yawning cavern casts a dreadful shade:
> Nor the fleet arrow from the twanging bow,
> Sent with full force, could reach the depth below."

The ravenous creature that haunted here was, men say, a daughter of the sea-god Phorcys, on whom a jealous witch had worked woe, mixing in her bath maleficent herbs to change her into a twelve-footed and six-headed monster, greedy to prey on all that came within reach of her yelping jaws and rows of gnashing teeth. Circe had advised Odysseus to make no show of fight against such a fell foe; but he, ever too venturesome, put on his armour and took his stand at the prow as if to defy that cruel hag. Keenly scanning the rock well, at first he could see nothing of her as they shot through the gloomy strait; but when they shrank away from the yawning mouth of Charybdis to hug the opposite side, suddenly she darted out her six heads, and in a trice Odysseus saw six of his best men snatched up into the air, screaming and stretching their hands for help in vain, as she hauled them into the mouth of the cave: never in all his adventures did he see a more grisly sight!

But with that the escaped from danger, for now the scared sailors rowed clear through those jaws of death; and soon they saw loom ahead the great three-cornered island, on which they could hear the lowing and bleating of the Sun-god's herds. Mindful of warnings given him both by Tiresias and by Circe, Odysseus ordered his crew to row on without touching here; but they, weary of hard toil, would no longer obey, and Eurylochus insolently spoke for the others that, not being made of iron, they must go on shore for a night's rest. Odysseus had to give way; yet, before mooring in a harbour they found on the rocky coast, he made them all take a solemn oath not to meddle with the god's cattle; then they landed to cook their supper and to sleep away their grief for those six comrades so miserably lost.

Next morning they should have been off betimes, had not a sudden tempest risen through the night, in face of which they dared not put out to sea; and for a whole month blew contrary winds to keep them imprisoned on the island. Soon came to an end the corn and wine with which Circe had given them; then the men wandered here and there, trying to catch fish or snare birds; and many a hungry eye was cast on the fat herds of the Sun-god which they had sworn not to touch.

They seemed like to starve, when Odysseus sought a solitary place in which to pray to the gods alone. While his back was turned, the mutinous Eurylochus stirred up the rest to lay hands on the sacred cattle, for, said he, no god could send them a punishment worse than dying by inches of famine. On coming back, their captain was startled by the smell of roast meat, and to his wrathful dismay he found the sailors gorging themselves on carcasses which they had butchered in guise of a sacrifice. It was too late for him to forbid, nor did his greedy men heed the prodigies that appeared to rebuke their crime, for the very hides of the dead beasts rose and walked, and the joints on the spits lowed as if still alive. For a week they kept up the impious banquet, in spite of all entreaty or warning; till at last came a blink of fine weather to tempt them to their doom.

Meanwhile, Hyperion the Sun-god had made loud complaint in heaven, threatening to forsake the sky and to shine henceforth down in Hades among the dead, unless he were granted vengeance upon those insolent men that had ravaged his beloved herds. Zeus appeased him by promising swift punishment; and Poseidon had kept an angry eye on that crew ever since the blinding of his Cyclops son. So no sooner were they out of sight of land, than the storm burst upon them afresh. The first squall blew out their mast to crush the steersman in its toppling over; and as the broken hulk tossed ungoverned upon the waves, from the dark sky shot a thunderbolt that shivered it to pieces.

Every man was swallowed up by the raging sea, save only Odysseus, who contrived to catch hold of the mast, and to tie it with other wreckage, making a raft on which he floated back towards Scylla and Charybdis. Here he was like to have been sucked down, but he caught hold of a fig tree that overhung the rock of Charybdis, and held on till the raft bobbed up below his feet, vomited out again by the black whirlpool. Once more clinging to it he drifted away; and for nine days was carried by winds and waves, whither he knew not, till the tenth night washed his raft on shore.

The hero came thus stranded on the island of Ogygia, where dwelt the divine nymph Calypso, daughter of Atlas. She, like Circe, was an enchantress, but her charms lay in lovely looks and loving eyes; and her wooded island home was as beautiful as its mistress. To a shipwrecked mariner the grotto in which she lived might well seem a blessed haven.

"Around, thick groves their summer-dress
Wore in luxuriant loveliness—
Alder and poplar quiver'd there,
And fragrant cypress tower'd in air.
And there broad-pinion'd birds were seen,
Nesting amid the foliage green;
Birds, which the marge of ocean haunt—
Gull, prating daw, and cormorant;
And there, the deep mouth of the cave
Fringing, the cluster'd vine-boughs ware.
Sprung from near sources, bright and gay
Four limpid fountains urge their way
Diveryent, o'er the parsley'd mead,
Where the sweet violet droops its head—
A scene, should gods survey the sight,
E'en gods might gaze on with delight!"

—Wrangham

To this solitary abode Calypso welcomed Odysseus with kindness, soon warming into love for the guest who, time-worn and toil-scarred, was still a goodly man in her soft eyes. So well she loved him that she would have him never leave the island; and at first the hero was content to rest here from his weary wanderings. So months sped by, and years, as in a dream. A spell of immortal beauty seemed laid upon Penelope's husband, so that he forgot all but the passing hours of happiness. Yet as time went by, he remembered his own rough island; and often, stealing apart from his charmer, would sit by the shore alone, to gaze over the waves with wistful thoughts of home.

Meanwhile at Ithaca his father Laërtes and his wife Penelope had heavy hearts, vainly hoping his return. The suitors of the faithful queen grew more and more urgent, living insolently in the house of Odysseus, and wasting his substance, since now they had no fear to see him back. The lad Telemachus had been growing up to be like his father; but for long he was too modest to withstand the riotous crew making themselves at home, as if already his inheritance had passed to a stepfather. Then there came a day when Athena breathed into him the spirit to rebuke those self-invited guests, and to declare that he meant being master in his own house. And when they jeered at the youth, with threats and complaints of Penelope's obduracy, he suddenly announced his intention of taking ship for the mainland, there to seek out news of his father. If he could hear of him as still alive, he would put up with the suitors for one year more; but if Odysseus were certainly dead, he himself would insist on his mother making her choice among them, as at liberty to marry again.

She herself had practised craft against the importunity of the suitors. Some god inspired her, as she thought, to set up a loom for weaving a great and splendid web to be seemly shroud for old Laërtes; and not till it was ended, she told them, would she be free to wed. Ceaselessly her fingers worked at it, but every night she sat up by torchlight, privily undoing the labour of the day. The tale came to be told in Hades by one of those long-deceived suitors, at last sent to his doom.

> "We wooed the wife of Odysseus, the lord so long away,
> And unto that loathly wedding said she neither yea nor nay,
> But the black doom and the deathday devised for us the while;
> Yea in our heart she devised us moreover this same guile;
> With a web that was great and mighty her loom in the house did she gear,
> A fine web, full of measure, and thus bespake us there.
>
> "'O younglings, ye my Wooers, since the godlike Odysseus is dead,
> Await ye abiding the wedding till I to an end have sped
> This cloth, for fear the warp-threads should waste and come to nought.
> 'Tis a shroud for the lord Laërtes 'gainst the day when he shall be caught
> At the last by the baleful doom of Death, the Outstretcher of men:
> Lest the women of Achaeans through the folk should blame me then,
> —Lo the man of many possessions he lieth lacking a shroud!'
>
> "So she spoke, for the while prevailing o'er our hearts the high and proud,
> And thenceforth o'er that web the mighty by daylight still she wrought;
> But ever by night undid it when the candles thereto she had brought.
>
> Three years she beguiled the Achaeans, and the thing by guile did hide,
> But when came on the fourth year and the seasons came in their tide,
> By all the waning of moons and the many days fulfilled,
> Then one of the women told us, who in the guile was skilled,
> And we found her there unweaving the noble web of cloth;
> And so to an end must she bring it perforce and exceeding loth."
>
> —William Morris

That device being treacherously disclosed, she had no further excuse for putting off the choice pressed upon her. If her true-loved husband came home, it must be soon or never. So she waited in prayers and tears, while young Telemachus secretly sailed away to Greece, inspired and accompanied by Athena in disguise of his honest guardian Mentor.

Landing at Pylos, he sought out old Nestor, who had much to tell of the Trojan war, but could not tell what had become of Odysseus. Nestor's son, Pisistratus, drove him on to Sparta, to be there courteously received by Menelaüs and Helen, now reconciled after their long divorce. Menelaüs was not without tidings of his famous comrade. He himself had made a wandering voyage home, in the course of which it was his fortune to come upon Proteus, the wise old man of the sea, whose knowledge had to be wrung from him by force. When Menelaüs and his companions, disguised in seal skins, caught that keeper of Poseidon's herds, basking on the shore, he changed in their hands to a lion, a leopard, a boar, and a serpent in turn, now melting into a fountain, now springing up as a tree; but to those bold enough to hold him fast under all his transformations, he was bound to tell truth at the end. Thus constrained, he had let Menelaüs know how Odysseus was a prisoner in Calypso's cave, vainly longing to go free from her flowery charms. Having heard of his father as still alive, Telemachus made haste back to Ithaca, where the suspicious suitors, on learning his absence, were now plotting an ambush to fall upon him as he reached home.

Mentor had abandoned him on the journey, resuming the divine form of Athena, who went about a greater service to this house which she had taken under her charge. When now for seven years Odysseus had lain in Calypso's isle, half-entranced, half-yearning to escape, the maiden goddess pled his cause in a council of Olympus, from which only Poseidon was absent. That insatiable persecutor of the much-enduring man having gone off to enjoy a hecatomb offered him by the Ethiopians, the other gods were easily moved to pity for such a hero, and Zeus himself now remembered how dutiful in prayers and offerings Odysseus had been during the days of his prosperity. So while Athena went back to earth as counsellor of Telemachus, Hermes was sent to Calypso, bearing a supreme command that her guest should be let go and furthered on his voyage homewards.

Ill-pleased was Calypso with this injunction, which she dared not disregard. Yet when she sought out Odysseus sitting homesick on the shore, to tell him how his heart's wish might now be gratified, she still would have tempted him to stay, reminding him of the trials and perils of the sea, promising to share with him her own immortality, if he could forget that mere woman Penelope, who surely did not rival herself in beauty. His first idea of her tidings had been that they were too good to be true, and that there must be some trick under her offer to let him build a boat for leaving the island; but she swore by the Styx, mightiest oath of the gods, that no harm was intended him: he was verily free to go, if he could bear to leave her. Then it wrung her heart to hear him answer with kindling eye—

> "Goddess and mistress, be not wroth with me
> Herein: for very well myself I know
> That, set beside you, wise Penelope
>
> "Were far less stately and less fair to view,
> Being but mortal woman, nor like you
> Ageless and deathless: but yet even so
> I long and yearn to see my home anew;

And through all days I see that one day shine:
But if amid the ocean bright as wine
Once more some God shall break me, then once more
With steadfast purpose would my heart incline

"Still to endurance, and would suffer still,
As ofttimes I have suffered, many an ill
And many a woe in wave or war; and now
Let this too follow after, if it will."

—Mackail

Much as it went against her heart, Calypso did all she could to speed his departure. She gave him tools to cut down trees, with which he built a raft, and her own garments she brought to make sails for it, and stored his little craft with victuals and skins of wine and water; and she raised for him a softly favouring breeze, when on the fifth day he launched forth, too ready to see the last of that charming hostess.

3 New Friends in Need

Once out at sea, his sailor-craft came back to Odysseus, long as he had lain idle on land. Steering heedfully by the Pleiades and the North Star, for seventeen days he never shut his eyes nor took his hand from the helm, till the eighteenth dawn showed him welcome land ahead. But now Poseidon, returning from his banquet among the Ethiopians, spied out that lonely voyager, and made haste to work him ill. The god lashed up the sea with his trident, calling forth storm winds from every quarter to wrestle round the little raft and whirl it about.

"Would that I had died illustriously among the heroes of Troy!" was Odysseus' thought, as he felt his frail craft breaking up beneath him.

A kindly sea nymph, perching on the wreck in form of a gull, advised him to take to swimming; but though already half-drowned, the poor sailor tried to stick to his raft as long as she would hold together, for he feared some new trick being played upon him by mischievous gods. Before long, however, he saw nothing else for it but to throw off his garments and plunge among the waves; and that sea nymph Leucothea, who, in mortal form, had been Ino, daughter of Cadmus, cast over him a magic scarf that bare up his stalwart body. When Poseidon saw him beaten about, he made no more ado, but drove home in his chariot, chuckling over the perilous plight of one to whom he owed such a grudge.

And now indeed the hero had been lost but for the aid of Athena, who laid all the winds but one, and let that carry him steadily towards the land. Two days and two nights he kept himself afloat on the swell; and when the third morning broke, a joyful sight of wooded hills close by gave him strength to strike out for dry ground. But it was no easy matter to get on shore, for before him stretched a sheer wall of surf-beaten rocks, rising suddenly from deep water. Dashed against the sharp edges, to which he would have clung with his bleeding hands, he found himself sucked back by the waves before he could get firm hold or footing to climb beyond their reach. There was nothing for it but to swim a little way out, and keep on along the coast till he came off the mouth of a river. Praying the god of this stream to receive him as a suppliant, he turned into its quiet channel, where at last he was able to drag himself ashore, so battered out of breath and strength that he lay in a swoon, and only after a little was able to kiss the ground in token of thankfulness.

But not yet did he seem safe. Night was drawing on, and the chill wind numbed his weary nakedness. He crawled into a wood for shelter, and made himself a bed of dry leaves, to forget his troubles in such sleep as falls on men who for long have not dared close an eye.

> "As some poor peasant, fated to reside
> Remote from neighbours, in a forest wide,
> Studious to save what human wants require,
> In embers heaped preserves the seeds of fire:
> Hid in dry foliage thus Ulysses lies
> Till Pallas poured soft slumbers on his eyes."

Now the island where he had this time come on shore was Scherië, inhabited by the rich Phaeacians, a people better known as traders than as warriors, whose city and the palace of their king Alcinous stood not far from that river mouth that gave the hero refuge. Softly and sumptuously they lived, yet their women folk, high and low, were not too proud for housewifely cares. That night, as Nausicaä, the king's daughter, lay asleep, a dream sent by Athena put into her head to see after a great washing of linen, that all things might be ready for her marriage feast, now that she had no lack of suitors. So in the morning she asked her father to let her have a mule wagon, which she loaded with the foul clothes of the family, and drove off with her maids to the river bank for a long day's work.

Turning out the mules to graze, this bevy of girls set the garments soaking in cisterns of fresh water, and vied with each other in the trampling them under their white feet, as seemed task fit for a king's daughter who hoped to be mistress of a lordly home. When the cleansed apparel had all been wrung out and spread to dry on the sunny beach, they bathed and anointed themselves; then, after taking their dinner in the open air, began to play at ball by way of pastime,

Nausicaä singing to them while they waited for the sun to finish their work. None of these sportive maidens guessed how a shipwrecked man was sleeping in the wood close by; nor did their merry noise disturb the tired Odysseus till late in the day, when, on a ball thrown amiss falling into the river, they all raised such a shrill clamour that he woke up with a start.

Peering out of his covert, at first he was ashamed to show himself near this troop of girls, without a rag on him as he stood. But he must not lose such a chance of succour in such hard plight, so he plucked a leafy branch to make a screen for his body, and thus strangely arrayed came forth to view. At the sight of a naked man, all bruised and brine-stained, with famine in his eye, these handmaidens might well shriek and run for it, as from a savage lion, Nausicaä alone standing fast, for she had a princely nature, and could guess that the desti- tute stranger meant her no harm.

Slenderly graceful like a palm tree, she stood, then, to listen while, accosting her with as much reverence as if she were a goddess – and so indeed she seemed to him by her pitiful looks – Odysseus told his tale of twenty days spent on the sea that had flung him at last to shore, and besought her for any scrap or wrap of clothing she had to spare, and for guidance to the nearest town, if she wished heaven to grant her a good husband and a happy home.

Once she had made sure that this was no fierce ruffian, but an honest man in distress, Nausicaä answered him kindly, calling back her maids, with orders to bring him a shirt and a cloak and a pot of oil. With these, going a little apart, he washed off the ooze and slime from his limbs. When he had dressed himself he looked another man, of whom Nausicaä thought she would wish no better for her spouse. But now modesty and the fear of scandal prompted her not to be seen in company with so handsome a foreigner. The clean clothes having been packed up, while Odysseus was refreshed with meat and drink from her store, she bid him then follow the wagon that would show him the way to her father's house.

Thus guided, he entered the walled city of the Phaeacians, wondering at its greatness and its busy harbour; still more, when Athena, in the shape of a little girl, led him to the palace gate of the king. Never in all his wanderings had he seen such magnificence!

> "Resplendent as the moon, or solar light,
> Alcinous' palace awed the o'erdazzled sight.
> On to its last recess, a brazen wall
> That from the threshold stretch'd, illumined all;
> Round it of azure steel a cornice roll'd,
> And every gate, that closed the palace, gold.
> The brazen threshold golden pillars bore,
> A golden ringlet glitter'd on the door,
> The lintel silver, and to guard his gate,

Dogs in a row, each side, were seen to wait,
In gold and silver wrought, by Vulcan made,
Immortal as the god, and undecay'd.
From the far threshold, to its last retreat,
Ranged round the wall, rose many a lofty seat,
With fine-spun carpets strew'd, by virgins wrought,
Where, as each newborn day new pleasures brought,
Phaeacia's chiefs, from thought and care released,
Sat throned, and lengthen'd the perpetual feast.
Stood on bright altars golden youths, whose hands
Lit through the night the guests with flaming brands:
And fifty maids administering around,
Some, the ripe grain beneath the millstone ground,
Some whirl'd the distaff, and the fleeces wove
Swift as the leaves that shake the poplar grove:
And ever as they plied their radiant toil,
The glossy web shone like transparent oil.
Nor less expert their course the seamen kept,
Than through the loom the female shuttle swept,
The gift of Pallas, who had there combined
The skilful hand with the inventive mind.
Without the court, yet nigh the city's bound,
A garden bloom'd, four-acred, wall'd around;
Tall trees there grew, the red pomegranate there,
Each glossy apple, and each juicy pear,
Sweet figs, and living olives: none decay'd
Or in the summer blaze, or winter shade;
While western winds unfolding every flower,
Here gemm'd with buds the branch, there fill'd with fruits the bower."

—Sotheby

For a little, Odysseus stood abashed on the brazen threshold, hardly venturing to enter so sumptuous an abode, for Nausicaä, driving on ahead, had taken herself off to the women's chambers. But, encouraged by the advice she had given him, he passed in, then on to the hall where Alcinous was banqueting with his lords. For the queen Arete he made, and bowing before her, clasped her knees with a humble entreaty for succour to a man in sore need. This done, he sat down in the ashes by the hearth, as became a supplicant.

Astonished by his sudden appearance among them, the guests stared upon him in silence, till one of the oldest spoke to remind the king what was due to misfortune. Thus prompted, Alcinous rose to give the stranger his hand and lead him to a seat of honour, where food and wine were quickly set before him, and a silver bowl into which from a golden ewer one of the serving maids poured clear water to lave his fingers.

This king and his people were so hospitable to a guest, as remembering how they might entertain some god unawares. They did not much trouble the castaway with questions while he ate and drank heartily after his long fast; yet before being shown to a snug bed outside the hall, he told the king and queen of his shipwreck, and how he had been found destitute on the shore by Nausicaä. Arete had guessed something of this when she recognized the clothes he wore as the work of her own looms. All he begged now was to be sent home across the sea, to which Alcinous readily agreed without even asking his name or country, for the Phaeacians were such skilled mariners that it would be easy for them to steer to any point.

Next day, while a ship was being fitted out for him, Alcinous and his lords did their best to entertain the stranger. The more he saw of him the more the king liked his guest's looks; now that he was rested and refreshed, Odysseus had such a stately manner that he might well be taken for a king, if not for a disguised god. When, still keeping his name secret, he declared himself only a mortal man, Alcinous pressed him to stay in Scherië, as his son-in-law, if he chose; nor was the modest Nausicaä loath to have him for a husband; but all the his mind was set on home, and the Phaeacians had too much courtesy to keep him against his will.

At the games held in his honour, the stranger would have been content to look on; but when rudely challenged by the best Phaeacian athlete, he caught up a quoit of extraordinary size and hurled it far beyond the mark of any other competitor. Warmed by such easy victory, he even began to boast, offering to box or wrestle or shoot with any of them, except the king's son, with whom, as his host, he did not care to contend; only, he granted, they could beat him at running, since his legs were still weak and stiff from the sea. Wondering what champion this might be, the Phaeacians spoke no more of matching themselves against him. Indeed they were not so good at feats of strength as at singing and dancing and the like diversion, fonder of feasting, too, than of rough frays.

After the games came a banquet, when the blind bard Demodocus was fetched to spice the fare with songs of love, such as the idle Phaeacians heard gladly; but their unknown guest, sending him a mess of meat from his place, bespoke in turn the tale of Troy's fall. That, then, the bard sang so stirringly, and so loudly extolled the son of Laërtes, as first among heroes of fame, that Odysseus could not keep back his tears. Alcinous, sitting beside him, noted how he turned his head to weep; then this kindly host cut short the song that moved in his guest such painful memories.

"Who are you and where are you from, to grieve for the fate of Troy?" he asked; and the answer was—

"I am Odysseus."

Amazed were the king and his lords to hear how this needy stranger, who had sat silent among them, was none other than that illustrious hero vanished for years from the knowledge of men. Eagerly they sought to learn all that had befallen him through those weary years; and half the night he kept them listening to a tale of adventures that would make matter for many minstrels.

But now it seemed as if his troubles were indeed near an end. For if the Phaeacians had been friendly and serviceable to the nameless castaway, they had nothing too good for the renowned warrior. Already they had given him bounteous gifts; and furthermore at the king's bidding they heaped up for him a treasure of gold and bronze vessels and goodly raiment, to be loaded upon the ship that should bear him home without delay. Alcinous himself visited it to see everything made taut and trim. Once more the guest was royally entertained with feast and song; but all day his eyes turned to the sun, as if to speed its setting, for no tired ploughman ever longed so much to come to an end of his furrows. And when darkness gave signal for departure, over a farewell cup he invoked blessings on Alcinous and his people, then joyfully went down to the harbour to get on board. The sailors spread a soft couch for him in the stern that he might sleep out the short voyage to Ithaca. No sooner had they loosed their hawser and dipped their oars in the gleaming surf, than the island born chief was rocked into a deep slumber, and knew not how

"As all together dash four stallions over the plains
At the touch of the whistling lash, at the toss of the glancing reins,
 And they bound through the air, and they fly, as upborne on the wings of the wind—
So was the stern tossed high as the good ship leapt, and behind
Rushing the dark wave sped of the manifold-roaring sea;
And unswervingly onward she fled: so swiftly, so surely went she,
Not the falcon could match her, whose flight is the fleetest of all things that fly,
So fast did she cleave and so light she rode over the waves tossing high,
As onward the hero she bore who in wisdom was like to a god,
Who had suffered affliction before, heart-troubles, a weariful load,
In battles of warring men, and on waves of the troublesome sea:
Yet peaceful slept he then, from their very remembrance free."

—A. S. Way

Odysseus had not yet awoke when at dawn the ship sighted Ithaca, its shores well known to the Phaeacian mariners. The crew ran their prow ashore in a sheltered cove, marked by a sea-hollowed rock that made a sacred haunt of the Naïads. Quietly they lifted his couch to lay him on the sand; and nearby, about the roots of an overshadowing olive tree, they piled up the gifts bestowed upon him by their countrymen. There they left him still sleeping, while they rowed back to Scherië.

But Poseidon frowned to see his foe thus brought safely home, whom he had meant to afflict a while longer, though it was the will of Zeus that in the end he should reach Ithaca. The sea-god went off to complain to his brother how those presumptuous Phaeacians had crossed his purpose; and the careless king of Olympus gave him full leave to punish them. So he did by turning the ship into a rock just as it was steering back into port; and there it stood rooted in the sea, like a mountain overhanging the city of Alcinous, who for doing such friendly service to a stranger was forced to make a sacrifice of twelve choice bulls that might appease the offended deity.

4 The Return to Ithaca

When Odysseus woke up to find himself alone, the air was dark with mist hiding all the landmarks of his native island, so that he feared the sailors must have treacherously set him on shore in some strange country. Even when he saw and counted his rich presents laid out safe under the olive tree, he could not believe but that a trick had been put on him. As sorrowfully he paced the beach, crying out upon his hard fate, and upon himself for having trusted the glib-tongued Phaeacians, there approached him through the mist what seemed a young and comely shepherd, whom he hastened to meet.

It was in truth his divine protectress, Athena, who in playful mood took this shape to guide him; and she too had sent the mist to conceal his arrival from the enemies that filled his home. So pleased was he to see anyone, that he saluted the seeming shepherd with the regard due to a god, begging him to say what country this might be.

"He must be a stranger indeed," was the reply, "not to know Ithaca, a small and rugged island, yet famed as far away as Troy!"

Glad as he was to hear himself at home after all, the crafty Odysseus had not wholly shaken off his distrust; so he thought well to tell a lame and lying tale of how he came to be here, deserted by dishonest shipmates, who yet had not robbed him of his treasure.

The young shepherd listened with a smile, all at once vanishing from his sight, where the goddess now stood before him in her own majestic form, and laughingly reproached him for his crafty lies, of which indeed he would soon have much need.

In reply, the hero might well complain of her fickle guardianship: now she came to his aid in one or another shape; then again she left him suffering under the worst strokes of fate; and even now, for all he could be sure, she might be cheating him with some false hope. The astute Athena explained that she had to beware of offending her uncle Poseidon, whose heart was still hot against Odysseus for blinding that one-eyed son of his. But to show herself truly his friend, she blew away the mist, then at once he could recognize the familiar scenes of his own island, falling on his knees to salute this native earth, with thanks to the sea nymphs that had wafted him home at last.

First helping him, like the prudent goddess she was, to hide away his treasure in the cave of the Naïads, she sat down with him below the olive tree to let him know how matters stood in his house, taken possession of by a greedy crowd of suitors for his wife's hand, and they would give her true husband no kindly welcome. Penelope, he heard with joy, was still faithful to him, though she had always much ado to put off their importunity. Telemachus had left home in search of his father, and the suitors were plotting to rid themselves of the heir on his return; but the goddess undertook to bring him quickly and safely back. Meanwhile, she advised Odysseus to take refuge with Eumaeüs, the keeper of his swine, and thence to spy out the state of his enemies before revealing his identity. The better to escape their malice, he must be transformed as a lowly beggar.

> "She spake, then touch'd him with her powerful wand.
> The skin shrunk up, and wither'd at her hand.
> A swift old age o'er all his members spread.
> A sudden frost was sprinkled on his head.
> Nor longer in the heavy eye-ball shin'd
> The glance divine, forth beaming from the mind.
> His robe, which spots indelible besmear,
> In rags dishonest, flutters with the air.
> A stag's torn hide is lapp'd around his reins.
> A rugged staff his trembling hand sustains;
>
> And at his side a wretched scrip was hung,
> Wide-patch'd, and knotted to a twisted thong.
> So look'd the chief, so mov'd, to mortal eyes
> Object uncouth, a man of miseries;
> While Pallas, cleaving the wild fields of air,
> To Sparta flies, Telemachus her care."

Thus disguised, Odysseus took a rough mountain track that led him to the spacious pens in which hundreds of swine were kept under charge of old Eumaeüs, a servant ever true to the memory of his master, and full of grudge against the usurping guests who daily devoured his fattest boars. As this honest swineherd sat cutting himself sandals out of a hide, a loud barking hailed the approach of a stranger, on whom four dogs, wild as wolves, flew out so fiercely that he might have been torn in pieces had crafty Odysseus not at once sat down to disconcert their onset; then Eumaeüs rushed out to drive them away with stones.

He for his part showed no want of kindness to one he took for a beggar. He led the unknown man into his hut, strewed for him a couch of rushes with a hide laid on the top, and made haste to kill and cook two young sucking-pigs to set before him with barley meal and wine. While Odysseus ate hungrily, Eumaeüs went on lamenting over his master, whose absence kept him poor, and abusing the suitors that consumed the pick of his herd, so that he could do no better for a guest. Odysseus asked that much-missed master's name, of whom a wanderer like himself might have heard some news. Nay, growled the swineherd, he had heard enough of lying tales brought by beggars from all quarters, seeking Penelope's bounty on pretence of having known her husband. Let who will believe them: the great Odysseus, the best master that ever was, must long ago have made food for fishes or vultures; else why did he not come back to set things right at home?

"Not so!" cried the beggar. "Poor as I am, I hate lying; and I make bold to swear that this year – indeed, before another month be out – Odysseus shall come back to his own!"

The swineherd shook his head, like one who had too often heard such promises; and would talk no more on a painful theme. Now that the guest had supped, he asked his name and how he came to Ithaca. For all his professed hatred of lying, Odysseus was a good hand at a fable: hereupon he told a long one, making himself out a Cretan, and inventing a string of mishaps that had brought him into slavery and cast him naked on this unknown island. In the course of his adventures, he declared, he had heard of Odysseus as bound for home with great wealth. Did Eumaeüs still not believe? Let them make a bargain, then. If Odysseus came back, the swineherd should give him a cloak and shirt and send him on to his own home; if not, he was willing to be pitched over a cliff as example to other lying beggars.

Heaven forbid! exclaimed the host, that he should so use a man who had eaten under his roof-tree. And soon again he showed himself as hospitable as rough of speech. For at evening the under-herdsmen came home driving in the grunting and squealing swine to be shut up for the night; then their master bid them pick out the fattest boar to make a fit feast for this stranger. Before they all sat down together to meat, Eumaeüs piously burned the bristles of the beast as a sacrifice, praying the gods for his lord's safe return; and when he cut the flesh into portions, one was set apart for Hermes, the conductor of souls. The guest was honoured with the juiciest slices, and made a second hearty meal with the rest, before they all lay down to rest.

Then crafty Odysseus again thought of a trick for putting his host's kindness to further proof. He told another tale of how, lying before the walls of Troy one cold night, he got Odysseus to send one of the soldiers running off on a message to the fleet, that he himself might borrow this man's cloak. Eumaeüs took the hint to lend the half-naked beggar a warm covering for his bed of skins in front of the fire. Outside, it was blowing and raining, dark as pitch; but, while his underlings slept under cover, the keeper, wrapped in a weather-proof mantle, and armed with sword and javelin, spent all night in the open air, to keep good watch over his absent master's flock. This trusty fellow was a slave stolen in childhood by Phoenician traders, and sold to Laërtes of Ithaca, to whom and to his son he showed by careful service his gratitude for kind usage. So he told Odysseus next day, when the disguised stranger heard of his old father as still alive, though sorely grieving for the son whose disappearance had been the death of his mother.

Still playing on the swineherd's goodwill, Odysseus talked of going up to the town, presenting himself in Penelope's halls, appealing to her kindness, or offering himself as servant to those suitors that were said to be eating her out of house and home. As if such proud lords would care to have a ragged beggar about them! blurted out Eumaeüs. No, no, the stranger could do no better than stay where he was for a while; times were not so bad but that there was something going for an honest guest: he could pay his welcome by telling stories of his wandering life, till Telemachus came home, who would be sure to prove openhanded to a man in need.

And Telemachus was not long in coming, having been speedily brought back from Sparta by Athena, who also warned him how the suitors had laid an ambush for him; so that instead of sailing straight to the town harbour, he landed on a lonely shore of Ithaca, and on foot made first for the swineherd's hut. Eumaeüs and his new friend were cooking their morning meal when they heard steps that set the dogs barking as for a stranger; then at the open door stood the form of a noble youth to bring the swineherd to his feet with cries of hearty welcome. He kissed his young master as one from the dead, weeping tears of joy; and the first question of Telemachus was whether Penelope had yet been forced into a marriage with one of the suitors. No, Eumaeüs could assure him; she still remained shut up in her chamber, mourning ever her absent lord.

Glad of that news, Telemachus entered the hut, and let the swineherd take his spear. The ragged vagrant would have risen to give him place; but the young master courteously bid him keep his seat. When he sat down to eat, waited on by Eumaeüs, he asked who this stranger might be; and the swineherd repeated the tale told him by Odysseus. Telemachus looked grave to hear that a needy beggar had waited his return in hope of relief. What could he do for the poor, indeed, who was hardly master at his own house? He also advised the man not to go near those insolent intruders: let him stay where he was, and Telemachus would send down some food and clothes for him.

Eumaeüs presently went off to tell Penelope of her son's safe return. Father and son were left together, yet not alone, for Athena stood at the door, visible only to Odysseus and to the dogs that shrunk cowering and whining away. She beckoned him forth; she whispered to him that the time was come to reveal himself to his son; she touched him with her wand to undo that lowly disguise. So the grey, hobbling, toothless beggar strode back into the hut a well-clad stalwart form, erect and black-bearded, in the prime of life, at sight of whom Telemachus cast down his eyes in amazement, uttering a prayer as to one of the gods.

"No god am I, but thy father so long lamented!"

So spoke the hero, embracing his son with tears of joy; but to Telemachus it seemed too good to be true, and he cried:

> "'My father,' saidst thou? 'No, thou art not he,
> But some Divinity beguiles my soul
> With mock'ries, to afflict me still the more;
> For never mortal man could so have wrought
> By his own pow'r; some interposing God
> Alone could render thee both young and old;
> For old thou wast of late, and foully clad,
> But wear'st the semblance, now, of those in heav'n!'
> To whom Ulysses, ever wise, replied,
> 'Telemachus! it is not well, my son!
> That thou should'st greet thy father with a face
> Of wild astonishment and stand aghast.
> Ulysses, save myself, none comes, be sure.
> Such as thou see'st me, num'rous toils achieved
> And woes sustain'd, I visit once again
>
> My native country in the twentieth year.
> This wonder Athenaean Pallas wrought,
> She cloth'd me even with what form she would,
> For so she can. Now poor I seem and old.
> Now young again, and clad in fresh attire.
> So easy is it to the Pow'rs above
> T'exalt or to debase a mortal man.'"
>
> —Cowper

At last made to understand that his long-lost father stood before him in flesh and blood, Telemachus was so overcome with joy that they might have sat weeping in one another's arms all day. But the wary Odysseus knew that it was a time for deeds rather than words. Hastily telling how he had come to be landed on

Ithaca, he questioned the youth as to the number of the suitors who were vexing his wife and eating up his substance. Alas! Telemachus told him, they were too many and too bold to be driven away. Leave that to him and to the help of the gods, said Odysseus: let his son do as now directed. He must go home without a word of his father's return, even to Penelope. Later, Eumaeüs would bring the disguised beggar to his own house; then, however he might be insulted or ill-used by the suitors, Telemachus should bridle his feelings till the hour of reckoning came.

> "And though they deal upon me sore despite,
> Even in mine own house, let thy soul forbear!
> Ay, though with missiles they would wound outright,
> And drag me from the doors by feet and hair,
> Calmly look on, and let thy soul forbear!
> Yet from their folly bid them still relent,
> And strive to turn them with a gentle prayer,
> Albeit I know that they will not repent,
> So surely their dark hour of doom stands imminent."
>
> —Worsley

By and by, Eumaeüs came back from the house, where Penelope had heard with joy of her son's return; but that made ill hearing for the suitors when they knew how he had slipped through their snares. The swineherd was not yet to be trusted with the secret, so Athena had once more transformed his master into an old cripple in rags. Telemachus spent the night with them; and next morning, when he went to his mother, he bid Eumaeüs bring the man to the town to try his luck at begging: he himself had too much trouble of his own to look after poor people. So he said, exchanging secret smiles with his father, whom he feigned to treat so lightly.

Soon afterwards, Eumaeüs followed with the stranger, leaning on a staff, bearing a wallet on his bent back, and to all appearance a right mendicant. As they drew near to the town, over which rose the high walls of its lord's abode, they fell in with Melantheus the goatherd, driving along the best of his flock to feast the suitors, whose favour he cared for more than his true master's weal. This rude fellow had nothing to give the old beggar but contemptuous words, even fetching Odysseus a kick as he passed, which the hero endured meekly, though he had half a mind to fell the churl with his staff. Eumaeüs cried shame on the insolent fellow, who would have to mend such manners if ever their master came to his own again. Melantheus answered with much coarse abuse, declaring that they would see no more of Odysseus, as sure as that Telemachus would soon be killed by the suitors. He hastened on to join the revels of those new friends; while the other two more slowly approached the great house, where a sound of music and a savoury smell of cooking showed what was going on within.

But here the master of this house did not pass unmarked by one old friend. Near the gate lay a worn-out dog that pricked up its ears and raised its head at his voice, only to fall dead in the effort of crawling forward to lick his hand.

"It was Argus, Odysseus' hound; himself had reared him of yore
Yet or ever his pleasure he found in the chase, unto Ilium's shore
Was he gone; yet the dog long ago with the young men wont to fare
Through the woodland pursuing the roe and the mountain-goat and the hare.
But he lieth a cast-off thing – for far away now is the king –
Where in front of the doors the dung of the mules and the kine from the stalls
Had been swept in heaps and flung, till the time should come for the thralls
To spread it forth on the tilth-lands broad of Odysseus the king.
There lieth Argus in filth, all vermin-festering.
Yet now, as his dying eyes behold Odysseus appear,
He is moving his tail as he lies for joy; he is drooping the ear:
But his strength is utterly gone, and he cannot crawl more near.
And Odysseus looking thereon must turn him away; for the tear
Sprang to his eye, but he wiped it unmarked of the swineherd, and said: 'Eumaeüs,
   'tis passing strange, this hound in the litter laid.
Grand is his frame, yet what he hath been I do not know,
Whether fleetness in running he had to match this goodly show,
Or was but as the dogs that be pampered with dainties from feastful boards,
And are nurtured for vain fair-seeming by pride-uplifted lords.'
And Eumaeüs the swineherd spake to the beggar-king and replied:
'Of a surety this is the hound of a king that afar hath died.
If his frame were but now as of old, and his deeds as the deeds of yore,
When Odysseus left him, passing away unto Troy-land shore,
Thou wouldst marvel beholding the fleetness and strength this dog showed then.
There was never a beast that escaped through the depth of the forest-glen,
Whatsoever he chased; for he followed with scent unerring the track.
But evil hath compassed him now; for the lost will never come back,
And the heedless women folk tend him not, but they leave him to lack.
Yea, thralls, when they feel no longer the hand of their lord and the might,
Have no more will to render him honest service aright.
For the half of the manhood of man Zeus Thunderer taketh away
When his feet are caught in the net of the bondage-bringing day."

—A. S. Way

When they entered the hall, Eumaeüs was beckoned by Telemachus to a seat at the banquet, while Odysseus held himself back near the door, as beseemed the humble part he was playing. There his son sent him a portion of bread and meat, which he ate sitting apart, and at first passed without notice, the eyes of all being fixed on a bard who was cheering their feast with song. When his strains came to an end, the old beggar rose to go round the table with bent head and outstretched hands, not so much for what he should get, as to test the disposition of these usurpers of his home. Most of them gave him something, as well they might be liberal with what was another's, so that soon he had his wallet stuffed with bread and meat. But Melantheus the goatherd again reviled him and the swineherd who had brought him; and Antinous, the most insolent of the suitors, called for him to be turned out of the house, where this man behaved as if already its master. In vain, with a supplicant whine, Odysseus stooped to flatter the haughty lord, telling one of those false tales of which he had so many, making himself out a once-rich man, who would never in his own prosperity have turned the poor from his door; then, taking another tone, he went on to upbraid the selfish churl who grudged him a morsel of bread not his own. This so enraged Antinous that he flung his footstool at the beggar, who bore the blow without moving, and went back to his place at the threshold audibly praying to whatever gods cared for the poor, that Antinous might come to the bad end of one who despised misfortune.

Antinous still fumed and threatened, heedless of Telemachus, sitting in silent fury to see his father thus used in his own house. But other suitors took shame for their comrade's rudeness; and one of them openly rebuked him for so serving a poverty-stricken man, who for all they knew might be a god in disguise. And when word was brought to Penelope in her chamber how Antinous had insulted a supplicant under her roof, she too was indignant at such a breach of hospitality. Through Eumaeüs she sent for the beggar to partake her bounty, the more readily as she heard that he professed to have known Odysseus. And, just then, Telemachus happened to sneeze so loudly that it resounded through the whole house, which his mother took for an omen of good news; and was still more eager to hear what the stranger might have to tell.

Odysseus, for his part, showed no haste to meet his wife, perhaps as remembering a warning given him in Hades by the ghost of Agamemnon, that had some cause not to trust woman's faith. He excused himself for not at once obeying Penelope's summons, promising to come to her at sunset, when he might be able to slink unnoticed through the crowd of revellers, and then their talk would stand in less danger of interruption. For the present, while Eumaeüs went back to his pigs, he himself remained in the hall, keenly watching those enemies of his home, all unaware who was among them.

Now there came up a real beggar, Irus by name, a greedy drunken braggart, well known as doing odd jobs about the place. He was ill-pleased to see another of the same trade here before him, and at once began to abuse this stranger, and talk of turning him out. Odysseus answered that there was room for both of them, and that the other might not find it so easy to turn him out. Deceived by his modest speech, Irus grew louder and more abusive; and the mischievous suitors egged him on, taking it for fine sport to set these two by the ears. Antinous laughingly proposed a fight between them, the prize to be a goat's paunch full of blood and fat, which was already put down at the fire for supper. The jovial crew would not listen to Odysseus' protest that he was a broken-down old man, unable to stand against a sturdy young fellow. Well then, since they would have it, he was ready to fight Irus, if he could be sure of getting fair play. That Telemachus promised him, and so did the rest.

Irus had been willing enough to try for an easy victory, but the stranger, stripping off his rags, disclosed such sturdy limbs that everyone saw he could make a better fight of it than had been expected. The more the boaster looked at this stalwart form the less he liked it; and now he was for backing out, even had to be dragged by force into the ring made for them in the courtyard. Trembling, he stood before the opponent who knew that he could kill him with a single blow of his fist. But, not to unmask himself by putting forth all his strength, Odysseus merely knocked the fellow down so that blood ran out of his mouth, and he lay spluttering and sprawling on the ground amid the brutal laughter of his backers. He dared not again stand up to the old man, who dragged him out by the foot, propped him up against the wall, with his staff in his hands and his torn cloak hung about him like a scarecrow, contemptuously bidding him stay there to keep off dogs and pigs.

When he himself came to sit meekly down in his former place at the door, as if he had done nothing out of the way, the suitors were inclined to treat such a doughty beggar with more consideration. Antinous brought him the promised prize; and Amphinomus, of nobler nature than the rest, gave him some bread into the bargain, and pledged him in a cup of wine, wishing him better fortune. That kindness moved Odysseus to tell the young lord that he knew his father, a worthy man, for whose sake he would drink to him with some good counsel.

> "Then hear my words, and grave them in thy mind!
> Of all that breathes, or grov'lling creeps on earth.
> Most man is vain, calamitous by birth.
> Today, with power elate, in strength he blooms.
> The haughty creature on that power presumes.
> Anon from Heaven a sad reverse he feels.
> Untaught to bear, 'gainst Heaven the wretch rebels,
> For man is changeful, as his bliss or woe;
> Too high when prosperous, when distress'd too low.
> There was a day when, with the scornful great,
> I swell'd in pomp and arrogance of state,
> Proud of the power that to high birth belongs,

And us'd that power to justify my wrongs.
Then let not man be proud; but firm of mind,
Bear the best humbly, and the worst resign'd.
Be dumb when Heaven afflicts; unlike yon train
Of haughty spoilers, insolently vain,
Who make their queen and all her wealth a prey;
But vengeance and Ulysses wing their way.
Oh! may'st thou, favour'd by some guardian power,
Far, far be distant in that deathful hour;
For sure I am, if stern Ulysses breathe,
These lawless riots end in blood and death."

Now attention was withdrawn from the old beggar by the appearance of Penelope in the hall, who came to rebuke her son for allowing such a disturbance and letting a stranger be ill-treated in his house. Bitterly Telemachus answered that it was no fault of his: what could he do against all those masterful wooers of hers who made themselves so much at home? Willingly would he see every one of them served as Irus had been. As he spoke, the self-invited guests came flocking around her, each pressing his suit with flattering compliments. Indeed Athena had for the nonce made Penelope look more beautiful than ever in their eyes; and Antinous spoke out for the rest that they would by no means take themselves off till she had chosen one of them as a husband.

"Alas!" sighed the queen, "care and affliction may well have marred my charms; yet how can I hold out against you longer? My dear lord, setting forth for Troy, charged me, if he came not back, to keep myself unwed till Telemachus' beard was grown. The time has come; and soon I must choose among you, though never again can I be happy in a husband. But yours makes strange manner of wooing. A suitor is bound to offer presents, rather than to live riotously at the expense of her he loves."

At this reproach the aspirants to her hand were eager to vie with one another in generosity. Each sent his servant for some precious gift to lay before her, one offering a richly embroidered garment, one a string of amber beads, one a pair of glittering ear-rings, another a costly necklace, and so forth. Penelope had all their presents taken up to her chamber, to which she presently retired without noticing the beggar, who chuckled to see how his prudent wife had the art to spoil those spoilers.

When she was gone, the suitors fell to singing and dancing by torchlight; and Odysseus was content to hold the torches for them in his own hall, still mocked and insulted by the lusty revellers. One of them, Eurymachus, scornfully asked what work he could do, and if he were too lazy to take a servant's place, instead of strolling about the country as a useless beggar. To this the hero boldly replied—

"I wish, at any work we two were tried,
In height of spring-time, when heaven's lights are long,
I a good crook'd scythe that were sharp and strong,
You such another, where the grass grew deep,
Up by day-break, and both our labours keep
Up till slow darkness eased the labouring light,
Fasting all day, and not a crumb till night;
We then should prove our either workmanship.
Or if, again, beeves, that the goad or whip
Were apt t'obey before a tearing plow,
Big lusty beasts, alike in bulk and brow,
Alike in labour, and alike in strength,
Our task four acres, to be till'd in length
Of one sole day; again then you should try
If the dull glebe before the plow should fly,
Or I a long stitch could bear clean and even.
Or lastly, if the Guide of earth and heaven
Should stir stern war up, either here or there,
And that at this day I had double spear,
And shield, and steel casque fitting for my brows;
At this work likewise, 'midst the foremost blows,
Your eyes should note me, and get little cause
To twit me with my belly's sole applause."

—Chapman

The man who was so ready to rail at other idlers, he ended, might talk big among those that knew no better; but if Odysseus came to the house, its wide gates would be too narrow for this vaunter's haste to be off.

Eurymachus was so angry on being thus spoken back to, that he flung a stool at the impudent beggar, but only managed to hit the cup-bearer and spill a jug of wine, while Odysseus took refuge beside Amphinomus. The uproar was now past bearing, and Telemachus begged of the drunken crew that they would have done with it. Amphinomus backed him up in declaring that it was, indeed, time for bed. So after a parting cup of wine and water, and a drink offering to the gods, they all went off, each to his own quarters, leaving father and son alone together.

No sooner were they unwatched than Odysseus bade Telemachus help him in hiding away the arms and armour that hung round the hall. If the suitors missed them, excuse might be made that the bright metal was begrimed by smoke, or that weapons were as well out of the way of men like to fall quarrelling over their wine. Only a couple of swords, spears, and shields were left at hand, ready for their own use when the time came. This done, his father sent the youth to bed, he himself sitting up to talk to Penelope.

All being at last quiet, Penelope came down into the hall with her maids, who cleared the disordered banquet-board, and made up the fire, beside which their mistress sat on her chair of ivory inlaid with silver. One of the maids spoke sharply to Odysseus, and would have turned him out; but Penelope rebuked her, ordering a seat to be set for the old beggar, that she might hear what he had to tell of the husband ever in her mind.

Strange to say, sitting with him in the firelight, she did not know that long-parted spouse, nor did she recognize his voice when she began by asking who and whence he was, and he put the question off by declaring himself a man of sorrows, who would fain not recall his past. Yet she took him at once into her confidence, explaining her woeful plight, and the device by which she had so long warded off the importunity of her suitors, weaving diligently at that costly web but by night secretly undoing the labour of the day.

Glad as he was to learn her faithfulness, not yet would Odysseus reveal to this patient wife that her widowhood was at an end. With his wonted craft, he spun a story of how he came from Crete, and how he had there made acquaintance with Odysseus, nor did her emotion stir him to betray himself.

> "She listened, melting into tears
> That flowed as when on mountain height the snow,
> Shed by the west-wind, feels the east-wind's breath,[2]
> And flows in water, and the hurrying streams
> Are filled, so did Penelope's fair cheeks
> Seem to dissolve in tears — tears shed for him
> Who sat beside her even then. He saw
> His weeping wife, and pitied her at heart;
> Yet were his eyes like iron or like horn,
> And moved not in their lids; for artfully
> He kept his tears from falling."
>
> —W. C. Bryant

Twenty years had passed, ran his tale, since he thus saw Odysseus; and in proof he described the very mantle that chief wore and the gold brooch fastening it, which with fresh tears she could remember as her parting gifts. But quite lately he had heard of her husband as on his way home, well and wealthy; and he called the gods to witness his firm belief that ere long she would see the long-lost one restored to her.

"So may it be!" sighed Penelope; "and if thy good news come true, it shall not go without reward."

With that she would have bidden her maids spread a soft bed for the stranger;

but he laughed off all such luxury as unfit for a hardy sailor. No maids to wait on him, unless same elderly woman to wash his feet! Penelope gave him to the charge of Eurycleia, the head of her household, who put him to confusion by remarking how like he was to Odysseus in figure and in voice. This old servant had been his own nurse, and he had to hide his face from the firelight lest she should know him. But as she was bathing his legs in warm water, she found on his knee the scar given him in youth by a wild boar, a wound she herself had dressed and could not now mistake it. In her surprise she let his foot fall, upsetting the bath. For a moment amazement tied her tongue, then she would have cried out her

Penelope
After the statue by R. J. Wyatt

master's name, had he not caught her by the throat, drawing her close to whisper a command of silence. He was indeed Odysseus, come to cleanse his house of its foes, but on pain of her life she must not disclose him yet. The joyful old crone promised secrecy, and without a word fetched more hot water to finish her task; after which he went to warm himself at the fire, taking care to hide that scar beneath his rags.

There, before she left the hall, Penelope again addressed him. She told how, lying in bed, turning over in her sad mind whether to remain true to the memory of Odysseus, or to rid her son's heritage of this locust swarm of suitors, if she let herself be led off by one of them as his wife, she had fallen into a dream in which she saw her flock of fat geese scattered and slain by an eagle swooping from the skies. Her guest readily interpreted that dream as a presage of Odysseus being at hand to harry the greedy suitors. But she shook her head, saying how false dreams came through the gate of ivory, as well as true ones through the gate of horn. Another device, she let him know, had come into her mind. One of her husband's feats had been to send an arrow straight through twelve axe-heads set up in a row. To this test she proposed to invite the suitors before another sun set; then whichever of them could bend the great bow of Odysseus and rival his unerring aim, him she would take for her new lord.

Let her so do without delay, replied the stranger, for he took on himself to say that before any one of that crew could bend his bow, Odysseus himself would be among them.

Penelope declared herself so pleased by his counsels that she could have stayed up all night to listen to him; but sleep was needful to mortals. Leaving her guest, then, to the care of the servants, she went to the chamber in which night by night she had bedewed her lonely couch with tears ever since Odysseus left her for that woeful war.

It was long before Odysseus could sleep on the bull's hide and heap of sheepskins where old Eurycleia wrapped him up with a warm coverlet. Lying in the silent hall, he heard outside the wanton laughter of the maidservants, debauched by those insolent interlopers; and his heart burned to understand into what disorder they had brought his house. He could hardly restrain himself from springing up to make an end to such unseemly riot; but he tried to keep patient for one more night.

> "Bear up, my soul, a little longer yet;
> A little longer to thy purpose cling!
> For, in the day when the dire Cyclops ate
> Thy valiant friends, a far more horrible thing
> Thou didst endure, till wit had power to bring
> Thee from that den where thou did'st think to die."
>
> —Worsley

And as he tossed from side to side, scheming how he, one against so many, should avenge himself on the spoilers of his wife and son, Athena stood over him, assuring him of her aidance, and shedding the balm of forgetfulness upon his fevered eyes. So he slept that night in his own home.

❧

5 The Day of Doom

That night Penelope awoke from a dream of her husband; then grief to think that soon she must take a less worthy spouse made the house resound with her weeping. Thus roused, at daybreak, Odysseus stepped forth into the open air, and lifting his hands to heaven, prayed Zeus for some sign of favour. The response was a peal of thunder that cheered not his heart alone. In the outer court, where the suitors had been wont to take pastime by casting quoits or hurling spears at a mark, he stood beside the mill at which twelve women were kept hard at work grinding corn for that insatiate company: one of them, weaker than the rest, had been up all night at her task, but now she paused in it to exclaim—

"Thunder from a clear sky is a lucky omen: would it might mean the last time those tyrants of mine are to feast in the house of Odysseus!"

The hero overheard her, and took her words too for a good omen. Now sunrise set all the household astir. The maids lit the fires, swept and sprinkled the floors, wiped the tables, and cleaned the vessels under the eye of old Eurycleia. Some of them came out to fetch water from the fountain, while menservants fell to chopping firewood. Today was to be a feast in honour of Apollo, when it behoved to have everything of the best.

Up came Eumaeüs driving in three fat pigs for the banquet; he greeted Odysseus kindly, and asked how it fared with him among the rude suitors. Next came Melantheus with his goats, who still growled at the beggar, promising him a taste of his fist, if he did not go off to beg elsewhere. Odysseus bowed his head without a word. More friendly was a third cattle-herd, Philoetius, who, after saluting the stranger, guessed him to be one that had seen better days.

"No, he reminds me of our good master, who perhaps is wandering about in like rags, if he is still in the land of the living. So must I go on rearing his cattle to be devoured by a crew that care neither for gods nor men! I have often thought of running away; but the hope holds me that Odysseus may yet come back to send them packing."

"Friend," murmured the hero, "I vow by Zeus that you shall see Odysseus slaying these usurpers."

249

"Gladly would I lend a hand," answered the faithful herdsman; and Eumaeüs, too, prayed that he might see that day.

Telemachus, having risen and dressed, still feigned not to notice his father, though he carefully enquired from Eurycleia as to the guest's entertainment. Soon arrived the suitors who had been plotting to kill the young master. But, as they hatched their plot, an eagle with a dove in its claws flew by on the left, and this Amphinomus took for an unfavourable omen; so they agreed to spare Telemachus for the present, giving themselves up to another day of revelry.

After due sacrifices they sat down to dinner and were waited on by the herdsmen. Telemachus had seated his father at a table apart, where he got his portion of meat and wine served to him like the rest; and today the young master plainly bid the suitors that they know that this was his house, in which he would not have a guest insulted. In spite of such a warning, one ribald fellow named Ctesippus jestingly flung an ox foot at the old beggar, who ducked his head with a bitter smile, and it hit the wall. Had it not missed, exclaimed Telemachus, he would have run Ctesippus through with his spear: let them kill him at once, if they pleased; but he could no longer bear to see his house turned upside down by them.

So bold was his tone, that for a little the suitors sat rebuked, till one of them, Agelaus, spoke up for the rest. If Telemachus were so anxious to get rid of them, why did he not persuade his mother to choose a new husband, now that there was no chance of her seeing Odysseus again? To this the young man protested that he did not hinder his mother from making a choice, but neither would he press her to leave his own house. That quarrel passed off, for the suitors now grew warm with wine; and Athena was at work stealing their wits. They took to mad laughter till they cried, then in their bleared eyes the meat before them seemed gory, as some dark shade of coming ill fell on their heedless hearts. One of those who sat at table was the seer Theoclymenus, who had come with Telemachus from Sparta, and he suddenly started up with a cry.

"'What is the fate of evil doom
Now threatening you, unhappy race?
I see that night in thickest gloom
Wraps every limb, and form, and face.

"'Out bursts like fire the voice of moan,
Drowned are your cheeks with sorrow's flood;
And every wall and pillared stone
Is soaked and dabbled in your blood.

"'Through hall and porch, full many a ghost
Crowds towards the mansion of the dead;
The sun from out the heavens is lost,
And clouds of darkness rushing spread.'

"He ceased, and they with jocund cheer
Into glad peals of laughter broke.
Eurymachus addressed the seer,
And thus in taunting accent spoke.

"'Mad is the new-come guest. 'T is meet
Instant to take him from our sight,
And lead him to the public street
Since he mistakes the day for night.'

"Then thus replied the seer divine:
'From thee no guide shall I request,
For eyes, and ears, and feet, are mine,
And no weak soul inspires my breast.

"'Then from this fated house I go;
Swift comes the destined vengeance on;
None shall escape the deadly blow
Of all the suitors – no, not one.'"

—William Maginn

He burst out, foreseeing the tragedy at hand; while the youngest suitors sneered at Telemachus:

"Strange guests has this house! First we sit down with an idle beggar, then with a fellow who sets up for a diviner. Let us ship off the pair of them to sell as slaves for what they will fetch!"

Telemachus said not a word, but kept an eye on his father, awaiting the signal for action. And the suitors, little aware what a supper was in store for them, went on with their day-long banquet, till it was broken up by Penelope's appearance in the hall. She bore the huge bow and quiver, stored away for years, that had been given her husband by a hero of old; and behind her the handmaids carried in a chest full of steel and bronze axes. All eyes turned upon the lady, who, standing by a pillar of the hall, her face hidden by a veil, gave forth mistressfully—

"Hearken to me, ye arrogant suitors, who day by day
Afflict mine house with devouring and drinking its wealth alway,
While my lord hath been long time gone: and through all this weary tide
Could your false hearts find for your lips no word-pretence beside,
Save this, that each of you sorely desired to win me his bride.
Come, suitors – for this is the contest appointed your wooing to end—
I will set you the mighty bow of Odysseus the hero divine:
Whosoe'er of you all with his hands shall the bow most easily bend,
And shoot through the rings of the axes twelve ranged all in line,
Him will I follow, forsaking this beautiful home of mine—

251

Dear home, that knew me a bride, with its wealth of abundant store!
I shall never forget it; in dreams I shall see it for evermore."

—A. S. Way

With this she bade Eumaeüs set up the axe-heads in a row, as he began to do in spite of the tears the sight of his master's bow brought to his eyes. Antinous jeered at the swineherd's soft-heartedness; but Telemachus carried out that charge for him, proudly then declaring that he himself must be first to make the trial.

"And if I can accomplish it," quoth he, "with none of you shall my mother go away from this house."

Two, three times he strove to string the stiff bow, but could not bend it. A fourth effort might have hitched the cord into its notch, but at a sign from Odysseus, he gave it up for the others to show their more manly strength.

It was agreed that they should try in turn, going from left to right in the order of their seats at table. And the first to take the bow in hand was Leiodes, a priest, the gentlest and most modest of the suitors, but no man of muscle, and his weak arms soon threw it down in despair. Antinous laughed at so feeble an attempt, yet, seeing that this would be no easy task for the sturdiest of them, he called on Melantheus to light a fire in the court and to bring a ball of lard, to warm and grease the tough wood. But for all they could do to make it supple, one after another tried in vain to bend the bow of Odysseus.

Unable to look on unmoved, Eumaeüs had gone outside with his fellow herd Philoetius. Odysseus followed them to ask—

"Were some god to bring back Odysseus, are you the men to stand by him against those spoilers of his house?"

"Would the gods gave us to prove our fidelity!" was their answer; but they stared when now he told them that he himself was Odysseus.

Not till he pulled aside his rags to show them that well-remembered scar of the boar's tusk, did they recognize their travel-worn master; and they fell upon him with tears and kisses. But this was no time for idle joy. He charged Eumaeüs to see that the bow came lastly into his own hands, then to shut the doors of the women's apartments and keep them out of the way, while Philoetius was at once to bar the outer gates that none should escape.

Followed by those faithful servants, he went back into the house, where Antinous and Eurymachus, the most arrogant of the suitors, were now trying in turn the ordeal that baffled them like the others. Eurymachus was overcome by shame at his failure, but Antinous was for putting off the trial till next day. This feast day of Apollo, he said, was better spent in drinking and making offerings to that heavenly archer, who to-morrow might grant them more strength and skill.

As the wine again went round, out stepped that ragged beggar, demanding the bow that he might try whether adversity had unstrung his sinews.

"Is the fellow drunk!" cried scornful Antinous, rebuked by Penelope, whose will was that this stranger too should have his chance. Thereupon Telemachus stood up to announce that he only had the right to say who should handle his father's bow. He asked his mother to leave the hall and keep to her own apartments with the women: such disputes were for a man to settle.

When Penelope had retired, Eumaeüs was for bringing the bow to Odysseus, but the suitors raised so high an outcry that he would have put it down, had not Telemachus hotly ordered him not to mind them. The bow, then, was given to the beggar, who at once began handling it carefully and lovingly, turning it over to make sure the horns had not been worm-eaten in all those years. The suitors took for certain he could make nothing of it; but to their consternation he strung it as lightly as a bard tunes his lyre, and twanged the tight cord so that it twittered like a swallow at his touch. At that moment there came a peal of thunder overhead to stir up his heart; but the suitors turned pale, as the seeming beggar fixed an arrow on the bowstring, and without rising from his seat, he shot it straight through the heads of the twelve axes, not one missed.[3]

"Your guest, Telemachus, has not put you to shame!" he cried exultingly.

With proud glance he gave a signal that brought the eager youth to his side, sword and spear in hand, while, as if by magic, the beggar stood up in appalling might.

> "Then fierce the hero o'er the threshold strode
> Stripped of his rags, he blazed out like a god.
> Full in their face the lifted bow he bore
> And quivered deaths, a formidable store.
> Before his feet the rattling shower he threw,
> And thus terrific to the suitor-crew:
> 'One venturous game this hand has won today,
> Another, princes, yet remains to play!'"

Therewith he let fly the first deadly shaft. Antinous had raised a cup of wine to quench his dismay, when it struck him on the throat, and he rolled over, dragging the table and the meats on it to the floor, where the wine mingled with his blood, such a slip was there between the cup and the lip. The other suitors started to their feet, still not fully aware what a fate was upon them all, and they angrily cried out at the man who had killed their comrade, by mischance as they thought, till they heard his voice above the uproar.

"Dogs, did you think Odysseus dead? You have wasted my substance, you have debauched my servants, you have sought to take my wife. Now shall you die, as enemies of gods and men!"

At the very name of Odysseus that trembling band shrank before him; and Eurymachus, speaking for the rest, would have softened the hero's rage.

"We have indeed done you wrong," he confessed. "But Antinous was foremost in the trespass that has cost him his life. Spare us, and we will make amends, paying for our misdeeds in gold and bronze and oxen."

"All that you own is too little to make amends for what you owe me," was the fierce answer. "But I shall take payment in full. You must fight for your lives, forfeit to my vengeance."

When they saw that there was no hope of mercy, the terrified suitors had to stand on their defence. They looked vainly for the arms hung round the hall, which through the night had been hidden. Drawing their swords, they caught up the overturned tables to serve as shields, and rushed in a body upon Odysseus. But their leader Eurymachus fell with an arrow in his heart; and when Amphinomus took his place, Telemachus brought him too to the ground, transfixed by a spear; then the rest drew back to take hurried counsel and to look about for some way of escape.

While Odysseus held them in check with his arrows, Telemachus hastened to bring from the storeroom arms for Eumaeüs and Philoetius. The traitor Melantheus, having stolen along back ways, was doing the same for the enemy; but his fellow herds caught him in the storeroom, and hung him helplessly to the rafters to await further punishment. Odysseus had kept on shooting down the suitors one by one, so long as his arrows lasted.

They fled back into the courtyard as far as might be out of reach of his deadly aim; and he took his stand at a postern, their only way of escape, soon with three well-armed men at his side, indeed four, for Athena appeared by him in the likeness of his old friend Mentor. Before long, indeed, she took a more shadowy form, soaring up to hover above the fight, warding off the spears of the foemen from Odysseus, or flashing dismay into their eyes with her terrible aegis.

Still outnumbering that little band, they huddled together at the farther end of the court, like cattle tormented by flies, and let themselves be slain helplessly as doves by vultures. Leiodes the priest fell at the knees of Odysseus praying for mercy, as aforetime he had prayed that the hero might never return; but his prayers did not avail him. More fortunate was Phemius the bard, who pleaded, nor in vain, that he had been forced into singing for the godless crew. Medon the herald also was spared at the request of Telemachus, to whom in his boyhood this man had been kind, and he had warned Penelope of the suitors' plot against her son. These two fearfully clung to the altar of Zeus, but the rest lay gasping in their blood, like a net full of fish drawn on the beach; and Odysseus went from one quivering corpse to another to make sure that they would trouble him no more.

When all was over, he sent Telemachus to call Eurycleia. She found her master ranging up and down like a lion over the prey; and when she saw the ground strewn with the enemies of his house, the old nurse raised an exultant cry, at once silenced by Odysseus—

"Women, experienced as thou art, control
Indecent joy, and feast thy secret soul.
To insult the dead is cruel and unjust,
Fate and their crime have sunk them to the dust."

What he sought from her was to know which of the servants had been misled by the suitors. Of fifty maids that made the household, she pointed out twelve as unfaithful to their duty and their mistress. These he ordered to be hanged; and Melantheus, too, was now put to a cruel death for taking the part of his master's foes. Lastly, the executioners washed their hands and feet; then Odysseus had fire lit and sulphur burnt on it to purify his house from the reek of blood.

This done, the doors were unlocked, behind which Penelope and her maids had been shut up safe from harm. They came forth astonished to find the house cleansed from its plague; but not even yet could Penelope believe that the ragged and gore-grimed beggar was her husband: only some god, she thought, could have so dealt with that throng of oppressors. In vain Telemachus besought her to speak to his father. She turned away her eyes and stood dumb for amazement.

Odysseus bid the bard Phemius strike his lyre to set the servants dancing, sounds of revelry that brought a crowd about the house outside, little aware what had gone on within, but taking it that Penelope's wedding was come at last. Meanwhile, the hero retired with old Eurycleia to the bath, from which he came forth washed and anointed, in goodly clothes, looking like a god indeed, for Athena had breathed over him an air of more than manly beauty.

Still Penelope was hard of belief that it could be her own husband who sat down before her. To try him, she ordered Eurycleia bring out the bed of Odysseus from his chamber.

"No," said he, "there is no man living can move that bed, unless some god aid him. For I built this house round an olive tree, and the stump I dressed to be the post of my bridal bed, as is known only to me and to you."

That proof broke down Penelope's lingering disbelief. She threw her arms round her husband's neck, with tears, kisses, and excuses for having been so slow to own him.

"'Frown not, Odysseus; thou art wise and true!
But God gave sorrow, and hath grudged to make
Our path to old age sweet, nor willed us to partake

"'Youth's joys together. Yet forgive me this,
Nor hate me that when first I saw thy brow
I fell not on thy neck, and gave no kiss,
Nor wept in thy dear arms as I weep now.
For in my breast a bitter fear did bow
My soul, and I lived shuddering day by day,

Lest a strange man come hither, and avow
False things, and steal my spirit, and bewray
My love; such guile men scheme, to lead the pure astray.'

"Sweet as to swimmers the dry land appears,
Whose bark Poseidon in the angry sea
Strikes with a tempest, and in pieces tears,

And a few swimmers from the white deep flee,
Crested with salt foam, and with tremulous knee
Spring to the shore exulting; even so
Sweet was her husband to Penelope,
Nor from his neck could she at all let go
Her white arms, nor forbid her thickening tears to flow."

—Worsley

Much had the so-long-sundered pair to hear and tell between them. The whole night would not have been enough for the story of twenty years, had not Athena drawn out their rapturous hours by her guardian care, holding back the fleet steeds of Eos beneath the ocean, to lengthen the night after that day when Odysseus came to his own.

6 The End of the Odyssey

But not yet were the hero's trials at an end. Next day he went to visit his aged father Laërtes, who lived at a farm some way from the town. Odysseus found him working alone in his vineyard, sorrily dressed and bowed down by years of grief for his lost son. Tears filled the wanderer's eyes to see him so woebegone; yet this crafty man, after his wont, must needs play on broken heart-strings by a freshly feigned tale. He went up to the half-blind greybeard with a story of his having met with his son in distant lands; but when Laërtes piteously lamented him as one dead and gone, he could not bear to keep up that deceit.

"Do you not know me?" he cried, throwing his arms round the old man's neck. "I am Odysseus himself!"

But now Laërtes was slow to trust the good fortune despaired of so long. Not till his son had let him see that scar of the boar's tusk would he believe; and all doubt left him, when Odysseus pointed out in the orchard the trees his father had given him in childhood to be his very own. Then Laërtes thanked heaven that the gods still lived to do justice on earth; and joy so worked on his withered heart, that after changing those mean clothes, as sign of mourning laid aside, he seemed to have grown years younger in an hour.

With his household he sat down to feast in honour of his son's return; but soon the merrymaking was disturbed. News having spread of the suitors' fate, their kinsmen and friends had gathered at the house of Odysseus to bear away the dead bodies to their homes in Ithaca and the adjacent isles. Amid their lamentations, they cried loudly for revenge, and the father of Antinous stirred them up against the returned hero who had worked such woe to them and theirs. Others spoke for peace, saying that the dead men had brought their doom upon themselves; but, while half of the crowd dispersed to their own homes, the rest hurried off to fall upon Odysseus in his father's house.

At the noise of their approach, the servants of Laërtes flew to arms, the old man himself donning armour he could hardly bear. They sallied forth to meet the foe, with Odysseus at their head, and by his side Telemachus eager to show himself worthy son of so brave a father. Already the spears had begun to whiz and to clang upon helmet and shield, when Zeus sent a thunderbolt to stay their hands, and an awful voice forbade further slaughter. Thereupon Athena herself appeared in the form of Mentor between the hostile bands, who at her command dropped their arms to make a covenant of atonement and goodwill.

So ends the story of Homer's Ody*ssey;* but other legends tell of further adventures in which the hero vanished. His death, it had been prophesied, should come out of the sea; and after so many wanderings he may well have found it hard to live on land at ease. In Hades, Tiresias had enjoined on him a penance whereby he might appease the anger of Poseidon: he must seek out a people that never saw the sea, nor knew of ships, nor tasted salt; he should go among them bearing an oar which the simple folk would mistake for a winnowing fan; and upon this sign he was to sacrifice a ram, a boar, and a bull to that offended deity, with offerings to the other gods: thus he might end his days in peace and honour.

We hear nothing of how this penance was performed, but only that, once more deserting Penelope and giving up his kingdom to Telemachus, the bold Odysseus again sailed to tempt fortune on unknown seas. Later bards had glimpses, as in a vision, of how it may have fared with him in some new world of waters and enchanted islands. Tennyson imagines for us what must have been the dauntless and restless mind of such a hero in his shortening days.

> "My mariners,
> Souls that have toil'd and wrought, and thought with me—
> That ever with a frolic welcome took
> The thunder and the sunshine, and opposed
> Free hearts, free foreheads – you and I are old;
> Old age hath yet his honour and his toil;
> Death closes all: but something ere the end

257

Some work of noble note, may yet be done,
Not unbecoming men that strove with Gods.
The lights begin to twinkle from the rocks:
The long day wanes: the slow moon climbs: the deep
Moans round with many voices. Come my friends,
'Tis not too late to seek a newer world.
Push off and sitting well in order smite
The sounding furrows; for my purpose holds
To sail beyond the sunset and the baths
Of all the western stars, until I die.
It may be that the gulfs will wash us down:
It may be we shall touch the Happy Isles,
And see the great Achilles, whom we knew.
Tho' much is taken much abides; and tho'
We are not now that strength which in old days
Moved earth and heaven; that which we are, we are;
One equal temper of heroic hearts,
Made weak by time and fate but strong in will
To strive to seek, to find and not to yield."

[1] (p. 218) As in the case of the *Iliad*, translations not otherwise marked are from Pope.

[2] (p. 246) It is hardly necessary to point out that the poet has not our insular climate in view.

[3] (p. 253) Commentators have puzzled themselves over the shape of the axe-heads through which this shot had to be made, whether rings, curved notches, the gap between two-headed axes, or what. There is also controversy as to the arrangement of the house: we may best conceive of the banqueting hall as a roofed space or cloister opening at one side upon an inner courtyard in which the axes were set up, beyond which again came an outer enclosure. As to the geography of the poem, *savants* who have variously mapped the hero's course, seem to forget that poets hold masters' certificates to navigate seas of fancy.

Hero and Leander

The Trojan land had tales of love as well as of war. Who has not heard of Leander, bold youth of Abydus, he that wooed fair Hero, Aphrodite's priestess at her shrine on the Thracian shore? Many lovers sighed for a maid fit to rank among the Graces; yet she smiled upon none but Leander, who lived at once so near and so far from her temple-dwelling at Sestus. For the strong tide of the Hellespont rolled between them night and day; and their eyes strained across it to catch each other's smiles thrown in vain from Europe to Asia.

But all-powerful love can find a way over the wildest water. At the close of each day, as Hesperus led in the stars, Leander stole down beside the Mysian strand, his eager eyes watching for the light of a torch with which Hero nightly beckoned him through the darkness to her sea-washed tower. That was signal for him to plunge into the waves, swimming swift and strong athwart the sundering current till, guided by that friendly gleam, he came safe across to rest in the arms of his Thracian bride. When dawn spread in the eastern sky, he anointed his limbs afresh with oil, and, all aglow from a parting kiss, swam back to Abydus, "himself the pilot, passenger and bark".

So he did throughout the summer weather, night by night, and all went well. Then came rough winter, bringing clouds and chills and tempests, and alas!

> "That night of stormy water
> When Love, who sent forgot to save
> The young, the beautiful the brave,
> The lonely hope of Sestus' daughter.
> Oh! when alone along the sky
> Her turret torch was blazing high,
> Though rising gale and breaking foam
> And shrieking sea-birds warned him home,
> And clouds aloft and tides below,
> With signs and sounds forbade to go—
> He could not see, he would not hear,
> Or sound or sign foreboding fear;

His eye but saw that light of love,
The only star it hailed above;
His ear but rang with Hero's song
'Ye waves, divide not lovers long!"

—Lord Byron

That stout swimmer had not shrunk from the roaring billows, on which for once he was tossed astray, now dragged down below the black water, now heaved up to catch a glimpse of the beacon that should be his guiding star. His breath failed him; his strokes grew feebler; chill spray and blinding foam hooded his eyes bent longingly towards the flickering torch. Suddenly it went out, when, through the howl of the storm, he might well-nigh have heard Hero's exclamation where she stood vainly trying to shield the light with her robe.

Anxiously she watched out the dark night, at once hoping and fearing that Leander had not ventured his perilous passage. But when, by the first gleam of day, she looked forth from her tower, it was to see his white body washed upon the rocks below, and the sullen foam stained by his blood. With one miserable cry, tearing off her priestly vestments, she leaped into the waves, to die beside her lover and be united to him in fame.

The Last Watch of Hero
From the painting by Lord Leigton P.R.A.

Cupid and Psyche

1 Aphrodite's Rival

Once upon a time a king and queen had three fair daughters, of whom the two eldest at fit time came to wed princely suitors. But the youngest, Psyche, was so wondrously beautiful that no one dared woo her, who seemed worthy rather of adoration. Men gazed at her from afar as at a goddess, and the rumour went that this was no mortal maiden, but Aphrodite herself revealed on earth to show her matchless charms in flesh and blood.

So eager was all the world to behold this prodigy, that far and wide the altars of the true goddess stood cold and silent, her chief shrines at Cnidus, Paphos, and Cythera deserted by the crowds flocking to strew flowers under the feet of Psyche. The jealous Aphrodite, seeing herself neglected for such a rival, called on her son to avenge her with his mischievous arrows.

"Inflame her heart with love, but with hottest love for the meanest wretch alive, so that together they may come to poverty and sorrow!"

Young Cupid needed not the kisses and caresses with which she would have coaxed him to such an errand. Ever too ready to play his cruel tricks, he promised to do his mother's bidding, and flew off to work harm for Psyche. But at the first sight of her beauty he was so amazed that he dropped on his foot the shaft he had made ready for her, and so became wounded by the enchantment of his own weapon. Himself unseen, he loved this mortal as hotly as he thought to make her love some unworthy man.

> "From place to place Love followed her that day,
> And ever fairer to his eyes she grew,
> So that at last when from her bower he flew,
> And underneath his feet the moonlit sea
> Went shepherding his waves disorderly,
> He swore that of all gods and men no one
> Should hold her in his arms but he alone;

That she should dwell with him in glorious wise
Like to a goddess in some paradise;
Yea, he would get from Father Jove this grace
That she should never die, but her sweet face
And wonderful fair body should endure
Till the foundations of the mountains sure
Were molten in the sea; so utterly
Did he forget his mother's cruelty."

—William Morris

Meanwhile it grieved Psyche's parents that so many came to wonder at but none to wed their youngest daughter, left at home like a virgin-widow, lamenting her too renowned charms. The anxious father sought an oracle of Apollo to know how she should find a husband; and the answer filled him with dread. On the top of a high rocky mountain, he was told, he must leave his daughter alone in bridal array. There should she be wooed by one of whom the very gods stood in fear: she whom men likened to Aphrodite was worthy of no common mate.

Hard was it to part with their daughter thus; but her parents dared not disobey the oracle. At nightfall they led her up the mountain, with a wedding train that seemed rather a funeral, for the light of the torches burned dim, and the songs of the bridesmaids turned to dirges, and poor Psyche was fain to dry her tears with her bridal veil. But having resigned herself to this strange fate as the will of the gods, she strove to comfort her weeping friends. The top of the mountain reached, they quenched the torches, and with tearful farewells left the maiden alone at dead of night as if borne here to her tomb.

When all were gone, Psyche stood shuddering in the chill darkness, so full of fear that she had almost called them to stay, or hurried after their footsteps while still heard on the mountain side. But soon came a gentle Zephyr that softly wrapped her about and carried her away to lay her on a bed of scented flowers, where all the rest of the night she slept off her sadness and weariness.

Daylight awoke her to look round in wonder. Close at hand, she saw a grove of tall trees, through which flowed a crystal stream, and on its banks stood a house so noble that it appeared the home of a god. The roof of costly woods was borne up by golden and ivory pillars; the floor was paved with coloured marbles, and the walls glowed with pictures inlaid in gems and precious metals. When Psyche ventured to enter, she found vast inner halls, more and more splendid and filled with treasures from every part of the earth. Everywhere was lit by a gleam of gold shining like the sun. What seemed most marvellous, all these riches were unguarded, every door stood open, and no living form came to view, as she went, lost in astonishment at the wealth of their unknown lord.

"Who can it be that owns so many rich and beautiful things!" she cried out at length; and soft voices answered her, though as yet she saw no human form.

"All are yours, Psyche! And we are your servants, appointed to wait on you. Command us as you wish, and it shall be done."

When she was tired of wandering through the palace, and feasting her eyes on its beauty, Psyche took courage to try what such invisible attendants could do for her. Having refreshed herself by bathing in a bath of silver, she took her place at a golden table that was at once spread with the finest fare; then as she ate and drank, soft music arose and a choir of sweet voices filled the room where she sat alone.

So the day passed by as in a dream; and when night fell, she would have lain down on a soft couch spread for her by those unseen hands. Now was she aware of a shadow by her side, and had almost cried out for terror. But her fears were kissed away as she found herself warmly embraced in the darkness, and heard a voice murmuring in kindest tones—

"Dear Psyche, I am the husband chosen for you by destiny. Ask not my name, seek not to see my face; only believe in my love, and all will be well with us!"

The very sound of his voice and the very touch of his hand won Psyche's heart to this unseen bridegroom. All night he told her of his love, and before day-light dawned, he was gone, since so it must be, promising with a kiss to return as soon as darkness fell.

Thus it was, night after night, that went by in tender speeches and endearments; yet never could she see her lover's face.

2 The Jealous Sisters

Psyche rejoiced in the love of this husband who came to her only by night; but sad were the long days through which she had to live alone. She soon wearied of wandering about her splendid house that seemed like a gilded cage; the daintiest food did not please her so long as no one shared it; the sunlit hours went too slowly by in sighing for the darkness that should bring back the joy of her life. In vain she begged him not to leave her by day, when she might see his face.

"It may not be," he whispered, and sealed her lips with kisses. "A dire danger threatens you, if you should know who or what I am. Be content to trust in my love, that is ever yours."

Strive as she might to be content, still poor Psyche pined in that daily solitude; and she besought her unseen husband to let her have at least a visit from her sisters to cheer her in his absence.

"Dearest Psyche!" cried he, "I fear they will come to do you harm. Already they seek you on the rocky crest where you were last seen of men; but they bring hate and peril for our love."

Yet she wept and entreated, till in the end he gave her leave to see her sisters, making her promise to tell them nothing about himself. So next morning, when he vanished with daylight, the same Zephyr that had wafted Psyche to this beautiful valley, was charged to catch up her two sisters and bring them to the house in which she lived alone with invisible attendants.

Glad was she to see them again, and not less amazed were they by the riches and adornments of her new home. But when eagerly they questioned her as to the master of all this wealth, she put them off with short answers. Her husband, she said, was a handsome young prince who stayed out all day hunting in the woods. And lest she should be tempted by their curiosity to say more, she made haste to dismiss the sisters with costly presents before the hour that should bring him to her arms.

But they, filled with envy of her good fortune, came back next day set on knowing who could be that great lord so much richer than their own husbands. With caresses they again sought to worm the secret out of her; and this time, forgetting what she had said of him before, she gave out her husband as a grey-bearded merchant, whose affairs called him often away from home. Nor did the sisters fail to note how she contradicted herself, so letting them understand she had something to hide.

Again dismissed with rich presents, the jealous elders were hotter than ever to know the secret of Psyche's marriage. They guessed that this husband of hers must be no mere man, and enviously railed at her for making a mystery of his real name. So they hatched a plot, of which he was well aware, for that night he murmured in her ear—

"Dearest one, beware of thy sisters. Tomorrow they will tempt you to look on me; but that would be the end of our happiness."

With tears and kisses Psyche vowed she would rather die a hundred times than disobey his least wish; and when left alone in the morning, she was determined to keep her secret. But soon came the sisters, who now coaxed and threatened her by turns, till in her confusion she owned to not having told them the truth. At last they pressed her to a confession that she had never seen this bridegroom who visited her only by dark night, and that she knew not even his name.

"Dear sister," said they, "it is as we feared. Believe us, who are older and wiser, and mean thy welfare. That false bridegroom is in truth a loathly monster that dared not meet the eye, lest love should be changed to horror. For all his fair words, his purpose is to devour thee secretly; and such will soon be Psyche's fate unless she act by our counsel."

"What shall I do?" cried Psyche, wringing her hands, for she believed their false words, knowing not why her husband should otherwise remain ever unseen.

"Have ready a lamp and a sharp knife," they bid her. "As soon as he is asleep, light the lamp, then the sight of the monster's hateful form will steel your hand to drive the knife to his cruel heart. Thus only can you save your own life."

Earnestly urging her to follow their counsel without delay, her sisters left Psyche tossed in mind like the waves of the sea. She doubted whether to obey them or her own heart. She at once loved her unseen husband and hated the monster they pictured him to be. But as night drew near, she made ready the lamp and the knife, with which she hoped to find courage to save herself from the threatened destruction.

As always, her husband came home with the darkness, and after embracing Psyche, lay down in bed. Curiosity now aiding dread, she made up her mind at least to see what shape he bore. When his breathing told that he was asleep, she rose to light the lamp; then holding it up in one hand and the sharp knife in the other, she stole softly to his side.

A cry had almost burst from her lips, as the lamp-gleam showed the sweetest and loveliest of monsters, Cupid himself in the bloom of youthful beauty, with ambrosial locks curling about his rosy cheeks, and snow-white shoulders on which his wings were softly folded like flowers. At such a sight the knife dropped from Psyche's trembling hand. Beside him lay his bow and quiver, whence she drew out one of the golden-tipped arrows, and in examining it pricked her finger, instantly inflaming her blood with new love for a husband no longer unseen.

Bending over this sleeping form, she would have hastily stooped to kiss him, when in her agitation she let a drop of hot oil fall from the lamp upon his shoulder. Roused by the pain, Cupid sprang up, and at a glance understood all.

"Ah, Psyche!" he exclaimed, "you have ruined our love. Why listen to your treacherous sisters rather than to my warning? Now we must part for ever!"

In tearful entreaties she sank before him, and sought to clasp his knees; but he spread his wings and flew into the air without a look of forgiveness. At the same moment, the enchanted palace vanished about her like a dream, then Psyche stood alone in the cold darkness calling vainly for the love she had lost, with his last words ringing in her ears.

> "Farewell! though I, a god, can never know
> How thou canst lose thy pain, yet time will go
> Over thine head, and thou mayst mingle yet
> The bitter and the sweet, nor quite forget,
> Nor quite remember, till these things shall seem
> The wavering memory of a lovely dream."
>
> —William Morris

❧

3 Penance and Pardon

Psyche's first thought, as she turned away from the scene of her lost happiness, was to die in despair. Coming to a river bank, she threw herself into its black water; but the pitiful stream washed her ashore on the further side, and she wandered on, hardly knowing where she went. She passed through the cities where lived her sisters; and these jealous women would have persuaded her that she had done well to follow their advice, since love was a cruel monster, for all the fair shapes he could take. Yet, on hearing truly how it had gone with her, the sisters in turn stole away to the top of that high mountain, each hoping that she herself might be chosen for the bride of a god. Far otherwise it fared with them, when, one after the other, they were caught up by a strong wind and dashed to destruction over the misty cliffs.

Meanwhile Psyche went her way alone through the world, everywhere seeking in vain for her vanished love. He, fevered by the pain of his burnt shoulder, or rather by the same grief as gave Psyche no rest by night and day, had taken refuge in his mother's chamber, and lay sick of a wound he dared not own. But a telltale bird whispered in Aphrodite's ear how Cupid had deigned to love a mortal, and hot was her anger to learn that this was none other than the very maid boasted on earth as her rival.

In sore anger the resentful goddess tended her son with rating and upbraiding. She threatened to take away his arrows, to unstring his bow, to quench his torch and to clip his wings, that he might no more fly about playing mischievous pranks on gods and men. And though she could not bring herself to punish him as he deserved, all the more eagerly she sought out Psyche for her vengeance. In vain her sister goddesses strove to appease her, making excuses for that wilful boy, reminding her that he must not be treated always as a child, asking who might choose a bride if not the god of love, and why marriage should be hateful in her family of all others.

Their jests but stirred the mother of Cupid to further wrath. By leave of Zeus, she sent down Hermes to proclaim through the world that whoever sheltered Psyche should be punished as an enemy to the gods, but seven kisses from Aphrodite herself were offered as reward to whoever gave her up. This proclamation reached poor Psyche's own ears, when, tired of the bootless search for her husband, she was ready to throw herself on his mother's mercy; and, going from one temple to another, some kinder goddess gave her counsel to seek forgiveness at the queen of Love's. Having none other refuge in her hapless plight, as a humble supplicant she approached the halls of Aphrodite, where she had no sooner told her name than one of the servants dragged her by the hair into her mistress's presence.

"At last!" the goddess greeted her with mocking laughter. "At last, you have come to greet your mother-in-law! Or is it to visit that husband of yours, that lies sick through your hurting? I have had trouble enough to catch you; but now you shall not go without learning what it is to rival Aphrodite."

Tearing her clothes for rage, she gave over Psyche to be scourged by sore tormentors who stood ready to obey her will. All day, the offended goddess cast about for means of wreaking her spite against the unwelcome daughter-in-law, who next morning was called to where Aphrodite had mixed up together a heap of wheat, barley, millet, peas, beans, and other seeds.

"Behold!" was her scornful greeting. "An ill-favoured face like yours can earn a husband only by industry; so I will try you at work. Sift me all these seeds, laying each kind apart; and let me see it done by evening."

With this the goddess went off in richest array to a wedding feast, leaving her daughter-in-law a task which she soon gave up as hopeless, and sat down to await fresh chastisement, since so it must be. But a little and took pity on her despair, and called out a troop of his kind to help Cupid's bride. Diligently they ran and carried all day, separating and sorting the different seeds, then vanished when the work was done.

At nightfall Aphrodite came back from the feast, wreathed with roses, scented with odours, and flushed with wine. Darkly she frowned to see how the task had been accomplished.

"This is no work of yours!" she cried, flinging to Psyche a crust of bread, and leaving her to sleep on the bare earth, while the goddess retired to her own luxurious couch. She had taken care to have her son locked up in an inner chamber, lest he and his bride should come to know how near they were to each other.

Next morning Psyche was roused betimes by her tyrant, who led her in sight of a rocky hill, and showed her a thicket at the top, about which fed a flock of wild sheep with fleeces shining like gold.

"They are untamed as lions," Aphrodite told her, "but I must needs have a handful of their golden fleece. Fetch it for me before the sun sets."

In silence Psyche set out on this errand; but soon she thought of throwing herself from the rocks rather than venture to handle such wild beasts, that could hence be seen butting at each other fiercely with their great horns. Then as she looked down upon a deep pool which seemed fit for a grave, the nymph of that fountain spoke from its depths.

"Psyche, defile not with your death my sacred water! I know what troubles you, and can give helpful counsel. Now, in the heat of the sun, the wild creatures play and fight, and it would be dangerous to come near their sharp horns and their venomous teeth. But when they are tired, they will lie down to sleep in the shade; then you may safely steal up to where they have left their fleecy gold, torn by thorns or hanging to the branches."

She took this good advice, and when the sheep lay down to rest, she was able to gather off the thorns a whole lapful of their golden wool, which she brought back long before evening. But obedience still gained her no favour.

"I will try your courage and strength where there will be none to help," said Aphrodite. "Behold that cloudy mountain, from whose crest flows a black stream that waters the Stygian marsh and falls into the fiery river of Cocytus. Haste to fill this crystal urn from its icy source, then bring it back to me before sunset."

Psyche took the urn, and patiently set out on her errand, from which soon she never thought to come back alive. For as she toiled upwards, she saw how the way was guarded by fearsome dragons that from afar glared at her with burning eyes and hissed out of their swelling throats. And the cold stream was its own guard, falling over the slippery cliffs in cataracts that, as they dashed into a dark abyss, warned her back with angry voices.

"What are you doing here? Away, or be swept from our path!"

Long before she got near the top, Psyche sank down like a stone, too much dismayed even for tears.

But a friend was at hand. Overhead hovered the eagle of Zeus, that, mindful how Cupid had guided its course when sent to fly away with Ganymede from Mount Ida, was now willing to serve his hapless bride.

"Weak and unknowing one," screamed the royal bird, as it swooped down upon the mountain side, " can you hope to steal a drop from that sacred spring, or even to approach it? The very gods, indeed Zeus himself, hold its black water in dread. But give the task to me."

She let the urn be snatched away in the eagle's claws, and swiftly it soared over the heads of the spitting dragons, and above the boiling cataracts, into clouds that darkly wrapped the summit; then soon it came back with the urn filled from Stygian springs. Psyche thankfully took it, to carry it carefully down without spilling a drop. Yet not a whit was her mistress appeased.

"Are you, then, a witch, or wicked enchantress, so lightly to finish such perilous tasks?" said Aphrodite mockingly. "But you shall be tried still further, my darling, and learn what it is to have the goddess of love for a foe!"

Aphrodite compelled Psyche to further suffering[1], but those trials had an end. When Cupid got to hear of his mother's cruelty, that made him love Psyche all the more. Escaping secretly from his sick-chamber, he flew up to Olympus, and besought Zeus to favour his wedding with a daughter of men.

" Are you one to ask indulgence at my hands!" said that father of the gods, stroking the lad's smooth face. "On which of us, pray, have you not played those

Cupid and Psyche
From the marble sculpture by Canova

tricks of yours? I myself have been turned into a bull, a swan, or what not, through your frolicsome roguery. But we cherish you kindly as the spoilt child of Olympus, for all your faults; and if I grant your prayer, be mindful of the grace you have ill deserved."

Forthwith Zeus sent out Hermes to summon a meeting of the gods, to which Aphrodite must come among the rest on pain of high displeasure; and Psyche, too, was brought in with downcast eyes that lit up at the sight of her lost lover among the radiant band. When all were assembled, the father of heaven thus addressed them—

"Gods and goddesses, you all know this tricksy boy, who has grown up among us, and whose wild pranks I have often had to chastise. Now he is of an age to settle down, with his wanton restlessness fettered in chains of marriage. He has chosen a bride among the daughters of men, to whom he has plighted his troth for weal or woe. What is done, is done; and so be it! You, mother of love," he turned to Aphrodite, "do not grudge this alliance with a mortal. To make her the equal of her spouse, I raise her among the gods: henceforth let none despise a child of heaven; and you, Psyche, take from me the gift of immortality in reward of your faithful love."

With this he held a goblet of nectar to her trembling lips. Psyche drank the wine of the gods; but the charm of deathlessness that ran through her veins was not such a strong cordial as to find Cupid's arms once more thrown round her, in full light of day. All the gods hailed their union; for even Aphrodite ceased to frown when she saw her son's pouting face now bright with smiles, nor could she scorn a daughter-in-law welcomed to Olympus.

So now their wedding feast was held in the home of the gods. Hephaestus cooked the dishes; Dionysus and Ganymede filled the wine cups. The Seasons wreathed the guests with blooming flowers; the Graces scattered perfumes; the Muses sang sweetly to Apollo's lyre; and who but proud Aphrodite herself led the dance! After all their troubles, Cupid and Psyche were made happy; and their first child was a daughter named Joy. Nor was this last of the immortals the least among them in the eyes of generations to come, and in the honour of poets for her that had no priest.

> "O brightest! though too late for antique vows,
> Too, too late for the fond believing lyre,
> When holy were the haunted forest boughs,
> Holy the air, the water, and the fire;
> Yet even in these days so far retired
> From happy pieties, thy lucent fans,
> Fluttering among the faint Olympians,
> I see, and sing, by my own eyes inspired.
> So let me be thy choir, and make a moan
> Upon the midnight hours;
> Thy voice, thy lute, thy pipe, thy incense sweet
> From swinged censer teeming;
> Thy shrine, thy grove, thy oracle, thy heat
> Of pale-mouthed prophet dreaming."
>
> —John Keats

---

[1] (p. 268) In Apuleius, Psyche's last ordeal is being sent to Hades to seek for Aphrodite a blush of Persephone's beauty. This episode may be here omitted, as repeating the experiences of Orpheus and other adventurers in the nether-world, while the heroine also repeats her fault of curiosity, for, like Pandora, she opens the casket containing the charm, that would have been lost but for Cupid's interference as she lay overcome by a swoon.

The Ring of Polycrates

Of all men in the world none seemed to be more fortunate than Polycrates, tyrant of Samos. That rich island he had mastered by force; and there for a time he reigned along with his two brothers, till having slain one of them and banished the other, he made himself its sole ruler. For long all prospered with him. No day passed but brought news of some victory to his fleet, or some ship came sailing back to the harbour laden with slaves and booty. So mighty grew his power that he hoped to make himself lord of the sea, and of all Ionia, where no city had so many galleys or so well-armed soldiers as Samos.

In the flush of his triumphs, Polycrates offered himself as an ally to Amasis, the great king of Egypt, who at first welcomed his friendship, but soon sent him this message.

"A man ever fortunate has much to fear. None rise to such power as yours without making enemies, and so long as one of them lives, he cannot be secure. No, the gods themselves are jealous of men with whom all goes too well; good and ill by turns make the common lot of mortals. I never heard of any so great as to have no cares, who yet came to a happy end. It were well for you, then, to choose out your richest treasure and offer it as a sacrifice to the gods, that still they may forbear to lay on you tribute of adversity."

Pondering on this counsel, the tyrant judged it wise. After surveying his treasures, he chose out from them an emerald seal-ring of great price, as what he would least like to lose; and this it seemed best to sacrifice. He put out to sea in a sumptuous galley, whence, in the eyes of his courtiers and guards, he solemnly threw the ring into deep water, trusting it might buy him the favour of the gods.

Before reaching home, he grudged that costly gem, and for days he sat reproaching himself for having thrown it away. A week had not passed when a poor fisherman brought to the palace a large fish which he thought worthy to be a present for the lord of Samos, who accepted it as his due. Then soon his servants came running to him with his sparkling ring, found inside the fish when it came to be cut up.

Polycrates took this for a sign his luck would ever be unbroken. He wrote joy-

271

fully to Amasis how he had followed his counsel, but how the gods had given back the precious offering. In answer, to his astonishment, the wise king sent a herald renouncing alliance with him as one who seemed destined to some signal calamity.

Yet the tyrant in his pride would take no warning. It is told of him that, gathering together all who murmured against his rule in Samos, he sent them in a fleet to help Cambyses, king of Persia, in his war on Egypt, since its king shrunk from his friendship. But these exiles, instead of fighting for one they hated, sailed over to Greece, and at Sparta sought aid against their tyrant. Then the Spartans, whose way was to be short in speech as strong in deeds, mocked at the long oration with which the eloquent strangers appealed to them.

"We have forgotten the beginning of it, and do not understand the end," was their answer to the Samian speech.

The men of Asia, then, thinking they no knew how to address these Laconians in their own manner, came back with an empty sack, and this time said no more than "The sack wants meal!" But still the laconic Spartans found fault with this speech as too long: to say "meal" would be enough for them, when the sack was shown empty.

In the end, however, they agreed to send an expedition against Polycrates, whose rich spoils the men of Sparta did not despise, for all that they professed to value no money but what was of iron. But they failed to conquer Samos; or, as some say, Polycrates bought them off with a cheat of lead money cunningly gilded.

Now the tyrant's pride and confidence were unbounded. He thought himself invincible, yet after all he was to come to ruin through his covetousness. The Persian ruler Oroetes, jealous of his wealth and power, wrote from Magnesia, proposing alliance and offering Polycrates a great treasure to help him in his conquests. The greedy lord of Samos sent a servant to see this treasure, to whom were shown eight chests filled with stones, but covered at the top with gold, ready for Polycrates to take away. He, on this report, could not be hindered from visiting the false Oroetes, though oracles and omens were adverse, and though his daughter begged him to stay at home, since in a dream she had seen him raised in the air, washed by Zeus, and anointed by the sun.

But Polycrates took this dream to presage an exaltation, of which he made sure. He went to Oroetes, who, having got him into his hands, ordered him to be straightway crucified. So came to be washed by the sky and anointed by the sun a man who thought he had nothing to fear from heaven or earth.

Croesus

The Lydians are said to have been the first people who coined money; and their king Croesus had gathered so much gold that his name became a proverb for wealth. It is told that when Solon visited him at Sardis, the king showed this wise Greek over his treasure chambers, expecting to be admired as the most fortunate of men. But Solon looked coldly on all his display of riches, and bid him know that no man could be called happy till his death. Croesus had cause thereafter to remember another saying of Solon, that his gold might be taken away by one who had more iron. Having in mind to make war on Cyrus, the king of Persia, he sent rich gifts to the oracle of Delphi, seeking to learn if this undertaking would turn out prosperously for him. The oracle gave answer that his war against Persia would overthrow a great empire. So it was when he himself came to be overthrown, and passed under the power of Cyrus with all his kingdom.

But even before the conquest of Lydia by the Persians, Croesus was to learn how gold is no sure shield against calamity. He had two sons, one of whom was deaf and dumb, but the other, named Atys, such a youth as made his father's pride and joy. One night Croesus dreamt that Atys would be wounded to death by an iron weapon. This dream so much troubled him, that he would no longer allow his favourite son to lead the Lydian army; he found him a wife to keep him at home; and all kinds of swords, spears, and other arms hung up in the palace he had stored away in a secret place, lest by accident any deadly point or edge might hurt the beloved Atys, who for his part, like a young man of courage and spirit as he was, took it ill that he should be so carefully guarded against harm.

Soon after his marriage, there came tidings of a huge wild boar ravaging the mountain region of Mysia. The Mysians sought help from the king against this terrible monster; and he sent them a band of picked hunters and hounds. Atys was eager to make one of this party, protesting that otherwise he should be taken for a coward by the people, with his old comrades in war and the chase, even with his new-wed wife. So hard he pressed for leave, that Croesus had to explain his refusal by relating to him the dream in which he had seen his son slain by iron.

273

"A boar's tusks are not of iron!" cried the young man lightly; and gave his father no peace till he unwillingly agreed to let Atys go on that hunt.

To guard him the more surely, he gave Atys in special charge of a brave warrior named Adrastus, grandson of Midas, who had taken refuge at the court of Croesus, banished from home on account of having accidentally killed his own brother. Grateful to the Lydian king for having harboured him in distress, Adrastus promised faithfully to watch over Atys and to answer for his safety with his own life.

The hunters set out in high spirits; they tracked the boar to its haunt; they closed round it in a circle, each keen to be foremost in striking it with spear or javelin. The boar fell under a shower of darts, but one went amiss. As Atys pressed in before the rest, he was pierced by the spear of Adrastus, and died according to his father's dream.

Miserable was the grief of Croesus when he heard how his dream had come true; and most wretched was this rich king as he met the mournful train that brought the body of his son. With it came Adrastus, who fell on his knees and stretched out his hands, supplicating the bereaved father to take his life in atonement. For all Croesus' affliction, he pitied and pardoned the remorseful man who unwittingly had worked the will of fate. But the remorseful Adrastus could not forgive himself, and he offered up his own life as a sacrifice upon the tomb of Atys, thus untimely taken before the Persian conqueror taught Croesus how truly Solon had spoken: *Call no man happy till his death.*

The Treasury of Rhampsinitus

Rhampsinitus of Egypt was another king of such great riches as might well put him in fear of robbery. To guard them safely he had built a strong treasure-house, of which he kept the key, and believed that no man could enter but himself. But the mason who built it had left one stone loose, which might easily be moved from the outside to let him in by stealth whenever he pleased: so are tyrants served.

When this man came to die, he told his two sons the secret of the stone, that they might rob the covetous king at will, by such an inheritance to live at ease and support their mother. Night after night, then, they stole into the treasury, and brought out as much gold as they could carry away. For a time their thieving went unnoticed, till at last Rhampsinitus began to suspect that some furtive hand must be at the heaps of money he found dwindling day by day; and to catch the thief he had man-traps set within the walls.

All unaware, the brothers came next night to turn the stone as before; then the first of them that pushed in, found himself held fast in a trap, from which no struggling could break him loose. Having nothing else for it, and expecting no mercy from the king, he bid his brother cut off his head, that it should never be known who the robbers were, nor need he, the living man, be brought into suspicion. The brother, unwilling as he was, did so, since so he must: he killed the unlucky companion of his adventure, and hastened away, carrying away the head that might have told a tale against them both.

Great was the king's astonishment to find a headless body in his trap; but the stone having been carefully replaced, he could not guess how the man had got in, nor even who he was, still less who had taken away the head. In this quandary, Rhampsinitus ordered the corpse to be hung up to a wall in public view, and sentinels set beside it, charged to seize and bring before him anyone that showed signs of grief over this dead man, whose friends or kindred might thus betray themselves.

But the robber's mother already knew his fate, and could not bear to let his body hang unburied, a gazing-stock for the people. She bid her surviving son fetch it away at all risks, else she would inform the king how he had broken into the treasury. Since the tearful woman would have it, he set his wits to work on some plan of cheating the sentinels, and hit upon this. With the money he had stolen, he bought a string of asses and loaded on them skins full of wine, to drive them by the wall on which his brother's body hung; then as he came past the watchful guard, he contrived to let the wine run out at the necks of the skins.

At the sight of wine flowing freely, the soldiers pressed forward to catch it in their drinking-vessels. At first the owner pretended to be angry, and all at a loss what to do with his leaky skins; but soon he made friends with the thirsty sentinels, desiring them to drink at will, rather than let the wine go to waste. So they did, drinking cup after cup till man by man they reeled over in drunken slumber. It being now dark, there was no one to hinder him taking his brother's body down; but before carrying it home, he shaved half the beards and the right cheeks of the heavily sleeping sentinels, leaving them thus marked for derision.

So bold grew this man that he came making love to the king's own daughter, who coaxed him into boasting that it was he who had robbed the treasury and cheated the guards. Hearing this in the dark, she would have seized him by the arm to give him up to her father; but the cunning fellow under his cloak had hidden one of the dead man's arms, which she now grasped to find it come away in her hand, while the thief slipped away without letting her see his face.

Rhampsinitus was so set on finding out who this bold and clever man could be that, all other efforts being in vain, he at last proclaimed full pardon and reward for him on disclosing himself. Trusting this promise, the man confessed himself to the king, who was so taken by his shrewdness as to give him his daughter in marriage and make him guardian of the treasury he had robbed.

The Lover's Leap

Sappho, famed as a poetess through the old Greek world, was a daughter of Lesbos, famous also for its wine. Her brother Charaxus, carrying wine to Egypt, is said to have ransomed from slavery and married Rhodopis, "the rosy cheeked", whom Sappho celebrated in an ode; and this woman, slave as she was, grew so rich that one of the pyramids passed for her monument. But another tale is told of Rhodopis and her fortune: that, as she was bathing in the Nile, an eagle caught up one of her sandals and carried it away over the fields of Egypt, to drop it into the lap of the king as he sat on his throne at Memphis; then the beauty of that sandal so took his heart that he sent out far and wide till he found the owner to make her his queen, after whose death he built a pyramid in memory of her.

Sappho had many lovers; but the one she loved best of all, she loved in vain. Between the islands of Lesbos and Chios plied a ferryman named Phaon, who was one day loosing his boat to set forth, when up came a hobbling old crone begging a passage, for love not for money, as she had nothing to pay him.

"In with you and welcome!" said Phaon, giving no more heed to this bundle of rags, as it seemed, huddled up among his other passengers.

The sun shone on a smooth sea, and a gentle wind filled the sail to carry the boat over without stroke of oar, as if some heavenly power wafted it on its way.

Then as the rest stepped on land, that old woman turned to thank Phaon for his kindness. But lo! she was old and bent no more; she showed fair and – proud and richly clad, manifest now to the amazed ferryman as no other than Aphrodite, queen of love, who addressed him with a radiant smile.

"For the service you have done me, I give you a boon not to be bought by all the gold in the world: be for ever young and beautiful, as befits one whose life is lit by my favour."

She breathed upon him, and in an instance Phaon felt himself another man. Fresh young blood throbbed from his heart; his wrinkled and sun-tanned cheeks grew smooth; the burden of years fell away from him; and he stood up the loveliest youth in Lesbos. They tell, too, how the goddess gave him an alabaster box of ointment, which was a charm to work on every woman that saw him, so that all the island's daughters could not but love him. But some say that the spell bestowed upon him lay in the root of a certain plant.

Too soon the eyes of Sappho were drawn to the transformed ferryman; and too surely her heart was caught in the spell of his blooming face. Forgetting her earlier sweethearts, she loved none but Phaon; and none like him. But alas! he loved her not again, for Aphrodite in making his face young and beautiful, had left his heart untouched. Friendly to man and woman, he would have no maid's devotion; and he turned away with a laugh from the passionate sighs which Sappho was skilled to put into song. When to songs and sighs his ears proved deaf, neither words nor tasks could soothe her longing.

> "As o'er her loom the Lesbian maid
> In love-sick languor hung her head
> Unknowing where her fingers strayed
> She weeping turned away and said—
>
> "'Oh, my sweet mother, 'tis in vain,
> I cannot weave as once I wove,
> So wildered is my heart and brain
> With thinking of that youth I love.'"
>
> —Thomas Moore

In vain, striking her lyre to the verses we still call Sapphics, she invoked the goddess who had wasted on Phaon that boon of beauty—

> "Splendour-throned Queen, immortal Aphrodite,
> Daughter of Jove, Enchantress I implore thee
> Vex not my soul with agonies and anguish;
> Slay me not Goddess!
> Come in thy pity – come, if I have prayed thee;
> Come at the cry of my sorrow; in the old times
> Oft thou hast heard, and left thy father's heaven
> Left the gold houses,
> Yoking thy chariot. Swiftly did the does fly,
> Swiftly they brought thee, waving plumes of wonder—
> Waving their dark plumes all across the aether[1]
> All down the azure.
>
> So once again come, Mistress; and, releasing
> Me from my sadness, give me what I sue for,
> Grant me my prayer and be as heretofore now
> Friend and protectress."
>
> —Edwin Arnold

In vain she would have lured Phaon with her sweetest songs; she had to sing of him to the winds.

"Peer of gods he seemeth to me, the blissful
Man who sits and gazes at thee before him
Close beside thee sits and in silence hears thee
Silverly speaking
Laughing love's low laughter. Oh this, this only
Stirs the troubled heart in my breast to tremble!
For should I but see thee a little moment,
Straight is my voice hushed;
Yea, my tongue is broken, and through and through me
'Neath the flesh impalpable fire runs tingling;
Nothing see mine eyes and a noise of roaring
Waves in my ear sounds;
Sweat runs down in rivers, a tremor seizes
All my limbs, and paler than grass in autumn,
Caught by pains of menacing death, I falter,
Lost in the love-trance."

—J. A. Symonds

In vain for her came the shades of evening, so kindly to man and cattle.

"Oh Hesperus! thou bringest all good things—
Home to the weary, to the hungry cheer,
To the young bird the parent's brooding wings,
The welcome stall to the o'erlaboured steer;
Whate'er of peace about our hearthstone clings,
Whate'er our household gods protect of dear,
Are gathered round us by thy look of rest;
Thou bring'st the child too, to the mother's breast."

—Lord Byron

In vain, when the unresponsive loved one went far out of reach of her endearments, she wrote to call him back to Lesbos.

"Gods, can no prayers, no sighs no numbers move
One savage heart, or teach it how to love?
The winds my prayers, my sighs, my numbers bear;
The flying winds have lost them all in air.
Or when, alas, shall more auspicious gales
To these fond eyes restore thy welcome sails?
If you return, ah, why these long delays?
Poor Sappho dies while careless Phaon stays.
O launch the bark, nor fear the watery plain:
Venus for thee shall smooth her native main.
O launch thy bark, secure of prosperous gales:
Cupid for thee shall spread the swelling sails.

279

If you will fly – (yet ah, what cause can be,
Too cruel youth, that you should fly from me?)
If not from Phaon I must hope for ease,
Ah, let me seek it from the raging seas:
To raging seas unpitied I'll remove;
And either cease to live or cease to love."

—Ovid, translated by Alexander Pope

At last, growing old in despair, she could no longer endure the pangs of her despised love. Then as now, the sea broke upon a tall white cliff, crowned by a temple of Apollo, from which love-lorn maidens were wont to hurl themselves, to cure this and all other ills. Here, dressed in virgin white, she came to end her life, yet hoping against hope maybe that the waves might bear her to Phaon's side. Singing her last song, Sappho took the fatal leap, to be seen no more of men, among whom will never be forgotten the name and fate of one celebrated as the Tenth Muse.

Sappho
From the painting by L. Alma Tadema R.A.

[1] (p. 278) air.

Er Among the Dead

Plato[1] relates this tale of Er, a brave warrior of Pamphylia, who falling in battle had been laid on the pile to be burned, since he showed no sign of life. But there his body remained uncorrupted till the twelfth day, when, to the amazement of his friends, he rose as from the dead and told them how it had gone with him in the world of the Shades.

His soul, passing out of the body, had found itself among a crowd of others in a wonderful scene, where two chasms opened down through the earth, and two other passages led upwards to heaven. Here sat the judges who pronounced every man's sentence. The souls of the just were bidden take the heavenly way, each bearing in front a scroll that was his title to blessedness; while on the backs of the rest were hung records of their evil deeds; and they had to descend underground. But when it came to Er's turn, the judges decided that he should bear back to our world a report of what he saw and heard among the dead.

He saw, then, how the newly dead went their separate ways by one of the two openings upwards and downwards, while through the other two kept rising back to earth hapless shades, covered with filth and dust, and to meet them came from heaven a shining stream of pure souls. On the plain between they mingled, recognizing those whom they had known during life, and eagerly exchanging news, the just full of joy, but the evildoers tearfully lamenting what they had borne for a thousand years. Er learned that each crime done in the flesh must be expiated during a tenfold term of shadowy life; that the most dreadful chastisements were for the impious and for parricides, and the richest rewards for those who had benefited their fellow men. He heard asked and told the fate of Ardiaeus, a tyrant of his own country, who a thousand years before had killed his father and his elder brother among other crimes. As the souls that so long ago came down with this malefactor were at last released from their penance, they had shuddered to see how the chasm closed before him, and how he, along with others of like guilt, was dragged back by hideous fiery forms to be bound head and foot, flayed with scourges, and torn through blood-dripping thorns before being again cast back into the depths of Tartarus.

281

The souls now destined to return to earth remained for a week in this place; then on the eighth day they set out for a pillar of light that after four days' march came into view glowing like a rainbow, but more brilliant and more ethereal. This light is the axis of heaven and earth; and in the midst of it hangs by chains the adamantine spindle of Necessity, which she turns on her knees to keep whirling eight variously coloured circles that are the courses of the sun, the moon, the planets, and the fixed stars. With each circle whirls a Siren, chanting on a single note, so that their eight voices mingle in harmony to make the music of the Spheres.

Around the throne of Necessity, at equal distances sat her three daughters, the Fates – Lachesis, Clotho, and Atropos – robed in white and wearing fillets on their heads. Their voices kept time with the Sirens: Lachesis sang the past, Clotho the present, Atropos the future; while from time to time all three touched the spindle to keep it turning. The souls had first to present themselves before Lachesis, ranged in order by a herald or minister who, placing on her knees the lots to be drawn for each, made proclamation to them all.

"Thus says the virgin Fate, daughter of Necessity: wandering souls, you are about to enter a new body of life. Each may choose his own lot in turn; but the choice will be irrevocable. Virtue has no respect of persons; it cleaves to who honours it, and flies from the despiser. On your own heads be your fortune: the gods take for it no blame."

First they had to draw lots for the order which they should choose, except only Er, bidden to stand by and watch. The same priest then strewed on earth before them all the conditions of human life, from tyranny to beggary, fame, beauty, riches, poverty, health, sickness, these fates either unmingled or a blending of good or evil. There were animal lives, too, mixed up with men's and women's. That minister of the fates now urged the souls not to choose hastily, since the last had as good a chance as the first.

But he who came foremost eagerly seized on the greatest sovereignty that offered itself; then, having looked closer into this lot, found that he was destined to devour his own children, among other enormities, whereon he cried out bitterly, accusing for such a choice fortune, the gods, everything but his own folly. This soul had come from Elysium, and had formerly lived in a well-ordered state, where he owed his virtue rather to custom and disposition than to wisdom. So indeed not a few of the souls from Elysium went wrong in their choice, for want of experience in the evils of life. On the other hand, those released from the world below had often been schooled by their own sufferings and those of others to be more considerate. Thus it happened that most of the souls now exchanged a good for an evil lot, or the contrary.

Er was struck both by pity and amusement to note how strangely the souls made their choice, guided apparently by some recollection of their former life.

The Three Fates
From the painting *A Golden Thread* by J. M. Strudwick

He saw Orpheus pick out the body of a swan, as if in hatred of the women who had torn him to pieces, not caring to owe his birth to such a one. He saw a swan choose the human figure, and other birds become musicians, while Thamyris took for himself the form of a nightingale. One soul chose to be a lion: this was Ajax, son of Telamon, who had never got over his rage when the arms of Achilles were awarded to another; and he would not be a man again. He was followed by Agamemnon, whose former fate also had soured him against mankind, so now he selected the life of an eagle. Atalanta, admiring the honour in which strength of body was held, chose to become an athlete outright. The soul of Epeus, maker of the Trojan Horse, preferred the lot of a woman clever with her fingers; and the buffoon Thersites, who came up among the rest, was turned into a monkey. Odysseus came last of all; and he, remembering the past mishaps that had sickened his soul of adventurousness, carefully searched out and at last found, in an out-of-the-way corner, a quiet simple life which all the other souls had despised; then he exclaimed that had he had the first choice, he would have asked no better.

When all the souls had made their choice, in the same order they passed before Lachesis, who gave to each the guardian genius that should accompany him through life and carry out the destiny bound up with his chosen lot. This genius led them to Clotho, that with a turn of the spindle she should confirm their choice. Each soul had to touch the spindle, and next was brought up to Atropos, twisting the thread between her fingers to make unbreakable what had been spun by Clotho. Lastly they defiled before the throne of Necessity, the soul and its genius side by side.

Thence they passed on to the bare plain of Lethe, where no tree shaded them from a scorching heat. The night was spent by the river of Forgetfulness, whose waters can be borne away in no vessel. From its stream each must drink, and some rashly drank too deep, so as to lose all memory of what had gone before. Thereupon they fell asleep, but towards midnight burst out a din of thunder and earthquake, by which the souls were roused to be scattered here and there like shooting stars to the different spots where they should be reborn. As for Er, he had not been suffered to drink of Lethe, yet he knew not how his soul came back to his body; but all at once, opening his eyes next morning, he found himself alive stretched out on his funeral pyre.

[1] (p. 281) This seems an artificial myth, composed for Plato's *Republic* by way of moral; but it may be based on some old story, and in name of the hero has been found a hint of *Zoroaster*.

Damon and Pythias

(After Schiller)

The halls of Dionysius
Had Damon sought with hidden steel,
But, seized and bound by watchful guards,
Must needs his stealthy aim reveal.
Bold was the desperate man's reply:
"I would have freed the commonweal!"
Then short the tyrant's sentence—"Die!"

"Behold me ready for my fate,
Nor would I crave my life from thee;
Yet wert thou pleased to grant respite,
My sister's wedding day to see,
Pythias, my friend, will lie in bail—
Three days I ask, and only three—
He braves thy vengeance, should I fail."

Sour smiled the lord of Syracuse,
And answered after hasty thought:
"The boon I grant – so let it be,
Yet by thy surety's peril bought:
Beyond the term if thou delay,
He to the shameful cross is brought,
And thus thy guilt is done away."

His friend he seeks and tells his need:
"So thou wilt pledge thy life for mine,
Three days of grace have I to pay
The forfeit of my rash design.

285

Thou know'st the cause; thou know'st my faith—
Ere the third sun hath ceased to shine,
I win thee back from bonds and scaith."

His friend embraced him silently,
And to the tyrant's dungeon sped.
Then Damon to his sister's home
Hath ta'en his way, and seen her wed;
But the third morning's early dawn
Rouses him from his restless bed,
While a dear life still lies in pawn.

All through that night, the mountain tops
Had been beset with storms of rain.
The springs welled up, the brooks rushed down,
The anxious traveller toiled in vain;
Hourly he saw the river swell,
And, ere the bridge his haste could gain,
Its arch in crashing ruin fell.

Dismayed he wandered by the brink,
And gazed upon the further shore:
He cried aloud, no answer came,
Only the torrent's echoing roar;
He looked around, no help saw he,
No bridge, no boat to bear him o'er
That stream fast growing to a sea.

Kneeling, with tears and lifted hands
To heaven he raised his piteous cry.
"Oh, stem, ye gods, the sundering flood!
Let me but pass!—the moments fly;
And, when the clouded sun goes down,
For me my trustful friend must die,
Should I have failed to reach yon town!"

But still the waters rush and roar,
Still mounts the sun with watery beam,
Then Damon, fearless in despair,
Plunges into the swollen stream,
And struggles through its whirling tide,

Till, favoured by the will supreme,
He wins across to grasp the side.

He gained firm ground, and hurried on;
But while his thanks to Jove he spoke,
From shelter of a gloomy wood
What crew of savage outlaws broke!
They barred his path, that robber band,
And, menacing with murderous stroke,
Bade the belated traveller stand.

"What would ye? Forfeit to the king
My life; nought else have I to take!"
Suddenly from the nearest hand
He snatched a heavy knotted stake,
To fall on them with maddened cry:
"No pity, then, for Pythias' sake!"
Three he strikes down, the others fly.

Soon, as the sun shines hotly forth,
He flags beneath its scorching ray;
Fainting he strives to stagger on,
But sinks upon his knees to pray:
"Twice aided thus in desperate strait,
Shall I now perish by the way,
And leave my friend to such a fate!"

And hark! there gathers, hard at hand,
A purling murmur on his ear.
And see! from out the barren rock
A fountain's silvery spray appear,
Trickling into a green-set pool.
The grateful waters, crystal clear,
His fevered limbs refresh and cool.

When now the sunset gleams aslant
Through leafy screens, and on the meads
Each tree draws out a lengthening shade,
Two travellers from the town he heeds,
For words that chill his heart with dread
He hears them say as past he speeds,
"Soon Pythias to the cross is led!"

What inward goadings urge him on!
What anxious tremblings wing his feet!
At length, the towers of Syracuse,
Gilt with the evening's glory, greet
His eager eyes; but at the gate,
Comes hurrying forth his lord to meet,
The faithful servant, Philostrate.

"Back! Back! Thy life thou still mayst save,
But for thy friend thou com'st too late.
By now he hangs in writhing throes;
From hour to hour did hope await
Thy coming, and his steadfast faith
The tyrant's scoff could not abate:
Now hope and trust are lost in death."

"Is it too late? Can I not save?
In vain did Pythias hold me true?
Yet shall no tyrant mock at love,
If doom our comradeship renew!
Boast not that friendly faith hath failed,
Thou cruel king! For one, let two
Victims upon the cross be nailed."

The dusk draws on. Lo! by the gate
That fearsome engine raised on high,
Whereto rough ropes and brutal hands
Are binding Pythias to die.
The guards, the gaping crowd give way—
"Hold, butchers, hold! See, here am I,
The man for whom in plight he lay!"

The friends fell in each other's arms;
Wondered the people all to see.
They wept for mingled joy and grief,
Nor any eye from tears was free.
This tale men carried to the king,
And some touch of humanity
Stirred him before his throne to bring

Damon and Pythias. Long he gazed,
Astounded, on them: "Ye the art

Have found to teach me trust is true,
And unto mercy move my heart.
If such the love of friends, let me
With your fair fellowship have part,
And in so strong a bond join Three!"

---

¹ In Schiller's ballad, which a little expands the classical story, the names of the heroes stood originally Moerus and Selinuntius; and by Cicero Pythias is named Phintias; but this translation presents them in the nomenclature that has become most famous.

Rhoecus

(James Russell Lowell)

Hear now this fairy legend of old Greece,
As full of freedom, youth, and beauty still
As the immortal freshness of that grace
Carved for all ages on some Attic frieze.

   A youth named Rhoecus, wandering in the wood
Saw an old oak just trembling to its fall,
And, feeling pity of so fair a tree,
He propped its gray trunk with admiring care,
And with a thoughtless footstep loitered on.
But, as he turned, he heard a voice behind
That murmured Rhoecus!" 'T was as if the leaves
Stirred by a passing breath, had murmured it,
And, while he paused bewildered, yet again
It murmured " Rhoecus!" softer than a breeze.
He started, and beheld with dizzy eyes
What seemed the substance of a happy dream
Stand there before him, spreading a warm glow
Within the green glooms of the shadowy oak.
It seemed a woman's shape, yet all too fair
To be a woman, and with eyes too meek
For any that were wont to mate with gods.
All naked like a goddess stood she there,
And like a goddess all too beautiful
To feel the guilt-born earthliness of shame.

"Rhoecus, I am the Dryad of this tree,"
Thus she began, dropping her low-toned words

Serene, and full, and clear, as drops of dew;
"And with it I am doomed to live and die;
The rain and sunshine are my caterers,
Nor have I other bliss than simple life;
Now ask me what thou wilt, that I can give,
And with a thankful joy it shall be thine."

   Then Rhoecus, with a flutter at the heart,
Yet, by the prompting of such beauty, bold,
Answered: "What is there that can satisfy
The endless craving of the soul but love?
Give me thy love, or but the hope of that
Which must be evermore my spirit's goal.
"After a little pause she said again,
But with a glimpse of sadness in her tone,
"I give it, Rhoecus, though a perilous gift;
An hour before the sunset meet me here."
And straightway there was nothing he could see
But the green glooms beneath the shadowy oak,
And not a sound came to his straining ears
But the low trickling rustle of the leaves,
And far away upon an emerald slope
The falter of an idle shepherd's pipe.

   Now, in those days of simpleness and faith,
Men did not think that happy things were dreams
Because they overstepped the narrow bourn
Of likelihood, but reverently deemed
Nothing too wondrous or too beautiful
To be the guerdon of a daring heart.
So Rhoecus made no doubt that he was blest,
And all along unto the city's gate

Earth seemed to spring beneath him as he walked,
The clear, broad sky looked bluer than its wont,
And he could scarce believe he had not wings,
Such sunshine seemed to glitter through his veins
Instead of blood, so light he felt and strange.

   Young Rhoecus had a faithful heart enough,
But one that in the present dwelt too much

And, taking with blithe welcome whatsoe'er
Chance gave of joy, was wholly bound in that,
Like the contented peasant of a vale,
Deemed it the world, and never looked beyond.
So, haply meeting in the afternoon
Some comrades who were playing at the dice,
He joined them and forgot all else beside.

The dice was rattling at the merriest,
And Rhoecus, who had met but sorry luck,
Just laughed in triumph at a happy throw,
When through the room there hummed a yellow bee
That buzzed about his ear with down-dropped legs
As if to light. And Rhoecus laughed and said,
Feeling how red and flushed he was with loss,
"By Venus! does he take me for a rose?"
And brushed him off with rough, impatient hand.
But still the bee came back, and thrice again
Rhoecus did beat him off with growing wrath.
Then through the window flew the wounded bee,
And Rhoecus tracking him with angry eyes,
Saw a sharp mountain-peak of Thessaly
Against the red disc of the setting sun,—
And instantly the blood sank from his heart,
As if its very walls had caved away.
Without a word he turned, and, rushing forth,
Ran madly through the city and the gate,
And o'er the plain, which now the wood's long shade,
By the low sun thrown forward broad and dim,
Darkened well nigh unto the city's wall.

Quite spent and out of breath he reached the tree,
And, listening fearfully, he heard once more
The low voice murmur "Rhoecus!" close at hand:
Whereat he looked around him, but could see
Nought but the deepening glooms beneath the oak.
Then sighed the voice, "Oh, Rhoecus! nevermore
Shalt thou behold me or by day or night,
Me, who would fain have blessed thee with a love
More ripe and bounteous than ever yet
Filled up with nectar any mortal heart:

But thou didst scorn my humble messenger,
And sent'st him back to me with bruised wings.
We spirits only show to gentle eyes.
We ever ask an undivided love;
And he who scorns the least of Nature's works
Is thenceforth exiled and shut out from all.
Farewell! for thou canst never see me more."

   Then Rhoecus beat his breast, and groaned aloud,
And cried, "Be pitiful! forgive me yet
This once, and I shall never need it more!"
"Alas!" the voice returned, " 't is thou art blind,
Not I unmerciful; I can forgive,
But have no skill to heal thy spirit's eyes;
Only the soul hath power o'er itself."
With that again there murmured "Nevermore!"
And Rhoecus after heard no other sound,
Except the rattling of the oak's crisp leaves,
Like the long surf upon a distant shore,
Raking the sea-worn pebbles up and down.
The night had gathered round him: o'er the plain
The city sparkled with its thousand lights,
And sounds of revel fell upon his ear
Harshly and like a curse; above, the sky,
With all its bright sublimity of stars,
Deepened, and on his forehead smote the breeze:
Beauty was all around him and delight,
But from that eve he was alone on earth.

Cephalus and Procris

(Thomas Moore)

A Hunter once in that grove reclined
   To shun the noon's bright eye,
And oft he wooed the wandering wind
   To cool his brow with its sigh.
While mute lay even the wild bee's hum,
Nor breath could stir the aspen's hair,
His song was still "Sweet air, oh come!"
While Echo answered " Come, sweet air!"

But, hark, what sounds from the thicket rise!
   What meaneth that rustling spray?
"'T is the white-horned doe," the Hunter cries,
   "I have sought since break of day!"
Quick o'er the sunny glade he springs,
The arrow flies from his sounding bow;
"Hilliho – hilliho!" he gaily sings,
While Echo sighs forth "Hilliho!"

Alas, 't was not the white-horned doe
   He saw in the rustling grove,
But the bridal veil, as pure as snow,
   Of his own young wedded love.
And, ah, too sure that arrow sped,
For pale at his feet he sees her lie;—
"I die, I die," was all she said,
While Echo murmured, " I die, I die!"[1]

---

[1] Our poet hardly brings out all the points of this story; amore comprehensive account can be found in the entry for Cephalus on p.344 of the dictionary section.

Tithonus[1]

(Alfred Tennyson)

The woods decay, the woods decay and fall,
The vapours weep their burthen to the ground,
Man comes and tills the field and lies beneath,
And after many a summer dies the swan.
Me only cruel immortality Consumes:
I wither slowly in thine arms,
Here at the quiet limit of the world,
A white-hair'd shadow roaming like a dream
The ever silent spaces of the East,
Far-folded mists, and gleaming halls of morn.

Alas! for this gray shadow, once a man—
So glorious in his beauty and thy choice,
Who madest him thy chosen, that he seem'd
To his great heart none other than a God!
I ask'd thee, "Give me immortality".
Then didst thou grant mine asking with a smile,
Like wealthy men who care not how they give.
But thy strong Hours indignant work'd their wills,
And beat me down and marr'd and wasted me,
And tho' they could not end me, left me maim'd
To dwell in presence of immortal youth,
Immortal age beside immortal youth,
And all I was, in ashes. Can thy love,
Thy beauty, make amends, tho' even now,
Close over us, the silver star, thy guide,
Shines in those tremulous eyes that fill with tears
To hear me? Let me go: take back thy gift.

Why should a man desire in any way
To vary from the kindly race of men,
Or pass beyond the goal of ordinance
Where all should pause, as is most meet for all?

A soft air fans the cloud apart; there comes
A glimpse of that dark world where I was born.
Once more the old mysterious glimmer steals
From thy pure brows, and from thy shoulders pure,
And bosom beating with a heart renew'd.
Thy cheek begins to redden thro' the gloom,
Thy sweet eyes brighten slowly close to mine,
Ere yet they blind the stars, and the wild team
Which love thee, yearning for thy yoke, arise,
And shake the darkness from their loosen'd manes,
And beat the twilight into flakes of fire.

Lo! ever thus thou growest beautiful
In silence, then before thine answer given
Departest, and thy tears are on my cheek.

Why wilt thou ever scare me with thy tears,
And make me tremble lest a saying learnt,
In days far-off, on that dark earth, be true?
"The Gods themselves cannot recall their gifts."

Ay me! ay me! with what another heart
In days far-off, and with what other eyes
I used to watch – if I be he that watch'd—
The lucid outline forming round thee; saw
The dim curls kindle into sunny rings;
Changed with thy mystic change, and felt my blood
Glow with the glow that slowly crimson'd all
Thy presence and thy portals, while I lay,
Mouth, forehead, eyelids, growing dewy-warm
With kisses balmier than half-opening buds
Of April, and could hear the lips that kiss'd
Whispering I knew not what of wild and sweet,
Like that strange song I heard Apollo sing,
While Ilion like a mist rose into towers.

Yet hold me not for ever in thine East:
How can my nature longer mix with thine?
Coldly thy rosy shadows bathe me, cold
Are all thy lights, and cold my wrinkled feet
Upon thy glimmering thresholds, when the steam
Floats up from those dim fields about the homes
Of happy men that have the power to die,
And grassy barrows of the happier dead.
Release me, and restore me to the ground;
Thou seest all things, thou wilt see my grave:
Thou wilt renew thy beauty morn by morn;
I earth in earth forget these empty courts,
And thee returning on thy silver wheels.

---

[1] Tithonus was Priam's brother, beloved by Eos (the Dawn), who procured for him the gift of immortality, but without enduring youth, so that he became a prototype of Swift's *Struldbrugs*.

Laodamia¹

(William Wordsworth)

"With sacrifice before the rising morn
Vows have I made, by fruitless hope inspired;
And from the infernal gods, mid shades forlorn,
Of night, my slaughtered lord have I required:
Celestial pity I again implore;
Restore him to my sight – great Jove, restore!"

So speaking, and by fervent love endowed
With faith, the suppliant heavenward lifts her hands;
While, like the sun emerging from a cloud,
Her countenance brightens, and her eye expands;
Her bosom heaves and spreads, her stature grows;
And she expects the issue in repose.

O terror! what hath she perceived? O joy!
What doth she look on? whom doth she behold?
Her hero slain upon the beach of Troy?
His vital presence – his corporeal mould?
It is – if sense deceive her not – 'tis he!
And a god leads him – winged Mercury!

Mild Hermes spake – and touched her with his wand
That calms all fear: "Such grace hath crowned thy prayer,

Laodamia! that at Jove's command
Thy husband walks the paths of upper air:
He comes to tarry with thee three hours' space;
Accept the gift – behold him face to face!"

Forth sprang the impassioned queen her lord to clasp,
Again that consummation she essayed;
But unsubstantial form eludes her grasp
As often as that eager grasp was made.
The phantom parts but parts to re-unite,
And re-assume his place before her sight.

"Protesilaüs, lo! thy guide is gone!
Confirm, I pray, the vision with thy voice:
This is our palace – yonder is thy throne:
Speak, and the floor thou tread'st on will rejoice.
Not to appal me have the gods bestowed
This precious boon – and blessed a sad abode."

"Great Jove, Laodamia, doth not leave
His gifts imperfect: spectre though I be,
I am not sent to scare thee or deceive;
But in reward of thy fiddity.
And something also did my worth obtain;
For fearless virtue bringeth boundless gain.

"Thou know'st, the Delphic oracle foretold
That the first Greek that touched the Trojan strand
Should die; but me the threat could not withhold:
A generous cause a victim did demand;
And forth I leapt upon the sandy plain;
A self-devoted chief – by Hector slain."

"Supreme of heroes – bravest, noblest, best!
Thy matchless courage I bewail no more,
Which then, when tens of thousands were depressed
By doubt, propelled thee to the fatal shore;
Thou found'st – and I forgive thee – here thou art—
A nobler counsellor than my poor heart.

"But thou, though capable of sternest deed,
Wert kind as resolute, and good as brave;
And he, whose power restores thee, hath decreed
That thou should'st cheat the malice of the grave;
Redundant are thy locks, thy lips as fair
As when their breath enriched Thessalian air.

"No spectre greets me, no vain shadow this:
Come, blooming hero, place thee by my side!
Give, on this well-known couch, one nuptial kiss
To me, this day a second time thy bride!"
Jove frowned in heaven; the conscious Parcae threw
Upon those roseate lips a Stygian hue.

"This visage tells thee that my doom is past:
Know, virtue were not virtue if the joys
Of sense were able to return as fast
And surely as they vanish.
Earth destroys Those raptures duly – Erebus disdains:
Calm pleasures there abide – majestic pains.

"Be taught, O faithful consort, to control
Rebellious passion; for the gods approve
The depth, and not the tumult, of the soul;
A fervent, not ungovernable love.
Thy transports moderate; and meekly mourn
When I depart, for brief is my sojourn."

"Ah, wherefore? Did not Hercules by force
Wrest from the guardian monster of the tomb
Alcestis, a re-animated corse,
Given back to dwell on earth in vernal bloom?
Medea's spells dispersed the weight of years,
And Aeson stood a youth mid youthful peers.

"The gods to us are merciful – and they
Yet further may relent: for mightier far
Than strength of nerve and sinew, or the sway
Of magic potent over sun and star,
Is love, though oft to agony distressed,
And though his favourite seat be feeble woman's breast.

"But if thou goest I follow – " "Peace!" he said—
She looked upon him and was calmed and cheered;
The ghastly colour from his lips had fled;
In his deportment, shape, and mien, appeared
Elysian beauty, melancholy grace,
Brought from a pensive, though a happy place.

He spake of love, such love as spirits feel
In worlds whose course is equable and pure;
No fears to beat away – no strife to heal—
The past unsighed for, and the future sure:
Spake of heroic arts in graver mood
Revived, with finer harmony pursued:

Of all that is most beauteous—imaged there
In happier beauty; more pellucid streams,
An ampler ether, a diviner air,
And fields invested with purpureal gleams;
Climes which the sun, who sheds the brightest day
Earth knows, is all unworthy to survey.

Yet there the soul shall enter which hath earned
That privilege by virtue. "Ill," said he,
"The end of man's existence I discerned,
Who from ignoble games and revelry
Could draw, when we had parted, vain delight
While tears were thy best pastime, day and night:

"And while my youthful peers, before my eyes,
(Each hero following his peculiar bent)
Prepared themselves for glorious enterprise
By martial sports, or, seated in the tent,
Chieftains and kings in council were detained;
What time the fleet at Aulis lay enchained.

"The wished-for wind was given; I then revolved
The oracle, upon the silent sea;
And, if no worthier led the way, resolved
That, of a thousand vessels, mine should be
The foremost prow in pressing to the strand,
Mine the first blood that tinged the Trojan sand.

"Yet bitter, ofttimes bitter, was the pang
When of thy loss I thought, beloved wife!
On thee too fondly did my memory hang,
And on the joys we shared in mortal life,
The paths which we had trod – these fountains – flowers;
My new-planned cities, and unfinished towers.

"But should suspense permit the foe to cry,
'Behold, they tremble! haughty their array,
Yet of their number no one dares to die!'
In soul I swept the indignity away:
Old frailties then recurred: but lofty thought,
In act embodied, my deliverance wrought.

"And thou, though strong in love, art all too weak
In reason, in self-government too slow;
I counsel thee by fortitude to seek
Our blest reunion in the shades below.
The invisible world with thee hath sympathized;
Be thy affections raised and solemnized.

"Learn by a mortal yearning to ascend
Towards a higher object. Love was given,
Encouraged, sanctioned, chiefly for that end:
For this the passion to excess was driven—
That self might be annulled: her bondage prove
The fetters of a dream, opposed to love."

Aloud she shrieked! for Hermes reappears!
Round the dear shade she would have clung – 'tis vain.
The hours are past – too brief had they been years;
And him no mortal effort can detain:
Swift, toward the realms that know not earthly day,
He through the portal takes his silent way,
And on the palace floor a lifeless corse she lay.

By no weak pity might the gods be moved;
She who thus perished, not without the crime
Of lovers that in reason's spite have loved,
Was doomed to wander in a grosser clime,
Apart from happy ghosts – that gather flowers
Of blissful quiet mid unfading bowers.

Yet tears to human suffering are due;
And mortal hopes defeated and o'erthrown
Are mourned by man, and not by man alone,
As fondly he believes. Upon the side
Of Hellespont (such faith was entertained)
A knot of spiry trees for ages grew

From out the tomb of him for whom she died:
And ever, when such stature they had gained
That Ilium's walls were subject to their view,
The trees' tall summits withered at the sight;
A constant interchange of growth and blight!

---

[1] Laodamia was the daughter of Acastus and the wife of Protesilaüs. Protesilaüs was the first of the Greeks to be killed by the Trojans, and Laodamia prayed that he be allowed back from the underworld for three hours. When that three hours was up she died with Protesilaüs. She is briefly mentioned in The Gathering at Aulis from The Tale of Troy

Arethusa

(Percy Bysshe Shelley)

Arethusa arose
From her couch of snows
In the Acroceraunian mountains,—
From cloud and from crag,
With many a jag,
Shepherding her bright fountains.
She leapt down the rocks
With her rainbow locks
Streaming among the streams:—
Her steps paved with green
The downward ravine
Which slopes to the western gleams:
And gliding and springing,
She went, ever singing,
In murmurs as soft as sleep;
The Earth seemed to love her,
And Heaven smiled above her,
As she lingered towards the deep.

Then Alpheus bold,
On his glacier cold,
With his trident the mountains strook;
And opened a chasm
In the rocks;—with the spasm
All Erymanthus shook.
And the black south wind
It concealed behind
The urns of the silent snow,

And earthquake and thunder
Did rend in sunder
The bars of the springs below:
The beard and the hair
Of the river God were
Seen through the torrent's sweep,
As he followed the light
Of the fleet nymph's flight
To the brink of the Dorian deep.

"Oh, save me! Oh, guide me!
And bid the deep hide me,
For he grasps me now by the hair!
"The loud Ocean heard,
To its blue depths stirred,
And divided at her prayer;
And under the water
The Earth's white daughter
Fled like a sunny beam;
Behind her descended,
Her billows, unblended
With the brackish Dorian stream:—
Like a gloomy stain
On the emerald main
Alpheus rushed behind,—
As an eagle pursuing
A dove to its ruin
Down the stream of the cloudy wind.

Under the bowers
Where the Ocean Powers
Sit on their pearled thrones:
Through the coral woods
Of the weltering floods,
Over heaps of unvalued stones:
Through the dim beams
Which amid the streams
Weave a net-work of coloured light;
And under the caves,
Where the shadowy waves
Are as green as the forest's night:—

Outspeeding the shark,
And the sword-fish dark,
Under the ocean foam,
And up through the rifts
Of the mountain clifts
They passed to their Dorian home.

And now on their fountains
In Enna's mountains,
Down one vale where the morning basks
Like friends once parted
Grown single-hearted,
They ply their watery tasks.
At sun-rise they leap
From their cradle steep
In caves of the shelving hill;
At noon-tide they flow
Through the woods below
And the meadows of Asphodel;
And at night they sleep
In the rocking deep
Beneath the Ortygian shore;—
Like spirits that lie
In the azure sky
When they love but live no more.

Cupid's Trick

(Anacreon – translated by Thomas Moore)

'T was noon of night, when round the pole
The sullen Bear is seen to roll;
And mortals, wearied with the day,
Are slumbering all their cares away:
An infant, at that dreary hour,
Came weeping to my silent bower,
And wak'd me with a piteous prayer,
To shield him from the midnight air.
"And who art thou," I waking cry,
"That bid'st my blissful visions fly?"
"Ah, gentle sire!" the infant said,
"In pity take me to thy shed;
Nor fear deceit: a lonely child
I wander o'er the gloomy wild.
Chill drops the rain, and not a ray
Illumes the drear and misty way!"

I heard the baby's tale of woe;
I heard the bitter night-winds blow,
And sighing for his piteous fate,
I trimm'd my lamp and op'd the gate.
'T was Love! the little wandering sprite,
His pinion sparkled through the night.
I knew him by his bow and dart;
I knew him by my fluttering heart.

Fondly I take him in, and raise
The dying embers' cheering blaze;

Press from his dank and clinging hair
The crystals of the freezing air,
And in my hand and bosom hold
His little fingers thrilling cold.

And now the embers' genial ray
Had warm'd his anxious fears away;
"I pray thee," said the wanton child,
(My bosom trembled as he smil'd,)
"I pray thee let me try my bow,
For through the rain I've wander'd so,
That much I fear, the midnight shower
Has injur'd its elastic power."
The fatal bow the urchin drew:
Swift from the string the arrow flew;
As swiftly flew as glancing
And to my inmost spirit came!
"Fare thee well," I heard him say,
As laughing wild he wing'd away;
"Fare thee well, for now I know
The rain has not relax'd my bow;
It still can send a thrilling dart,
As thou shalt own with all thy heart!"

Dictionary of
Classical Mythology

A

Abaris the Scythian in Greek mythology, a priest of APOLLO to whom the god gave a golden arrow on which to ride through the air. This dart ('the dart of Abaris') rendered him invisible; it also cured diseases and gave oracles. Abaris is said to have given it to the philosopher Pythagoras.

Abas in Greek mythology, the twelfth king of Argos, the son of LYNCEUS (1) and Hypermnestra, grandson of DANAÜS and father of ACRISIUS and PROETÜS, and, in some accounts, of IDMON. He was given his grandfather's shield, which was sacred to HERA and the sight of which was capable of subduing people.

Abdera an ancient Greek city on the Thracian coast, east of the river Nestus, the birthplace of the philosophers Democritus, Anaxacoras and Protagoras. Despite this, its inhabitants became proverbial for dullness and stupidity. According to Greek mythology, it was founded by HERACLES in honour of his friend ABDERUS.

Abderus in Greek mythology, a friend of HERACLES, devoured by the horses of DIOMEDES, king of THRACE. Diomedes gave him his horses to hold, and they devoured him.

Absyrtus *or* **Apsyrtus** in Greek mythology, a son of AEËTES, king of COLCHIS and brother of MEDEA. When Medea fled with JASON she took Absyrtus with her, and when she was nearly overtaken by her father she murdered her brother, cut his body in pieces and strewed them on the road so that her father would be detained by gathering the limbs of his child.

Abydus in Greek mythology a city situated on the Asian side of the HELLESPONT which was allied with the city of TROY in the TROJAN WAR. It is better known as the home of LEANDER.

Acacetus one who does nothing badly. It was a name given to HERMES because of his eloquence.

Acamas *see* **Demophon**.

Acarnania the most westerly portion of northern Greece, bounded on the north by the Ambracian Gulf, on the northeast by Amphilochia, on the west and

311

southwest by the Ionian Sea and on the east by AETOLIA. One of the original independent states of ancient Greece, its inhabitants, the Acarnanians, were considered to be behind the other Greeks in civilization, living by robbery and piracy.

Acastus in Greek mythology, a son of PELIAS, king of IOLCUS. He was one of the ARGONAUTS and also took part in the CALYDONIAN BOAR hunt. His wife, Astydamia, fell in love with PELEUS.

Acestes according to Virgil's *Aeneid*, in a trial of skill Acestes the Sicilian discharged his arrow with such force that it took fire ('the arrow of Acestes').

Achaea *see* **Achaia**.

Achaeans *or* **Achaians** one of the four races into which the ancient Greeks were divided. In early times they inhabited a part of northern Greece and of the PELOPONNESUS. They are represented by Homer as a brave and warlike people, and so distinguished were they that he usually calls the Greeks in general Achaeans. Afterwards they settled in the district of the Peloponnesus, called ACHAIA (2) after them and forming a narrow belt of coast on the south side of the Gulf of CORINTH.

Achaeus in Greek mythology, son of XUTHUS and CREÜSA (1), and consequently the brother of ION and grandson of HELLEN. He returned to THESSALY and recovered the dominions of which his father had been deprived.

Achaia *or* **Achaea** (1) a district in the south of THESSALY in which PHTHIA and HELLAS were situated. It appears to have been the original home of the ACHAEANS, who were hence called Phthiotan Achaeans to distinguish them from the Achaeans in PELOPONNESUS. It was from this part of Thessaly that ACHILLES came, and Homer says that the subjects of this hero were called MYR-MIDONS, HELLENES and ACHAEANS.

Achaia *or* **Achaea** (2) a district in PELOPONNESUS where the ACHAEANS settled.

Achates in Greek mythology, a companion of AENEAS in his wanderings subsequent to his flight from TROY. He is always distinguished in Virgil's *Aeneid* by the epithet *fidus*, 'faithful', and has become typical of a faithful friend and companion.

Acheloüs the largest river in Greece, which rises in Mount Pindus and flows mainly north-south to the Ionian Sea. In Greek mythology, it was regarded as the ruler and representative of all fresh water in HELLAS and was worshipped as a mighty god throughout Greece. The river-god is celebrated on account of his combat with HERACLES for the possession of DEÏANEIRA. Acheloüs first attacked Heracles in the form of a serpent, and on being worsted assumed the shape of a bull. Heracles wrenched off one of his horns, which forthwith became a cornucopia, or horn of plenty. This legend alludes apparently to some efforts made at an early period to check the ravages of the inundations of the river and by thus damming it creating a land of plenty.

Achemon *or* **Achmon** and his brother Basalus in Greek mythology, two CERCOPES who were forever quarrelling with each other. One day they saw HERACLES asleep under a tree and insulted him, but Heracles tied them by their feet to his club and walked off with them, heads downwards, like a brace of hares. Everyone laughed at the sight, and it became a proverbial cry among the Greeks, when two men were seen quarrelling 'Look out for Melampygos!' (i.e. Heracles).

Acheron the ancient name of several rivers in Greece and Italy, all of which were connected by legend with the lower world. The principal was a river of Thesprotia in EPIRUS (the 'River of Sorrows), which passes through Lake Acherusia and flows into the Ionian Sea. Homer speaks of Acheron as a river of the lower world, and late Greek writers also use the name to designate the lower world.

Acherontian Books the most celebrated books of augury in the world. They are the books which the Etruscans received from TAGES.

Acherusia a cavern on the borders of PONTUS, in Greek mythology said to lead down to the infernal regions. It was through this cavern that HERACLES dragged CERBERUS to earth.

Achilles a Greek legendary hero, the chief character in Homer's *Iliad*. His father was PELEUS, ruler of PHTHIA in THESSALY, his mother the sea-goddess THETIS. When only six years of age he was able to overcome lions and bears. His guardian, CHEIRON the Centaur, having declared that TROY could not be taken without his aid, his mother, fearing for his safety, disguised him as a girl, and introduced him among the daughters of LYCOMEDES of Scyrus. Her desire for his safety made her also try to make him invulnerable when a child by anointing him with ambrosia, and again by dipping him in the River STYX, from which he came out proof against all wounds except in the heel by which she had held him. When his hiding place was discovered by ODYSSEUS, Achilles promised his assistance to the Greeks against Troy. Accompanied by his close friend, PATROCLUS, he joined the expedition with a body of followers (MYRMIDONS) in fifty ships, and occupied nine years in raids upon the towns neighbouring Troy, after which the siege proper commenced. On being deprived of his prize, the maiden BRISEÏS, by AGAMEMNON, Achilles refused to take any further part in the war, and disaster attended the Greeks. Patroclus persuaded Achilles to allow him to lead the Myrmidons into battle dressed in his armour, and when Patroclus was slain by HECTOR, Achilles vowed revenge on the Trojans, and forgot his anger against the Greeks. He attacked the Trojans and drove them back behind their walls, slaying them in great numbers. He chased Hector, who fled before him three times round the walls of Troy, slew him, and dragged his body at his chariot wheels, but afterwards gave it up to King PRIAM, who had come in person to beg for it. He then performed the funeral rites of Patroclus, with which the *Iliad* closes. He was killed in a battle at the Scaean Gate of Troy by an arrow from the bow of PARIS, which struck his vulnerable heel. In discussions on the origin of Homeric poems the term *Achilleid* is often applied to those books of the *Iliad* in which Achilles is prominent, and which some suppose to have formed the original nucleus of the poem.

Acis in Greek mythology, a beautiful shepherd of Sicily, loved by GALATEA and crushed to death by his rival, the Cyclops POLYPHEMUS. His blood, flowing from beneath the rock which crushed him, was changed by Galatea into a river bearing his name, and renowned for the coldness of its water.

Achmon see **Achemon**.

Acrisius in Greek mythology, son of ABAS and twin brother of PROETÜS, with whom he is said to have quarrelled even in the womb, and father of DANAË. After the death of Abas, he expelled Proetüs from his inheritance, but Proetüs, supported by IOBATES, returned and Acrisius was compelled to give him TIRYNS while he kept ARGOS.

acropolis the citadel or chief place of an ancient Greek city, usually on an eminence commanding the town. The Acropolis of ATHENS contained some of the finest buildings in the world, such as the Parthenon, Erechtheum, etc.

Actaeon in Greek mythology, son of Autonoë, a great hunter who was turned into a stag by ARTEMIS for looking on her when she was bathing and torn to pieces by his own dogs.

Actor *see* **Eurytion**.

Admetus in Greek mythology, king of PHERAE in THESSALY, and husband of ALCESTIS, who gave signal proof of her love by consenting to die in order to prolong her husband's life.

Adonis originally a deity of the Phoenicians but borrowed into Greek mythology. He was represented as being a great favourite of APHRODITE, who accompanied him when engaged in hunting, of which he was very fond. He received a mortal wound from the tusk of a wild boar, and when the goddess hurried to his assistance she found him lifeless, whereupon she caused his blood to give rise to the anemone flower. The worship of Adonis, which began in Phoenicia was afterwards widely spread round the Mediterranean. He is the reproductive principle, nature's decay in winter and its revival in spring.

Adonis a small river rising in Lebanon and flowing to the Mediterranean. When in flood it is tinged with a red colour, and so is connected with the legend of ADONIS.

Adrasteia *see* **Ida**; **Titans**.

Adrastus in Greek mythology, a king of ARGOS, whose daughter married POLYNEICES of THEBES, who had been exiled from his native city by his brother ETEOCLES. Adrastus led the expedition of the SEVEN AGAINST THEBES to restore his son-in-law to his right, and, as had been foretold by AMPHIARAUS, was the only who survived. Ten years later he led the six sons of the heroes who had fallen to a new attack on Thebes, the war of the EPIGONI. This attack was successful, but a son of Adrastus fell, and the father died of grief.

Aea a name given by very early writers to COLCHIS as residence of AEËTES.

Aeacus in Greek mythology, son of ZEUS and AEGINA, born on the island of AEGINA, of which he became the ruler. His sons TELAMON and PELEUS abandoned the island, Telamon going to SALAMIS and Peleus to PHTHIA. After his death Zeus made him a judge of the shades in HADES with MINOS and RHADAMANTHUS.

Aechmodius *see* **Echetus**.

Aeëtes in Greek mythology, a son of HELIOS, brother of CIRCE, PASIPHAË and PERSES (3). He was married to EIDYIA, by whom he had two daughters, MEDEA and Chalciope, and one son, ABSYRTUS. He was king of COLCHIS at the time when PHRIXUS brought there the GOLDEN FLEECE. At one time he was expelled from his kingdom by his brother Perses, but was restored by his daughter Medea.

Aegaeon *see* **Briareus**.

Aegean Sea that part of the Mediterranean which washes the eastern shores of Greece and the western coast of Asia Minor.

Aegeus in Greek mythology, son of PANDION (2), king of ATHENS and Pylia. Pandion had been expelled from his kingdom by the Metionids, but Aegeus with his brothers PALLAS (3), NISUS and LYCUS (3) restored him, and Aegeus being the eldest succeeded. Neither of his first two wifes bore him children. He ascribed this misfortune to the anger of APHRODITE and to conciliate her introduced her worship at Athens. Afterwards he begot THESEUS by AETHRA (1) at Troezen. When Theseus had grown to manhood he went to Athens and defeated the fifty sons of his uncle Pallas, who had deposed Aegeus and also wished to exclude Theseus from the succession. Aegeus was restored, but died soon after. When Theseus went to Crete to deliver Athens from the tribute it had to pay to MINOS, he promised his father that on his resturn he would hoist white sails as a signal of his safety. On his approach to the coat of ATTICA he forgot his promise, and his father, who was watching on a rock on the coast, on seeing the black sails thought that his son had perished and threw himself into the sea, which according to some traditions received from this event the name of the AEGAEAN SEA. MEDEA, who was believed to have spent some time at Athens on her return from CORINTH to COLCHIS, is said to have become mother of a son, Medos, by Aegeus.

Aegialeia an ancient town of SICYON, its name derived either from AEGIALEUS (2) or from a brother of PHORONEUS and first king of Sicyon, to whom the foundation of the town was ascribed.

Aegialeus (1) in Greek mythology, a son of ADRASTUS and Amphithea or Demoanassa. He was the only one of the EPIGONI who was killed.

Aegialeus (2) in Greek mythology, a son of INACHUS and the Oceanid MELIA, from whom the part of PELOPONNESUS afterwards called ACHAIA (2) derived its name of AEGIALEIA.

Aegina in Greek mythology, the daughter of the river-god, ASOPUS. ZEUS carried her to the island of Oenone or Oenopia, where she bore him a son, AEACUS. The island took her name.

Aegina a mountainous Greek island in the Gulf of Aegina, south of Athens, triangular in form. It was one of the most celebrated islands in Greece. In Greek mythology it was called Oenone or Oenopia and received the name of Aegina from AEGINA, who there bore ZEUS a son, AEACUS. At this time Aegina was uninhabited, and Zeus changed the ants of the island into people, the MYRMIDONS, over whom Aeacus ruled.

Aegipan *see* **Delphyne**.

aegis in Greek mythology, the shield of ZEUS, according to Homer, but according to later writers and artists a metal cuirass or breastplate, in which was set the head of the Gorgon MEDUSA, and with which ATHENA is often represented as being protected. In a figurative sense the word is used to denote some shielding or protecting power.

Aegisthus in Greek mythology, a son of THYESTES and cousin of AGAMEMNON, king of MYCENAE. He became the lover of the queen, CLYTEMNESTRA, with whom he killed Agamemnon. He helped Clytemnestra rule Mycenae for seven years, and was slain with her by ORESTES, the son of Agamemnon.

Aegyptus in Greek mythology, a son of BELUS (1) and twin brother of DANAÜS. Belus assigned to Danaüs the sovereignty of Libya and to Aegyptus he gave Arabia. Aegyptus also subdued the country of Melampodes, which he called Aegypt after his own name. All his fifty sons except LYNCEUS (1) were killed by their brides, the daughters of DANAÜS. *See* DANAÏDES.

Aello *see* **Harpies**.

Aeneas the hero of Virgil's *Aeneid*, a Trojan, who, according to Homer, was, next to HECTOR, the bravest of the warriors of TROY. When Troy was taken and set on fire, Aeneas, according to Virgil, with his father, son, and wife CREÜSA (2), fled, but the latter was lost in the confusion of the fight. Having collected a fleet, Aeneas sailed for Italy, but after numerous adventures he was driven by a tempest to the coast of Africa, where Queen DIDO of CARTHAGE received him kindly and would have married him. ZEUS, however, sent HERMES to Aeneas and commanded him to sail to Italy. While the deserted Dido ended her life on the funeral pile, Aeneas set sail with his companions, and after some further adventures by land and sea reached the country of King LATINUS, in Italy. The king's daughter LAVINIA was destined by an oracle to wed a stranger, this stranger being Aeneas, but had been promised by her mother to TURNUS, king of the RUTULI. The result was a war, which was ended by Aeneas slaying Turnus and marrying Lavinia. *See also* ROME.

Aeneïd *see* **Virgil**.

Aeolian Islands a group of volcanic islands in the Tyrrhenian Sea. One of the islands, Strongyle is an active volcano and in Roman mythology was considered the home of VULCAN.

Aeolians one of the four races into which the ancient Greeks were divided, orginally inhabiting the district of Aeolis, in THESSALY, from which they spread over other parts of Greece. In Greek mythology they are represented as descendants of AEOLUS, the son of HELLEN. In early times they were the most numerous and powerful of the HELLENES, chiefly inhabiting northern Greece and the western side of PELOPONNESUS, although latterly a portion of them went to LESBOS and TENEDOS and the northwest shores of Asia Minor, where they possessed a number of cities.

Aeolus (1) in Greek mythology, the god of the winds, which he kept confined in a cave in the AEOLIAN ISLANDS, releasing them when he wished or when he was commanded by the superior gods.

Aeolus (2) in Greek mythology, a son of HELLEN, to whom Hellen is said to have left his kingdom in THESSALY and from whom the AEOLIANS were descended.

Aerope *see* **Atreus**; **Nauplius** (3).

Aeropus *see* **Echemus**.

Aeschylus the first of the three great tragic poets of Greece, the others being SOPHOCLES and EURIPIDES. He was born at Eleusis, in Attica, 525 BC, died in Sicily 456. Only seven of his tragedies are extant: *The Persians, Seven against Thebes, Suppliants, Prometheus, Agamemnon, Choephori*, and *Eumenides*, the last three forming a trilogy on the story of ORESTES.

Aesculapius *or* **Asclepius** in Greek mythology, the god of medicine. He was afterwards adopted by the Romans. He is usually said to have been a son of APOLLO and CORONIS (1). He was worshipped in particular at EPIDAURUS, in the PELOPONNESUS, where a temple with a grove was dedicated to him. The sick who visited his temple had to spend one or more nights in the sanctuary, after which the remedies to be used were revealed in a dream. Those who were cured offered a sacrifice to Aesculapius, commonly a cock. He is often represented with a large beard, holding a knotty staff, around which is entwined a serpent, the serpent being specially his symbol.

Aeson in Greek mythology, son of Cretheus and heir to the throne of IOLCUS, and father of JASON. Usurped by his half-brother, PELIAS, he sent Jason to CHEIRON the Centaur for protection.

Aeson *or* **Aesonis** a town of Magnesia in Thessaly, the name of which is derived from AESON, the father of JASON.

Aethalia the ancient name of the island of ELBA.

Aether in Greek mythology, the personification of the clear upper air breathed by the OLYMPIANS, son of EREBUS and his sister NYX.

Aethices a barbarous Epirot clan, who lived by robbery, placed by Strabo on the Thessalian side of Pindus. They are mentioned by Homer, who relates that the CENTAURS, expelled by Peirithoüs from Mount Pelion, took refuge among the Aethices.

Aethra (1) in Greek mythology, a daughter of King Pittheus of Troezen. BELLEROPHON sued for her hand but was banished from CORINTH before the nuptials took place. She later became the mother of THESEUS by AEGEUS. She went to ATTICA from where she was carried off to LACEDAEMON (2) by CASTOR AND POLLUX and became a slave of HELEN, with whom she was taken to TROY. At the taking of Troy she came to the camp of the Greeks where she was recognized by her grandsons, and DEMOPHON, one of them, asked AGAMEMNON to free her. Agamemnon accordingly sent a messenger to Helen to request her to give up Aethra. This was granted, and Aethra became free again.

Aethra (2) in Greek mythology, a daughter of OCEANUS by whom ATLAS fathered the twelve HYADES and a son, Hyas.

Aetna, Mount *see* **Etna, Mount**.

Aetolia a western division of northern Greece, separated on the west by the River ACHELOÜS from ACARNANIA and washed by the Corinthian Gulf on the south. It was one of the original independent states of Greece. In Greek mythology MELEAGER slew the CALYDONIAN BOAR here.

Aetolus in Greek mythology, a hero who invaded the country of DORUS (2) and his brothers, killed them and founded AETOLIA.

Agamemnon in Greek mythology, son of ATREUS, king of MYCENAE and ARGOS, brother of MENELAÜS, and commander of the allied Greeks at the siege of TROY. Returning home after the fall of Troy, he was treacherously assassinated by his wife, CLYTEMNESTRA, and her lover, AEGISTHUS, Agamemnon's cousin. He was the father of ORESTES, IPHIGENIA, and ELECTRA.

Aganippe (1) in Greek mythology, the daughter of the river-god Parmesses, or Termessos, and nymph of a fountain on Mount Helicon, which was sacred to the MUSES, and which had the property of inspiring with peotic fire whoever drank from it.

Aganippe (2) in Greek mythology, the name often given to the wife of ACRISIUS and mother of DANAË.

Agave a daughter of CADMUS, king of THEBES, and sister of SEMELE. She was the wife of ECHION (1), one of the SPARTI, and mother of PENTHEUS. For her abuse of Semele, who died when pregnant with DIONYSUS by ZEUS, she was driven mad by the gods and tore her son, Pentheus, to pieces. An exile from Thebes, she travelled to ILLYRIA where she married the king, Lycotherses. She later killed him so that her father, Cadmus, might become the king of ILLYRIA. *See also* INO.

Agdistus *see* **Cybele**.

Agenor (1) in Greek mythology, a hero, king of Phoenicia and father of EUROPA and CADMUS, Phoenix, Cylix, THASUS and PHINEUS. When Europa was carried off by ZEUS, Agenor sent his sons in search of her and enjoined them not to return without her. As Europa was not to be found, none of them returned, and all settled in foreign countries.

Agenor (2) in Greek mythology, a brother of IASUS and PELASGUS. After their deaths he invaded their lands and thus became king of ARGOS.

Agenor (3) in Greek mythology, one of the bravest among the Trojans, slain by NEOPTOLEMUS.

ages of man *see* **races of man**.

Aglaia *or* **Aglaea** in Greek mythology, wife of HEPHAESTUS and one of the three GRACES, the other two being Euphrosyne and Thalia.

Agorious *see* **Oxylus**.

Agrianome *see* **Oicles**; **Oileus**.

Agrius *see* **Oeneus**.

Ajax in Greek mythology, son of TELAMON, a Greek hero and king of SALAMIS (1) who sailed with twelve ships to join the fight against TROY. He is represented by Homer as the boldest and handsomest of the Greeks after ACHILLES. He had more than one combat with HECTOR, against whom he was well matched. On the death of Achilles, when his arms, which Ajax claimed, were awarded to ODYSSEUS, he became insane and killed himself. This is the subject of Sophocles' tragedy *Ajax*. Shakespeare used him in *Troilus and Cressida*.

Ajax the Less in Greek mythology, son of OILEUS, king of Locris, and a champion on the Greek side in the TROJAN WAR. At the fall of TROY he entered the shrine of ATHENA and seized CASSANDRA. He lost his life during his homeward voyage, either by shipwreck or by a flash of lightning sent by Athena, who was offended at the violation of her temple.

Alba Longa a city of LATIUM, according to tradition built by ASCANIUS, the son of AENEAS, three hundred years before the foundation of ROME, at one time the most powerful city of Latium. It ultimately fell under the dominion of Rome, when the town was destroyed, it is said. *See also* HORATII.

Albula, River the ancient name of the River TIBER.

Alcaeus *see* **Electryon**.

Alcathous in Greek mythology, a son of PELOPS and Hippodamia, (1) brother of ATREUS and THYESTES, and father of Iphinoë, Periboea, Automedusa and others. When MEGAREUS offered his daughter and his kingdom to whoever should slay the Cythaeronian lion, Alcathous undertook the task, conquered the lion and became king of Megara. He rebuilt the walls of MEGARA with the aid of APOLLO.

Alcestis in Greek mythology, wife of ADMETUS, king of THESSALY. Her husband was ill, and, according to an oracle, would die unless someone made a vow to meet death in his stead. This was secretly done by Alcestis, and Admetus recovered. After her death HERACLES brought her back from the infernal regions.

Alcidamea *see* **Bunus**.

Alcinous king of the PHAEACIANS, a son of NAUSITHOUS and grandson of POSEIDON. On their return from COLCHIS the ARGONAUTS came to the island where Alcinous lived with his queen, Arete, and were hospitably received. When the Colchians in their pursuit of the Argonauts also arrived and demanded that MEDEA be handed over to them, Alcinous declared that if she was still a virgin she would be restored to them, but if she was already the wife of JASON he would protect her. The Colchians were obliged, by the contrivance of Arete, to depart without Medea, and the Argonauts continued their voyage homewards. ODYSSEUS was shipwrecked on the island of Alcinous, and Homer's description of his palace and his dominions, the way in which Odysseus is received, the entertainments given to him, and the stories he related to the king about his own wanderings occupy a considerable portion of the *Odyssey*.

Alcmaeon in Greek mythology, a son of AMPHIARAUS and ERIPHYLE and the brother of Amphilochus, Eurydice and Demonassa. Before Amphiaraus set out with the SEVEN AGAINST THEBES, he enjoined his sons to kill their mother as soon as they should be grown to adulthood. Alcmaeon commanded the EPIGONI and slew LAODAMUS. After the fall of Thebes he killed his mother, possibly with Amphilochus, for which deed he was made mad by the FURIES.

Alcmene *or* **Alcmena** in Greek mythology, the wife of AMPHITRYON and the mother of HERACLES by ZEUS and of IPHICLES by Amphitryon. The love affair of Zeus and Alcmene has been the subject of comedies, notably by Plautus and Molière. HERA, jealous of Alcmene, delayed the birth of Heracles for seven days that EURYSTHEUS might be born first and thus be entitled to geater rights, according to a view of Zeus himself. After the death of Amphitryon, Alcmene married RHADAMANTHUS, son of Zeus.

Alecto in Greek mythology, one of the three FURIES, the others being Megaera and Tisiphone.

Alector in Greek mythology, king of Argos and father of IPHIS. He was consulted by POLYNEICES as to the manner in which AMPHIARAUS might be compelled to take part in the expedition of the SEVEN AGAINST THEBES.

Aleus *see* **Lycurgus** (2); **Nauplius** (3).

Alexander *see* **Paris**.

Allcidocus *see* **Oxylus**.

Aloeus in Greek mythology, a son of POSEIDON and Canace. He married IPHIMEDEIA, the daughter of TRIOPAS (1), who was in love with Poseidon and had two sons by him, OTUS AND EPHIALTES.

Alope in Greek mythology, a daughter of Cercyon, king of ELEUSIS, who was seduced by the god POSEIDON to whom she bore a son, Hippothoon. She was afraid of what her father would do if he found out about the baby and so abandoned him. The child survived, being suckled by mares, and was found by shepherds. The shepherds were surprised at the magnificence of the child's clothing and took the child to the king. Cercyon recognized the clothing as having been made by his daughter and left the child to die, having killed Alope. Again the child was saved by being suckled by mares. On growing to manhood, Hippothoon asked THESEUS, king of Athens, to appoint him king of Eleusis. Theseus, who had already killed Cercyon in a quarrel in self-defence, agreed to the request. Like Hippothoon, Theseus was a son of Poseidon.

Alphaea *see* **Britomartis**.

Alpheias *see* **Alpheus**.

Alpheus *or* **Alpheius** (now Rufia) the largest river of PELOPONNESUS, flowing westwards into the IONIAN SEA. In Greek mythology, Alpheus appears as a celebrated river-god, like all the river-gods the son of OCEANUS and TETHYS. The fact that in its upper reaches the river flows underground probably gave rise to the fable that Alpheus flowed beneath the sea and attempted to mingle its waters with the fountain of ARETHUSA on ORTYGIA. Hence Ovid's name for Arethusa is Alpheias.

Althaea in Greek mythology, a daughter of Thestius and Eurythemis. She was the wife of her uncle, OENEUS, king of CALYDON, and the mother of MELEAGER and DEÏANEIRA. In the course of the CALYDONIAN BOAR Hunt, Meleager killed some of his mother's brothers in a quarrel. Althaea is said to have put a curse on her son and caused his death by burning a charred piece of wood, knowing that Meleager was doomed to die when it was burned to ashes. Having taken revenge on her son for her brothers' deaths, she then took her own life in remorse.

Alxior *see* **Oenomaus**.

Amarynceus *see* **Diores**.

Amazons in Greek mythology, the name of a community of women, who permitted no men to reside among them, who fought under the conduct of a queen, and who long constituted a formidable state. They were said to burn off the right breast so that it might not impede them in the use of the bow – a legend that arose from the Greeks supposing the name was from *a*, 'not', *mazos*, 'breast'. It is probably from *a*, 'together', and *mazos*, 'breast', the name meaning, therefore, 'sisters'. Several nations of Amazons are mentioned, the most famous being those who dwelt in PONTUS and who built EPHESUS and other cities. Their queen, HIPPOLYTA, was killed by HERACLES, who took from her the girdle of ARES. They attacked ATTICA in the time of THESEUS. They came to the assistance of TROY under their queen, Penthesilea, who was slain by ACHILLES.

Ambracia (modern Arta) a gulf, town and river in northwest Greece. The town stands on the River Arta, which for a considerable distance above its mouth formed a part of the boundary between Greece and Turkey. In Greek mythology, the town was founded by Ambrax, son of Thesprotus, or by Ambracia, daughter of Augeas.

Amor in Roman mythology, a name for Cupid, the god of love, equivalent to the Greek Eros.

Amphiaraus a son of Oicles and Hypermnestra, the daughter of Thestius, he was a seer, descended on his father's side from the seer Melampus. He was among the hunters of the Calydonian Boar and was said to have deprived it of one eye. He married Eriphyle, sister of Adrastus, and was the father of Alcmaeon, Amphilochus, Eurydice and Demonassa. When he married Eriphyle he swore that he would abide by her decision on any point in which he should differ in opinion from Adrastus. When he was asked by Adrastus, therefore, to join the Seven against Thebes, although he foresaw the outcome he was nevertheless persuaded by his wife to join his friends, Eriphyle having been enticed to induce her husband by the necklace of Harmonia which Polyneices had given her. On leaving Argos, Amphiaraus enjoined his sons to avenge his death on their heartless mother. During the war against Thebes, Amphiaraus fought bravely, but was pursued by Periclymenus and fled towards the river Ismenius. Here the earth opened up before he was overtaken by his enemy, and swallowed up Amphiaraus together with his chariot, but Zeus made him immortal. He was worshipped as a hero and had a sancturary at Argos.

Amphidamus *see* **Lycurgus** (2).

Amphion in Greek mythology, son of Zeus and Antiope (1), daughter of Nycteus, and husband of Niobe. He had miraculous skill in music, being taught by Hermes or, according to others, by Apollo. In poetic legend he is said to have availed himself of his skill when building the walls of Thebes—the stones moving and arranging themselves in proper position at the sound of his lyre. He was assisted by his twin brother, Zethus.

Amphissa *see* **Echetus**.

Amphissus *see* **Dryope**.

Amphithamus *see* **Nasamon**.

Amphithea *see* **Deïpyle**; **Opheltes**.

Amphitrite in Greek mythology, daughter of Oceanus and Tethys, or of Nereus and Doris, and wife of Poseidon, represented as drawn in a chariot of shells by Tritons, with a trident in her hand. In the Homeric poems she is the personification of the Sea, and her marriage to Poseidon is alluded to in a number of scenes depicted on ancient monuments.

Amphitryon in Greek mythology, king of Thebes, grandson of Perseus and husband of ALCMENE. During his absence from home in order to punish the murderers of his wife's brothers (*see* ELECTRYON), Alcmene was seduced by ZEUS in the disguise of Amphitryon, who himself returned home the next day.

Amulius in Roman mythology, a king of ALBA LONGA and brother of NUMITOR. In order to acquire the throne, he drove his brother from power, killed his nephews, and forced his niece REA SILVIA to be a Vestal Virgin (*see* VESTA) so that she would not bear sons to threaten his position. When twin sons, ROMULUS AND REMUS, were born to her by MARS, Amulius had them put in a basket on the Tiber so that they would die. However, they survived and later killed Amulius before restoring their grandfather Numitor to the throne.

Amyclae a town of ancient Greece, the chief seat of the Achaeans in Laconia, a short distance from SPARTA, by which it was conquered about 800 BC. It was one of the most celebrated cities of PELOPONNESUS in the heroic age. In Greek mythology, it was founded by AMYCLAS and was the home of TYNDAREUS and of CASTOR AND POLLUX, who are hence called *Amyclaei Fratres*.

Amyclas in Greek mythology, a son of LACEDAEMON and SPARTA, and father of HYACINTH by Diomede. He was king of LACONIA and was regarded as the founder of AMYCLAE.

Amycus *see* **Bebryces**.

Amymone *see* **Nauplius** (1).

Amythaon *see* **Bias**.

Anadyomene (Greek 'she who comes forth') a name given to APHRODITE when she was represented as rising from the sea.

Anaphe a small mountainous island in the south of the Greek Archipelago, east of THERA. In Greek legend, it was called Membliarus from the son of CADMUS of this name, who came to the island in search of EUROPA. It was celebrated for the temple of APOLLO, the foundation of which was acribed to the ARGONAUTS because Apollo had shown them the island as a place of refuge when they were overtaken by a storm.

Anaurus, River a small river in MAGNESIA, in THESSALY, flowing past IOLCOS into the Pagasean Gulf. According to legend, JASON lost one of his sandals in it.

Anaxabia *see* **Pylades**.

Anaxarete *see* **Iphis** (3).

Anaxo *see* **Electryon**.

Anchiale *see* **Dactyls**.

Anchises in Greek mythology, the father by APHRODITE of the Trojan hero AENEAS, who carried him off on his shoulders at the burning of TROY and made him the companion of his voyage to Italy. This voyage, which is not mentioned in the Homeric legend, is described by Virgil in his *Aeneid*. He died at Drepanum in Sicily.

Ancus Marcius according to Roman tradition, the fourth king of Rome, who succeeded TULLUS HOSTILIUS in 638 and died in 614 BC. He was the son of the daughter of NUMA POMPILIUS, and sought to imitate his grandfather by reviving the neglected observances of religion. He is said to have built the wooden bridge across the Tiber known as the Sublician, constructed the harbour at Ostia and built the first Roman prison.

Andraemon (1) in Greek mythology, the husband of GORGE, daughter of OENEUS, and father of THOAS. When TYDEUS delivered Oeneus, who had been imprisoned by the sons of Agrius, he gave the kingdom to Andraemon as he was already too old to rule.

Andraemon (2) a son of OXYLUS and husband of DRYOPE.

Andromache in Greek mythology, daughter of EËTION and wife of HECTOR, and one of the most attractive women of Homer's *Iliad*. The passage describing her parting with Hector, when he was setting out to battle, is well known and much admired. On the taking of TROY, her son was hurled from the wall of the city, and she herself fell to the share of NEOPTOLEMUS, who took her to EPIRUS where she bore him three sons. She afterwards married HELENUS, a brother of Hector.

Andromeda in Greek mythology, daughter of the Ethiopian king CEPHEUS and of CASSIOPEIA. Cassiopeia having boasted that her daughter surpassed the NEREÏDS, if not HERA herself, in beauty, the offended goddesses prevailed on their father, POSEIDON to afflict the country with a horrid sea monster, which threatened universal destruction. To appease the offended god, Andromeda was chained to a rock but was rescued by PERSEUS and after death was changed into a constellation. The legend forms the subject of tragedies by both Euripides and Sophocles, and Ovid introduced it into his *Metamorphoses*.

Antaea *see* **Stheneboea**.

Antaeüs in Greek mythology, the giant son of POSEIDON and GE, who was invincible so long as he was in contact with the earth. HERACLES grasped him in his arms and stifled him suspended in the air, thus preventing him from touching the earth.

Antenor in Greek mythology, a Trojan hero who advised HELEN to return to MENELAÜS.

Anteros in Greek mythology, the god of mutual love. According to some, however, Anteros is the enemy of love, or the god of antipathy. He was also said to punish those who did not return the love of others.

Antianeira *see* **Erchion** (2).

Anticleia *see* **Laërtes**.

Antigone (1) in Greek mythology, the daughter of OEDIPUS and JOCASTA, celebrated for her devotion to her brother POLYNEICES, for burying whom against the decree of King CREON she suffered death. She is the heroine of Sophocles' *Oedipus at Colonus* and his *Antigone*; also of Racine's tragedy *Les Frères Enemis*.

Antigone (2) in Greek mythology, a daughter of Eurytion of Phthia and wife of Peleus, by whom she became the mother of Polydora. When Peleus had killed Eurytion and fled to Acastus at Iolcus, he drew on himself the hatred of Astydamia, the wife of Acastus. As a result of this Astydamia sent a message to Antigone in which she lied that Peleus was on the point of marrying Sterope, a daughter of Acastus. When she heard this, Antigone hanged herself.

Antigone (3) in Greek mythology, a daughter of Laomedon and sister of Priam. She boasted of excelling Hera in the beauty of her hair and was punished for her presumption by being changed into a stork.

Antilochus in Greek mythology, a son of Nestor, distinguished among the younger heroes who took part in the Trojan War by beauty, bravery and swiftness of foot. He was slain by Memnon, but Achilles avenged his death.

Antimachus *see* **Deïphobus**.

Antinous *see* **Eupeithes**.

Antiope (1) in Greek mythology, daughter of Nycteus, king of Thebes. Zeus was attracted by her beauty and came to her in the guise of a satyr. Antiope conceived twin sons, Amphion and Zethus, by this union and, scared of her father's wrath, when her condition became obvious she fled from Thebes and went to Sicyon, where she married King Epopeus. Another version of the legend has it that Epopeus seduced and abducted Antiope.

Antiope (2) in Greek mythology, an Amazon, a sister of Hippolyte, who married Theseus. When Attica was invaded by the Amazons, Antiope fought with Theseus against them and died the death of a heroine by his side.

Aonia in ancient geography, a name for part of Boeotia in Greece, containing Mount Helicon and the fountain Aganippe, both haunts of the Muses.

Aphaea *see* **Britomartis**.

Aphareus in Greek mythology, a son of the Messenian king Perieres and Gorgophone. He had three sons, Peisus, Lynceus and Idas. He received Neleus, the son of Cretheus, and Lycus, the son of Pandion (2), who had fled from their countries into his dominions. To the former he gave a tract of land in Messenia.

Aphrodite in Greek mythology, the goddess of erotic love and marriage, counterpart of the Roman Venus. She was supposed to have sprung from the sea foam surrounding the severed parts of Uranus, although according to Homer she was the daughter of Zeus and Dione. A festival called Aphrodisia was celebrated in her honour in various parts of Greece, but especially in Cyprus.

Apollo in Greek mythology, son of Zeus and Leto, who, being persecuted by the jealousy of Hera, after tedious wanderings and nine days' labour, was delivered of him and his twin sister, Artemis, on the Island of Delos. Skilled in the use of the bow, Apollo slew the serpent Python on the fifth day after his birth. Afterwards, with his sister, Artemis, he killed the children of Niobe. He aided

Zeus in the war with the Titans and the giants. He destroyed the Cyclops because they had forged the thunderbolts with which Zeus killed Apollo's son and favourite Aesculapius. According to some traditions he invented the lyre, although this is generally ascribed to Hermes. The brightest creation of polytheism, Apollo is also the most complex, and many aspects of the people's life were reflected in his cult. He was originally the sun-god, and although in Homer he appears distinct from Helios (the sun), yet his real nature is hinted at even here by the epithet *Phoebus*, that is, 'the radiant' or 'beaming'. In later times the view was almost universal that Apollo and Helios were identical. From being the god of light and purity in a physical sense, he gradually became the god of moral and spiritual light and purity, the source of all intellectual, social, and political progress. He thus came to be regarded as the god of song and prophecy, the god that wards off and heals bodily suffering and disease, the institutor and guardian of civil and political order, and the founder of cities. His worship was introduced in Rome at an early period, probably in the time of the Tarquins. Among the ancient statues of Apollo that have survived, the most remarkable is the Apollo Belvedere in the Vatican at Rome. This statue was discovered at Frascati in 1455 and purchased by Pope Julian II, the founder of the Vatican museum. It is a copy of a Greek statue of the third century BC and dates probably from the reign of Nero.

Apollodorus a Greek writer who flourished about 140 BC. Among the numerous works he wrote on various subjects, the only one extant is his *Bibliothece,* which contains a concise account of the mythology of Greece down to the heroic age (*see* RACES OF MAN).

Apollonius of Rhodes (Apollonius Rhodius) a Greek rhetorician and poet, flourished about 230 BC. Of his various works only the *Argonautica* survives. It is an epic poem dealing with the story of the ARGONAUTS' expedition.

apple of discord *see* **Eris**; **golden apple**.

Apsyrtus *see* **Absyrtus**.

Apulia a region in the southeast of Italy on the Adriatic. In Greek mythology, it was settled by Diomedes (1), who founded its principal cities.

Aquarius *see* **Ganymede**.

Arachne in Greek mythology, a maiden from Lydia who presumptuously challenged Athena to a weaving contest. Athena, out of jealousy, changed her into a spider.

Arcadia the central and most mountainous portion of the Peloponnesus, the inhabitants of which in ancient times were celebrated for simplicity of character and manners. Their occupation was almost entirely pastoral, and thus the country came to be regarded as typical of rural simplicity and happiness. In Greek mythology, the Arcadians derived their name from Arcas, a son of Zeus. The lyre is said to have been invented here by Hermes, and the syrinx, the musical instrument of the shepherds, was the invention of PAN, the tutelary god of Arcadia.

Arcas in Greek mythology, the ancestor and eponymous hero of the Arcadians, from whom the region of ARCADIA and its inhabitants derived their name. He was the son of ZEUS by CALLISTO, a companion of ARTEMIS. After the death or metamorphosis of his mother, Zeus gave the child to MAIA. Arcas became afterwards by Leaneira or Meganeira, the father of ELATUS and Apheidas.

Arceisius *see* **Laërtes**.

Arcesilaus *see* **Battus**.

Archemorus *see* **Opheltes**.

Arctophylax, Arctos *see* **Ursa Major**.

Ardea an ancient city of LATIUM, situated on a small river near the sea, south of Rome. According to one legend, it was founded by a son of ODYSSEUS and CIRCE, but others represent it as founded by DANAË, mother of PERSEUS. It appears in the story of AENEAS as the capital of the RUTULI.

Areas *see* **Oenomaus**.

Arene *see* **Gorgophone**; **Idas and Lynceus**.

Areopagus the oldest of the Athenian courts of justice, an assembly having a position more august than an ordinary court, and in its best days exercising a general supervision over public morals. It obtained its name from its place of meeting, on the Hill of ARES, near the Acropolis or citadel of Athens.

Ares in Greek mythology, the god of war whose Roman counterpart is MARS. The son of ZEUS and HERA, he is represented as terrible in battle but not as invulnerable, since he was wounded at various times by HERACLES, DIOMEDES, and ATHENA. He is represented as a youthful warrior of strong frame, either naked or clothed with the chlamys. He was a lover of APHRODITE, by whom he had several children, and of others. The chief seats of the worship of Ares were in THRACE and Scythia.

Arete *see* **Nausicaä**.

Arethusa in Greek mythology, a daugher of NEREUS and Doris and a nymph changed by ARTEMIS into a fountain in order to free her from the pursuit of the river-god ALPHEUS. This fountain was said to exist in the small Island of ORTYGIA, near Syracuse, and was fabled to have a subterranean connection with the River Alpheus in Greece.

Arge *see* **Opis**.

Argeia *see* **Polyneices**.

Arges *see* **Cyclops**; **Titans**.

Argives *or* **Argivi** the inhabitants of ARGOS. It is a term used by Homer and other ancient authors as a generic appellation for all the Greeks.

Argo in Greek mythology, the ship of the ARGONAUTS.

Argolis *see* **Argos**.

Argonautica *see* **Apollonius of Rhodes.**

Argonauts in Greek mythology, fifty Greek heroes who performed a hazardous voyage to COLCHIS, a far-distant country at the eastern extremity of the BLACK SEA, in the ship *Argo* under the command of JASON. PELIAS, the usurping king of IOLCUS, to get rid of his nephew Jason, sent him to fetch the GOLDEN FLEECE that was preserved in Colchis suspended upon a tree and under the guardianship of a sleeplesss dragon. Jason caused ARGUS (3) to build a ship of fifty oars and gathered together the bravest heroes from all parts of Greece, including HERACLES, CASTOR AND POLLUX, MELEAGER, ORPHEUS and THESEUS. They sailed by LEMNOS, along the coast of THRACE, up the HELLESPONT and over the Black Sea, encountering many adventures, such as passing safely betwen the CLASHING ROCKS. When they arrived at Colchis, King AEËTES promised to give up the fleece on condition that Jason should yoke to a plough two fire-breathing bulls and should sow the dragon's teeth not already sown by CADMUS in THEBES. From the king's daughter MEDEA, who had fallen passionately in love with Jason, he obtained, under promise of marriage, a charm against fire and steel, which enabled him to destroy all the warriors who sprang up from the land sown with the dragon's teeth. With Medea's help he stupefied the guardian dragon, seized the fleece, and embarked in the *Argo* accompanied by Medea. Despite pursuit by Aeëtes and the charms of the SIRENS and of storms that drove them to Crete and elsewhere, the Argonauts arrived safely at Iolcus, and Jason dedicated the *Argo* to POSEIDON at CORINTH.

Argos a town of Greece, in the north-east of the PELOPONNESUS, between the Gulfs of AEGINA and NAUPLIA or ARGOS. The town and the surrounding territory of Argolis were famous from the legendary period of Greek history onwards. Here, besides Argos, was MYCENAE, where AGAMEMNON ruled. In the plain of Argos was the Lernean marsh, home of the HYDRA slain by HERACLES.

Argus (1) the third king of ARGOS, a son of ZEUS and NIOBE from whom Argos and Argolis derived their names.

Argus (2) *or* **Argus Panoptes** in Greek mythology, a fabulous being, said to have had a hundred eyes, placed by HERA to guard IO. Argus was slain by HERMES, who either stoned him or charmed him to sleep with the music of his flute and then cut off his head. Hera put his hundred eyes in the tail of the peacock, her favourite bird. From him comes the term 'argus-eyed', applied to one who is exceedingly watchful.

Argus (3) the builder of the ARGONAUTS' ship, *Argo*.

Ariadne in Greek mythology, a daughter of MINOS, king of Crete. She gave THESEUS a ball of thread to conduct him out of the labyrinth after his defeat of the MINOTAUR. Theseus promised to marry her but abandoned her on the island of Naxos, where she was found by DIONYSUS, who married her.

Arimaspians in Greek mythology, a people who lived in the extreme northeast of the ancient world. They were said to be one-eyed and to carry on a perpetual war with the gold-guarding griffins, whose gold they endeavoured to steal.

Arion (1) an ancient Greek poet and musician, born at Methymna, in LESBOS, flourished about 625 BC. He lived at the Court of Perinder of CORINTH, and afterwards visited Sicily and Italy. Returning from Tarentum to Corinth with rich treasures, the avaricious sailors resolved to murder him. APOLLO, however, having informed him in a dream of the impending danger, Arion in vain endeavoured to soften the hearts of the crew by the power of music. He then threw himself into the sea, when one of a shoal of dolphins, which had been attracted by his music, received him on his back and bore him to land. The sailors, having returned to Corinth, were confronted by Arion and convicted for their crime. The lyre of Arion and the dolphin that rescued him became constellations in the heavens. A fragment of a hymn to POSEIDON, ascribed to Arion, is extant.

Arion (2) in Greek mythology, a divine horse which POSEIDON, in the form of a horse, fathered on DEMETER while she was in the shape of a mare in order to escape from Poseidon's pursuit of her. Another story says the horse was created by Poseidon in his contest with ATHENA. From Poseidon the horse passed through the hands of ONCIUS, HERACLES and ADRASTUS. *See also* SEVEN AGAINST THEBES.

Aristeas in Greek mythology, a personage represented to have lived over many centuries, disappearing and reappearing by turns.

Aristomachus *see* **Oxylus**.

Arnaeus *see* **Irus**.

Artemis in Greek mythology, a divinity, identified with the Roman DIANA. She was the daughter of ZEUS and LETO and was the twin sister of APOLLO, born on the island of DELOS. She is variously represented as a huntress with bow and arrows; as a goddess of the nymphs, in a chariot drawn by four stags; and as the moon-goddess, with the crescent of the moon above her forehead. Probably originally a pagan fertility goddess, she became a maiden divinity, never conquered by love, except when ENDYMION made her feel its power. She demanded the strictest chastity from her worshippers, and she is represented as having changed ACTAEON into a stag, and caused him to be torn in pieces by his own dogs, because he had secretly watched her as she was bathing. The Artemisia was a festival celebrated in her honour at DELPHI. The famous temple of Artemis at EPHESUS was considered one of the wonders of the world, but the goddess worshipped there was very different from the huntress goddess of Greece, being of Eastern origin, and regarded as the symbol of fruitful nature.

Ascanius *or* **Iulüs** in Greek mythology, the son of AENEAS and CREÜSA (2), and the companion of his father's wanderings from TROY to Italy. *See also* IULÜS.

Asclepius *see* **Aesculapius**.

Asia in Greek mythology, a daughter of OCEANUS and THETYS, who became by IAPETUS the mother of ATLAS, PROMETHEUS and EPIMETHEUS. According to some traditions, the continent of Asia derived its name from her.

Asopus the name of several rivers in Greece, of which the most celebrated is in BOEOTIA. The river-god Asopus, father of AEGINA, is associated with a river of PELOPONNESUS, which flows through Sicyonia to the Gulf of CORINTH.

asphodel a favourite plant among the ancients, who were in the habit of planting it round their tombs. In Greek religion it is associated with PERSEPHONE, the dead, and the underworld.

Assaracus *see* **Ilus** (2).

Asteria in Greek mythology, a daughter of the TITAN Coeus and PHOEBE (2). She was beloved by ZEUS, and in order to escape from him she metamorphosed into a quail, threw herself into the sea and was here metamorphosed into the island of Asteria or Ortygia, afterwards called DELOS.

Asterion (1) in Greek mythology, a Cretan king who married EUROPA after she had been carried to Crete by ZEUS. He also brought up her three sons by Zeus, MINOS, SARPEDON and RHADAMANTHUS.

Asterion (2) in Greek mythology, a river-god of the River Asterion in Argos

Asterope *see* **Oenomaüs**.

Astraea *or* **Astraia** in Greek mythology, the daughter of ZEUS and THEMIS and the goddess of justice. During the GOLDEN AGE she dwelt on earth, but on that age passing away she withdrew from the society of men and was placed among the stars, where she forms the constellation VIRGO. The name was given to one of the asteroids, discovered in 1845.

Astraeus *see* **Notus**.

Astyanax in Greek mythology the son of HECTOR and ANDROMACHE who was thrown from the walls of the city of TROY after ODYSSEUS warned the Trojans that no descendant of King PRIAM should be allowed to live. According to one version NEOPTOLEMUS took the child from his mother and hurled him to his death.

Astydameia *see* **Acastus**; **Peleus**.

Astyoche *see* **Ialmenus**.

Atalanta *or* **Atalante** in Greek mythology, a famous huntress of ARCADIA who took part in the CALYDONIAN BOAR hunt. She was to be obtained in marriage only by him who could outstrip her in a race, the consequence of failure being death. Melanion, one of her suitors, obtained from APHRODITE three GOLDEN APPLES, which he threw behind him, one after another, as he ran. Atalanta stopped to pick them up and was not unwillingly defeated. There was another Atalanta belonging to BOEOTIA. In this case the suitor who won her was Hippomenes, but otherwise the two cannot be distinguished.

Ate in Greek mythology, the goddess of hate, injustice, crime and retribution, daughter of ZEUS according to Homer, but of ERIS according to Hesiod.

Athamas in Greek mythology, son of Aeolus, brother of Sisyphus and king of
Orchomenus (2) in Boeotia. At Hera's command, he married Nephele, who
bore him two children, a son, Phrixus, and a daughter, Helle. His second wife,
Ino, plotted against Phrixus, but Nephele was able to save them by using the
ram with the golden fleece.

Athena *or* **Pallas Athene** a Greek goddess, identified by the Romans with
Minerva, the representative of the intellectual powers. She is one of the
greater Greek divinities, forming with Zeus and Apollo the supreme triad in
Greek mythology. According to the legend, Zeus, when he had attained supreme power after his victory over the Titans, chose for his first wife Metis
('wisdom'), but being advised by both Uranus ('heaven') and Ge ('earth'), he
swallowed her when she was pregnant with Athena. When the time came that
Athena should have been born, Zeus felt great pains in his head and caused
Hephaestus to split it with an axe, whereupon Athena sprang forth with a
mighty war shout and in complete armour. Her father was the greatest, her
mother the wisest of the gods. She is literally born of both and so their qualities
harmoniously blend in her. She is personified reason, the wisdom of the divine
father, while Apollo, also beloved of Zeus, is his mouth, the revealer of his
counsel. In her character of a wise and prudent warrior she was contrasted with
the fierce Ares. In the war of Zeus against the giants she assisted her father
with her counsel, killed the giant Pallas (2) and buried Enceladus under the
island of Sicily. In the wars of the mortals she aided and protected heroes distinguished for their wisdom as well as their valour. In the Trojan Wars she
favoured the Greeks. She is the patroness of agriculture, the inventor of the
plough and rake, the first to introduce the olive into Attica, and (in harmony
with her character as the personification of active wisdom) to teach men the
use of almost all the implements of industry and art. Philosophy, poetry and
oratory are also under her care. She was the special patroness of the state of
Athens, protecting its liberties by her power and wisdom. She maintained the
authority of law and justice in her courts, and was believed to have instituted
the court of justice (the Areopagus). In the images of the goddess she is always
dressed, generally in a Spartan tunic with a cloak over it and wearing a gold
helmet adorned with figures of different animals. Her aegis, the round Argolic
shield, has in its centre the head of Medusa. Her face is beautiful, earnest and
thoughtful, and the whole figure majestic.

Athens in ancient times the capital of Attica and centre of Greek culture, now
the capital of Greece; situated in the central plain of Attica, near the Gulf of
Aegina, an arm of the Aegean Sea running in between the mainland and the
Peloponnesus. In mythology, it was founded by Cecrops, and thus also bore
the name Cecropia. The name of Athens is derived from Athena, who from
earliest times was the city's patron goddess. The city was extended by Theseus.

Atlantis a large mythical island which, according to Plato, existed in the Atlantic over against the Pillars of Hercules (Straits of Gibraltar), was the home of a great nation, and was finally swallowed up by the sea in an earthquake nine thousands years before his time, at the end of a long contest with the Athenians. The gardens of the HESPERIDES and the Islands of the Blessed were referred to the same region. The legend has been accepted by some as fundamentally true, but others have regarded it as the outgrowth of some early discovery of the New World.

Atlas in Greek mythology, son of the Titan IAPETUS and CLYMENE (1), and brother of PROMETHEUS and EPIMETHEUS. He was the father of the PLEIADES and the HYADES. As leader of the TITANS, he attempted to storm the heavens, and for this supreme treason was condemned by ZEUS to bear the vault of heaven on his head and hands in the neighbourhood of the HESPERIDES at the western extremity of the earth, where day and night meet, on the mountains in the northwest of Africa still called by his name. His name is given to a collection of maps and charts, because Gerard Mercator in the sixteenth century used the figure of Atlas bearing the globe on the title page of such a work.

Atreus in Greek mythology, a son of PELOPS and HIPPODAMIA, grandson of TANTALUS and elder brother of THYESTES. He was married first to Cleola, who bore him Pleisthenes, then to Aerope, who had been wife of his son Pleisthenes and who bore him AGAMEMNON and MENELAÜS, and lastly to Pelopia, daughter of his brother Thyestes. Having to flee for the murder of his half-brother Chrysippus, he came with Thyestes to MYCENAE where he married Aerope, daughter of EURYSTHEUS, king of Mycenae, whom he succeeded. Aerope was seduced by Thyestes who, when banished for this outrage, sent Pleisthenes to kill Atreus, but Atreus killed the youth instead, unaware that he was his own son. In revenge Atreus gave a banquet ostensibly to celebrate the brothers' reconciliation at which Thyestes partook of the flesh of his own sons whom Atreus had killed. Thyestes fled in horror, and the vengeance of heaven, in the shape of famine, fell on Atreus for his atrocity. Advised by the oracle to call Thyestes back, he went in search of him, and at the court of King Thesprotus married his third wife, Pelopia, whom he believed to be a daughter of Thesprotus but who was really a daughter of Thyestes and at the time with child by him. This child, AEGISTHUS, afterwards slew Atreus when commissioned by him to slay Thyestes. The tragic events connected with the family of Pelops provided plots for some of the great Greek dramatists.

Atropos *see* **Fates**.

Atthis *see* **Erechtheus**.

Attica one of the independent states of HELLAS, or ancient Greece, the capital of which was ATHENS. The territory was triangular in shape, with Cape Sounium (Colonna) as its apex and the ranges of Mounts CITHAERON and Parnes as its base. On the north these ranges separated it from Boeotia; on the west it was bounded by Megaris and the Saronic Gulf; on the east by the Aegean. Its most marked physical divisions consisted of the highlands, midland district, and coast district, with the two plains of Eleusis and Athens. The Cephissus and Ilissus, though small, were its chief rivers; its principal hills, Cithaeron, Parnes, Hymettus, Pentelicus, and Laurium. According to tradition the earliest inhabitants of Attica lived in a savage manner until the time of Cecrops, who came with a colony from Egypt, taught them all the essentials of civilization, and founded Athens. One of Cecrops' descendants founded eleven other cities in the regions around, and there followed a period of mutual hosility. Theseus united these cities in a confederacy, with Athens as the capital. After this union of the several states, the whole of Attica shared in the fortunes of Athens.

Atys *or* **Attis** in classical mythology, the shepherd lover of Cybele, who, having broken the vow of chastity which he made her, castrated himself.

Atys in Asia Minor a deity with somewhat the same character as Adonis.

Auge *see* **Nauplius** (3); **Telephus**.

Augeas *or* **Augeias** in Greek mythology, son of Phorbas or of Helios and king of the Epeans in Elis. He had 3,000 head of oxen in his stables, which had not been cleaned for thirty years. Heracles was commissioned by Eurystheus to cleanse the Augean stables in one day and was promised as payment a tenth part of the oxen. He accomplished the task by turning the courses of the rivers Peneus and Alpheus through the stables. Augeas refused to pay the stipulated wages, whereupon Heracles killed him.

Aurora in Roman mythology, the goddess of the dawn, the equivalent of the Greek Eros.

autochthones the earliest known or aboriginal inhabitants of a country.

Automedusa *see* **Iolaüs**; **Iphicles**.

Autonoë *see* **Ino**.

Auxo *see* **Horae**.

B

bacchanalia *or* **dionysia** feasts in honour of Bacchus or Dionysus, characterized by licentiousness and revelry, and celebrated in ancient Athens. In the processions were bands of bacchantes of both sexes, who, inspired by real or feigned intoxication, wandered about rioting and dancing. They were clothed in fawn-skins, crowned with ivy, and bore in their hands *thyrsi*, that is spears entwined with ivy, or with a pine-cone stuck on the point. These feasts passed

from the Greeks to the Romans, who celebrated them with still greater disso-
luteness till the Senate abolished them in 187 BC.

bacchants or bacchanals *see* **maenads**.

bacchante a person taking part in revels in honour of BACCHUS. *See also*
BACCHANALIA; MAENAD.

Bacchus one of the names among the Greeks and the usual name among the
Romans for DIONYSUS, the god of wine. Originally an epithet or surname, it did
not occur in Greek writers until after the time of Herodotus, and its use is generally confined to the god in his more riotous aspects. His worship was
introduced into Rome from Greece and was amalgamated with the worship of
LIBER, an old Italian deity who presided over planting and fructification.

Balius *see* **Xanthus**.

Basalus *see* **Achemon**.

Bateia (1) in Greek mythology, daughter of TEUCER, king of the land which became known as TROY. She was married to DARDANUS, by whom she had two
sons, ILUS and Erichthonius. The son of the latter, TROS, gave his name to Troy,
and a town near Troy was named in Bateia's honour.

Bateia (2) *see* **Icarius** (1).

Baton in Greek mythology, the charioteer of AMPHIARAUS who with him was
swallowed up by the earth after the battle of SEVEN AGAINST THEBES. He was
worshipped as a hero and had a sanctuary at ARGOS.

Battus legendary founder of the Greek colony of CYRENE in Libya, about 650 BC.
There were eight rulers of the family founded by him, bearing alternately the
names Battus and Arcesilaus.

Baucis and Philemon in Greek mythology, an elderly husband and wife who
were peasants of BITHYNIA. They entertained ZEUS and HERMES in their humble
hillside hut after the two gods, in the guise of mortals, were refused hospitality
by everyone else in the region. The gods sent a flood to cover the town at the
foot of the hill to punish the inhabitants for their lack of hospitality. The peasants' hut was turned into a shrine by the gods and the old couple were asked to
make a wish. Their wish was to spend the rest of their lives at the temple and
that they should die together with neither of them outliving the other. Their
wish was granted and when they died toether they were changed into two
trees, an oak and a linden, which grew side by side.

Bear Mountain (now known as Kapidagi) a mountainous region on the Mysian
coast of the Sea of MARMARA said in Greek mythology to have been inhabited
by earthly monsters with six arms. They were killed by HERACLES and the
ARGONAUTS after attacking the *Argo*.

Bebryces in Greek mythology, a tribe who lived towards the eastern side of the
Sea of MARMARA and were noted for their warlike characteristics. In a dispute
with the MARIANDYNIANS over ownership of the territory which divided their

lands HERACLES sided with the Mariandynians for a time, and the Bebryces lost some of the land. However, on the departure of Heracles, they won some of it back again under the leadership of their king, Amycus. He was killed in a boxing match against Polydeuces when the ARGONAUTS visited the territory.

Bellerophon *or* **Hipponous** in Greek mythology, a hero who, having accidentally killed his brother, fled from CORINTH to PROETÜS, king of Argos, whose wife, STHENEBOEA, fell in love with him. Being slighted by him, she persuaded her husband to send him to her father, IOBATES, king of LYCIA, with a letter urging him to put to death this man who had insulted his daughter. Iobates, not wishing to do so directly, imposed on him the dangerous task of conquering the CHIMAERA, a monster that was ravaging the Lycian countryside. Bellerophon, mounted on PEGASUS, a gift from ATHENA, overpowered the monster. Iobates then sent him on an expedition against his enemies, the Solymi, who were routed by Bellerophon and then against the AMAZONS. Once again Bellerophon was victorious, and Iobates, desperate to kill him, sent a band of his Lycian soldiers to ambush him. Bellerophon killed all of them, and as a reward Iobates gave up his attempt to kill Bellerophon and afterwards gave him his daughter Philonoë in marriage and shared his kingdom with him. Bellerophon attempted to soar to heaven on the winged horse Pegasus. ZEUS was angry at his arrogance and sent a gadfly to sting Pegasus so that the horse reared and caused Bellerophon to fall to the earth, where he wandered about blind, or lame (legends differ as to which) and alone, having been spurned by the gods, until he died.

Bellona in Roman mythology, the goddess of war and companion of MARS. She is described by the poets as being armed with a scourge, her hair dishevelled and a torch in her hand. She may originally have been a SABINE deity, worship of her being brought to Rome by Sabine settlers. In Rome a temple was erected to her at the Campus Martius.

Belus (1) in Greek mythology, a son of POSEIDON by Libya or Eurynome. He was a twin brother of AGENOR and father of AEGYPTUS and DANAÜS. He was believed originally to be the ancestral hero and national god of several eastern countries who became mixed up with Greek myths.

Belus (2) in Greek mythology, the father of DID. He conquered Cyprus and then gave it to TEUCER.

Bia in Greek mythology, the personification of might and force, represented as the offspring of STYX and the Titan PALLAS, held in some legends to be a son, in others to be a daughter. Together with his brother CRATOS, the personification of strength, Bia helped HEPHAESTUS to nail PROMETHEUS to a cliff. Bia and Cratos together were a symbol of the absolute power of ZEUS, and in company with their brother and sister, ZELUS and NIKE, were always beside ZEUS.

Bias in Greek mythology, son of Amythaon and Idomene and brother of

MELAMPUS. He married PERO, daughter of NELEUS. Her father had stipulated that anyone who married his daughter would first have to bring him the oxen of IPHICLES and Melampus arranged this on behalf of his brother. Melampus is also said to have acquired for Bias a third of the kingdom of ARGOS. Bias's second wife was IPHIANASSA.

Bistonians *or* **Bistones** a Thracian tribe, said by some legends to have been located on the south shore of THRACE east of the River Nestos, where they gave their name to Lake Bistonis, and by others to have been located in the Thracian Chersonese with Polymestor having been one of their kings.

Bithynia an ancient territory in the northwest of Asia Minor, on the Black Sea and Sea of MARMARA, at one time an independent kingdom, afterwards a Roman province. The legend of BAUCIS AND PHILEMON is based in Bithynia.

Black Corcyra an island named after CORCYRA, daughter of the Phliasian river-god ASOPUS, as was Corcyra, now Corfu. Situated off the Croatian coast the island is now called Korcula.

Black Sea a sea situated between Europe and Asia and connected with the Mediterranean by the BOSPORUS, Sea of MARMARA and HELLESPONT. The Black Sea was called Euxine by the ancients and the area is rich in myth. COLCHIS lay at the eastern end of the Black Sea, and the Crimean Peninsula was the home of the TAURIANS. The ARGONAUTS entered the Black Sea through the Bosporus and escaped from it by sailing up the Ister, now the Danube.

Boeotia one of the independent states of Hellas, or ancient Greece, lying between ATTICA and PHOCIS, and bounded east and west by the Euboean Sea and the Gulf of CORINTH respectively. The whole country is surrounded by mountains, on the south Mounts CITHAERON and Parnes, on the west Mount HELICON, on the north Mount PARNASSUS and the Opuntiuan Mountains, which also closed it in on the east. The northern part is drained by the CEPHISSUS, the waters of which formed Lake Copais (in ancient times also called Cephissus); the southern by the ASOPUS, which flows into the Euboean Sea. The inhabitants were AEOLIANS, and most of the towns formed a kind of republic, of which THEBES in the southeast was the chief city. The other major city was ORCHOMENUS in the northwest, on the shore of Lake Copais. Since refinement and cultivation of mind never made such progress in Boeotia, 'Boeotian' was used by the Athenians as a synonym for dullness.

Bona Dea in Roman mythology, a goddess worshipped from earliest time exclusively by women. A prophetic deity with a sanctuary in the Aventine, she revealed her oracles only to women, and men were not even allowed to know her name. Bona Dea means 'good goddess', and the goddess was also called FAUNA. Legend has it that she was related to the god FAUNUS, but the legends differ as to whether she was his sister, wife or daughter. She is variously depicted as being connected with chastity, fertility and healing.

Boötes *or* **Philomelus** in Greek mythology, the son of DEMETER and IASION who, being robbed of all his possessions by his brother, invented the plough and cultivated the soil. He was translated to heaven with the plough and yoke of oxen under the name of Boötes ('ox-driver'), which is still borne by a constellation beside the Great Bear (or Wain). According to others, Boötes was the son of CALLISTO (*see* URSA MAJOR) and to yet others the winemaker ICARIUS (2).

Boreades an epithet meaning 'sons of BOREAS'. ZETES AND CALAÏS are often referred to by it.

Boreas in mythology, the name of the north wind as personified by the Greeks and Romans and said to be the son of Astraeus and EOS. His home was in THRACE in a cave in Mount HAEMUS. He carried off and married OREITHYIA, a daughter of ERECHTHEUS, who would have opposed the match since the Athenians hated the Thracians. Later, during the Persian war he showed favour to the Athenians by destroying the Persian ships and saving the Athenians from invasion. He had two winged sons, ZETES AND CALAIS, and two daughters, CLEOPATRA (2), who became the wife of PHINEUS, and Chione. He is also supposed to have fathered twelve stallions by mares belonging to Erichthonius, a king of TROY. Boreas is sometimes represented in art as having serpent tails instead of feet, especially when depicted as carrying off Oreithyia.

Borus in Greek mythology, a son of PERIERES who married POLYDORA, daughter of PELEUS.

Bosporus *or* **Bosphorus** the strait joining the BLACK SEA with the Sea of MARMARA, called also the Strait of Constantinople. The Cimmerian Bosporus was the ancient name of the strait that leads from the BLACK SEA into the Sea of AZOV. There was also in ancient times a kingdom of the name of Bosporus situated on both sides of the strait.

Brasiae a town on the coast of northern LACONIA connected with one of the legends relating to the birth of DIONYSUS. According to this legend, SEMELE, having been seduced by ZEUS, gives birth to Dionysus and is locked with her baby in a chest by her father CADMUS, king of THEBES, who did not believe the story of the seduction. The chest was flung into the sea and was washed up at Brasiae where Semele was found to be dead but the baby alive. INO is then said to have reached Brasiae in the course of her wanderings and takes care of the infant Dionysus in a cave.

Brass Race *see* **Races of Man**.

Brauron a town in eastern ATTICA, whose name was derived from the ancient hero of the name Brauronian. ARTEMIS was worshipped here, the ancient statue of the goddess supposedly being the one stolen from the TAURIANS by ORESTES and IPHIGENEIA.

Brazen Race *see* **Races of Man**.

Briareus *or* **Aegaeon** in Greek mythology, a giant with a hundred arms and fifty heads, who aided ZEUS in the great war waged with the TITANS and was rewarded by Cympola, daughter of ZEUS. He was the son of POSEIDON or GE and URANUS. *See also* ETNA.

Briseïs in Greek mythology, the concubine of ACHILLES who abducted her from LYRNESSUS after he had plundered the city and killed her husband, parents and brothers. AGAMEMNON, on the loss of his own concubine, Chryseïs, took Briseïs from Achilles, thereby starting a quarrel between Achilles and Agamemnon, which led to Achilles refusing to fight with the the Greeks. On the death of PATROCLUS, Achilles relented and agreed to fight and Briseïs was returned to him.

Britomartis a Cretan goddess and the daughter of ZEUS and Carme, daughter of Eubulus. She was associated with hunting and with fishermen. There were several points of resemblance between her and ARTEMIS, who loved her and is said to have assumed her name. Thus in some legends the two goddesses have become identified. Britomartis was loved by MINOS, king of Crete, who pursued her relentlessly. Weary of his advances, she threw herself into the sea. Legends differ as to whether she was saved by falling into the nets of some fishermen or whether she died and became immortal, being made a goddess by Artemis. As a goddess in Crete she was given the name DICTYNNA, a name which was also later sometimes given to Artemis. She was also worshipped by AEGINA where she was known as Aphaea.

Bromios in Greek mythology, a name given to DIONYSUS, meaning 'thunderer'.

Brontes *see* **Cyclops**; **Titans**.

Broteas (1) in Greek mythology, a son of TANTALUS (1), king of Phrygia, who is supposed to have carved the oldest image of CYBELE on a rock named Coddinus which was north of Mount Sipylus. ARTEMIS drove him mad because of his refusal to worship her, and he leapt into a fire and died, believing himself in his madness to be immune to flames. According to some legends Broteas was the father of TANTALUS (2), the first husband of CLYTEMNESTRA.

Broteas (2) in Roman mythology, a son of VULCAN and MINERVA who was so upset by taunts about his exteme ugliness that he burned himself.

Brygeians *or* **Brygi** in Greek mythology, a tribe in EPIRUS who with the support of ARES defeated the Thesprotians led by ODYSSEUS.

Bull of Minos *see* **Minotaur**.

Busiris a mythical Egyptian king, a son of POSEIDON and Lysinianassa, daughter of EPAPHUS. In the course of a severe drought he sacrificed strangers to his land to ZEUS on the advice of a seer. He was defeated and killed by HERACLES.

Butes (1) in Greek mythology, a son of BOREAS. His father forced him into exile because of his hostile treatment of his step-brother, LYCURGUS (1), king of THRACE, and he went to the island of Strongyle, later called Naxos, with a band of followers. Having no women in their party they tried to carry off a group of women who were celebrating a festival of Dionysus at Thessaly. Butes took Coronis, who complained to Dionysus. The god then drove Butes mad, and he leapt into a well and was killed.

Butes (2) in Greek mythology, an Argonaut and son of Teleon or Poseidon and Zeuxippe, daughter of the river-god Eridanus. When the Argonauts passed by the Sirens on their homeward journey, Butes leapt overboard and swam towards them as they sang on the island of Anthemoessa. Aphrodite took pity on him and saved him by taking him to Lilybaeum in Sicily where she bore him a son, Eryx.

Butes (3) in Greek mythology, a son of Pandion (1), king of Athens, and Zeuxippe, he has become confused with Butes (2) the Argonaut and may be the same person. He was a twin brother of Erechtheus, and he married his brother's daughter, Chthonia. After the death of Pandion he obtained the office of priest of Athena and of Poseidon Erechtheus.

Buthrotum a port in Epirus opposite the island of Corcyra founded by the Trojan Helenus who was taken there after the fall of Troy by Neoptolemus.

Byblis and Caunus in Greek mythology, Byblis was a daughter of Miletus and Eidothea or Cyaneë and twin sister of Caunus. There are two different versions of the legend relating to brother and sister. According to one, Caunus had feelings of love for Byblis which were more than brotherly and went away to Lycia when he could not get over these. His sister went to look for him and finally killed herself by hanging herself on her girdle when she could not find him. From her tears sprang the well Byblis. According to another legend Byblis had feelings of passion for her brother and confessed these to him. He was horrified and fled to the country of Leleges, and Byblis hanged herself. There are various variations on these legends. The Phoenician city of Byblus is said by some to be named after Byblis.

Byblus *or* **Byblos** (now called Jebail) an ancient maritime city of Phoenicia, a little north of Beirut. It was famous as the birthplace of Adonis or Tammuze, of whose worship it became the centre.

C

Cabiri *or* **Cabeiri** deities or deified heroes worshipped in the ancient Greek islands of Lemnos, Imbros and Samothrace, and also on the neighbouring coast of Troy in Asia Minor.

Cadmus in Greek mythology, the son of Agenor (1) and Telephassa, grandson of Poseidon and brother of Europa. When Europa was carried off by Zeus, he was sent by Agenor in quest of her and told not to return without her. His search was in vain, and the oracle at DELPHI told him to abandon it and instead to follow a cow of a certain kind which he would meet and build a city where it would lie down. Cadmus found the cow in PHOCIS, followed her to BOEOTIA and built there the city of THEBES. Intending to sacrifice the cow to ATHENA, he sent some men to the nearby well of ARES for water, but they were killed by the dragon, a son of Ares, who guarded it. Cadmus then slew the dragon and sowed its teeth in the ground. From these sprang up armed men who slew each other until only five were left. They became the SPARTI, the progenitors of the Theban families. Athena assigned to Cadmus the government of Thebes, and Zeus gave him HARMONIA for his wife. All the gods of OLYMPUS were at the marriage, and Cadmus gave Harmonia a peplus and necklace that he had received from HEPHAESTUS or Europa. They had one son, POLYDORUS, and four daughters, INO, SEMELE, Autonoë and AGAVE. Subsequently Cadmus and Harmonia left Thebes and conquered ILLYRIA. Other legends ascribe the introduction of the Phoenician alphabet into Greece to Cadmus. The solar mythologists identify him with the sun-god. *See also* AGAVE.

caduceus the winged staff of HERMES, which gave the herald the power to fly. Originally a simple olive branch, its stems were afterwards formed into two snakes twisted round it, and several tales were devised by mythologists to explain this, as that Hermes having found two snakes fighting, divided them with his rod and thus they came to be used as an emblem of peace. It was the staff or mace carried by heralds and ambassadors in time of war. It was not used by the Romans. Many magical virtues were ascribed to the caduceus. In Homer, Hermes touches the souls of the dead with it and so lulls them to sleep before carrying them to the underworld. It is also seen in the hands of ARES, DIONYSUS, HERACLES, DEMETER and APHRODITE. The rod represents powers; the serpents, wisdom; and the two wings, diligence and activity.

Caenis *or* **Caenus** *see* **Elatus** (2).

Calaïs *see* **Zetes**.

Calchas in Greek mythology, a seer, son of Thestor, who was attached to the Greek forces during the TROJAN WAR. His reputation was such that AGAMEMNON went to him in person to persuade him to join their expedition. He is said to have foretold the length of the siege and to have predicted that Troy could not be won without the help of ACHILLES while Achilles was still a child. When the fleet was detained at Aulis by adverse winds, he demanded the sacrifice of IPHIGENEIA. He is said to have died at Colophon from chagrin at being surpassed in soothsaying by one Mopsus.

Calliope in Greek mythology, one of the MUSES. She presided over eloquence, heroic poetry, and knowledge in general. She is said to have been the mother of ORPHEUS by APOLLO or OEAGRUS.

Callirrhoë *see* **Ganymede**; **Ilus** (2).

Callisto in Greek mythology, a huntress and companion of Artemis, who was loved by Zeus and was mother of Arcas by him. To hide his liaison from Hera, Zeus metamophosed Callisto into a bear, and she was slain by Artemis during a hunt. Zeus gave Arcas to Maia to be brought up, and Callisto was placed among the stars as Arctos (*see* Ursa Major).

Calydon the ancient capital city of Aetolia in northern Greece, ruled by Oeneus and celebrated in Greek mythology on account of the ravages of the Calydonian Boar.

Calydonian Boar in Greek mythology, a terrible boar sent by Artemis to lay waste Calydon, the land of Oeneus, who had omitted a sacrifice to her and who was absent on the Argonauts' expedition. No one dared to face the monster until Meleager, the son of Oeneus, with a band of heroes pursued and slew him. The Curetes laid claim to the head and hide, but were driven off by Meleager. Later accounts make Meleager summon to the hunt heroes from all parts of Greece, among them Atalanta, who gave the monster the first wound.

Calypso in Greek mythology, a nymph, a daughter of Atlas, who inhabited the wooded island of Ogygia, on the shores of which Odysseus was shipwrecked. She promised him immortality if he would consent to marry her, but after a seven years' stay she was ordered by the gods to permit his departure. Calypso bore Odysseus two sons, and on his departure died of grief.

Camenae in Roman mythology, goddesses or nymphs identified with the Muses. They were worshipped from early times.

Canis Major ('the greater dog') a constellation of the southern hemisphere containing Sirius, the brightest star. **Canis Minor** ('the lesser dog') is a constellation in the northern hemisphere, immediately above Canis Major, the chief star in which is Procyon. The dog represented in the larger constellation is said to have been the hound of Orion, or Maera, the dog of Icarius (2). Alternatively, Maera is sometimes held to have been the dog repesented in the smaller constellation.

Capaneus in Greek mythology, one of the Seven against Thebes. He scaled the walls of Thebes during the siege and said that he would set fire to the city even if Zeus opposed it. As a punishment for his arrogance, Zeus sent a thunderbolt to kill him. His son, Sthenelus (2) was one of the Epigoni.

Capys *see* **Ilus** (2).

Caria an ancient country in the southwest corner of Asia Minor. The original inhabitants may have been Lelegians, who were subjects of Crete and manned the ships of Minos. Later it was partly settled by Greek colonists, chiefly Dorians. Cnidus, Halicarnassus and Miletus were among the chief towns.

Carme *see* **Britomartis**.

Carmenta *see* **Evander**.

Carnabos *see* **Ophiuchus**.

Carpo *see* **Horae**.

Carthage a Phoenician city on the north coast of Africa, the capital of one of the great empires of the ancient world, situated on a peninsula at the northeast corner of the region now known as Tunis. In mythology, it was founded by DIDO.

Cassandra in Greek mythology, a daughter of PRIAM and HECUBA and twin sister of HELENUS. The two children were left one night in the sanctuary of APOLLO, and during their sleep their ears were touched and purified by two snakes so that they could understand the meaning of the language of birds and thus know the future. Cassandra afterwards attracted the love of Apollo by her beauty, and he taught her the secrets of prophecy, but, displeased by her rejection of his suit, he laid upon her the curse that her prophecies should never be believed. She frequently foretold the fall of TROY and warned her countrymen in vain against the stratagem of the horse. When Troy was taken, she fled to the temple of ATHENA, but was torn from the altar by AJAX THE LESS and ravished in the temple. She fell, as part of his share of the booty, to AGAMEMNON, who, in spite of her warnings, carried her with him as his slave to MYCENAE, where they were both murdered by CLYTEMNESTRA. The name is now often used of one who takes gloomy views of the political or social future.

Cassiopeia a conspicuous constellation in the northern hemisphere, situated next to CEPHEUS and often called the Lady in her Chair. It was said to represent Cassiopeia, the wife of Cepheus, king of Ethiopia, in a chair but on her back and with her feet in the air. This was meant to be a punishment for her pride in thinking that either she or her daughter, ANDROMEDA, was more beautiful than the NEREÏDS.

Castalia a fountain on the slope of PARNASSUS, a little above DELPHI, in PHOCIS, sacred to APOLLO and the MUSES. Those who visited the temple at Delphi would wash their hair in the fountain, but those who needed to be purified from murder bathed their whole body. Its waters were supposed to give poetic inspiration to those who drank from it. The name was due to Castalia, daughter of ACHELOUS, who threw herself into the fountain to escape the pursuit of Apollo.

Castor and Pollux (also called **Dioscuri**, 'sons of Zeus') in Greek mythology, twin divinities, sons of TYNDAREUS, king of SPARTA, and LEDA, and so brothers of HELEN of Troy. According to a later tradition, they were the sons of ZEUS and Leda. Castor was mortal, but Pollux was immortal. The former was particularly skilled in breaking horses, the latter in boxing and wrestling. Both received divine honours at Sparta as patrons of mariners. One story tells that when Castor, the mortal, was killed, Pollux prayed Zeus to let him die with him, and was permitted either to live as his immortal son in OLYMPUS or to share his brother's fate and live one day in heaven with the gods, the other among the shades. Zeus placed the brothers among the stars as Gemini, and their names are attached to the principal stars in that constellation.

Castra *see* **Idas and Lynceus**.

Catalogues of Women *or* **Eoiae** a fragmentary catalogue of Greek mythological heroines. It has been pieced together from brief passages quoted or summarized by ancient writers.

Catreus *see* **Nauplius** (3).

Caunus *see* **Byblis**.

Cebren *see* **Oenone**.

Cecrops in Greek mythology, the founder of Athens and the first king of Attica, sometimes represented as half man and half dragon. He was said to have taught the savage inhabitants religion and morals, made them acquainted with the advantages of social life and instituted marriage and the worship of the gods, and introduced agriculture, navigation and commerce. By the later Greeks he was represented as having led a colony to Attica from Egypt about 1440 or 1500 BC.

Cedalion *see* **Orion**.

Celaeno *see* **Nycteus**.

Celeus in Greek mythology, a king of Eleusis and husband of Metaneira, by whom he had two sons, Demophon and Triptolemus. *See also* Eleusinian Mysteries.

Centaurs in Greek mythology, beings represented as half man, half horse. The earliest references to them, however, merely represent them as a race of wild and savage men inhabiting the mountains and forests of Thessaly. The most ancient account of the Hippocentaurs, sometimes considered as distinct but more often confused with the Centaurs, is that they were the offspring of Magnesian mares and Centaurus, himself the offspring of Ixion and a cloud. Mythology relates the combat of the Centaurs with the Lapiths, which arouse at the marriage feast of Peirithoüs and took place in Thessaly or Arcadia. This fight is sometimes put in connection with a combat of Heracles with the Centaurs. It ended in the Centaurs being expelled from their country and taking refuge on Mount Pindus on the frontiers of Epirus. The most famous Centaur was Chiron, the teacher of Achilles and other heroes. The Centaur Nessus is also famous in ancient mythology. Chiron and Pholus are the good Centaurs, while the others are represented as lustful and savage. In art, the Centaurs were represented as men from the head to the loins, with the rest of the body that of a horse.

Centaurus *see* **Centaurs**.

Cephalonia *or* **Kephallenia** a mountainous island of Greece, the largest of the Ionian Islands, west of the Morea, at the entrance of the Gulf of Patras. Its earliest inhabitants were probably Taphians, and it is said to have derived its name from CEPHALUS, who made himself master of the island with the help of AMPHITRYON.

Cephalus in Greek mythology, a son of DEION, ruler of PHOCIS, and and husband of PROCRIS. Eos was in love with Cephalus, but he resisted her because of a vow that he and Procris had made to remain faithful to each other. Eos advised Cephalus not to break his vow until Procris had broken hers. She then meta-morphosed Cephalus into a stranger bearing rich gifts with which to tempt Procris, who was induced by these to break the vow. When she recognized her husband, she fled to Crete where either ARTEMIS or MINOS made her a present of a dog, LAELAPS, and a spear, which were never to miss their object. Procris returned home disguised as a youth and went out hunting with Cephalus. When he saw the excellence of her dog and spear, he tried to buy them from her, but she refused to part with them for any price except love. When he promised to love her, she revealed herself to him and they were reconciled. As, however, she still feared the love of Eos, she always jealously watched Cephalus when he went out hunting, and on one occasion he killed her by acci-dent with the never-erring spear. Subsequently AMPHITRYON came to Cephalus and persuaded him to give up his dog to hunt the Teumessian vixen which was ravaging the Cadmean territory. Cephalus is said to have committed suicide by leaping into the sea from Cape Leucas, on which he had built a temple of APOLLO, in order to atone for having killed his wife.

Cepheus (1) in Greek mythology, a king of Ethiopia and husband of CASSIOPEIA, father of ANDROMEDA and father-in-law of PERSEUS. His name was given to a constellation of stars in the nothern hemisphere surrounded by Cassiopeia, URSA MAJOR, Draco and Cygnus.

Cepheus (2) in Greek mythology, a son of Aleus, brother of LYCURGUS (2) and an ARGONAUT from TEGEA in ARCADIA, of which he was king. He had twenty sons and two daughters. Nearly all his sons perished in an expedition that they had undertaken with HERACLES.

Cephissus, River the name of two rivers in Greece. The Cephissus in ATTICA rises on the western slope of Mount Pentelicus and the southern side of Mount Parnes and flows past ATHENS into the Saronic Gulf. The Cephissus in BOETIA flows into Lake Copais. The river-god Cephissus was the father of NARCISSUS by the nymph Leirope.

Cerberus in Greek mythology, a son of ECHIDNA and TYPHON, the dog-monster that guarded HADES, variously described as having a hundred, fifty, and three heads, with a serpent's tail and a mane consisting of the heads of various snakes. Homer mentions him simply as the dog of Hades. ORPHEUS charmed him with the magic of his lyre, and he was subdued by HERACLES, who, as the last test of his strength, snatched Cerberus from the halls of Hades.

Cercopes in Greek mythology, a band of dwarf-like creatures who lived in Lydia. They were noted for their habit of stealing. and were either killed or captured by HERACLES. The ancient Greeks believed monkeys to be degraded men. The Cercopes were changed into monkeys for attempting to deceive ZEUS.

Cercyon *see* **Alope**.

Ceres in Roman mythology, a goddess corresponding to the Greek DEMETER. She was the daughter of SATURN and RHEA, and the mother of PROSERPINE and BACCHUS. She was the goddess of the earth from the aspect of bringing forth fruits, and she especially watched over the growth of grain and other plants. The Romans celebrated in her honour the festival of the Cerealia (12th to 19th April) with games in the circus. Ceres was always represented in full attire, her attributes being ears of corn and poppies, and her sacrifices consisting of pigs and cows.

Cerynes *see* **Deïphontes**.

Cerynitian hind in Greek mythology, a golden-horned deer which was sacred to ARTEMIS. One of the tasks of HERACLES was to capture it alive.

Cestus in Greek mythology, a girdle worn by APHRODITE or VENUS, endowed with the power of exciting love towards the wearer. It was borrowed by HERA when she desired to win the love of ZEUS.

Ceto in Greek mythology, a sea monster, the daughter of GE and PONTUS and mother of the GORGONS.

Cetus (The Sea-Monster or The Whale) a constellation. It was said to represent the monster sent by POSEIDON to devour ANDROMEDA as a punishment for her mother's arrogance (*see* CASSIOPEIA).

Chalciope *see* **Aeëtes; Eidyia**.

Chalybes a tribe inhabiting a part of the southern coast of the BLACK SEA. They were famous for their work in iron and were warlike.

Chaos in old theories of the earth, the void out of which sprang all things or in which they existed in a confused, unformed shape before they were separated into kinds. Some ancient writers make it the original source of all; others mention along with it GE, TARTARUS and EROS, the rough outlines of heaven and earth proceeding from Chaos while the organization and perfecting of all things was the work of Eros. Later writers represent it as that confused shapeless mass out of which the universe was formed into a cosmos, or harmonious order. One writer makes Chaos the mother of EREBUS and NYX.

Chariclo *or* **Naïs** *see* **Chiron**.

Charites the Greek name for the GRACES.

Charon in Greek mythology, the son of EREBUS and NYX. It was his task to ferry the dead over the rivers of the infernal regions, for which he received an obolus, or farthing, which accordingly was usually put into the mouth of the deceased. If this rite was neglected, Charon refused to convey the soul across, and it was doomed to wander restlessly along the shores of ACHERON. He was represented as an old man, with a gloomy aspect, matted beard and tattered garments.

Charybdis an eddy or whirlpool in the Strait of MESSINA, celebrated in ancient times and regarded as the more dangerous to navigators because in endeavouring to escape it they ran the risk of being wrecked upon SCYLLA, a rock opposite to it.

Chimaera in Greek mythology, a fire-breathing monster, the foreparts of whose body were those of a lion, the middle of a goat, and the hind part of a dragon. She was the daughter of ECHIDNA and TYPHON, and devastated Lycia until killed by BELLEROPHON. The name has come to be used for something imaginary.

Chieron *or* **Chiron** in Greek mythology, son of CRONOS and PHILYRA, and husband of Naïs or Chariclo, the most famous of the CENTAURS. He lived at the foot of Mount PELION in THESSALY, and was famous throughout all Greece for his wisdom and acquirements, particularly for his skill in healing, hunting, music and prophecy. The greatest heroes of the time—DIONYSUS, JASON, HERACLES, ACHILLES, etc—were represented as his pupils. He died by being accidentally wounded by one of the poisoned arrows of his friend Heracles.

Chione *see* **Boreas**; **Oreithyia**.

Chios *or* **Scio** an island belonging to Greece, in the AEGEAN SEA, separated from the coast of Asia Minor by a channel. It is one of the places that contended for the honour of having given birth to Homer.

Chiron *see* **Cheiron**.

Chloris *see* **Neleus**; **Pero**.

Chlorus *see* **Pelasgus**.

Chromius *see* **Neleus**.

Chryseïs *see* **Briseïs**; **Homer**.

Chrysomallus *see* **golden fleece**.

Chrysopeleia in Greek mythology, a wood NYMPH who was one day in great danger as the oak tree which she inhabited was undermined by a mountain torrent. ARCAS, who was hunting in the neighbourhood, discovered the situation, led the torrent in another direction and secured the tree by a dam. Chrysopeleia became by Arcas the mother of ELATUS (1) and Apheidas.

Chryssipus *see* **Laïus**.

Chthonia *see* **Butes** (3).

chthonian deities in Greek mythology, spirits of the earth or underworld.

Chthonius *see* **Nycteus**; **Sparti**.

Ciconian Women *see* **Hebrus**.

Cilicia in ancient geography, the region of Asia Minor between Pamphylia and

Syria, lying south of Mount Taurus. In early ages it was ruled by its own kings, the people, who were probably akin to Syrians and Phoenicians, being notorious pirates.

Cinna *see* **Niobe** (2).

Circe in Greek mythology, a sorceress, the daughter of HELIOS and the ocean nymph PERSE. She lived in the Island of Aeaea and around her palace were numbers of human beings whom she had changed into the shapes of wolves and lions by her drugs and incantations. She changed twenty-two of the companions of ODYSSEUS into swine after making them drink enchanted wine. Odysseus, protected by the herb MOLY that HERMES had given him, remained uninjured by her drugs and compelled her to restore his companions. Odysseus remained with her for a year, and when he departed, she instructed him how to avoid the dangers that he would encounter on his homeward voyage. Ovid relates how, when Circe was jealous of SCYLLA, whose love was sought by GLAUCUS, she poured the juice of poisonous herbs into that part of the sea where her rival was accustomed to bathe and so changed her into a hideous monster.

Cithaeron, Mount (modern Elatea) a mountain of Greece, which, stretching northwest, separates BOEOTIA from MEGARIS and ATTICA. On its northern slope stood the city of Plataea.

Clashing Rocks two rocks on either side of the northern entrance of the Bosporus. They were called the Symplegades and were sometimes called the Cyanean ('dark blue') Rocks. They were said to clash together when the wind blew strongly. The ARGONAUTS with the help of ATHENA successfully negotiated them.

Cleio *see* **Clio**.

Cleola *see* **Atreus**.

Cleopatra (1) *or* **Alcyone** in Greek mythology, a daughter of IDAS and Marpessa and wife of MELEAGER. She is said to have hanged herself after her husband's death or to have died of grief.

Cleopatra (2) in Greek mythology, daughter of BOREAS and OREITHYIA, and the first wife of PHINEUS.

Clio *or* **Cleio** in Greek mythology, one of the nine MUSES, a daughter of ZEUS and MNEMOSYNE. The Muse of history and epic poetry, she is represented as sitting with a half-opened scroll in her hand and a casket for holding manuscripts at her feet.

Clonio *see* **Nycteus**.

Clotho in Greek mythology, that one of the three FATES, or Parcae, whose duty it was to put the wool for the thread of life round the spindle, while that of LACHESIS was to spin it, and that of ATROPOS to cut it when the time had come.

Clymene (1) in Greek mythology, a daughter of OCEANUS and THETYS, and the wife of IAPETUS, by whom she became the mother of ATLAS, PROMETHEUS and others.

Clymene (2) in Greek mythology, a daughter of Minyas (*see* MINYANS) and the wife of PHYLACUS, by whom she became the mother of IPHICLUS and Alcimede.

Clymene (3) in Greek mythology, the daughter of King Catreus of Crete who sold her to NAUPLIUS (3), who married her.

Clytemnestra in Greek mythology, a daughter of King TYNDAREUS and LEDA, and wife of AGAMEMNON. During the absence of her husband in the TROJAN WAR, she became the mistress of AEGISTHUS, and with him murdered Agamemnon on his return from Troy. Together with her lover she governed MYCENAE for seven years. Her son ORESTES killed them both.

Clytoneus *see* **Nauplius** (2).

Cocytus, River a river of ancient EPIRUS, a tributary of the ACHERON, in Greek mythology, supposed to be connected with the lower world. Homer makes it a branch of STYX; Virgil makes the Acheron flow into the Cocytus.

Codrus in Greek mythology, the last king of ATHENS. Having learned that the enemies of his country would be victorious, according to the declaration of an oracle, if they did not kill the Athenian king, he voluntarily entered their camp, provoked a quarrel, and was slain. The grateful Athenians abolished the royal dignity, substituting that of archon, regarding no one worthy to be the successor of Codrus. His son Medon was the first archon, chosen for life.

Coeus *see* **Phoebe** (2); **Titans**.

Colchian Dragon *see* **Echidna**.

Colchis the ancient name of a region at the eastern extremity of the BLACK SEA, resting on the Caucasus, famous in Greek mythology as the destination of the ARGONAUTS, and the native country of MEDEA. The principal coast town was Dioscurias (the Roman Sebastopolis).

Corcyra in Greek mythology, a daughter of the river god ASOPUS, with whom POSEIDON fell in love. He carried her off to the most northerly of the Ionian Islands, which was called Corcyra after her.

Corinth a once celebrated city-state on the isthmus of the same name which unites PELOPONNESUS with northern Greece. It commanded an advantageous position, and its citadel, the Acro-corinthus, rendered it a strong fortress. Originally a Phoenecian colony, according to legend an Aeolian dynasty was founded there by SISYPHUS, whose cunning and love of gain may typify the commercial enterprise of the early maritime population who replaced the original inhabitants. Under the sway of Sisyphus and his descendants, Corinth became one of the richest and most powerful cities in Greece. Sisyphus had two sons, GLAUCUS (3) and Ornytion. From the line of Glaucus came BELLEROPHON, who was worshipped with heroic honours at Corinth, and whose exploits were a favourite subject among the Corinthians. The figure of the winged horse PEGASUS, which Bellerophon caught at the fountain of Peirene on the Acro-corinthus, is constantly found on the coins of Corinth and her colonies. Bellerophon settled in Lycia, and the descendants of Ornytion continued to rule at Corinth until overthrown by the DORIANS.

Corinth, Gulf of *or* **Gulf of Lepanto** a beautiful inlet of the Mediterranean between the PELOPONNESUS and northern Greece, having the Isthmus of Corinth closing it in on the east.

Coronis (1) in Greek mythology, a daughter of PHLEYGAS and mother of AESCULAPIUS by APOLLO. She became the lover of ISCHYS while she was pregnant, so Apollo, wishing to punish her faithlessness, caused ARTEMIS to kill her and Ischys.

Coronis (2) *see* **Butes** (1).

Corybants in Greek mythology, male attendants of CYBELE. Their rites included dances during which they clashed spears and shields.

Corycian Cave *see* **Delphyne**.

Cos *or* **Kos** an island in the AEGEAN SEA, on the coast of Asia Minor.

Cottus *see* **Hundred-handed**.

Cranaus *see* **Erechtheus**.

Cratos in Greek mythology, the personification of strength, a son of URANUS and GE and brother of BIA, NIKE and ZELUS.

Creon the brother of JOCASTA and successor to OEDIPUS as king of THEBES.

Cretan Bull in Greek mythology, a bull that was sacred to POSEIDON. MINOS prayed to Poseidon for his assistance when he claimed the throne of Crete. Poseidon sent a bull from the sea with instructions that Minos should sacrifice it to him. Minos sacrificed a less fine bull in its place. As an act of vengeance, Poseidon caused the wife of Minos, PASIPHAË, to give birth to a monster by the bull, the MINOTAUR. After this the bull roamed CRETE. Capturing it alive was the seventh labour of HERACLES.

Crete a large mountainous island in the Mediterranean, north of the African coast. High mountains, covered with forests, run through the whole length of the island in several ranges. The island was colonized at a very early period by Egyptians and Anatolians and was the 'cradle' of pre-Greek or Aegean civilization, which has two phases, Minoan and Mycenaean. Minoan refers to the island culture and is named after MINOS, while Mycenaean, a late phase of Minoan, is so called because it is well represented at MYCENAE. About 1400 BC the palace of Knossos was sacked, probably by Mycenaeans aided by Achaeans, and the dynasty of Minos ended. Large numbers of Cretans appear to have migrated. A colony of them settled in CYPRUS, and it may be that the classical legend of the expedition of Minos to SICILY, and the subsequent Cretan expedition to avenge his death, refer to attempts made to found colonial settlements in Sicily and Italy. The king of Crete who fought in the TROJAN

WAR was evidently subject to Mycenae. The chief divinity of Crete appears to have been the mother goddess who had links with RHEA, DEMETER, ATHENA and APHRODITE. Offerings were made to her in cave sanctuaries. The dove and serpent were connected with her cult. There was also a group of three goddesses. A double-axe symbol of a deity was honoured, and in late times it was connected with the son of the mother goddess, the 'Cretan Zeus' or 'Zeus of the Double-axe'.

Cretheus *see* **Iolcus**; **Neleus**.

Creüsa (1) in Greek mythology, the daughter of ERECHTHEUS, wife of XUTHUS and mother of ACHAEUS and ION. She is also said to have been loved by APOLLO, who is sometimes said to be the father of Ion.

Creüsa (2) in Greek mythology, a daughter of PRIAM and HECUBA, and the wife of AENEAS and mother of ASCANIUS and IULÜS. She was lost in their flight from TROY. When Aeneas returned to seek her, she appeared to him as a ghost, consoled him, revealed to him his future fate and told him she was kept back the great mother of the gods and was obliged to let him depart alone.

Creüsa (3) *see* **Glauce**.

Crius *see* **Titans**.

Crommyonian Sow in Greek mythology, a wild pig named Phaea, said to have been the offspring of ECHIDNA and TYPHON, which ravaged the town of Crommyon on the Isthmus of CORINTH until it was destroyed by THESEUS.

Cronos, Cronus *or* **Kronos** in Greek mythology, a son of URANUS and GE (Heaven and Earth) and youngest of the TITANS. He was the ruler of the world after Uranus was deprived of it, and was in turn deposed by ZEUS in the War of the Titans. Cronos was thought by the Romans as identical with their SATURN.

Cumean Sibyl *see* **sibyl**.

Cupid *or* **Amor** in Roman mythology, the god of love, corresponding to the Greek EROS. He is variously said to be the son of VENUS by MARS, JUPITER or MERCURY. He is represented as a winged boy, naked, armed with a bow and a quiver full of arrows. His eyes are often covered so that he shoots blindly. His darts could pierce the fish at the bottom of the sea, the birds in the air, and even the gods in OLYMPUS.

Curetes in Greek mythology, the attendants of RHEA. They were supposed to have saved the infant ZEUS from his father CRONOS, and then to have become a sort of bodyguard of the god. Their number is sometimes given as ten, although in Greek art only three are usually represented. The ceremonies in connection with the cult of the Curetes consisted principally in performing the Pyrrhic dance, a kind of war dance. The ancients themselves confused the Curetes with other rather similar beings—the CORYBANTES and CABEIRI—and modern research has been unable to clear up the confusion. *See also* TITANS.

Curiatii *see* **Horatii**.

Cyanean Rocks *see* **Clashing Rocks**.

Cyaneë *see* **Byblis and Caunus**.

Cyathus *or* **Eunomus** *see* **Oeneus**.

Cybele, Agdistis *or* **Dindymeme** originally a goddess of the Phrygians, the Great Mother Deity, and, like Isis, the symbol of the moon. From Asia Minor her cult spread to THRACE and the islands, and finally to Greece and to Rome. Her worship was celebrated with a violent noise of instruments and rambling through fields and woods, and her priests were eunuchs in memory of ATYS. The Greeks identified her with their ancient earth goddess RHEA, whose worship seems to have originated in CRETE where she is associated with the CURETES. Among the Romans she was considered as identical with OPS, the wife of SATURN and mother of JUPITER. The Roman priests of Cybele were often called Galli. In later times she was represented as a matron seated on a throne adorned with a mural crown (in reference to the improved condition of men arising from agriculture and their union into cities) with lions crouching to the right and left, or sitting in a carriage drawn by lions.

Cyclades *or* **Kyklades** the principal group of islands in the Greek Archipelago, so named from lying round the sacred island of DELOS in a circle. The largest islands of the group are Andros, Paros, Mykonos, NAXOS, Melos, and Thera (or Santorini). They are of volcanic formation and generally mountainous.

Cyclops *or* **Cyclopes** (literally 'round-eyed', in English the word is used as a singular or a plural) a fabled race of one-eyed giants, variously described in Greek mythology. According to Homer, they were a wild, lawless and impious race of giants inhabiting the sea coasts of SICILY, the most prominent of whom is POLYPHEMUS. Although Homer does not directly call them one-eyed, he expressly describes Polyphemus as such, and later writers attribute this peculiarity to the rest. Another version has them as the three Cyclops, Brontes, Steropes and Arges, each with an eye in the middle of his forehead. These are the three sons of URANUS and GE (Heaven and Earth), belonging to the TITANS, who forged thunderbolts for ZEUS. Hurled into TARTARUS by their father, they were saved by their mother. They helped CRONOS to usurp the government of heaven, but Cronos threw them back to Tartarus, from which they were again released by Zeus, whose servants they now became. Finally they were slain by APOLLO because they forged the thunderbolt with which Zeus killed AESCULA-PIUS. Later tradition placed their workshop in Mount ETNA or in the volcanoes of LEMNOS and Lipari, and made them the slaves of HEPHAESTUS.

Cyllen in Greek mythology, a son of ELATUS (1), from whom Mount Cyllene was believed to have received its name.

Cyllene (modern Ziria) a mountain of Arcadia in southern Greece. It is the fabled birthplace of HERMES.

Cympola *see* **Briareus**.

Cynortas *see* **Oebalus**.

Cynthia, Cynthius surnames respective of ARTEMIS and APOLLO, from Mount Cynthus on the island of DELOS, on which they were born.

Cyprus an island lying on the south of Asia Minor, and the most easterly in the Mediterranean. The chief features of its surface are two mountain ranges, both stretching east and west. The Cypriot or Paphian goddess, answering to the Phoenician Astarte or Ashtaroth, was worshipped by the Greeks as APHRODITE. DIDO stopped at Cyprus and carried off from there eighty virgins to be the wives of her followers in their new home at CARTHAGE.

Cyrene (1) in Greek mythology, a nymph of Mount PELION who was loved by APOLLO. He carried her to Libya, where CYRENE derived its name from her. She became by Apollo the mother of IDMON.

Cyrene (2) *see* **Diomedes** (1).

Cyrene in ancient times a celebrated city in Africa, near the north coast, founded by BATTUS and named after CYRENE (1).

Cythera *or* **Kithera** a Greek island in the Mediterranean, south of the Morea, from which it is separated by a narrow strait. It is mountainous and barren, although some of the valleys are fertile. In Greek mythology ancient Cythera is mentioned as the sacred abode of APHRODITE.

Cyzicus *see* **Doliones**.

D

Dactyls in Greek mythology, beings whose name means literally 'fingers'. Their number is variously given as three, five, ten or even a hundred. Born on Mount IDA in CRETE and said to be the sons of the nymph Anchiale, they are credited with the discovery of iron and the art of smelting. They are connected with the worship of RHEA and that of CYBELE.

Daedalus (literally the 'cunning worker') in Greek mythology, an architect and sculptor, said to have lived three generations before the TROJAN WAR. An Athenian of royal race, he killed his nephew and pupil, TALUS (2), in envy at his growing skill and had to flee to CRETE, where he is credited with building for MINOS the famous labyrinth to confine the MINOTAUR. He was imprisoned by Minos but escaped with the help of Queen PASIPHAË and invented wings for himself and his son ICARUS with which to fly across the sea. He himself flew safely across the AEGEAN, but Icarus foolishly flew too near the sun, the heat of which melted the wax that fastened his wings to him and he was drowned in the Icarian Sea. Daedalus himself made his way to SICILY. Some accounts

made him first alight at Cumae, where he dedicated his wings to APOLLO and
built a temple to the god.

daimon *or* **daemon** in mythology, a kind of spirit usually associated with a particular place or object, such as a tree, stream, mountain, etc. Numbered among
the daimons are NYMPHS, SATYRS, RIVER-GODS and PENATES.

Damastes *see* **Procrustes**.

Danaë in Greek mythology, daughter of ACRISIUS, king of ARGOS. She was shut
up by her father in a tower, as there was a prophecy that her son would kill her
father. ZEUS, who loved her, descended to her in a shower of gold and thus
gained access to her. She bore him a son, PERSEUS. Acrisius next put both
mother and child into a chest and set it adrift on the sea. The chest, however,
drifted ashore on the island of SERIPHUS in the CYCLADES, and Danaë and her
child were saved. She remained on the island until Perseus had grown up and
become a hero famous for his exploits, then she accompanied him to Argos.
On his arrival, Acrisius fled, but was subsequently slain accidentally by
Perseus at Larissa. Correggio, Rembrandt and Titian have made the story of
DANAË's union with Zeus the subject of famous paintings.

Danaïdes in Greek mythology, the fifty daughters of DANAÜS, who were all condemned with the exception of one (Hypermnestra) eternally to pour water into
a vessel full of holes. Hypermnestra allowed her husband, LYNCEUS (1), to escape. This was their punishment for murdering their husbands, the sons of
AEGYPTUS, on their wedding night.

Danaüs in Greek mythology, the son of BELUS and twin brother of AEGYPTUS,
originally ruler of Libya. Fearing his brother, he fled to ARGOS with his fifty
daughters, the DANAÏDES. Here he became king of Argos, after a dispute with
Gelanor which was settled by the people of Argos in favour of Danaüs after a
wolf rushed among a herd of cattle and killed an ox, which they took to be an
omen. The fifty sons of Aegyptus followed Danaüs to Argos and under the
pretence of friendship sought the hand of his daughters in marriage. Danaüs
consented, but on the wedding night he gave his daughters each a dagger and
urged them to murder their bridegrooms in revenge for the treatment he had
received from Aegyptus. All did so, except one.

Daphne the Greek name for laurel, in Greek mythology a NYMPH loved by
APOLLO. Deaf to the wooing of the god and fleeing from him, she beseeched
ZEUS to protect her. Her prayer was heard, and at the moment Apollo was
about to encircle her in his arms she was changed by her mother, GE, into a
laurel, a tree thereafter consecrated to the god.

Dardania the area around or including TROY. It was called after DARDANUS (1),
who became ruler of the land and who was the son-in-law of TEUCER (1), the
first king.

Dardanus (1) in Greek mythology, son of ZEUS and ELECTRA (3), the daughter of

353

ATLAS. He was the mythical ruler of DARDANIA and the Dardanians, who are identified with the Trojans, and is regarded as being the ancestor of the Trojans. Originally a king in ARCADIA, he migrated to SAMOTHRACE and from there to Asia where TEUCER (1) gave him the site of his town, Dardania. He married BATEIA, a daughter of Teucer, and his grandson was the eponymous hero TROS, who removed his grandfather's PALLADIUM to TROY.

Dardanus (2) in Greek mythology, a king of the Scythians and father of IDAEA (2), whom he condemned to death because of crimes that she committed against her stepsons.

Dascylus (1) in Greek mythology, a king of the MARIANDYNIANS who received assistance from HERACLES in defeating his enemies.

Dascylus (2) in Greek mythology, son of LYCUS (4), king of the MARIANDYNIANS, and grandson of DASCYLUS (1). He acompanied the ARGONAUTS on their journey as far as the Thermodon so that they would be treated in a friendly manner by the allies of the Mariandynians.

Dawn in Roman mythology was represented as AURORA and in Greek mythology as EOS.

Death *see* **Thanatos**.

Degmenus *see* **Oxylus**.

Deïaneira in Greek mythology, a daughter of ALTHAEA and OENEUS, king of CALYDON, and sister of MELEAGER. She was the wife of HERACLES. She killed herself after she accidentally killed him with a poisoned potion which she believed to be a harmless love potion given to her by the centaur NESSUS.

Deïdameia (1) in Greek mythology, a daughter of BELLEROPHON and wife of EVANDER, by whom she became the mother of SARPEDON.

Deïdameia (2) in Greek mythology, a daughter of LYCOMEDES in the island of Scyrus. When ACHILLES was concealed there in woman's dress, Deïdamia became by him the mother of NEOPTOLEMUS and, according to others, also of Oneirus.

Deïdameia (3) in Greek mythology, the wife of PEIRITHOÜS, who is commonly called Hippodamia.

Deion *or* **Deïoneus** in Greek mythology, a son of AEOLUS and Enarete, king of PHOCIS and husband of DIOMEDE (1), by whom he became the father of Asteropeia, Aenetus, Actor, PHYLACUS and CEPHALUS. After the death of his brother, Salmoneus, he took his daughter TYRO into his house and gave her in marriage to Creutheus.

Deioneus *see* **Dia**.

Deïphobus in Greek mythology, son of PRIAM, king of TROY, and HECUBA, who married HELEN after the death of PARIS. On the fall of Troy to the Greeks, he is said in some legends to have been killed by MENELAÜS. According to other legends he was killed by Helen or was killed in battle.

Deïphontes in Greek mythology, son of Antimachus and husband of Hyrnetho, daughter of Temenus, a leader of the HERACLIDS who became king of Argos. The sons of Temenus were jealous of Deïphontes and his influence on their father. They overthrew Temenus and tried to kidnap their sister from her husband. In the ensuing struggle Deïphontes killed one of the brothers, Cerynes, but Hyrnetho was acidentally killed by her brother, Phalces. Deïphontes erected a sanctuary to her memory in an olive grove in EPIDAURUS, where he had lived with her.

Deïpyle in Greek mythology, a daughter of ADRASTUS and Amphithea, wife of TYDEUS and mother of DIOMEDES (2).

Delia in Greek mythology, a surname sometimes applied to ARTEMIS and formed from the island of DELOS, her birthplace.

Delos an island of great renown among the ancient Greeks. In Greek mythology, it was at first a floating island, but was fixed to the bottom of the sea by ZEUS in order that it might become a safe place for LETO for the birth of APOLLO and ARTEMIS. It was a centre of the worship of Apollo and the site of a famous oracle. It is the central and smallest island of the CYCLADES, in the AEGEAN SEA. At first the island, occupied by the IONIANS, had kings of its own, who also held priestly office. It subsequently became the common treasury of the Greeks. Its festivals were visited by strangers from all parts of Greece and Asia Minor.

Delphi an ancient Greek town, originally called Pytho, the seat of the famous oracle of APOLLO. It was situated in PHOCIS, on the southern side or PARNASSUS, north of the Gulf of CORINTH. The oracles were delivered through the mouth of a priestess who was seated on a tripod above a subterranean opening, from which she received the vapours ascending from beneath, and with them the inspiration of the Delphian god. The oracular replies were always obscure and ambiguous but they served, in earlier times, in the hands of the priests, to regulate and uphold the political, civil and religious relations of Greece. The oracle was celebrated as early as the ninth century BC, and continued to have importance till long after the Christian era, being at last abolished by the Emperor Theodosius. People came to consult it from all quarters, bestowing rich gifts in return. The spendid temple thus possessed immense treasures, and the city was adorned with numerous statues and other works of art.

Delphinus (The Dolphin) a small constellation that in Greek mythology is identified with the dolphin that saved the life of ARION and with his lyre.

Delphinius in Greek mythology, a surname or epithet applied to APOLLO. It is derived either from the fact that he is said to have killed the dragon DELPHYNE or from the fact that he is said to have assumed the shape of a dolphin to lead Cretan colonists to DELPHI.

Delphyne a mythical monster who was half serpent and half woman and who was given the task of guarding the sinews of ZEUS in the Corycian Cave after

Typhon had severed these. Hermes and Aegipan succeeded in stealing the sinews from the cave to give them back to Zeus. Delphyne is said to have been killed by Apollo.

Deluge *see* **Deucalion**.

Demeter *or* **Deo** in Greek mythology, one of the twelve principal deities, the great mother-goddess, goddess of corn or of the earth and its fruitfulness. By the Romans she was called Ceres. She was the daughter of Cronos and Rhea, but her main claim to fame is as the mother of Persephone by Zeus. While gathering flowers in the Nysian plain, Persephone was carried off by Hades. Demeter wandered for some time in search of her daughter, and when she learned where she had been taken, she left Olympus in anger and dwelt on earth among men, bringing blessings in her train. At length Zeus sent Hermes to bring Persephone back, and both mother and daughter returned to Olympus. As Persephone had eaten part of a pomegranate in the underworld, she was obliged to spend one-third of the year in her husband's gloomy kingdom, returning to her mother for the rest of the year.

demigod *see* **Races of Man**.

demon a spirit or immaterial being of supernatural but limited powers, especially an evil or malignant spirit. Among the ancient Greeks the name was given to beings similar to those called angels in the Bible.

Demonice *or* **Demodoce** in Greek mythology, daughter of Agenor and Epicaste who was the mother of several children by Ares.

Demophon *or* **Demophoön** (1) in Greek mythology, a son of Theseus and Phaedra and brother of Acamas. Legend has it that the two brothers went to the Trojan war on the side of the Greeks and, while there, rescued their grandmother, Aethra (1), who had been previously abducted to become a servant of Helen. According to another legend, Demophon was going to marry Phyllis, the daughter of the Thracian king, Sithon. While he was on a journey to Attica she is said to have assumed that he had abandoned her and to have taken her own life and become a tree which grew buds and leaves when Demophon returned and pressed it to his bosom. Demophon is also presented as having defended the family of Heracles against Eurystheus.

Demophon *or* **Demophoön** (2) in Greek mythology, a son of Celeus and Metaneira who was brought up by Demeter. She fed him with her own milk and ambrosia and gave him no human food. She also placed him in a fire every night so that he would become immortal. The story goes on to relate that his mother disturbed the goddess one night, protesting at the treatment of the child, and Demophon burned to death.

Dendrites in Greek mythology, an epithet applied to Dionysus indicating his connnection with trees.

Deo another name for Demeter.

Despoina in Greek mythology, the daughter of DEMETER and POSEIDON, conceived while Demeter had turned herself into a mare while being pursued by Poseidon. He became a stallion and mounted her. Despoina means 'mistress' or 'ruling goddess' and occurs as the epithet of several goddesses, such as APHRODITE and PERSEPHONE.

Deucalion (1) in Greek mythology, a son of PROMETHEUS. He was the king of PHTHIA and was the husband of PYRRHA. When ZEUS sent a flood to destroy mankind Deucalion took his father's advice and built a ship and stocked it with stores of provisions. Deucalion and Pyrrha were saved from the flood and sailed around for nine days before reaching Mount PARNASSUS. They felt very lonely and asked the oracle of THEMIS to help them restore mankind. They were advised to throw the bones of their mother behind them and correctly interpreted this as an instruction to throw the stones of mother-earth behind them. The stones thrown by Deucalion became men and those thrown by Pyrrha became women. Deucalion and Pyrrha were the parents of HELLEN, ancestor of the HELLENES.

Deucalion (2) in Greek mythology, a son of MINOS and PASIPHAË, and one of the ARGONAUTS and one of the hunters of the CALYDONIAN BOAR. He was the father of IDOMENEUS.

Dexames in Greek mythology, a king of OLENUS and father of DEÏANEIRA, who married HERACLES after having been saved by him from a forced marriage to the Centaur, EURYTION (2).

Dia (1) *or* **Eioneus** in Greek mythology, a daughter of Deioneus and mother of PEIRITHOÜS by her husband, IXION, according to one legend, or according to another, by ZEUS. Peirithoüs is said to have received his name from the fact that Zeus when he attempted to seduce Dia ran around her in the form of a horse.

Dia (2) in Greek mythology, an epithet given to HEBE or GANYMEDE.

Dia an early name of the island Naxos.

Diana in Roman mythology, an ancient Italian goddess, in later times identified with the Greek ARTEMIS, with whom she had various attributes in common, being the virgin goddess of the moon and of the hunt, and as such associated with the crescent moon, bow, arrows, and quiver. The name is a feminine form of JANUS. She seems to have been originally the patron divinity of the SABINES and LATINS. She was worshipped especially by women, as presiding over births, no man being allowed to enter her temple.

Dicte, Mount a mountain in CRETE in which the infant ZEUS is said to have been sheltered. It is also said to have been the home of the HARPIES.

Dicte a NYMPH from whom Mount DICTE is said to have received its name.

Dictynna in Greek mythology, an epithet applied to the Cretan goddess, BRITOMARTIS, thought by some to mean 'lady of the nets', by others to mean 'she of mount Dicte'.

Dictys in Greek mythology, a fisherman who became king of SERIPHUS, brother of POLYDECTES and son of MAGNES (1).

Dido *or* **Elissa** in Greek mythology, the reputed founder of CARTHAGE. She was the daughter of a king of TYRE, called by some BELUS, by others Metten or Matgenus. After her father's death, her brother murdered her husband, SICHAEUS, with the intention of obtaining his wealth. However, Dido, accompanied by many Tyrians of her party, fled with all the treasure over the sea, and landed on the coast of Africa, not far from the Phoenician colony of Utica, where she built a citadel called Byrsa ('the hide of a bull') on a piece of ground which she had bought from the Numidian king, IARBAS. The meaning of the word Byrsa gave rise to the legend that Dido bought as much land as could be encompassed with a bullock's hide. Once the agreement was concluded, she cut the hide into small thongs, and thus enclosed a large piece of ground, on which she built the city of CARTHAGE. To avoid being compelled to marry Iarbas, she stabbed herself on a funeral pile, and after her death was honoured as a deity by her subjects. The story is told by Virgil, with many inventions of his own, in the *Aeneid*. He ascribes the death of Dido to her unrequited passion for AENEAS, but many of the ancient writers realized that he had committed an anachronism in making her contemporary with the Trojan prince. More than three hundred years separated the fall of TROY (1184 BC) from the founding of Carthage (853 BC).

Dike *see* **Virgo**.

Dindymene *see* **Cybele**.

Dindymus, Mount a mountain near the ancient city of Gordium and a place much favoured by the goddess CYBELE who was called DINDYMENE in recognition of this fact. The ARGONAUTS sacrificed to her on the mountain.

Diomede (1) *see* **Deion**.

Diomede (2) *see* **Diomedes** (2).

Diomedes (1) in Greek mythology, the son of ARES and Cyrene, and king of the BISTONES in THRACE, who fed his horses on human flesh, and used to throw all strangers who entered his territories to those animals to be devoured. He was killed by HERACLES, who carried off the horses.

Diomedes (2) *or* **Diomede** in Greek mythology, one of the heroes at the siege of TROY, the son of TYDEUS and DEÏPYLE, and king of ARGOS, one of the suitors of HELEN. He was one of the EPIGONI, and after Helen was carried off, he took part in the expedition against Troy, in which his courage and the protection of ATHENA rendered him one of the most distinguished heroes. He was the bravest, after ACHILLES, of all the Greeks who took part in the TROJAN WAR. He vanquished in fight HECTOR and AENEAS, and even APHRODITE and ARES, when they took the field on the Trojan side, were attacked and wounded by him. Three times he attacked APOLLO. In the games instituted by Achilles in honour of PATROCLUS, he gained the prize in the chariot race and worsted AJAX in single combat. By carrying off the horses of RHESUS from the enemies' tents, by aiding ODYSSEUS in the removal of PHILOCTETES from LEMNOS and carrying off the PALLADIUM on which the fate of Troy depended, he fulfilled three of the conditions on which alone Troy could be conquered. Finally he was one of the heroes concealed in the WOODEN HORSE by which the capture of Troy was at length accomplished. Different accounts were given of his life thereafter. According to one, on returning to Argos, to the crown of which he had succeeded after the death of ADRASTUS, he found that his wife had been unfaithful in his absence, whereupon he sailed to Italy and there married the daughter of DAUNUS and lived to a good old age.

Dione in Greek mythology, a female TITAN, a daughter of OCEANUS and TETHYS or perhaps of URANUS and GE. She is held in some legends to be the mother of APHRODITE, daughter of ZEUS.

dionysia *see* **bacchanalia**.

Dionysus the original Greek name of the god of wine, the name BACCHUS, by which he was also called both by the Greeks and the Romans, being at first a mere epithet or surname. The worship of Dionysus, who was originally the god of vegetation and not until the time of Homer the god of wine, was borrowed by the Greeks from the Thracians. When adopted as a Greek god he was naturally made the son of ZEUS, the sky from which falls the rain that makes vegetation grow. His mother, SEMELE, was destroyed before his birth because of her folly in begging Zeus to visit her in all his majesty of thunder and lightning. Dionysus was born from the thigh of Zeus, making his paternity doubly sure, so was called the 'twice born'. When wine became known it was regarded as the gift of Dionysus, and from that came his title as god of wine. He was said to be the first to teach the cultivation of the vine and the preparation of wine. To spread the knowledge of his invention he travelled over various countries, receiving honours as he went. Drawn by lions (some say panthers, tigers, or lynxes), he began his march, which resembled a triumphal procession. Those who opposed him were severely punished, but on those who received him hospitably he bestowed rewards. His love was shared by several, but only ARIADNE, whom he found deserted upon NAXOS, became his wife and a sharer of his immortality. In art he is represented with the round, soft, and graceful form of a maiden rather than with that of a young man. His long waving hair is plaited behind in a knot and wreathed with sprigs of ivy and vine leaves. He is usually naked; sometimes he has a loose mantle hung negligently round his shoulders; sometimes a fawn-skin hangs across his breast. He is often accompanied by SEILENUS, BACCHANTES, SATYRS, etc. *See also* BACCHANALIA.

Diores in Greek mythology, a son of Amarynceus who was killed by the Thracian leader Pieros during the TROJAN WAR.

Dioscuri *see* **Castor and Pollux**.

Dirae in Roman mythology, one of the names under which the FURIES were known to the Romans.

Dirce in Greek mythology, daughter of HELIOS and wife of LYCUS, a king of THEBES. AMPHION and ZETHUS, sons of ANTIOPE, tied Dirce to a bull because of her cruel treatment of their mother. She was killed by the bull, and in the spot where she died on Mount CITHAERON DIONYSUS, of whom she was a devoted follower, caused a spring to burst forth in her memory.

Dis in Roman mythology, a contraction of **Dives**, a name sometimes given to PLUTO, god of the underworld.

Dius in Greek mythology, a king of ELIS who resisted OXYLUS's usurpation but failed to keep his throne.

Dodona a celebrated place of ancient Greece, in EPIRUS, where one of the most ancient Greek oracles was located. It was a seat of ZEUS (surnamed the Pelasgian), whose communications were announced to the priestesses in the rustling of the leaves on its oak tree and the murmuring of water which gushed forth from the earth.

Doliche *see* **Icaria**.

Doliones a Mysian tribe who, in Greek mythology, gave hospitality to the ARGONAUTS. Their king, Cyzicus, was killed when the Argonauts attacked the Doliones by mistake and his subjects renamed their capital city after their dead king.

Dolius in Greek mythology, an elderly slave of PENELOPE given by her father to her on her marriage to ODYSSEUS, and who was her gardener. When Odysseus returned from his travels Dolius and six of his sons were faithful to him and took his side against the Ithacan relatives of the suitors. His seventh son, MELANTHEUS, took the side of the relatives and was killed.

Dolon in Greek mythology, the son of Eumedes, who was a Trojan herald. He spied for the Trojans on the Greeks hoping to be rewarded by the chariot and horses of ACHILLES. He was soon captured by ODYSSEUS and DIOMEDES and gave them information about the Trojan camp to ensure his safety but they killed him.

Dolphin, The *see* **Delphinus**.

Dorians one of the three great branches of the Greek nation who migrated from THESSALY southwards, settling for a time in the mountainous district of DORIS in Northern Greece and finally in PELOPONNESUS. Their migration to the latter was said to have taken place in 1104 BC, about eighty years after the fall of TROY, and as among their leaders were Temenus, Cresphontes and Aristodemus, three descendants of HERACLES, it was known as 'the return of the Heraclidae' ('descendants of Heracles'), who had come to recover the territory taken from their ancestors by EURYSTHEUS. The Dorians ruled SPARTA with great renown as a strong and warlike people, although less cultivated than the other Greeks in arts and letters. Their laws were severe and rigid, as typified in the codes of the great Doric legislator MINOS.

Doris *see* **Galatea** (1); **Nereïds.**

Doris in ancient times a small and mountainous region of northern Greece, at one time the home of the DORIANS.

Dorus (1) in Greek mythology, the ancestor of the DORIANS, said to have been a son of HELLEN and the nymph Orseis. When Hellen divided the Greek lands among his three sons, Dorus, AEOLUS (2) and XUTHUS, Dorus received the region around PARNASSUS.

Dorus (2) son of APOLLO. With his brothers, Laodocus and POLYPOETES, he was killed by AETOLUS when he invaded their country.

Doso in Greek mythology, a name given to DEMETER.

Drepane the island which was home to the PHAEACIANS. The name means 'sickle', and legend has it that the island's name comes from the sickle with which CRONOS castrated his father, URANUS. Another legend has it that the name derives from the sickle of DEMETER, the goddess of corn, who had once lived on the island and who had taught the TITANS to plant corn.

Dryad in Greek mythology, a wood NYMPH, supposed to be a deity of trees. Each particular tree or wood was the home of its own special dryad.

Dryas *see* **Lycurgus** (1); **Tereus**.

Dryope in Greek mythology, a daughter of King Eurytus. APOLLO took the shape of a tortoise and then of a serpent in order to seduce her. Soon afterwards she married ANDRAEMON (2)but bore Apollo a son, Amphissus.

Dryopians *or* **Dryopes** a people who originally lived in the valley of the River SPERCHEIUS. They were called after Dryops, a son either of the river-god Sperchius or of APOLLO. They were driven from their land by HERACLES, some emigrating to Asine and later to MESSENIA. Others settled in Styra.

E

Earth-born Monsters *or* **Gegenees** in Greek mythology, a tribe of giants each of whom had six arms. They lived on BEAR MOUNTAIN on the Mysian coast and mounted an attack on the ARGONAUTS, who destroyed them.

Echemus in Greek mythology, son of Aeropus and grandson of of CEPHEUS. He succeeded LYCURGUS (2) to the throne of ARCADIA. He was the husband of Timandra, daughter of TYNDAREUS and LEDA, but she deserted him to go off with PHYLEUS after bearing Echemus a son, Laodocus. Echemus, while helping the Arcadian forces defend the PELOPONNESUS against the HERACLIDS, killed Hyllus, the son of HERACLES, in single combat, after which the Heraclids undertook not to repeat their attempted invasion of Peloponnesus within the next fifty or a hundred years.

Echetus in Greek mythology, a king of Epirus who was noted for his terrible cruelty. Such was his cruelty that he blinded his own daughter, Metope or Amphissa, and compelled her to grind grains of bronze in a dungeon as a punishment for having taken a lover. He promised his daughter that he would restore her sight if she could grind the bronze into flour. Her lover Aechmodicus was cruelly mutilated.

Echidna in Greek mythology, a daughter of TARTARUS and GE, or of CETO and PHORCYS, or of STYX and Peiras. She was a monster, being half-maiden and half serpent, who lived in a cave and ate passers-by. By TYPHON she became the mother of CHIMAERA, the HYDRA, CERBERUS and the many-headed dog ORTHUS. She was also the mother of the SPHINX, the NEMEAN LION, the Colchian dragon and perhaps SCYLLA (2). She was not immortal although she never grew old and was killed in her sleep by ARGUS PANOPTES.

Echion (1) in Greek mythology, one of the SPARTI, the five survivors of the group of armed men that sprang up from the teeth of ARES' sacred dragon at Thebes sown by CADMUS. He was the husband of AGAVE, daughter of Cadmus, and the father by her of PENTHEUS, who succeeded Cadmus to the throne.

Echion (2) in Greek mythology, son of HERMES and Antianeira and twin brother of Erytus, with whom he took part in the CALYDONIAN BOAR hunt and in the expedition of the ARGONAUTS in which he acted as a spy.

Echo in Greek mythology, a mountain NYMPH (one of the Oreads). Legend relates that by her talking she detained HERA, when the latter sought to surprise ZEUS among the mountain nymphs. To punish her the goddess deprived her of speech, unless first spoken to. She subsequently fell in love with NARCISSUS, and because he did not reciprocate her affection, she pined away until nothing was left but her voice.

Ectenes in ancient Greece, a tribe native to the region of THEBES which was completely wiped out by a terrible plague. Their king was OGYGUS.

Edonians *or* **Edoni** a tribe of Thracia who lived in the region of Mount PANGAEUS. Their king, LYCURGUS (1), persecuted DIONYSUS and his followers. He was subjected to a terrible punishment—such as being torn apart by horses—when his subjects were told by an oracle that the severe drought which affected their land had been sent by the gods because of the crimes of their king.

Eëtion in Greek mythology, a king of Hypoplacian Thebes in the Troad and father of ANDROMACHE and Podes. He was an ally of the Trojans, and he and his seven sons were killed by ACHILLES in one day.

Egeria in Roman mythology, a nymph who received divine honours. NUMA POMPILIUS is said to have received from her the laws which he gave to the Romans.

Egypt the country around the river Nile named after AEGYPTUS, a son of King BELUS (1), the scene of many Greek myths.

Eidothea *see* **Byblis and Caunus**.

Eidyia *or* **Idyia** in Greek mythology, a daugter of OCEANUS and TETHYS, who married AEËTES, king of AEA (COLCHIS), and mother of MEDEA and Chalciope and possibly ABSYRTUS.

Eileithyia in Greek mythology, daughter of ZEUS and HERA, who became the goddess of childbirth, although there is some confusion with ARTEMIS here. When she was kindly disposed she would hasten a birth, but when she was angry she delayed the birth and protracted labour.

Eioneus (1) in Greek mythology, a son of MAGNES (1) and one of the suitors of HIPPODAMIA. He was slain by OENOMAUS.

Eioneus (2) *see* **Dia**.

Elatus (1) in Greek mythology, a son of ARCAS possibly by the nymph CHRYSOPELEIA. He married Laodice and was the father of STYMPHALUS, Aepytus, CYLLEN, and Pereus. He is often called the father of ISCHYS, the lover of CORONIS, but this is probably from confusion with ELATUS (2). Elatus received Mount CYLLENE as his share of his father's kingdom. He protected the Phocians and the Delphic sanctuary against the Phlegyans. He founded the town of Elateia.

Elatus (2) in Greek mythology, a Lapith prince and father of Caenis (later Caenus) and POLYPHEMUS (2), both of whom took part in the expedition of the ARGONAUTS. He is sometimes confused with ELATUS (1), and there is in particular confusion as to which one was the father of ISCHYS.

Elba an island off the west coast of Italy, known in classical times as Aethalia or Ilva. It was a stopping point of the ARGONAUTS on their return journey.

Electra (1) in Greek mythology, a daughter of AGAMEMNON and CLYTEMNESTRA. After the murder of her father by her mother and her mother's lover, AEGISTHUS, she helped her brother ORESTES and PYLADES to kill Clytemnestra and Aegisthus. She married Pylades and bore him two sons, Medon and Strophius. One legend has it that Electra was told that her sister, IPHIGENIA, had sacrificed their brother Orestes to ARTEMIS, and she snatched up a firebrand with the intention of putting out her sister's eyes. Fortunately Orestes appeared at that point alive and well. Electra is the principal character in a number of classical tragedies, such as Sophocles's *Electra* and Euripides's *Electra*.

Electra (2) in Greek mythology, a sister of CADMUS from whom the Electrian gate at Thebes was said to have received its name.

Electra (3) in Greek mythology, daughter of ATLAS and Pleione. She was one of the PLEIADES and lived on the island of Samothrace. By ZEUS she was the mother of DARDANUS (1) and possibly of HARMONIA (3), and one legend has it that the dim star among the Pleiades constellation is Electra, who lost her brilliance with grief either when her son Dardanus was killed or when TROY was sacked.

Electra (4) in Greek mythology, daughter of OCEANUS and TETHYS and the wife of THAUMAS, a Titan, by whom she bore IRIS and the HARPIES.

Electris a mythical island of Greece said to have been named for ELECTRA (3).

Electryon in Greek mythology, son of PERSEUS and ANDROMEDA who inherited the throne of MYCENAE from his father. He married Anaxo, the daughter of Alcaeus, by whom he had a daughter, ALCMENE, and several sons. He also had a son, LICYMNIUS, by Midea, a Phrygian woman. While his sons were tending their father's herd they were attacked by a party of TAPHIANS, the sons of Pterelaus, a descendant of Electryon's brother, Mestor. Only Licymnius and Everos, who was guarding the Taphian ships, survived. Electryon was killed in a quarrel with his son-in-law, AMPHITRYON, either accidentally or deliberately, and STHENELUS (1) banished Amphitryon and seized the throne. Amphitryon avenged Electryon's sons on the Taphians.

Eleusinian Mysteries the sacred rites observed in ancient Greece at the annual festival of DEMETER or CERES, so named from their original seat in ELEUSIS. According to the Homeric hymn to Demeter, the goddess, while wandering in search of PERSEPHONE, came to Eleusis, where she was hospitably received by King Celeus. He directed the establishment of a temple in her honour, and showed the use of grain to TRIPTOLEMUS and other princes. As a preparation for the greater mysteries celebrated at Athens and Eleusis, lesser Eleusinia were celebrated at Agrae on the Ilissus. The greater Eleusinia were celebrated September-October, beginning on the fifteenth of the month and lasting nine days. The celebrations, which were varied each day, consisted of processions between Athens and Eleusis, torch-bearing and mystic ceremonies attended with oaths of secrecy. They appear to have symbolized the old conceptions of death and reproduction, and to have been allied to the orgiastic worship of DIONYSUS (Bacchus).

Eleusis next to ATHENS, the most important town of ancient ATTICA, on the Bay of Eleusis, opposite Salamis. It was famous as the chief seat of the worship of CERES, whose mystic rites were performed here with great pomp and solemnity from earliest times. *See also* ALOPE.

Elis a maritime state of ancient Greece in the west of the PELOPONNESUS, bordering on ACHAEA, ARCADIA and MESSENIA, and watered by the Rivers ALPHEUS and Peneus. It was famed for the excellence of its horses. Of its capital Elis (now Kloskopi) there are few traces. OLYMPIA, where the famous games were held, was near the Alpheus.

Elissa *see* **Dido**.

Elysium *or* **Elysian Fields** in Greek and Roman mythology, the regions inhabited by the blessed after death. They are placed by Homer at the extremities of the earth. Plato located them at the antipodes, and others in the Fortunate Islands (the Canaries). They were at last supposed to be in the interior of the earth, where Virgil described them as being. In the *Odyssey*, Homer describes Elysium as a place where the blessed led a life of tranquil enjoyment in a perfect summer land, where the heroes, freed from all care and infirmities, renewed their favourite sports. In the *Iliad*, however, he gives a sombre view of the state of the departed souls. ACHILLES, although in Elysium, is made to envy the life of the meanest hind on earth.

Enarete *see* **Magnes** (1); **Sisyphus**.

Enceladus in Greek mythology, a son of TARTARUS and GE, and one of the hundred-armed giants who made war upon the gods. He was killed, according to some, by ZEUS, by a flash of lightning and buried under Mount ETNA. According to others he was killed by the chariot of ATHENA. In this flight Athena threw the island of Sicily on him.

Endymion in Greek mythology, a huntsman, a shepherd, or a king of Elis, who is said to have asked of ZEUS, or to have received as a punishment, eternal sleep. Others relate that SELENE or ARTEMIS conveyed him to Mount Latmos in Caria, and threw him into a perpetual sleep in order that she might enjoy his society whenever she pleased. Endymion is also supposed to be a personification of the sun, or of the plunge of the setting sun into the sea, as in Keats's *Endymion*.

Enna *see* **Athena**.

Eoiae *see* **Catalogues of Women**.

Eos in Greek mythology, the goddess of the dawn. *See* AURORA.

Epaphus in Greek mythology, a son of ZEUS and Io, who was born on the River Nile after the long wanderings of his mother. He was then hidden by the CURETES, at the request of HERA, but Io afterwards found him in Syria. He subsequently became king of Egypt, married MEMPHIS or, according to others, CASSIOPEIA, and built the city of Memphis in Egypt. He had one daughter, Libya, from whom the African country received its name.

Epeirus *see* **Epirus**.

Epeius *see* **wooden horse**.

Ephesus an ancient Greek city of LYDIA, in Asia Minor. It was a sacred city from an early period and became famous for its temple of ARTEMIS, called Artemision, the largest and most perfect model of Ionic architecture and reckoned one of the seven wonders of the world.

Ephialtes *see* **Otus**.

Epicasta *see* **Jocasta**.

Epidaurus a town and seaport of ancient Greece, situated in ARGOLIS, in the PELOPONNESUS, particularly celebrated for its magnificent temple of AESCULAPIUS, which stood on an eminence not far from the town. It had also temples of ARTEMIS, DIONYSUS, APHRODITE, and HERA.

Epigoni ('heirs' or 'descendants') in Greek mythology, the sons of the SEVEN AGAINST THEBES, who ten years later conducted a war against Thebes to avenge their fathers. This is called the war of the Epigoni. According to some traditions, this war was undertaken at the request of ADRASTUS, the only survivor of the seven heroes. Those who took part were AEGIALEUS (1), son of Adrastus, DIOMEDES (2), son of Tydeus, Promachus, son of Parthenopaeus, STHENELUS (2), son of CAPANEUS, THERSANDER, son of POLYNEICES, and Eurylus, under the command of ALCMAEON and supported by a considerable band of ARGIVES. A Theban force under Laodamas protecting the city was defeated, with the death on the Argive side of Aegialeus, and the city put under siege. TEIRESIAS persuaded the Thebans to quit the town with their wives and children, and the Argives took possession of it and razed it to the ground. The Epigoni sent a portion of the booty and Manto, the daughter of Teiresias, to Delphi and then returned to Peloponnesus.

Epimetheus in Greek mythology, the son of IAPETUS, brother of PROMETHEUS and ATLAS, and husband of PANDORA. Epimetheus may be translated as 'afterthought', and Prometheus as 'forethought'.

Epirus *or* **Epeirus** the ancient name of a part of northern Greece, extending between ILLYRIA and the Ambracian Gulf and from the Ionian Sea to the chain of Pindus. The ACHERON was one of its principal rivers, and the chief towns were DODONA and AMBRACIA.

Epistrophus *see* **Iphitus** (1).

eponym a mythical person created to account for the name of a tribe or people. Thus TROS is the eponymous hero of Troy, Italus was assumed as ancestor of the Italians, etc.

Epopeus in Greek mythology, a son of POSEIDON who went from Thessaly to Sicyon where he succeeded in the kingdom. He carried away from Thebes the beautiful ANTIOPE (1), the daughter of NYCTEUS, who therefore made war on Epopeus. The two hostile kings died of the wounds that they received in the war.

Erato in Greek mythology, one of the nine MUSES, whose name signifies 'loving' or 'lovely'. She presided over lyric and especially amatory poetry, and is generally represented crowned with roses and myrtle, and with the lyre in the left hand and the plectrum in the right in the act of playing.

Erebus in Greek mythology, the son of CHAOS (darkness) and father of AETHER and HEMERA (day). The name Erebus was also given to the infernal region.

Erechtheus *or* **Erichthonius** in Greek mythology, an Attic hero, said to have been the son of HEPHAESTUS and Atthis, daughter of Cranaus, the son-in-law and successor of CECROPS. He was brought up by ATHENA, who placed him in a chest, which was entrusted to the three daughters of Cecrops. In defiance of orders, they opened the chest, and discovering a child entwined with serpents, were seized with madness and threw themselves down the most precipitous part of the ACROPOLIS. When Erechtheus became king of ATHENS, he instituted the Panathenaea, and in his honour a fine temple, the Erechtheum, was built on the Acropolis. In some representations of him he is depicted as half snake, so that he was one of the autochthones, the earth-born ancestors of the Athenians.

Erichthonius (1) *see* **Erechtheus**.

Erichthonius (2) *see* **Bateia** (1); **Boreas**.

Eridanus the name of various rivers in ancient Greece and Europe, including the River Po. In Greek mythology, the river-god associated with this river is a son of OCEANUS and TETHYS and father of ZEUXIPPE. He is called the king of rivers, and on its banks amber was found.

Erigone (1) in Greek mythology, a daughter of ICARIUS (2). She was seduced by DIONYSUS when he came into her father's house.

Erigone (2) in Greek mythology, a daughter of AEGISTHUS and CLYTEMNESTRA, and by ORESTES the mother of PENTHILUS.

Erinyes *see* **Furies**.

Eriopis *see* **Oileus**.

Eriphyle in Greek mythology, the wife of AMPHIARAUS, whom she betrayed for the sake of the necklace of HARMONIA.

Eris in Greek mythology, the goddess of discord, the sister of ARES, and, according to HESIOD, daughter of NYX (night). Not being invited to the marriage of Peleus, she revenged herself by means of the GOLDEN APPLE of discord.

Eros in Greek mythology, the god of love, whom the Romans called CUPID.

Erysichthon *see* **Triopas** (1).

Erytus *or* **Eurytus** a son of HERMES and Antianeira and brother of ECHION (2). He was one of the ARGONAUTS.

Erytus *or* **Eurytus** *see* **Echion** (2).

Eryx (modern San Giuliano) an ancient city and a mountain in the west of Sicily. The mountain rises direct from the plain. On the summit in ancient times stood a temple of VENUS said to have been built by Eryx, son of APHRODITE by BUTES (2). Eryx is also said to have received HERACLES on his visit to this part of Sicily and to have taken part in a wrestling match with him, in which he was defeated.

Eteocles in Greek mythology, a son of OEDIPUS, king of THEBES and brother of POLYNEICES, ANTIGONE (2). After their father's banishment from Thebes, Eteocles usurped the throne to the exclusion of his brother, an act which led to an expedition by POLYNEICES and six others against Thebes. This war is known as the SEVEN AGAINST THEBES, and forms the basis of Aeschylus's *The Seven against Thebes*. The two brothers fell by each other's hand.

Eteoclus in Greek mythology, a son of IPHIS and one the SEVEN AGAINST THEBES. He had to make the attack upon the Neïtian gate. He was killed by a Theban champion.

Ethiopia *or* **Aethipia** in ancient geography, the country lying to the south of Egypt, but its limits were not clearly defined. It was vaguely spoken of in Greek and Roman accounts as the land of the Ichthyophagi or 'fish-eaters', the Macrobii or 'long-livers', the Troglodytes or 'dwellers in caves', and of the Pygmies or 'dwarf races'. In ancient times its history was closely connected with that of Egypt.

Etna *or* **Aetna, Mount** the greatest volcano in Europe, a mountain in Sicily that dominates the whole northeast part of the island. In mythology, the remarkable phenomena exhibited by Etna were ascribed to the struggles of the giant TYPHON (or ENCELADUS according to some), who had been buried under the mountain by ZEUS after the defeat of the giants. Others assigned it as the workshop of VULCAN (HEPHAESTUS), although other traditions placed this in the AEOLIAN ISLANDS. The mountain was supposed to have received its name from a nymph, Aetna, the daughter of URANUS and GE, or, according to others, of BRIAREUS. In some accounts it was consecrated to Zeus, but later to Vulcan.

Etruria the name given in ancient times to that part of Italy which corresponds partly with modern Tuscany and was bounded by the Mediterranean, the Apennines, the River Magra, and the TIBER. The name of Tusci or Etrusci was used by the Romans to designate the race of people inhabiting this country, but the name by which they called themselves was Rasena (or perhaps more correctly Ta-rasena). After a long struggle with Rome, Etruscan power was completely broken by the Romans in a series of victories. The Etruscans were specially distinguished by their religous institutions and ceremonies, which reveal gloomy and mystic tendencies. Their gods were of two orders, the first nameless, mysterious deities, exercising a controlling influence in the background on the lower order of gods, who manage the affairs of the world. At the head of these is a deity resembling the Roman JUPITER (in Etruscan Tinia). VULCAN was Sethlans, BACCHUS Phuphluns, and MERCURY Turms.

Etruscans *see* **Etruria**.

Euboea a Greek island, the second largest island of the AEGEAN SEA. It is separated from the mainland of Greece by the narrow channels of Egripo and Talanta. It was peopled in early historic times chiefly by tribes from Thessaly and by Ionic Greeks, and afterwards by colonists from Athens. It was believed to have derived its name from Euboea, a daughter of ASOPUS.

Eubulus *see* **Britomartis**.

Eumedes *see* **Dolon**.

Eumenides *see* **Furies**.

Euneus in Greek mythology, a son of JASON by HYPSIPYLE, in LEMNOS, from where he supplied the Greeks with wine during the TROJAN WAR. He purchased Lycaon, a Trojan prisoner, from PATROCLUS for a silver urn.

Eunomus *or* **Cyatheus** *see* **Oeneus**.

Eupeithes in Greek mythology, a nobleman of Ithaca, father of Antinous. Once when he had attacked the Thesprotians, the allies of the Ithacans, ODYSSEUS protected him from the anger of the Ithacan people. When Odysseus returned home after his long wanderings, Eupeithes wanted to avenge the death of his son, who had been one of PENELOPE'S suitors and was slain by Odysseus. He accordingly led a band of Ithacans against Odysseus but died in the struggle, killed by LAËRTES.

Euphorbas *see* **Patroclus**.

Euphorion *see* **Helen**.

Euphrosyne in Greek mythology, one of the GRACES.

Euripides the last of the three great Greek writers of tragedies, the others being AESCHYLUS and SOPHOCLES. He was born about 480 BC and died 406 BC. Seventeen tragedies have survived. His most notable plays are *ALCESTIS*, *MEDEA*, *ORESTES* and *The Trojan Women*, the last of which describes the fate of the captive Trojan women after the Greek victory over Troy. Euripides adopted a more rationalist, questioning approach to the gods and their divine affairs than his great predecessors and was clearly more concerned with the business of everyday human beings.

Euripus in ancient geography, the strait between the Island of Euboea and Boeotia in Greece.

Europa in Greek mythology, the daughter of AGENOR, king of the Phoenicians, and the sister of CADMUS. Tradition relates that she was abducted by ZEUS, who for that occasion had assumed the form of a white bull and swam with his prize to the island of Crete. Here Europa bore him three sons, MINOS, SARPEDON (1), and RHADAMANTHUS.

Europa in ancient geography the known world around the Mediterranean, named after EUROPA.

Eurotas in Greek mythology, a son of Myles and grandson of Lelex. He was the father of SPARTE, the wife of LACEDAEMON, and is said to have carried the waters stagnating in the plain of Lacedaemon into the sea by means of a canal and to have called the river that arose there from after his own name.

Eurybia *see* **Ge**.

Eurydice (1) in Greek mythology, the wife of ORPHEUS.

Eurydice (2) in Greek mythology, one of the DANAIDES.

Eurydice (3) in Greek mythology, daughter of ADRASTUS and wife of ILUS, mother of Themiste and LAOMEDON.

Eurydice (4) in Greek mythology, a daughter of Lacedaemon and wife of Acrisius.

Eurydice (5) in Greek mythology, a daughter of Clymenus and wife of Nestor.

Eurydice (6) in Greek mythology, the wife of Lycurgus (3) and mother of Archemorus.

Eurydice (7) in Greek mythology, the wife of Creon, king of Thebes.

Euryganeia *see* **Ismene** (1).

Eurylus *see* **Epigoni**.

Eurynome in Greek mythology, a daughter of Oceanus. When Hephaestus was expelled by Hera from Olympus, Eurynome and Thetis received him in the depths of the sea. Before the time of Cronos and Rhea, Eurynome and Ophion had ruled in Olympus over the Titans, but after being conquered by Cronos, she had sunk down into Tartarus or Oceanus. By Zeus she was the mother of the Graces or of Asopus.

Eurystheus in Greek mythology, a king of Mycenae and persecutor of Heracles. When Heracles killed his wife and children in a fit of madness, he was compelled by the Delphic oracle to serve Eurystheus for twelves years and perform a series of tasks or labours. Eurystheus chose the most difficult tasks that he could think of since he wished to get rid of Heracles.

Euryte *see* **Oeneus**.

Eurythemis *see* **Althaea**.

Eurytion (1) in Greek mythology, king of Phthia. When Peleus was expelled from his dominions, he fled to Eurytion, who purified him and whose daughter Antigone (2) he married, but in shooting at the Calydonian Boar, Peleus inadvertently killed his father-in-law.

Eurytion (2) in Greek mythology, a Centaur who fled during the fight of Heracles with the Centaurs. He was later killed by Heracles in the dominions of Dexamenus, whose daughter, Dexames, Eurytion was on the point of making his wife.

Eurytion (3) *see* **Orthus**.

Eurytus (1) in Greek mythology, a son of Melaneüs and Stratonice and king of Oechalia. He was a skilful archer and married to Antioche. He was proud of this skill and is said to have instructed Heracles in the art. He organized an archery contest for the hand of of his daughter Iole, which Heracles won.

Eurytus (2) *see* **Dryope**.

Eurytus (3) *see* **Erytus**.

Euryvale (1) *see* **Gorgons**.

Euryvale (2) *see* **Orion**.

Euterpe in Greek mythology, one of the Muses, considered as presiding over lyric poetry, the invention of the flute being ascribed to her. She is usually represented as a virgin crowned with flowers, having a flute in her hand.

Euxine Sea (*Pontus Euxinus*) the ancient name for the BLACK SEA.

Evadne *see* **Iphis**.

Evander in Greek mythology, son of HERMES by an Arcadian NYMPH, called by the Romans Carmenta or Tiburtis. About sixty years before the TROJAN WAR he is said to have led a Pelasgian colony from ARCADIA to Italy, and to have landed on the banks of the TIBER and near the foot of the Palatine Hill. Here he built a town, naming it Pallantium after the one in Arcadia. Virgil represents him as being still alive when AENEAS arrived in Italy after the sack of Troy and as having sent him aid under his son Pallas, who was killed by TURNUS.

Evarete *see* **Oenomaus**.

Evenus *see* **Idas and Lynceus**.

Everos *see* **Electryon**.

F

Fates in Greek and Roman mythology, the inexorable sisters who were engaged in spinning the thread of human life. In Greek mythology, the name CLOTHO ('the spinner') was probably at first common to them all, constituting an ultimate monotheistic element—the vague Unity binding together and dominating the crowd of Olympian deities. To Homer, who in every instance save one speaks of Fate in the singular, Fate was not a deity but merely a personification, the destinies of men being determined by the will of the gods. According to later Greek writers the gods too were subject to the control of the Fates, and they were three in number: Clotho, the spinner of the thread of life; Lachesis, who determines the lot of life; Atropos, the inevitable, all three referring to the same subject from different points of view. The Fates knew and predicted what was yet to happen. They were usually represented as young women of serious aspect, Clotho with a spindle, Lachesis pointing with a staff to the horoscope of man on a globe, and Atropos with a pair of scales, or a sundial, or an instrument to cut the thread of life.

Fauna in Roman mythology, the female complement of FAUNUS, also called BONA DEA. Her name is now used to designate animals of a particular region or of a particular geological period. Flora is the term used for vegetation.

Fauns in Roman mythology, rural deities or demi-gods, inhabiting forests and groves and differing little from SATYRS. Their form was principally human, but with a short goat's tail, pointed ears, projecting horns and sometimes also with cloven feet. All terrifying sounds and appearances were ascribed to them.

Faunus in Roman mythology, an ancient king who instructed his subjects in agriculture and the management of flocks and was afterwards worshipped as the god of fields and of shepherds, somewhat like PAN, with whom he became associated and whose attributes he acquired. He was the son of PICUS and the grandson of SATURN. FAUNA was his female counterpart.

Faustulus in Roman mythology, the chief shepherd of AMULIUS, uncle of REA SILVIA, the mother of ROMULUS AND REMUS. It was he who found the twin boys when they had been put in a basket on the Tiber and had been tended by a wolf. He took them home to his wife, Larentia, who reared them.

Fishes, The *see* **Pisces.**

Flora in Roman mythology, the goddess of flowers and spring, and also of exuberant youthful vitality, whose worship was established at Rome from earliest times. Her festival, the Floralia, was celebrated at the end of April with much licentiousness. She is represented as a flower-crowned maiden in the full bloom of beauty. Her name is now used to designate the plant species of a particular region or of a particular geological period. Fauna is the term used for animals.

Fortuna in Roman mythology, the goddess of chance or success, corresponding to the Greek Tyche. She was the daughter of OCEANUS or a sister of the FATES. She differed from the Fates in that she worked without rule, giving or taking away at her own pleasure and dispensing joy or sorrow indifferently. Greek artists generally depicted her with a rudder, emblem of her guiding power, or with a globe, or wheel or wings as a symbol of her mutability. The Romans proudly declared that when she entered their city she threw away her globe and put off her wings and shoes to indicate that she meant to dwell with them for ever. Later she is represented with a bandage over her eyes and a sceptre in her hand, and sitting or standing on a wheel or globe.

Furies in Roman mythology, three winged maidens who dwell in the depths of TARTARUS, daughters of Earth or of Night (called Erinyes or Eumenides in Greek mythology). They were originally personifications of the curses pronounced upon guilty criminals. The crimes which they punished were failing to honour father and mother, perjury, murder, and violation of the laws of hospitality or of the rights of suppliants. They were supposed to be able to destroy all peace of mind, and to be able to make their victim either childless or have ungrateful or wicked children. They were regarded also as goddesses of Fate, somewhat like the FATES, and they had a share in the grim providence which led the doomed into the way of calamity. A part of their function was also to hinder man from acquiring too much knowledge of the future. Their number is usually three, and their names Alecto, Megaera and Tisiphone, but sometimes they appear as one, and in the *Eumenides*, the concluding play of AESCHYLUS's *Oresteia*, there is a chorus of twelve furies on the stage. This describes the reconciliation between the older gods and the newer ones, and ends with the

Furies consenting to share a sanctuary with ATHENA. Aeschylus describes them as being dressed in black, having serpents in their hair, and blood oozing from their eyes. Later poets and sculptors represented them in the form of winged virgins wearing hunting garb, bearing torches in their hands and with a wreath of serpents round their heads. Gradually they came to be considered goddesses of the infernal regions, who punished crimes after death but seldom appear on earth. In Athens their worship, which, like that of the other infernal deities, was conducted in silence, was held in great honour. The sacrifices offered to them consisted of black sheep and a mixture of honey and water, no wine being offered. The turtle dove and the narcissus were sacred to them.

G

Gabii a town east of Rome which the mythical king Lucius TARQUINUS conquered without a single battle. This was because of the treachery of his son Sextus.

Gaea *see* **Ge**.

Galanthis in Greek mythology, a Theban attendant present at the birth of HERACLES. The goddess EILEITHYIA was preventing the birth from taking place and Galanthis tricked her into lifting the spell that was responsible for this. In revenge the goddess turned Galanthis into a weasel.

Galatea (1) in Greek mythology, the daughter of NEREUS and Doris, who rejected the suit of the Cyclops POLYPHEMUS and gave herself to the Sicilian shepherd ACIS. The monster, having surprised them, crushed Acis beneath a rock.

Galatea (2) in Greek mythology, a daughter of EURYTIUS and wife of Lamprus at Phaestus in CRETE. Her husband, wanting a son, ordered that if she should give birth to a daughter she must kill the infant. Galatea did give birth to a daughter but could not comply with her husband's cruel command and instead disguised the child as a boy under the name of Leucippus. When the child had grown up, Galatea, dreading the discovery of the secret and her husband's anger, took refuge with her daughter in a temple of LETO and prayed to the goddess to change the girl into a youth. Leto granted the request.

Galatea (3) in Roman mythology, the name of a statue said to have been endowed with life by VENUS in answer to the prayer of the sculptor PYGMALION. The story, which is derived from Ovid's *Metamorphoses*, is the subject of comedies by W. S. Gilbert and George Bernard Shaw.

Galli *see* **Cybele**.

Ganymede *or* **Ganymedes** in Greek mythology, an exeptionally handsome youth who was the son of TROS and of Callirrhoë, daughter of SCAMANDER. ZEUS sent his eagle to carry him off from Mount IDA to OLYMPUS, where he held the office of cup-bearer to the gods in succession to HEBE. Zeus gave Tros a pair of divine horses as a compensation for his loss, and comforted him by informing him that Ganymede had become immortal and free from all earthly ills. He was later also represented as the god of the fertilizing and life-giving Nile. Greek astronomers placed him among the stars under the name of Aquarius ('the water-bearer'). He was a favourite subject of ancient art.

Ge *or* **Gaea** in Greek mythology, the earth or the earth goddess. The equivalent in Roman mythology was TELLUS or Terra. Ge is said to have been born from CHAOS, having as siblings TARTARUS and EROS. Although she did not have a mate, she gave birth to URANUS, Ourea and PONTUS, respectively the sky, the mountains and the sea. Thereafter she married Uranus and gave birth to the CYCLOPS, the TITANS, and the HUNDRED-HANDED (or Hecatoncheires). Because of their extreme strength and their extreme ugliness Uranus very much disliked Cyclops and the Hundred-handed and hid them in Ge's body, thereby giving her intense pain. She was very angry and persuaded one of her sons, the Titan CRONOS, to castrate Uranus as she lay with him with a sickle which she had made for the purpose. From the drops of the blood of Uranus which fell to the earth Ge bore the FURIES, the GIANTS and the MELIAE or Ash NYMPHS. Later she gave birth to NEREUS, Thaumas, PHORCYS, CETO and Eurybia, their father being Pontus. Many of the offspring of Ge were monsters, different legends ascribing different monstrous offspring to her. For example she gave birth to Echidna and TYPHON by her brother Tartarus. Typhon became a formidable enemy of ZEUS.

Gegeneës *see* **Earth-born monsters.**

Gelanor *see* **Danaüs**.

Gemini (the Twins), the third sign of the Zodiac. The constellation Gemini was supposed to represent CASTOR AND POLLUX, the two brights stars of the constellation being named Castor and Pollux. Another versions says that they are IASION and TRIPTOLEMUS.

Genii in Roman mythology, the protecting spirits who were supposed to accompany every created thing from its origin to its final decay. They belonged not only to people, but to all things animate and inanimate, and especially to places. Not only had every individual his genius, but also the whole people. The statue of the national genius was placed in the vicinity of the Roman forum and is often seen on the coins of the emperors Hadrian and Trajan. The genius of an individual was represented as a figure in a toga, with the head veiled and the cornucopia or patera in the hands, while local genii appear under the figure of serpents eating fruit set before them.

Gerenia a city in Messenia or Laonia on the southern coast of Messenia, whose people were renowned horse-breeders. NESTOR, son of the king of Pylus, NELEUS, was reared by them and so was saved from the fate experienced by his brothers at the hands of HERACLES.

Geryon *or* **Geryones** in Greek mythology, a king of Erytheia, who had three heads or the body of three men from the waist down. He was the son of the Gorgon MEDUSA. He had herds of man-eating cattle, and was killed when trying to retrieve them from HERACLES who had driven them off.

Giants in Greek mythology, beings of monstrous size, with hid- eous countenances and with the tail of a dragon. They lived in volcanic districts, having been banished there after an unsuccessful attempt upon heaven, when the gods, with the assistance of Heracles, imprisoned them under Etna and other volcanoes. They are said to have been of mingled heavenly and earthly descent and to have sprung from the blood that fell from the slain URANUS upon the earth, GE, which was their mother. Their reputed origin, like where they live, points to the idea of the electrical and volcanic convulsions of nature, which they obviously typify.

Glauce *or* **Creüsa** in Greek mythology, the daughter of CREON, king of Corinth. She was to marry JASON but at the wedding she was killed when she tried on a poisoned robe that Jason's jealous divorced wife, MEDEA, had sent as a present.

Glaucus (1) in Greek mythology, a son of MINOS and PASIPHAË, who as a child drowned in a large jar of honey. The seer Polyidus of Argos revived him with the aid of a serpent, which revealed a herb effective for the purpose.

Glaucus (2) in Greek mythology, a minor sea-god who gave good advice to the ARGONAUTS. He was originally a fisherman who was transformed into a sea-god after eating a strange herb. He fell in love with SCYLLA, who was then beautiful. When she rejected him, he asked CIRCE for help, but she fell in love with him. On being rejected by him she was furious and poisoned the water in which Scylla as a sea-nymph often swam. Because of this Scylla was turned into a terrible monster.

Glaucus (3) in Greek mythology, a son of SISYPHUS and MEROPE, and a king of Ephyra (Corinth), who married Eurynome, daughter of NISUS. Sisyphus was hated by ZEUS, who swore that although Sisyphus would rear children he would never father his own. As a result of this Sisyphus reared BELLEROPHON who was unbeknownst to him the result of a union between EURYNOME and POSEIDON. He was eaten by his horses after losing a chariot race to IOLAÜS and his ghost scared horses in Corinth in revenge.

Glaucus (4) in Greek mythology, captain, with SARPEDON (2), of the Lycian forces at TROY, noted for his bravery. He was the son of Hippolochus and was killed by AJAX while trying to retrieve the corpse of ACHILLES. When he was about to be engaged in combat with DIOMEDES (2), the Greek general, he and his enemy discussed their ancestors before embarking on the fight. On discovering that OENEUS, grandfather of Diomedes, had once entertained BELLEROPHON, grandfather of Glaucus, the two abandoned the fight and exchanged armour as an act of friendship, the relationship of guest/host being important in Greek mythology.

Golden Age that early mythological period in the history of almost all races, depicted as having been of primeval innocence and enjoyment, in which the earth was common property, and brought forth spontaneously all things necessary for happy existence, in which people did not engage in warfare. while beasts of prey lived at peace with other animals. The Romans referred this time to the reign of SATURN.

golden apple in Greek mythology, a prize for beauty which was to be awarded to a goddess by PARIS. It had its origins in the wedding of PELEUS to THETIS, which all the gods attended except ERIS, goddess of strife, who was not invited because of her propensity for making trouble. When she went to it without invitation she was not allowed to enter and in spite she threw a golden apple, inscribed 'for the fairest', into the wedding group. Immediately it was claimed by three of the goddeses, HERA, ATHENA and APHRODITE, each of whom considered herself the fairest and each of whom assumed that the apple was meant for her. As Eris had planned, a quarrel broke out, and ZEUS ordered HERMES to turn the problem over to Paris, son of PRIAM, king of Troy, and thought to be the most handsome man in the world, who was tending a flock of sheep on Mount Ida. It was assumed that he would be impartial, but each of the goddesses immediately tried to bribe him with tempting rewards if he would select her as the fairest. Hera promised to make him ruler of the world, Athena promised him that he would always be the victor in war and Aphrodite, goddess of love, promised him the love of the most beautiful woman in the world. Paris decided to accept Aphrodite's bribe and declare her the fairest. The woman who was considered to be the most beautiful woman in the world was HELEN, daughter of TYNDAREUS, the former king of SPARTA, and married to MENELAÜS. Paris persuaded Helen to go off with him and the event gave rise to the TROJAN WAR.

golden bough in Greek mythology, a magical bough of a tree near Cumae. AENEAS took this bough from the tree, having taken the advice of the Cumaean SIBYL, before his descent into the Underworld so that it would help him gain access to it. It was intended as a gift for PERSEPHONE. The phrase was used as the title of Sir James Frazer's enterprising and comprehensive work on comparative religion.

golden fleece in Greek mythology, the fleece made of gold of the ram Chrysomallus. The ram had rescued PHRIXUS from death as a youth and had flown through the air with him to AEA, the capital of Colchis, a land situated at the farthest end of the BLACK SEA. Phrixus sacrificed the ram and nailed its fleece to a tree in a grove sacred to ARES, where the fleece was guarded by a dragon that never slept. Whoever wished to take the fleece would not only have to get past the dragon but would have to persuade AEËTES, the king of Colchis, to allow the golden fleece to leave the country. The king had been warned by an oracle that he would hold the throne of Colchis only as long as the golden fleece remained in the sacred grove. It was in quest of this golden fleece that JASON undertook the ARGONAUTS' expedition to Colchis, he having been tricked into acquiring the golden fleece by PELIAS, who had deposed Jason's father as king of THESSALY. When the Argonauts came to Colchis for the fleece, MEDEA put the dragon to sleep and Jason carried the fleece away. Medea was in love with Jason at the instigation of HERA, who hated Pelias and wanted him destroyed. She thought that Medea was the most likely to be able to undertake this destruction but knew that she would be unwilling to make the long journey to Thessaly. Medea did make the journey as Jason's wife and did help Jason destroy Pelias.

Golden Race *see* **Races of Man**.

Gordius in Greek mythology, a peasant who became king of PHRYGIA. The Phrygians were seeking a king and were informed by the oracle at DELPHI that they were to choose the first person they met riding on an ox cart towards the temple of ZEUS. That person was Gordius, who was duly elected king. He afterwards dedicated his cart and yoke to Zeus in the acropolis of Gordium (a city named after himself) and tied the knot of the yoke in so skilful a manner that an oracle declared that whoever should unloose it would be ruler of all Asia. When Alexander the Great came to Gordium, he cut the knot in two with his sword and applied the prophecy to himself. From this legend comes the phrase 'to cut the Gordian knot', i.e. to solve a problem or end a difficulty in a vigorous or drastic way.

Gorge in Greek mythology, a daughter of OENEUS and ALTHAEA, who married ANDRAEMON and became the mother of THOAS, leader of the Aetolian forces during the TROJAN WAR. According to some legends she was also the mother of PERIBOEA by Oeneus, her own father, this having been brought about because ZEUS had decreed that Oeneus should fall in love with his daughter.

Gorgons in Greek mythology, three monsters whose names were Stheno, Euryale and Medusa, daughters of PHORCYS and CETO. They were all immortal, except Medusa. Their hair was said to be entwined with serpents, their hands were of brass, their bodies were covered with impenetrable scales, their brazen teeth were as long as the tusks of a wild boar, and they turned to stone all those who looked upon them. According to later legends, Medusa was originally a very beautiful maiden. Having become a mother by POSEIDON in one of

ATHENA'S temples, the virgin goddess changed her hair into serpents, which gave her so fearful an appearance that whoever looked on her was turned to stone. Medusa was killed by PERSEUS, and her head was afterwards placed on the AEGIS of ATHENA. From her blood the winged horse PEGASUS is supposed to have sprung.

Gorgophone in Greek mythology, the only daughter of PERSEUS and ANDROMEDA. A great deal of confusion is attached in legend to the question of her husbands. She is supposed to have married PERIERES, to whom she bore APHAREUS and LEUCIPPUS, and OEBALUS, king of Sparta, to whom she bore three sons, TYNDAREUS, HIPPOCOÖN and ICARIUS, and two daughters, Arene and Peirene. She was the grandmother of CLYTEMNESTRA.

Graces in Greek mythology, the divine personifications of grace, gentleness and beauty, usually described as daughters of ZEUS and EURYNOME and as being three in number, AGLAIA (brilliancy), Thalia (the blooming) and Euphrosyne (mirth). The earliest conception seems to have been but one aspect of APHRODITE, the divsion into a plurality of beings coming later. Homer mentions them in the *Iliad* as handmaidens of HERA (Juno), but in the *Odyssey* as those of APHRODITE (Venus), who is attended by them in the bath, etc. He conceived them as forming a group of goddesses, whose duty it was to make sure that the gods and goddesses were happy. The three Graces are usually represented slightly draped or entirely nude, either locked in each other's embrace, or hand in hand.

Graeae in Greek mythology, the grey women, two hags called Enyo and Pemphredo or Pephredo, who were the daughters of of PHORCYS and CETO and sisters of the GORGONS and of ECHIDNA and Ladon. Their name derives from the fact that they had grey hair from birth. They had only one eye and one tooth between them and these were stolen by PERSEUS. According to some legends the hags were three in number, the third being called Deino.

Gratioe the Roman name for the GRACES.

Great Mother *see* **Cybele**; **Rhea**.

Greek mythology the ancient religion of the Greeks with a great number of divinities, many of whom were personifications of natural powers, or of phenomena of the external world, or personified feelings. Thus there were gods corresponding to Earth and Heaven, the Ocean and Night. The Romans, when they became acquainted with the literature and religion of the Greeks, identified the Greek deities with those of their own pantheon. In this way the Greek and Roman deities came to be confused, and the names of the latter even came to supersede those of the former. The supreme ruler among the gods was ZEUS (Roman JUPITER), the son of CRONOS (Roman SATURN), who, after the subjugation of the TITANS and GIANTS, ruled in OLYMPUS while his brother PLUTO reigned over the lower world (HADES) and POSEIDON (NEPTUNE) ruled in the sea. Similar reverence was paid to HERA (JUNO), the sister and wife of Zeus and the queen of Heaven, to the virgin ATHENA (MINERVA), to the two children of LETO (LATONA), namely, APOLLO, the leader of the MUSES, and his sister, the huntress ARTEMIS (DIANA), the goddess of the moon, to the beautiful daughter of Zeus, APHRODITE (VENUS), the goddess of love, to ARES (MARS), the god of war, HERMES (MERCURY), the herald of the gods, and others. In addition, there was an innumerable host of inferior deities (NYMPHS, NEREÏDS, TRITONS, SIRENS, DRYADS, etc) who presided over woods and mountains, fields and meadows, rivers and lakes. There was also a race of heroes or demigods, such as HERACLES (HERCULES) and PERSEUS, tracing their origin from Zeus and forming a connecting link between gods and men, while on the other hand the SATYRS formed a connecting link between the race of men and the lower animals.

The priests were keepers of sacred things, of rites, symbols and images. They showed how a god was to be worshipped, but it was not their office to teach theological doctrine, or even as a rule to exhort people to religious duty. The true teachers of religion were the poets and other writers (see Aeschylus, Hesiod, Homer, Euripides, Sophocles). No degree of consistency is to be found in them, however, the personality and local origin of a writer largely moulding his views. A belief in the justice of the gods as manifested in the punishment of all offences against them was central. The man himself might escape, but his children would suffer, or he might be punished in a future state. The gods are also represented as being holy and truthful, although they are in innumerable other passages described as being themselves guilty of the grossest vices, and likewise as prompting humans to sin and deceiving them to their own destruction. In their general attitude towards humans, the gods appear as inspired by a feeling of envy or jealousy. Hence they had constantly to be appeased, and their favour won by sacrifices and offerings. Certain classes were, however, under the peculiar protection and favour of the gods, especially strangers and suppliants.

The Greeks believed that the gods communicated their will to humans in various ways, but above all by means of ORACLES, the chief of which were those of Apollo at DELPHI, and of Zeus at DODONA. Dreams ranked next in importance to oracles, and divination by birds, remarkable natural phenomena, sneezing, etc, was also practised.

griffin *or* **gryphon** a fabulous monster commonly represented with the body, the feet, and claws of a lion, and the head and wings of an eagle. The native country of the griffins was supposd to be India or Scythia, and it was alleged that they guarded the gold in the mountains. Amongst the Greeks it appears on antique coins and as an ornament in classical architecture.

Gyes *see* **Hundred-handed**.

H

Hades in Greek mythology, originally the name of the king of the lower or invisible world, afterwards called PLUTO (*see also* PERSEPHONE), but in later times, it is applied to the region itself. According to the belief of the ancients, the departed spirits of good and bad alike went to the halls of Hades.

Haemon in Greek mythology, a son of PELASGUS and father of Thessalus. The ancient name of THESSALY, Haemonia or Aemonia, was believed to have been derived from him.

Haemones *see* **Iolcus**.

Haemus in Greek mythology, a son of BOREAS and OREITHYIA, who was married to RHODOPE, by whom he became the father of HEBRUS. As he and his wife presumed to assume the names of ZEUS and HERA, both were metamorphosed into mountains.

Haemus, Mount the range of mountains in THRACE, now called the Balkans. The name is derived from the Greek word for blood (*haima*), the explanation being that TYPHON is said to have lost a great deal of blood there when ZEUS pelted him with thunderbolts.

hamadryads in mythology, NYMPHS who presided over woods and trees.

Hare, The *see* **Lepus**.

Harmonia in Greek mythology, daughter of ARES and APHRODITE, or of ZEUS and ELECTRA (3), and wife of CADMUS. On her marriage, she received a necklace worked by HEPHAESTUS from Cadmus, or it may have been given to her by Aphrodite or ATHENA. POLYNEICES inherited the necklace and gave it to ERIPHYLE to induce her to persuade her husband, AMPHIARAUS, to accompany the SEVEN AGAINST THEBES.

Harpies in Greek mythology, ancient goddesses who were considered as ministers of the vengeance of the gods. Their parentage, ages, appearance, names and number are very differently given by the poets. In the Homeric poems they are ministers of untimely death, 'snatchers', and personfications of the angry winds. Others represent them as two young virgins of great beauty, called Aëllo and Ocypete, daughters of THAUMAS and ELECTRA (4), and sisters of IRIS. Three are sometimes recognized by later writers, who call them variously daughters of POSEIDON or of TYPHON and vie with each other in depicting them under the most hideous forms, covered with filth and polluting everything in contact with them. They are often represented as being birdlike with female faces. The most celebrated tradition regarding the Harpies is connected with the blind Phineus, whose meals they carried off as soon as they were spread for him, a plague from which he was delivered by the Argonuats, on his engaging to join in their quest. Zetes and Calaïs attacked the Harpies, but spared their lives on their promising to cease molesting Phineus. In Roman mythology, Virgil locates them in the Strophades.

Harpius *see* **Oenomaüs**.

Hebe in Greek mythology, the goddess of youth, and the cup-bearer to the gods, until replaced by Ganymede. She was a daughter of Zeus and Hera, who, according to one version of the legend, gave her as a wife to Heracles after he was deified, to whom she bore two sons, Alexiares and Aniketos. According to Homer she remained a virgin. In the arts she presents the nectar, under the figure of a charming young girl, her dress adorned with roses, and wearing a wreath of flowers. In Rome she was worshipped as Juventas, personifying the eternal youth of the city. She is represented in art as caressing an eagle.

Hebrus, River the ancient name of an important river in Thrace, now the boundary between Greece and Turkey. In Greek mythology, the river-god Hebrus was the son of Haemus and Rhodope. When Orpheus was killed by the Ciconian women his head and lyre floated down the Hebrus.

Hecabe *see* **Hecuba**.

Hecate in Greek mythology, an ancient goddess whose powers were various. She could bestow wealth, victory and wisdom; good luck on sailors and hunters; prosperity on youth and on flocks. She was afterwards confused with other divinities, such as Demeter, Artemis and Persephone (Proserpina), and finally became especially an infernal goddess and was invoked by magicians and witches. Dogs, honey and black female lambs were offered to her at places where three roads met. She was often represented with three bodies or three heads, with serpents round her neck. Her festivals were celebrated annually at Aegina (2). One legend says she is the mother of Medea.

Hecatoncheires *see* **Hundred-handed**.

Hector in Greek mythology, the eldest son of Priam and Hecuba, the bravest of the Trojans, whose forces he commanded. His wife was Andromache. His exploits are celebrated in the *Iliad*, where he is portrayed as the ideal of a warlike hero, brave to the last degree, yet faithful and tender alike as husband, father and son. One of the finest passages in the Iliad describes his parting with Andromache. He holds the same rank among the Trojans as Achilles does among the Greeks. After bearing the main burden of the war, he was slain by Achilles, enraged at the death of his beloved friend Patroclus. The body of Hector was dragged at the chariot wheels of the conqueror round the tomb of Patroclus, but afterwards it was delivered to Priam for a ransom. Priam gave it a solemn burial.

Hecuba *or* **Hecaba** in Greek mythology, the second wife of Priam, king of

TROY, to whom she bore nineteen children, including HECTOR, PARIS, CASSANDRA, CREÜSA (2)and TROILUS. During the TROJAN WAR she witnessed the destruction of all her sons, with the exception of HELENUS, and at last saw her husband murdered before her eyes by Pyrrhus (*see* NEOPTOLEMUS). After the fall of Troy she was given as a slave to ODYSSEUS, and, according to one form of the legend, in despair leaped into the HELLESPONT. EURIPIDES and others describe her as a tender mother, a noble princess and a virtuous wife, exposed by fate to the most cruel sufferings.

Heleius *or* **Helius** in Greek mythology, son of PERSEUS and ANDROMEDA. He joined AMPHITRYON in war against the Teleboans and received from him the islands of the TAPHIANS. He founded the city of Helos in Argolis.

Helen *or* **Helena** in Greek mythology, the most beautiful woman of her age. She was daughter of ZEUS by LEDA, wife of the Spartan king, TYNDAREUS, and owed her more than mortal loveliness to her divine origin. At the age of ten she was carried off by THESEUS and PEIRITHOÜS, but was soon recovered by her brothers CASTOR AND POLLUX, of whom the latter was half an immortal like herself. She was sought in marriage by all the noblest Greek princes. By the advice of ODYSSEUS, her suitors were bound by oath to respect her choice of husband, and to maintain it even by arms. She chose MENELAÜS and bore him the fair HERMIONE. When she was carried off by PARIS, son of PRIAM of TROY, through the connivance of APHRODITE, Menelaüs mustered all the Greek princes to revenge the wrong and thus the ten years' TROJAN WAR began. After the death of Paris, not long before the fall of the city, she married his brother Deiphobus, and she is said to have betrayed him to Menelaüs and so regained her husband's love. On the fall of Troy she returned to Sparta with Menelaüs. There they lived the rest of their lives and were buried together at Therapnae in Laconia, although, according to a prophecy in the Odyssey, they were not to die but to be translated to ELYSIUM. Another story makes Helen survive Menelaüs and be driven out of the Peloponnesus by his sons. She fled to Rhodes and was there tied to a tree and strangled by Polyxo, a crime expiated only by the Rhodians building a temple to her under the name of Helena Dendritis. Yet another tradition makes her marry ACHILLES on the island of Leuce and bear him a son, Euphorion.

Helenus in Greek mythology, a Trojan soothsayer, son of PRIAM and HECUBA, twin brother of CASSANDRA, and husband of ANDROMACHE after HECTOR's death. He foretold the destiny of AENEAS, and welcomed the latter in Epirus, where he ruled after the death of NEOPTOLEMUS.

Helice in Greek mythology, the wife of ION. The town of Helice in Achea on the gulf of Corinth was founded by Ion, who named it after her.

Helicon, Mount (now Sagara) a mountain range of Greece, in the west of Boeotia, in some sense a continuation of the range of PARNASSUS. It was the favourite seat of the Muses, who, with Apollo, had temples here. In it also were the fountains of Aganippe (1) and Hippocrene, whose waters were reputed to give poetic inspiration.

Helios in Greek mythology, the god of the sun (the Roman Sol), son of the Titan Hyperion and Theia, and brother of Eos and Selene. He was said to dwell with Eos in the ocean behind Colchis, from which he issued in the morning and to which he returned at night. He later began to be identified with Apollo, but the identification was never complete. His worship was widely spread, and he had temples in Corinth, Argos, Troezen and Elis, but particularly in Rhodes, the Colossus of which was a representation of Helios. The island of Trinacria (Sicily) was also sacred to Helios, and here his daughters, Phoetusa and Lampetia, kept his flocks of sheep and oxen. It was customary to offer up white lambs or boars on his altars. The animals sacred to him were horses, wolves, cocks and eagles.

Hellas the Greek name for Greece ('Greece' being the Roman name).

Helle in Greek mythology, sister of Phrixus. She left her home with him on the back of a miraculous ram that could fly and that had a golden fleece. They were escaping from their stepmother, Io, who was trying to persuade their father to sacrifice Phrixus. Helle lost her grip on the ram as they flew over the strait between Europe and Asia, and she fell into the water. Thereafter the stretch of water was called Hellespont, 'sea of Helle'.

Hellen in Greek mythology, son of Deucalion and Pyrrha, and founder by his three sons, Dorus, Aeolus and Xuthus, of the four great branches of the Greek people, or Hellenes.

Hellenes the people of Greece. The earliest inhabitants of Greece were the Pelasgians, of whom little is known. They were succeeded by the Hellenes, or Greeks proper, who may have been a Pelasgian tribe. To the early period of their occupation of Greece belongs its mythology. The Hellenes were divided into four chief tribes—the Aeolians, occupying the northern parts of Greece (Thessaly, Boeotia, etc); the Dorians, occupying originally a small region in the neighbourhood of Mount Eta; the Achaeans, occupying the greater part of the Peloponnesus; and the Ionians, occupying the northern strip of the Peloponnesus and Attica. Of the four, the Ionians were most influential in the development of Greece. The distribution of the Hellenic tribes was greatly altered by the migration of the Dorians.

Hellespont the ancient name for the Dardanelles, the strait between the Aegean Sea and the Sea of Marmara. It gained its name from the legend of Helle.

Hemera in Greek mythology, day and the goddess of day. She was born from Erebus (darkness) and Nyx (night). She emerged from Tartarus as Nyx left it and returned to it as he was emerging from it.

Hephaestus *or* **Hephaistos** in Greek mythology, the son of Hera, the god of fire and smithying, patron of all those who worked in iron and metals, identified by the Romans with their VULCAN. He is represented by Homer as lame, walking with the aid of a stick. His character is good-tempered, affectionate and compassionate. There is also an element of the comic connected with him. His gait and ungainly figure provoked the laughter of the gods, yet he was himself given to practical jokes. He fixed his residence in LEMNOS, where he built himself a palace, and raised forges to work metals. The CYCLOPS of Sicily were his workmen and attendants, and with him they manufactured not only the thunderbolts of ZEUS, but also arms for the gods and the most celebrated heroes. His forges were supposed to be under ETNA. APHRODITE was the wife of Hephaestus, although according to the *Iliad*, he was married to AGLAIA, one of the GRACES. He was concerned in the myths of the birth of the first woman, PANDORA, and the birth of ATHENE, and ERECHTHEUS claimed Hephaestus as his father.

Hera in Greek mythology, an ancient goddess, identified by the Romans with their Juno, the sister and wife of ZEUS (Jupiter), and daughter of CRONOS and RHEA. She was the goddess of marriage, childbirth and menstruation. The poets represent Zeus as an unfaithful husband and Hera as an obstinate and jealous wife, the result of which was frequent strife between them. As the goddess of lawful marriage, she persecuted the illegitimate offspring of her consort Zeus, such as HERACLES and DIONYSUS. She conspired against Zeus, who made reprisal by hanging her up from heaven with golden fetters on her hands and a couple of anvils on her feet. In consequence she subsequently preferred to thwart him secretly rather than defy him openly. She took the part of the Greeks in the TROJAN WAR as she hated the Trojans because PARIS awarded the fatal GOLDEN APPLE of discord to APHRODITE. She is the mother of HEPHAESTUS, the god of fire, of ARES, the god of war, of EILEITHYIA, of HECATE and of HEBE. She was worshipped in all Greece, but her principal seats were at ARGOS and SAMOS. The companions of Hera were the NYMPHS, GRACES and HORAE. IRIS was her particular servant. Among animals, the peacock, the goose, and the cuckoo were sacred to her. Her usual attribute is a royal diadem on her head. The festivals in her honour were called Heaea. The principal ones were those celebrated every fifth year at Argos, which city was considered to be especially under her protection.

Heracles in Greek mythology, the most celebrated hero or semi-divine personage of Greek mythology, called Hercules by the Romans. He was the son of ZEUS by ALCMENE, the wife of AMPHITRYON. The name Heracles is explained as 'renowned through HERA'. He was brought up at THEBES, and before he had completed his eighth month strangled two snakes sent by the jealous HERA to devour him. His tutor was the Centaur CHEIRON. Early in life he had, at the command of Zeus, to subject himself for twelve years to the will of

EURYSTHEUS, king of Argos, on the understanding that after he had acquitted himself of this duty he should be counted among the gods. He therefore went to MYCENAE, and performed at the bidding of Eurystheus the tasks known as the twelve labours of Heracles. These were: (1) to kill a lion which ravaged the country near Mycenae; (2) to destroy the Lernaean HYDRA; (3) to capture, alive and unhurt, a stag famous for its incredible swiftness, its golden horns, and brazen feet; (4) to capture alive a wild boar which ravaged the neighbourhood of Erymanthus; (5) to clean the stables of AUGEAS, where 3000 oxen had been confined for many years; (6) to kill the birds which ravaged the country near the Lake Stymphalus, in Arcadia, and ate human flesh; (7) to bring alive into Peloponnesus the CRETAN BULL, which laid waste the Island of Crete; (8) to obtain the mares of DIOMEDES (1), which fed upon human flesh; (9) to obtain from HIPPOLYTE, the queen of the Amazons, a girdle which she had received from ARES (Mars); (10) to kill the monster GERYON, king of Gades, and bring to Argos his numerous flocks, which fed upon human flesh; (11) to obtain apples from the garden of the HESPERIDES; (12) the last and most dangerous of all, to bring from the infernal regions the three-headed dog CERBERUS. Besides these labours, he also achieved of his own accord others equally celebrated. He killed a sea monster that ravaged TROY, and when the mares promised him as reward for killing the monster were denied him he destroyed Troy. His love of horses also led him to kill IPHITUS, although his guest. He assisted the gods in their wars against the GIANTS, and it was through him alone that Zeus obtained the victory. Having attempted to plunder the temple at DELPHI, he became engaged in conflict with APOLLO, and was punished by being sold to OMPHALE, queen of LYDIA, as a slave. She eventually freed him and married him. On his return to Greece, he became the husband of DEÏANEIRA, who unwittingly brought about his death by giving him a tunic poisoned with the blood of the Centaur NESSUS, which she innocently believed would retain for her Heracles's love. The poison took effect when the garment was put on, and was fatal. Therefore Heracles placed himself on a burning pile on Mount ETA, was received up into heaven, and being there reconciled to Hera, received her daughter HEBE in marriage. In ancient works of art Heracles is generally represented as naked, with strong and well-proportioned limbs, He is sometimes covered with the skin of the Nemaean lion, and holds a knotted club in his hand, on which he often leans. The myth of Heracles is believed by many writers to represent the course of the sun through the twelve signs of the zodiac. His marriage with Hebe was explained even by the ancients as symbolic of the renewing of the sun's course after its completion.

Heraclids *or* **Heracleidae** in its widest sense, all 'the descendants of HERACLES', but more particularly applied to those who, founding their claims on their supposed descent from the great hero (to whom ZEUS had promised a portion of the land), were said to have joined the Dorians in the conquest of the Peloponnesus. Several expeditions were undertaken for this purpose, the last and greatest occurring eighty years after the Trojan War. The chiefs of the invaders defeated Tisamenus, son of Orestes and grandson of Agamemnon, and took possession of the Peloponnesus.

Heraean Games in ancient Greece, games held specifically for women every four years at Olympia. The contestants took part in the race wearing a dress with one shoulder bared and their hair hanging loose. The prizes were crowns of wild olive and portions of a cow sacrificed to Hera. The Heraean Games are thought to be older than the Olympic Games and to have been inaugurated by Hippodamia in honour of Hera in gratitude to the goddess for assisting her in getting Pelops as her husband.

Hercules the Roman name for Heracles.

Hermaphroditus in Greek mythology, the son of Hermes and Aphrodite, born on Mount Ida and brought up by naïads. He rejected the love of the nymph Salmacis, but the latter, embracing him, prayed to the gods to unite her to her lover for ever. The two finally formed a being half male and half female.

Hermes in Greek mythology, the son of Zeus and Maia, the daughter of Atlas. He was born in Arcadia, and soon after his birth left his cradle and invented the lyre by stringing the shell of a tortoise with three or seven strings. The lyre, however, he accorded to Apollo, with whom it was ever after identified. Hermes also invented the the flute and syrinx. The ancients represent Hermes as the herald and messenger of the gods. He conducted the souls of the departed to the lower world and had the closely related function of bringing dreams to mortals. He was the ideal embodiment of grace, dignity and persuasiveness, but also of prudence, cunning, fraud, perjury, theft, and robbery. His cunning was frequently of service both to the gods and the heroes, and even to Zeus himself. Later writers ascribe to him the invention of dice, music, geometry, etc. He was worshipped in all the cities of Greece, with Arcadia the chief place of his worship, his festivals being called Hermoea. In monuments he is represented as in the flower of youth, or in the full power of early manhood. He often appears with small wings attached to his head and ankles. Among his symbols are the cock, the tortoise, a purse, etc, and especially his winged rod, the caduceus. The Romans identified Hermes with their own Mercury.

Hermione in Greek mythology, the daughter of Menelaüs and Helen. She was nine years old when her mother left her to go with Paris to Troy. She is said to have been promised in marriage both to Neoptolemus and Orestes. According to one legend she married Neoptolemus and then Orestes after his death.

Hero in Greek mythology, a priestess of Aphrodite at Sestos, on the coast of Thrace. She was loved by Leander, whose home was at Abydos, across the Hellespont. Hero's office and her parents' will forbade their union, but

Leander every night swam across the Hellespont, guided by a lamp that burned on the top of a tower on the seashore. One stormy night the light was blown out and Leander was drowned, and his body washed ashore. Hero, when she saw his dead body at daybreak, was overcome with anguish and threw herself down from the tower into the sea and perished.

heroes in Greek mythology, the kings, princes, generals, leaders, all brave warriors, and men who excelled in strength, courage, wisdom and experience. Many of these had, on account of such qualities, an origin half human, half divine, and were honoured after their death with a kind of adoration or inferior worship. These heroes and demigods were recognized as the special patrons or protectors of particular countries, cities or families, and temples and altars were raised to them.

Heroic Age *see* **Races of Man**.

Hesiod the father of Greek didactic poetry, who lived probably in the eighth century BC. His most important work is *Works and Days*, which contains many well-known passages, such as the story of PANDORA. The *Theogony* is an attempt to systematize mythology, and gives an account of the creation, a history of Zeus and Cronos and a list of women who married gods. It also deal with the war between the gods and TITANS.

Hesione in Greek mythology, a daughter of LAOMEDON and sister of PRIAM. When Troy was visited by a plague and a monster because of Laomedon's breach of promise, in order to get rid of these calamities, Laomedon chained Hesione to a rock in accordance with the command of an oracle, where she was to be devoured by wild beasts. HERACLES, on his return from the expedition against the AMAZONS, promised to save her if Laomedon would give him the horses that he had received from ZEUS as a compensation for GANYMEDE. Laomedon again promised but did not keep his word. Hesione was afterwards given as a slave to TELAMON, by whom she became the mother of TEUCER (2). Priam sent ANTENOR to claim her back, and the refusal on the part of the Greeks is mentioned as one of the causes of the TROJAN WAR.

Hesperides in Greek mythology, certain NYMPHS who lived in gardens, of rather uncertain locality, as guardians of the golden apples that grew there and which HERA had recieved from GE on her marriage with ZEUS. They were assisted in the charge by a dragon, Ladon. Some legends place the gardens in an island of the ocean far to the west. It was the eleventh labour of HERACLES to kill the dragon and bring the golden apples of the Hesperides, but they were afterwards restored by ATHENA.

Hestia in Greek mythology, the hearth and the goddess of the hearth. The equivalent Roman goddess was VESTA. Hestia was the goddess associated with general household activities and the community generally. She was a daughter of CRONOS and RHEA.

Hiarbas *see* **Iarbas**.

Hippocentaurs *see* **Centaurs**.

Hippocoön in Greek mythology, a king of Sparta, son of OEBALUS and GORGOPHONE, who refused to purify HERACLES after he murdered IPHITUS. He caused further offence by killing OEONUS, a relative of Heracles. In revenge Heracles killed Hippocoön and his twelve sons.

Hippocrene ('The Horse's Fountain') a spring on Mount HELICON, a mountain in BOEOTIA, consecrated to the MUSES, the waters of which possessed the power of poetic inspiration. It is said to have risen from the ground when struck by the hoofs of PEGASUS.

Hippodamia (1) in Greek mythology, the beautiful daughter of OENOMAÜS, king of Pisa in ELIS. It had been predicted to her father that he should be slain by his future son-in-law. He therefore stipulated that every suitor of his daughter should run a chariot race with him, and that death should be the consequence of defeat. At length PELOPS bribed the king's charioteer and thus succeeded in reaching the goal before Oenomaus, who, in despair, killed himself. Hippodamia became by Pelops the mother of ATREUS and THYESTES.

Hippodamia (2) *see* **Deïdameia**.

Hippolochus *see* **Glaucus** (4).

Hippolyte (1) in Greek mythology an AMAZON queen, the daughter of ARES and Otrera. The ninth labour of HERACLES was to retrieve *Hippolyte's belt.* On meeting Heracles aboard his ship, Hippolyte agreed to give him the belt without resistance, but HERA, posing as an Amazon, persuaded Hippolyte's followers that their queen was being kidnapped. The Amazon women attacked the ship and Heracles killed Hippolyte, believing that she had betrayed him.

Hippolyte (2) in Greek mythology a daughter of Cretheus, who was a son of AEOLUS (2). By some accounts it was Hippolyte who was the wife of ACASTUS and who fell in love with PELEUS.

Hippolytus in Greek mythology, son of THESEUS and ANTIOPE (2), queen of the AMAZONS. His stepmother, PHAEDRA, fell in love with him and made accusations about him to his father in order to revenge herself for his indifference. Theseus cursed his son and requested POSEIDON to destroy him. One day, therefore, when Hippolytus was riding his chariot along the coast, Poseidon sent a bull from the sea. The horses were frightened, upset the chariot and dragged Hippolytus until he was dead. His innocence was afterwards established, and Phaedra killed herself. Hippolytus was restored to life by AESCULAPIUS, and according to Italian traditions, ARTEMIS placed him, under the name of VIRIBUS, under the protection of the nymph EGERIA in the grove of Aricia in LATIUM where he was honoured with divine worship.

Hippomedon *see* **Seven against Thebes**.

Hippomenes *see* **Atalanta**; **Megareus**; **Onchestus**.

Hipponous (1) in Greek mythology, the original name of the hero BELLEROPHON. He received the name Bellerophon because he had killed Bellerus, a distinguished Corinthian.

Hipponous (2) *see* **Oeneus**; **Olenus**.

Hippothoon *see* **Alope**.

Hodoedocus *see* **Oileus**.

Homer the name given by the Greeks to the (traditionally blind) author of the two great Greek epics, the *Iliad* and the *Odyssey*. Of Homer's date and birthplace nothing was known to the Greeks. Many cities claimed to be his birthplace, mostly in the islands and in early Greek colonies in Asia, and it is probable that he was born on Chios and lived in the eighth century BC. The *Iliad* deals with an episode of the TROJAN WAR: the wronging of ACHILLES by AGAMEMNON in the matter of the captive maiden Chryseïs, the wrath which Achilles feels and shows at that, and the consequences and final appeasement of his wrath. The Greeks suffer disaster through his withdrawing himself from the Trojan fight. PATROCLUS, his close friend, is slain by the Trojan champion, HECTOR, son of PRIAM. Achilles was roused to slay Hector in revenge, and the poem ends with the ransoming of Hector's body by his father. The *Odyssey* tells of the wanderings and adventures of ODYSSEUS in the course of his return to Ithaca after the capture of Troy, and of what had meanwhile gone on in his house, where PENELOPE, his wife, was besieged by suitors. Finally, it relates how Odysseus and his son TELEMACHUS, whom he had left an infant when he set out for Troy, encountered and slew the suitors, and how husband and wife were reunited. The capture of Troy is related. incidentally. The *Iliad* breaks off before that point is reached.

Horae in Greek mythology, the goddesses of the seasons and the order of nature. At Athens they were originally two: Thallo and Carpo. Elsewhere they were at first three, Thallo, Carpo and Auxo, and afterwards their number increased to four. They are represented as maidens carrying the different products of the seasons.

Horatii in Roman mythology, three brothers who, in the reign of TULLUS HOSTILIUS, were selected to fight three Alban brothers (the Curiatii), the champions of ALBA Longa, in order to decide the supremacy between Rome and Alba. Victory went to Rome, and the only surviving Horatius was triumphantly conducted back to the city. His sister, however, had been betrothed to one of the Curiatii, and her obvious grief so enraged Horatius that he stabbed her in the heart. For this he was condemned to death, but his father and the people begged him off. He lived to destroy Alba and carry its inhabitants to Rome. The myth points to the close relationship that existed between Rome and Alba Longa and to the internecine struggle that probably took place before the latter was incorporated in the political organization of the former.

Horatius Cocles in Roman mythology, a hero of ancient Rome and descendant of the surviving HORATII, who, with Titus Herminius and Spurius Lartius, formed the 'dauntless three' who in 507 BC held the Sublician bridge against the army of Lars Porsena of Latium while the Romans broke it down behind them. When this was nearly finished, Horatius sent his two companions back, and as the bridge fell he plunged into the Tiber with his armour and safely reached the opposite bank.

Hundred-handed *or* **Hecatoncheires** in Greek mythology, three giants each with fifty heads and one hundred arms. Their names were BRIAREUS, Gyes and Cottus. Their father, URANUS, was jealous of their supreme strength and hid them within their mother, GE, to her great pain. When Ge persuaded CRONOS to castrate Uranus, the god kept the Hundred-handed locked up in TARTARUS with the CYCLOPS. They were released temporarily to help ZEUS fight the TITANS but were returned to Tartarus to be guardians of the Titans now imprisoned there.

Hyacinth *or* **Hyacinthus** in Greek mythology, a son of AMYCLAS, king of Sparta, and Diomede, or of Perius and the Muse CLIO. He was an extremely handsome young man and the first man to be loved by another man. The bard Thamyris fell in love with Hyacinth. APOLLO and ZEPHYRUS were also in love with him. Zephyrus became jealous because Hyacinth favoured Apollo and caused his quoit to strike and kill the youth while they were at play. A flower sprang up from the blood of the dying youth, and the flower was called hyacinth.

Hyades in Greek mythology, daughters of ATLAS and the nurses and guardians (three, five or seven in number) of the young DIONYSUS. ZEUS converted them into stars and transplanted them to the heavens where they form the head of the constellation TAURUS. Their rising with the sun was held in Greece to mark the beginning of the rainy season.

Hydra in Greek mythology, a celebrated monster which infested the neighbourhood of Lake Lerna in Argolis in the PELOPONNESUS. Some writers make it the offspring of STYX and the TITAN PALLAS (1), and others of ECHIDNA and TYPHON. Some accounts give it a hundred heads, others fifty, others nine, with an equal number of mouths that discharged a subtle and deadly venom. As soon as one of these heads was cut off, two immediately grew up if the wound was not stopped by fire. It was one of the labours of HERACLES to destroy this monster, and this he effected with the assistance of IOLAUS, who applied a burning iron to the wounds as soon as one head was cut off.

Hygieia in Greek mythology, the goddess of health, daughter of AESCULAPIUS. Her temple was placed near that of Aesculapius, and her statues were even erected in it. She is represented as a youthful maiden with a bowl in her hand, from which she is feeding a snake, the symbol of healing. In 293 BC, her cult was introduced into Rome, where she was known as Valetudo or Salus.

Hyllus *see* **Echemus**; **Nausithous**; **Sthenelus** (1).

Hymen *or* **Hymenaeus** originally the Greek name of the bridal song that was sung by the companions of the bride as she went from her father's house to that of the bridegroom. In Greek mythology, it came to be used for the god of marriage. He is said to be the son of APOLLO and a MUSE, or less often as the son of DIONYSUS and APHRODITE. No marriage took place without his being invoked to sanction it. He is described as a youth with wings having around his brows the flower of the herb marjoram, in his left hand the flame-coloured nuptial veil, in his right the nuptial torch, and on his feet golden sandals. He is a taller and more serious EROS, and is accompanied by song and dance.

Hyperboreans in Greek mythology, the name given in early legends to a people whose land was generally supposed to lie in the extreme northern parts of the world, 'beyond (*hyper*) BOREAS' or the North Wind, and so were not exposed to its blasts. As the favourites of APOLLO, they enjoyed an earthly paradise, a bright sky, a perpetural spring, a fruitful land, unbroken peace, and everlasting youth and health.

Hyperenor *see* **Sparti**.

Hyperion (1) in Greek mythology, a TITAN, son of URANUS and GE, and father of HELIOS, SELENE and EOS. Homer and later writers apply the name to Helios himself.

Hyperion (2) *see* **Megara**.

Hypermnestra *see* **Danaïdes**; **Danaüs**.

Hypnos in Greek mythology, sleep and the god of sleep, called Somnos by the Romans. He was a son of NYX (night) and a brother of THANATOS (death).

Hyppolyte *or* **Hippolyta** in Greek mythology, a queen of the Amazons who was vanquished and killed by HERACLES in pursuit of his ninth labour, to obtain the belt given to her by ARES.

Hypsipyle in Greek mythology, queen of Lemnos who saved her father when the women of LEMNOS vowed to kill all the men. She put her father in either a chest or a boat and set him adrift on the sea. He reached the island of Oenoë. Later she was a nurse to the infant OPHELTES. She was mother of EUNEUS and Deipylus by JASON

Hyrnetho *see* **Deïphontes**.

I

Iacchus in Greek mythology, an obscure deity sometimes described as DEMETER's son, sometimes as her husband. Other legends describe him as being a son of PERSEPHONE identical with Zagreus and some as the son of

Dionysus, with whom he is sometimes confused. He was honoured at the Eleusinian Mysteries with Demeter and Persephone.

Ialmenus in Greek mythology, a son of Ares and Astyoche. He and his brother were joint kings of Minyan Orchomenus (2). They were both Argonauts, and both sought the hand of Helen. They were the leaders of thirty ships to the Trojan War.

Ianthe *see* **Iphis** (2).

Iapetus in Greek mythology, a Titan and a son of Ge and Uranus. He was the father either by the Oceanid Clymene (1) or Asia of Atlas, Menoetius, Prometheus and Epimetheus.

Iarbas *or* **Hiarbas** a king of Numidia in North Africa. He is said to have sold the site of Carthage to Dido and later wooed her. It was his prayer to Jupiter that led to Aeneas's desertion of Dido.

Iasion in Greek mythology, a son of Zeus and Electra (3), daughter of Atlas. He left his homeland in Samothrace to go to Thebes to attend the wedding celebrations of Cadmus and Harmonia, whom some legends claim was the sister of Iasion. The goddess Demeter fell in love with him and had an affair with him. The result of this union was a son, Plutus, who became a minor deity connected with agriculture. In some legends Iasion was killed by Zeus for daring to lie with a goddess. Others say that he was killed by his team of horses and with Triptolemus became the constellation Gemini. According to one legend Iasion and Demeter had another son, Philomelus, who was made into the constellation Boötes for his invention of the plough.

Iasus (1) in Greek mythology, a son of Phoroneus and brother of Pelasgus and Agenor, or Arestor.

Iasus (2) in Greek mythology, a king of Argos and son of Argus Panoptes and Ismene, daughter of Asopus or of Triopas (2). He is said by some to have been the father of Io.

Iasus (3) in Greek mythology, a son of Lycurgus (2), king of Arcadia. According to some legends he was the father of Atalanta by Clymene (2), daughter of Mynas. Since he wanted only male children he left the child Atalanta to die of exposure. However she was rescued by hunters having been suckled by a bear. When she grew to adulthood she was reunited with her father, who is reputed to have devised the foot race that preserved her virginity.

Icaria an island in the Aegean Sea. In Greek mythology, when Icarus fell to his death in the Icarian Sea his body was washed up on the shores of the island of Doliche. There Heracles found it, buried it and renamed the island Icaria in memory of Icarus. Dionysus was captured by pirates from Icaria.

Icarius (1) in Greek mythology, a son of Perieres and Gorgophone, or of Oebalus and the nymph Bateia. According to some legends he and his brother Tyndareus were expelled from Sparta and were reinstated by Heracles. According to another legend Icarius helped his brother Hippocoön expel their brother Tyndareus from Sparta. The nymph Peroboea bore him two daughters, Penelope and Ipthime, and also five sons, among whom were Perileus or Perilaus, who may have been the accuser of Orestes at his trial on the Areopagus. Odysseus arrived in Sparta in order to pay court to Penelope. One legend says that Icarius organized a foot race as a way of deciding which suitor would win Penelope's hand. Other legends say that Tyndareus, brother of Icarius, interceded on behalf of Odysseus with Icarius. In any event Odysseus won Penelope. Icarius, upset at the idea of his daughter leaving, tried to persuade Odysseus to settle in Sparta with Penelope. When Odysseus refused to comply with this request, Icarius followed his chariot pleading with Penelope to stay. Odysseus told Penelope that he wished her to go with him willingly or not at all, that she must choose between him and her father. In response Penelope veiled her face, a gesture by which Icarius deduced that she wished to accompany Odysseus. When his daughter left Icarius erected a statue of Modesty.

Icarius (2) in Greek mythology, an Athenian who was taught the art of vine culture by Dionysus because of the hospitality which he and his daughter, Erigone (1), had shown to the god. Icarius made some wine and loaded his wagon with wineskins full of wine, taking with him his dog, Maera, and set out. On meeting some shepherds he gave them some wine. They drank this undiluted with water and, not being used to wine drinking, they fell into a drunken stupor. When they recovered from this they deduced that, in view of their stupor, the stranger had tried to poison them. In revenge for this they beat Icarius to death with clubs, threw his body into a well and hurried away. Maera howled by his master's grave and thus led Erigone to it. She had been out anxiously looking for her father. She was so upset at the death of her father that she killed herself by hanging herself from the tree that grew over the well. The dog, Maera, killed himself by jumping into the well. The god Dionysus was furious at the deaths of those who had shown kindness to him. He devised a plan to avenge their deaths by making Athenian girls mad and causing them to hang themselves from trees. Anxious to discover the reason for this, the Athenian leaders consulted the oracle and were told about the murder of Icarius. They apprehended the murderers and punished them. In memory of Icarius and Erigone they established certain rites in their honour to take place at the grape festival. As part of these rites Athenian girls swung from trees in swings in imitation of Erigone. Dionysus honoured Icarius and his daughter and dog by making them all constellations. Icarius became Boötes, Erigone Virgo and Maera is the Dog Star (*see* Canis Major). When the island of Ceüs suffered from a severe drought that accompanied the intense heat during the rise of the Dog Star, Apollo advised the inhabitants to sacrifice to the ghost of Icarius. It is thought that the murderers of Icarius had fled to Ceüs.

Icarus in Greek mythology, the son of DAEDALUS, who ignored his father's advice not to fly too near the sun when he was escaping, with his father, from a prison in CRETE by means of wings made of wax and feathers. When he did go too near the sun the wax of his wings melted and he plunged into the sea south of Samos, an area now called the Icarian Sea in his memory. His body was washed up on the island of Doliche. It was buried by HERACLES and the island was renamed ICARIA.

Ida in Greek mythology, a NYMPH of Mount IDA in CRETE. She was a daughter of MELISSEUS and sister of Adrasteia. With her sister she nursed the infant ZEUS. *See also* TITANS.

Ida, Mount (modern Idhi) (1) in ancient geography, a mountain range in Asia Minor, extending from PHRYGIA through MYSIA into the Troad, at the foot of which lay the city of Troy. It is the scene of many ancient Greek legends. The southern part of the range was called Gargarus, and here there was a temple of CYBELE, from which she is known as the Idaean Mother. From Mount Ida flow several streams, as the Granicus, Simöeus and SCAMANDER.

Ida, Mount (2) in ancient geography, the middle and highest summit of the mountain chain that divides the Island of CRETE from east to west. In Greek mythology, ZEUS was brought up and educated here.

Idaea (1) in Greek mythology, a NYMPH of Mount IDA near Troy. TEUCER (1), king of the region of Troy, was said to have been a son of Idaea and SCAMANDER, a local river-god. Teucer's daughter, BATEIA (1), was one of the ancestors of the royal Trojan line.

Idaea (2) in Greek mythology, the second wife of PHINEUS. By Idaea, Phineus had two sons, Thynius and and Mariandynus. Idaea disliked the sons of Phineus by his first marriage, and she made accusations against them. These were believed by their father, who tortured and imprisoned them. They were rescued by the ARGONAUTS. In disgrace Idaea was sent home to her father, DARDANUS (2), who condemned her to death.

Idaean Mother a name given to CYBELE, who had a temple on Mount IDA (1).

Idaeus in Greek mythology, the herald of the Trojan forces at the time of the TROJAN WAR. It was he who drove the mule cart that carried PRIAM on his secret journey to try to persuade ACHILLES to give him HECTOR's body.

Idas and Lynceus in Greek mythology, sons of APHAREUS, king of MESSENIA. Idas and his younger brother LYNCEUS (2) were inseparable. Idas was strong and bold, but Lynceus was possessed of an unusual gift. He had such sharp powers of vision that he could even see what was hidden in the earth. Both brothers took part in the CALYDONIAN BOAR hunt and were both ARGONAUTS. Idas tended to be rather arrogant and insolent, which got him into trouble on the *Argo*. He also showed this arrogance by abducting Marpessa, daughter of Evenus, despite being well aware of the fact that APOLLO was wooing her. According to some legends, Idas was able to escape with Marpessa at a very rapid pace because he had been lent a winged chariot by POSEIDON. He was, at any rate, too fast for Evenus, who failed to catch up with Idas and his daughter and drowned himself in the river Lycormas, which then became known as the river Evenus. Apollo, however, was swift enough to catch up with Idas and fought with him for Marpessa. ZEUS intervened in the fight, separated the contenders and told them to leave it to Marpessa to decide between them. She, because she felt that Apollo being so powerful would one day desert her, chose Idas. They married, and she bore him a daughter, CLEOPATRA (1), who became the wife of MELEAGER. Idas went on to invade Teuthrania in Mysia while TEUTHRAS was on the throne, but he was driven back by Telephus and Parthenopaeus. Later Idas and Lynceus were involved in a dispute with CASTOR AND POLLUX, who had been with them both on the Calydonian Boar hunt and on the expedition of the Argonauts. The quarrel led to the deaths of all four contenders.

Idmon in Greek mythology, one of the ARGONAUTS and a son of CYRENE (1) and APOLLO, or, according to some legends, ABAS. Idmon was a seer, having been taught the arts of prophecy, augury and the divining of omens. Idmon knew that if he joined the expedition of the Argonauts he would not survive the expedition. A native of ARGOS, he joined the crew of the *Argo* despite this forewarning. When the Argonauts stopped near Mariandynus on the southern shore of the Black Sea, Idmon was killed by a boar. His fellow Argonauts spent three days mourning his passing and planted an olive tree on his grave. Much later Apollo ordered the people who colonized Heracleia to found their city around the olive tree and to honour Idmon who would be their protector.

Idomene *see* **Bias**.

Idomeneus in Greek mythology, a king of Crete and a son of DAEDALUS and grandson of MINOS. During the TROJAN WAR he was the leader of a Cretan force of eighty ships. Despite the fact that he was considerably older than most of the other Greek leaders, he fought boldly and bravely. After the fall of Troy he returned safely to his home in Crete only to discover that his wife, Meda, had had an affair with Leucus, NAUPLIUS (1) having encouraged her in this. Leucus was both ambitious and ruthless, and killed both Meda and her daughter. He seized control of ten Cretan cities and drove out Idomeneus. He and his followers sailed for Italy and settled in the part of the country which forms the 'heel' of Italy, the Sallentine Plain.

Idyia *see* **Eidyia**.

Iliad *see* **Homer**.

Ilione in Greek mythology, the eldest daughter of PRIAM and HECUBA. She was the wife of Polymestor, king of the Thracian Chersonese, and bore him a son. As well as bringing up her own son she was responsible for the rearing of her young brother, Polydorus.

Ilissus *or* **Ilisus, River** a stream located near ATHENS. In Greek mythology, BOREAS carried off OREITHYIA, daughter of ERECHTHEUS, from the banks of the Illisus.

Ilium *see* **Troy**.

Illyria *or* **Illyricum** a name formerly rather loosely applied to a large tract of country on the east side of the Adriatic, the ancient Illyrians being the ancestors of the modern Albanians. Piracy was carried on by the Illyrians, whose kings were therefore embroiled in quarrels with the Romans, which ended in their subjugation in 228 BC. After the murder of CADMUS'S successor, Cadmus, his wife, HARMONIA, and their daughter AGAVE settled in Illyria, as did many of the people of THEBES when they were driven from Thebes by the EPIGONI.

Ilus (1) in Greek mythology, the elder son of DARDANUS, king of DARDANIA, and BATEIA, daughter of TEUCER. Since Ilus died without having fathered any children, his brother succeeded to the throne of Dardania on his death. Ilus is sometimes confused in some legends with ILUS (2), after whom Ilium is called.

Ilus (2) in Greek mythology, a king of TROY who gave his name to Ilium. He was the son of TROS, who gave his name to Troy, and Callirrhoë, daughter of the river-god SCAMANDER. He left Dardania, where his brother Assaracus, was king and went to PHYRGIA. In the Games there Ilus won a wrestling match and was awarded a prize of fifty youths and fifty young women. At the same time he received a dappled cow from the king of Phrygia, who ordered him to found a city where it lay down. The king of Phrygia was acting under instuctions from an ORACLE. Ilus was led by the cow to a hill which was sacred to ATE. There he built a city and called it Ilium after himself, its inhabitants being the young people whom he had won as a prize. As Ilus was praying to ZEUS, the PALLADIUM dropped to the earth from the sky right in front of his tent. Ilus built a temple for it, and a saying came into being that Ilium would be invulnerable as long as the Palladium remained in the city. Ilus married Eurydice (3), daughter of ADRASTUS, and fathered LAOMEDON and Themiste. His daughter, Themiste, married Capys, son of Assaracus, the brother of Ilus. At his death Ilus was succeeded as king by his son, Laomedon.

Ilus (3) in Greek mythology, a king of Thesprotian Ephyra who was descended from MEDEA. His family were skilled in the art of making poisons and he had inherited the art. He offended ODYSSEUS by refusing to sell arrow poison to him.

Ilva *see* **Elba**.

Inachus the chief river of Argos, in Greek mythology often personified as a god. He was a son of of the Titans OCEANUS and TETHYS. When HERA and POSEIDON were engaged in a dispute over possession of Argolis, ZEUS asked Inachus and two other rivers, CEPHISSUS and ASTERION, to adjudicate. They decided in favour of Hera. In revenge Poseidon dried up the rivers so that they could flow freely only when it rained. According to some legends, Inachus was not a god but the first king of ARGOS. He is said to have named the river Inachus after himself and to have been the first person to worship Hera. His wife was a MELIA, an ash-nymph. They had two sons, PHORONEUS and AEGIALEUS (2), and a daughter, Io. Io told her father about some erotic dreams that were being sent to her by Zeus. The oracles of DELPHI and DODONA told Inachus to exile her. He obeyed their instructions, and she was exiled and turned into a heifer. After this Inachus sat down and wept in his cave, the legend being that his tears were the source of the river of the name.

Ino in Greek mythology, a daughter of CADMUS, king of Thebes, and HARMONIA. She was a sister of SEMELE and with her siblings, AGAVE and Autonoë, told everyone that Semele was lying when she claimed that ZEUS was the father of the child whom she was expecting. After the death of Semele and after the second birth of the baby, DIONYSUS, from the thigh of Zeus, Ino was asked by HERMES to rear the child as a girl so that HERA would be deceived. By this time Ino had married ATHAMAS, king of ORCHOMENUS (2). When suffering from divine madness, Ino helped Agave to tear to pieces her son PENTHEUS, king of Thebes. Athamas had been married before—to NEPHELE by whom he fathered PHRIXUS and HELLE. Ino was very jealous of them and plotted to destroy them. They were saved by flying away on a miraculous ram that could fly and had a GOLDEN FLEECE.

Io in Greek mythology, the daughter of INACHUS, the river god of Argos and its first king. She was beloved by ZEUS, who sent her erotic and seductive dreams. When she told her father, he consulted the oracle, who advised him to exile her or else a thunderbolt from Zeus would destroy his people. Reluctantly he exiled her. There are several versions of the rest of the story. One legend has it that HERA knew about the designs that Zeus had on Io and turned her into a white heifer to protect her and thwart the designs of Zeus. Another legend suggests that Io was fleeing from Zeus when he was spotted by Hera. He changed Io into a white heifer to hide his embarrassment. Hera asked Zeus for the gift of the heifer, and Zeus had to comply with her request in case Hera inquired further. When Zeus sent HERMES to steal the heifer, Hera sent the many-eyed ARGUS PANOPTES to guard her. Io was tied to an olive tree in the grove at MYCENAE, and Argus watched her night and day, at least some of his eyes being always open. Eventually, according to some legends, Hermes disguised himself as a goatherd who lulled Argus to sleep with his stories and tunes on his pipes. Hermes, who was noted for his cunning, then cut off Argus's head as he slept. Hera had to think up another way to keep Zeus from Io and sent a gadfly to sting the heifer and drive her out of Argolis. Io then began her wanderings. Various routes have been ascribed to these wanderings, but she is eventually supposed to have reached the Nile near the Egyptian city of

Canobus or Memphis. There Zeus went to her and she conceived a child by the union that took place. Io resumed human shape and gave birth to a son, EPAPHUS. At Hera's request the child was kidnapped by the CURETES, whom Zeus killed in revenge. Epaphus had been taken to Syria where Io found him being nursed by the queen of Byblus. Io returned with her son to Egypt and married King Telegonus and established the worship of DEMETER there.

Iobates in Greek mythology, a king of Lycia who married his daughter, STHENEBOEA, to PROËTUS and restored him to power in ARGOS. He then tried to get rid of BELLEROPHON but changed his mind and gave him the hand of his daughter Philonoë.

Iolaüs in Greek mythology, a son of IPHICLES and Automedusa, daughter of ALCATHOUS. He was the nephew of HERACLES and his charioteer and frequent companion. Iolaüs assisted Heracles in the execution of several of his labours; indeed he played such a major part in the destruction of the HYDRA that EURYSTHEUS refused to accept this as one of the labours that Heracles had done alone. Iolaüs tried to save the children of Heracles from the persecution of Eurystheus. He is said to have prayed to the gods to make him young again so that he could protect his dead uncle's family. He was temporarily rejuvenated and able to kill Eurystheus and behead him.

Iolcus an ancient city of MAGNESIA in THESSALY, at the head of the gulf of Pagasae. It was founded by Cretheus, one of the sons of AEOLUS (2), and he was also its first ruler. The rightful heir to the throne of Iolcus was the son of Cretheus, AESON, but he was deprived of the throne by PELIAS, his half-brother, who went on to rule the country for many years. Iolcus was captured by the ARGONAUTS under JASON, who was the son of Aeson, after MEDEA had tricked the daughters of Pelias into killing him. Jason turned over the throne to the son of Pelias, ACASTUS. Another Argonaut, PELEUS, visited Iolcus. The wife of Acastus fell in love with him, but he rejected her advances. To get her revenge she told her husband that Peleus had raped her, and he tried to kill Peleus but he failed. With the help of Jason, Peleus attacked and destroyed Iolcus and gave the throne to Haemones. According to one legend Acastus survived and later either he or his sons banished Peleus from Phthia.

Iole in Greek mythology, a daughter of EURYTUS (1), king of Oechalia, promised by her father to anyone who could defeat him in an archery competition. When he was defeated by HERACLES, he refused to honour his promise. Later Eurytus was killed by Heracles who then took Iole as his concubine. On discovering that Heracles had taken a concubine, his wife, DEÏANEIRA, sent him a poisoned robe which caused his death.

Ion in Greek mythology, a son of CREÜSA (1), wife of XUTHUS, by either Xuthus or APOLLO. Apollo had visited Creüsa in a cave, and when she gave birth to a son she left him to die in the same cave. The god, however, had the child taken to DELPHI and there had him educated by a priestess. When the boy had grown up, Xuthus and Creüsa came to consult the oracle about the means of obtaining an heir, the answer was that the first human being whom Xuthus met on leaving the temple would be his son. Xuthus met Ion and recognized him as his son, but Creüsa, thinking him to be a son of her husband by a former lover, gave him a cup filled with the poisonous blood of a dragon. Ion, however, before drinking poured out on the ground a libation to the gods, and a pigeon that drank of it died on the spot. Ion was on the point of killing Creüsa when a priestess interfered and explained the situation. Mother and son thus became reconciled. Ion later married HELICE, daughter of Seilnus, king of Aegialeia in the northern PELOPONNESUS, and after the king's death succeeded to the throne. Thus the Aegialeans became IONIANS.

Ionia that part of the seaboard of Asia Minor which was inhabited by Ionian Greeks, a beautiful and fertile country opposite the Islands of Samos and Chios, which also belonged to it. According to tradition, the Greek colonists came over from ATTICA after the death of CODRUS, the last king, led by the sons of Codrus, Neleus and Androclus, who were dissatisfied with the abolition of royalty and the appointment of their eldest brother Medon as archon. Here they founded twelve towns, which, though mutually independent, formed a confederacy for common purposes. These included Phocaea, EPHESUS, MILETUS, etc, and afterwards SMYRNA.

Ionian Islands a chain of Greek islands in the Ionian Sea, extending along the western and southern shores of Greece, of which the largest are Corfu, CEPHALONIA, Zakinthos and Cerigo, others being ITHACA and Paxos. All are extremely mountainous. The Ionian Islands often figure in the ancient history of Greece, but only individually.

Ionian Sea the sea that lies between southern Italy and Sicily on the west and Greece, from EPIRUS to the PELOPONNESUS on the east. It may have been named after the IONIANS who were said to have once inhabited Peloponnesus.

Ionians a Greek-speaking people called after ION, son of XUTHUS or APOLLO who succeeded to the throne of Aegialus in the northern PELOPONNESUS. At the time of the DORIAN invasion the Ionians were driven out of the Peloponnesus and fled to ATTICA. Thereafter many emigrated to the CYCLADES or to Asia Minor. They founded or conquered several cities in the land later called IONIA.

Iphianassa (1) in Greek mythology, a daughter of PROËTUS and STHENEBOEA and granddaughter of IOBATES, who was cured of madness by MELAMPUS and married his brother, BIAS as his second wife.

Iphianassa (2) in Greek mythology, a daughter of AGAMEMNON and CLYTEMNESTRA. According to some legends she is identified with IPHIGENEIA.

Iphicles *or* **Iphiclus** in Greek mythology, the son of ALEMENE and AMPHITRYON, the twin and half brother of HERACLES. Heracles was the son of ZEUS. When the babies were in their crib, two snakes entered it and were strangled by Heracles. Iphicles married Automedusa, daughter of ALCATHOUS, king of Megara, and she bore him a son, IOLAÜS. Iphicles later married the younger daughter of CREON. He took part in the CALYDONIAN BOAR hunt and may have died fighting against the sons of HIPPOCOÖN.

Iphiclus in Greek mythology, the son of PHYLACUS, king of Phylace, and Clymene (2), daughter of Minyas (*see* MINYANS). He was a famous runner. JASON was the son of Iphiclus' sister, Alcimede.

Iphigeneia *or* **Iphigenia** in Greek mythology and poetry, daughter of AGAMEMNON and CLYTEMNESTRA. To avert the wrath of ARTEMIS, whom Agamemnon had enraged and who detained at Aulis the Greek fleet that had been prepared for the TROJAN WAR, Iphigeneia was to be sacrificed on the altar, but a stag was miraculously substituted for her, and she was conveyed in a cloud to Tauris (Crimea). She became priestess there to Artemis, and saved her brother ORESTES when on the point of being sacrificed. The story of Iphigeneia is the subject of two plays by EURIPIDES, of one by Racine and another by Goethe.

Iphimedeia in Greek mythology, a daughter of TRIOPAS (1) who married POSEIDON's son ALOEUS, but she fell in love with Poseidon and took to walking by the sea and pouring sea water into her lap. Poseidon came to her, and she bore him two giant sons, OTUS AND EPHIALTES. She also bore a daughter, Pancratis, to her husband. Mother and daughter while taking part as bacchants in a revel were abducted by Thracian pirates to Strongyle (Naxos). Otus and Ephialtes attacked the island and rescued them.

Iphinoë *see* **Megareus**.

Iphis (1) in Greek mythology, a king of ARGOS and a son of ALECTOR, and the person who urged POLYNEICES to bribe ERIPHLYE with HARMONIA's necklace. He was the father of ETEOCLUS and of Evadne, who married CAPANEUS. The latter died with Iphis in the war against Thebes (*see* SEVEN AGAINST THEBES) and the kingdom was left to STHENELUS (2), son of CAPANEUS.

Iphis (2) in Greek mythology, the daughter of Ligdus and Tele-thusa. Ligdus of Phaestus in Crete told his wife when she was already pregnant that she would have to bear him a son and that he would not be able to support a daughter. If one were born to them she would have to be killed. His wife, Telesthusa, was a votary of Isis (the Egyptian name of Io), and the goddess appeared to her before the baby was born wih promises to help her. However, Telethusa went on to give birth to a daughter. In an effort to save her, Telethusa dressed the baby girl in boy's clothes and named her Iphis. Surprisingly she got away with the deception until her daughter was thirteen. At that point her father betrothed his supposed son to Ianthe. Telethusa tried all manner of delaying tactics and, just as it seemed hopeless, the goddess, Isis, transformed Iphis into a boy.

Iphis (3) in Greek mythology, a Cypriot youth who hanged himself from the doorpost of the house of Anaxarete, whom he loved desperately but who had rejected him. During his funeral procession Anaxerete was turned to stone.

Iphitus (1) in Greek mythology, a son of Naubolus, king of Phocis, and an ARGONAUT. He was the father of SCHEDIUS (1) and Epistrophus, who is said to have been the leader of the Phocian forces to the TROJAN WAR.

Iphitus (2) in Greek mythology, a son of EURYTUS (1), king of Oechalia. When Eurytus promised his daughter to anyone who defeated him at archery and then reneged on his promise when HERACLES won, Iphitus took the side of Heracles. Later, however, he was killed by Heracles, who threw him from the walls of Tiryns, possibly because they had quarrelled over stolen mares belonging to Eurytus. For this crime he was smitten with a terrible disease which could be cured only by selling himself into slavery.

Ipthime *see* **Icarius** (1).

Iris in Greek mythology, the swift golden-winged messenger of the Olympian gods in the *Iliad*, the office of HERMES in the *Odyssey*. Iris was originally the personification of the rainbow. She is represented with wings attached to her shoulders and a herald's staff in her left hand, representative of her office of messenger. She is represented as the daughter of THAUMAS and ELECTRA (4), and sister of the HARPIES. According to legend she was the wife of ZEPHYRUS and the mother of EROS.

Iron Race *see* **Races of Man**.

Irus in Greek mythology, a beggar from Ithacus, christened Arnaeus. It was his practice to beg from the suitors of PENELOPE, and when he saw an aged beggar in his area, Irus threatened him, not knowing that the supposed beggar was ODYSSEUS in disguise. Odysseus felled Irus with one blow, although Irus was much younger than him, in a boxing match that was arranged by the suitors.

Ischys in Greek mythology, a son of ELATUS (2) and lover of CORONIS (1). He was killed by ARTEMIS at APOLLO's request.

Islands of the Blessed *see* **Races of Man**; **White Island**.

Ismene (1) in Greek mythology, a daughter of OEDIPUS, by JOCASTA or Euryganeia. In *Antigone* by Sophocles she is afraid to take part in the illegal burial of POLYNEICES but later offers to die with her sister for committing the deed.

Ismene (2) in Greek mythology, a daughter of ASOPUS and Metope and wife of ARGUS by whom she became the mother of IASUS and IO.

Ithaca (modern Ithaki) one of the IONIAN ISLANDS on the west of Greece, a long narrow island lying between the mainland and CEPHALONIA. It is mountainous and the coast is steep and rocky. Ithaca was the royal seat of ODYSSEUS, and is minutely described in the *Odyssey*. It is one of the most famous sites in mythology.

Itoni in Greek mythology, a Lydian tribe who caused much trouble to Omphale, queen of Lydia until Heracles subdued them.

Iülus in mythology, the son of Aeneas and Creüsa (2). He was originally called Ilus and was often called Ascanius. With Aeneas he fought against the forces of Turnus. He founded the city of Alba Longa. The Julian line of Roman emperors takes its name from him.

Ixion in Greek mythology, a king of the Lapiths in Thessaly and father of Peirithoüs. He married Dia, the daughter of Deioneus, and caused the death of his father-in-law. He prayed for forgiveness to Zeus, who pardoned him and invited him to his table. Ixion then tried to seduce Hera, and for his wickedness was chained to a fiery wheel, which rolled for ever in the sky.

J

Jana *see* **Janus**.

Janus in Roman mythology, a god, after whom the first month of the year was named. He was held in great reverence by the Romans, greater even than that of Jupiter, and was represented with two faces, one looking forward, the other backward. All doors, passages and beginnings were under his care. His principal festival was New Year's Day, when people gave each other presents. The temple of Janus, which was open in time of war and closed in time of peace, was shut only three times in the long space of 700 years—once in the reign of Numa Pompilius, again after the first Punic War, and the third time under the reign of Augustus. Vespasian also closed it in AD 71. There was also a goddess, Jana, although she never became prominent in the state religion.

Jason in Greek mythology, the elder son of Aeson, a grandson of Aeolus (2). The half-brother of Aeson, Pelias, usurped Aeson as heir to the throne of Iolcus. Aeson was afraid for his life and for the life of the son that was born to him. To preserve the infant's life, he and his wife pretended that the baby had died and sent him to Cheiron the Centaur for protection. The Centaur named the child Jason and reared him in his cave on the mountain of Pelion, east of Iolcus. When Jason was a man, he set out for Iolcus to depose Pelias. Legend has it that Pelias, who did not have the courage to kill Jason, asked Jason what he would do if an oracle said that a certain man would kill him. Jason replied that he would order the person who was supposedly going to kill him to go and bring back the golden fleece. (Phrixus had flown to Colchis on the back of a mirculous ram and had nailed to a tree in the grove of Ares the ram's golden fleece where it was guarded by a dragon which never slept). Pelias ordered

Jason to do this, making the excuse that the Delphic oracle had revealed to him that the gods of the Underworld had issued a directive that the spirit of Phrixus must be brought back from the foreign land of Colchis to Thessaly and with it the golden fleece. Jason choose the most courageous of the young nobles from the Greek cities and instructed ARGUS to build a ship with the help of ATHENA. The ship was called the *Argo*. During the expedition Jason was under the protection of HERA, whom he had carried over a stream when she was in the guise of an old woman and who hated Pelias. Hera thought that MEDEA would be clever enough to overthrow Pelias, but Medea lived in COLCHIS, a long way from Iolcus. Hera enlisted the help of APHRODITE to cause Medea to fall in love with Jason so that she would return to Iolcus with him and depose Pelias. Jason succeeded in getting the golden fleece, and the ARGONAUTS returned. Meanwhile, Pelias had killed Jason's father and brother. On his return to Iolcus with Medea as his wife, he and Medea avenged the murder of his parents and his brother by putting Pelias to death. He did not take possession of his throne, but, according to one legend, went to Corinth, where, he lived with Medea for some time until he married GLAUCE (or Creüsa), daughter of CREON, and put away Medea and her children. Medea killed his new wife. Different accounts are given of his death. One of these is that he was killed by a wooden beam that fell from the wreckage of the *Argo* as he sat in it. Medea and Jason had two sons, Mermerus and Pheres, and Jason had previously had sons, EUNEUS and either Nebrophonus or Deipylus by HYPSIPYLE, queen of Lemnos.

Jocasta *or* **Epicasta** in Greek mythology, a daughter of MENOECEUS, who married LAïUS when he became king of Thebes. Laïus was warned by an oracle that a son born to him would kill him. When Jocasta gave birth to a son they left the baby to die of exposure on Mount Cithaeron, but he was saved by shepherds and brought up by the king of Corinth, Polybus, and his wife, Merope, in Corinth. When he became a young man, OEDIPUS, as he was called, was warned by the Delphic oracle that he would kill his father and marry his mother. In order to prevent this coming true, he did not return to Corinth. When he left DELPHI he met Laïus without knowing who he was and killed him in a quarrel. He then went to Thebes, where the people were trying to get rid of the SPHINX who was asking a riddle of passers-by and killing them when they could not answer it. Oedipus solved the riddle that she put to him, and she threw herself from a rock. As a reward he was given the hand of Jocasta by CREON, her brother, and was made king of Thebes. Jocasta and he had two sons, ETEOCLES and POLYNEICES, and two daughters, Antigone and ISMENE (1). Because of this unconsciously incestuous relationship, a plague was sent by the gods to Thebes. When Oedipus was informed by the seer TEIRESIAS that he had murdered his father and married his mother, one legend has it that Jocasta hanged herself and Oedipus gouged out his own eyes.

judgment of Paris *see* **golden apple**.

Juno in Roman mythology, the principal goddess, sister and wife of JUPITER, the equivalent of the Greek HERA. She was the queen of heaven, and under the name of Regina (queen) was worshipped in Italy at an early period. She bore the same relation to women that Jupiter did to men. She was regarded as the special protectress of whatever was connected with marriage and with women. She was also the guardian of the national finances. A temple, which contained the mint, was erected to her under the name of Juno Moneta on the Capitoline.

Jupiter in Roman mythology, the supreme deity, the same as the Greek ZEUS, and the Sanskrit Dyaus ('the sky'), the second part of the word being the same as the Latin *pater*, 'father'. As the supreme deity Jupiter received from the Romans the title of *optimus maximus* (best greatest), and as the deity presiding over the sky he was considered as the originator of all the changes that took place in the sky. From him accordingly proceeded rain, hail and the thunderbolt, and he it was that restored serenity to the sky after it had been obscured by clouds. Hence the epithets of Pluvius ('rainy'), Tonans ('thundering'), etc, were applied to him. The most celebrated of his temples was that on the Capitoline Hill, dedicated to him as Jupiter Optimus Maximus, jointly with JUNO and MINERVA. He was represented with a sceptre as a symbol of his supreme authority. He maintained the sanctity of oaths, he was the guardian of all property, and every Roman was believed to be under his protection, and that of his consort, Juno, the queen of heaven. He was associated with the colour white. White animals were offered up to him in sacrifice, his priests wore white caps, and his chariot was represented as drawn by four white horses.

Juventas in Roman mythology, the goddess of youth, who was identified with the Greek goddess HEBE, whose name also meant truth.

K

Ker in Greek mythology, a spirit associated with death, which is often represented as a woman with talons and fangs. The Keres carried off dead bodies to HADES. They were said to be the daughters of NYX (night) and to be sisters of Moros (doom), THANATOS (death), and HYPNOS (sleep).

Kore in Greek mythology, a name given to PERSEPHONE, a goddess of the Underworld and the daughter of ZEUS and DEMETER. She had been carried off by HADES and had to spend part of the year with him and the rest with her mother. Her annual return from Hades coincided with the sprouting of crops in spring, as though the earth were returning to life again after winter.

Kos *see* **Cos**.

Kronos *see* **Cronos**.

Ktesios in Greek mythology, a spirit who guarded storerooms. Sacred objects representing him were placed in all storehouses to protect them. He is identified with ZEUS.

L

Labdacus in Greek mythology, a son of the Theban king POLYDORUS and grandson of CADMUS. His father died when Labdacus was young, and he was placed under the guardianship of NYCTEUS and afterwards under that of LYCUS. When he reached manhood Lycus surrendered the government to him, and on the death of Labdacus, which occurred soon after, Lycus again undertook the guardianship of his son LAÏUS.

Labyrinth a structure with numerous intricate winding passages, which render it difficult to find the way through it. The Cretan labyrinth was said to have been constructed by DAEDALUS for King MINOS to contain the MINOTAUR. There were other labyrinths at LEMNOS and Samos.

Lacedaemon in Greek mythology, a son of ZEUS by TAŸGETE, who was married to SPARTE, the daughter of EUROTAS, by whom he became the father of AMYCLAS, Eurydice (4) and Asine. He was king of the country which he called after his own name, Lacedaemon, while he gave to his capital the name of his wife, SPARTA.

Lacedaemon the ancient name of LACONIA. *See also* SPARTA.

Lachesis *see* **Fates**.

Laconia the southernmost part of the PELOPONNESUS. Its chief city was SPARTA or Lacedaemon. It was one of the largest of the ancient Greek regions.

Ladon in Greek mythology, a hundred-headed snake, the offspring of TYPHON and ECHIDNA. It was immortal and helped the HESPERIDES to guard the apples in their garden.

Laelaps in Greek mythology, a hound which some legends say was given by ZEUS to to EUROPA as a watchdog, decreeing that it would catch anything or anyone that it pursued. ARTEMIS, or Europa's son MINOS, gave the hound to PROCRIS, and she gave it to her husband, CEPHALUS. In turn he lent it to AMPHITRYON, who used it to try to catch the Teumessiam vixen. This proved a real problem since HERA had decreed that the vixen would never be caught. In the face of this dilemma Zeus turned both animals to stone.

Laërtes in Greek mythology, king of ITHACA and the only son of Arceisius, or of

CEPHALUS and PROCRIS. He is said to have been one of the ARGONAUTS. He conquered the city of Nericus and married Anticleia, who bore him ODYSSEUS. He was too old to protect PENELOPE when she was being pursued by suitors during Odysseus's absence, but she pretended to be weaving a shroud for him to give herself more time. Laërtes was still alive when Odysseus returned, and he killed EUPEITHES.

Laestrygonians *or* **Laestrygones** in Greek mythology, cannibal giants who lived in a city called Telepylus. Several ships of ODYSSEUS's fleet, although not his, were crushed with a huge stone by the giants who speared the sailors and ate them.

Laïus in Greek mythology, a king of Thebes whose father, LABDACUS, died while he was young. He was placed under the guardianship of LYCUS, and on the death of the latter when the throne was usurped by AMPHION and Zethus, was obliged to take refuge with PELOPS in the Peloponnesus. Laïus fell in love with Chryssipus, the king's extremely handsome, illegitimate son, and took him back to Thebes after the death of Amphion and Zethus. Laïus married JOCASTA and was advised to have no children because a child of his would kill him. When he had a son, he left him to die of exposure on Mount Cithaeron, but the child, OEDIPUS, was rescued and later killed his father and married his mother without knowing who they were.

Lampetia in Greek mythology, a daughter of HELIOS by the nymph NEAERA. After her birth she and her sister Phaetusa were carried to Sicily in order to watch over the herds of their father.

Laocoön in Greek mythology, a priest of APOLLO among the Trojans, who married against the will of the god, who warned the Trojans against taking the WOODEN HORSE into the city of Troy and threw his spear at it. For one or both of these reasons he was killed, along with his two sons, by two enormous serpents sent by APOLLO, which came up out of the sea. It has been a popular subject for poets, but it is chiefly known as the subject of an ancient sculpture discovered in Rome in 1506.

Laodamas in Greek mythology, a son of ETEOCLES and king of Thebes. In his reign the EPIGONI marched against Thebes. Laodamas led an army against them and slew their leader, AEGIALEUS (1), but was himself killed by ALCMAEON.

Laodamia in Greek mythology, the daughter of ACASTUS and wife of PROTESILAÜS. Her husband was the first of the Greeks to fall by a Trojan hand, being killed as he leapt on shore from his ship. Laodamia prayed to the gods to give him back to her for only three hours. Her prayer was granted and HERMES led him back to the upper world. When the moment to return came, Laodamia died with him.

Laodice *see* **Elatus** (1).

Laodocus *see* **Dorus** (2); **Echemus**.

Laomedon in Greek mythology, a king of Troy for whom APOLLO and POSEIDON undertook to build a wall round Troy. When he refused to pay them, they punished him by sending a plague and a sea monster to his land. HERACLES saved HESIONE on the understanding that Laomedon would give him his arms but the king reneged on the bargain. Heracles returned after the completion of his labours and killed Laomedon, leaving PRIAM, son of Laomedon, on the throne.

Laphystius, Mount a Boeotian mountain west of Lake Copais. In Greek mythology, It was on this mountain that ATHAMAS was preparing to sacrifice his son PHRIXUS when the miraculous flying lamb wih the GOLDEN FLEECE came to take him and his sister HELLE away to safety.

Lapiths *or* **Lapithae** in Greek mythology, a tribe of northern Thessaly famous for their battle against the CENTAURS.

Larentia *see* **Faustulus**.

lares in Roman mythology, a class of tutelary spirits or deities (domestic and public). All the household lares were headed by the *lar familiaris*, who was revered as the founder of the family. In the mansions of the rich, the images of the lares had their separate apartment. When the family took their meals, some portion was offered to the lares, and on festive occasions they were adorned with wreaths. *See also* LEMURES; MANES; PENATES.

Larissa *see* **Pelasgus**.

larvae *see* **lemures**.

Latins *or* **Latini** the ancient inhabitants of Latium in Italy. In very early times the Latins formed a league of thirty cities, of which ALBA LONGA, said to have been built by ASCANIUS, became the head. ROME was originally a colony of Alba, and thus the language of the Romans is known as the Latin language.

Latinus in Roman mythology, king of Laurentum, after whom the area of Latium was named. He was defeated by AENEAS, who married his daughter LAVINIA and succeeded as king of Laurentum.

Latium the ancient name applied to a district of central Italy on the Tyrrhenian Sea, extending between ETRURIA and Campania, and inhabited by the LATINS, Volsci and Aequi.

Latona the Roman name for LETO.

Laurentum the land ruled by LATINUS, father of LAVINIA, south of ROME.

Lavinia in Roman mythology, the daughter of LATINUS. When AENEAS went to Italy after the burning of TROY with his followers, he overcame the local tribes under the leadership of TURNUS from Ardea or under that of Latinus. Aeneas married Lavinia and became king of the region and named the city which he founded near Laurentum as Lavinium. His followers from Troy agreed to give up the name of Trojans and start speaking the local language. On the death of Aeneas, Lavinia acted as regent until his son, Ascanius, became king. When Lavinium expanded as a city, Ascanius decided to found another city further inland. This he called ALBA LONGA. Acsanius's descendants, thirteen generations on, were NUMITOR and AMULIUS. Numitor's daughter, REA SILVA, was the mother by MARS of ROMULUS AND REMUS.

Lavinium a city south of Rome, according to tradition built and named by AENEAS after his wife, LAVINIA, daughter of LATINUS. Thirty years after the city was built, Ascanius founded ALBA Longa.

Leander *see* **Hero**.

Leaneira *see* **Elatus** (1).

Leda in Greek mythology, the wife of the Spartan king TYNDAREUS. By ZEUS, who came to her in the form of a swan, she was the mother of CASTOR AND POLLUX. In another story she was the mother by Zeus of Pollux and HELEN, and by Tyndareus of Castor and CLYTEMNESTRA.

Leirope *see* **Narcissus**.

Lelegians *or* **Leleges** a division of the earliest inhabitants of Greece, who lived in the Aegean Islands and were powerful during the Minoan domination. They were driven to CARIA in Asia Minor, where they became known as Carians.

Lemnos the most northerly island of the Greek Archipelago, between the HELLESPONT and Mount Athos. It was sacred to HEPHAESTUS and was said to contain a volcano, Mosychlus, which was regarded as his workshop.

lemures in Roman mythology, the general term for all spirits of the dead, of whom the good were honoured as lares and the bad (larvae) were feared as capable in their night journeys of exerting a malignant influence upon mortals. The festival called Lemuria was held on the 9th, 11th and 13th of May, and was accompanied with ceremonies of washing hands, throwing black beans over the head, etc, and the pronunciation, nine times, of the words 'Begone, you spectres of the house!' which deprived the lemures of their power to harm.

Leonteus *see* **Polypoetes**.

Lepus (The Hare) a constellation. The hare was said to have been put in the sky by HERMES in honour of the fact that the hare was so fleet of foot. The people of Leros introduced hares to the island and became overrun by them because they reproduced so quickly. They finally drove them into the sea.

Lerna *or* **Lerne** *see* **Hydra**.

Lesbos (now Mytilene) a Greek island of the Aegean group. It is mountainous but exceedingly fertile. The island was famous in ancient times as a centre of Greek life and civilization. It formerly contained nine cities, the chief being Mytilene.

Lethe in Greek mythology, the River of Oblivion, one of the streams of the lower regions, whose water had the power of making those who drank of it forget the whole of their former existence. Souls before passing into ELYSIUM drank to forget their earthly sorrows; souls returning to the upper world drank to forget the pleasures of Elysium.

Leto in Greek mythology, daughter of the Titan Coeus and PHOEBE and the mother of APOLLO and ARTEMIS. She was one of the early loves of ZEUS, and HERA was jealous of her. She was worshipped chiefly in Lycia, Delos, Athens and other cities of Greece. The Romans called her Latona.

Leucippus (1) in Greek mythology, a son of PERIERES and GORGOPHONE and brother of APHAREUS, and prince of Messenia. He is mentioned among the hunters of the CALYDONIAN BOAR, and the Boeotian town of Leuctra is said to have derived its name from him.

Leucippus (2) *see* **Oenomaüs**.

Leucus *see* **Idomeneus**.

Liber in Roman mythology, an ancient god of fertiliity. *See* BACCHUS.

Libera in Greek mythology, an ancient fertility goddess.

Libya *see* **Epaphus**.

Licymnius in Greek mythology, a son of ELECTRYON and the Phrygian slave Mideia, and a half-brother of ALCEMENE. He was the father of OEONUS. He was a friend of HERACLES, whose son Tlepolemus slew him, according to some unintentionally and according to others in a fit of anger.

Ligdus *see* **Iphis** (2).

Linus in Greek mythology, the personification of a dirge or lamentation, and described as a son of APOLLO or OEAGRUS and a MUSE, probably CALLIOPE, or of Amphimarus and URANIA.

Locris *or* **Locri** an ancient people of Greece, descended, according to Aristotle, from the LELEGIANS.

Lotis in Greek mythology, a nymph who gave her name to a tree. She was turned into a tree for her protection when she was being pursued by PRIAPUS.

Lotus-eaters *or* **Lotophagi** in Greek mythology, the name of a people inhabiting a portion of Cyrenaica in Northern Africa, who lived on the fruit of the lotus tree, from which they also made wine. According to Homer, they received ODYSSEUS and his followers hospitably, but the sweetness of the fruit induced such a feeling of happy languor that they ceased to desire to return to their native land.

lotus a name applied to a number of different plants, from the lotus famous in Greek legend. One of these is *Zizyphus lotus*, a native of northern Africa and southern Europe. Some think this was the food of the LOTUS-EATERS, although others consider it to have been the date or the berry of the *Rhamnus lotus*.

Lucina in Roman mythology, goddess of light, a title given to DIANA as the goddess who presided over childbirth.

Lucretia in Roman mythology, the wife of Tarquinius Collatinis, who was outraged by Sextus, son of TARQUINIUS SUPERBUS, king of Rome. She summoned her husband and a group of friends and, after making them take a solemn oath to drive out the hated race of Tarquins from the city, stabbed herself. Her death was the signal for the revolution by which the Tarquins were expelled and a republic formed.

Luna in Greek mythology, the goddess of the moon.

Lusi an ancient town of ARCADIA, in the foothills of the Aroanian Mountains. It had a temple of ARTEMIS, which was founded by PROËTUS, whose daughters were cured here of their madness by MELAMPUS.

Lycaon (1) in Greek mythology, a son of PELASGUS by Meliboea, the daughter of OCEANUS. He was king of ARCADIA, a civilized one by some accounts, a barbarian by others. By several wives he became the father of a large number of sons, fifty by some accounts, twenty-two by others.

Lycaon (2) in Greek mythology, a son of PRIAM and Laothoe, who was taken by ACHILLES and sold as a slave to EUNEUS. He was ransomed but on encountering Achilles again was slain by him.

Lycaon (3) *see* **Orchomenus** (1).

Lycia an ancient maritime province in the south of Asia Minor, bounded by Caria on the west, Pamphylia on the east, and Pisidia and PHRYGIA on the north. It was colonized by the Greeks at a very early period, and its historical inhabitants were Greeks, although with a mixture of aboriginal blood. The Lycians were prominent in the TROJAN WAR.

Lycomedes a king of the Dolopians on Scyrus, father of DEIDAMEIA (2), grandfather of NEOPTOLEMUS. When THESEUS came to Scyrus, Lycomedes, dreading the influence of the stranger on his own subjects, thrust him down a rock.

Lycotherses *see* **Agave**.

Lycurgus (1) in Greek mythology, a king of the EDONIANS of THRACE. When DIONYSUS came to his country with his MAENADS, Lycurgus drove them away, and he was later punished. Opinions vary as to what form the punishment took. Some say that he was blinded by ZEUS, others that he was driven mad by Dionysus and cut off his own feet, or hacked to death his son, Dryas. A famine was sent to Thrace to punish him, and his people are said to have thrown him to man-eating horses on Mount PANGAEUS.

Lycurgus (2) in Greek mythology, a king of ARCADIA who ruled the kingdom for his elderly father, Aleus, while his brothers, CEPHEUS (2) and Amphidamus, went on the Argonauts' expedition.

Lycurgus (3) in Greek mythology, a brother of ADMETUS and king of NEMEA. He was the father of OPHELTES.

Lycus (1) in Greek mythology, son of Chthonius, one of the SPARTI, brother of NYCTEUS and king of THEBES.

Lycus (2) in Greek mythology, a king of THEBES who marched against SICYON, the king of which, EPOPEUS, had married ANTIOPE (2), niece of Lycus, when she fled to Sicyon when pregnant by ZEUS. Epopeus was either killed or died of a wound, and Lycus took Antiope back to Thebes.

Lycus (3) a son of PANDION (2) and brother of AEGEUS, NISUS and Pallas. He was expelled by Aegeus and took refuge in the country of the Termili with SARPEDON (1). That country was afterwards called Lycia after him.

Lycus (4) son of DASCLYUS (1) and king of the MARIANDYNIANS was connected with HERACLES and the ARGONAUTS.

Lydia an ancient and powerful kingdom of Asia Minor, which extended eastward from the Aegean and comprised Paphlagonia (BLACK SEA littoral), BITHYNIA, MYSIA (at the HELLESPONT), Lydia Proper, LYCIA, PHRYGIA and part of Cappadocia. Sardis was the capital. Its first mythical dynasty was founded by ATYS (2), who was worshipped there along with CYBELE and the Babylonian gods Tammuz and Istar.

Lyra (The Lyre) a constellation, the lyre in the sky being that used by ORPHEUS.

Lyrnessus a city near Troy, to which AENEAS fled when ACHILLES drove him from Mount IDA. Achilles sacked the city.

Lynceus (1) a son of AEGYPTUS and husband of Hypermnestra, daughter of DANAÜS, who, alone among the DANAÏDES, spared her husband's life. Danaüs thereupon kept her in strict confinement but was afterwards prevailed upon to give her to Lynceus who succeeded him on the throne of Argos.

Lynceus (2) in Greek mythology, a son of APHAREUS and Arene and brother of IDAS. He was one of the ARGONAUTS, famous for his keen sight. He is also mentioned among the hunters of the CALYDONIAN BOAR and was slain by POLLUX.

Lysinianassa *see* **Busirus**.

M

Maeander *or* **Maeandrus** in Greek mythology, a son of OCEANUS and TETHYS, and the god of the River Maeander in PHRYGIA. The winding course of the river is the origin of the English word meander.

maenads in Greek mythology, female votaries of the god DIONYSUS. The maenads took part in orgiastic rites and encouraged other women to do so also.

Maera in Greek mythology, the dog of ICARIUS (2) who was placed in the constellation CANIS MAJOR by DIONYSUS.

Magnes (1) in Greek mythology, a son of AEOLUS and Enarete, who was the father of POLYDECTES by a NAÏAD.

Magnes (2) in Greek mythology, a son of ARGUS (1) and Perimele from whom MAGNESIA derived its name.

Magnesia in ancient Greece, a coastal area of eastern THESSALY which contains Mount PELION and was the home of the CENTAURS.

Maia (1) in Greek mythology, the oldest of the PLEIADES and daughter of ATLAS and Pleïone. In a grotto of Mount Cyllene in ARCADIA she became by ZEUS the mother of HERMES. ARCAS, the son of Zeus by CALLISTO, was given to her to be reared.

Maia (2) *or* **Majesta** in Roman mythology, a divinity mentioned in connection with VULCAN, regarded by some as his wife. She later became identified with MAIA (1), but it is more probable that Maia was an ancient name of BONA DEA.

Malis the southern part of THESSALY. The Malians went to the TROJAN WAR under the leadership of PHILOCTETES, but the Greeks abandoned him at LEMNOS.

manes *or* **di manes** in Roman mythology, the souls or ghosts of the dead, to whom were presented offerings of victims, wine, milk, garlands of flowers, etc. The offerings were made at funerals and at the Parentalia, or Fralia, commemorative ceremonies held by the Romans in February. A similar worship of ghosts or ancestral spirits prevails among many races.

Mantius *see* **Oicles**.

Manto *see* **Epigoni**.

Marathon in Greek mythology, the hero eponymous of the Attic town of Marathon. According to some traditions, he was a son of EPOPEUS and, being driven from PELOPONNESUS by the violence of his father, went to Attica. After his father's death he returned to Peloponnesus, divided his inheritance between his two sons, Sicyon and Corinthus, and then settled in Attica.

Marathon a town of ancient Greece in ATTICA, northeast of ATHENS, said to have been founded by MARATHON. Here XUTHUS, who married the daughter of ERECHTHEUS, is said to have reigned, and here the HERACLEIDAE took refuge when driven out of Peloponnesus, and defeated EURYSTHEUS. It is also celebrated in the legends of THESEUS, who conquered the CRETAN BULL that devastated the plain of Marathon around the town.

Mariandynians *or* **Mariandyni** a tribe inhabiting an area of the BLACK SEA, whose king, DASCYLUS, was assisted by HERACLES in conquering his enemies.

Mariandynus *see* **Idaea**.

Marmara *or* **Marmora, Sea of** (ancient Propontis) the sea separating Asia Minor from Europe. It communicates with the BLACK SEA by the BOSPORUS, and with the AEGEAN and Mediterranean by the Dardanelles (HELLESPONT).

Marpessa *see* **Idas and Lynceus**.

Mars in Roman mythology, the god of war and of husbandry, at an early period identified with the Greek ARES, a deity of similar attributes. Like JUPITER, he was designated *Pater*, 'father', and was regarded in particular as the father of the Roman people, ROMULUS AND REMUS being the fruit of his union with RHEA SYLVIA. Several temples at ROME were dedicated to him, and the Campus Martius, where the Romans practised athletic and military exercises, was named in his honour. The month of March, the first month of the Roman year, was also named in his honour and was sacred to him. His service was celebrated not only by particular *flamines* devoted to him, but by the College of the Salii, or priests of MARS, who danced in complete armour. As the tutelary god of Rome he was called *Mars Quirinus*, and for his special care of Roman citizens he was called *Quirites*. In his character as the god of war he was called *Gradivus* (the striding) and as the rustic god *Silvanus*. The wolf and the woodpecker were sacred to him.

Mecisteus in Greek mythology, one of the SEVEN AGAINST THEBES, who is said to have won the contests at OEDIPUS's funeral games.

Meda *see* **Idomeneus**.

Medea *or* **Medeia** in Greek mythology, daughter of AEËTES, king of COLCHIS, and of the OCEANID Idyia, or of HECATE. When JASON, the leader of the ARGONAUTS, came to Colchis in search of the GOLDEN FLEECE, she fell in love with the young hero, helped him to obtain the fleece, and fled with him. She prevented her father from pursuing by killing her brother ABSYRTUS and strewing the sea with his limbs. She avenged her husband on the aged PELEUS by persuading his daughters to cut him in pieces and boil him in order to make him young again. Medea lived with Jason for ten years, until he discarded her in favour of GLAUCE (or Creüsa), daughter of CREON, king of CORINTH. In revenge she sent Glauce a bridal robe which enveloped her in consuming flame, and thereafter she slew her own children by Jason. She fled to Athens in a chariot drawn by dragons, which she obtained from HELIOS. There she was received by AEGEUS, to whom she bore Medos, but afterwards being compelled to flee from Athens, she took Medos to Aria, the inhabitants of which were thenceforth called Medes. She finally became immortal and married ACHILLES in ELYSIUM. The story of Medea was a favourite theme of ancient tragedians, but only Euripides's masterpiece is extant.

Medon *see* **Electra** (1).

Medos *see* **Medea**.

Medusa *see* **Gorgons**.

Megaera in Greek mythology, one of the three FURIES, the others being Alecto and Tisiphone.

Megapenthes (1) in Greek mythology, a son of PROËTUS, king of ARGOS. He exchanged his dominion for that of PERSEUS so that the latter received TIRYNS instead of Argos. He is said to have afterwards killed Perseus.

Megapenthes (2) in Greek mythology, son of MENELAÜS by an Aetolian slave, Pieris or Teridae. Menelaüs brought about a marriage between Megapenthes and a daughter of ALECTOR. According to one tradition, after the death of his father Megapenthes expelled HELEN from ARGOS and she fled to Polyxo at RHODES.

Megara the principal city on the Isthmus of CORINTH, so called because of the *megaras*, or shrines, that Car, son of PHORONEUS and the founder of Megara, built to DEMETER. Twelve generations later, Lelex came from Egypt and gave the inhabitants the name of LELEGIANS. Lelex was succeeded by his son Cleson, and he by his son PYLAS, whose son SCEIRON (2) married the daughter of PANDION (2), king of ATHENS. But NISUS, the son of Pandion, disputing with Sceiron the possession of Megara, AEACUS, who had been called in as arbiter, assigned the kingdom to Nisus and to Sceiron the command in war. Megarian tradition suppresses an account of a capture of the city during the reign of Nisus by MINOS. According to Boeotian tradition, in the reign of Pylas, Pandion being expelled from Athens by the METIONIDAE, fled to Megara, married the daughter of Pylas and succeeded his father-in-law. When the Metionidae were driven out of Athens and the dominions of Pandion were divided among his four sons, Nisus, the youngest, obtained Megara, and the city was called Nisa after him. When Minos attacked Nisus, MEGAREUS, son of POSEIDON, came from ONCHESTUS in BOEOTIA to assist Nisus and was buried in the city, which was called Megara after him. Through the treachery of his daughter SCYLLA, Nisus perished, and Minos obtained possession of the city and demolished its walls. They were subsequently restored by ALCATHOUS, son of PELOPS, who came from ELIS. In this work he was assisted by APOLLO. It was further related that Hyperion (2), the son of AGAMEMNON, was the last king of Megara and that after his death a democratic form of government was established.

Megareus in Greek mythology, a son of Onchestus (1) or of POSEIDON, Hippomenes, APOLLO or AEGEUS by Oenope. He was a brother of Abrote, the wife of NISUS. According to a Boeotian tradition, Megareus with his army went to the assistance of Nisus, king of MEGARA, against MINOS, but he fell in battle and was buried at Megara which was called after him for its previous name had been Nisa. According to a Megarian tradition, which discarded the account of an expedition of Minos against Megara, Megareus was the husband of Iphinoë, the daughter of Nisus, and succeeded his father-in-law. His two sons died before him so he left Megara to ALCATHOUS.

Megaris a small mountainous state of ancient Greece, between ATTICA and the Isthmus of Corinth. Its capital was MEGARA.

Melampus in Greek mythology, one of the great seers. He is said to have been able to understand the language of birds and animals. He was devoted to his brother BIAS. He cured IPHICLUS of impotence in return for a herd of cattle belonging to the young man's father, Phylacus. NELEUS, the father of Pero (1), whom Bias wanted to marry, was demanding the cattle in exchange for his daughter's hand in marriage.

Melanion *see* **Atalanta**.

Melanippus in Greek mythology, a Theban champion in the war against ARGOS. He killed two of the SEVEN AGAINST THEBES.

Melantheus *or* **Melanthius** in Greek mythology, son of Dolius and the chief goatherd of Odysseus, who sided with the suitors of Penelope even after his master returned. He was mutilated and left to die as a punishment for his treachery.

Meleager the son of Oeneus, king of Calydon and Althaea. He distinguished himself in the Argonauts' expedition and more particularly at the Calydonian Boar hunt, where he killed the Boar and gave its skin as the highest token of his regard for Atalanta. During the hunt he quarrelled with some of his uncles, and as a result his mother brought about his death.

Melia in Greek mythology, a nymph, a daughter of Oceanus, who became by Inachus the mother of Phoroneus and Aegialeus (2) or Pegeus. By Seilenus she became the mother of the Centaur Pholus and by Poseidon of Amycus. She was carried off by Apollo and became by him the mother of Ismenius and of the seer Tenerus.

Meliae in Greek mythology, nymphs of the manna ash trees, who were said to have sprung from the blood of the castrated Uranus.

Melisseus in Greek mythology, an ancient king of Crete who, by Amalthea, became the father of the nymphs Adrasteia and Ida, to whom Rhea entrusted the infant Zeus to be brought up.

Melpomene in Greek mythology, the Muse who presides over tragedy, daughter of Zeus and Mnemosyne. She is generally represented as a young woman, with vine leaves surrounding her head and holding in her hand a tragic mask.

Membliarus *see* **Anaphe**.

Memnon in Greek mythology, a hero mentioned in the Homeric poems as the beautiful son of Eos (the morning), and in the post-Homeric accounts as the son of Tithonus and step-nephew of Priam, whom he assisted at the siege of Troy. He slew Antilochus, but was himself slain by Achilles. His mother was filled with grief at his death, which Zeus endeavoured to soothe by making her son immortal. The name of Memnon was afterwards connected with Egypt, and was attached to a statue still standing at Thebes, being one of the two known from their size as 'the Colossi'. This statue, known as 'the vocal Memnon', was celebrated in antiquity as emitting a sound every morning at the rising of the sun, which was perceived as the voice of Memnon hailing the newly risen Eos. The sound was perhaps contrived by the priests, although some think it was owing to expansion caused by heat. Both statues seem originally to have been about 70 feet high.

Memphis in Egyptian mythology, daughter of the god Nile who married Epaphus who founded the city of Memphis which he named after his wife.

Memphis the ancient city of Egypt, on the left bank of the Nile, at the apex of the Delta, in Greek mythology, said to have been founded by Epaphus and named after Memphis.

Menelaüs in Greek mythology, a son of Atreus and Aerope, younger brother of Agamemnon and husband of the beautiful Helen, with whom he received the kingdom of Sparta or Lacedaemon. His wife having been abducted by Paris, son of Priam, king of Troy, he summoned the Greek princes to avenge the affront and himself led sixty ships to the siege of Troy. After its conquest he returned with Helen to his native land in a roundabout voyage which led him to Cypria, Phoenicia, Egypt, and Libya during a period of eight years.

Menestheus in Greek mythology, a king of Athens held to be the first demagogue according to some legends. He roused the people of Athens against the king of the time, Theseus, who was then detained in Hades. He is said to have encouraged Castor and Pollux, brothers of Helen, to invade Athens to take back their sister. This they did and put Menestheus on the throne before going away. He was one of the Greek leaders in the wooden horse at Troy. There is dispute about his later fate.

Menoeceus (1) in Greek mythology, a Theban grandson of Pentheus and father of Hipponome, Jocasta and Creon.

Menoeceus (2) in Greek mythology, a grandson of Menoeceus (1) and son of Creon. In the war of the Seven against Thebes, Teiresias declared that the Thebans would conquer if Menoeceus would sacrifice himself for his country. Menoeceus accordingly killed himself outside the gates of Thebes.

Menoetius in Greek mythology, a son of Iapetus and Clymene (1) or Asia, and a brother of Atlas, Prometheus and Epimetheus. He was killed by Zeus with a flash of lightning in the fight of the Titans and thrown into Tartarus.

Mercury in Roman mythology, the name of a god, identified in later times with the Greek Hermes. In representing Hermes he was regarded as the son of Jupiter and Maia, and was looked upon as the god of eloquence, of commerce, and of robbers. He was also the messenger, herald and ambassador of Jupiter. As a Roman god he was merely the patron of commerce and gain.

Mermerus in Greek mythology, a son of Jason and Medea, killed by his mother.

Merope (1) in Greek mythology, a daughter of Atlas, one of the Pleiades and the wife of Sisyphus of Corinth, by whom she became the mother of Glaucus (3). In the constellation of the Pleiades she is the seventh and the least visible star because she is ashamed of having had intercourse with a mortal man.

Merope (2) in Greek mythology, a daughter of Oenopion in Chios. She was loved by Orion, who was in consequence blinded by her father.

Merope (3) *see* **Periboea**.

Messenia an ancient state of Greece located in the southern part of the Peloponnesus. Its capital was Messene. Its earliest inhabitants are said to have been Lelegians but after five generations Aeolians came there under Perieres, a son of Aeolus, who was succeeded by his son Aphareus.

Messina, Strait of the channel separating Italy from Sicily, and connecting the

Tyrrhenian with the Ionian Sea. It is deep and the current is strong, and it is almost certain that SCYLLA AND CHARYBDIS were situated here.

Mestor *see* **Electryon**.

metamorphosis any marked change of form, shape, or structure. In ancient mythology the term is applied to the frequent transformations of human beings into beasts, stones, trees, fire, water, etc.

Metaneira in Greek mythology, the wife of CELEUS and mother of TRIPTOLEMUS, who received DEMETER on her arrival in ATTICA.

metempsychosis *or* **reincarnation** the belief that the souls of the dead are reborn in the bodies of other men or animals. In Greek mythology, it was a feature of the worship of DIONYSUS and ORPHEUS. Mentions of it in Roman mythology are all from Greek sources.

Metionidae in Greek mythology, the sons of Metion, a son of ERECHTHEUS and Praxithea and husband of Alcippe. They expelled their cousin PANDION (2) from his kindgom of ATHENS but were themselves afterwards expelled by the sons of Pandion.

Metis in Greek mythology, the personification of prudence, described as a daughter of OCEANUS and THETYS. At the instigation of ZEUS, she gave CHRONOS the emetic that caused him to vomit up his children. She was the first love and wife of Zeus, from whom she had at first endeavoured to withdraw by metamorphosing herself in various ways. She prophesied to him that she would give birth first to a girl and afterwards to a boy, to whom the rule of the world was destined by fate. For this reason Zeus devoured her when she was pregnant with ATHENA and afterwards he himself gave birth to his daughter, who issued from his head.

Metope *see* **Echetus**.

Midas in Greek mythology, the son of GORDIUS and CYBELE, pupil of ORPHEUS and king of PHRYGIA, whose request that whatsoever he touched should turn to gold was granted by DIONYSUS. In this way even his food became gold, and it was not until he had bathed in the Pactolus that the fatal gift was transferred to the river. Another legend is that, in a musical contest between PAN and APOLLO on the flute and the lyre, Midas, who was umpire, decided in favour of the former, whereupon the angry Apollo bestowed upon the presumptuous critic a pair of ass's ears. He hid the deformity under his Phrygian cap, but could not hide it from his barber, who felt the burden of the secret he could not reveal so heavily that he dug a hole in the ground and whispered into it, 'King Midas has ass's ears'. He then filled up the hole and his heart was lightened, but out of the ground sprang a reed which whispered the shameful secret to the breeze.

Midea *see* **Electryon**.

Miletus in Greek mythology, a son of APOLLO and Areia of CRETE. Being loved by MINOS and SARPEDON (1), he attached himself to the latter and fled from

Minos to Caria in Asia Minor where he built a town which he called after his own name.

Miletus an ancient city of Caria, Asia Minor, situated near the mouth of the MAEANDER, one of the chief Greek cities of Asia Minor. Its earliest inhabitants were either Carians, or LELEGIANS who were later augmented by Cretan settlers introduced by SARPEDON (1).

Milky Way known to the Greeks as *galaxias kyklos*, 'milky circle'. The name is said to have been derived from a myth in which HERA, furious at being tricked into suckling HERACLES, who was not her child, tore her breast from the infant's mouth and her milk squirted across the sky.

Minerva in Roman mythology, a daughter of JUPITER, and one of the great divinities of ancient Rome. She was looked upon as the patroness of all arts and trades, and her annual festival, called Quinquatrus, lasted from the 19th to the 23rd of March inclusive. This goddess was believed to protect warriors in battle, and to her was ascribed the invention of numbers and of musical instruments, especially wind instruments. At Rome a temple was built for Minerva by Tarquin on the Capital, where she was worshipped along with Jupiter and JUNO; and there was also a temple of the Aventine dedicated to herself alone. This deity is supposed to be of Etruscan origin, and her character has much in common with the Greek goddess ATHENA.

Minos in Greek mythology, a ruler of CRETE, said to have been the son of ZEUS and EUROPA, and a brother of RHADAMANTHUS and SARPEDON (1). He was father by PASIPHAË of DEUCALION, ARIADNE and several others. During his lifetime he was celebrated as a wise lawgiver and a strict lover of justice, and after his death he was made, with AEACUS and Rhadamanthus, one of the judges of the internal world. The story evidently contains reminiscences of Cretan supremacy in the Aegean. This theory is supported by recent discoveries, which tend to prove the existence of a powerful kingdom of CRETE during the Mycenaean Age.

Minotaur in Greek mythology, the offspring of PASIPHAË and the CRETAN BULL, for which she had conceived a passion through the contrivance of POSEIDON. The queen placed herself in an artificial cow made by DAEDALUS, and so became the mother of a monster said to to have had the body of a man with the head of a bull. It fed on human flesh, on which account MINOS, husband of Pasiphaë, shut him up in the labyrinth of Daedalus, and there fed him at first with criminals, but afterwards with youths and maidens yearly sent from Athens as a tribute. The Minotaur was slain by THESEUS with the help of ARIADNE.

Minyans *or* **Minyae** in Greek mythology, an ancient race of heroes at ORCHOMENUS (2), Iolcus and other places. Their ancestral hero, Minyas, is said to have migrated from THESSALY in the northern parts of Boeotia and there to have established the powerful race of Minyans with the capital of

Orchomenus. The greater part of the ARGONAUTS were descended from Minyans, and the descendants of the Argonauts founded a colony in LEMNOS which was called Minyae.

Mnemosyne in Greek mythology, daughter of URANUS and GE, and by ZEUS the mother of the nine MUSES.

Moirai the Roman name for the FATES.

moly in Greek mythology, a magical herb given by HERMES to ODYSSEUS, which he used as an antidote to the charms of CIRCE.

moon in classical mythology, the moon is seen as a goddess while the sun is a god. SELENE, LUNA and DIANA are goddesses of the moon.

Mopsus *see* **Calchas**.

Moros *see* **Ker**; **Nyx**.

Morpheus in Roman mythology, the son of sleep and the god of dreams. He is so named because he shapes or moulds the dreams that visit the sleeper. He is represented as an old man with wings, pouring sleep-inducing vapour out of a horn.

Mother Deity *see* **Cybele**.

Mother of the Gods *see* **Rhea**.

Muses in Greek mythology, the daughters of ZEUS and MNEMOSYNE, who were, according to the earliest writers, the inspiring goddesses of song, and according to later ideas divinities presiding over the different kinds of poetry, and over the sciences and arts. Their original number appears to have been three, but afterwards they are always spoken of as nine: CLIO, the muse of history; EUTERPE, the muse of lyric poetry; Thaleia, the muse of comedy and of merry or idyllic poetry; MELPOMENE, the muse of tragedy; Terpsichore, the muse of choral dance and song; ERATO, the muse of erotic poetry and mimicry; Polymnia or Polyhymnia, the muse of the sublime hymn; URANIA, the muse of astronomy; and CALLIOPE, the muse of epic poetry. They were first honoured amongst the Thracians, and as Pieria around OLYMPUS was the original seat of that people, it came to be considered as their native country and they were therefore called Pierides. They are often represented as the companions of APOLLO and as singing while he played on the lyre at the banquets of the Immortals. Various legends ascribed to them victories in musical competitions, particularly over the SIRENS. Among the places sacred to them were the fountains of AGANIPPE and HIPPOCRENE on Mount HELICON, and CASTALIA on Mount PARNASSUS.

Mycenae a very ancient city of ARGOLIS, built on a craggy height in the Peloponnesus. It is said to have been founded by PERSEUS, and before the TROJAN WAR to have been the residence of AGAMEMNON, in whose reign it was regarded as the leading city in Greece. It was destroyed by the inhabitants of Argos about 468 BC and never again rose to its former prosperity. Its ruins are extremely interesting for their antiquity and grandeur. Among them are the Lion Gate, the vaulted beehive tomb called the Treasury of Atreus, the city wall and a great rambling palace.

Mycene in Greek mythology, a daughter of INACHUS and wife of Arestor from whom MYCENAE was believed to have derived its name.

Myrmidons *or* **Myrmidones** an ancient Greek people of THESSALY, who accompanied ACHILLES to the TROJAN WAR. They are said to have emigrated into Thessaly under the leadership of PELEUS and to have colonized the island of AEGINA. ZEUS peopled Thessaly by transforming the ants into men (in Greek, *myrmix* means 'ant'). The term has come to signify the followers of a daring and unscrupulous leader, or the harsh and unfeeling agents of a tyrannical power.

Mysia in ancient geography, a country in the extreme northeasterly corner of Asia Minor, on the modern Aegean, HELLESPONT and Sea of MARMORA. The Mysi were a Thracian people who migrated into Asia. The TROAD was one of the subdivisions of Mysia.

Mysteries certain rites and ceremonies of ancient Greece and Rome, known only to, and practised by, congregations of certain initiated people at appointed times and in strict seclusion. The most important Mysteries were the ELEUSINIAN and Themsophorian, both representing, each from a different point of view, the rape of PERSEPHONE and DEMETER's search for her. In addition there were those of ZEUS of CRETE, of BACCHUS, CYBELE and APHRODITE, the two latter to do with procreation but celebrated in diametrically opposed ways, the former culminating in self-mutilation of the worshippers, the latter in prostitution. There were also the Mysteries of ORPHEUS, who was considered the founder of all Mysteries, and of other gods and goddesses, like HERA, MINERVA, DIANA and HECATE. Towards the end of the classical periods, the mysteries became public orgies and eventually were banned

N

naïads in classical mythology, the NYMPHS of fresh water, i.e. lakes, fountains, rivers and streams, as opposed to NEREIDS, nymphs of the sea, and OCEANIDS, nymphs of the ocean, i.e. the boundary round the world.

Nais *or* **Chariclo** *see* **Chiron.**

Narcissus in Greek mythology, the son of the NYMPH Leirope by the river-god CEPHISSUS. The young Narcissus was extremely handsome but was excessively vain and self-centred. ECHO pined away to a mere voice because her love for him went unrequited. NEMESIS determined to punish him for his coldness of heart, and caused him to drink at a certain fountain in which he saw his own image. He was so taken with his own beauty and fell so much in love with himself that he pined away because he was unabe to embrace himself. The gods transformed him into the flower which still bears his name. His name lives on on English in the word 'narcissistic', meaning full of self-love.

Nasamon in Greek mythology, a son of the Cretan Amphithemis and the NYMPH of Lake Tritonis, who gave his name to a Libyan tribe, the Nasamonians.

Naubolis *see* **Iphitus** (2).

Naupactus a port at the entrance to the Gulf of ARGOLIS from which the HERACLIDS embarked on their invasion of the PELOPONNESUS.

Nauplia a seaport near the head of the Gulf of ARGOLIS, home of NAUPLIUS (1), who founded the city. It was the port and arsenal of Argos.

Nauplius (1) in Greek mythology, a son of POSEIDON and Amymone, a native of ARGOS and reputed founder of NAUPLIA. He was a famous navigator who was said to deal in slave trafficking and he was said to have discovered the constellation of URSA MAJOR.

Nauplius (2) in Greek mythology, a son of Clytoneus and a descendant of the navigator NAUPLIUS (1), and an ARGONAUT. Nauplius was an Argivi who offered to steer the *Argo* after the death of TIPHYS. He is liable to be confused with his ancestor.

Nauplius (3) a king of EUBOEA. He was asked by King Aleus of TEGEA either to drown or sell his daughter Auge after she had been seduced by HERACLES. He sold her to TEUTHRAS, king of Teuthrania. He was asked by King Catreus of CRETE to perform a similar function and sell his daughters Aerope and CLYMENE (3) in view of the fact that he had been warned by an ORACLE that he would be killed by one of his children. Although Nauplius carried out his instructions with regard to Aerope and sold her to ATREUS or Pleisthenes, he elected to marry Clymene himself. Clymene bore him three sons, Palamedes, OEAX and Nausimedon. Nauplius was also involved in avenging the death of Palamedes when he was stoned to death by the Greeks at Troy. He sailed to each of the Greek cities and persuaded the wives of the Greek leaders – CLYTEMNESTRA, MEDA, and the wife of DIOMEDES (2) – to commit adultery. He also lit a fire on the Euboean Cape of Caphareus to induce the captains of the Greek ships to make for there when they were caught in a storm. Many of the ships were wrecked, with considerable loss of life. Those Greeks who reached the shore safely were killed by Nauplius.

Nausicaä in Greek mythology, daughter of ALCINOUS and Arete. When ODYSSEUS was shipwrecked he asked her help, and she told him how to get the assistance of her parents. Her father suggested to Odysseus that he marry her but he refused because he was married already.

Nausimedon *see* **Nauplius** (3).

Nausithoüs in Greek mythology, son of Poseidon and Periboea and king of the Phaecians. His people were lovers of peace and disliked being harassed by their neighbours, the Cyclops. So that they could obtain peace Nausithous took them to the faraway island of Scherie or Drepane, usually identified with Corcyra (Corfu). He helped the son of Heracles, Hyllus, to found his own city. Nausithous had two sons, Alcinous and Rhexenor, and Alcinous succeeded to the throne on the death of Nausithoüs.

Naxos the largest and most important island of the Cyclades group, in the Aegean Sea midway between the coasts of Greece and Asia Minor. In ancient times it was also called Strongyle and Dia. The wine of Naxos was famous, and on this account the island was celebrated in the legends of Dionysus, and especially in those relating to Ariadne.

Neaera in Greek mythology, a nymph and the mother of Lampetia and Phoethusa by Helios.

Neleus in Greek mythology, a king of Pylus. He was the son of Tyro by Poseidon and had a brother, Pelias. Tyro wanted rid of the boys as she was about to marry Cretheus, king of Iolcus. She left them to die of exposure, but they were found by horsemen and brought up by them. When they discovered who they really were, they sought out their stepmother, Sidero, who had treated Tyro badly, and Pelias killed her. Later Neleus and Pelias quarrelled, and Neleus was driven out of Iolcus by his brother. He went to Messenia, which was ruled by his cousin Aphareus, who gave him some of the coastal territory to rule. This territory included the city of Pylus. The founder of the city was still living there, but Neleus banished him and made Pylus his own capital. The city and Neleus prospered, and he became a powerful ruler. He married Chloris, daughter of Amphion, who bore him a daughter, Pero, and twelve sons, of whom three were Nestor, Chromius and Periclymenus. Neleus insisted that his daughter marry a man who would bring her the cattle of Iphiclus from Phylace in Thessaly. The brother of Bias, the seer Melampus, brought the cattle and thus won Pero (2) for Bias. Neleus had seized the property of Melampus when he was away getting the cattle, and this he now had to return. Meanwhile Heracles had killed Iphitus and went to Neleus to be purified of his crime. Because he was a friend of Iphitus's father, Neleus refused. Afterwards Heracles conquered Pylus and killed Neleus, his wife and eleven of his sons. Nestor escaped death because he was away at the time, and he succeeded to the throne.

Nemea a city in northern Argolis. When the forces of the Seven against Thebes were passing through Nemea and accidentally contributed to the death of the infant Opheltes, they instituted the Nemean Games in his honour. The Nemean Lion roamed the area round the city until it was killed by Heracles.

Nemean Games ancient Greek games held in the valley of NEMEA in Argolis, where HERACLES is said to have killed the NEMEAN LION. They recurred ordinarily every second year, and were similar in character to the other Greek games. They were instituted in honour of the infant OPHELTES by the SEVEN AGAINST THEBES. The victors received crowns of parsley in memory of the bed of parsley that Opheltes had lain on.

Nemean Lion in Greek mythology, a monster which was the offspring of ECHNIDA and TYPHON. Some legends say that it was suckled by SELENE, the moon goddess, and others that it was nursed by HERA. It was killed by HERACLES as the first of his labours, and he then wore its skin. Hera immortalized the lion in a constellation.

Nemesis in Greek mythology, the personification of the righteous anger of the gods, the goddess of retribution for evil deeds or undeserved good fortune. The goddess was said to be a daughter of NYX (night). According to one legend ZEUS fell in love with Nemesis. She rejected his advances and assumed various shapes in order to avoid him. When she became a goose Zeus became a swan and raped her.

Neoptolemus *or* **Pyrrhus** in Greek mythology, a son of ACHILLES by Deidameia. Achilles was brought up at the court of LYCOMEDES, king of the Aegean island of SCYRUS, because his mother, THETIS, wanted to keep him away from the TROJAN WAR. He had an affair with the daughter of Lycomedes, DEÏDAMEIA, who bore him a son named Pyrrhus. After the death of Achilles in the Trojan conflict, the Greeks were informed by the seer HELENUS, whom they had captured at Troy, that the city of Troy would not be taken unless three conditions were fulfilled. These were that the bones of PELOPS must be brought to Troy, that PHILOCTETES, who owned the bow and arrows that had been the property of HERACLES, must fight on the Greek side against Troy, and that the son of Achilles must also fight on the Greek side. ODYSSEUS and PHOENIX came to Scyrus to take Pyrrhus to Troy and gave him the armour of Achilles. Pyrrhus fought bravely in the Trojan War and was one of the Greeks who hid in the WOODEN HORSE. He killed PRIAM, king of Troy, and when the ghost of his father asked for the blood of Priam's daughter, he sacrificed her on his father's grave. When the Trojan captives were distributed, ANDROMACHE, the widow of Hector, was given to Neoptolemus, as by this time Pyrrhus was more commonly called, meaning literally 'young soldier'. By Andromache he became the father of several sons. Legends disagree about what happened to Neoptolemus after the Trojan War. Some indicate that he reached home safely unharmed, others that Thetis saved him from the storms that destroyed many of the Greek ships on their homeward journey, and others that he travelled home by land in response to a warning from Thetis. Some legends say that he did not return to Phthia, his father's homeland, but that he conquered EPIRUS and ruled there.

Nephele in Greek mythology, the first wife of ATHAMAS, king of Boeotian ORCHOMENUS (2), who bore him a son, PHRIXUS, and a daughter, HELLE. Athamas took a second wife who plotted for the downfall of Phrixus. She persuaded Athamas to sacrifice his son, but Nephele took a miraculous ram that had been given to her as a present by HERMES, and the two children flew away on the ram's back, the GOLDEN FLEECE.

Neptune in Roman mythology, the chief sea-god. When the Greek mythology was introduced into Rome, he was completely identified with the Greek POSEIDON, all the traditions relating to whom were transferred by the Romans to their own deity. In art he is usually represented as an old man with copious hair and a beard, and armed with a trident. The horse and the dolphin are his symbols.

Nereïds *or* **Nereïdes** in mythology, sea-NYMPHS, daughters of NEREUS and Doris, daughter of OCEANUS and TETHYS, and constant attendants on POSEIDON or NEPTUNE. Fifty in number, they are represented as riding on sea-horses, sometimes in human form and sometimes with the tail of a fish. They were distinguished on the one hand from the NAÏADS, the nymphs of fresh water, and on the other from the OCEANIDES, the nymphs of the ocean.

Nereus in Greek mythology, a sea-god, the father of the NEREÏDS. He was the son of PONTUS (Sea) and GE (Earth). In the ancient works of art, and also by the ancient poets, he is represented as an old man, with a wreath of sedge, sitting upon the waves with a sceptre in his hand.

Nessus in Greek mythology, a CENTAUR who was driven from ARCADIA by HERACLES. He set up as a ferryman on the Aetolian River Evenus. DEÏANEIRA, the bride of Heracles, was taken by Nessus in his ferry while he left Heracles to struggle across the water alone. When Nessus tried to rape the girl, Heracles shot him. When he lay dying he cunningly persuaded Deïaneira to make a love potion of his blood and semen. He knew, although she did not, that his blood contained HYDRA venom from the arrow with which Heracles had shot him. It was this potion that later caused the death of Heracles.

Nestor in Greek mythology, one of the Greek heroes at TROY, son of NELEUS, king of Pylos, and Chloris. He escaped destruction when HERACLES slew all his brothers, and married Eurydice (5), by whom he became the father of a numerous family. In his youth he was distinguished for valour, taking part in wars with the Arcadians and the CENTAURS, in the hunting of the CALYDONIAN BOAR and in the ARGONAUTS' expedition, and in his advanced age for wisdom. Although he was an old man when the expedition against Troy was undertaken, he joined it with sixty ships. He is noted as the wisest adviser of the chiefs at Troy, after the fall of which he retired to Pylos, where he lived to a great age.

Nicostratus in Greek mythology, a son of MENELAÜS and either HELEN or a slave girl. He and his brother, MEGAPENTHES, in some legends were responsible for banishing Helen from SPARTA after the death of their father. Neither of them inherited their father's throne. Instead ORESTES' claim was recognized.

Nike in Greek mythology, the goddess of victory, the daughter of STYX and PALLAS (1). In Roman mythology she is called VICTORIA. She was rewarded by ZEUS with permission to live in OLYMPUS for readily coming to his assistance in the war with the TITANS. Her brothers were CRATOS, BIA and ZELUS. There is a temple to her on the Acropolis of Athens. She is represented as resembling ATHENA but has wings and carries a palm or wreath and is engaged in raising a trophy or in inscribing the victory of the conqueror on a shield.

Niobe (1) in Greek mythology, the daughter of TANTALUS (1), king of LYDIA, and wife of AMPHION, king of THEBES. Proud of her numerous progeny, she provoked the anger of APOLLO and ARTEMIS by boasting to their mother LETO, who had no other children but those two. She was punished by having all her children put to death by those two deities. She herself was metamorphosed by ZEUS into a stone (on Mount Sipylus, Asia Minor) which shed tears during the summer. This fable has afforded a subject for art.

Niobe (2) in Greek mythology, a daughter of PHORONEUS and the NYMPH Teledice or Cinna, and the first mortal lover of ZEUS. By Zeus she bore ARGUS and, according to some legends, PELASGUS.

Nisus *or* **Nysus** in Greek mythology, a king of MEGARA and a son of ARES or of Deion or of PANDION (3), the king of ATHENS who became king of Megara. PALLAS (3) and LYCUS (3) were his brothers and AEGEUS his half-brother. All three brothers assisted their half-brother to regain the kingdom of Athens from which their father had been driven. The right of Nisus to the throne of Megara was disputed by SCEIRON (2), the son of Pandion's predecessor. AEACUS was asked to arbitrate and decided in favour of Nisus. MINOS of CRETE attacked the city of Megara, and SCYLLA, a daughter of Nisus who had fallen in love with him, helped him. Nisus had been given a warning that his life depended on his retaining a single red lock in the middle of his forehead. Scylla cut it off while her father slept, but Minos showed her no gratitude. Legends differ as to whether Minos drowned her or whether she drowned herself. Nisus on his death was turned into an osprey.

Notus in Greek mythology, the south wind, said to have been a son of EOS and Astraeus and a brother of BOREAS and ZEPHYRUS, although, unlike his brothers, he was rarely personified or referred to as a god.

Numa Pompilius in the legendary history of ROME, its second king. He was of Sabine origin and was universally revered for his wisdom and piety. Unanimously elected king by the Roman people, he soon justified by his conduct the wisdom of their choice. After dividing the lands that ROMULUS had conquered, he proceeded, with the assistance of the nymph EGERIA, who gave him interviews in a grove near the city, to draw up religious institutions for his subjects.

His reign lasted for thirty-nine years and was a golden age of peace and happiness.

Numitor in the legendary history of Rome, a king of ALBA Longa. When he was deposed by his brother, AMULIUS, he was restored to the throne with the help of ROMULUS AND REMUS.

Nycteïs *see* **Nycteus**; **Polydorus**.

Nycteus in Greek mythology, a king of THEBES, and brother of LYCUS. They were the sons of Chthonius, one of the SPARTI, or of Hyrieus by the NYMPH Clonia, or of POSEIDON by the Pleiad Celaeno. They were brought up in EUBOEA but had to flee from there when they killed PHLEGYAS, king of Orchomenus (1). They were made citizens of Thebes because they were friendly with King PENTHEUS. The successor of Pentheus, POLYDORUS, married Nycteis, daughter of Nycteus. She bore him a son, LABDACUS, but Polydorus died before the child grew up, and Nycteus was made regent. Nycteus had another daughter, ANTIOPE (1). ZEUS was attracted by her beauty and seduced her in the guise of a SATYR. Antiope conceived a child by this union, and when her condition became obvious she fled from Thebes and went to SICYON, where she married King EPOPEUS. One legend has it that Nycteus committed suicide out of shame. Another has it that Epopeus seduced and abducted Antiope and that Nycteus marched against him, was wounded and went back home to die.

Nyctimene in Greek mythology, a daughter of Epopeus, king of LESBOS. She was raped by her father and hid in the woods becaused she was so ashamed. ATHENA felt sorry for her and turned her into an owl, which does not come out in daylight.

Nyctimus in Greek mythology, a king of ARCADIA. His forty-nine brothers were destroyed by ZEUS but he was saved by GE. He is assumed to have been killed in the flood sent by Zeus.

nymph in Greek mythology female divinities of inferior rank, inhabiting the sea, streams, groves, meadows and pastures, grottoes, fountains, hills, valleys and trees. Among them different classes were distinguished, particularly the OCEANIDS, daughters of OCEANUS (nymphs of the great ocean which flows around the earth), the NEREÏDS, daughters of NEREUS (nymphs of the inner depths of the sea, or of the Inner Sea, i.e. the Mediterranean), Potameides (river nymphs), NAÏADS (nymphs of fountains, lakes, brooks and wells), Oreads (mountain nymphs), Napoeoe (nymphs of valleys) and Dryads or Hamadryad (forest nymphs, who were believed to die with the trees in which they dwelt). They were imagined as beautiful maidens, not immortal, but always young, who were considered as tutelary spirits not only of certain localities, but also of certain races and families. They occur generally in connection with some other divinity of higher rank, and they were believed to be possessed of the gift of prophecy and of poetical inspiration.

Nysa the mountain on which DIONYSUS was reared by NYMPHS, of uncertain location.

Nysus *see* **Nisus**.

Nyx in Greek mythology, night and the goddess of night, called Nox by the Romans. She was born out of CHAOS together with EREBUS (darkness), GE (earth), TARTARUS, and EROS (love). By Erebus she is the mother of Aether (upper air) and HEMERA (day). Without a mate she spawned Moros (doom), THANATOS (death), HYPNOS (sleep), the FATES and NEMESIS. She saved her son Hypnos when ZEUS was going to expel him from OLYMPUS.

O

Oceanids *or* **Oceanides** *see* **nymphs**; **Oceanus**.

Oceanus in Greek mythology, the eldest of the TITANS, regarded as the god of the ocean. The god Oceanus married his sister TETHYS and by her became father of all river-gods and of the three thousand Oceanids or ocean NYMPHS. He and Tethys also reared the goddess HERA, the daughter of their sister RHEA. Oceanus did not join his brother Titans in opposing ZEUS when he usurped URANUS. Oceanus was also the river that issued from the Underworld and flowed in a circular stream around the earth. The Greeks considered the earth as a flat circle surrounded by a river (Oceanus). The term 'ocean' was thus applied specially to the Atlantic, in contradistinction to the Mediterranean Sea.

Ocnus in Greek mythology, one of the damned in HADES. His punishment was continually to plait a rope of straw that was eaten by a she-ass as rapidly as Ocnus could plait it.

Ocypete *or* **Okypete** *see* **Harpies**.

Odius in Greek mythology, a Greek herald at the TROJAN WAR. He was part of the embassy that AGAMEMNON sent to placate ACHILLES.

Odysseus in Greek mythology, king of the island of ITHACA and one of the Greek heroes who engaged in the war against TROY. In Roman mythology he is called ULYSSES. In returning to his own country after the siege he had many adventures. He visited the country of the LOTUS-EATERS in North Africa, the CYCLOPS in Sicily (*see also* POLYPHEMUS), and the island of Aeolus, king of the winds. He also reached the island of AEAEA, where CIRCE changed (temporarily) his companions into swine; and visited the infernal regions, where he consulted the soothsayer TEIRESIAS on how to return to his country. He succeeded in passing in safety the coast of the SIRENS, and successfully negotiated the joint dangers of SCYLLA AND CHARYBDIS. He remained for seven years on OGYGIA with the nymph CALYPSO after losing all his men and at last, after an absence of twenty years, returned to Ithaca. Here he found his palace occupied and his property wasted by suitors for the hand of his wife PENELOPE, people having assumed that he, Odysseus, was dead. With the aid of his son, TELEMACHUS, he put them to death. He lived about sixteen years after his return. These adventures of Odysseus are the subject of Homer's *Odyssey*.

Odyssey *see* **Homer**.

Oeagrus in Greek mythology, a king of THRACE, the father of ORPHEUS and Linus by the Muse CALLIOPE.

Oeax in Greek mythology, son of NAUPLIUS (1) and Clymene, who hated the ARGIVES for their unjust execution of his brother Palamedes at Troy by stoning him. He may have been the cause of CLYTEMNESTRA plotting AGAMEMNON's death since he told her that Agamemnon was bringing home a Trojan concubine. Later he tried to persuade the Argives to banish ORESTES after he murdered his mother.

Oebalus in Greek mythology, a king of Sparta who was a son of Cynortas or of his son PERIERES. He married GORGOPHONE, widow of the Aeolid Perieres, and the daughter of PERSEUS. Either she or the NAÏAD bore him TYNDAREUS, HIPPOCOÖN and ICARIUS (1).

Oechalia an ancient Greek city whose location is uncertain.

Oedipus *or* **Oedipodes** in ancient Greek mythology, son of the Theban King LAÏUS and his queen JOCASTA. He was left to die of exposure on Mount Cithaeron as an infant with his feet pierced through—on account of an oracle saying that Laïus would be killed by his son—but he was saved by a shepherd, who named him Oedipus because of his swollen feet, and was brought up at the court of CORINTH by Periboea (2), wife of Polybus, king of Corinth. Believing Corinth to be his native land, he left his foster-parents because the Delphic ORACLE had advised him that he was destined to slay his father and commit incest with his mother. On his way to THEBES to escape his fate, he met on a narrow road in Phocis the chariot of King Laïus. The charioteer ordered him out of the way, and a quarrel ensued in which he unknowingly killed Laïus. In the meantime, the SPHINX had appeared near Thebes and was asking a riddle of everyone who passed by, putting to death all who failed to solve it. In despair, the Thebans offered the kingdom, together with the hand of the queen, to whoever should deliver them from the monster. Oedipus offered himself, whereupon the Sphinx asked, 'What creature alone changes the number of its feet? In the morning it goes on four feet, at midday on two, in the evening three feet. And with the fewest feet, it has ever the strength and swiftness.' Oedipus replied that it was man, at which the Sphinx threw herself headlong from the rock on which she sat. Having solved the riddle, Oedipus became king of Thebes and married his mother, Jocasta. She bore him two sons, ETEOCLES AND

POLYNEICES, and two daughters, ANTIGONE and ISMENE. According to legend a plague was sent to Thebes, and CREON, brother of Jocasta, was sent to the Delphic oracle to inquire its cause. He was told by the oracle that the plague had been sent because the murderer of Laïus was living unpunished in the city. An enquiry was launched by Oedipus, and the shepherd who had saved Oedipus when he was left to die as an infant gave evidence, as did the person who was with Laïus when he died. On realizing the truth and what he had done, Oedipus gouged out his own eyes, and Jocasta killed herself. The details of Oedipus's later life are uncertain. One legend has it that he was exiled and wandered for many years as an outcast, accompanied only by his daughter Antigone. Before leaving Thebes he is supposed to have cursed his sons.

Oeneus in Greek mythology, a king of CALYDON and a son of Porthaon (or Portheus) and Euryte. He married ALTHAEA, daughter of Thestius, by whom he had MELEAGER, GORGE, and other sons and daughters. Oeneus was a very generous ruler and welcomed guests, being noted for his hospitality. When DIONYSUS visited his court and Oeneus suspected that the god had designs on his wife, Althaea, he left the country for a time, supposedly to attend to some religious rituals and left Althaea alone with the god by whom she conceived DEÏANEIRA. Dionysus gave his host the gift of vine culture in recognition of his somewhat unusual hospitality. Oeneus gave HERACLES Deïaneira's hand in marriage, despite the fact that, while a guest of Oeneus, he had killed Cyathus or Eunomus, the young cup-bearer to the king, for some minor misdemeanour. Oeneus incurred the wrath of ARTEMIS by forgetting to ask her to a harvest festival. The goddess took revenge for this accidental insult by sending a giant boar which caused destruction to the crops and people of Calydon. Oeneus appealed to the bravest men from other cities to come and help him get rid of the boar. The CALYDONIAN BOAR hunt was organized under the leadership of Meleager and they succeeded in killing the boar. However, a quarrel arose which resulted in Meleager's death. After her son's death, Althaea killed herself, and Oeneus later married PERIBOEA (1), having conquered OLENUS, where her father, Hipponous, was king. Periboea bore him two sons, Olenias and TYDEUS, although some legends indicate that it was Gorge, his own daughter, who bore Tydeus by him. Tydeus was exiled from Calydon after he killed someone, and the sons of Agrius deposed Oeneus and threw him in prison. Tydeus returned and rescued his father, killed his enemies and took Oeneus back to Argos with him. The name Oeneus may be derived from the Greek word for wine (*oinos*) since Oeneus is said to have introduced vine-growing in Calydon.

Oenoë in Greek mythology, a water NYMPH who gave her name to the island of Oenoe. She bore Sicinus, after whom the island of that name (Zykinthos) was called.

Oenomaus in Greek mythology, a king of Pisa in ELIS and son of Alxior or Areas and Harpius or the Pleiad Asterope. He was the father of HIPPODAMIA and LEUCIPPUS (2). Legends differ as to the identity of his wife. Some say that he was married to Evarete, but others say that Asterope was his wife rather than his mother, as some legends claim. Oenomaus killed all of the suitors of Hippodamia until he himself was killed by PELOPS.

Oenone (1) in Greek mythology, NYMPH of Mount IDA and a daughter of the river-god of the River Cebren. She was skilled in the art of healing and learned the art of prophecy from RHEA. She was the wife of PARIS until he went to win the hand of HELEN. When Paris was severely wounded by PHILOCTETES, he went to Mount Ida to get Oenone to heal his wounds, but in view of his rejection of her for Helen she refused. She reversed her decision, but it was too late to save his life. She was extremely remorseful when he died and hanged herself.

Oenone (2) *or* **Oenopia** *see* **Aegina** (1).

Oenopion in Greek mythology, a son of DIONYSUS and ARIADNE and king of the island of CHIOS which was a wine-growing area. The island was colonized by Oenopion, who originally came from Crete. ORION, the giant, wanted to marry MEROPE (2), daughter of Oenopion, but her father kept putting off the wedding, and Orion raped her. In revenge, Oenopion blinded Orion and banished him. Later Orion's sight was restored, and he returned to the island. Anxious for Oenopon's safety, the people of Chios hid him in an underground chamber until Orion left the island,.

Oeonus in Greek mythology, a son of LICYMNIUS. When he was attacked by a dog belonging to the sons of HIPPOCOÖN, he threw a stone at it. In revenge they killed him. In turn his death was avenged by HERACLES, his cousin, who killed Hippocoön and all his sons.

Oeta, Mount a mountain range northeast of AETOLIA which HERACLES climbed to get to his funeral pyre when he was dying.

Ogyges *see* **Ogygus**.

Ogygia in Greek mythology, the name given by Homer in the *Odyssey* to the island inhabited by the nymph CALYPSO. He describes it as the central point or navel of the sea, far from all other lands. ODYSSEUS reached it after being borne at sea for eight days and nights after he had escaped from Charybdis (*see* SCYLLA AND CHARYBDIS), and that when he left it again he sailed for seventeen days and nights in an easterly direction until he came to the land of the PHAEACIANS.

Ogygus *or* **Ogyges** in Greek mythology, one of the kings of BOEOTIA and the ruler of the ECTENES, who inhabited the region of THEBES. His people are said to have died of the plague, and some legends indicate that he did also. Thebes was sometimes known as Ogygia.

Oicles in Greek mythology, king of ARCADIA, son of either Mantius or Agrianome and father of AMPHIARAUS.

Oileus in Greek mythology, son of Hodoedocus and Agrianome and one of the ARGONAUTS. He was loved by APOLLO. He was the father of AJAX THE LESS by Eriopis.

Okypete *or* **Ocypete** *see* **Harpies**.

Olenias *see* **Oeneus**.

Olenus a city on the Gulf of Patra of which DEXAMES was one of the kings. Olenus was conquered by OENEUS, king of CALYDON, when Hipponous (2) was king. Oeneus married PERIBOEA(1), daughter of Hipponous.

Olympia a locality in Greece, the scene of the OLYMPIC GAMES, a valley of the River ALPHEUS, lying in the middle portion of the ancient district of ELIS, in the western part of the PELOPONNESUS. As a national sanctuary of the Greeks, collected here were thousands of statues of the gods and of victors in the games, treasure-houses, temples, tombs, and treasures of Greek art.

Olympians in Greek mythology, the gods and goddesses who occupied OLYMPUS.

Olympic Games the great national athletic festivals of the ancient Greeks, so called from being held at OLYMPIA. In legend, they were founded by HERACLES in a celebration of a victory, but their existence is only clearly recorded from 776 BC, when they were established as a national festival, but their origin goes far back beyond that date. They were held every fifth year, or rather in the first month after the lapse of four years from the previous celebration, and lasted five days. In its early days the festival was one of local interest only, organized and taken part in by the Peloponnesians. Later other Greek states were attracted to the games, and the assembly became pan-Hellenic. Women were excluded even from being present, upon pain of death, although it is clear that this rule was not always strictly observed, for women are known to have taken part on some occasions, and to have received the victor's crown. Previous to the games all intending competitors had to spend ten months of severe training. The first day of the festival appears to have been devoted to the offering of sacrifices, and to the classing and arranging of the competitors by the judges, previously sworn to strict impartiality and to the rejection of bribes. On this day there were also contests for the trumpeters. The second day was allotted to boys, who contested in wrestling, boxing, and foot- and horse-racing. Their place was taken on the third day by men, who engaged in similar events. On the fourth day took place the pentathlon, or five-fold contest, the events of which included running, leaping, wrestling, throwing the discus, and throwing the spear. These were followed by horse- and chariot-races, with contests for the heralds. The proceedings terminated on the fifth day with further sacrifices, processions, banquets to the victors, and the presentation of the crowns. These last, the sole rewards, were of no intrinsic value, being merely wreaths of twigs gathered from a sacred olive tree believed to have been planted by

HERACLES—which grew in the Altis, but these simple prizes were greatly coveted, and winning them brought much honour.

Olympus the ancient name of several mountains or chains of mountains. The most famous of them was situated between and Macedonia, and was the highest mountain in ancient Greece, its eastern side fronting the sea. It was regarded as the chief abode of the gods, and the palace of ZEUS was supposed to stand on its broad summit. According to legend, it was formerly connected with OSSA but was separated from it by an earthquake, allowing a passage for the River Peneus through the narrow vale of TEMPE to the sea. The abode of the gods was later transferred to heaven.

Omphale in Greek mythology, a queen of LYDIA, a daughter of Iardanus. and mother of Lamus. She became queen of Lydia on marrying Tmolus, king of Lydia, and became queen in her own right on his death. Omphale bought HERACLES when he was sold into slavery. He was involved in many adventures while in her service. He destroyed a huge snake that was wreaking destruction in part of Lydia, he killed the outlaw Syleus and his daughter, and razed the city of the ITONI to the ground. Some legends indicate that Omphale forced him to wear womanish clothes during his servitude. After three years in slavery Heracles was freed by Omphale. According to some legends she married him.

omphalos a sacred stone at DELPHI supposed to mark the centre of the world.

Onca *or* **Onga** in mythology, a Phoenician goddess who was equated with the Greek goddess ATHENA. There was a shrine to Onca at THEBES, the worship of the Phoenician goddess having been brought to Greece by CADMUS.

Onchestus in Greek mythology, a son of POSEIDON and founder of the city of ONCHESTUS.

Onchestus a Boeotian city on Lake Copais. It was celebrated for its grove dedicated to POSEIDON. In this grove there was a fight which led to a long-drawn-out feud between Onchestus and THEBES, a feud which eventually led to the rise of Thebes and the decline of Onchestus. According to one legend, Hippomenes, son of MAGAREUS, a king of Onchestus, won the hand of ATALANTA.

Oncius *or* **Oncus** in Greek mythology, a son of APOLLO and a king of Thelpusa. He gave his horse, ARION, to HERACLES.

Opheltes in Greek mythology, a son of LYCURGUS (3), king of Nemea, and Amphithea or Eurydice (6). His father had been warned by an ORACLE not to put Opheltes on the ground before the child could walk. The child's nurse, HYPSIPYLE, was asked for directions by the SEVEN AGAINST THEBES, and when she was showing them the way to a spring she had to put Opheltes down. She did not lay him on the ground but on a thick bed of parsley. Nevertheless, harm came to the child. He was killed by the snake that guarded the spring. The Seven against Thebes buried Opheltes under the name of Archemorus, a name meaning 'beginning of doom', having been told by a seer, AMPHIARAUS, that the death of the child was the beginning of the path to their destruction. The NEMEAN GAMES were founded in honour of Opheltes by ADRASTUS.

Ophion in Greek mythology, an ancient god whom some legends indicate ruled OLYMPUS with the Oceanid EURYNOME before being defeated by CRONOS and falling into OCEANUS.

Ophiuchus (The Serpent-bearer) one of the ancient northern constellations, representing a man holding a serpent which is twined about him. Legends differ as to the origin of Ophiuchus. Some say it is HERACLES killing a Lydian snake for OMPHALE when he was her slave, others that it is AESCULAPIUS, who was usually depicted with a snake.

Opis *or* **Upis** in Greek mythology, perhaps a name given to ARTEMIS. Opis is said to have been a HYPERBOREAN maiden who went to DELOS with her friend, Arge, at the same time as Artemis and APOLLO. According to some legends, Opis was raped by ORION, who was then killed by Artemis in revenge.

Ops in Roman mythology, a goddess of plenty, equated with the Greek goddess RHEA and with CYBELE.

Opus an ancient city whose inhabitants claimed that DEUCALION (1) and PYRRHA settled there after being saved from the flood.

oracle the response delivered by a deity or supernatural being to a worshipper or inquirer, and also the place where the response was delivered. These responses took the form of divine inspiration, either on a person, as in the dreams of the worshipper in the temples, or by its effect on certain objects, as the tinkling of the cauldrons at DODONA, the rustling of the sacred laurel, the murmuring of streams, or by the actions of sacred animals. Oracles were limited to a particular place and could not be moved. The most renowned of the Greek oracles was the Delphic oracle (*see* DELPHI). Sacrifices were offered by the inquirers, who walked with laurel crowns on their heads and delivered in questions inscribed on lead tablets. The response was deemed infallible and was usually dictated by justice, sound sense, and reason. Other oracles of APOLLO were at Abae in Phocis and in DELOS. Zeus had oracles at OLYMPIA and Dodona, and those of other deities existed elsewhere. There was also a secondary class of oracles of heroic or prophetic persons, the two most celebrated of which were those of the seers AMPHIARAUS and Trophonius. The oracle of Amphiaraus was situated at Oropus in Attica. Those who consulted it fasted a whole day, abstained from wine, sacrificed a ram to Amphiaraus and slept on the skin in the temple, where their destiny was revealed by dreams. The oracle of Trophonius was at Lebadea in BOEOTIA and was given in a cave into which the votary descended, bathed and anointed, holding a honeyed cake.

Orchomenus (1) in Greek mythology, a son of Lycaon, said to have founded the Arcadian towns of ORCHOMENUS (1) and Methydrium.

Orchomenus (2) in Greek mythology, a king of ORCHOMENUS (2). He is in some legends a son of Minyas (*see* MINYANS) and in some is the father of Minyas and son of ZEUS.

Orchomenus (1) an Arcadian city, whose founder is said to have been called after its founder, one of the sons of Lycaon (3).

Orchomenus (2) the principal city of northern BOEOTIA, situated at the north-western corner of Lake Copais where it was joined by the CEPHISSUS. It was an extremely wealthy city and the centre of MINYAN power. It sent thirty ships to the TROJAN WAR. Its government was thoroughly aristocratic, and was involved in several wars with the democratic THEBES. The rise of Thebes probably contributed to its decline.

Orcus in Roman mythology, a name for PLUTO and for his kingdom.

oread *see* **nymphs**.

Oreithyia in Greek mythology, a daughter of ERECHTHEUS and Praxithea. She was abducted by BOREAS, the north wind, as she danced by the River ILISSUS. He took her to Sarpedon's Rock in THRACE and raped her. She bore him two daughters, Chione and Cleopatra (2), and two sons, ZETES AND CALAÏS.

Orestes in Greek mythology, the son of AGAMEMNON and of CLYTEMNESTRA. When his father was murdered, he was saved from a similar fate by his sister ELECTRA (1). He was sent to Phocis, where he formed an intimate friendship with PYLADES, the son of King Strophius. He was then called upon by the ORACLE at DELPHI to avenge his father, and hastened to MYCENAE, where he slew Clytemnestra and AEGISTHUS. For this murder he was relentlessly pursued by FURIES, and only succeeded in appeasing those terrible goddesses by carrying out the instructions of the Delphic oracle to bring back the statue of ARTEMIS from Tauris to ARGOS. He recovered his father's kingdom at Mycenae, slew NEOPTOLEMUS and married his wife HERMIONE, daughter of MENELAÜS, who had been formerly promised to himself. Orestes also ruled over Argos on the death of its king. Orestes is the hero of several Greek tragedies.

orgies secret rites or customs connected with the worship of some gods, such as the secret worship of DEMETER and the festival of DIONYSUS, which was accompanied with many customs of mystic symbolism and much licence. From this comes the modern sense of drunkenness and debauchery.

Orion in Greek mythology, a giant who was a hunter and is said to have been extremely handsome. Legends differ as to his origins but he is held to have been the son of Euryale, daughter of MINOS, and of POSEIDON. He married Side but she boasted that she was more beautiful than HERA and was punished for her arrogance by being sent to HADES. He then went to the island of Chios and asked for MEROPE's (2) hand in marriage. She was the daughter of the king of Chios, OENOPION. It is said that the king kept postponing the date of the wedding, and Orion raped Merope. In revenge Oenopion blinded him while he slept and banished him from the island. Since his father, Poseidon, had given Orion the power to walk on the sea he was able to go northwards to LEMNOS. There HEPHAESTUS had a smithy, and he gave Orion his servant, Cedalon, to be his guide. Orion carried the boy on his shoulders and asked to be directed east to where the sun rose. There HELIOS, the sun god, cured his blindness. When he was cured he returned to Chios to exact vengeance on Oenopion, but his people hid him in an underground chamber. Failing to find his enemy, Orion went off to CRETE to hunt with ARTEMIS. There are various and differing legends about the relationship between Orion and Artemis. According to one she fell in love with him. APOLLO, brother of Artemis, resented this and tricked Artemis into shooting with an arrow what seemed to be a black object floating on the surface of the sea. It was in fact the head of Orion swimming in the sea, and she killed him accidentally. Artemis is then said to have placed Orion in the sky as a constellation in recognition of their friendship. According to other legends, Artemis shot Orion for challenging her to a game of quoits or for trying to rape either her or the HYPO-BOREAN maiden OPIS. In another legendary explanation of his death, Orion is stung to death by a giant scorpion that GE sent to punish him for boasting that he could kill all animals on the earth. After his death Artemis asked ZEUS to place him in the sky as the constellation which bears his name. The constellation is considered to represent the figure of a man with a sword hanging from his belt. The principal stars are four, forming a large quadrilateral representing the right and left shoulders, right knee and left foot, and three in a slanting line representing the belt. The middle star in the sword is a mutiple star, surrounded by the Great Nebula. Being a hunter, Orion is accompanied by a dog, the constellation CANIS MAJOR.

Ornytion *see* **Corinth**.

Orpheus in Greek mythology, a hero and legendary singer, the chief representative of the art of song. He is also represented as the founder of a religious sect. Orpheus was the son of OEAGRUS, king of THRACE, or of APOLLO, and the Muse CALLIOPE. He is credited with the application of music to the worship of the gods. Some legends indicate that Apollo taught him to play the lyre and others that it was the MUSES. In either event he played it so well so that he moved not only people and the beasts, but the woods and rocks with its melody. Orpheus is at the centre of a number of legends. In one, having lost his wife Eurydice (1) by the bite of a serpent, he descended to HADES to try and get her back. His music so moved the infernal deities Hades and PERSEPHONE that they allowed her to return to earth, on condition that her husband, whom she was to follow, would not look back until they had reached the upper world. Love or doubt, however, drew his eyes towards her, and she was lost to him for ever. His death is sudden and violent. According to some accounts, it was the thunderbolt of ZEUS that killed him because he revealed the divine MYSTERIES.

According to others, it was DIONYSUS, who, angry at Orpheus refusing to worship him, caused the MAENADS to tear him to pieces, which pieces were collected and buried by the Muses at the foot of OLYMPUS. Others again said he met his death at the hands of a band of furious Thracian women who divided his limbs between them, either from excessive madness of unrequited love or from anger at his drawing their husbands away from them. In another legend he is represented as one of the ARGONAUTS. He is said to have kept the rest of the Argonauts from being too unruly by his playing, He introduced the Argonauts to the Samothracian mysteries on the outward journey and on the return journey drowned out with the playing of his lyre the singing of the SIRENS guaranteed to seduce all sailors.

Orseis *see* **Dorus**; **Xuthus**.

Orthus *or* **Orthrus** in Greek mythology, a two-headed dog and an offspring of TYPHON and ECHIDNA. In company with his master, Eurytion (3), he guarded the cattle of GERYON in Erytheia. HERACLES killed both Orthus and Eurytion and stole the cattle.

Ortygia the original name of the island of DELOS or the name of an island nearby it.

Ossa, Mount the ancient name of a mountain in MAGNESIA on the east side of THESSALY, near PELION and separated from OLYMPUS by the vale of TEMPE. In Greek mythology, Ossa was the seat of the CENTAURS and GIANTS and was one of the three mountains that OTUS AND EPHIALTES piled up to form a structure that would enable them to storm heaven.

Otreus in Greek mythology, a king of PHRYGIA who fought with PRIAM of Troy against the AMAZONS.

Otus and Ephialtes in Greek mythology, twin giants, sons of IPHIMEDEIA, daughter of TRIOPAS (1), and wife of ALOEUS. She fell in love with his father, POSEIDON, and poured water into her lap until she conceived her two sons. The twins were not only very large and very strong but they were very arrogant and unruly. They tried to storm heaven by heaping Mount OSSA on Mount OLYMPUS and Mount PELION on Mount Ossa, They also captured ARES, the god of war, and kept him in a brass jar. He was eventually rescued by HERMES. As punishment for their behaviour one legend indicates that APOLLO shot them. Another indicates that Apollo sent a deer between them and that while trying to pierce the deer with their spears, they killed each other instead. They founded the city of Ascra at the base of Mount HELICON and may have been the first to worship the MUSES, although these were then three in number, not nine. In HADES the twins continued to be punished for their misdeeds and were bound back to back with snakes to a pillar on which a screech owl sat.

Ourea *see* **Ge**.

Ovid (Publius Ovidius Naso), Roman poet, born 43 BC, died AD 17. His best-known work is the *Metamorphoses*, a long poem that relates all the mythological tales which have to do with TRANSFORMATIONS. It begins with the transformation of CHAOS into Cosmos, and ends with the metamorphosis of Julius Caesar into a star.

Oxylus in Greek mythology, a king of ELIS and son of Andraemon or of HAEMON. He was a native of Aetolia but was banished from his native land for killing his brother Thermius or else a man named Allcidocus. During the invasion of Pelopennsus the leaders of the HERACLID, the sons of Aristomachus, engaged him as a guide on condition that he was rewarded with the kingship of Elis. There was already a king of Elis, DIUS, but he agreed to let the rights to the throne be decided by the outcome of a single combat between an Aetolian slinger, Pyrchaechmes, on the side of Oxylus and an Eleian archer, Degmenus, on the side of Dius. Pyrchaemes won and so Oxylus was declared king of Elis. On the advice of an oracle, he asked Agorius, great-grandson of ORESTES, a descendant of the famous Elian king PELOPS, to share the throne of Elis, and the city prospered.

P

paean in Greek, a hymn to APOLLO or to other gods, or a song in praise of heroes. A paean was sung before a battle in honour of ARES (Mars), and after a victory, in praise of Apollo. The word is derived from Paean, an ancient Greek god of healing, afterwards identified with Apollo. In the hymns to Apollo the phrase *Io paean* was frequently repeated, and hence these hymns were also called *paeans*.

Palamedes *see* **Nauplius** (3); **Oeax**.

Palladium in Greek mythology, a wooden image of PALLAS (4) Athene which is said to have fallen from heaven and to have been preserved in Troy. The Trojans believed that their city would be invincible so long as it contained the Palladium. ODYSSEUS and DIOMEDES (2) stole it and so helped to secure victory for the Greeks. The Romans pretended that it was brought to Italy by AENEAS, and preserved in the temple of VESTA at Rome, but several Greek cities claimed to possess it.

Pallas (1) in Greek mythology, one of the TITANS, a son of Crius and Eurybia and brother of Astraeus and PERSES (1). He was married to STYX by whom he became the father of ZELUS, CRATOS, BIA and NIKE.

Pallas (2) in Greek mythology, a giant who in a fight with the gods was slain by ATHENA and flayed by her.

Pallas (3) in Greek mythology, a son of the Athenian king PANDION (2) and a brother of AEGEUS, NISUS and LYCUS. He was slain by his nephew THESEUS.

Pallas (4) in Greek mythology, the epithet most commonly applied to ATHENA, as Pallas Athene. The word may be an early Greek word for a girl.

Pan in Greek mythology, a rural divinity, the god of shepherds, represented as old, with two horns, pointed ears, a goat's beard, goat's tail, and goat's feet. Sometimes he appeared to travellers, startling them with sudden fear, from which has come the word 'panic'. During the heat of the day he would sleep in shady woods and was very angry if his slumber was disturbed by hunters. He was patron of all occupied in the care of cattle and bees, and in hunting and fishing. The worship of Pan originally existed in ARCADIA, and was first introduced into ATHENS after the battle of MARATHON, in which it was asserted that he had assisted the Athenians. His festivals were called by the Greeks Lycoea. He was identified by the Romans with FAUNUS, and his festivals there were known as the Lupercalia. He was afterwards regarded by some philosophers as the all-supporting god of nature, and personified the universe. He is also represented as fond of music and of dancing with the forest NYMPHS and invented the syrinx, or pandean pipes.

Pancratis *see* **Iphimedeia**.

Pandarus in Greek mythology, the leader of the forces of Zeleia in Lycia at the TROJAN WAR. He went to the war on foot as a bowman, being, next to PARIS, the best of the Greek archers.

Pandion *see* **Butes** (3); **Nisus**.

Pandion (1) in Greek mythology, a son of Erichthonius, the king of Athens by the NAÏAD Pasithea. He was married to ZEUXIPPE by whom he became father of PROCNE and PHILOMELA and of the twins ERECHTHEUS and BUTES (3). In a war against LABDACUS, he called upon TEREUS of Daulis in Phocis for assistance and afterwards rewarded him by giving him Procne in marriage. It was in his reign that DIONYSUS and DEMETER were said to have come to Attica.

Pandion (2) in Greek mythology, a son of CECROPS and Metiadusa and a king of Athens. Being expelled from Athens by the METIONIDAE, he fled to MEGARA and there married Pylia, the daughter of king PYLAS. When the latter, following a murder, emigrated to PELOPONNESUS, Pandion obtained the government of Megara. He became the father of AEGEUS, PALLAS (3), NISUS, LYCUS and a natural son, OENEUS, and also of a daughter who was married to SCIRON (2).

Pandora in Greek mythology, the first woman on earth, made from clay by HEPHAESTUS, and sent by ZEUS to mankind in vengeance for PROMETHEUS's theft of heavenly fire. Each of the gods gave her some gift fatal to man. According to later accounts, the gods gave her a box full of blessings for mankind, but on her opening the box they all flew away, except hope. EPIMETHEUS, brother of Prometheus, married her.

Pangaeus, Mount a mountain in western THRACE where in Greek mythology LYCURGUS (1) was torn to pieces by horses when his treatment of the MAENADS brought famine to the land.

Paphos two ancient cities in Cyprus—Old Paphos, on a hill near the southwestern coast, and New Paphos (modern Baffa), to the northwest and on the shore. APHRODITE was said to have risen from the sea at Old Paphos.

Parcae the Greek name for the FATES.

Paris also called Alexander, in Greek mythology the second son of PRIAM, king of Troy, by HECUBA. His mother dreamed before his birth that she had brought forth a firebrand, which was interpreted to mean that he would cause the destruction of Troy. To prevent this, the child was exposed on Mount IDA, where he was discovered by a shepherd, who brought him up a his own son. Here his grace and courage commended him to the favour of OENONE, a NYMPH of Ida, whom he married. An accident having revealed his parentage, Priam became reconciled to his son. At the marriage of PELEUS and THETIS, a dispute arose whether HERA, ATHENA or APHRODITE was the most beautiful, and as such entitled to the GOLDEN APPLE, Paris was chosen as judge. Hera promised him wealth if she won and Athena promised him military renown and wisdom, but he decided in favour of Aphrodite, who had promised him the fairest woman in the world for this wife—hence the animosity which the other two goddesses later displayed against the Trojans. Subsequently he visited SPARTA, the residence of MENELAÜS, who had married HELEN, the fairest woman of the age, whom Paris persuaded to elope with him. This led to the siege of Troy, at the capture of which he was wounded by a poisoned arrow. He went to Mount Ida to be cured by Oenone, but she avenged herself for his unfailthfulness to her by refusing to help him, and he returned to Troy to die. An arrow from his bow caused the death of ACHILLES. *See also* WOODEN HORSE.

Parmesses *or* **Termessos** in Greek mythology, a river-god, father of AGANIPPE.

Parnassus, Mount a mountain of Greece, situated in Phocis, northwest of Athens. It has two prominent peaks, the higher of which was dedicated to the worship of DIONYSUS. The rest of the mountain was sacred to APOLLO and the MUSES. On its southern slope was situated DELPHI and the fountain of CASTALIA.

Parthenon the temple of ATHENA at Athens, situated on the Acropolis and probably the most perfect specimen of Greek architecture.

Parthenopaeus *see* **Idas and Lynceus**.

Parthenos *see* **Virgo**.

Pasiphaë in Greek mythology, the wife of MINOS and mother by the CRETAN BULL of the MINOTAUR.

Patrae the ancient name of Patras, a seaport of Greece, in the northwest of the Morea, on the gulf of the same name. It was one of the twelve cities of the ACHAEAN Confederacy of ancient Greece and is the only survivor. The Gulf of

Patras lies between the northwest part of the Morea and northern Greece, and communicates on the east with the Gulf of LEPANTO.

Patroclus in Greek mythology, the friend of ACHILLES, whom he accompanied to the TROJAN WAR. His success was at first brilliant, but, APOLLO having stunned him and rendered him defenceless, he was slain by Euphorbus and HECTOR.

Pegasus in Greek mythology, a winged horse, said to have sprung from the trunk of Medusa when she was slain by PERSEUS. He is said to have received his name because he first appeared beside the springs (*pegai*) of OCEANUS. He afterwards ascended to heaven to carry the thunder and lightning of ZEUS. BELLEROPHON had sought in vain to catch Pegasus for his combat with the CHIMAERA, and at length was advised by the seer Polyidus (2) of Corinth to sleep in the temple of MINERVA. The goddess appeared to him in his sleep and gave him a golden bridle with which he caught him and with his help overcame the Chimaera. Later writers made Pegasus the horse of the MUSES, as he had created the sacred well HIPPOCRENE, on Mount HELICON, with a single kick of his hoof.

Peiras *see* **Echidna**.

Peirene *see* **Gorgophone**.

Peirithoüs in Greek mythology, a king of the LAPITHS and a son of IXION by DIA. He waged a war against the CENTAURS and helped THESEUS carry off the AMAZON Antiope and later HELEN. He tried to carry off PERSEPHONE, queen of the underworld, and was bound with chains to a stone seat by her husband HADES. He remained a prisoner in the underworld.

Pelasgians the earliest inhabitants of Greece and the islands. They were succeeded by the HELLENES.

Pelasgus in Greek mythology, the mythical ancestor of the PELASGIANS, different origins being accorded to him in different parts of the country occupied by the Pelasgians. To the Arcadians he was either an autochthon or a son of ZEUS by NIOBE (2) and became the father of LYCAON (1) by the OCEANID Meliboea, the NYMPH Cyllene or DEÏANEIRA. In ARGOS he was believed to have been a son of TRIOPAS (1) and Sois and a brother of Iasus, Agenor and Xanthus, or a son of PHORONEUS. The ARGIVES also believed that he taught the people agriculture and that he received DEMETER at Argos on her wanderings. In THESSALY Pelasgus was described as the father of Chlorus or as the father or grandfather of HAEMON or again as a son of POSEIDON and Larissa.

Peleus in Greek mythology, a king of Phthia in THESSALY. He was a son of AEACUS, king of AEGINA and Endeis. He and his brother TELAMON killed their half-brother and were banished by their father when he discovered the crime. He went to Phthia, where he was purified of his crime and married ANTIGONE (2), daughter of the king, EURYTION (1). He joined the CALYDONIAN BOAR hunt with his father-in-law and accidentally killed him. He did not go back to Phthia for fear of what would happen. Instead he went to IOLCUS and was purified by King ACASTUS. He repelled the advances of the wife of ACASTUS, and she sent word to Antigone that Peleus was going to marry Acastus's daughter, Sterope. Antigone killed herself. Acastus was told by his wife that Peleus had tried to rape her, and Acastus plotted to get rid of him. He contrived to leave him unarmed on Mount PELION, where the CENTAURS would get him, but CHEIRON, king of the Centaurs, spared his life. He later killed Astydamia, wife of Acastus, and returned to Phthia where he became king.

Pelion, Mount a mountain of ancient Greece, in THESSALY, near the sea. In Greek mythology, in the war of the TITANS with the gods the former piled Pelion upon OSSA to aid them in climbing to OLYMPUS.

Pelias in Greek mythology, a king of IOLCUS who became one of the most powerful Greek kings of his time and had rather a violent nature. He killed his half-brother, AESON, and banished his brother NELEUS to get the throne. He was killed by JASON, son of Neleus, after he had tricked him into going on the quest for the GOLDEN FLEECE.

Pellonia in Roman mythology, a goddess who was believed to assist mortals in warding off their enemies.

Pelopia *see* **Atreus**.

Peloponnesus the peninsula which formed the southern part of ancient Greece, HELLAS proper being north of the isthmus of Corinth. Among its most important cities were SPARTA and ARGOS. After war with MESSENIA, Sparta acquired supremacy over the others states and disputed the supremacy with ATHENS in the Peloponnesian War.

Pelops in Greek mythology, son of TANTALUS, king of LYDIA. He married HIPPODAMIA, a daughter of King OENOMAUS of Elis, and succeeded his father-in-law in that kingdom by conquering him in a chariot race, establishing the house of AGAMEMNON. PELOPONNESUS received its name from him. Of his sons by Hippodamia, ATREUS and THYESTES are the most famous.

Pelor *see* **Sparti**.

penates *or* **di penates** in Roman mythology, gods of the storeroom and kitchen. The images of these gods were kept in the *penetralia*, or central part of every house, each family having its own penates and the state its public penates. The LARES were included among the penates but were not the only penates, for each family had generally only one lar whereas the penates are usually spoken of in the plural. Their worship was closely connected with that of VESTA.

Penelope in Greek mythology, the wife of ODYSSEUS and mother of TELEMACHUS. During the protracted absence of Odysseus, he was generally regarded as dead, and Penelope was surrounded by a host of suitors, whom she put off on the pretext that before she could make up her mind she must first finish a shroud that she was weaving for her aged father-in-law, LAËRTES. To gain time, she undid by night the work she had done by day. When the suitors had discovered this device, her position became more difficult than before, but fortunately Odysseus returned in time to rescue her and slay the importunate wooers who had been living riotously and wasting his property.

Penthesilea *see* **Amazons**.

Pentheus in Greek mythology, a son of Echion (1) and Agave, and successor of Cadmus as king of Thebes, formerly Cadmeia. He refused to do homage to Dionysus and refused to allow the women of the country to join in the revels of the bacchants. He was pulled to pieces by his mother and her sisters, who in a fit of madness thought he was a wild boar.

Penthilus in Greek mythology, a son of Orestes and Erigone (2), who is said to have led a colony of Aeolians to Thrace.

Pereus *see* **Elatus**.

Periboea (1) in Greek mythology, a daughter of Hipponous, king of Olenus, and wife of Oeneus. She was the mother of Olenias and possibly of Tydeus.

Periboea (2) *or* **Merope** in Greek mythology, wife of Polybus and the foster-mother of Oedipus.

Periclymenus *see* **Neleus**.

Perieres a king of Messenia and husband of Gorgophone, daughter of Perseus, by whom he had two sons, Aphareus and Leucippus (1). He was also the father of Borus and Pisus. Some legends make him the father of Tyndareus and Icarius (1), but others indicate that these were the offspring of Gorgophone by her second husband, Oebalus.

Perileus *or* **Perilaus** *see* **Icarius** (1).

Pero (1) in Greek mythology, the mother of the river-god Asopus by Poseidon.

Pero (2) in Greek mythology, a daughter of Neleus and Chloris, who was married to Bias and celebrated for her beauty.

Peroboea *see* **Icarius** (1).

Perse in Greek mythology, a daughter of Oceanus and wife of Helios, by whom she became the father of Aeëtes and Circe. She is sometimes called the mother of Pasiphaë.

Persephone in Greek mythology, a goddess of the underworld, the only child of Zeus and Demeter. She was abducted by Hades and was found by Demeter after an unceasing quest, but she had to remain a third of the year with Hades and the rest of the year with her mother. In Roman mythology she is called Proserpine.

Perses (1) in Greek mythology, a son of the Titan Crius and Erybia, and husband of Asteria by whom he became the father of Hecate.

Perses (2) in Greek mythology, a son of Perseus and Andromeda who is described as the founder of the Persian nation.

Perses (3) in Greek mythology, a son of Helios and Perse and brother of Aeëtes and Circe.

Perseus in Greek mythology, king of Mycenae and Tiryns and son of Zeus and Danaë. Perseus promised to bring the head of the Gorgon Medusa to King Polydectes. It was a virtually impossible task because escape after an attack was impossible since her sisters could fly. With the help of nymphs who gave him a pair of winged sandals and a cap of darkness which made him invisible. He received a sword of adamant from Hermes. Polydectes and his court were turned to stone when he brought the head back.

Phaea *see* **Crommyonian Sow.**

Phaeacians in Greek mythology, a seafaring people who lived on the island of Scherie or Drepane. They were led there by their king, Nausithous, a son of Poseidon, after being driven out of Hypereia by the Cyclops.

Phaedra in Greek mythology, a daughter of Minos, king of Crete, and Pasiphaë. Her unrequited love for Hippolytus, son of Theseus, led to his death and her suicide.

Phaëthon (1) a frequent title of Helios and subsequently used as his name.

Phaëthon (2) in Greek mythology, a son of Helios, famous for his unfortunate attempt to drive his father's chariot. Scarcely had he seized the reins than the horses, perceiving his weakness, ran off and, approaching too near Earth, almost set it on fire. Earth cried to Zeus for help, and he struck down Phaëthon with a thunderbolt into the Eridanus or Po. His sisters, the Heliades, who had harnessed the horses of the Sun, were changed into poplars and their tears into amber.

Phalces *see* **Deïphontes.**

Pherae an ancient city of Thessaly, near Mount Pelion. In Greek mythology, it was the royal seat of Admetus and Alcestis, and afterwards, under the rule of tyrants, became a controlling power of the whole of Thessaly, and for long made its influence felt in the affairs of Greece.

Pheres *see* **Jason.**

Philoctetes in Greek mythology, a famous archer, the friend and armour-bearer of Heracles, who bequeathed him his bow and poisoned arrows. As one of the suitors of Helen, he led seven ships against Troy, but being bitten in the foot by a snake (or, according to one story, wounded by his own arrows), he fell ill. As his wound gave forth an unendurable stench, the Greeks left him on the island of Lemnos, where for ten years he spent a miserable life. But an oracle declared that Troy could not be taken without the arrows of Heracles, so Odysseus and Neoptolemus were despatched to bring Philoctetes to the Greek camp where, healed by Aesculapius or his sons, the restored hero slew Paris and helped powerfully in the taking of Troy. After the war he settled in Italy.

Philomela or **Philomena** in Greek mythology, a daughter of Pandion and Zeuxippe who, after being raped by her brother-in-law Tereus was metamorphosed into a nightingale or swallow.

Philomelus in Greek mythology, a son of IASION and DEMETER and brother of PLUTUS. He is said to have invented the wagon. As a reward for his ingenuity his mother, on his death, placed him in the sky as the constellation BOÖTES.

Philonoë in Greek mythology, a daughter of IOBATE, king of Lycia, and wife of BELLEROPHON.

Philyra in Greek mythology, a daughter of OCEANUS and TETHYS, who bore a child by CRONOS. Her son was CHEIRON, who had the body of a horse from the waist down. He became king of the CENTAURS. Philyra was so ashamed at the sight of her son that she asked ZEUS to turn her into a tree, and she became a linden tree.

Phineus in Greek mythology, king of Salmydessus and husband of CLEOPATRA (2), daughter of BOREAS. His second wife, IDAEA, made him torture or blind his sons by Cleopatra, and they were rescued by the ARGONAUTS. Phineus may have been blinded as a punishment by them, but he may already have been blind. He is noted for having his food snatched away by the HARPIES every time that he tried to eat.

Phlegyas in Greek mythology, a son of ARES and a very warlike leader. He became king of Andreis, later ORCHOMENUS (2), and called the region Phlegyantis. He was killed by NYCTEUS.

Phocis one of the original states of ancient Greece, west of BOEOTIA in northern Greece. The greater part of it consisted of the mountain range of PARNASSUS and it possessed the famous oracle of DELPHI. The Phocians waged the Sacred or Phocian War over the use of a piece of land belonging to the temple of Delphi, but it ended disastrously for them. Twenty-one of their twenty-two cities were destroyed and the inhabitants parcelled out among the hamlets.

Phoebe (1) an epithet of ARTEMIS.

Phoebe (2) in Greek mythology, a female TITAN, a daughter of URANUS and GE. She was the mother of LETO and ASTERIA by her brother Coeus.

Phoebus an epithet, and subsequently a name, of APOLLO. It referred both to the youthful beauty of the god and to the radiance of the sun when latterly Apollo became identified with HELIOS.

Phoenix in Greek mythology, a king of the Dolopians. As a young man he took part in the CALYDONIAN BOAR hunt and was in charge of the young ACHILLES. As an old man, he accompanied Achilles to the TROJAN WAR, having persuaded him to join the battle, and tried to persuade him to rejoin the war after he quarrelled with AGAMEMNON and withdrew. He remained with Achilles, and at the end of the war set out for home with NEOPTOLEMUS, son of Achilles.

Phoetusa in Greek mythology, daughter of HELIOS and NEAERA.

Phorbas (1) in Greek mythology, a king of THESSALY, According to some legends he was immortalized as the constellation OPIUCHUS, the Serpent-bearer.

Phorbas (2) *see* **Augeas**.

Phorcys in Greek mythology, a sea-god, a son of Pontus and GE. By his sister CETO, a sea monster, he fathered a series of monsters, such as the Gorgon ECHIDNA, and LADON, the snake. He may have fathered SCYLLA (2).

Phoroneus in Greek mythology, a son of INACHUS, a river-god. The city of ARGOS was originally called Phoronea after him. He was the father of NIOBE (2) and Car, the founder of MEGARA. The ARGIVES claimed that he, and not PROMETHEUS, discovered fire.

Phrixus in Greek mythology, a son of ATHAMAS and NEPHELE. His father's second wife, INO, forced her husband to sacrifice his son, but just as the boy was about to die, a ram with a GOLDEN FLEECE appeared and carried off him and his sister, HELLE. Phrixus reached Aea, capital of Colchis, and the ram told him to sacrifice it and hang its golden fleece on an oak tree in a grove sacred to ARES. This fleece was the object of JASON'S quest for the golden fleece. *See* HELLESPONT.

Phrygia in ancient geography, a country in Asia Minor, stretching along the shores of the HELLESPONT and Troad. Its early history is mythological, with GORDIUS and MIDAS as its kings. On the death of ADRASTUS, the royal family became extinct, and it became a province of LYDIA.

Phthia the principal city of PHTHIOTIS or ACHEA in southern Thessaly and the adopted home of PELEUS.

Phthiotis the southeast corner of Thessaly and the home of ACHILLES.

Phylacus in Greek mythology, a king of Phylace and father of IPHICLUS and ALCIMEDE, mother of JASON. *See also* MELAMPUS.

Phyleus in Greek mythology, king of Dulichium, who was exiled from his native Elis by his father. He was later given the throne of Elis by HERACLES because of his help in protesting against the treatment of Heracles by AUGEAS, the father of Phyleus. Timandra is said to have deserted ECHEMUS for him.

Phyllis in Greek mythology, a daughter of the Thracian king, Sithon. See DEMOPHON.

Picus an old sylvan deity in Italy, who was represented with the head of a woodpecker and presided over divination.

Pierus in Greek mythology, a king of Pella in Macedonia. The region of Pieria round OLYMPUS is named after him. He was closely associated with the MUSES and introduced worship of them to Thespiae in BOEOTIA. He was the father of HYACINTH by the Muse CLIO.

Pisces (The Fishes) a constellation. The two fish are APHRODITE and EROS, who leapt into the River Euphrates and became fish to escape the monster TYPHON.

Pisus *see* **Perieres**.

Planctae *see* **Wandering Rocks**.

Pleiades the so-called 'seven stars' in the neck of the constellation TAURUS (2). Ancient Greek legends associate the Pleiades with the seven daughters of AT-

LAS and the NYMPH Pleione, fabled to have been placed as stars in the sky, possibly to save them from pursuit by Orion. Their names are ELECTRA (3), Maia, Taÿgete, Alcyone, Celaeno, Sterope (the invisible star) and MEROPE (1).

Pleïone *see* **Pleiades**.

Pleisthenes *see* **Atreus**; **Nauplius** (3).

Pleuron in Greek mythology, a son of AETOLUS and Pronoë, and brother of CALYDON, was married to Xanthippe, by whom he became the father of Agenor, Sterope, Stratonice, and Laophonte. He is said to have founded the town of Pleuron in Aetolia.

Pluto in Greek mythology, originally only a surname of HADES, as the giver or possessor of riches, the third son of CRONOS and RHEA, and the brother of ZEUS and RHEA. He obtained the sovereignty of the underworld and ruled the spirits of the dead. He married PERSEPHONE, daughter of DEMETER, after carrying her off from the plains of Enna. He assisted his brothers in their wars against the TITANS, and received from the CYCLOPS, as a reward for delivering them from TARTARUS, the helmet that made him invisible, which he lent to HERMES in the wars against the Titans and to PERSEUS in his fight with the GORGON.

Plutus in Greek mythology, a god of wealth, the son of DEMETER and IASION. He was commonly represented as a boy bearing a cornucopia.

Podarge in Greek mythology, one of the HARPIES and mother of XANTHUS AND BALIUS by ZEPHYRUS.

Podes *see* **Eëtion**.

Pollux *or* **Polydeuces** *see* **Castor and Pollux**.

Polybus in Greek mythology, a king of CORINTH and husband of Merope (3). He was the foster-father of OEDIPUS. *See also* JOCASTA.

Polydectes in Greek mythology, a king of SERIPHUS, son of Magnes (1) and brother of DICTYS. He was turned to stone by PERSEUS.

Polydeuces *see* **Pollux**.

Polydora in Greek mythology, a daughter of PELEUS and ANTIGONE (1) and wife of BORUS. She was the mother of MENESTHEUS by the river-god SPERCHEIUS.

Polydorus in Greek mythology, a son of CADMUS and HARMONIA. He was king of THEBES and husband of Nycteïs by whom he became the father of LABDACUS.

Polyidus (1) *or* **Polyeidus** in Greek mythology, a seer of ARGOS. *See* GLAUCUS (1).

Polyidus (2) in Greek mythology, a seer of CORINTH. *See* PEGASUS.

Polymester *see* **Bistonians**; **Ilione**.

Polyneices *or* **Polynices** in Greek mythology, brother of ANTIGONE (2) and son of OEDIPUS and cursed by him. He and his brother, ETEOCLES, were meant to rule THEBES in alternate years, but Eteocles refused to relinquish the throne, and Polyneices sought the help of ADASTRUS, king of Thebes, whose daughter, Argeia, Polyneices married. This led to the expedition by the SEVEN AGAINST THEBES. Polyneices and Eteocles killed one another in single combat.

Polypemon *see* **Procrustes**.

Polyphemus (1) in Greek mythology, the most famous of the Cyclops, who is described as a cannibal giant with one eye in his forehead, living alone in a cave of Mount Etna and feeding his flocks on that mountain. Odysseus and his companions, having been driven upon the shore by a storm, unwarily took refuge in his cave, and Polyphemus killed and ate four of the strangers. Odysseus, however, intoxicated the monster with wine, and as so on as he fell asleep, forced out his one eye with the blazing end of a stake. He then escaped from the cave with his companions. Polyphemus was the despised lover of the nymph Galatea.

Polyphemus (2) in Greek mythology, a son of Elatus (2) and an Argonaut. He was abandoned by the Argonauts with Heracles in Mysia and founded the city of Cius. In his youth he fought against the Centaurs.

Polypoetes in Greek mythology, brother of Dorus and son of Peirithoüs. He was a great warrior, and with Leonteus he led forty ships to the Trojan War.

Polyxo *see* **Helen**.

Pomona in Roman mythology, the goddess of fruit and the wife of Vertumnus. She was usually represented with a basket of fruit, or with fruit in her bosom.

Pontus in Greek mythology, a personification of the sea and described as a son of Ge and as the father of Nereus, Thaumas, Phorcys, Ceto and Erybia by his own mother.

Porthaon *or* **Portheus** *see* **Oeneus**.

Poseidon in Greek mythology, son of Cronos and brother of Zeus and Pluto. He was god of the sea, of earthquakes and of horses. The Roman equivalent was Neptune.

Ppeiras *see* **Echidna**.

Praxithea *see* **Oreithyia**.

Priam in Greek mythology, son of Laomedon and king of Troy at the time of the Trojan War. His name means 'the ransomed' and was given to him on account of his having been ransomed by his sister Hesione from Heracles, into whose hands he had fallen. His second wife was Hecuba, by whom he had many children. The best known of these are Hector, Paris, Helenus, Troilus, Creüsa (2) and Cassandra. He was too old to take an active part in the war. After Hector's death he went to the tent of Achilles to beg the body for burial.

Priapus in Greek mythology, a Phrygian god. of fertility, son of Dionysus and Aphrodite. He was represented as being very ugly and satyr-like with huge genitals.

Procne in Greek mythology, a daughter of King Pandion of Athens and Zeuxippe. She was the wife of Tereus and the sister of Philomela. She metamorphosed into a nightingale or a swallow after discovering that her husband had raped her sister.

Procris in Greek mythology, a daughter of Erechtheus and wife of CEPHALUS. MINOS or ARTEMIS gave her the hound LAELAPS. Because of the anger of PASIPHAË, wife of Minos, she returned to Athens and gave the dog to her husband, Cephalus.

Procrustes ('the Stretcher') in Greek mythology, the surname of a robber of ancient times, named Polypemon or Damastes. He had two beds, one short and the other long, and boasted that they would fit everybody. If his victims were too short for the bed, he stretched them to death, while if they were too tall, he cut off their feet or legs. THESEUS served him in the same way.

Proëtus in Greek mythology, a son of Abas and twin brother of Acrisius (*see* DANAË). In a dispute between the two brothers for the kingdom of ARGOS, Proëtus was defeated and expelled. He fled to IOBATES in Lycia and married his daughter STHENEBOEA by whom he had three daughters and a son, MEGAPENTHES. Iobates restored Proëtus to his kingdom by armed force, and Acrisius then agreed to share it, surrendering TIRYNS to him. When BELLEROPHON came to Protëus to be purified for a murder that he had committed, Stheneboea fell in love with him. As Bellerophon refused to comply with her desire, she charged him before Proëtus with having made improper proposals to her. Proëtus then sent Bellerophon to Iobates with a letter in which Iobates was asked to murder Bellerophon.

Promachus *see* **Epigoni**.

Prometheus in Greek mythology, one of the TITANS, brother of ATLAS and of EPIMETHEUS, and the father of DEUCALION. His name means 'forethought', as that of his brother Epimetheus signifies 'afterthought'. He gained the enmity of ZEUS by bringing fire from heaven to men, and by conferring other benefits on them. To punish this offence, Zeus caused Prometheus to be chained by HEPHAESTUS on a rock of the Caucasus (the eastern extremity of the world, according to the notions of the earlier Greeks), where his liver, which was renewed every night, was torn by a vulture or an eagle. He was ultimately saved by HERACLES.

Pronoë *see* **Pleuron**.

Propontis the ancient name of the Sea of Marmara, from being before or in advance of the Pontus Euxinus or BLACK SEA.

Proserpina the Roman name of PERSEPHONE.

Protesilaüs *see* **Laodamia**.

Proteus (1) in Greek mythology, king of Egypt who succeeded Pharos. HERMES brought HELEN to him for her protection during the TROJAN WAR. There is some confusion between him and PROTEUS (2), 'the old man of the sea'.

Proteus (2) in Greek mythology, a minor sea-god, sometimes called the 'old man of the sea', who was in charge of POSEIDON's herd of seals. In an effort to persuade Proteus to tell him how to get back to Sparta when he became stranded on the Egyptian island of Pharos after the Trojan War, Menelaüs disguised himself and three of his followers as seals and bound the old man up when he was asleep. Despite changing himself into various shapes, such as a lion, a leopard and a snake, Proteus failed to free himself and was forced to give Menelaüs directions. There is some confusion between him and Proteus (1).

Psyche in Greek mythology, a beautiful daughter of an unknown king. Aphrodite was jealous of her and asked Eros to make Psyche fall in love with a lowly person. Apollo's oracle told Psyche's father that she must marry an evil spirit on a lonely mountain top. When she was on the mountain she was wafted by the west wind to a beautiful palace and an unknown lover or husband who always left at dawn. She was not to try to find out his identity. She must not look at his face, Her two older sisters persuaded her that he was a serpent and gave her a light to see him and a knife to kill him. When she looked at Eros he fled, leaving her inconsolable. To punish her, Aphrodite gave her a variety of difficult tasks. Eventually she was overcome by a death-like sleep and Zeus made her immortal and married her to Eros.

Pterelaus *see* **Electryon**.

Pygmalion in Greek mythology, a king of Cyprus, who, disgusted with the debaucheries of his countrywomen, took an aversion to the sex. According to Ovid, he made an ivory image of a maiden, fell in love with his own work, and entreated Aphrodite to endow it with life. His prayer was granted, and the maiden became his wife. W.S. Gilbert's drama of *Pygmalion and Galatea* is founded on this story.

Pylades in Greek mythology, son of Strophius (1), king of Phocis, and Anaxabia, the sister of Agamemnon, after whose murder by Clytemnestra, their son Orestes, being carried secretly to the court of Strophius, formed the friendship with Pylades which has become proverbial. He assisted Orestes in murdering Clytemnestra, and eventually married his sister Electra (1).

Pylas in Greek mythology, a king of Megara, who, after having slain his uncle, founded the town of Pylos in Peloponnesus and gave Megara to Pandion (2), who had married his daughter Pylia.

Pyramus and Thisbe according to Ovid, young Assyrian lovers who lived next to each other and fell in love. Their parents would not allow them to see each other, and they spoke to each other through a chink in the adjoining wall. One night they decided to disobey their parents and meet at the tomb of King Ninus. Thisbe arrived first but was frightened away by a lioness, which then tore her cloak up with his bloody jaws as she had dropped it while running. Pyramus thought that she had been killed when he arrived and killed himself with his sword. Thisbe returned and also killed herself with his sword.

Pyrchaechmes *see* **Oxylus**.

Pyrrha in Greek mythology, a daughter of Epimetheus and Pandora, the first mortal-born woman. *See* Deucalion.

Pyrrhus *see* **Neoptolemus**.

Python in Greek mythology, a dragon that guarded the oracle of Delphi, a son of Ge. He lived in the caves of Mount Parnassus but was killed by the infant Apollo who then took possession of the oracle.

Q

Quirinus in Roman theology, a surname of Romulus after he had been raised to the rank of a divinity. Hence Quirinalia, a festival in honour of Romulus, held annually on the thirteenth day before the calends of March, that is, 17th February. Quirinus is the third great god, ranking next to Jupiter and Mars.

R

Races of Man in Greek mythology, the gods created five races of man, the ages in which they lived being called the five ages of man. The first race was a Golden Race living in a Golden Age under the rule of Cronos. Members of this race led happy lives and died in peace, becoming on their death guardian spirits of mortals. The next race was a Silver Race living in a Silver Age. Members of this race did not lead such good or contented lives as those of the Golden Age and were so unappreciative of the work of the gods that the Olympians destroyed them. The next race was a Brazen or Brass Race. This race did not last very long because they were so warlike that they were soon all killed. Next came a race of demigods, who lived in what is called the Heroic Age. It is this age that is most usually celebrated in Greek mythology. The war of the Seven against Thebes and the Trojan War claimed the lives of many of these, and the rest went to live a happy existence in the Islands of the Blessed ruled over by Cronos, who by then had been deposed from Olympus. The fifth race is the present one, the Iron Race, and the worst one, with members of it leading wicked lives. Legend has it that the Iron Race will be destroyed by Zeus when babies emerge from their mothers' wombs already old. Legend does not indicate whether the end of the iron race would be the end of mankind, the gods having given up on mortals.

Rea Silvia in Roman mythology, the daughter of Numitor, king of Alba Longa and the mother of twin boys, Romulus and Remus. Their father was Mars, who seduced her although she was a Vestal Virgin (*see* Vesta). She had been appointed a Vestal Virgin because her uncle, Amulius, who had deposed her father from the throne, did not wish her to bear any children who would be heirs to the throne and thus prevent his claim to it. When her sons were born, he threw her in prison and put the babies in a basket which was put in the River Tiber in the hope that they would die of exposure. They were saved and suckled by a wolf and reared by the wife of Faustulus, the shepherd who found them by the river.

Regina *see* **Juna**.

reincarnation *see* **metempsychosis**.

Remus *see* **Romulus and Remus**.

Returns, The a name given to the homeward or return journey of the Greek leaders at the end of the Trojan War. The Greek word was *Nostoi*.

Rhadamanthus *or* **Rhadamanthys** in Greek mythology, the son of Zeus and Europa, and brother of Minos, king of Crete, whom he assisted in his kingly duties and whose jealousy he aroused by his inflexible integrity, which earned for him the admiration of the Cretans. Because of this jealousy, Rhadamanthus subsequently fled to Boeotia, where he married Alcmene. After his death he became, on account of his supreme love of integrity and justice, one of the three judges of the lower world with Minos and Aeacus.

Rhamnusia in Greek mythology, a name given to the goddess Nemesis. The name is derived from the town of Rhamnus, a town in Attica which was the chief centre of her worship.

Rhea *or* **Rheia** in Greek mythology, one of the female Titans, the equivalent of the Roman goddess, Ops, the daughter of Uranus and Ge, sister and wife of Cronos, and mother of Hestia, Demeter, Hera, Hades, Poseidon and Zeus. She received the title of 'Mother of the Gods', and 'Great Mother', being subsequently identified with Cybele.

Rhesus in Greek mythology, a son of of Strymon, the river-god, and one of the Muses. He was king of Thrace and an ally of the Trojans against the Greeks. Dolon, the Trojan spy, having been caught by the Greeks, tried to gain favour by taking them to Rhesus's camp, where they killed him and drove off his valuable horses. Dolon's attempts at ingratiating himself were in vain, and he was murdered by the Greeks. After his death Rhesus became an oracular spirit dwelling in caves near the the silver mines of Thrace.

Rhexenor in Greek mythology, a son of Nausithous, a king of the Phaeacians, who was killed by Apollo.

Rhodas *see* **Triopas** (1).

Rhode *or* **Rhodos** in Greek mythology, a nymph and a daughter of Poseidon and

AMPHITRITE, who gave her name to the island of RHODES. She bore seven sons to HELIOS, the sun god, who had claimed the island for his own as it rose from the sea.

Rhodes an island in the Aegean Sea, off the southwest coast of Asia Minor, crossed by a mountain range. Rhodes was much celebrated in antiquity, being called after the NYMPH, RHODE, wife of the sun god, HELIOS, who had claimed the island for his own as it rose from the sea. It was settled by DORIANS from Greece, and the Rhodians soon became an important maritime people.

Rhodope in Greek mythology, the NYMPH of a Thracian well, the wife of HAEMUS and mother of Hebrus. She is mentioned among the playmates of PERSEPHONE.

Rhodope, Mount the ancient name of a range of mountains now situated on the border between Greece and Bulgaria. Its highest peak is Muss Allah. In Greek mythology, it is the mountain from which DIONYSUS threw LYCURGUS (1), the Edonian king, to his panthers below.

Rhone (Rhodanus), River the European river that rises in Switzerland and flows through southern France to the Mediterranean. It was possibly the river that the ARGONAUTS sailed down having sailed up the ERIDANUS, thought to be the river Po, from the Adriatic. It is thought that they might have taken a wrong route north originally, going by the river Rhine before going by the Rhone.

river-gods in Greek mythology, a DAIMON associated with a river and considered to be the son of OCEANUS and TETHYS. There were some three thousand, the most famous of which are ACHELOÜS and ASOPUS. They were represented as vigorous men with beards and a pair of horns on their brows as a symbol of strength.

Roman mythology the body of myths connected with the deities of Rome. Unlike Greek mythology, in early Roman mythology there were no picturesque legends, Roman gods and goddesses betraying fewer of the failings by which those of Greece often sink to human level. The Romans took a more practical and objective approach to religion and religious worship, striking a rural and domestic note and worshipping especially gods of nature, like FAUNUS, and those who shielded the house and family, like the LARES. Every thing and every action had its corresponding deity, even such day-to-day processes as ploughing, harrowing, etc. As Rome grew as a power, however, its mythology began to be created and state deities like JUPITER came to the fore. After Jupiter, the head of the divine world became MARS, the defender of the city, father of ROMULUS and of the Roman people, and QUIRINUS, the deified Romulus. Closer contact with Greece brought the importation and absorption of Greek mythology until the two became totally intermingled.

Rome in modern times the capital city of Italy situated on the River Tiber. In mythology, it was founded by ROMULUS and succeeded LAVINIUM and ALBA Longa as the major city of the region. Rome became a great city but, having no women, the male citizens abducted some women from the Sabine tribe who lived in the mountains. This led to war, and when it was ended the Romans and some of the Sabines joined together to form a single political unit. Power was based in Rome but shared by Romulus and Titus Tatius, the king of the Sabines. Titus was killed as the result of a quarrel, and Romulus reigned alone, although the Sabines retained some control. After the death of Romulus, NUMA POMPILIUS, who was a Sabine, ruled Rome and brought peace and law to a warlike city. The next king, TULLUS HOSTILIUS, was warlike and engaged in several wars. He also forced the people of ALBA Longa to move to Rome. Near the end of his reign, Rome was struck by a great plague. Later kings of Rome included ANCUS MARCIUS and Lucius Tarquinus Priscus, an Etruscan born of a Greek father, who named as his successor Servius Tullus, whose mother had been a Latin captive. He was a good ruler, and Rome flourished, particuarly the common people in it. His son-in-law Lucius Tarquinius Superbus had him assassinated and declared himself king. He reigned for twenty-five years by force. but he was overthrown in an uprising caused by the rape of LUCRETIA by Tarquinius's son Sextus, the rebellion being led by Lucius Junius Brutus. The Romans expelled the Etruscan Tarquins and declared Rome a republic.

Romulus and Remus in Roman mythology, the twin sons of MARS and REA SILVIA, daughter of NUMITOR, who had been appointed as a Vestal Virgin by AMULIUS, her uncle, so that she would not be able to bear children who could be heirs to the throne and prevent Amulius from ruling. When Rea Silvia was made pregnant on being seduced by Mars, Amulius was furious, and her sons were born, he threw her in prison and put the babies in a basket on the River Tiber so that they would die. However, Romulus and Remus were washed up on the shore and were suckled by a wolf until they were rescued by FAUSTULUS, who took them home to his wife Larentia for her to rear them. When they became men, Romulus and Remus were the leaders of a band of shepherds. and were held to be very brave. When their true identity was discovered, Numitor was overjoyed. Romulus and Remus killed Amulius and restored Numitor to the throne. The two brothers then decided to build a new city of their own, but each wanted to call this after himself. The brothers left this difficult decision to the gods, who were to suggest some form of contest. The details of this are unclear, but in any event Remus was killed. According to one legend, Remus was killed by Romulus or one of his men for jumping over the wall that Romulus had just laid out as the wall of his city. On the death of Remus, Romulus built the new city himself and named it Rome after himself. Rome became a great city but, having no women, the male citizens abducted some women from the Sabine tribe who lived in the mountains. This led to war, and when it was ended the Romans and some of the Sabines joined together to form a single political unit. Power was based in Rome but shared by Romulus and Titus Tatius, the king of the Sabines. Titus was killed as the result of a quarrel and Romulus reigned alone again, although the Sabines retained some control.

Rutulians *or* **Rutuli** in Roman mythology, a tribe living in LATIUM who went to war against AENEAS and his TROJAN companions.

S

Sabines *or* **Sabini** an ancient people widely spread in Middle Italy, allied to the LATINS and already an important nation prior to the foundation of ROME. Originally they were confined to the mountain districts to the northeast of Rome, and their ancient capital was Amiternum.

Salamis (1) an island of Greece, in the Gulf of Aegina, close to the shore of ATTICA. The island is said to have obtained its name from Salamis, a daughter of ASOPUS. TELAMON, son of AEACUS, fled there after the murder of his half-brother Phocus and became king of the island. His son AJAX accompanied the Greeks with twelve Salmacian ships to the TROJAN WAR.

Salamis (2) *see* **Tiryns**.

Salmacis *see* **Hermaphroditus**.

Salmoneus *see* **Neleus**.

Salus *see* **Hygieia**.

Samos a mountainous Greek island in the Aegean Sea, near the coast of Asia Minor. It was inhabited in antiquity by Ionian Greeks, and had an important position among the Greek communities as early as the seventh century BC.

Samothrace a mountainous Greek island in the north of the Aegean Sea. Homer describes POSEIDON as viewing the events of the TROJAN WAR from its highest point. It was the chief seat of the worship of the CABIRI, and DARDANUS stayed there before he went to Troy.

Sarpedon (1) in Greek mythology, a son of ZEUS and EUROPA, and a brother of MINOS and RHADAMANTHUS. After a quarrel with Minos over MILETUS, he took refuge with Cilix, whom he assisted against the Lycians, and afterwards he became king of the Lycians. ZEUS granted him the privilege of living three generations.

Sarpedon (2) a son of ZEUS and a Lycian prince and grandson of SARPEDON (1). In the TROJAN WAR he was an ally of the Trojans and distinguished himself by his valour. He was slain at Troy by PATROCLUS. APOLLO, at the command of Zeus, cleaned and anointed his body, which was carried to Lycia by Sleep and Death for an honourable burial.

Saturn in Roman mythology, an agricultural god popularly but erroneously identified with the Greek god CRONOS and by a further error sometimes identified with Time. His reign was supposed to have been the GOLDEN AGE. His emblem was a sickle, the origin of Time's scythe.

Saturnalia a festival held by the Romans in honour of SATURN, during which the citizens, with their slaves, gave themselves up to unrestrained freedom and mirth. Under the Caesars it lasted seven days, from 17th to 23rd December. While it continued, no public business could be transacted, the law courts were closed, the schools kept holiday, and slaves were freed from restraint. Masters and slaves even changed places, so that while the servants sat at table, they were waited on by their masters and their guests. In the last days of the festival presents were sent by one friend to another.

satyrs in Greek mythology, a class of woodland divinities. In later times they were inseparably connected with the worship of DIONYSUS (Bacchus) and representing the luxuriant vital powers of nature. The satyrs appear in works of art as half-man and half-goat, with horns on the head, and a hairy body with the feet and tail of a goat. They are often portrayed with a cup or a thyrsus in their hand and shown sleeping, playing musical instruments or dancing with nymphs.

Scamander *or* **Scamandrus** a river rising on Mount IDA and crossing the plain of TROY. In Greek mythology, its river-god was the father of TEUCER and Callirrhoë and grandfather of GANYMEDE.

Sceiron *or* **Sciron** (1) in Greek mythology, a robber who haunted the frontier between ATTICA and Megaris and not only robbed travellers who passed through the country but compelled them, on the Sceironian Rock, to wash his feet, during which operation he kicked them with his feet into the sea. At the foot of the rock there was a tortoise that devoured the bodies of his victims. He was slain by THESEUS in the same manner in which he had killed others.

Sceiron *or* **Sciron** (2) in Greek mythology, a son of PYLAS and grandson of Lelex. He was married to the daughter of PANDION (2) and disputed with her brother NISUS the government of MEGARA. But AEACUS, who was chosen umpire, decided that Nisus should have the government and Sceiron the command in war.

Schedius (1) in Greek mythology, a son of IPHITUS (1) and HIPPOLYTE, who commanded the Phocians in the TROJAN WAR. He was slain by HECTOR.

Schedius (2) in Greek mythology, a son of Perimedes, likewise a Phocian who was killed at TROY by HECTOR.

Scylla (1) in Greek mythology, a daughter of King NISUS of MEGARA, who, because of her love of MINOS cut off the red hair from her father's head and thereby caused his death. When Minos deplored what she had done, she drowned herself. She is often confused with SCYLLA (2).

Scylla (2) **and Charybdis** two rocks in the Strait of MESSINA between Italy and

Sicily which were considered highly dangerous to navigators. In Greek mythology, one legend has it that there dwelt in the middle of the rock nearer Italy a fearful monster called Scylla, who barked like a dog, had twelve feet, six long necks and mouths, each of which contained three rows of sharp teeth. The opposite lower rock contained a hugh fig tree under which dwelt Charybdis, who three times every day swallowed the waters of the sea and threw them up again. Another legend says that Scylla was a beautiful maiden who often played with the sea nymphs and was loved by the god GLAUCUS (2). He applied to CIRCE for some means of making her return his love, but Circe was jealous of her and threw magic herbs in the well in which she bathed and so metamorphosed her in such a manner that the upper part of her body remained that of a woman while the lower part was changed into the tail of a fish or serpent surrounded by dogs. Another tradition relates that Scylla was loved by POSEIDON, and that AMPHITRITE, from jealousy, changed her into a monster. HERACLES is said to have killed her because she had stolen some of the oxen of GERYON, but PHORCYS is said to have restored her to life. Charybdis is described as a daughter of Poseidon and GE, and as a voracious woman who stole oxen from Heracles and was hurled by the thunderbolt of ZEUS into the sea where she retained her voracious nature.

Scyrus *or* **Scyros** (modern Skiros) an island in the Aegean Sea and one of the northern SPORADES. It frequently appears in Greek mythology. Here THETIS concealed ACHILLES in woman's attire among the daughters of LYCOMEDES to save him from the fate that awaited him at TROY. It was here too that Pyrrhus, the son of DEÏDAMEIA (2) by Achilles, was brought up and was fetched from thence by ODYSSEUS to the TROJAN WAR. According to another tradition, Scyrus was conquered by Achilles, and this conquest was connected with the death of THESEUS. After Theseus had been driven out of ATHENS, he retired to Scyrus, where he was first hospitably received by Lycomedes but was afterwards treacherously hurled into the sea from one of the rocks in the island. It was to revenge his death that PELEUS sent Achilles to conquer the island.

Seilenus *or* **Silenus** in Greek mythology, the foster-father and constant companion of DIONYSUS, and a leader of the SATYRS. He was represented as a robust old man, generally in a state of intoxication and riding on an ass, carrying a cantharus, or bottle.

Seirenes *see* **Sirens**.

Selene in Greek mythology, the goddess of the moon, daughter of HYPERION, and sister of HELIOS (the sun) and EOS (the dawn). She was also called Phoebe, and in later times was identified with ARTEMIS. According to a popular legend, ENDYMION, her lover, lay sunk in eternal sleep in a cave on Mount Latmos, where he was nightly visited by Selene. In art she is often represented as a beautiful woman with large wings, a long robe, and a coronet.

Selinus *see* **Seilenus**.

Semele in Greek mythology, a daughter of CADMUS by HARMONIA, and beloved by ZEUS. Jealous of her husband's mistresses, HERA persuaded Semele to entreat her lover to attend her with the same majesty as he approached Hera. As he had sworn to gratify her every wish, Zeus, although horrified at this request, came to her accompanied by lightning and thunderbolts, when Semele was instantly consumed by fire. DIONYSUS was her son by Zeus. *See also* AGAVE.

Seriphus *or* **Seriphos** an islet of the CYCLADES. In Greek mythology, it is the island where DANAË and PERSEUS were washed ashore in the chest in which they had been put by ACRISIUS, where Perseus was brought up, and where he afterwards turned the inhabitants to stone with the GORGON's head.

Serpent-holder, The *see* **Ophiuchus**.

Servius Tullius the sixth king of Rome. In Roman mythology, he was the son of a slave and was favoured by the gods, especially the goddess FORTUNA. During his lifetime she would visit him secretly as his spouse, and after his death his statue was placed in her temple and remained unhurt when the temple itself was once destroyed by fire. He was given as a slave by TARQUINIUS PRISCUS to Tanaquil, his wife, who recognized the future destiny of the boy and had him raised as part of the royal family. He married Tarquinius's daughter, and on the death of his father-in-law he was raised to the throne. His reign was noted for the establishment of civil rights and institutions, and he extended and beautified the city.

Seven against Thebes a group of champions under the leadership of ADRASTUS, king of ARGOS. With their troops they marched against THEBES with the aim of getting the throne of Thebes back for POLYNEICES from his brother ETEOCLES. Eteocles had broken an agreement that, after the deposition of OEDIPUS, Polyneices and Eteocles should have the throne of Thebes in alternate years. The force included MECISTEUS, brother of Adrastus, CAPANEUS, nephew of Adrastus, AMPHIARAUS, brother-in-law of Adrastus, Hippomedon, another relative of Adrastus, ETEOCLUS and Parthenopaeus, one of the Arcadian chieftains. These with Adrastus made up the Seven, and they were joined by Polyneices himself and Tydeus, son of OENEUS, king of Calydon. When the force marched against Thebes, Adrastus assigned a champion to each of the seven gates of Thebes. As the seer Amphiaraus had foretold, the whole force from Argos was killed, except Adrastus himself. He was carried by his divine horse, ARION, from the field of battle. Capaneus was killed by a thunderbolt from ZEUS when he shouted as he scaled the walls of Thebes that not even the god himself could prevent him from burning the city. Mecisteus and Eteoclus were both killed by Theban champions, Parthenopaeus died when a huge stone crushed his skull, and Tydeus and MELANIPPUS killed each other in single combat. Amphiaraus was saved from death at a Theban's hands when Zeus split the earth with a thunderbolt and swallowed up him and his chariot. Polyneices and Eteocles killed each other in single combat, thus fulfilling the curse of their father, Oedipus. With both Polyneices and Eteocles dead, their uncle, CREON, became king of Thebes. Ten years later sons of the Seven avenged their fathers as the EPIGONI.

Sextus *see* **Oenoë**.

sibyl in Greek and Roman mythology, the name of certain women endowed by APOLLO with the gift of prophecy. Their number is variously stated, but is generally given as ten. Of these the most celebrated was the Cumaean sibyl (from Cumae in Campania). She was consulted by AENEAS before he descended into the underworld. She is said to have written in Greek verses the collection of prophecies known as the Sibylline books, three of which she sold to TARQUINIUS SUPERBUS.

Sichaeus *or* **Sychaeus** in Greek mythology, a wealthy Phoenician and husband of DIDO, who was treacherously murdered by her brother, who was anxious to secure his treasures.

Sicily the large triangular island at the southwestern extremity of Italy, from which it is separated by the narrow strait of MESSINA. Its highest point is the active volcano of ETNA, in the east of the island. Its earliest inhabitants were the Iberian Sicani, from Iberia (Spain), and the Siculi, from Italy, followed by the Phoenicians and Greeks, who entered the island in the eighth century BC, founded the great cities of Syracuse, Agrigentum and Messina, and spread their influence and culture over the whole island.

Sicinus *see* **Oenoë**.

Sicyon one of the most ancient cities of Greece, said to have existed under the name of AEGIALEIA or Aegiali long before the arrival of PELOPS in Greece. It was also called Mecone, under which it is celebrated as the 'dwelling place of the blessed' and as the spot where PROMETHEUS instituted the Hellenic sacrifices and deceived ZEUS. Its name Aegialeia is said to come from Aegialeius, a son of INACHUS. It was conquered by AGAMEMNON.

Side *see* **Orion**.

Sidero in Greek mythology, the stepmother of TYRO who was killed by PELIAS at the altar of HERA.

Silenus *see* **Seilenus**.

Silvanus *or* **Sylvanus** in Roman mythology, a god of the fields and forests, who is also called the protector of the boundaries of fields. He is represented as carrying the trunk of a cypress. His Greek counterpart is PAN.

Silver Age, Silver Race *see* **Races of Man**.

Sinon in Greek mythology, a young relative of ODYSSEUS whom he accompanied to TROY. There Sinon allowed himself to be taken prisoner by the Trojans and opened the WOODEN HORSE.

Sirens *or* **Seirenes** in Greek mythology, sea NYMPHS who by their singing fascinated those who sailed by their island and then destroyed them. When ODYSSEUS approached their island, on the advice of CIRCE he took the precaution of stuffing the ears of his companions with wax, while he bound himself to the mast, and so they escaped. When the ARGONAUTS passed by the Sirens, the Sirens began to sing, but in vain for ORPHEUS rivalled and surpassed them. As it had been decreed that they should live only until someone, hearing their song, should pass by unmoved, they threw themselves into the sea and became formidable rocks.

Sisyphus a mythical king of CORINTH, son of AEOLUS (2) and Enarete. He was married to MEROPE (1) and became by her the father of GLAUCUS (3) and others. He promoted navigation and commerce but was fraudulent and avaricious. For his wickedness he was severely punished in the lower world, being obliged to roll a heavy stone to the top of a hill, on reaching which it would always roll back again, thus rendering his punishment eternal.

Sithon *see* **Demophon**; **Phyllis**.

Smyrna one of the most celebrated and most flourishing cities in Asia Minor, on the Gulf of Smyrna. In mythology, it was founded by an Amazon called Smyrna or Myrrhe, who had previously conquered EPHESUS. It is one of the reputed birthplaces of HOMER.

Sois *see* **Pelasgus**.

Sol *see* **Helios**.

Somnos *or* **Somnus** in Roman mythology, the equivalent of HYPNOS.

Sophocles Greek dramatist born *c.*496 and died *c.*406 BC. He was the most popular of the three great Athenian tragedians, the others being AESCHYLUS and EURIPIDES. His characters are plausible, have recognizable human failings, and their tragic situations have a strong element of pathos. Seven of his many plays are extant, including *Oedipus Rex*, *Oedipus at Colonus* and *Antigone*.

sown men *see* **Sparti**.

Sparta in Greek mythology, a daughter of EUROTAS (1) and wife of LACEDAEMON, by whom she became the mother of Amyclas and Eurydice (4). From her the the city of SPARTA was believed to have derived its name.

Sparta *or* **Lacedaemon** a city of ancient Greece, the capital of LACONIA and of the Spartan state, and the chief city in the PELOPONNESUS, in the Eurotas Valley. Sparta was a scattered city, actually a union of five villages, and was always unwalled. Unlike ATHENS, it was plainly built and had few notable public buildings.

Sparti (literally 'the sown men') in Greek mythology, the name given to the armed men who sprang from the dragon's teeth sown by CADMUS and who were believed to be the ancestors of the oldest families in THEBES. They were ECHION (1), Udaeus, Chthonius, Hyperenor and Pelor.

Spercheius, River a river in the south of THESSALY. The Dryopians lived along the upper part of its course. In Greek mythology, its river-god became the father of MENESTHEUS by POLYDORA, the daughter of PELEUS, and he is also mentioned in connection with ACHILLES.

Sphinx in Greek mythology, a daughter of ORTHUS and CHIMAERA, or of TYPHON and ECHIDNA, or of Typhon and Chimaera, or a natural daughter of LAÏUS. She was a monster renowned for posing an unanswerable riddle that she learnt from the MUSES or that Laïus taught her. She is represented as having the winged body of a lion and the breast and upper part of a woman. *See also* JOCASTA; OEDIPUS.

Sporades the general name for a group of small islands in the Greek Archipelago, lying scattered to the east of the CYCLADES. The principal islands are Scio or Chios, SAMOS, Cost, RHODES, LESBOS and Patmos.

Sterope *see* **Peleus**.

Stheneboea *or* **Antaea** in Greek mythology, a daughter of IOBATES and wife of PROËTUS. She was in love with BELLEROPHON, who later married her sister.

Sthenelas *see* **Tiryns**.

Sthenelus (1) in Greek mythology, a son of PERSEUS and ANDROMEDA and husband of Nicippe, by whom he became the father of Alcinoë, Medusa and EURYSTHEUS. When his brother ELECTRYON was killed by AMPHITRYON, Sthenelus seized Mycenae for himself. He was slain by Hyllus, the son of HERACLES.

Sthenelus (2) in Greek mythology, a son of CAPANEUS and Evadne. He was one of the EPIGONI who took THEBES and commanded the Argives under DIOMEDES (2) in the TROJAN WAR, being the faithful friend and companion of Diomedes. He was one of the Greeks concealed in the WOODEN HORSE, and at the distribution of the booty, he was said to have received an image of a three-eyed ZEUS which was afterwards shown at ARGOS.

Stheno *see* **Gorgons**.

Strophius (1) in Greek mythology, king of Phocis, son of Crisus and father of Astydameia and PYLADES.

Strophius (2) in Greek mythology, son of PYLADES and ELECTRA.

Stymphalanian birds man eating birds that infested a lake near the city of STYMHALUS. The sixth labour of HERACLES was to rid the lake of these birds.

Stymphalus in Greek mythology, a son of ELATUS and Laodice. PELOPS, who was unable to conquer him in war, murdered him by stratagem and cut his body in pieces. For this crime Greece was visited with a famine, which however was averted by the prayer of AEACUS. Also a city in ARCADIA named after Stymphalus; reputed to be the first home of HERA, it was one of her cult centres.

Styx in Greek and Roman mythology, the name of the principal river in the lower world, around which it flows seven times. The river is described as a branch of OCEANUS, flowing from its tenth source, and the COCYTUS is a branch of the Styx. Styx is described as a daughter of Oceanus and TETHYS, and as a nymph she dwelt at the entrance of HADES in a lofty grotto that was supported by silver columns. By PALLAS, STYX became the mother of ZELUS, NIKE, BIA and CRATOS. She was the first of the immortals to take her children to ZEUS to help him against the TITANS, and in return her children were allowed to live with Zeus for ever and Styx herself became the divinity by whom the gods took the most solemn oaths. When one of the gods was to take an oath by Styx, IRIS fetched a cup full of water from the Styx, and the god, while taking the oath, poured out the water. Zeus became by her the father of PERSEPHONE and Peiras the father of ECHIDNA.

Sybaris an ancient Greek city of lower Italy, on the Gulf of Tarentum, the first Greek colony, in mythology said to be founded by AJAX. It rapidly rose to an extraordinary degree of prosperity, and the inhabitants were proverbial for their luxury and voluptuousness.

Sychaeus *see* **Sichaeus**.

Symplegades *see* **Clashing Rocks**.

Syrinx in Greek mythology, an Arcadian NYMPH who, being pursued by PAN, fled into the River Ladon, and at her own request was changed into a reed of which Pan then made his pipes.

T

Tages in Roman mythology, a grandson of JUPITER.

Taking of Oechalia, The a lost epic poem which dealt with the capture of EURYTUS'S city by HERACLES, his abduction of IOLE, and possibly his death.

Talaus in Greek mythology, a son of BIAS and PERO who sailed with the ARGONAUTS. He was king of ARGOS and father of ADRASTUS, Parthenopaeus, Pronax, Mecisteus, Aristomachus and Eriphyle.

Talthybius in Greek mythology, the chief herald of the Greek forces in the TROJAN WAR. According to legend it was his fate to perform unpleasant duties, such as telling HECUBA that her daughter Polyxena had been sacrificed by the Greeks and going with ODYSSEUS to bring IPHIGENEIA to Aulis, even though she knew that she was to be sacrificed there.

Talus (1) in Greek mythology, a giant made of brass who guarded CRETE. According to some legends he was the last survivor of the brass age (*see* RACES OF MAN).

Talus (2) in Greek mythology, a son of Perdix, the sister of DAEDALUS. He was a disciple of Daedulus and invented several mechanical instruments. Daedalus, incensed by envy, thrust him down the rock of the Acropolis at ATHENS.

Tanaquil the wife of Lucius TARQUINUS PRISCUS, the fifth king of Rome. She was an Etruscan woman who urged her husband to move to Rome to further her ambitions. She was skilled in the art of augury, the observation and interpretation of omens.

Tantalus (1) in Greek mythology, a son of ZEUS, and king of PHRYGIA, LYDIA, ARGOS or CORINTH, who was admitted to the table of the gods, but who had forfeited their favour either by betraying their secrets, by stealing ambrosia from heaven, or by presenting to them his murdered son PELOPS as food. His punishment consisted in being placed in a lake whose waters receded from his lips when he attempted to drink, and of being tempted by delicious fruit overhead which withdrew when he attempted to eat. Moreover, a huge rock for ever threatened to fall and crush him.

Tantalus (2) in Greek mythology, a son of THYSTES or BROTEAS. He was the first husband of CLYTEMNESTRA before she married AGAMEMNON.

Taphians the inhabitants of the Taphian Islands and Cephallenia off the coast of Arcarnania who were descended from POSEIDON. Originally called Teleboans, they made their living mainly by piracy. When ATHENA visited TELEMACHUS at ITHACA, she assumed the form of Mentes, the leader of the Taphians.

Taraxippus in Greek mythology, a round altar located near a very dangerous spot on the racecourse at OLYMPIA. The altar was thought to mark a tomb of someone whose ghost haunted the racetrack. Whose ghost it was was not clear although many suggestions were made. Horses were often thrown for no reason near the altar during chariot races, and sacrifices were made at the start of races to propitiate the ghost and ensure the safety of the horses. Taraxippus means 'horse-scarer'.

Tarpeia *see* **Tarpeian Rock**.

Tarpeian Rock a precipitous rock forming part of the Captoline Hill at Rome over which people convicted of treason to the State were hurled. It was so named from Tarpeia, a Vestal Virgin (*see* VESTA) and daughter of the governor of the citadel on the Capitoline, who, coveting the golden bracelets worn by the SABINE soldiers, opened the gate to them on the promise of receiving what they wore on their left arms. Once inside the gate, they threw their shields upon her, instead of the bracelets. She was buried at the base of the Tarpeian Rock.

Tarquinius, Sextus *see* **Tarquinius Superbus**.

Tarquinius Priscus, Lucius the fifth King of Rome, supposed to have reigned from 616 to 578 BC. The family of Tarquinius was said to have been of Greek extraction, his father, Demaratus, being a Corinthian who settled in Tarquinii, one of the chief cities of Etruria. Having removed with a large following to Rome, Tarquinius became the favourite and confidant of the Roman king ANCUS MARTIUS, and at his death was unanimously elected his successor. He made war with success on the LATINS and SABINES, from whom he took numerous towns. His reign was distinguished by the construction of the Cloaca Maxima, the Forum, the wall round the city, and the Capitoline Temple. He was killed by assassins employed by the sons of Ancus Martius.

Tarquinius Superbus, Lucius the last of the legendary kings of Rome, and son of Lucius TARQUINIUS PRISCUS, who reigned from 534 to 510 BC. He abolished the privileges conferred on the plebeians by his father, banished or put to death the senators whom he suspected, never filled up the vacancies in the senate, and rarely consulted that body. He continued the great works of his father, and advanced the power of Rome abroad by wars and alliances. By the marriage of his daughter with Octavius Mamilius of Tusculum, the most powerful of the Latin chiefs, and other political measures, he caused himself to be recognized as the head of the Latin confederacy. In 510 BC, a conspiracy broke out by which Tarquinius and his family were exiled from Rome, an infamous action of his son Sextus being part of the cause of the outbreak (*see* LUCRETIA). He tried repeatedly, without success, to regain his power, and at length died at Cumae in 495 BC.

Tartarus in Greek mythology, a deep and sunless abyss as far below HADES as earth is below Heaven. According to legend an anvil would fall for nine days in order to reach it. It was closed by iron gates, and in it ZEUS imprisoned the rebel TITANS. who had warred with the gods. They were guarded by the HUNDRED-HANDED. Later writers describe Tartarus as the place in which the spirits of the wicked receive their due punishment. Sometimes the name is used as synonymous with Hades, or the lower world in general. It is also used as a personification of the region, who is said to have issued from CHAOS together with GE and EROS. He is said to have been the father by Ge of the monsters TYPHON and ECHIDNA.

Tartessus an ancient city near Gades (now Cadiz) in Spain. HERACLES returned to HELIOS his golden boat here after stealing the cattle of GERYON.

Tatius, Titus a king of the SABINES who led his troops against Rome to take vengeance on the abduction of the Sabine women by the Romans (*see* ROME). At the end of the conflict ROMULUS agreed to share power with Tatius jointly over the Romans and the Sabines.

Taurians the inhabitants of the Tauric Chersonese, the penisula on the north coast of the BLACK SEA, now known as the Crimea. They were at one time ruled by PERSEUS and later by Thoas (2). They were a barbaric people who sacrificed strangers.

Taurus (1) in Greek mythology, a Cretan noble who was the leader of MINOS's navy. He won many prizes for prowess at the Games but was defeated by THESEUS.

Taurus (2) (The Bull) one of the twelve signs of the zodiac and a constellation. Its brightest star represents the eye of the Bull and is named Aldebaran. The bull was placed among the stars to commemorate ZEUS carrying off EUROPA to Crete in the form of a bull. Close by is the group of stars called the HYADES. The constellation also contains the cluster of the PLEIADES.

Taÿgete in Greek mythology, a daughter of ATLAS and the OCEANID Pleione, the nymph of Mount Taÿgetus. ZEUS fell in love with her, and although ARTEMIS turned her into a doe to protect her, Zeus captured her and fathered a child, LACEDAEMON, by her. To thank Artemis for her help, Taÿgete inscribed the golden horns of a doe with the name of the goddess. This doe is said to have been the CERYNITIAN HIND which HERACLES captured as his third labour.

Taÿgetus, Mount a range of mountains that divided MESSENIA from LACONIA. It was named after its resident nymph, TAŸGETE.

Tegea a city of southeast ARCADIA, the principal city of Arcadia. in early times. It was often in conflict with SPARTA in later times.

Teiresias *or* **Tiresisas** in Greek mythology, a Theban seer who was changed into a woman as a youth when he killed a female snake when it was coupling with its mate. Seven or eight years later he killed a male snake when it was coupling with its mate, and he was turned back into a male. He was called upon by HERA and ZEUS as arbitrator in their dispute as to whether a man or a woman most enjoyed sex since he had experience of being both sexes. He said that women received most satisfaction, and Hera was so annoyed that she blinded him. Zeus was pleased and granted him long life and the gift of prophecy. It was Teiresias who revealed that OEDIPUS was the killer of his father and that he had committed incest with his mother. He died after drinking from the spring of TELPHUSA.

Telamon in Greek mythology, son of AEACUS and a brother of PELEUS. He emigrated from Aegina to SALAMIS and had as his second wife PERIBOEA or Eriboea, a daughter of ALCATHOUS, by whom he became the father of AJAX. He was one of the hunters of the CALYDONIAN BOAR and a member of the ARGONAUTS' expedition. He is said to have been a great friend of HERACLES and to have joined him in his expedition against LAOMEDON of Troy, which city he was the first to enter. Heracles gave him Theaneira or Hesione, a daughter of Laomedon, by whom he became the father of TEUCER and Trambelus. On this expedition Telamon and Heracles also fought against the Meropes in Cos on account of Chalciope, the daughter of Eurypylus, the king of the Meropes, and against the giant Alcioneus, on the isthmus of Corinth. He also accompanied Heracles on his expedition against the AMAZONS and slew Melanippe.

Telchines in Greek mythology, sorcerers of RHODES. The Telchines were the sons of Thalatta (sea) and the first inhabitants of Rhodes. With the OCEANID, Capheira, they nursed the infant POSEIDON at the request of his mother to prevent his father, CRONOS, from swallowing him. The Telchines could change their shape, and they were able to bring on rain, hail and snow. They are said to have invented the art of making statues of the gods.

Teledice *see* **Niobe** (2).

Telegonus (1) in Greek mythology, the son of ODYSSEUS and CIRCE who killed his father when he was old without knowing who he was until it was too late. He later married PENELOPE.

Telegones (2) *see* **Io**.

Telemachus in Greek mythology, the son of ODYSSEUS and PENELOPE, who was an infant when his father went to TROY, and in his absence of nearly twenty years he grew up to manhood. After the gods in council had determined that Odysseus should return home from the island of Ogygia, ATHENA, assuming the appearance of Mentes, king of the TAPHIANS, went to ITHACA and advised Telemachus to eject the troublesome suitors of his mother from his house and to go to Pylos and SPARTA to gather information concerning his father. Telemachus followed the advice, but the suitors refused to go, and Athena, in the form of Mentes, accompanied Telemachus to Pylos. There they were hospitably received by NESTOR, who also sent his own son to conduct Telemachus to Sparta. MENELAÜS received him kindly and communicated to him the prophecy of Proteus concerning Odysseus. From Sparta Telemachus returned home and on his arrival found his father with the swineherd Eumaeus. As Athena had metamorphosed Odysseus into a beggar, Telemachus did not recognize his father until the latter disclosed to him who he was. Father and son now agreed to punish the suitors, and when they were slain or dispersed, Telemachus accompanied his father to the aged LAËRTES.

Telephassa *see* **Cadmus**.

Telephus in Greek mythology, a son of HERACLES and Auge, the daughter of King Aleus of TEGEA. He was reared by a hind and educated by King Corythus in ARCADIA. When he had grown up, he consulted the Delphic ORACLE as to who his mother was. He was ordered to go to King TEUTHRAS in MYSIA. There he found his mother and was kindly received. He married Argiope, the daughter of Teuthras, whom he succeeded on the throne of Mysia.

Telethusa *see* **Iphis** (2).

Tellus *or* **Terra** in Greek mythology, the earth and the goddess of the earth, the equivalent of the Greek GE. She is often mentioned in contrast with JUPITER, the god of heaven, and connected with DIS and the MANES.

Telphusa in Greek mythology, a spring near Haliartus in BOEOTIA and the NYMPH of the spring. The spring was the site of an ancient oracle. TEIRESIAS died when he drank Telphusa's water.

Temenus *see* **Deïphontes**.

Tempe, Vale of a valley of Northern Greece, in THESSALY, on the River Peneus, in a gorge between Mount OLYMPUS on the north and Mount OSSA on the south.

Tenedos a Greek island in the Aegean Sea, on the west coast of Asia Minor, southwest of the HELLESPONT. The Greeks are said to have waited there before returning to Troy after the Trojans had taken the WOODEN HORSE into their city.

Tereus in Greek mythology, a son of ARES and king of the Thracians in Daulis, later Phocis, or of Megaris. PANDION (1), king of ATTICA, called on the help of Tereus against an enemy and gave him his daughter PROCNE in marriage. Tereus became by her the father of Itys, and then hid Procne in the country and told her sister PHILOMELA that Procne was dead and so seduced her. When Philomela learned the truth, Tereus took out her tongue. She made the truth known by weaving a message into a peplus that she sent to Procne. Procne then killed her own son, Itys, placed his flesh in a dish before Tereus and fled with her sister. Tereus pursued them with an axe, and when the sisters were overtaken they prayed to the gods to change them into birds. Procne became a nightingale, Philomela a swallow and Tereus a hoopoe.

Termessos *see* **Parmessos**.

Terpsichore in Greek mythology, one of the nine MUSES. She was a daughter of ZEUS and MNEMOSYNE.

Terra *see* **Tellus**.

Tethys in Greek mythology, a female TITAN, a daughter of GE and URANUS. She married her brother OCEANUS and became the mother of all the river-gods and their sisters, the OCEANIDS. During the war between the Titans and the gods she took care of her niece HERA in her house at the ends of the earth.

Teucer (1) in Greek mythology, the first king of TROY, a son of the river-god SCAMANDER and IDAEA (1), a NYMPH of Mount Ida. DARDANUS of Samothrace married his daughter BATEIA (1) and was his successor.

Teucer (2) in Greek mythology, son of TELAMON and HESIONE, and the best archer with the Greek forces in the TROJAN WAR. He would have shot HECTOR if ZEUS had not broken his bowstring. On his return from the war, Telamon refused to receive him in SALAMIS because he had not avenged the death of his brother AJAX. Because of a promise of APOLLO, Teucer sailed in search of a new home, which he found in the island of CYPRUS, which was given to him by BELUS, king of Sidon. There he founded the town of Salamis.

Teumissian vixen *see* **Cephalus**; **Laelaps**.

Teuthras in Greek mythology, king of MYSIA, who received Auge, the daughter of Aleus, and brought up her son TELEPHUS. From him the town of Teuthrania in Mysia was believed to have received its name.

Thaleia in Greek mythology, one of the nine MUSES, a daughter of ZEUS and MNEMOSYNE.

Thalia in Greek mythology, one of the GRACES.

Thallo *see* **Horae**.

Thamyris *see* **Hyacinth**.

Thanatos in Greek mythology, death and also the personification of death, the offspring of NYX. He lived with his brother HYPNOS in TARTARUS.

Thasus in Greek mythology, a son of POSEIDON or AGENOR, one of the Phoenicians in search of EUROPA.

Thasus the most northerly island in the Aegean Sea, a few miles south of the Macedonian coast. It was said to be first settled by Phoenecians led by THASUS.

Thaumus in Greek mythology, a son of PONTUS and Ge, and by the Oceanid ELECTRA (4), the father of IRIS and the HARPIES.

Thebes a city of ancient Greece, the principal city of BOEOTIA, midway between the Corinthian Gulf and the Euboean Sea. In Greek mythology, it was founded by CADMUS, was the native city of TEIRESIAS and the reputed birthplace of HERACLES and DIONYSUS. The five SPARTI were the ancestors of its noble families. When Cadmus became old, his grandson PENTHEUS became king, and after his death Cadmus went to Illyria and POLYDORUS became king. Polydorus was succeeded by his son LABDACUS, who left at his death an infant son, LAÏUS. The throne was usurped by LYCUS, whose brother NYCTEUS was the father of ANTIOPE (1), who became by ZEUS the mother of twin sons, AMPHION and ZETHUS. Nycteus having died, Antiope was exposed to the persecutions of her uncle Lycus and his cruel wife, Dirce, until at length her two sons revenged her wrongs, became kings of Thebes and fortified the city. After Amphion and Zethus, Laïus, father of OEDIPUS, became king of Thebes. When Oedipus was expelled from the city, ETEOCLES and POLYNEICES quarrelled for the throne, and this quarrel led to two sieges of Thebes, the SEVEN AGAINST THEBES and the War of the EPIGONI. This second siege was again led by Adastrus and consisted of the sons of the seven heroes of the first. The Epigoni gained a victory and thus became masters of Thebes, placing THERSANDER, son of Polyneices on the throne.

Theia in Greek mythology, a female TITAN, a daughter of GE and URANUS. She married her brother HYPERION and was the mother of EOS, HELIOS and SELENE.

Themis in Greek mythology, a female Titan, daughter of Ge and URANUS. She was goddess of order, law and justice among the Greeks. She was the second wife and chief adviser of ZEUS.

Themiste *see* **Ilus**.

Thera (modern Santorini) a volcanic island north of CRETE. In Greek mythology it was said to have grown from a clod of Libyan earth given by TRITON to the ARGONAUT Euphemus, who threw it into the sea from the *Argo*, having been instructed to do so in a dream.

Thermius *see* **Oxylus**.

Thersander in Greek mythology, a son of POLYNEICES and Argeia and one of the EPIGONI. After having been made king of THEBES, he went with AGAMEMNON to TROY and was slain in that expedition.

Thersites in Greek mythology, a Greek soldier in the TROJAN WAR noted for his ugliness and for his mocking and criticism of the Greek leaders. ACHILLES killed him and the killing led to a dispute among the Greeks. Achilles sailed to LESBOS to offer sacrifice to APOLLO.

Theseus in Greek mythology, a king of ATHENS and famous hero. He was the unacknowledged son of AEGEUS by AETHRA (1), the daughter of Pittheus of Troezen in PELOPONNESUS, although other traditions say he was the son of POSEIDON and Aethra. Brought up by his mother, when he reached maturity he set off for Athens, taking with him the sword and sandals that had been left with his mother by Aegeus. Eager to emulate HERACLES, he went by land, displaying his prowess by destroying the robbers and monsters that infested the country, including PROCRUSTES and the CROMMYONIAN SOW. At Athens Aegeus recognized Theseus because of the sword he was carrying and acknowledged him as his son and successor. Many notable deeds are told of Theseus, such as the slaying of the MINOTAUR. When the time came when the Athenians had to send to MINOS their tribute of seven youths and seven maidens for the monster, Theseus offered himself as one of the youths. When they arrived at CRETE, ARIADNE, the daughter of MINOS, fell in love with Theseus and gave him a sword, with which he slew the MINOTAUR, and a ball of thread by which he found his way out of the labyrinth. Having rescued the victims, Theseus set sail, carrying off Ariadne. Most myths speak of Theseus as losing or abandoning Ariadne on the island of Naxos. He was generally believed to have had by her two sons, Oenopion and Staphylus. As the vessel in which they sailed approached ATTICA, they neglected to hoist the white sail that was to have been the signal that the expedition had had a successful end, an omission that led to the death of Aegeus.

Another of his adventures was his expedition against the AMAZONS. He is said to have assailed them before they had recovered from the attack of Heracles and to have carried off their queen, ANTIOPE. The Amazons in their turn invaded Attica and penetrated into Athens itself, the final battle in which Theseus overcame them being fought in the middle of the city. By Antiope Theseus was said to have had a son, HIPPOLYTUS or Demophon, and after her death to have married PHAEDRA. Theseus figures in almost all the ancient heroic undertakings. He was one of the ARGONAUTS, he joined in the hunt of the CALYDONIAN BOAR, and aided ADRASTUS in recovering the bodies of those slain at THEBES. He had a close friendship with PEIRITHOÜS and helped him against the CENTAURS. Aided by Peirithoüs, he carried off HELEN from SPARTA while she was a girl and placed her in the care of Aethra. In return he assisted

Peirithoüs in his attempt to carry off PERSEPHONE from the lower world. Peirithoüs perished in the enterprise, and Theseus was kept imprisoned until rescued by Heracles. Meanwhile, CASTOR AND POLLUX had invaded Attica and carried off Helen and Aethra. MENESTHEUS also tried to incite the people against Theseus, who on his return found himself unable to re-establish his authority and retired to Scyrus, where he met a treacherous end at the hands of LYCOMEDES.

Thesprotus *see* **Atreus**.

Thessalus in Greek mythology, a son of JASON and MEDEA. who managed to escape the murder that befell his brother.

Thessaly a northeastern area of Greece, mainly consisting of a rich plain enclosed between mountains and belonging almost entirely to the basin of the River Peneus which traverses it from west to east, and falls into the Aegean through the Vale of TEMPE. Its major cities in ancient times were Larissa, Pharsalus and Pherae, which were frequently at feud with one another.

Thestius *see* **Althaea; Oeneus**.

Thestor *see* **Calcas**.

Thetis *or* **Thetys** in Greek mythology, a divinity, a daughter of NEREUS and Doris, and therefore one of the NEREIDS. She was brought up by HERA and when she reached maturity, ZEUS and Hera gave her, against her will, in marriage to PELEUS, by whom she became the mother of ACHILLES. POSEIDON and Zeus himself are said to have sued for her hand, but when THEMIS declared that the son of Thetis would be more illustrious than his father, both suitors desisted. Her nuptials with Peleus were celebrated on Mount PELION and were honoured by the presence of all the gods except ERIS or Discord, who was not invited and who, to avenge the slight, threw in among them the GOLDEN APPLE of discord.

Thisbe *see* **Pyramus**.

Thoas (1) in Greek mythology, a son of ANDRAEMON (1) and GORGE and king of Calydon and Pleuron in AETOLIA. He went with forty ships against Troy in the TROJAN WAR.

Thoas (2) in Greek mythology, a son of Borysthenes and king of the TAURIANS, into whose dominions IPHGENIA was carried by ARTEMIS when she was to have been sacrificed.

Thrace the south-easternmost region of Europe, separated from Asia by the Propontis, and its two narrow channels, the Bosporus and the HELLESPONT. From earliest historic times Thrace was a convenient ground for contending kings, statesmen and nations to settle their differences by the sword, and, as a highway out of the east into the west, it passed under the sway of many rulers. For the Greeks, who founded a number of maritime settlements but did not attempt to explore the hinterland, Thrace was a barren northern land and formed, with Europa, Libya and Asia, the whole of the known world. The designation was subsquently narrowed down to embrace only the region south of the Haemus mountain chain, and east and northeast of Macedonia.

Thyestes in Greek mythology, son of Pelops and Hippodamia, and grandson of Tantalus (1). He seduced the wife of his brother Atreus, who, in revenge, served up to him the body of his own son at a feast.

Thynius *see* **Idaea** (1).

thyrsus a pole which was carried by maenads and satyrs while taking part in revels associated with Dionysus. It was tipped with a pine cone and was twined with ivy or grapevine.

Tiber, River a river of Italy, rising in the Apennines in Tuscany, and flowing into the Mediterranean. It traverses the city of Rome.

Timandra *see* **Echemus**; **Phyleus**.

Tiphys in Greek mythology, a son of Agnius or of Phorbas and Hyrmine, of Siphae or Tiphae in Boeotia, was the helmsman of the *Argo* on the Argonauts' expedition.

Tiresias *see* **Teiresias**.

Tiryns a very ancient ruined city of Greece, in the Peloponnesus, in the plain of Argolis, near the sea. In Greek mythology, it derived its name from Tiryns, the son of Argos, and its foundation was ascribed to Proëtus. Megapenthes, the son of Proëtus, ceded Tiryns to Perseus, who transmitted it to Electryon. Alcmene, the daughter of Electryon, married Amphitryon, who succeeded to the crown but was expelled by Sthenelas, king of Argos. Their son Heracles afterwards regained possession of Tiryns, where he lived for many years.

Tisiphone in Greek mythology, one of the three Furies, the others being Alecto and Megaera.

Titans in Greek mythology, the sons and daughters of Uranus (Heaven) and Ge (Earth). They were twelve in number, six sons and six daughters. They were Oceanus, Coeus, Crius, Hyperion, Iapetus, Cronos, Theia, Rhea, Themis, Mnemosyne, Phoebe (2) and Tethys. Uranus, the first ruler of the world, threw his sons, the Hundred-handed (Briareus, Cottus, Gyes) and the Cyclops (Arges, Steropes and Brontes), into Tartarus. Ge, indignant at this, persuaded the Titans, except Oceanus, to rise against their father. Cronos castrated Uranus and threw the part into the sea and from the drops of his blood arose the Furies. The Titans then deposed Uranus, liberated their brothers from Tartarus and raised Cronos to the throne. But he again threw the Cyclops into Tartarus and married his sister Rhea. He had been foretold by Ge and Uranus, however, that he would be dethroned by one of his own children, so after their birth he swallowed successively his children Hestia, Demeter, Hera, Pluto and Poseidon. When Rhea became pregnant with Zeus, she went to Crete, gave birth to the child in a cave in Mount Dicte and entrusted him to the Curetes and the daughters of Melisseus, the NYMPHS Adrasteia and IDA, to be brought up. The armed Curetes guarded the infant and struck their shields with their spears so that Cronos could not hear the voice of the child. Rhea gave Cronos a stone wrapped in cloth which he swallowed, believing it be be his newly born son. When Zeus had grown up, he called on the help of Thetis, the daughter of Oceanus, who gave Cronos a potion which caused him to bring up the stone and the children he had swallowed. United with his brothers and sisters, Zeus now waged war against Cronos and the ruling Titans. This war was carried on in Thessaly, the Titans occupying Mount Othrys and the sons of Cronos Mount Olympus, and lasted ten years. At length, Ge promised Zeus victory if he would deliver the Cyclops and the Hundred-handed from Tartarus. Zeus accordingly slew Campe, who guarded the Cyclops, and the latter provided him with thunder and lightning. Pluto gave him a helmet and Poseidon a trident. The Titans were then overcome and hurled down into a cavity below Tartarus.

Tithonus in Greek mythology, a son of LAOMEDON and brother of PRIAM. By the prayers of EOS, who loved him, he obtained from the gods immortality but not eternal youth, in consequence of which he completely shrunk together in his old age.

Triopas (1) in Greek mythology, a son of POSEIDON and Canace, a daughter of AEOLUS, or of HELIOS and Rhodos, and the father of IPHIMEDEIA and Erysichthon. He is also called the father of PELASGUS. He expelled the Pelasgians from the Dotian plain but was himself obliged to emigrate and went to CARIA, where he founded Cnidus. Erysichthon was punished by DEMETER with insatiable hunger because he had violated her sacred grove.

Triopas (2) in Greek mythology, a son of Phorbas and the father of IASUS, Agenor and Messene.

Triptolemus in Greek mythology, a prince of ELEUSIS, son of CELEUS and Metaneira and the brother of DEMOPHON. To make up for the loss of Demophon, DEMETER bestowed many favours on Triptolemus, including a chariot with winged dragons and seeds of wheat. He took to the skies and spread and sowed grain all over the earth. He was a great hero in the ELEUSINIAN MYSTERIES.

Triton in Greek mythology, the name of certain sea-gods. They are variously described, but their body is always a compound of the human figure above with that of a fish below. They carry a trumpet composed of a shell, which they blow at the command of POSEIDON to soothe the waves.

Troad an area of Asia Minor which took its name from its main city, TROY.

Troïlus in Greek mythology, a son of HECUBA and either PRIAM or APOLLO. He was ambushed and killed by ACHILLES during the TROJAN WAR.

Trojan horse *see* **wooden horse**.

Trojan War in Greek mythology, a war waged against the city of Troy by a league of Greek leaders. The war is said to have had its origins in the beauty contest caused by the goddess ERIS and her throwing of the golden apple. The walled city of Troy succeeded in withstanding the Greek forces for ten years, but the city fell owing to the Greek's trick with the wooden horse.

Tros in Greek mythology, the king after whom TROY was named. He was a grandson of BATEIA (1) and DARDANUS and removed his grandfather's PALLA-DIUM to Troy. His son GANYMEDE was carried off by ZEUS to be cup-bearer to the gods.

Troy an ancient city in the TROAD in Asia Minor, south of the HELLESPONT. It was the scene of the ten years' siege by the Greeks in the TROJAN WAR.

Tullus Hostilius the third legendary king of Rome and successor to NUMA POMPILIUS. He was a warlike monarch, in whose reign took place the combat of the HORATII and Curiatii.

Turnus in mythology, a son of DANAÜS and Venilia and king of the RUTULIANS at the time of the arrival of AENEAS in Italy. He was related to Amata, the wife of King LATINUS. ALECTO, by the command of HERA, stirred him up to fight against Aeneas after his landing in Italy. He was defeated and killed by Aeneas.

Twins, The *see* **Gemini**.

Tyche in Greek mythology, the personification of chance or luck, the equivalent of the Roman FORTUNA.

Tydeus in Greek mythology, a son of OENEUS, king of Calydon, who assisted ADASTRUS in the Argive expedition against Thebes, the SEVEN AGAINST THEBES, in the attempt to help POLYNEICES get back the throne of THEBES.

Tyndareus in Greek mythology, a king of SPARTA and husband of LEDA, although legends vary as to which of her many children he fathered. He was probably the father of CLYTEMNESTRA but probably not the father of HELEN, who was probably the daughter of ZEUS. In his youth he was expelled from Sparta by HIPPOCOÖN, but was restored to the Spartan throne by HERACLES, who killed Hippocoön. He asked the advice of ODYSSEUS about selecting a suitor for Helen. Following this advice, he made each of the suitors swear to abide by his decision and to punish anyone who thereafter tried to take Helen away from her husband, a ritual that led to the TROJAN WAR. MENELAÜS was selected as the husband of Helen. *See also* GOLDEN APPLE.

Typhon *or* **Typhoeus** in Greek mythology, a monster, a son of GE and TARTARUS, described sometimes as a destructive hurricane and sometimes as a fire-breathing giant a hundred heads, fearful eyes and terrible voices. He was able to speak the language of animals and people. He tried to overthrow the gods but was killed, after a fearful struggle, by ZEUS with bolts of lightning. He was buried in TARTARUS under Mount ETNA.

Tyre one of the most celebrated cities of ancient Phoenicia, and with the older city of Sidon, a great trading market. It was built partly on an island and partly on the mainland. It was the home of DIDO, who fled after the murder of her husband by her brother.

Tyro in Greek mythology, the wife of Cretheus and the beloved of the river-god Enipeus in THESSALY, in the form of whom POSEIDON appeared to her and became by her the father of PELIAS and NELEUS. By Cretheus she was the mother of AESON, Pheres and Amythaon.

Tyrrhenian Sea the name given to that part of the Meditrranean Sea which is enclosed between the Islands of Corsica and Sardinia on the west, the Italian Peninsula on the east, and Sicily on the south.

U

Udaeus *see* **Sparti**.

Ulysses *or* **Ulixes** the Latin name of ODYSSEUS.

Underworld *see* **Hades**.

Upis *see* **Opis**.

Urania in Greek mythology, one of the nine MUSES, a daughter of ZEUS and MNEMOSYNE, said to have borne a son, Linus, by a son of POSEIDON, Amphimarus.

Uranus in Greek mythology, the sky and the god of the sky. He was the son of GE, the earth, and by her the father of the TITANS, CYCLOPS, and Hecatoncheires, the HUNDRED-HANDED. He hated his children and confined them in TARTARUS within the body of the earth, causing much distress to Ge. On the instigation of Ge, CRONOS, the youngest and wiliest of the Titans planned to overthrow and destroy his father. Ge gave him a sickle and while Uranus was lying with Ge, Cronos castrated him and flung the severed parts into the sea. APHRODITE grew from the foam that surrounded these. The FURIES, the GIANTS and the MELIAE were spawned from the blood that fell on the ground. He was overthrown by Cronos.

Ursa Major (The Great Bear); **Ursa Minor** (The Lesser Bear) constellations in the northern sky. Ursa Major is the Roman name, called Arctos in Greek. It was held in legend to be the nymph CALLISTO, who had been turned into a bear. Ursa Major is followed in the sky by Arctophylax, 'bear-keeper', who was the son of Callisto. Callisto is said to have been greatly disliked by HERA, who persuaded her foster mother, TETHYS, never to allow Ursa Major to set in the ocean.

V

Valetudo *see* **Hygieia**.

Veii an Etruscan city north of ROME. Its citizens, the Veientes, were frequently at war with Rome in the early years of its existence.

Venus in Roman mythology, the name of the goddess of love, called by the Greeks APHRODITE. She surpassed all other goddesses in beauty, and hence received the GOLDEN APPLE which was to be awarded to the most beautiful by PARIS. She was the wife of VULCAN, but also bestowed her love on the gods MARS, BACCHUS, MERCURY, and NEPTUNE, and the mortals ANCHISES and ADONIS. The myrtle, rose, poppy, apple, and other fruits were sacred to her, as were the dove, sparrow, swan, swallow, ram, hare, and tortoise. In ROME several temples were erected to her under different names. In art she was originally represented draped, in later times nude. The scene of her arising from the sea was sculpted by Phidias on the base of the statue of ZEUS at OLYMPIA, and one of the most famous pictures of Apelles represented the same subject. The Venus of Capua and the Venus of Milo represent her as Venus Victrix, with one foot on a helmet and raising a shield.

Vergil *see* **Virgil**.

Vertumnus *or* **Vortumnus** in Roman mythology, a god of fertility, particularly with regard to crops and the changing of the seasons. He is said to have been able to change his shape. He assumed the shape of an old woman who pleaded with the fruit goddess, POMONA, to accept the love of Vertumnus, Pomona being unaware that it was actually Vertumnus who was doing the pleading. Pomona accepted his love.

Vesta in Roman mythology, the goddess of the hearth, the Roman equivalent of the Greek HESTIA. She was worshipped, along with the PENATES, at every family meal, when the household assembled round the hearth, which was in the centre of the room. Her public sanctuary was in the Forum, and the sacred fire was kept constantly burning in it by the Vestal Virgins, her priestesses. The Vestal Virgins are said to have been established by NUMA. There were at first four, and afterwards six of them. They were taken in when they were from six to ten years of age and compelled to be virgins for thirty years, the term of their service, after which they were allowed to marry. They were treated with great honour and respect and had important public privileges. The punishment of a Vestal Virgin who broke her vow of chastity was burying alive. Theodosius abolished the practice of the Vestal Virgins in AD 394.

Vestal virgins *see* **Vesta**.

Virbius in Roman mythology, a minor god and companion of DIANA. He was a king of Aricia and favourite of Diana and when he died she called him to life and entrusted him to the care of the nymph EGERIA. The fact of his being a favourite of Diana seems to have led the Romans to identify him with HIPPOLYTUS who, according to some traditions, had established the worship of Diana.

Virgil *or* **Vergil** (Publius Vergilius Maro) the national poet of Rome, born 70 BC, died 19 BC. His works include his masterpiece, the *Aeneid*, an epic poem in twelve books that charts the progress of AENEAS from the fall of TROY to the founding of the Roman state.

Virgo (The Virgin) a constellation. It is not clear who the virgin in question was, although there have been many suggestions. She is variously described as being ASTRAEA or Dike (justice), Tyche (fortune), Parthenos, a daughter of APOLLO, or ERIGONE (2), daughter of CLYTEMNESTRA and AEGISTHUS.

Volscians *or* **Volsci** an ancient Italian tribe who delt in LATIUM, on both sides of the River Liris (Garigliano). Their principal city was Corili, from which Coriolanus derived his name. After having several times endangered ROME, they were conquered and disappeared from history.

Vortumnus *see* **Vertumnus**.

Vulcan in Roman mythology, the god who presided over fire and the working of metals and patronized handicraftsmen of every kind. By some writers he is said to have been born lame, but others attribute his lameness to his having been thrown from OLYMPUS. He was equated with the Greek god HEPHAESTUS. His name is remembered in the word volcano.

W

Wandering Rocks (Planctae) in Greek mythology, mobile rocks in the sea that destroyed ships that attempted to pass between them. The ARGONAUTS passed through them safely with the help of the NEREIDS, the sea nymphs. ODYSSEUS, however, chose to avoid them when he was about to encounter them near the island of the SIRENS and took an alternative route which involved encountering SCYLLA AND CHARYBDIS.

water-bearer, The *see* **Ganymede**.

Whale, The *see* **Cetus**.

White Island an island in the BLACK SEA said in legend to have been one of the Islands of the Blessed where some of the Greek heroes lived in eternal happiness after their adventures in the TROJAN WAR.

Women of the Sea in Greek mythology, a name given to some followers of DIONYSUS. Known as the Haliae, the women went to ARGOS to support Dionysus in a war with PERSEUS. The latter defeated them and killed most of them. Dionysus later made peace with the people of Argos.

wooden horse in Greek mythology, a cunning device thought up by the Greeks to gain entrance to TROY undetected. The plan to get the Trojans to open their gates was conceived either by ODYSSEUS or Epeius. Epeius, who was a skilled craftsman, built a large wooden model of a horse with the help of ATHENA from wood cut from trees on Mount IDA. The interior of the model horse was hollow and large enough to contain a considerable number of men. When the horse was complete, a number of the Greek leaders under the command of Odysseus climbed inside the horse. Meanwhile the rest of the Greeks packed up camp and sailed away, giving the impression to the Trojans that they had given up the struggle against them. In fact they sailed only as far as the offshore island of TENEDOS. They had left the wooden horse on the shore. When they thought that the Greeks had gone, the Trojans took the opportunity to leave their city, which had been under siege for so long. They were surprised to see the wooden horse but relieved to read the inscription on it. It read 'For their return home the Greeks dedicate this thanks offering to Athena'. There was dispute among the Trojans as to what should be done with the wooden horse. Some wished to destroy it or break into it. Others wanted to take it into their city. Because it had associations with a goddess, they thought that they should not destroy it, and some of them thought that taking care of an offering to Athena might bring them good fortune. CASSANDRA, who was noted for telling true prophecies that no one would believe, warned the Trojans that there were spears inside the horse, but they ignord her. Some of them even ignored it when LAOCOÖN, a priest of APOLLO, agreed with the warning and threw his spear at the horse. Others were more suspicious. The Greeks had anticipated these suspicions and had left behind Sinon, a young relative of Odysseus, with arms bound up and with clothes in tatters. When he was captured by shepherds and brought to PRIAM, king of Troy, he told a story about how CALCHAS, a Greek seer, plotted with Odysseus, with whom Sinon had quarrelled, to interpret an oracle to the effect that Sinon must be sacrificed to the gods to ensure a safe return home for the Greeks. Sinon had succeeded in escaping just before the Greeks left. He was extremely plausible and convincing, and the Trojans believed him and trusted him. On being asked about the meaning of the wooden horse, Sinon told them that the Greeks had angered Athena by stealing the PALLADIUM, an image sacred to Athena, from the Trojan citadel. Calchas had advised the Greeks to build a wooden horse to appease Athena and then leave for home. They had deliberately made it too large to be taken through the gates of Troy in case the Trojans received good luck from it and attacked

Greek cities. The seer had also said that if the Trojans destroyed the horse Athena would be angry with them and Troy would be destroyed. The Trojans believed this story, especially because two serpents swimming in the sea snatched and ate the two young sons of Laocoön and then Laocoön himself, and the Trojans interpreted this as a punishment sent by Athena for Laocoön throwing a spear at the horse. In fact it was supposed to be a punishment sent to his priest by APOLLO for some other misdemeanour. The Trojans tore down part of their city walls to admit the wooden horse. They then celebrated their supposed victory over the Greeks by eating and drinking. Sinon is said to have released the Greeks inside the horse, and the Greek fleet returned. The Greeks left the ships and entered Troy. The carousing Trojans were easily defeated.

Xanthe in Greek mythology, one of the daughters of OCEANUS.

Xanthippe in Greek mythology, the wife of PLEURON.

Xanthus in Greek mythology, a son of TRIOPAS (1) and Oreasis, who was a king of the Pelasgians at ARGOS and afterwards settled in the island of LESBOS.

Xanthus and Balius in Greek mythology, the immortal horses of ACHILLES. They were the offspring of the Harpy PODARGE by ZEPHYRUS. The horses were given to PELEUS as a gift to celebrate his marriage to THETIS. Xanthus was given the power of speech by HERA in order to warn Achilles of his impending death. The FURIES immediately removed the powers for fear that Xanthus might reveal some more of the god's secrets to mortals.

Xanthus an ancient city of Asia Minor, the principal city of LYCIA, on the River Xanthus.

Xuthus in Greek mythology, a son of HELLEN by the nymph Orseis, and a brother of DORUS and AEOLUS (2). He was king of PELOPONNESUS, and the husband of CREÜSA (2), the daughter of ERECHTHEUS, by whom he became the father of ACHAEUS and ION. According to other legends, Xuthus, after the death of his father, was expelled from Thessaly by his brothers and went to Athens, where he married the daughter of Erechtheus. After the death of Erechtheus, Xuthus was chosen as arbitrator and decreed that the kingdom should be ruled by his eldest brother-in-law, CECROPS. As a result of this judgement Xuthus was expelled by the other sons of Erechtheus and settled at Aegialos in Peloponnesus. Xuthus is an important character in Euripides's *Ion*, a play which deals with the events surrounding the discovery that Ion is a son of Creüsa by APOLLO. Xuthus remained happy in the belief that he was the young man's father.

Z

Zacynthus one of the islands lying off the western coast of PELOPONNESUS near ITHACA. In Greek mythology, it was colonized by Zacynthus, son of DARDANUS, from Psophis in ARCADIA. Its inhabitants sent forces to fight the Trojans under the leadership of ODYSSEUS.

Zagreus *see* **Iacchus**.

Zelus in Greek mythology, the personification of zeal or strife, a son of the Titan PALLAS and STYX, the constant companion of ZEUS. He was the brother of Cratos, BIA and NIKE.

Zephyrus *or* **Zephyr** in Greek mythology, the west wind and god of the west wind, a son of Eos and Astraeus. He was the father of XANTHUS AND BALIUS, the immortal horses. In some legends he caused the death of HYACINTH because he was jealous of Hyacinth's love for APOLLO.

Zetes and Calaïs in Greek mythology, the twin sons of BOREAS, the north wind and god of the north wind. They were known as the Boreades and are depicted as having wings that sprouted either from their backs or from their heads and feet. Either their wings or their hair is depicted as being purple in colour. They voyaged with the ARGONAUTS and chased the HARPIES when they were attacking PHINEUS, king of Thracia, brother-in-law of Zetes and Calaïs.

Zethus in Greek mythology, son of ZEUS and ANTIOPE and brother of AMPHION.

Zeus in Greek mythology, the supreme divinity; the ruler of the other gods. He is generally treated as the equivalent of the Roman JUPITER, and was the son of CRONOS and RHEA, and brother of POSEIDON and HERA, the latter of whom was also his wife. Rhea, with her mother GE, tricked Cronos at the birth of Zeus by giving him a stone wrapped in swaddling clothes instead of the baby. This was because Cronos had been warned that he would be deposed by one of his children, just as he had deposed his father, URANUS. In order to get rid of his children he swallowed them. In the case of the infant Zeus it was the stone that he swallowed. For his protection the baby Zeus was hidden in a cave on Mount Dicte in CRETE. When he was an adult Zeus persuaded the Oceanid METIS to give his father, Cronos, an emetic, and he vomited up the brothers and sisters of Zeus whom he had previously swallowed. They then joined Zeus in his struggle against Cronos for control of OLYMPUS. He finally expelled his father and the dynasty of the TITANS, successfully opposed the attacks of the GIANTS and the conspiracies of the other gods, and became chief power in heaven and earth.

Zeuxippe in Greek mythology, a NAÏAD, daughter of ERIDANUS and the wife of PANDION (1), king of ATHENS. He was in fact her nephew. She bore him PROCNE and PHILOMELA and twin sons, ERECHTHEUS and BUTES (2).